THE
BADGER STATE

THE
BADGER STATE
A DOCUMENTARY HISTORY OF WISCONSIN

by
Justus F. *and*
Barbara Dotts Paul

William B. Eerdmans Publishing Company
Grand Rapids, Michigan

Library of Congress Cataloging in Publication Data

Main entry under title:

The Badger State.

Includes index.
1. Wisconsin—History—Addresses, essays, lectures.
I. Paul, Justus F., 1938– II. Paul, Barbara Dotts
F581.5.B32 1979 977.5'04 78-23340
ISBN 0-8028-7038-4

To our parents and our children

Acknowledgments

The people of the state of Wisconsin have long supported the collection, preservation, and display of materials that concern the state's past. Through the vigorous efforts of the State Historical Society of Wisconsin, documents and artifacts continue to be actively collected. This tradition began with Lyman C. Draper, first secretary of the Society, and continued with his successors. In the days before oral history became popular, Draper wrote letters to Wisconsin leaders and pioneers, urging them to record their experiences. He traveled to the homes of many Wisconsinites to transcribe their reminiscences when they were unable to write them down. Following Draper's example, the State Historical Society of Wisconsin has continued to excel in the collection and publication of historical materials on the state. We are indebted to the Society and Paul H. Hass, editor of the *Wisconsin Magazine of History,* for their generosity in making these materials available, and to George Talbot of the Society's Iconography Department for his assistance in obtaining most of the illustrations.

We also appreciate using the collections of the James H. Albertson Center for Learning Resources at the University of Wisconsin, Stevens Point; the McMillan Memorial Library, Wisconsin Rapids; and the Charles M. White Memorial Public Library, Stevens Point.

Many colleagues have assisted our search for source materials by sharing with us their knowledge of unique documents. We appreciate their help. Arthur M. Fish, Documents Librarian at the James H. Albertson Center for Learning Resources, has been particularly helpful. This project has been partially funded with a research grant from the University of Wisconsin, Stevens Point. We would also like to thank Stacie Clark for her clerical help in preparing the manuscript.

Contents

List of Illustrations

Preface

The purpose of a documentary history is to span the history of the subject with the use of individual documents that narrate and interpret the significant events of that history. In *The Badger State: A Documentary History of Wisconsin* we have attempted to trace the history of Wisconsin through a combination of contemporaneous, often firsthand accounts and scholarly, interpretive essays. Brief historical surveys are provided for each chapter and bibliographical introductions for each subgroup of materials. The editors hope that these preliminary statements will tie the materials together for the reader.

Intended for the general reading public as well as for the serious student of the state's history, *The Badger State* is organized chronologically for the most part, although topical overlapping in different chapters has been necessary at times. The basic outline of the book is patterned after the outline used by the standard textbook of Wisconsin history, Robert C. Nesbit's *Wisconsin: A History* (Madison, 1973). The editors feel that this organization is appropriate for at least two reasons. First, it is a good and useful organization. And second, since many high schools, colleges, and universities use Nesbit's text, this volume can be easily fitted into a course structured around its use.

From the earliest days of the Wisconsin Territory to the trials and drama of the 1960s and 1970s, the editors have selected materials that seemed to best depict the major events and developments in the state's history. The land, the peoples (both native and foreign-born), the development from territory to statehood, the crisis of the Civil War and related problems are covered in the first half of the book. In the second half, Wisconsin's transition from a wheat economy to a mixed agricultural-industrial economy is illustrated, as are the changing patterns of political development in the state. Wisconsin's ethnic heritage, an important factor in many aspects of the state's development, is given substantial coverage. Finally, the impact of the problems and progress of the twentieth century is illustrated in the later chapters.

The history of Wisconsin is not unlike that of other states of the upper Middle West except, perhaps, for the political developments of the Progressive-Socialist parties of the early twentieth century. Native Americans occupied the territory first, followed by white outsiders, including the French, the British, and finally, the Americans. As part of the original Northwest Territory, Wisconsin was the last segment to gain statehood. And, only a decade after attaining statehood, Wisconsin found itself in the Civil War. The Yankee origins of most Wisconsinites made it easy for them to support the Union.

After the war, the state—along with others in the Great Lakes–upper Midwest area—began a period of rapid maturation. Political and economic changes occurred with great rapidity in the tumultuous post-Civil War decades. By 1900 the state was no longer an unimportant wheat-producing state but a leader in both industry and diversified agriculture. Machinery, beer, timber, and dairy products brought wealth—and railroads—to the state. With some differences caused by changing conditions, this basic mixed economy has remained constant throughout the first three-quarters of the twentieth century.

Politically, the state's post-Civil War history was also turbulent. Reformism in the 1900–1920 period, both within the traditional two-party system and outside it—Robert LaFollette's Progressive party and the Milwaukee Socialists—brought national prominence to Wisconsin. After two world wars and the Great Depression, political unorthodoxy again brought national attention to Wisconsin when Republican Senator Joseph R. McCarthy became the most outspoken anti-Communist witch-hunter during the height of the Cold War in the 1950s. After the strain and pressures of the Vietnam era of the 1960s and early 1970s, calm returned, and Democratic majorities controlled much of the state's political machinery as the state neared the end of the 1970s.

* *

A final word on sources is necessary. The spelling, punctuation, and capitalization in some of the primary documents, such as early letters and diaries, do not conform to twentieth-century grammatical standards. In the interest of authenticity, we have printed those sources exactly as they were written. We have retained footnotes from the original sources, and occasionally added our own, when we felt it would be instructive to the reader to define a geographical location or the meaning of an expression. A book such as this one requires a substantial base of documentary and analytical information, and historians of Wisconsin are fortunate to have the library of the State Historical Society of Wisconsin. With its fine collection of materials covering nearly all aspects of the state's history, and with its publications, the earlier *Wisconsin Historical Collections* and the continuing *Wisconsin Magazine of History,* the historian has at his command a wealth of vital source materials. The state, its citizens, and historians of Wisconsin should all be grateful for the interest in and sensitivity to history long displayed by the Badger State.

Barbara Dotts Paul

University of Wisconsin, Stevens Point   Justus F. Paul

Chapter I
WISCONSIN TO 1775

Wisconsin was Indian land before 1775. Chippewa, Menominee, Winnebago, Sauk, Fox, and Miami all laid claim to parts of the land. Some tribes were almost sedentary, farming plots and remaining in a small area; others were nomadic, moving across the land according to the season and the hunting conditions.

Europeans first came to the shores of Lakes Michigan and Superior in search of water routes to the west. The abundance of fur-bearing animals attracted French Canadians, who established trading routes into Wisconsin and beyond by way of the St. Lawrence River and the Great Lakes. With them came the missionaries, impelled by their religion to bring Christianity to the Indians. From the American colonies along the eastern seaboard British and American frontiersmen ventured into the Old Northwest to compete in the fur trade.

The French-British rivalry in the colonies, in Europe, and on the ocean erupted into sporadic wars during the seventeenth and eighteenth centuries. Wisconsin, on the fringe of European influence, felt repercussions as Indian tribes took sides. Meanwhile, the Indian way of life was being eroded by the introduction of trade goods, firearms, liquor, and Christianity. Hostile bands who hindered traders going to or from the rendezvous were dealt with harshly.

By 1775, Wisconsin was a major trade route between the Great Lakes and the Mississippi Valley. Traders came up the Fox River from Green Bay, portaged to the Wisconsin River across a mile and a half of swamp, and traveled down the Wisconsin to where it joined the Mississippi at Prairie du Chien. From there the canoes could carry them north up the Mississippi into Sioux country or south to the posts of Cahokia and Kaskaskia. Traders brought European goods to exchange for furs at summer rendezvous where Indians would appear with their winter's harvest of furs. Green Bay and Prairie du Chien were typical meeting places. Small communities of old traders and their families grew up around these sites. Missionaries in Wisconsin mainly lived alone among the Indian tribes, wandering from village to village, trying to learn the native languages, but trying to change their religion and their culture. It was a discouraging business.

1: The Land and the River

Aldo Leopold, conservationist, and August Derleth, author, both wrote with love about Wisconsin. Leopold's essays on the land, especially in *A Sand County Almanac,* have been compared with those of Henry David Thoreau. Derleth, who grew up in the state, drew upon his experiences in his fiction and journals. Among his many books about Wisconsin is a history of the Wisconsin River, written in 1942. Others who have written about the state's natural beauty include Robert Gard (*This Is Wisconsin,* Spring Green, 1969; *The Trail of the Serpent,* Madison, 1973) and Fred L. Holmes (*Side Roads; Excursions Into Wisconsin's Past,* Madison, 1949). The Federal Writers Program produced *Wisconsin, A Guide to the Badger State* (New York, 1941), which is still useful, particularly for its topical bibliography. A more thorough discussion of the origins of Wisconsin's name is found in Virgil Vogel, "Wisconsin's Name: a Linguistic Puzzle," *Wisconsin Magazine of History,* XLVIII (Spring 1965), 181–186.

Marshland Elegy

ALDO LEOPOLD

A dawn wind stirs on the great marsh. With almost imperceptible slowness it rolls a bank of fog across the wide morass. Like the white ghost of a glacier the mists advance, riding over phalanxes of

From *A Sand County Almanac, With Other Essays on Conservation from "Round River"* (New York, 1966), pp. 95–101. Reprinted by permission of Oxford University Press.

tamarack, sliding across bogmeadows heavy with dew. A single silence hangs from horizon to horizon.

Out of some far recess of the sky a tinkling of little bells falls soft upon the listening land. Then again silence. Now comes a baying of some sweet-throated hound, soon the clamor of a responding pack. Then a far clear blast of hunting horns, out of the sky into the fog.

High horns, low horns, silence, and finally a pandemonium of trumpets, rattles, croaks, and cries that almost shakes the bog with its nearness, but without yet disclosing whence it comes. At last a glint of sun reveals the approach of a great echelon of birds. On motionless wing they emerge from the lifting mists, sweep a final arc of sky, and settle in clangorous descending spirals to their feeding grounds. A new day has begun on the crane marsh.

A sense of time lies thick and heavy on such a place. Yearly since the ice age it has awakened each spring to the clangor of cranes. The peat layers that comprise the bog are laid down in the basin of an ancient lake. The cranes stand, as it were, upon the sodden pages of their own history. These peats are the compressed remains of the mosses that clogged the pools, of the tamaracks that spread over the moss, of the cranes that bugled over the tamaracks since the retreat of the ice sheet. An endless caravan of generations has built of its own bones this bridge into the future, this habitat where the oncoming host again may live and breed and die.

To what end? Out of the bog a crane, gulping some luckless frog, springs his ungainly hulk into the air and flails the morning sun with mighty wings. The tamaracks re-echo with his bugled certitude. He seems to know.

Our ability to perceive quality in nature begins, as in art, with the pretty. It expands through successive stages of the beautiful to values as yet uncaptured by language. The quality of cranes lies, I think, in this higher gamut, as yet beyond the reach of words.

This much, though, can be said: our appreciation of the crane grows with the slow unraveling of earthly history. His tribe, we now know, stems out of the remote Eocene. The other members of the fauna in which he originated are long since entombed within the hills. When we hear his call we hear no mere bird. We hear the trumpet in the orchestra of evolution. He is the symbol of our untamable past, of that incredible sweep of millennia which underlies and conditions the daily affairs of birds and men.

And so they live and have their being—these cranes—not in the constricted present, but in the wider reaches of evolutionary time. Their annual return is the ticking of the geologic clock. Upon the

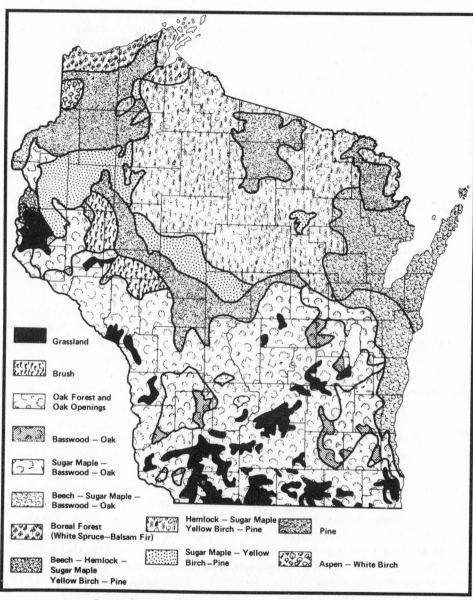

Grassland

Brush

Oak Forest and
Oak Openings

Basswood — Oak

Sugar Maple —
Basswood — Oak

Beech — Sugar Maple —
Basswood — Oak

Boreal Forest
(White Spruce—Balsam Fir)

Beech — Hemlock —
Sugar Maple
Yellow Birch — Pine

Hemlock — Sugar Maple
Yellow Birch — Pine

Sugar Maple — Yellow
Birch — Pine

Pine

Aspen — White Birch

From Collins, An Atlas of Wisconsin. Courtesy of American Printing and Publishing Co.

Original vegetation cover of Wisconsin

place of their return they confer a peculiar distinction. Amid the endless mediocrity of the commonplace, a crane marsh holds a paleontological patent of nobility, won in the march of aeons, and revocable only by shotgun. The sadness discernible in some marshes arises, perhaps, from their once having harbored cranes. Now they stand humbled, adrift in history.

Some sense of this quality in cranes seems to have been felt by sportsmen and ornithologists of all ages. Upon such quarry as this the Holy Roman Emperor Frederick loosed his gyrfalcons. Upon such quarry as this once swooped the hawks of Kublai Khan. Marco Polo tells us: 'He derives the highest amusement from sporting with gyrfalcons and hawks. At Changanor the Khan has a great Palace surrounded by a fine plain where are found cranes in great numbers. He causes millet and other grains to be sown in order that the birds may not want.'

The ornithologist Bengt Berg, seeing cranes as a boy upon the Swedish heaths, forthwith made them his life work. He followed them to Africa and discovered their winter retreat on the White Nile. He says of his first encounter: 'It was a spectacle which eclipsed the flight of the roc in the Thousand and One Nights.'

When the glacier came down out of the north, crunching hills and gouging valleys, some adventuring rampart of the ice climbed the Baraboo Hills and fell back into the outlet gorge of the Wisconsin River. The swollen waters backed up and formed a lake half as long as the state, bordered on the east by cliffs of ice, and fed by the torrents that fell from melting mountains. The shorelines of this old lake are still visible; its bottom is the bottom of the great marsh.

The lake rose through the centuries, finally spilling over east of the Baraboo range. There it cut a new channel for the river, and thus drained itself. To the residual lagoons came the cranes, bugling the defeat of the retreating winter, summoning the on-creeping host of living things to their collective task of marsh-building. Floating bogs of sphagnum moss clogged the lowered waters, filled them. Sedge and leatherleaf, tamarack and spruce successively advanced over the bog, anchoring it by their root fabric, sucking out its water, making peat. The lagoons disappeared, but not the cranes. To the moss-meadows that replaced the ancient waterways they returned each spring to dance and bugle and rear their gangling sorrel-colored young. These, albeit birds, are not properly called chicks, but *colts*. I cannot explain why. On some dewy June morning watch them gambol over their ancestral pastures at the heels of the roan mare, and you will see for yourself.

One year not long ago a French trapper in buckskins pushed his canoe up one of the moss-clogged creeks that thread the great marsh. At this attempt to invade their miry stronghold the cranes gave vent to loud and ribald laughter. A century or two later Englishmen came in covered wagons. They chopped clearings in the timbered moraines that border the marsh, and in them planted corn and buckwheat. They did not intend, like the Great Khan at Changanor, to feed the cranes. But the cranes do not question the intent of glaciers, emperors, or pioneers. They ate the grain, and when some irate farmer failed to concede their usufruct in his corn, they trumpeted a warning and sailed across the marsh to another farm.

There was no alfalfa in those days, and the hill-farms made poor hay land, especially in dry years. One dry year someone set a fire in the tamaracks. The burn grew up quickly to bluejoint grass, which, when cleared of dead trees, made a dependable hay meadow. After that, each August, men appeared to cut hay. In winter, after the cranes had gone South, they drove wagons over the frozen bogs and hauled the hay to their farms in the hills. Yearly they plied the marsh with fire and axe, and in two short decades hay meadows dotted the whole expanse.

Each August when the haymakers came to pitch their camps, singing and drinking and lashing their teams with whip and tongue, the cranes whinnied to their colts and retreated to the far fastnesses. 'Red shitepokes' the haymakers called them, from the rusty hue which at that season often stains the battleship-gray of crane plumage. After the hay was stacked and the marsh again their own, the cranes returned, to call down out of October skies the migrant flocks from Canada. Together they wheeled over the newcut stubbles and raided the corn until frosts gave the signal for the winter exodus.

These haymeadow days were the Arcadian age for marsh dwellers. Man and beast, plant and soil lived on and with each other in mutual toleration, to the mutual benefit of all. The marsh might have kept on producing hay and prairie chickens, deer and muskrat, crane-music and cranberries forever.

The new overlords did not understand this. They did not include soil, plants, or birds in their ideas of mutuality. The dividends of such a balanced economy were too modest. They envisaged farms not only around, but *in* the marsh. An epidemic of ditch-digging and land-booming set in. The marsh was gridironed with drainage canals, speckled with new fields and farmsteads.

But crops were poor and beset by frosts, to which the expensive ditches added an aftermath of debt. Farmers moved out. Peat beds dried, shrank, caught fire. Sun-energy out of the Pleistocene shrouded the countryside in acrid smoke. No man raised his voice against the waste, only his nose against the smell. After a dry summer not even the winter snows could extinguish the smoldering marsh. Great pockmarks were burned into field and meadow, the scars reaching down to the sands of the old lake, peat-covered these hundred centuries. Rank weeds sprang out of the ashes, to be followed after a year or two by aspen scrub. The cranes were hard put, their numbers shrinking with the remnants of unburned meadow. For them, the song of the power shovel came near being an elegy. The high priests of progress knew nothing of cranes, and cared less. What is a species more or less among engineers? What good is an undrained marsh anyhow?

For a decade or two crops grew poorer, fires deeper, wood-fields larger, and cranes scarcer, year by year. Only reflooding, it appeared, could keep the peat from burning. Meanwhile cranberry growers had, by plugging drainage ditches, reflooded a few spots and obtained good yields. Distant politicians bugled about marginal land, over-production, unemployment relief, conservation. Economists and planners came to look at the marsh. Surveyors, technicians, CCC's, buzzed about. A counter-epidemic of reflooding set in. Government bought land, resettled farmers, plugged ditches wholesale. Slowly the bogs are re-wetting. The firepocks become ponds. Grass fires still burn, but they can no longer burn the wetted soil.

All this, once the CCC camps were gone, was good for cranes, but not so the thickets of scrub popple that spread inexorably over the old burns, and still less the maze of new roads that inevitably follow governmental conservation. To build a road is so much simpler than to think of what the country really needs. A roadless marsh is seemingly as worthless to the alphabetical conservationist as an undrained one was to the empire-builders. Solitude, the one natural resource still undowered of alphabets, is so far recognized as valuable only by ornithologists and cranes.

Thus always does history, whether of marsh or market place, end in paradox. The ultimate value in these marshes is wildness, and the crane is wildness incarnate. But all conservation of wildness is self-defeating, for to cherish we must see and fondle, and when enough have seen and fondled, there is no wilderness left to cherish.

Some day, perhaps in the very process of our benefactions, perhaps in the fullness of geologic time, the last crane will trumpet his farewell and spiral skyward from the great marsh. High out of the clouds will fall the sound of hunting horns, the baying of the phantom pack, the tinkle of little bells, and then a silence never to be broken, unless perchance in some far pasture of the Milky Way.

The Wisconsin River

AUGUST DERLETH

Of the name, Wisconsin, and its meaning, there is speculation still. The first recorded printing of the name in its early form was in Père Marquette's *Journal,* which was published in 1681 in Paris. The priest spelled the name Meskousing, Miskous, and, on the map published with the *Journal,* Messc8sing—the 8 used in place of the *ou.* Of its Indian origin, there can be no question whatever. Writing in her *Old Forts and Real Folks,* published as recently as 1939, Susan Burdick Davis says that the second part of the word—"sing, sin, or san . . . was probably an Indian ending indicating 'place' or 'location.'" The second appearance of the river was on the 1683 map drawn by Father Hennepin; there it is spelled Ouisconsin, clearly indicative of the French pronunciation of the Indian name. Its evolution to Wiskonsan is obvious, this being the English spelling suggested by the French pronunciation of Ouisconsin. On July 4, 1836, the final change was brought about; Wiskonsan became Wisconsin, despite the objection of some substantial citizens to the use of *c* for *k;* and on January 30, 1845, the territorial legislature in a formal resolution fixed upon the spelling of 1836 as the authorized spelling for the territory and thus also for the river. The alternative spellings of the past, which are sometimes come upon— Ouisconsings, Miskonsing, Ouisconsink, Ouisconsinc, *et al,* are obviously only mutations of the earlier forms, Meskousing or Ouisconsin. The origin of La Salle's Meschetz Odéba is lost in history, and the name occurs nowhere else.

The matter of the meaning of the name is another argument altogether. The Chippewa on the headwaters of the Wisconsin called the river Wees-konsan, which, they explained, meant "the place of the gathering of waters." But there is also the belief that the word means "red cliff" to the Chippewa; this belief is recorded by Miss Davis, though her source is not given. As she points out, however, "where are there 'cliffs' of any importance along the Wisconsin River, with the exception of the Dells, and how red would we call these?" H. E. Cole, writing in *Baraboo, Dells, and Devil's Lake Region,* maintains that Wisconsin "is an Indian word, meaning 'wild, rushing river,'" while Marquette affirmed that the word meant "the river of flowery banks." Finally, as recorded by Carver, there is the meaning of "the river of a thousand isles."

From *The Wisconsin: River of a Thousand Isles* (New York, 1942), pp. 34–38. Reprinted by permission of Holt, Rinehart and Winston.

Courtesy of the State Historical Society of Wisconsin [WHi (X3) 33859]

The Wisconsin River with Rib Mountain in the background

Of these meanings, only two fit the facts, and one of these is questionable. Undoubtedly in the early days of the Wisconsin, the meadows and low places along the river abounded in flowers—but surely no less so than hundreds of other rivers. There are still count-less flowers along the river—the white and blue violets, the loose-strifes and lobelias, the blue flags and arrowleafs and yellow pond lilies, the ground nut and bonesets and all the yellow glory of the sunflower family, wild ginger and columbine and honeysuckle, puc-coon, spotted crane's-bill, thimbleweed, wild roses and scores of others. But there is one aspect of the river which has not changed from its earliest time to this—the islands. Truly, the Wisconsin is a river of a thousand isles.

Great and small, islands dot the Wisconsin from its headwaters to its mouth, some of them shifting sandbar islands, staying long enough to grow a few trees and shrubs before disappearing again, but most of them substantial bodies of land, heavily wooded, some-times so long that it is impossible to see from end to end, or even to ascertain that their nearer shore is not, indeed, the shore of the

Wisconsin itself. Some of them retain the appearance they must have presented to the earliest explorers: hung with grapevines, bittersweet, carrion berry, greenbrier; abounding with trees, many of them tremendous in girth, here and there still a right-angled tree, hoary with age now, once bent by a passing Indian to make a trail-marking tree. For that reason, I am inclined to believe that the translation of Wisconsin as meaning the stream or river of a thousand isles is to be preferred above all others.

. . . .

The Wisconsin rises on the summit of the Archaean watershed, in the waters of Lac Vieux Desert, a shallow lake nowhere more than nineteen feet deep, almost equally divided by the border of Michigan and Wisconsin. The water area is approximately 6,400 acres, and in Wisconsin, 2,698 acres lie in Vilas County. "The country in the vicinity of this beautiful lake is called, in Chippewa language, Katakittekon," writes Captain Thomas Jefferson Cram in the *Wisconsin Historical Collections,* "and the lake bears the same name. On South Island there is an old Indian potato-planting ground; hence the appellation of Vieux Desert, which, in mongrel French, means 'old planting-ground.' There is more reason for calling it Lac Vieux Desert than for the appellation Lake of the Desert." Despite its shallowness Lac Vieux Desert is a large lake, one of the largest in northern Wisconsin, and, while the country immediately around it is flat, hills are not far away. It has a shore line of forty miles, with many well-hidden bays and islands, and on the shores, many Indian mounds.

The Wisconsin flows from Lac Vieux Desert at the southwestern end of the lake and proceeds in a northerly and westerly direction as a stream from six to twelve feet wide through level country which was once valuable timberland, has now been replanted, and will again yield timber in the future, pine, hemlock, tamarack, and cedar predominating, though there are birch and maple varieties, poplar and linden also. It soon establishes a southerly direction, and meanders for all but a hundred miles of its more than 400-mile length almost due south, bending in a wide, gracious curve to westward from Stevens Point to Strong's Prairie and back to Portage, its most easterly point, where it lies slightly over a mile from the Fox River, and is joined to it by a canal for the purpose of navigation. From Portage it pursues a more southwesterly direction until it discharges into the Mississippi a few miles below Prairie du Chien. In the northern part of the state, the river is widened slowly by the waters of almost fifteen hundred lakes and lakelets, which lie in the region covered by the most recent glacial drift. In the Merrill area,

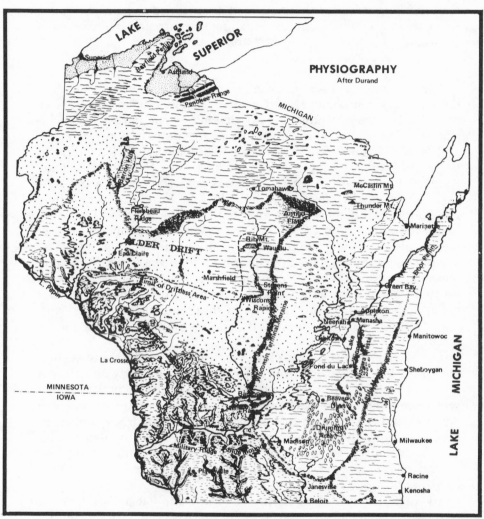

From Collins, An Atlas of Wisconsin. *Courtesy of American Printing and Publishing Co.*

The physiography of Wisconsin

where the tributaries have the familiar tree pattern, the river flows through a region of older glacial drift. From Stevens Point to Wisconsin Dells the Wisconsin winds through a sandy plain which is comparatively recent in origin, geologically writing, and from the Dells to the Sauk Prairie, flows through drift region. H. E. Cole, writing in *Baraboo, Dells, and Devil's Lake Region,* points out that "the work of erosion is so incomplete, at the present time the swamp lands in the vicinity of Portage have not yet been drained." From the Sauk Prairie to the mouth of the Wisconsin, the river passes through a fourth type of country: the driftless limestone region, a country of comparatively few swamps and lakes. If there is another river system which presents four such distinct types of drainage, I do not know of it.

2: Copper and Lead Mining

The ancient copper and lead mines of the Wisconsin Indians were powerful magnets for the French explorers. Louise Phelps Kellogg discusses these early mines in a chapter of her history on the French period in Wisconsin history. She also wrote a second volume on the British period, *The British Régime in Wisconsin and the Northwest* (Madison, 1935). See also Volume One of Milo M. Quaife's *Wisconsin: Its History and Its People, 1634–1924* (4 vols., Chicago, 1924).

Mining

LOUISE PHELPS KELLOGG

The first miners in the region of Wisconsin were the Indians. Archeologists have found clear evidence that an aboriginal mining industry of large proportions was located on the shores of Lake Superior. The belief that the American Indians did not utilize metals was abandoned years ago because of the proof afforded by the great number of copper implements and ornaments that have been found in Wisconsin. Our earlier scientists were astonished to find these prehistoric copper artifacts in such numbers upon our soil. Later search has resulted in more and more coming to light. Over twenty years ago a count was made and thirteen thousand copper pieces had been recovered from Wisconsin mounds and village sites. The chief collector of copper artifacts in Wisconsin expressed his belief

From *The French Régime in Wisconsin and the Northwest* (Madison, 1925), pp. 341–346, 358–361. Footnotes in the original omitted. Reprinted by permission.

that the copper articles manufactured by the North American Indians amounted to millions.

Copper implements and ornaments are likewise found in Ohio mounds, and in sites along the Atlantic coast plain as far south as Georgia and Florida. The manufacture of these metallic articles was formerly attributed to a pre-Indian race called the mound builders, who were thought to have been of a higher culture than the aborigines found by whites on the discovery of the western continent. Now that the theory of the mound builders as a separate race has been abandoned, it is freely admitted that the prehistoric Indians had sufficient skill to have been the manufacturers of the copper artifacts found in the mounds. None of these show signs of casting or of melting by fire. Modern Indians have not lost the art of fashioning copper without smelting. Plates as thin as those used in the making of ornaments may be beaten out and shaped with stones, and the edges of the metal hardened in the process. Indeed, it is probable that the prehistoric miners and artificers considered the copper nuggets only as a peculiar kind of stone.

The source of the prehistoric copper is not difficult to find. The glacial drift brought down into the northern Mississippi and Ohio valleys many small pieces of copper, which were seized upon by the Indian workers; but the chief source of their supply was the Lake Superior deposits. As early as 1848, when agents of the Minnesota Mining Company were prospecting in the northern peninsula of Michigan, they found hundreds of abandoned diggings along the copper lode. As mining in this region progressed, prehistoric workings were located over a range one hundred miles long and from three to five miles wide in Ontonagon, Houghton, and Keweenaw counties; these were soon discovered to have been opened on the richest parts of the lode, and the early prospectors profited by the sagacity of their remote predecessors. On the north shore of Lake Superior, also, Indian mines have been discovered, and the prehistoric workings on Isle Royale are the most extensive yet found. Numberless pits have been seen from which copper was taken, and excavations of another type seem to have been used by the prehistoric miners as dwellings. William H. Holmes, one of our leading archeologists, is convinced that the Lake Superior mines were worked by Indians for hundreds of years.

The methods employed by these primitive miners are shown by the remains that have been found. Stone hammers were evidently used, and with these copper masses were pounded until flakes were broken off. They cared little for large pieces of metal, since these were too refractory for their methods of transportation and manufacture. Evidences of the use of fire abound, but heat was used, not to melt the metal, but to loosen the rock strata in which it was embedded. After fires were built, water was dashed upon the heated rocks to crack them. In some of the deeper pits ladders have been found and wooden props on which small masses of metal were raised. Immense numbers of broken stone hammers and axes lie around these old workings, and everything testifies to the indefatigable industry of these primitive miners.

No studies have yet been made of the tribal affinities of these first miners on Lake Superior. Some archeologists hold that the region about this great lake was the primitive home of the great Siouan race, and that therefore the early miners must have belonged to this stock. Radisson, the first observer of the Lake Superior peoples, noted that some of his Siouan visitors wore in their ears crescents and stars of copper polished until it shone. On the other hand, few copper artifacts have been found on prehistoric Siouan sites, and even the Wisconsin Winnebago acquired the copper artifacts they had by intertribal trade, and not by manufacture. So few metallic remains have been found in Winnebago graves and village sites, that their recent historian definitely asserts that members of this tribe were never copper makers.

On the other hand, evidence is fast accumulating that the greater number of copper artifacts are to be found on Algonquian sites. In Wisconsin the richest finds of prehistoric copper have been made along the Lake Michigan littoral, on sites associated with the Menominee and Potawatomi villages of historic times. The Georgia and Ohio mounds in which copper ornaments have been found are thought to have been the burial places of Algonquian peoples. Most of the early explorers along the Atlantic coast found the aborigines they met supplied with copper ornaments, and these tribes were nearly all of the Algonquian stock. It seems then reasonable to suppose that the ancient miners of Lake Superior were the ancestors of the historic Algonquian tribes, all the more since the original home of this great race is thought to have been northwest of the Great Lakes, and that from this region they migrated east and south. Whether we can ever identify these primitive miners any more closely than to say that they were probably Algonquian is doubtful. The great branch of that race which now occupies the lands around Lake Superior—the Chippewa—was not there when the whites first came west. One tribe of the Chippewa was met at the Sault (hence their French name, Saulteurs), but they had come from farther east, and the whole trend of their migratory movement seems to have been a counter one from that of the primitive Algonquian. Moreover, the Chippewa knew nothing of mining methods. They were in possession of many copper nuggets, which they regarded as sacred and cherished "as household gods"; but although they acted as purveyors of the metal, they denied all knowledge of the ancient mines, declaring that these had existed before they came to Lake Superior.

Certain natural facts gave an impetus to the primitive use of Lake Superior copper; one was its color, which made it highly prized, for when polished it glowed almost like gold. "Red copper" it was always called by the first explorers. The second fact was its purity. Because of these qualities its use was widespread, and it early came to the notice of European adventurers. Fish, furs, and metals were the first resources of the New World to be sought and exploited. Mines were especially in demand because of the riches Spain had acquired in Central and South America.

. . . .

Lead, another metal found in abundance in Wisconsin, was known to prehistoric Indians, but was little prized. Galena has been found in mounds as far east as Ohio. But, considering the abundance of that ore and the ease with which it could be obtained, astonishingly few leaden artifacts have been found antedating historic times. It was occasionally used for net-bobs, for boatstones, and ornaments, such as beads. A few pipes, some turtle effigies, and a cone comprise the entire series of prehistoric leaden implements found in Wisconsin. Even its use to inlay catlinite pipes dates from historic times. The fact is that not until the use of firearms became common did the tribesmen come to covet lead; after they had many times exchanged beaver skins for pouches of leaden bullets, the idea occurred to them that they might obtain these articles on their own land, and save their beaver skins for other purchases.

The French, always alert for indications of mineral wealth, discerned signs of mines in southwest Wisconsin at a very early date. Radisson says that he heard of lead mines in the West, but his report is too vague to be reliable. Marquette thought he saw in 1673 traces of an iron mine on the south bank of the Wisconsin River. Tonty reported lead mines near the Mississippi, which were so rich that only a third part became refuse. It was Nicolas Perrot, however, who was the real discoverer of the lead mines, and it was due to his popularity with the Indians that the secret of the mines was made known to him. About 1690 a chief of the Miami presented Perrot with some lead, which he said came from "a very rich lead mine, which he had found on the banks of a stream which empties into the Missisipi." The chief would reveal its locality to his white friend if the latter would build a fort in the vicinity. Perrot affected to be uninterested, while secretly much pleased; finally after many solicitations he followed his guide and built a fort near the mine, some-where below the mouth of the Wisconsin. The exact site is not known; from Perrot's description of its rocky crevices it is supposed that the lode he worked was at the present Dubuque, and that his fort was on the eastern bank near Dunleith, Illinois.

Perrot's post at this place did not long exist, but it is believed that he taught the Indians some crude mining methods, which they used for many years. Perrot says that he taught them to cut out the ore from the rocks, and that by melting it was reduced one-half. Later, when the Indians worked a deep mine, they learned to use an in-clined plane, by which they carried down wood, built fires, poured water on the heated rocks, and dug out the mineral with all sorts of implements, such as buck horns, hoes, old gun-barrels, and the like. Most of the labor was performed by the squaws, who drew out the ore thus extracted in birch-bark "mococks," and then placed it in a crude furnace built of logs, set fire to the whole, and as the lead melted and ran down, scraped out a place large enough for it to settle and form the large flat pieces, known as "plats," in which it was transported. Each of these bars weighed from thirty to seventy pounds, and hundreds of tons of lead were made by these crude methods.

From Perrot's time throughout the entire French régime, the lead mines were worked more or less constantly both by Indians and by white *voyageurs,* who used the product to supplement the fur trade. When Le Sueur in 1700 ascended the Mississippi in his sailing ves-sel, he stopped long enough to take out a supply for his proposed fort, probably from Wisconsin mines. Had he but continued oper-ations in this region, instead of mounting to the Blue Earth River, he might have made his enterprise a success, and have supplied Louisiana with lead.

3: Missionaries

French missionaries who ventured into the Northwest sent regular reports to France, which were published annually in the *Jesuit Relations*. Louise Phelps Kellogg used Reuben Thwaites' edition (73 vols., Cleveland, 1896–1901) for her *Early Narratives of the Northwest, 1634–1699*, from which is taken Jean Claude Allouez's description of his mission to the Indians in the Green Bay area in 1669–1670. Allouez was a Jesuit who had spent seven years learning Indian languages and lore so that he could be an effective missionary. His reports show the work of a sensitive and expressive observer.

The second selection, again from Kellogg's *The French Régime in Wisconsin and the Northwest,* sums up the impact of the early missionaries on Wisconsin Indians. Additional materials may be found in the many collections of missionaries' writings. Useful biographies include *Samuel de Champlain, Father of New France* by Samuel Eliot Morrison (Boston, 1972); *Caesars of the Wilderness* by Grace Lee Nute (New York, 1943); *Jolliet: Some La Salle Journeys* by Jean Delanglez (Chicago, 1938); and *Marquette's Explorations: the Narratives Reexamined* by Raphael N. Hamilton (Madison, 1970).

Mission to the Wisconsin Indians, 1669–1670

JEAN CLAUDE ALLOUEZ

Of the Mission to the Ousaki.

The village of the Ousaki is the first where I began to give instruction. As soon as we were provided with a cabin there, I assembled

From Louise Phelps Kellogg, ed., *Early Narratives of the Northwest, 1634–1699* (New York, 1917), pp. 147–153. Reprinted by permission of Barnes & Noble Books, a division of Harper & Row, Publishers, Inc.

all the elders, to whom, after relating the news of the peace with the Iroquois, I expatiated on the purpose of my journey, which was naught else than their instruction. I explained to them the principal articles of our belief, which they heard with approval, appearing to me very well disposed toward Christianity. Oh, if we could succor them in their poverty, how flourishing our Church would be! The rest of that month, I labored for their instruction, and gave baptism to several sick children,—having the consolation of seeing one of these, some time afterward, leave the Church Militant, which had received him into the number of her children, to enter the Church Triumphant, there to sing eternally the mercies of God toward him, and to be an advocate for the conversion of the people of his nation.

Among those who had not heard about our mysteries were some irreligious persons, who made fun of them. God put into my mouth words wherewith to check them; and I hope that, strengthened by Grace, we shall, with time and patience, have the consolation of winning some of them to Jesus Christ. Those who are Christians have come punctually every Sunday to prayers and to instruction, where we have the *Pater* and *Ave* chanted in their language.

In the month of January I purposed to go and carry the Gospel to another village, but it was impossible for me to go and settle down among them. I tried to make up for this by frequent visits.

Of the Mission to the Pouteouatamis.

On the seventeenth of February I repaired to the village of the Pouteouatamis, which is eight leagues from this place, on the other side of the lake.[1] After walking all day without halting, we arrived there at sunset, sustained by some small bit of frozen meat that hunger made us eat. On the day after my arrival, they made us a present of all the fat of a bear, with many manifestations of affection.

On the nineteenth, I assembled the council, and, after relating the news, informed them of the purpose that had brought me to their country, reserving for the following day a fuller discourse on our religion. This I carried out with success and the divine blessing, causing them, of their own accord, to draw this conclusion, that, since the Faith was so necessary for avoiding Hell, they wished to pray, and hoped that I would procure them a missionary to instruct them, or else would myself stay and do them that kindness.

---

[1] The site of the Potawatomi village is thought to have been on the east shore of Green Bay, about six miles from the mouth of Fox River, not far from Point Sable. This seems to have been the village where Perrot also first encountered the Potawatomi.

In the days following, I visited all the cabins, and instructed the inmates very fully in private, with satisfaction on both sides. I had the consolation of conferring baptism there on two new-born babes and on a young man who was dying, who exhibited an excellent disposition.

On the twenty-third, we set out to return thence; but the wind, which froze our faces, and the snow, compelled us to halt, after we had gone two leagues, and to pass the night on the lake. On the following day, the severity of the cold having diminished, although very little, we continued our journey with much suffering. On my part, I had my nose frozen, and I had a fainting fit that compelled me to sit down on the ice, where I should have remained, my companions having gone on ahead, if, by a divine providence, I had not found in my handkerchief a clove, which gave me strength enough to reach the settlement.

At the opening of the month of March, the great thaws having begun, the savages broke up their settlements to go in quest of the means to sustain life, after being for some time pressed with hunger.

I was very sorry not to have been able to go through all the villages, by reason of the remoteness of some of them, and the little inclination of others to receive me. I resolved to try at least to establish Christianity firmly in a neighboring village, composed for the most part of Pouteouatamis. Calling the men together twice, I explained to them fully our mysteries and the obligation resting upon them to embrace our Faith; and that this was the sole reason that had brought me to their country in the autumn. They received very favorably all that I said to them, and I often visited them in their cabins, to inculcate in the inmates what I had taught them in public. I baptized some sick children there, and received great consolation in the assurance which certain persons gave me that, since hearing me five years ago at the Point of Saint Esprit, on Lake Superior, they had always invoked the true God. They said that they had been very appreciably protected by Him; that they had always succeeded in their hunting and fishing; that they had not been ill, and that, in their families, death did not occur so frequently as was usual before they adopted prayer. On another day, I taught the catechism to the girls and women, our cabin being entirely filled. These poor people are very well disposed, and show great good will; many of them question me on various matters, in order to receive instruction, propounding to me their difficulties, which arise only from their high idea of Christianity, and from their fear of not being able to fulfill its obligations. Our stay was not long, as hunger was pressing them, and they were forced to go in search of provisions. We withdrew full of consolation, praising and blessing God that His holy name had been respected, and the holy Faith well received, by these barbarian peoples.

On the 21st of that month, I took the sun's altitude, and found that this was about 46 degrees, 40 minutes; and its elevation from the pole, or the complement of the above, was about 43 degrees, 20 minutes.[2]

The ice did not break up here until the 12th of April, the winter having been extremely severe this year; and consequently navigation was much impeded.

On the 16th of April, I embarked to go and begin the mission to the Outagamis, a people of considerable note in all these regions. We slept at the head of the bay, at the mouth of the River des Puans, which we have named for Saint Francis.[3] On our way we saw clouds of swans, bustards, and ducks. The savages set snares for them at the head of the bay, where they catch as many as fifty in one night, this game seeking in autumn the wild oats that the wind has shaken off in the month of September.

On the 17th, we ascended the River Saint François, which is two, and sometimes three, arpents wide.[4] After proceeding four leagues, we found the village of the savages called Saky, whose people were beginning a work that well deserves to have its place here. From one bank of the river to the other they make a barricade by driving down large stakes in two brasses of water, so that there is a kind of bridge over the stream for the fishermen, who, with the help of a small weir, easily catch the sturgeon and every other kind of fish,—which this dam stops, although the water does not cease to flow between the stakes.[5] They call this contrivance *Mitihikan,* and it serves them during the spring and a part of the summer.

On the eighteenth we passed the portage called by the natives Kekaling,[6] our sailors dragging the canoe among rapids, while I walked on the river-bank, where I found apple-trees and vine-stocks in great numbers.

On the 19th, our sailors ascended the rapids for two leagues by the use of poles, and I went by land as far as the other portage,

[2]In 1902 a combined sun-dial and compass of French manufacture was found on the site of this village. It apparently dates from the seventeenth century, and on the reverse contains notes of the latitude of principal places in New France. It was with some similar instrument that Allouez took his observation. The true latitude is about 44° 31'.
[3]Fox River was first known as Rivière des Puans; after the removal of the Outagami or Fox Indians to its banks (about 1680) it acquired their name, which in varying forms it has since retained.
[4]The French arpent was an area a little larger than an acre, or about 220 feet square. The meaning is that the river is 400, or at times 600, feet wide.
[5]This primitive weir was at the rapids later called De Pere from the establishment there of the Jesuit mission. The place is now covered by a government dam.
[6]This rapid was at the site of the modern Kaukauna, which is a variation of the Indian name. In all early navigation of the Fox, these rapids had to be portaged.

which they call Ooukocitiming, that is to say, "the bank."[7] We observed on this same day the eclipse of the sun predicted by the astrologers, which lasted from noon until two o'clock; a third of the sun's disk, or nearly that, appeared to be eclipsed, the other two-thirds making a crescent.[8] We arrived in the evening at the entrance to Lake des Puans, which we have named Lake Saint François; it is about twelve leagues long and four wide, extends from the north-northeast to the south-southwest, and abounds in fish, but is uninhabited, on account of the Nadouecis, who are there held in fear.[9]

On the twentieth, which was Sunday, I said mass, after voyaging five or six leagues on the lake, after which we came to a river, flowing from a lake bordered with wild oats; this stream we followed, and found at the end of it the river that leads to the Outagamis, in one direction, and that which leads to the Machkoutenck, in the other. We entered this first stream, which flows from a lake;[10] there we saw two turkeys perched on a tree, male and female, resembling perfectly those of France—the same size, the same color, and the same cry. Bustards, ducks, swans, and geese are in great number on all these lakes and rivers, the wild oats, on which they live, attracting them thither. There are large and small stags, bears, and beavers in great abundance.

On the twenty-fourth, after turning and doubling several times in various lakes and rivers, we arrived at the village of the Outagamis.

This people came in crowds to meet us, in order to see, as they said, the Manitou, who was coming to their country. They accompanied us with respect as far as the door of the cabin, which we were made to enter.

This nation is renowned for being populous, the men who bear arms numbering more than four hundred; while the number of women and children there is the greater on account of the polygamy which prevails among them, each man having commonly four wives, some having six, and others as many as ten. Six large cabins of these poor people were put to rout this month of March by eighteen Iroquois from Tsonnontouan,[11] who, under the guidance of two fugitive Iroquois slaves of the Pouteouatamis, made an onslaught, and killed all the people, except thirty women whom they led away as captives. As the men were away hunting, they met

[7]Probably Grand Chute, at the site of the present city of Appleton.
[8]The solar eclipse of April 19, 1670, was total in the northernmost parts of North America. A description of the phenomena observed at Quebec occurs in this *Relation* just after the portion we extract.
[9]This lake still retains the tribal name Winnebago. It is the largest in Wisconsin, about thirty miles long by eleven miles at its widest part. The Nadouecis were the Sioux tribes.
[10]After crossing Lake Winnebago to the site of Oshkosh, the missionary entered upper Fox River; thence through Lake Butte des Morts, a widening of the stream, he reached the entrance of Wolf River, whose course he followed to the Outagami village.
[11]This is the Algonquian-French appellation of the Seneca tribe of the Iroquois confederacy.

with but little resistance, there being only six warriors left in the cabins, besides the women and children, who numbered a hundred or thereabout. This carnage was committed two days' journey from the place of our winter quarters, at the foot of the Lake of the Ilinioues, which is called Machihiganing.[12]

On the twenty-fifth, I called together the elders in a large assembly, with the purpose of giving them the first acquaintance with our mysteries. I began with the invocation of the Holy Ghost, to whom we had made our appeal during our journey, to pray for His blessing upon our labors. Then, when I had, by means of a present which I thought I ought to make them, dried the tears which the remembrance of the massacre perpetrated by the Iroquois caused them to shed, I explained to them the principal articles of our Faith, and made known the law and the commandments of God, the rewards promised to those that shall obey Him, and the punishments prepared by Him for those that shall not obey Him. They understood me without my having need of an interpreter, and that, too, with attention; but, oh, my God! what ideas and ways contrary to the Gospel these poor people have, and how much need there is of very powerful grace to conquer their hearts! They accept the unity and sovereignty of God, Creator of all things; for the rest, they have not a word to say.

An Outagami told me, in private, that his ancestor had come from Heaven, and that he had preached the unity and the sovereignty of a God who had made all the other gods; that he had assured them that he would go to Heaven after his death, where he should die no more; and that his body would not be found in the place where it had been buried, which was verified, said this Outagami, the body being no longer found where it had been put. These are fables which God uses for their salvation; for after the man had finished telling me everything, he added that he was dismissing all his wives, retaining only one, whom he could not change; and that he was resolved to obey me and pray to God. I hope that God will show him mercy. I tried to visit the people in their cabins, which are in very great number, sometimes for the purpose of instructing them in private, and at other times to go and carry them some little medicine, or, rather, something sweet for their little sick children, whom I was baptizing. Toward the end, they brought them to me voluntarily in the cabin where I lodged.

I spoke their language, in the assurance they gave me that they understood me; it is the same as that of the Satzi.[13] But alas, what difficulty they have in apprehending a law that is so opposed to all their customs!

[12]Lake Michigan. This Iroquois attack occurred near the site of Chicago.
[13]Misprint for Saki (Sauk).

Missionary Influence

LOUISE PHELPS KELLOGG

What were the causes of the decline in interest and enthusiasm, and the ultimate failure of the work begun with so much earnestness and supported with such zeal? In the first place, the interest in and enthusiasm for missionary effort suffered a sharp decline in France. This may have been due in part to the lack of the stimulus of the yearly volumes of *Jesuit Relations;* but the difficulty went deeper than that. The French crown was engaged in a struggle with the Papacy over the question of the regale, or the independence of the national church. The Jansenists, who were the strong opponents of Jesuitism, were very powerful in the latter half of the seventeenth century. Gallicanism was growing at the expense of Ultramontism. Fewer and fewer of the better class of French youths entered the Jesuit order; desire for sufferings and martyrdom in distant lands declined. The civil authorities of New France frequently deplored the lack of new missionaries. In 1683 only one arrived in Canada. The missions were poorly manned, and with the decline in numbers came a decline in the character and influence of the missionaries who did come. The missions became stereotyped; the tribes that had accepted Christianity brought their children to be baptized, occasionally attended mass and confession, but made no difference in their customary mode of life. Except by the token of a crucifix or a silver cross, a Christian savage was scarcely distinguishable from a pagan. For the Jesuit scheme did not involve civilizing the Indians. They did not as a rule encourage the use of the French language. As for the introduction of French customs and habits, they set their faces against these as a flint. The savages were to be maintained in their simplicity and ignorance, only to be taught to worship the true God.

This policy was opposed to the governmental plan for the native population. The French authorities advocated assimilation and civilization. They wanted the young Indians educated and taught to take their places in the body politic. The Jesuit opposition to this viewpoint, frequently covert, often declared, was one of the strongest reasons for the distrust of their order among the ablest of the Canadian governors and colonists. The Jesuits desired to preserve the West, especially, from exploitation, to cultivate their missions for the natives only, where the missionaries might rule supreme and keep their flocks from the demoralizing influence of the

From *The French Régime in Wisconsin and the Northwest* (Madison, 1925), pp. 172–178. Footnotes in the original omitted. Reprinted by permission of the State Historical Society of Wisconsin.

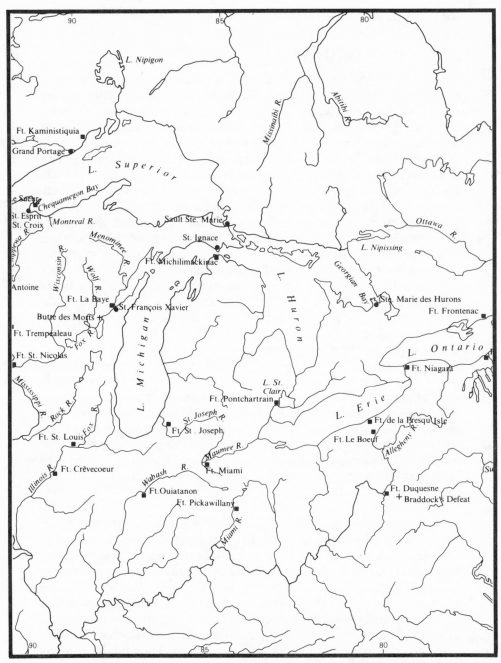

French settlements in the western Great Lakes area

lawless and licentious French traders, as well as from the domination of the French commandants. In other words, they wished to make a Paraguay of the great central valley of North America, an Indian kingdom wherein the missionaries would rule supreme.

There is no doubt that the missionaries had just cause of complaint of the debauchery introduced by the white traders among the simple savages. It was the same tale as that of missions everywhere; the white men's vices and the white men's liquor did more harm to the aborigines than all the teachings of the missionaries could do good. To their credit be it said, that the Jesuits everywhere and unalterably opposed the liquor traffic, the licentiousness of the *coureurs de bois,* and the unjust exploitation of the Indians by the traders. No doubt these conditions were great hindrances to the success of the western missions. But the failure had a deeper cause, in the character of the northwestern Indians and in their resistance to change and influence.

The Indian was very proud and independent, and was deeply satisfied with his own condition, customs, and beliefs. He showed no desire for imitation of a higher civilization, nor envy for the white man's mode of life. His invariable reply was that the Great Spirit had made the white man and the red man different; that what was good for the former was not good for the latter; let each go his separate way and preserve his own traditions. The missionaries, unable to influence the chiefs and warriors, turned to the women and children. Their reports are full of the piety of the young women and girls. This only increased the distance between the "black robe" and the men of the tribe. Their ideals were incompatible; every boy wished to become a great warrior; hatred of enemies was the highest tribal virtue; meekness and obedience were scorned. Even small children were not corrected, in order that they might grow up self-dependent and lead a free existence.

To the Indian the missionary was always a mystery; with the white trader who brought him goods and mingled with him on terms of equality he made friends. The trader's motives he understood and as a rule respected. The "black robe," on the other hand, was a being aloof. Try as he might he could obtain no comradeship with the Indian. The latter's complacency with his own manners and mode of life, especially with his religious conceptions, erected a barrier between him and this mysterious personage who made strange signs over dying babies, devoted hours to saying mass and to reading books the Indian could not understand. He felt certain that there must be some sinister motive in the conduct of this unasked-for guest. The missionary's meekness and patience only increased the Indian's contempt. Dislike and distrust either resulted in indifference and neglect or quickened into persecution. Seldom did the missionary gain any influence in the Indian councils; when he did it was as a white man, a messenger of Onontio, not as a "black robe," a servant of the white man's manitou. Thus the very virtues of each group rendered them contemptible to the other. The ideals of the North American Indian and the French Jesuit were incompatible; the former could not yield without denial of his highest motives. Thus the Jesuit never became in the Great Lakes region the father and leader of a band of faithful neophytes, as did the missionaries of South America and Mexico. The tribes most docile to missionary training, such as the Illinois, lost their manliness and sank in the aboriginal scale until they became the prey of more virile enemies and are now extinct. Some tribes, however, such as the Hurons and the mission Iroquois, retained their warlike qualities while nominally following Christian ceremonies. "Praying Indians," as they were called, they never became docile to missionary dictation.

What the missions might have become if continued as they were begun, by high-souled men of commanding genius, we cannot say; the red men might have been elevated to the Christian standard by substituting milder qualities for their outstanding barbaric virtues. As it was, the fierce independence and proud complacency of the Wisconsin tribesmen proved a barrier which the Jesuits could not overpass. The missions came and went, and the religion of the tribesmen was comparatively unchanged.

Not only the characteristics but the migrations of the Indians contributed to this result. La Salle in 1680 and Cadillac in 1701 changed the Indian geography of the Northwest. The Miami and Mascouten left Wisconsin forever; the Potawatomi moved south and east around Lake Michigan. At Mackinac but a remnant of the tribesmen that visited the chapels of St. Ignace remained at that place. The Fox wars broke up the missions for the Sioux and closed the mission house at De Pere, finally leading to abandonment by the missionaries of what is now Wisconsin. None of the Wisconsin tribes became Christian. For a century after the withdrawal of the last Jesuit missionary from Green Bay, no messenger of the Christian faith ever visited that region.

Yet, with all this seeming failure, the Jesuit missions must not be called valueless. Granted that their influence on the Indians was not permanent; nevertheless, the presence of the Jesuits in the western country tended toward civilization. As chaplains for the garrisons and the French expeditionary forces they filled a needed want; their presence acted as a restraint upon the lawless conduct of the French traders and *voyageurs*. At the time of treaty or council with the Indians they were frequently utilized as interpreters, and often as ambassadors from the governor to the tribesmen. The governors of the eighteenth century considered it good policy to maintain missionaries at these distant posts. They sometimes detected and reported incipient Indian conspiracies against French sovereignty. In a few cases their influence was sufficient to counteract these movements and to restrain the tribes within the French alliance. As white population grew around the frontier posts, the Jesuits gave to these settlers pastoral care, marrying, baptizing, and burying these people, even educating their children and acting as their guardians.

For present-day historians the reports of these trained and educated observers are invaluable. Their writings form the basis of our knowledge of Indian ethnology and linguistics; their descriptions are our best sources for primitive Wisconsin; even their scientific observations of eclipses, parhelia, tides, flora, and fauna are valuable. In map making many of these men were highly trained; their descriptions first disclosed our region to the world of geographers and savants, their enthusiastic accounts made France aware of the value of her possession on the upper lakes. Without the Jesuits our knowledge of early Wisconsin history would be fragmentary.

We are also indebted to them for examples of pure lives nobly devoted to an unselfish purpose. Whatever we of today think of their methods or their results, there is but one verdict for their motives. None would withhold the meed of praise for these men who, for the sake of conscience and a religious zeal, abandoned the comforts of civilization and plunged into a pathless wilderness, endured such hardships and sufferings as can hardly be imagined, and were prepared to lay down their lives rather than to be "disobedient to the heavenly vision." As long as courage, persistence, and zeal in a holy cause shall be considered noteworthy, so long will the story of the early missions of Wisconsin hold an honored place in its first history.

4: Fur Traders and Indians

Peter Pond, a New England trader, spent many years collecting furs from the Indians in Wisconsin. In his autobiography he describes his 1773–1774 trip up the Fox River, across the portage ("caring plas"), and down the Wisconsin to Prairie du Chien, and he records his experiences with the Winnebago ("Pewans") and Sauk ("Saukeas") Indians. Pond wrote phonetically. His unique spelling reflects his New England speech patterns; and because his capitalization is very erratic and internal punctuation nonexistent, double spaces have been used to indicate ends of sentences.

The second selection is Louis B. Porlier's account of a Menominee tribal memory related by the chief Sho-no-nee to illustrate how the predictions of Pontiac in 1763 had come true. The selection is also useful for its description of 1848 treaty negotiations with the Menominee. It is clear that the Menominee were frustrated by white pressure and unwilling to surrender more land.

A Trip Through Wisconsin, 1773–1774

PETER POND

at the End of two Days we aSended the fox River til we Came to a Villige which Lises on the East End of a Small Lake that Eties [empties] in to the fox River   these People are Cald Pewans [Puans] & the Lake By the Same Name   these People are Singelir from the

From "The Narrative of Peter Pond," in Charles Marvin Gates, ed., *Five Fur Traders of the Northwest*, pp. 34–42, reprint edition 1965 by the Minnesota Historical Society.

Rest of thare Nighbors thay Speake a Hard un Corth [uncouth] Langwige Scarst to be Larnt By Eney People thay will not aSosheat with or Convars with the other tribes Nor Intermarey among them I Enquird in to the Natral Histrey of these People when I was at Detroit of the Oldest and Most Entelaget french men Who had Bin aquanted with them for Meney Years the Information amounted to this that thay formely Lived west of ye Miseiarey [Missouri] River that thay Had Entarnal Disputes among themsel[ves] and Dispute with the Nations about them at Length thiare Nighber In Grat Numbers fel apon them and what was Saved flead acros the Misesurea to ye [e]astward and Over the Massappey and on to this Lake whare thay now live thare thay met with a tribe of Indans Who Suferd them to Seat Doun in it was as is Suposed the fox Nation who leved Near them the foxis was Drove from Detroit for thare Misbehaver which ware a proper People to aSist tham in thare flite I Beleve most of it thay are Insalent to this Day and Incline-ing Cheaterey thay will if thay Can Git Creadeat from the trader in the fall of ye Year to Pay in the Spring after thay Have made thare Hunt But When you mete them in Spring and Know them Parsen-eley ask for your Pay and thay will Speake in thare one Langwege if thay Speake at all Which is not to be understud or Other wase thay will Look Sulkey and Make you no answer and you lous your Dept [debt?] I was at Mackenac when Capt George Turnbull Cumanded Preaves to the aMarecan Reverlution and thare Came in a Cheafe with a Small Band of these[1] he Held a Counsel with them But he Could[not] Git an Intarpreter in the Plase that UndarStud them at Length the Captn Said that he Had a mind to sand for an Old Highland Solger that Spoke Leatels But the Hars[h] Langwege Perhaps he mite understand for it Sounded Much Like it the Land about them on the Lake is Exalant thar women Rase Corn & Beens Punkpins &c But the Lake aford no Varietey of fish thare wood Produse Sum Rabits & Partrageis a Small Quantatey of Vensen thay Live in a Close Connection among them selves We made But a Small Stay Hear and Past a Small Distans on this Lake and Entard the fox River a gane Which Leads up to the Cairing Plase of Ouiconstan [Wisconsin] we asendead that River til we Cam to a High Pece of Groand Whare that Nation yous to Entair thar Dead whin thay Lived in that Part[2] we stopt hear a while finding Sum of

[1]The period of Captain Turnbull's service as commandant of the post at Mackinac is not clear. He was sent to Detroit in 1766, where he remained in charge for three years, and apparently went from Detroit to Mackinac. Wisconsin Historical Collections, 18:312n.

[2]In the latter years of the seventeenth century the Fox Indians left their home on the upper Wolf River and built a village at this spot, near the site of the present Butte des Morts, Wisconsin. It is believed that the great mound found there was erected to cover the warriors, Foxes and Sauks, who were slain in the Battle of Butte des Morts (1733), an important engagement of the Second Fox War. Kellogg, *French Régime*, pp. 205, 332.

that Nation on the Spot who Came thare to Pay yare Resepct to thar Departed frend   thay Had a small Cag of Rum and seat Around the Grave thay fild thar Callemeat [calumet] and Began thare Saremony By Pinting the Stem of the Pipe upward then giveing it a turn in thare and then toward ye head of the Grave then East & West North & South after which thay smoake it out and fild it a Gane & Lade [it] By   then thay toock Sum Rum Out of the Cag in a Small Bark Vessel and Pord it on the Head of the Grave By Way of giveing it to thare Departed Brother   then thay all Drank them Selves Lit the Pipe Smokd and seam to Injoie themselves Verey well   thay Repeated this till thay the Sperit Began to Operrate and thare harts Began to Soffon   then thay Began to Sing a Song or two But at the End of Everey Song thay Soffend the Clay   after Sum tim Had Relapst the Cag hat Bin Blead often   thay Began to Repete the Saisfaction thay had with that frind while he was with them and How fond he was of his frinds while he Could Git a Cag of Rum and how thay youst to Injoy it togather   thay amused them selves in this manner til thay all fell a Crying and a woful Nois thay Mad for a while til thay thought wiseley that thay Could not Bring him Back and it would not Due to Greve two much that an application to the Cag was the Best way to Dround Sorrow & Wash away Greafe   The Moshan was sun Put in Execution and all Began to be marey as a Partey Could Bea   thay Contineued til Near Nite   Rite wen thay ware More then Half Drunk the men began to aproach the femals and Chat frelay and apearantly frindley   at Length thay Begin to Lean on Each other Cis & apeard Virey amoras   at Length two would Steapt a Sid in ye Eag [edge] of the Bushis   Prasently two more would Steap of But I Could Obsarve Clearley this Bisnes was first Pusht on By the women who mad thare Viseat to the Dead a Verey Pleaseing one in thare way   Wone of them who was Quit Drunk as I was By [my] Self Seating on the Ground obsarveing thare Saremones Came to me and ask me to take Share of Her Bountey in the Eag of the Bushis But I thought it was time to Quit and went about Half a mile up the Rive[r] to my Caneuees whare My men was Incampt But the Indans Neaver Came Nigh us thar the Men Menshan that thre[e] of the Women had bin at the Camp In the Night in Quest of Imploy; the nest Morning we Praseaded up the River which was Verey Sarpentine indea [indeed] till we Came to a Shallo Lake whare you Could Sea no water But Just in the Caneu track the Wild Oates was so thick that the Indans Could Scarse Git one of thare Small Canues into it to Geather it and the Wild Ducks Whe[n] thay Ris Maed a nois like thund[er]   we Got as meney of them as we Chose fat and Good   we Incampt hear would not undertake to Cros til Morning the water was two Deap

to wade and ye Bottom Soft the Rode narrow that it toock the Most
of ye next Day to get about three Miles With our Large Cannewes
the track was so nare   Near nite we Got to Warm Ground whare
we Incampt and Rest[?] Well after the fateages [fatigues] of the
Day   the Next Day we Proseaded up the River which was Slack
water But Verey Sarpentine   ye Have to go two Miles with out
Geating fiftey yards ahead so winding But Just at nite we reacht
within Site of ye Caring [carrying] plas and Incampt   Next morning
Near non we arived and unLoded our Caneues & toock them out of
the water to Dry that thay mite be liter on the Caring Plase—   An
acount of the fox River and its Neghbering Cuntrey   A Long its
Shores from the Moath to the Peuans Lake is A good Navagation
One or two Small Rapeds from that Lake the Water up to the
Caring plase is Verey Gental But Varey Sarpentine   In Meney Parts
In Going three Miles you due not advans one   the Bank is all most
Leavel With the Water and the Madoes on Each Side are Clear of
wood to a Grate Distans and Cloth with a Good Sort of Grass   the
Ope[n]ings of this River W[h]ich are Cald Lakes But thay are no
more than Large Opening   [In] these Plaseis the water is aboat four
or five feet deap with a Soft Bottom   these Plaseis Produseis the
Grateest Qantateys of Wild Rise of which the Natives Geather Grat
Qantaties and Eat what thay Have Ocation for & Dispose of the
Remainder to People that Pas & Repass on thare trad   this Grane
Looks in its Groth & Stock & Ears Like Ry and the Grane is of the
Same Culler But Larger and Slimer   when it is Cleand fit for youse
thay Boile it as we Due Rise and Eat [it] with Bairs Greas and Suger
But the Greas thay ad as it is Bileing which Helps to Soffen it and
make it Brake in the Same maner as Rise   when thay take it out of
thare Cittels [kettles] for yous thay ad a Lettle suger and it [is] Eaten
with fres Vonsen or fowls   we yoused it in the Room of Rise and it
Did verey well as a Substatute for that Grane   as it Busts it tarns
Out Parfectly White as Rise   Back from this River the Lands are as
Good as Can be Conseaved and Good timber But not Overthick   it
is Proverbel that the fires Which Ran th[r]ew these woo[d]s and
Meadoes Stops the Groth of ye wood and Destroise Small wood   I
Have Menshand the Vast Numbers of Wild Ducks which faten on
ye Wild Rise Eaverey fall   it would Sound two much Like a travelers Storey to Say What I Rearley Beleve from what I Have Sean
you Can Parchis them Verey Cheape at the Rate of two Pens Per
pese   if you Par[fer] Shuteing them your Self you may Kill what you
Plese—   An acound of the Portage of Osisconstan   the South End
of this Caring plase is Verey Leavel But in wet wather it is Bad On
acount of the Mud & Water which is two thirds of a Mile and then
the Ground Riseis to a Considerabel Hith and Cloth with fine Open

Wood & a Hansum Varder [verdure]   this Spot is Abot the Senter
of ye Portage and take up about a Quorter Part of it   the North End
is Low flat and Subject to Weat   it was on this Spot that Old
Pinneshon a french Man Imposed apon Carve[r] Respecting the
Indan haveing a Rattel Snake at His Call which the Indand Could
order into a Box for that Purpas as a Peat [pet]³   this frenchman
was a Solder in the troops that ware stasond at the Elenoas [Il-
linois] he was a Sentanal A[t] the Mageasean of Pouder   he De-
sorted His Post & toock his Boat up the Miseeurea among the
Indans and Spant Maney years among them   he Larnt Meney
Langeweg and from Steap to Step He Got among the Mondans
[Mandans] whare he found Sum french traders who Belongd to the
french facterey at fort Lorain on the Read River⁴   this facterey
Belong to the french traders of Cannaday   those People toock Pinneshon to the facterey with them and the Concarn took him into
thare Sarvis til the Hole Cuntrey Was Giveen up to the English and
he then Came in to thare Sarvis   the french Strove to take him afor
His Desarson But fald   However thay Ordred him to be Hung in
Efagea [effigy] Which was Dun; this is the a Count he Gives of
himselvef   I Have Hurd it from his one Lips Meney times as he has
bin Relateing his advant[ure]s to Others   He found Carver on this
Spot Going on Dissoverey in an Obscur[?] Mananer without un-
dirstanding orther [either] french or Indan & full of Enquirey threw
his Man who Sarved him as an Enterprar thought it a Proper Oper-
tunetey to ad Sumthing more to his adventers and Make his Bost of
it after which I have Haird Menea times   it hirt Cairver much
hearing such things & Puting Confadens in them   While he is Correct [correct?] He Give a Good a Count of the Small Part of the
Westarn Cuntrey he Saw But when he a Leude to Hearsase he flies
from factes in two meney Instansis—   After Two Day Hard Laber
We Gits Our Canues over the Caring Plase with all our Goods and
Incamp on the Bank of the River Oisconston & Gumd Our Canues
fit to Desend that Rive[r]—⁵   A Bout Midday we Imbark   the

³Jonathan Carver is chiefly deserving of note as the author of a book that aroused tremendous interest in America among European readers and writers. This work, *Travels through
the Interior Parts of North America,* describing his journeys of 1766–67 and his winter
among the Sioux on the St. Peter's (Minnesota) River, was first published in 1778, and in
numerous editions thereafter. Carver's Journal of the expedition is in the British Museum.
The Minnesota Historical Society has a photostatic copy. "Old Pinnashon," in Thwaite's
opinion, was Pennesha George, a trader. See Wisconsin Historical Collections, 1:41; 3:261–
263.
⁴Fort la Reine, mentioned also by Macdonell, was built in 1738 by La Vérendrye. Situated at
Portage la Prairie on the Assiniboine River, it served as an outpost from which expeditions
reached the Mandan country on the Missouri. See Lawrence J. Burpee, ed., *Journals and
Letters of Pierre Gaultier de Varennes de la Vérendrye and His Sons* (Publications of the
Champlain Society, Vol. 16, Toronto, 1927), p. 10.
⁵The fur trader's canoe was made of large pieces of birch bark stretched over a frame of
cedar. The seams were stitched with wattap or spruce roots and rendered watertight by a

River is a Gentel Glideing Stream and a Considabel Distans to the
first Villeag which Lise on the Side North   the River Runs near west
from the Portag to the Misseppey   its a Gentel Glideing Stream, as
we Desended it we Saw Meneey Rattel Snakes Swiming a Cross it
and Kild them, the Next Day we aRived at the Villeag whare we
tarread two Days[6]   this Beaing the Last Part of Septr these People
had Eavery artickel of Eating in thare way In abandans—

I Shall Give Sum acount of these People and the Cuntrey—   these
People are Cald Saukeas   thay are of a Good Sise and Well Dis-
post   Les Inclind to tricks and Bad mannars then thare Nighbers
thay will take of the traders Goods on Creadeat in the fall for thare
youse In winter and Exept [for] Axedant thay Pay the Deapt [debt]
verey well for Indans I mite Have Sade Inliteand Or Sivelisd Indans
which are in General Made wors By the Opration   thare Villeage is
Bilt Cheafely with Plank thay Hugh of [o]ut of wood that is ye
uprite   the top is Caseh [cased?] Over with Strong Sapplens Suffis-
ant to Suport the Ruf and Coverd with Barks which Makes them a
tite ruf   Sum of thare Huts are Sixtey feet Long and Contanes
Saverl fammalyes   thay Rase a Platform on Each Side of thare Huts
a Bout two feet High & about five feet Brod on which thay Seat &
Sleap   thay have no flores But Bild thar fire on the Ground in the
Midel of the Hut and have a Hole threw the Ruf for the Smoke to
Pas   In the fall of ye Year thay Leave these Huts and Go into the
Woods in Quest of Game and Return in the Spring to thare Huts
befou[r] Planting tim   the women Rase Grat Crop of Corn Been
Pumkens—Potatoes Millans and artickels   the Land is E[x]alant &
Clear of wood Sum Distans from the Villeage   thare [are] Sum
Hundreds of InHabbatan   thare amusements are Singing Daning
Smokeing matches Gameing and Feasting Drinking Playing the Slite
of Hand Hunting & thay are famas in Mageack   Thay are Not
Verey Gellas [jealous] of thare women   In Genaral the women find
Meanes to Grattafy themSelves with out Censent of the men   the
Men often jion war parteies with Other nations and Go aganst the
Indans on the Miseeure and west of that   Sume time thay Go Near
St Fee [Santa Fe] in New Maxeco and Bring with them Spanish
Horseis; I have Sean Meney of them   the River aford But a fue fish

---

generous application of gum, a resinous substance made from pine pitch. The canoes received
very hard usage and required gumming at frequent intervals.

[6]Carver reports this Sauk village as the largest Indian town he ever saw. Boasting a population of three hundred warriors, the settlement contained eighty large buildings besides a
number of farmhouses in the fields for the convenience of the squaws. The town was situated
on the north side of the Wisconsin River about forty miles below the end of the portage. It
was built in the decade between 1740 and 1750, and was occupied until the end of the
Revolutionary period, when a fear of the Chippewa drove the inhabitants to other homes
near the Mississippi. Carver's Journal; Louise P. Kellogg in Wisconsin Historical Society
Proceedings, 1907, pp. 143, 181; Wisconsin Historical Collections, 12:80.

thare woods aford Partragis a fue Rabeat Bairs & Deear are Plentey In thare Seasons, wild foul they have fue thare Religan is Like Most of the tribes thay a Low thare is two Sperits One Goods Who Dwelve a Bove the Clouds Superintends over all and helps to all the Good things we have and Can Bring Sicknes on us if He pleaseis and another Bad one who dwelves in the fire and air Eaverey whare among m[en] & Sumtimes Dose Mischef to Mankind Cortship & Mareages—[*two words illegible*] At Night when these People are Seating Round thare fiuer [fire] the Elderly one will be teling what thay Have Sean and Hard or Perhaps thay may be on Sum Intrest[ing] Subg[ec]t the famley are lis[ten]ing if thare be aney Young Garle in this Lodg or hut that any Man of a Differan Hut Has a Likeing for he will Seat among the Parson of his Arrant [errand] Being Prasent hea will watch an Opertunety & through [throw] a Small Stick at Hair if She Looks up with a Smile it is a Good Omen he Repets a Sacond tim Perhaps ye Garle will Return the Stick the Simtam [symptoms] ar Still Groing Stronger and when thay think Proper to Ly Doun to Slepe Each Parson Raps himself up in his One Blanket he takes Notis whar the Garl Seats for thare [she] sleep when all the famaley are Qui[e]t and Perhaps a Sleap he Slips Soffely in to Hut and Seats himself Down By her Side PresantLey he will Begin to Lift Her Blanket in a Soft maner Perhaps she may twish it Out of his hand with a Sort of a Sie & Snore to Gather But this is no Kiling Matter he Seats a while and Makes a Sacond Atempt She May Perhaps Hold the Blankead Doun Slitely at Length She turns Over with a Sith and Quits the Hold of the Blanket He then Creapes under and Geats as Close as he Can til allmost and than of[f] to his one Hut this Meathard [method] is Practest a Short [time] and then ye yong Indan will Go ahanting and [if] he is Luckey to Git meat he Cums and Informs the famely of it and whare it is he Brengs the tung and hart with him and thay Seat of after the Meat and Bring it Home this Plesis [pleases] and he Begins to Gro Bold in the famerly the Garl after that will not Refuse him under the Blanket he Will then Perhaps Stay about the famerley a Year and Hunt for the Old father But in this Intram he Gives his Consent that thay may Sleap toogther and when thay Begin to have Children thay Save what thay Can git for thare One youse and Perhaps Live In a Hut apart

Capture of Mackinaw, 1763: A Menominee Tradition

LOUIS B. PORLIER

On the 14th of October, 1848, Hon. William Medill, Commissioner of Indian Affairs, called a council at Poygan, Wisconsin, to negotiate a treaty with the Menomonee tribe of Indians. H. S. Baird was appointed Secretary to the Commissioner. On the morning of the day of the meeting, Osh-kosh came to our tent and said to Augustin Grignon, Sr., "I have been notified to attend the council; will you go with me?" Mr. Grignon replied that he would, and they both started towards the council-house. Immediately after I told Augustin Grignon, Jr. to call our men to put up our shanty so as to be in readiness for the annuity payment, which was to take place immediately after the treaty should be concluded. As soon as the shanty was up so they could get along without me, I told the younger Grignon that I was going over to listen to the council, and started towards the council-house.

Just before reaching the place of assembly, I saw Sho-no-nee, or Silver—one of the principal Menomonee chiefs, coming out of the council-house, and walking towards a group of Indians who were gathered at a short distance away. I followed him thither, as I knew that he would relate what had been said in the council. He seated himself on a log and they all thronged close around him, anxious to ascertain what was the business of the Commissioner.

In a laughing manner he replied: "You don't expect he has come to decorate your ears with silver ear-bobs? No, he comes here simply to get the balance of our country! Not being satisfied with what he has already obtained, he proposes to remove us across the Mississippi, which country he represents to be far better than ours; he says there is an abundance of all kinds of game there; that the lakes and the rivers are full of fish and wild rice." Several of those who were listening, here interrupted the speaker with evident anxiety, saying, "Why don't he go himself and live in such a fine country, where there is an abundance of everything? He is mistaken! and you ought to have told him at once not to say any more about it." Sho-no-nee replied: "That is what we did; but you know how the Ke-che-mo-co-man (or the Great Knife, as they name the American) never gets rebuked at a refusal; but will persist, and try over and over again till he accomplishes his purpose. I left our chief Osh-kosh

From Louis B. Porlier, "Capture of Mackinaw, 1763—A Menominee Tradition," *Wisconsin Historical Collections*, VIII (Madison, 1879), 227–231. Some footnotes in the original have been omitted.

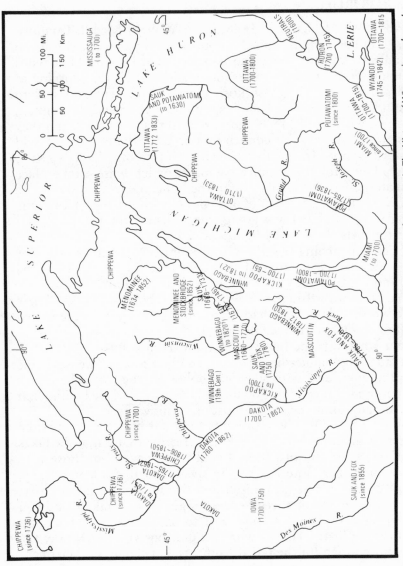

Indian tribes of the western Great Lakes area

Reprinted, with permission, from a map in The History of Wisconsin, volume I, copyrighted in 1973 by the State Historical Society of Wisconsin

to debate with him, and I will not adhere to any proposition he may make."

Sho-no-nee then made running remarks about different tribes of Indians who had been removed from their country to distant lands, referring especially to the Winnebagoes and the Pottowatamies; and in winding up his remarks, said: "We know by those who have come back from the country whither they have been removed to what dangers they are exposed;" and, after a pause, he added: "It is but the result of what Pontiac had foreseen and foretold." The by-standers inquired who Pontiac was, and what he had foreseen. Sho-no-nee then resumed by saying: "Pontiac lived before my time; but I will simply state to you what my ancestors have related to me in regard to him. He was, they told me, a noble-minded Indian; he had come to Milwaukee at one time,[1] and then and there had assembled different tribes of Indians, and addressed them as follows:

"My Friends! I have come here to consult you in behalf of our common cause. When the white man came across the ocean, and landed on our shores, he spoke with a sweet and silver-tongued mouth, saying that we had large possessions of land, and that he had none, and asked to be permitted to settle in a corner, and live with us like brothers. We received and admitted them as such; and they lived true to their proposition and promise, until they had gained strength. They then commenced to encroach upon us more and more. Their purpose is plain to me—that they will continue to encroach upon us, until they discover that they have sufficient power to remove us from our country to a distant land, where we will be confronted with all kinds of danger, and perhaps be annihilated. The time is not far distant when we shall be placed in a critical position. It is now in our power to force the whites back to their original settlements. We must *all join in one common cause,* and sweep the white men from our country, and then we shall live happy, and we shall have nothing more to do with the hated race. We shall have no unsatisfied desires, as we have an abundance of game in our forests—our rivers and lakes are teeming with all kinds of fish, fowl and wild rice—we shall live as did our forefathers; we shall with our furs and skins obtain all necessary supplies, and—be happy."

The inquiry was then made, what answer did Pontiac receive from the assembled nations. "Well," said Sho-no-nee, "with the

---

[1]See Grignon's *Recollections, Wis. Hist. Colls.,* III., 226, for some reference to this grand Milwaukee assemblage early in 1763. Sho-no-nee's tradition shows that Pontiac was its master-spirit, and probably his influence and eloquence so alienated those Indians from the English, that Col. De Peyster, sixteen years thereafter, denominated them as "those renegades of Milwaukee—a horrid set of refractory Indians."

exception of the Menomonees, they all joined with him, and placed themselves in readiness to take the war-path at the first warning. Mackinaw was the first point to be attacked; and after its capture, messengers were to be sent eastward, and the successive attacks would have been like a large prairie set on fire, with a strong wind spreading the flames in every direction, making the whole one solid mass of fire, destroying everything before it as it rushes along! And this would have been the result; but you are familiar with our customs in regard to incantations. The spirit that gave the power to the war-chief, required of him to make a sacrifice of the officers captured at Mackinaw, before taking any further step. The Chippewa war-chief[2] succeeded in capturing the post of Mackinaw; but before he could make the sacrifice, *the Bravest of the Brave* came and snatched the officers out of his hands—and the war-chief squatted down, foiled in his purpose." It was then asked, who was this *Bravest of the Brave?*—and why did the war-chief not stand his ground, and prevent him from rescuing the officers? "The Bravest of the Brave," said Sho-no-nee, "was Au-ke-win-ge-ke-taw-so, or Defender of his Country—Charles Langlade, the grand-father of Augustin Grignon—and he was too well known all over the western world for any one to dare oppose him."

The Poygan Council continued day after day. On the morning of the fourth day, H. S. Baird saddled his horse, and, as soon as he had had his breakfast, started for Green Bay as angry as he well could be, having lost all hopes that the treaty could be made. The vacancy of Secretary was filled by the appointment of Morgan L. Martin; and, when the council was adjourned at the close of the day, Mr. Martin came to our tent and said: "Mr. Porlier, I wish you would tell Mr. Grignon that he had better advise the chiefs to make a treaty while they have an opportunity. They ought to make the most advantageous one they can; for if they should persist in refusing to treat, the President can at his pleasure order their removal, without giving them another chance to make a treaty, and then it would be optional with him whether to give them anything or nothing, because it is provided in the existing treaty, that whenever the President should want their lands, they should relinquish their title— they only possessing such lands as hunting-grounds. The President has now sent a Commissioner to make a treaty, and they ought to embrace the opportunity to make the most favorable one they can; it is a matter of course that the Commissioner cannot give beyond his instructions, but he can give to the utmost limit."

[2]See Vol. VII., *Wis. Hist. Colls.,* pp. 188–91, for evidence that Match-e-ke-wis was the Chippewa chief who captured Mackinaw in 1763.

I told Mr. Grignon what Mr. Martin had advised. "Well," said Mr. Grignon, "tell Mr. Martin I will attend to it." Then Mr. Martin told me to go and see Osh-kosh, and to tell him that he wanted to see him on business, and further requested me at the same time to go and see the chiefs of the Shawano band, and state to them what Mr. Martin had said. I went on my mission, and after having given a full statement of Mr. Martin's views and advice, to the Shawano band, I suggested that they should call on the rest of the chiefs and have a consultation on the subject, and to do their best to promote the welfare of their nation, and to be prepared to meet the Commissioner in council the next day. They accordingly met in council with the Commissioner, and in the course of the day the treaty was concluded.

Chapter II
CIVILIZATION ENCROACHES

In 1775 the American colonies of Great Britain revolted for reasons that were not appreciated in the western wilderness. The Indians and French-Canadian fur-trapping families were content with British control of the area. Although no battles took place in Wisconsin, both sides recruited soldiers and sought allies among the inhabitants. It was common for allegiances to shift depending on the most persuasive gifts and promises. After the entry of the Spanish and French into the war on the side of the Americans, their representatives in Spanish Louisiana began to appeal to the Indian tribes also.

The end of the war left Wisconsin in American hands but not in its control; the British continued to man the forts inside the new northern border and to carry on the fur trade. In Wisconsin the trade was conducted by loose alliances of traders who knew the geography and had established good relations with the Indians by learning their languages and marrying into their tribes.

When the War of 1812 broke out, American troops ascended the Mississippi from St. Louis to build a fort at Prairie du Chien. A quickly assembled British army of engagés and Indians marched from Green Bay to take the fort. The ensuing battle was the only one fought in Wisconsin during the War of 1812. American Fort Shelby became British Fort McKay until the end of the war, when it was destroyed following British evacuation.

Recognizing the need for more control in the Northwest, the American government built forts at Green Bay and Prairie du Chien after that war. Troops and Indian agents had the difficult tasks of maintaining peace between tribes, regulating the fur trade, and shielding the Indians from predatory whites. The military frontier was a short but influential phase in Wisconsin history.

1: The American Revolution

Chief Black Bird, a Potawatomi from the western shore of Lake Michigan, was allied with the Americans and Spanish during the Revolutionary War, and his participation was extremely troublesome to the British. In the first selection Robert G. Carroon describes his activities. The second selection is a letter written in 1781 by Francisco Cruzat, the Spanish lieutenant governor of Upper Louisiana, exhorting the Sauk and Fox Indians to remain allies of Spain—and therefore of the Americans.

Chief Black Bird

ROBERT G. CARROON

The major figure in Milwaukee during the American Revolution was the Potawatomie chief known to his fellow tribesmen as Siggenauk, to the French as Le Tourneau, to the Spanish as El Heturno, and to the British and Americans as Black Bird. He was a firm ally of the Spanish and the Americans. He was personally acquainted with Francisco Cruzat, Spanish commandant at St. Louis, as well as the leader of the American forces in the West, George Rogers Clark, and was considered important enough to be mentioned in a report from Governor Patrick Henry to the Virginia delegation in Congress.

From Robert G. Carroon, "Milwaukee and the American Revolution," *Historical Messenger,* XXIX (Winter 1973), 118–142. Footnotes in the original omitted. Reprinted by permission of the Milwaukee County Historical Society.

Black Bird was present at the major councils of the Spanish and Americans and was the instigator of at least two engagements with the British and their Indian allies. So annoying were his activities on behalf of the "Bostonniens" (Bostonais or Americans) that the British made a concerted attempt to capture him and put an end to his machinations.

The headquarters of Black Bird during the American Revolution was the village of Potawatomies and other mixed tribes located on the bank of the Milwaukee River adjacent to the place where it entered Lake Michigan. The site was an important center for the fur trade and had been occupied by the Indians at least since 1674, when it was visited by Father Marquette; French traders were there by 1741 and the British by 1764. The Potawatomie settlement of Milwaukee apparently was the result of an emigration from a village near St. Joseph's (present day Niles, Michigan) in about 1769.

. . . .

The British themselves were fully aware of the enmity of the Milwaukeeans. Supplies were not plentiful at Michilimackinac, and the Indians were being urged to bring in corn and other provisions. But so pronounced was the enmity of the Indians that the British did not dare venture among them. "The Milwaky Indians," wrote Captain John Mompesson, commander of the troops at Michilimackinac under Sinclair, to De Peyster, "have not brought in any, neither can a trader be allowed to go amongst them, as they are at present not behaving in a proper manner." Black Bird was not content, however, to simply deny the British supplies; he intended, before the winter set in, to join in a raid to take what supplies the British did have. His resistance to the British also had the effect of discouraging further military efforts on their part after the St. Louis debacle. Francisco Cruzat wrote to Bernardo de Galvez, Governor of Louisiana, that there had been dissension among the British commanders and that, "These dissensions and the courageous resistance made against Langlade by the Indians El Heturno [Black Bird] and Naguihuen were responsible for the abandonment of the plan they had made to attack us at the time of the corn harvest." So apprehensive did the British become of a possible attack on Michilimackinac that they proceeded to move the fort from the mainland to Mackinac Island.

. . . .

This final campaign of the Milwaukee Indians in the American Revolution was by far their most ambitious. The Indians had planned for some time to make a major effort against the British.

The Milwaukee Chief, Naquiguen, had arrived in St. Louis by the second week in November, 1780, informing the Spanish that those Indians who had previously opposed them, particularly in the unsuccessful attack on St. Louis the previous May, were now ready to ally themselves with the Spanish, French, and Americans.

Black Bird arrived in St. Louis the day after Christmas with the news of the defeat of the French under Hamelin at St. Joseph's. The Chief urged the Spanish to mount an immediate attack on St. Joseph's, even though it was the dead of winter. He probably did this for at least two reasons. First, the defeat of Hamelin would be most embarrassing to him as the leader of pro-ally element in the Potawatomie tribe, and if he was to maintain his standing in the tribe, immediate retaliation was necessary. Secondly, Black Bird was fully aware of the well-stocked supply depot in St. Joseph's, and the temptation to seize this booty (accompanied by a sufficient force to retain it this time) was a great one. Black Bird and Naquiguen urged the Spanish to commence operations at once. "The savage . . . nations from Milwaukee to here, with whom I have been able to speak are favorably disposed to us," wrote Senor Malliet to Cruzat.

Francisco Cruzat was impressed by Black Bird's proposals and he made it quite clear that it was the Chief's initiative that influenced his decision to attack St. Joseph's. In reporting his action to Governor Galvez at New Orleans, Cruzat pointed out that he was forced to mount an attack on the British post because "not to have consented to the petition of El Heturno and Naquiguen would have been to demonstrate to them our inadequate forces" which might have resulted in the Indians changing sides and allying themselves with the British. An additional reason for the attack at this time, Cruzat maintained, was to deprive the British of supplies and to terrorize their Indian allies.

The detachment, consisting of sixty-five Spanish soldiers and sixty Indians, set out from St. Louis on January 2, 1781. Ascending the Mississippi and Illinois rivers, they gathered additional Indians and militia on the way. On January 20 the little army, commanded by Don Eugenio Purre and Black Bird, reached Lake Peoria, which they discovered to be frozen over. Hiding their canoes and caching those provisions they could not carry, the force marched overland for three hundred miles. They reached the bank of the St. Joseph River, opposite the fort and settlement, on the evening of February 11. The detachment remained hidden and sent in a Potawatomie scout named Laje, to caution the village Indians against aiding the British in the forthcoming attack. At seven o'clock the following morning the force crossed the frozen river on the ice and seized the fort. Complete surprise was achieved and not a man was lost. The garrison was made prisoner, the Spanish flag was run up, a proclamation of annexation was read, and the supplies found at the post were distributed among the rejoicing Indians. After occupying St. Joseph's for twenty-four hours the detachment marched out and made their way back to the Illinois reaching St. Louis on March 6, 1781. "The great chiefs El Heturno and Naquieguen, and all the Indians of their nations who went on the expedition, behaved so well," wrote Cruzat to Don Estevan Miro, Galvez's successor as Governor of Louisiana, "that they gave further evidence of their friendly inclination toward the Spaniards, and showed themselves worthy of the confidence which they desire shall be placed in their affection and sincerity. This is the reason why I have always treated them and received them as they deserve and as the conditions of the time require. . . ."

The expedition was obviously a great success. The Spanish and Indians achieved their objectives without the loss of a man. The Indians secured both honor and booty, wiping out former reverses in both categories. The Spanish were able to use the incident of flying the flag and issuing a proclamation to advance a claim to the eastern shore of the Mississippi, although the claim was later disallowed at the peace conference in Paris.

. . . .

The British, for their part, raged against the Spanish and the Indians in general, and the Milwaukee chiefs in particular. In a council held at Detroit on March 11, 1781, between the British and the Potowatomies, the latter apologized for not preventing the capture of St. Joseph's, and their spokesman, Assimut, stated, "They came to St. Joseph's at a time that all the Indians were yet at their hunt, excepting a few young men who were not sufficient to oppose one hundred white People and Eighty Indians led by Seguinack and Makewine who deceived them by telling them that it was the Sentiment of the Indians in general to assist the French and Spaniards. . . ." To these representations De Peyster answered that they should pay no attention to the "sugar mouthed Spaniards," and furthermore, "do not be afraid to trouble the lands because there are Indians foolish enough to join them—If you are afraid, I am not—Therefore to prevent yourselves the affront return to St. Joseph's and bring me the chiefs Seguinac and Makewine, or I will find others from Michilimackinac to do it. Do you know that they are the outcasts of their Nations—I once bought those Runnagade Chiefs off in hopes that they would return to a sense of their duty I now determined no longer to spare them." These threats on the part of the British were to no avail, and no attempt was made to seize the Milwaukeeans.

Message to the Sauks and Foxes, 1781

LIEUTENANT GOVERNOR FRANCISCO CRUZAT

MY DEAR CHILDREN THE SAUKS AND FOXES!—I am happy to have seen, in my house, your two principal chiefs, HUISCONSIN and MITASSE, and I listened to their words, this beautiful and clear day, with much pleasure. I found my ears to hear what they said to me, in the name of all of you.

MY DEAR CHILDREN!—I beg you to listen to my words, in your turn. Open, then, to day, your ears! It is the Master of the World who speaks through my mouth. Look up to the sky! you shall see that it is blue, and that I am not a liar; that I have not a sweetened mouth to deceive you. I talk to you as a good father, who loves his children, and desires to see them happy.

You know your ancient fathers, the French, with whom you have grown up, and come out of the earth, have, in all ages, loved the red complexion, and have harmed them only to punish the foolish who had dipped their hands in the blood of the whites. Recall, then, well in your minds, my children, what the two grand chiefs, Messrs. MONTCALM and MARIN said before their death—to adhere to the same tree, that they had always held to. Although that tree was a little bent, caused by a storm that had passed through your lands, yet you will see it one day erect, its branches rise and spread above all other trees. That period has now come. The tree I speak of, is your ancient father, the French. You see, my children, that he is up, that he does not wish to see the blood of his children, the red skin, shed. He extends his hand to you, without fear. Yes, my children, your fathers, the French and the Spanish, have always been but one; as you have heard it said, so you now see it. Know, then, when you

From "Lieut. Gov. Cruzat's Message to the Sauks and Foxes," *Wisconsin Historical Collections*, III (Madison, 1857), 504–505. Footnotes in the original omitted.

Courtesy of the Missouri Historical Society

Francisco Cruzat

shake hands with the French, you shake also with the Spanish; and when you shake hands with the Spanish, you also shake hands with the French—since those two nations are upon the earth to protect you, and to teach you the will of the Master of life. You well know, my children, that I have recommended you to remain quiet upon your lands, to provide for your wives and children, and not to take part in the war between the whites. I repeat again to day the same advice, remain quiet. I do not wish to see your blood flow into your rivers. But I wish that the waters of the Mississippi should remain clear and blue, and its channel be without any obstruction. Then, my children, be quiet. When you hear any thing evil said of your brethren the French and the Spaniards, come and tell me, as you have promised me. You shall have in me a good father, who will receive and embrace you, so long as you shall remain his children.

Your True Father, the Spaniard,   CRUZAT.
At St. Louis, of the Illinois, Nov. 20, 1781.

2: War of 1812

In his reminiscences the fur trader Thomas Anderson tells his version of the capture of Fort Shelby at Prairie du Chien. He was clearly unimpressed with the abilities of the nominal leader of the force, Colonel McKay.

The second selection is a letter from William Puthuff, Indian agent at Mackinac, to his superior, Lewis Cass, Governor of the Michigan Territory. Puthuff described Indian sentiments concerning the recent war, the unrest encouraged by the British on Drummond Island, and his opinion of John Jacob Astor.

Reginald Horsman has written another account of the conflict in "Wisconsin and the War of 1812," *Wisconsin Magazine of History,* XLVI (Autumn 1962), 3–15.

The Capture of Fort Shelby

THOMAS G. ANDERSON

My boat was repaired, and about the twentieth of March, 1814, I left the river St. Peter's, with full intent to return to the trade, not, of course, knowing what a kind Providence had in store for me.

Arriving at Prairie du Chien, I, as usual, deposited such articles as I would require for the next Winter's trade; and after feasting eight or ten days at my friend, Mons. Brisbois', on thickened milk and sugar, I started for Mackinaw. It being early in the season, and hard

From "Personal Narrative of Capt. Thomas G. Anderson," *Wisconsin Historical Collections,* IX (Madison, 1882), 192–196. Footnotes in the original omitted.

Courtesy of the SHSW [WHi (D485) 9761]

Captain Thomas G. Anderson

work for the men to stem the strong current of the Ouisconsin river, I permitted them to go on leisurely, stopping along the sand banks to collect turtles' eggs, which were excellent eating, and to kill rattle-snakes, some of which were very beautiful to behold—at a respectful distance—being about four feet long, with skin of a bright golden color, interspersed with ebony black heart-shaped spots.

But the eating of turtle's eggs was, after a few days, brought to a sudden termination. These eggs are somewhat less in size than a pigeon's. My cook brought me, as usual, a dozen for breakfast. On opening the first one, I observed something coiled in it, like a black hair; but how a hair could get inside of an egg, I could not make out. So I summoned the men to examine the phenomenon. They at once called out, "a snake." I was not aware till then that turtles' and rattlesnakes' eggs were quite similar; and that they both made their deposits in the sand, for the warmth of the sun to hatch; nor did I know how many young snakes I may have eaten. We had collected of the mixed kinds, and eaten at least a peck a day for the last five days, and I now regretted the discovery, for they were very good. But our stomachs revolted against them for further indulgence.

I spent a few days at Green Bay, with my friend, John Lawe. In short, I so dawdled away my time that nearly all the traders had arrived, and I did not reach Mackinaw until about the tenth of June. I made a splendid return: three hundred and thirty buffalo robes, and ten packs of beaver and other furs and peltries. For the robes I was offered, by the commanding officer of the fort, ten dollars each; but I had received a circular from my equipper in Montreal, Touissant Portier, advising me not to sell before his arrival, as he would give the highest market price.

The garrison at Mackinaw was commanded by Lieut. Col. Robert McDouall, of the Glengaries, with detachments of the Royal veterans, the Eighty-First and Newfound-land regiments, and a Sergeant's command of the Royal artillery. Being a poor Indian trader, it was, of course, not my business to seek acquaintance with such great men as army officers. However, before the end of a week after my arrival, I was roused up one morning by a gentleman, who informed me that two men in a little bark canoe had just arrived express from Prairie Chien, with the information that three boat loads of American soldiers had arrived there, and were building a fort at that place.

I jumped up, exclaiming, "We must go and take the fort." I dressed, and, on reaching the street, I found all astir, and alive to my views. I said: "All those who are willing to go, give me your

names." By sun-down, I had more than eighty volunteers, all traders' clerks and *engages,* save one, who had large interests at stake on
the Mississippi. It is true our enterprise appeared unwise, and very
doubtful of success, for our private means were too limited for a big
job of this kind. We had no stores of any description for such an
undertaking—no boats, provisions, arms, nor ammunition.

When Col. McDouall, in the course of the day, became aware of
my success, he was much pleased, and offered me any military
stores he could spare from his scanty stock. This good news inspired
our ambition. I was made a Captain, mounted a red coat, mustered
a couple of epaulettes and an old rusty sword, with a red cock
feather adorning my round hat. I was at once a Captain of pompous
dimensions, and lucky it was for Napoleon and his hosts, that they
were beyond the reach of *Anderson's Mississippi Volunteers.*

I was an entire stranger to the Commandant, and it would not
have been soldier-like in him to have entrusted valuable military
stores to a man without credentials. So the command of the expedition was placed nominally under a volunteer officer from Lower
Canada, Lieut. Col. McKay, whose entire knowledge of war matters consisted of his predilection for rum. Well, the island of Mackinaw was, in fact, under blockade, and in daily expectation of a
formidable attack. It would, therefore, have been unwise in the
Commandant to have granted us very many supplies from his limited stores; but knowing the vast importance of securing the services
of the North-Western tribes, and witnessing also the devoted enthusiasm of a jolly band of Canadian voyageurs, embodied in so
short a time—and that, too, by an old volunteer of the Revolutionary War, in defense of their country, inspired him with confidence in us, and were joyfully mustered into service as a part of his
command.

Col. McDouall assigned three gun-boats for our use—open ves-
sels which had been constructed at Not-ta-wa-saw-gun the Winter
before; one having a platform near the prow for a gun. A brass
three-pounder, and such other stores as he could prudently spare,
also one artillery man for a bombardier, and a worn-out soldier
from the veteran battalion. Finally we were ready, and started,
about the twentieth of June, 1814, on our expedition against Prairie
du Chien, with many a cheer, and hearty wish, for our success. We
made all haste to get out of the reach of the expected enemies' fleet
from below. At Green Bay some of the Menomonee tribe volunteered, and following us in their canoes, joined us at Winnebago
Lake. In fact, when we reached Prairie du Chien, about the twentieth of July, we had a host of followers of all nations, ages and
sexes.

We reached there about noon, and pitched out camp at a convenient place; and I went immediately with a flag of truce, demanding
their surrender. This they refused to do. I noticed that they had built
houses, and fenced them in with strong oak pickets, ten feet high,
with two substantial block-houses, with *chevaux de-frise,* and two
gun-boats at anchor near by. On my return to camp, we opened fire
on the fort, but to little effect upon their earthed-oak pickets. Their
six-pound shot, because of their bad powder, did not reach our
camp. Meanwhile, under shelter of the village buildings, the Indians
kept up a constant firing at the fort, cutting down their flag, and
wounding two of their men through the port-holes. Two of our
Indians were also wounded, but slightly. Thus ended the first day.

The next morning, we re-opened our fire upon the fort. Our shots
hit them, but they did not return the fire. So I ordered the bombardier to run his gun up, and attack the gun-boats. Only one returned
the fire, the [other] being empty. They gave shot for shot merrily. At
length my gunner cried out: "For God's sake, come and help me!" I
ran to him and found all his men had left him, and I said, "what can
I do?" "Take the trail of the gun, please, and enable me to lay it,"
he replied. The next shot from the boat rolled in between the wheels
of our gun, being a three-pound shot, having taken aim, saying:
"Will you return us this ball, sir?" "Yes," we replied; and loading
our gun with it, shot it off, and with it cut off their gunners' two
legs. This shut them up; they cut cable, and I ran to camp, ordering
our gun-boats ready to follow and capture their vessel, as it had all
their valuable stores on board.

But our commander, Col. McKay, rose from his snooze came
along rubbing his eyes, peremptorily ordering me to desist. One
word from me would have caused mutiny. The American boat
turned a point about a mile below, and landed to stop leakage, and
prevent their sinking.

Our cannon shot were now nearly all gone. So I got a quantity of
lead from the village, and with a couple of brick made a mould, and
cast number of three-pound leaden balls. Meanwhile, the Indians,
were bringing in balls which the Americans had by their short shots,
scattered about the prairie without effect. Our stores of provisions
were getting low, our ammunition exhausted, but the fort and its
contents we came to take, and must have them.

At day light the next morning, our gun was within one hundred
and fifty yards of the pickets, with a small fire making an iron shot
red hot. When they found themselves in a fair way to be burnt out,
they surrendered. We took sixty-five prisoners, several iron guns, a
small quantity of pork, flour, etc., together with a quantity of
whisky. The casks containing the liquor, I stove in, fearing the

Indians might get it. As they were thirsting for the blood of their enemies, and required some tact to keep their hands off from the American prisoners. We could not trust any of them inside the fort. The American empty boat was fitted up, and next morning at day light, the prisoners were on their way to St. Louis, on parole; escorted by one of our Lieutenants, [Brisbois] for a short distance.

Letter from Mackinac

WILLIAM H. PUTHUFF

MICHILLIMACKINAC 20th. June 1816

DR.—SIR—By return of the vessel Com. Perry, I gave you a hurried account of the situation of the agency here, my business has continued on the increase and kept me insessantly employed, on the 17 inst. I met 39 Ottaways from Green Bay 202 Chippeways from Lake Michigan, 584 Fallsawynes* from Green Bay and its dependencies, 167 Wynabagoes from Green Bay or near that place and 141 Sieux from the Neighbourhood of Praire du Chéne in Council the pipe of peace was presented to the Orators of each tribe or nation respectively in the name of their nations and on behalf of the whole collectively.

The council opened on the part of the Fallsawyne by Tomah their principal chief who professed on behalf of his tribe and the whole present, the most amicable sentiments and feelings toward us, and asked that we would send them traders to reside among and with them. Charged the British with having induced them to embark in the late war, expressed his regret at having done so, and observed that he was now going [to] tell them so and demand his *discharge* from them, that he had now done with them and would never again quit his great father the President of the United States, he was followed by Ech Chaguin a young man so called, or private

---

*Menominee (editors' footnote)

From Major William Henry Puthuff to Governor Lewis Cass, in "Fur Trade in Wisconsin," *Wisconsin Historical Collections*, XIX (Madison, 1910), 417–424. Footnotes in original omitted.

Orator for the Wynnebagoes a tribe of about 770 warriors living principally near Praire du Chéne and between there and Green Bay, who expressed the same wish in relation to the sending traders among them, but expressed no determined resolution to abandon the British acknowledged no wrong at the part of his people in the part they had taken during the late war nor made any promises or professions other than a wish to remain at peace and never again raise the Tomahawk. The Chippeway's expressed the same sentiments which had been advanced by the Falls-awynes, and the Sieux closed the council by a restoration of the sentiments, wishes, Professions and acknowledgements of the Falls and Chippeway's. I assured them that their Great Father the President of the United States, would comply with their request in sending traders among them, receive them under his protection and attend to their real wants etc. etc.

The Wynebagoes have no doubt many among them who are disaffected towards us, and cannot in my opinion be rely'd further than their weakness and want of support from the neighbouring tribes will justify. The Fallsawynes or a very decided majority of them, are decidedly favourably disposed to the Establishment of an American post at Green Bay, so are the Chippeways and Ottaway's in the vicinity of that place.

This day I have met in Council the Chiefs and head men of the Ottaways and Chippeways within my immediate agency, or near this Post. They have in the name of their respective tribes declared openly their determination forever to abandon the British Interest, have taken their American father by the hand, and have declared the determination never again to abandon us have acknowledged their error in having listened to other councils, stated that they were forced to take up the Tomahawk, were promised much and much disappointed, asked permission occasionally to visit Drummonds Island for the purpose of collecting their dues, and in a word, promised to conform strictly to our wishes in all things, and asked for advice, and orders. My answer was to assure them of our sincerity and the promises of protection we had accorded them, in the forgiveness of the past and necessity for their careful observance of their promises and professions for the future, this they most solemnly promised and pledged themselves it should be comply'd with.

I am sincerely of the opinion that no good grounds for a doubt of the sincerity of their professions exists, I think I can venture to pledge myself for them, that so long as a respectable force shall be kept at this post, they will decidedly adhere to us. I must beg leave again to repeat that they have been grossly deceived, they are sensible of it, and well disposed to return to their former habits of intimacy and friendship with us.

The issues here for the Indian Department have as will be seen by the subjoined report of Indians visiting this Post, far exceeded my expectation. I have been and shall continue to be as economical on that subject as possible. Many of the Indians from Lake Superior and its tributary streams may be expected to visit this Post shortly, several Canoes have this moment arrived, who report that many more may be immediately expected.

I expect to meet them collectively in Council in one or two days. the Potawatomies and neighbouring Indians from Chicagou and its vicinity will it is said soon visit us, by the next vessel I expect to be enabled to give you a particular account of their profession and requests, which I am inclined to believe will be similar to those of the Fallsawynes, Chippeways and Sieux. the Wynibagoes I am fully persuaded are the most hostile towards us of any tribes in this district of Country, and are encouraged in that hostility of feeling and disposition toward us, by certain traders Roulette, Grinois etc. who are now at the Green bay. I have good grounds for advancing this opinion and hope to succeed in arresting these fellows, who will be held to account for their ungenerous, Illiberal and Hostile conduct to an injured Country, who has but too long cherished reptiles of their description in its bosom in the character of traders, they will not easily escape the vigilence of this post. 4 Boats are almost constantly manned and cruising here for the purpose of intercepting all Boats, Canoes or other conveyances for Furs obtained without License in the Indian Country, my information on the subject of that trade, is general.

I am already apprized of every Trader who has thus gone into the Country and their place of trade, and the place where their Furs have been collected and probable time that they may be expected at the Foot of Lake Michigan. Colonel Chamber's exertions to arrest them is unremitting, nor will any of them in my opinion be enabled to escape, the subjoined list of seizures made here, will inform you of our vigilence, the mode I have adopted, at the request of the respective owners, in releasing Goods, Wares and Merchandize thus seized, as will appear by Bonds herewith transmitted, will, I hope meet your approbation   I was induced to adopt this mode from a belief that no injury would or could arise to the Country therefrom, and from a belief that the manner in which I have drawn up the Bonds (a copy of which I furnished Mr. Abbott—Notary Public and who has been employed to draw them up and have them signed pursuant to that Copy) will obviate any difficulty that might otherwise have arisen from the want of a regular process in releasing the goods so seized on this subject I wish for your opinion and advice by the first Opportunity.

. . . .

The Indians who have lately attended here in Council from Green Bay, Praire du Chéne etc., are now at Drummonds Island they have promised to call on their return and report what shall be said to them there, how sincere they may be in this promise, or how far their reports may be relied upon, is, perhaps in some degree doubtfull. Yet I am inclined to believe much important information may be collected from them. A party [of] Wynebagoes who had left this Post from [for] Drummonds Island the day or two previous to my arrival, have since returned here and proceeded on to their Summer residence near the Green Bay. They report that the British detained one Canoe of their Young Men, until they should hear from the King, when these young men, so detained are to return to their nation with the news. Many of the traders have been extremely active in the Chicago and Green Bay Countries, in souring the minds of the Indians, encouraging the disaffected, exciting their fears and preparing them to oppose the establishment of American posts at for one year longer in their Country.

The Wynebago Orator Ech-cha-gun made this request in private council, he stated that though his chiefs would not permit him to do so in Public, yet that it was their real sentiments and that they would have asked or made the same request in Public, had they not feared a refusal, and that their father would be angry at them for doing so.

His reasons were that many of his Young Men were dissatisfied and might strike our young men if they came among them too soon, that by the next summer his Young men could be reconcil'd and there would then be no danger to be apprehended from them. That their Chiefs and great men were sincere in their professions of friendship towards us, that they had used every means in their power to satisfy and quiet their young men, but had not as yet entirely succeeded, but by the next summer he had no doubt, they would be enabled to quiet them and therefore asked his great Father the President not to send his soldiers among them until the next summer. Shortly after this request had been thus made, many of the same tribe, who had received information of its nature and my Answer, called upon me to request that I would pay no attention to their Orator, that he was himself one of the most disaffected among them and had with many others endeavoured to form a Coalition of all the Indians in that district of country against us but had failed, as not a single nation even their own the Wynebagoes, would consent to it or agree again to raise the Tomahawk they were tired of the War and sincerely wished for peace, that there were some among them hostile toward us but that it was only a few who would not dare to acknowledge their hostility when we did come among them. The small party who left this previous to my coming 30 or 40 in number, made the same request in council with Col. Chambers, from these different and conflicting account, little doubt exists of the unfriendly disposition of a part of this tribe at least, how far it may or will be evinced by their conduct on the establishment of a Milty. post at Green Bay, I am not prepared to venture a decided opinion, but am inclined to the belief that a respectable Military force will, the moment it appears among them, Quiet all murmering and produce the most happy effects in restoring an amicable intercourse between those Indians and our Government and People. They have been told by the restless unprincipalled traders who are yet with them, that it was the intention of our Government to take the lands from them and drive them still farther back upon the extensive Wilderness between them and Pacific Ocean. That we were determined to take their fur, skins etc. for a mere nothing and a thousand reports have been industrious circulated among them by the restless and designing men. at Drummonds Island the Indians are informed that presents cannot as Yet be made them to a large amount because of the determination of the American Government to prevent British Traders from living or residing with the Indians, and thus deprived of their best friends and natural protectors, the Americans will rob them of any valuable presents which they should receive.

I mentioned these reports merely to shew the spirit which is so industriously attempted to be raised and encouraged on the part of individuals attached to the British Government, among the Indians. there is no reason however to believe that any serious evil will grow out of this mode of procedure, as the Indians openly profess to believe it only calculated to evade the promises made them by that Government and call them Liars.

I have seen a letter addressed by J. J. Astor to a Mr. Franks a British trader now at this place in which Mr. Astor expresses surprise and regret at the passage of a law forbidding British subjects from trading with Indians, within the American limits etc. but observes that power is vested in the President to grant special license for that purpose and that he Astor has dispatched a messenger to the President from whom he entertains no doubt that some may be procured and will be immediately forwarded to Mr. Franks and Mr. Astor's friends in the North west trade. I wish to god the President knew this man Astor as well as he is known here. Licenses would

Courtesy of the SHSW [WHi (X3) 21050]

Governor Lewis Cass of the Michigan Territory

not be placed at his descretion to be distributed among British subjects, Agents or Pensioners. I hope in god no such license will be granted, his British Friends here calculate confident on his success in this matter, that they may be disappointed is my most sincere wish, should they succeed incalculable evil will assuredly grow out of the measure.

I am Sir, Your most obt. and Hble. Servt.

WM. HENY. PUTHUFF

Ind. Agent Michillimackin[ac]

His Excellency L. Cass Gov. of M. Ty. etc.

The within despatch have been made up under the greatest possible pressure of business. Errors will I hope be excused.

3: Fur Trading and the American Factory System

The United States entered the fur-trading business in 1796, when Congress authorized the establishment of government trading posts, or factories, in frontier areas. Although the system enjoyed some successes, in the Northwest the entrenched private traders were too much competition. The first selection, by Royal B. Way, explains reasons for the failure of the government factories. A book-length study of the subject is Ora B. Peake's *A History of the United States Indian Factory System, 1795–1822* (Denver, 1954).

To illustrate the problems of the government factors, some correspondence between Major Matthew Irwin, Jr., factor at Green Bay, and his superior, Colonel Thomas L. McKenney, Superintendent of the Indian trade, makes up the second selection. Many other narratives and letters are to be found in the *Wisconsin Historical Collections* (31 vols., Madison, 1855–1931).

The third selection is Rhoda Gilman's summary of the decline of the fur trade and its impact on the Indian tribes who depended upon it.

United States Factory System

ROYAL B. WAY

With the war of 1812 and the signing of the treaty of Ghent in December, 1814, the British fur traders lost their former ascendency

From Royal B. Way, "United States Factory System for Trading With the Indians, 1796–1822," *Mississippi Valley Historical Review*, VI (Sept. 1919), 220–235. Footnotes in the original omitted.

on American soil. With the restoration of the important mart of Mackinac to the United States the British traders and Indian agents removed their military posts to the nearest possible sites within the British boundaries, Amherstburg opposite Detroit and Drummond Island just east of the Mackinac straits. There they inaugurated a systematic policy of flattery and gift-giving to the Indians with the hope of counteracting the American overtures and retaining their former hold upon the Indians. They did not despair, even, of regaining the northwest when the next expected clash of their country with the United States should occur. Friction naturally arose between the neighboring British and American agents, as the letters of William Henry Puthuff, the United States agent at Mackinac, testify.

Distressing times now befell the Wisconsin French traders who had been among the most faithful subjects of the British. Left by the treaty within the United States, they were still allied to the British by ties of custom, self-interest, and association. With an undefined status they found themselves neither British nor American citizens. Unable to obtain titles to the lands which they had inherited from their ancestors and had long cultivated, they were at the same time suspected and often harassed by officious American agents, their furs seized, their licenses revoked, and every possible obstacle placed in the path of the only method they had of earning a livelihood for their families. In their dilemma, John Jacob Astor, already a power in the Wisconsin trade, saw his opportunity. Having secured the passage by congress of an act April 29, 1816, by which foreigners were excluded from any participation in the fur trade within the United States except in subordinate capacities under American traders, he cleverly began through his agents to enlist the distressed French traders of Wisconsin in the service of his American fur company, which then succeeded to the interests of both the North West and Southwest companies. Within his field of operation he then began from his base at Mackinac to embrace the region of the Great lakes, the upper Mississippi, and the entire length of the Missouri, with headquarters at St. Louis. Having driven out the competing British traders by the exclusion law of 1816 he successfully defended his own practice of engaging foreigners in his service. His faithful lieutenant, Ramsay Crooks, had by 1819 induced the war department at Washington to clear up the disputed construction of the law in regard to Astor's use of foreigners and the territorial extent of licenses so that the St. Louis officials were directed to recognize the validity of the licenses of the American fur company's Mackinac traders.

During the same period the United States government was also extending both its posts and trading factories within the borders of Wisconsin and the northwest. In 1816 Fort Howard at Green Bay and Fort Crawford at Prairie du Chien, with Indian agencies auxiliary to both establishments, were founded. Then the government extended its factory system to the northwest as an aggressive movement to diminish the power and influence of the British traders. A new phase of the fur trade was thus begun. Thereafter government agents and private traders competed one with another for the trade of the Indians. With the bars down the traders became disorganized while a horde of adventurous Americans entered the lists against the old established trading families who were allied to the Indians by intermarriage and well trained in the efficient methods of the French and British régimes. With the gradual location of the factories alongside the American military posts numerous broils arose between the soldiers and the factors. While the treaties made by American officials with the Indian tribes at Portage des Sioux in 1815 and 1816 were made possible only by the threats of the Americans, the Winnebago as a whole refused to treat and remained for years sullen towards the United States. Down to 1825 the Wisconsin Indians made annual visits to Drummond Island and Amherstburg to consult with their wily British father and to receive their customary presents.

Nevertheless, the earnest efforts of the United States after 1815 to gain control of the northwest fur trade, to expel inhabitants unwilling to become American citizens, to build and garrison the forts, and to rehabilitate the government fur trading factories at first bade fair to achieve success; in particular the outlook for the factory system seemed for a time bright. Even British observers and interested parties prophesied beneficial effects from the fair dealings with the Indians. The Indians, it was said, who had at Green Bay paid fifteen dollars for a pound of tobacco and a dollar and a half for a thimble would readily recognize and appreciate the benevolence of a government that sold them articles at cost and paid them full market value for their furs.

Some features of the Indian trade, however, were overlooked by the United States when it inaugurated its cash system. The Indian, frequently improvident, had no reserve stock of necessities. He could not possibly go out on his winter hunt unless he was supplied in advance on unsecured credit with firearms, ammunition, clothing, and many sundries. He was accustomed to pledge to private traders who furnished the supplies the peltries he expected to gather. Naturally, when advancing goods at such risks, the trader charged the highest prices while he gave the Indian as little as possible for his furs on his return from the hunt. Knowing well how

George Catlin's painting *The Bane* shows
traders selling whiskey to Indians

shifty and uncertain the Indians were in all financial affairs, the trader sent clerks and voyageurs to follow many of his Indian debtors to their hunting grounds to secure on the spot all the peltry possible. The practice of stopping others in the forest and along the streams on their return to the summer villages became common. Almost wholly depleted of the results of their winter's hunt, the Indians reached Green Bay, Prairie du Chien, or the other posts with but few skins to sell to the government factors on a strict market basis.

The United States government failed to foresee and avoid another difficulty. Both the French and British officials had periodically made considerable presents to their Indian wards. Weapons, ammunition, utensils, clothing, ornaments, and liquor had been distributed with a free hand as annuities for the insurance of the Indians' good will. Not only were the United States factors not supplied with such presents for distribution, but they were even held to a very strict accountability for all goods in their hands so that there was no opportunity for well-placed American advertising. The Indians, of course, considered the factors contemptible for their parsimony and suspected them further of withholding gifts the government meant the Indians to have. Moreover, the Indians were unable to obtain any liquor from the factories because of the United States' prohibition of the traffic; at the same time, however, the government failed to enforce its prohibitive law in the case of private traders, thus giving a heavy advantage to the factors' rivals.

The square dealing at the factory soon lost its charm for the Indian when he found he could get neither the necessary credit, nor presents, nor liquor, for all three were obtainable at the unofficial trading posts. At the same time it was but natural for the Indians to hold in contempt a government that turned trader, especially when they often heard the private traders dub the government factors "Dam Yankee pedlars."

Further, the local agents of the great fur companies, such as the American, were often married to native women and had long lived in the region. Supported by a great corporation under the management of Americans who had strong influence at Washington, these agents were the foreign rivals of whom the government factors so bitterly complained in their reports.

The private traders did not stop with their efforts to oust the factories by competition alone. As early as 1816 St. Louis merchants made a direct appeal to congress to abolish the factories; in the next year began the series of attacks which resulted within five years in the overthrow of the system and the complete triumph of Astor's American fur company.

Green Bay Factory, 1817–1820

MATTHEW IRWIN, JR.

Major Irwin to Colonel McKenney.

GREEN BAY, *March 10, 1817.*

The opportunity of conveying this being immediate, leaves me but little time to state why so little business has been done at this Factory during the winter; and, without going into a detail of minor reasons, I believe the principal ones will be found to be these: 1st, the admission of many British traders, who have been accustomed to do business in this quarter, and who placed themselves in the most advantageous places for business within fifty, seventy, and one hundred miles of this; 2d, the hints given the Indians by these traders to follow them, lest the Americans might punish them for their recent bad conduct during the Late War; 3d, the practice (conducted secretly) of vending whisky; and 4th, the prejudices excited by the traders against our Factories.

I recognize among them many who were openly and highly instrumental in exciting the Indians of our Territory to rise in arms against us during the Late War. I think, if British traders are to be admitted to trade with Indians, regard should be had to their past, or, at least, a guarantee should be given for their future conduct.

The Indian agents in this quarter, contrary to custom, exact fifty dollars from each private trader, British or American, for each annual license, which is considered as a perquisite of office, notwithstanding they are salary officers.

Colonel McKenney to Major Irwin.

OFFICE OF INDIAN TRADE, *May 28, 1817.*

SIR:—Your letters of the 10th of March are before me; one covering an inventory of goods, furs, and cash on hand, and debts due the Factory; the other, two sets of salary and subsistence accounts for the last quarter of 1816; also, your letter of advice to Zadock Walker, Esq., which I have transmitted by this day's mail.

You have not stated what goods were exchanged or sold for the debts, and furs, and cash; no out-goings being specified, except the goods sold Colonel Chambers, in whose bill there is an error of $8; thirty yards of blue cloth at $4 being entered $1.12, instead of $1.20.

From Matthew Irwin, Jr. to Col. Thomas L. McKenney, in "The Fur Trade and Factory System at Green Bay, 1816–1821," *Wisconsin Historical Collections,* VII (Madison, 1876), 269–288. Footnotes in the original omitted.

When you furnish goods to an Indian Agent for the use of the Indians, it would be proper to take a draft for the amount and remit it to this office. Two hundred and eighty-nine dollars and forty-four cents appear to have been furnished the Indian Agent, and no draft accompanied your invoice.

You state that two hundred barrels of salt, a quantity of iron, brushes, turpentine, etc., were purchased by Major Wooley, at Pittsburg, and there is no invoice of them. There has been no account rendered of a purchase of iron. Invoices of the other articles are enclosed. I must beg the favor of you to adhere, in all respects, to the forms required by this office, and which, if you have never had them, shall be sent you. Errors, no matter how small, cause delays and give trouble. I must request your particular attention to the subject of your quarterly accounts, not only to render them punctually, but also to have them faultless and errorless; as far so, at least, as practicable.

I should like to hear of your prospects for trade; whether the Factory promises to increase in its operations. I am averse to a credit business, except so far as your letter of instructions warrants. I mention this to guard you. Great caution is required. Quick returns are all-essential to a vigorous prosecution of the trade; and I look for them from such establishment. If Factories are not well supported, it is evidence the Indians do not require them; and, it being a plan for their benefit, when they cease to require them, it becomes a duty to send the means of administering comforts amongst other tribes who need help. I hope you will do well at Green Bay. I feel the force of your remarks on British traders, and hope they will soon be expelled. I am aware of their pertinacious adherence to a system, which nothing but exertions, active and constant on your part, can check; and if they cannot be controlled, their influence can be lessened. Are there no means to detect those who sell whisky? If so, why not make examples of a few of them?

Such of the British traders as you recognize as having been hostile to us during the war, report to the Agent, and transmit me copies of your remonstrance, which I will take care, in case he should omit or forget to act, to hand in to the War Department. Specify in your statement that the Agent receives fifty dollars for issuing a license, and I will report upon it.

There is much risk in crediting goods to be carried amongst the Indians; the plan is a good one, if the risk were less. I have no objection to authorize you to send small parcels out to serve the Indians, never to amount to more than two thousand dollars, and this sum to be in sundry hands; not to repeat an advance to any one till the previous one is fully adjusted. But issue none except on security.

Major Irwin to Colonel McKenney.

GREEN BAY, *September 29, 1817.*

I have more than once given you my opinion in relation to the state of this Factory, and what it might probably accomplish; and I recollect I stated that it could supply the wants of all the Indians comprised in this district. In compliance with this belief, I made corresponding arrangements, after the receipt of your letter of the 28th (a copy of which is enclosed, marked No. 18,) of May last. Several applications were made by American citizens to obtain merchandise for the purpose of supplying the wants of the Indians; and presuming it to be the intention of the Government to have the Indians supplied by them, I encouraged, after the receipt of your said letter, the applications of Lewis Rouse and Thomas P. James, who incurred considerable expense in making the preparatory arrangements for that purpose.

They had, too, an assurance from the Indian Agent here that he would not license British subjects to trade where they intended to establish themselves. Mr. Rouse was to supply the Indians at or near the Ouisconsin, and Mr. James those at Menomonie River, and intended to send a person to Winnebago Lake. A few days previous to their departure for those places, information was received that a number of British traders, licensed by the Indian Agent at Mackinac, were on their way to trade with the Indians at the places to which Mr. Rouse and Mr. James intended going; and a confirmation of it soon after, came in a letter from the Governor of Michigan Territory to the Indian Agent at Mackinac, informing him that he had received a letter from the Secretary of War, stating that Mr. John Jacob Astor had purchased the whole of the interest in the late Southwest Company, and wishing every facility to be given him in carrying on his trade with the Indians; in consequence of which, the Governor directed the said Agent to license all persons that the agent of Mr. Astor should name to him. Mr. Astor's agent is a Mr. Crooks, a known and professed British subject, who named to the agent at Mackinac a number of persons, (all British subjects,) whom the Agent licensed. Several of them came to this place for the purpose of trading with the Indians at Ouisconsin, and other places.

This at once would have determined Mr. Rouse and Mr. James to abandon their undertaking; but they had engaged the necessary number of persons for the usual period, (six months,) and incurred other expenses. They, therefore, determined not to abandon their undertaking, although they feel persuaded it will eventually be a bad business, as they think they are not able to cope in business with old and experienced persons, personally acquainted with the Indians, etc.

Courtesy of the SHSW [WHi (X3) 1894]

Fort Howard, built on the west bank of the Fox
River in 1816, from an 1855 daguerreotype

Should they be correct, I fear it will be difficult to persuade other American citizens to undertake to supply the Indians in this quarter. Besides the British traders licensed to trade at the Ouisconsin, others were licensed by the Agent at Mackinac to trade at the Upper Mississippi and this place, at which, in the village alone, six are licensed; and all of them, with one exception, held commissions during the Late War, are influential with the Indians, and were named by me in my letter of the 24th of July last to the Indian Agent here, a copy of which I transmitted you.

The persons engaged by the American house of David Stone & Co. were British subjects; and they were, I understand, licensed by the Agent at Mackinac. Governor Clark last year directed the stoppage of British subjects entering the Mississippi; Governor Edwards requested the Agent at Chicago to prevent them from entering the Illinois. What reasons exist for allowing them to trade with the Indians in this quarter, I am at a loss to imagine.

It is well known it is not necessary to license British subjects to trade at Mackinac, as very little business is done there by the Indians; and if it were greater, the American storekeepers could attend to it. At Chicago, the Factory used to supply all the Indians in that quarter; and, it can be well established, that it is wholly unnecessary to license a single person at this place, for last year a British trader (Peter Grignon) supplied all the Indians at or near the Ouisconsin, and another (Peter Powell) those at Menomonie River; and the trade of this village was attended to by two or three British subjects, who, altogether, did not make twenty packs.

There appears a palpable incongruity in the manner of conducting the Indian trade; the factors are sent to supply the wants of the Indians, and the Indian Agents can adopt such measures as to defeat all their plans to that end. It is very certain that the authority vested in them to issue licenses is well calculated to destroy all the benefits that might be expected from the Factories; particularly, too, when they interfere with each other's districts, as in the case with the Agent at Mackinac, who is in the constant practice of licensing persons to trade here and on the Mississippi. I can promise nothing from this Factory while these irregularities exist. It was not expected that Mr. Astor would engage to do business with the Indians with none but British subjects, and those, too, so exceptionable in every particular.

Considering, then, that the plans which I might adopt next year for supplying the Indians are liable to be frustrated by the impediments which seem to be put in the way of the prosperity of the Factory, and the consequent injury it would do to the individuals I might engage for that purpose, I must beg you to decline sending any more merchandise here, unless the Secretary of War can correct the irregularities which I have alluded to. The truth is, the Factories require to be well supported before they can be of any utility; one of the first measures to which should be, the prohibition to grant licenses where the Factory can supply the necessities of the Indians.

. . . .

Major Irwin to Colonel McKenney.

GREEN BAY, *August 10, 1818.*
Seeing that the business of this Factory must, in some measure, be regulated by the various fluctuations which occur in the Indian trade, I reduced the prices of many of the goods on hand, particularly those first received, as I discovered that if I did not do it I should do little or no business, in consequence of a determination on the part of British traders to under sell the goods in the Factory. They put in practice a plan (suggested by Joseph Rolette) for preventing the factory from doing any business. It was this: each trader to advance a piece of stronds, with the usual assortment of other articles, (termed by them an assorted piece of strond,) to be sold at first cost:

and keeping a person employed to watch the arrival of the good Indians, and take them to the house where those goods were kept. It proved as they desired—successful; and will account, in some measure, for the little business I have done with the Indians.

. . . .

Colonel McKenney to the Secretary of War
[Courtesy copy sent to Major Irwin]

INDIAN TRADE OFFICE, *July 5, 1821.*

SIR: I have the honor respectfully to represent, that for three years last past the two Factories on the Lakes, one at Chicago, the other at Green Bay, have been in a measure useless to the Indians, and, in a pecuniary point of view, to the Government also. This state of things is owing entirely to the unsuitable provisions which exist for the regulation of the trade. Hordes of private adventurers, availing themselves of the looseness of the system, have crowded into those parts on account of the superiority of the furs which are taken there, and level all sorts of policy but their own, by the powerful agency which they derive from the free use of spirituous liquors as an article of their commerce; and after which the Indians, however afflicting they know the consequences to be, will go.

This view of the state of these two Factories should have been given thus formally before, had I not waited in the hope that Congress would have placed this trade under the guidance of suitable regulations, which, if done, would insure to the Government the harmony and attachment of these Lake Indians; and to the Indians all the consequences which the Government contemplated in the adoption of this just and humane branch of its policy. This hope, and the apprehension that a removal of the Factories (which, although they do but little in the way of trade, operate as a check to the traders,) might expose the Indians to oppression, seemed to authorize me in waiting for the final judgment of Congress in this matter. I am unable, however, on a review of this subject, to realize in the proceedings of the last Congress any additional disposition to place this item upon what I conceive its proper basis; and the continuation of the same inactivity which has hitherto characterized the business done at these two Factories promising to make inroads upon the fund allotted for the trade, I do not feel myself authorized further to delay a decision on the subject, and recommend it accordingly for the Executive approval; it is, to break up and discontinue the two Factories located at Chicago and Green Bay. In making this decision, however, I am led to it entirely from considerations growing out of the duty which my trust imposes on me, and which embraces an obligation binding on me to keep the capital from diminution, and not from consideration of *policy*. My opinion is, that an abandonment of these posts must tend to much excitement, and a corresponding alienation of feelings on the parts of the Indians from the Government, as well as to bloodshed. This, however, is a part of the case at which I feel myself authorized but incidentally to glance.

I propose, on breaking up the trading-houses at Chicago and Green Bay, to unite the stocks, so far as they may furnish suitable materials, and follow the military post with a Factory to the St. Peter's. The Government is not yet known in the exercise of its parental capacity in supplying the wants of the Indians in that region. In addition to the advantages which the Indians will derive from a Factory located at or near the military post, will be the active and abundant returns which will be received from it.

If this recommendation be approved, I will have to dispose of, at Chicago, the items enumerated in the inclosed invoice which are unsuited to a trade at St. Peter's, and which, supposing they may be useful in the event of a treaty with any tribes of Indians in that region, I propose to turn over to the Indian Department at cost and charges, and pass the amount to the debit of the Indian Department account with this office.

I have the honor to be, very respectfully, your obedient servant,
THOMAS L. McKENNEY,
Superintendent Indian Trade.

THE HON. SECRETARY OF WAR.

Wisconsin Fur Trade

RHODA R. GILMAN

[After the War of 1812—*eds.*]

What the Americans had won was the privilege of presiding over the closing years and final destruction of the Indian fur trade in this

From Rhoda R. Gilman, "The Fur Trade in the Upper Mississippi Valley," *Wisconsin Magazine of History*, LVIII (Autumn 1974), 3–18. Footnotes in the original omitted. Reprinted by permission of the State Historical Society of Wisconsin.

region. The seeds of that destruction were in the American hunger for land and the engulfing wave of white settlement. There is little solid evidence that the fur trade as a way of life for Indian people could not have continued, with some modifications, if it had been possible to guarantee them possession of the land and its resources. Although some fur-bearing species were permanently depleted by intensive hunting, the over-all figures on fur production in the Great Lakes-upper Mississippi region during the last half of the nineteenth century clearly show that animal resources on the whole held their own and even increased.

There is even less reason to assume that Indian societies were doomed to internal collapse from contact with Western civilization. By the end of the eighteenth century native Americans in the upper Mississippi Valley and Great Lakes region had reached in material terms what has been called a "pan-Indian culture." Nearly all the tools and implements used in their daily lives were manufactured in Europe, and the goods from which they made their clothes were also largely European. The limited range of things for which they had traded a century before had expanded. More sophisticated tools had been added to the list—such items as spring-operated animal traps, augers, nails, handsaws, corn mills, and burning glasses; clay pipes had replaced stone ones for nonceremonial occasions and imported tobacco had replaced that grown locally or the substitutes which had been smoked; horses had been introduced, and bits, bridles, and a variety of harness gear were in demand; silver ornaments had become popular—armbands, brooches, gorgets, earrings, and even cradleboard decorations. This so-called "trade silver" was part of a whole class of goods designed and manufactured by Europeans solely for the Indian market. Other examples were tomahawk pipes, wampum, and trade guns with enlarged trigger guards and serpent shaped sideplates of brass.

But in spite of this "pan-Indian" material sameness, other aspects of Native American culture remained little changed. A Winnebago was still different from a Chippewa—just as the use of mass-produced goods failed to make a Norwegian and an Italian into identical Europeans. Probably the best evidence for the inherent vitality of Indian societies is the extent to which some still retain their identities even under the pressures of the mid-twentieth century.

One widespread characteristic of Indian culture which persisted despite the new variety of goods available was indifference to acquiring wealth beyond the immediate need. This presented a problem for the aggressive white trader, who generally interpreted the lack of concern for material possessions as laziness. It was a major factor leading him to introduce liquor. Time and again traders testified that Indian people addicted to alcohol produced more furs than those who had not acquired the bitter craving and hunted only to make a living. Also recorded are frequent protests by Indian leaders against the deliberate pushing of liquor among their people. Alcohol was unquestionably a major factor in the fur trade, and addiction to it was wide-spread among both whites and Indians. There are innumerable lurid accounts of its effects but little evidence to support the claim that Indians could not resist it or that its ravages alone ever destroyed Indian society.

The traditional life of Indian peoples moved with the measured cycle of the seasons, and their adaptation to the fur trade did not change this greatly. Winter was still by necessity the time for hunting. Northern tribes like the Chippewa dispersed in small family groups through the frozen forests. If a trader's wintering post were nearby, supplies might be purchased occasionally and furs delivered to pay for credit extended in the fall, but if the trip were too long, this would wait until spring—perhaps to be accomplished on the way to the sugar bush. Summer was a time for gathering into larger bands or villages, for social and religious celebrations, for travel and trade, and sometimes for warfare. In early fall came the ricing season, then gardens were harvested, food was laid away, and winter supplies of ammunition, clothing, and other necessities were secured from the trader, possibly on credit. Among tribes in milder climates the pattern varied. There a whole band often united for an early winter hunt, traveling in search of game like deer or buffalo, returning to the village for the bitterest months, then leaving again in early spring to hunt muskrat or other furred game. Maple sugar or wild rice might be gathered, but the greatest reliance for food would be upon fields of corn, squash, melons, potatoes, and other crops.

As fur posts were opened throughout the region, these crops also gained importance in trade. Because transportation was difficult and every pound precious, fur traders relied upon buying as much of their food supply as possible from Indian people. Jonathan Carver reported that a Sauk village on the Wisconsin River raised "great quantities of Indian corn, beans, melons, &c, so that this place is esteemed the best market for traders to furnish themselves with provisions of any within eight hundred miles of it." Peter Pond noted that the Ottawa of L'Arbre Croche, Michigan, "rase Corn Beens and meney artickels which they youse in Part them salves and Bring the Remander to Market"—also that maple sugar, dried venison, and bear's grease formed a considerable part of the local trade at Mackinac. Wild rice was a major item of trade at the North West

Company post on the Snake River of east-central Minnesota in the winter of 1804–1805. Pemmican is still another example of an Indian food source which became vital to the operation of the fur trade, although its use in the Mississippi Valley was limited.

The fur trade itself also moved with the cycle of the seasons. Fall was the time to stock up and disperse to small wintering posts. Winter was a time of isolation and boredom, broken sometimes by visits to groups of customers living at a distance. Spring brought the gathering in and packing of furs and attention to canoes or other means of travel. With early summer came the trip to the rendezvous or nearest supply point, the settling of accounts, the paying of debts, the renewing of contracts, and the discussing of new plans and arrangements. Then there was the assembling of the next year's "outfit"—the purchase of goods, the hiring of men, and at last the departure once more for the hinterland.

This pattern varied immensely with the particular period and location. During the British years in the Mississippi Valley there were two stages: clerks, wintering partners, and small traders, along with many Indians, assembled at Prairie du Chien for the spring rendezvous. There the major traders formed a canoe brigade to carry the furs to Mackinac in late summer, returning to the Prairie with their supplies in early fall. Then they dispatched clerks to wintering locations and made arrangements with the smaller traders, to whom they might either sell at a markup or advance goods for a share of the profits.

During the early years of the American period this began to change. St. Louis developed rapidly as a supply point, and with the beginnings of steamboat traffic on the upper Mississippi in the 1820's more and more goods came up the river. Prairie du Chien itself then became the major distribution point for the area, and Mendota, opposite Fort Snelling at the mouth of the Minnesota River, became the local rendezvous for traders from the Minnesota Valley and beyond. Until 1842, however, furs from Prairie du Chien continued going to Mackinac and on to New York. The coolness of the climate was apparently still enough of an advantage to overcome the difficulties of transportation up the Wisconsin. With the failure of the American Fur Company in 1842 this also changed. Thenceforward furs went to the Chouteau Company warehouse in St. Louis.

. . . .

By 1830 white settlement was pushing into the valley from the south and blossoming legally and otherwise among the lead mines and around fur trade and military establishments at Fort Madison,

Rock Island, Prairie du Chien, Milwaukee, Green Bay, La Pointe, and Mendota. Already the Potawatomi Nation had signed away most of its land in Illinois, and within another year or two the Fox and Sauk under Black Hawk would be engaged in their final, despairing struggle against white aggression. The rest of the Indian population, long decimated by epidemic diseases, was still shrinking. Some kinds of game, like elk and buffalo, had been permanently depleted, and beaver was practically extinct in the area. The highly valued "fine" furs like marten, fisher, and otter were no longer shipped in large quantities, though their smaller cousin, the mink, remained plentiful. So did the lowly muskrat. In the 1830's it accounted for 95 per cent of the furs shipped from the upper Mississippi Valley, with deer skins second.

Those Indian people who depended for their whole living on selling furs faced poverty and even actual starvation. They were caught in a vicious circle of vanishing resources and therefore even greater dependence on expensive trade goods—often including food to get them through the winter. One trader observed during an especially bad season that there were plenty of fur-bearing animals but that his Indians were too weak to hunt them. Without food, guns, ammunition, and traps they could not hunt, and without hunting there would be no furs at all, so traders gave credit, hoping always for a better season that seldom came. There were few bands by this time that did not have their resident trader, and as debts mounted, the relationship became far more like employment at piece work than independent barter. It was a losing business, but one that neither the trader nor his customers could afford to quit.

Most of the losses appeared on the trader's books as unpaid Indian debts, which mounted from year to year. To some extent these losses were passed on when small traders received credit from their suppliers in the larger outfits. But the organization of the business generally placed the major risk on the subsidiary trader, just as he sought to place it on the Indian. As the years went by the American Fur Company paid liberal dividends while many of its small traders failed and were replaced by new men. What losses were passed on to the company were never written off—merely added to the mountain of Indian debts on the books.

It was these accumulated losses masquerading as bad debts for which the larger operators claimed reimbursement when the tribes of the upper Mississippi Valley were at last forced to give up their land to the United States Government. The politics of treaty making were delicate and involved, but Dousman and Sibley were equal to them, and both men collected handsomely. As Dousman told Sibley after traders had pocketed a subsidy of $310,000 under the 1837

Sioux, Chippewa, and Winnebago treaties: "Otherwise we were gone coons."

Fur was only a marginal part of the business in the few years that remained before all Indian people of the upper Mississippi Valley were confined to reservations. Instead of the rendezvous there was the annuity payment, and there the treaty story was continued: traders profited immensely and eventually collected most of the government money, either for payment of debts or new purchases.

After two hundred years the forms of adaptation by which Indian people had coped with the white man's commercial world had been thrust aside. The fur trade was compatible with traditional Indian life styles and skills, and its economics were viable as long as parity of power existed and Indian people had total access to the resources of their land. On his side, the white man argued that the land could be put to far more efficient use and when he had the power to take it, he did so.

4: The Military Frontier

Francis Paul Prucha has studied intensively the United States Army's role along the early nineteenth-century frontier. He has assessed the military contributions to settlement of the Northwest in *Broadax and Bayonet: The Role of the United States Army in the Development of the Northwest, 1815–1860* (Madison, 1953). His other books include *The Sword of the Republic: The United States Army on the Frontier, 1783–1846* (New York, 1969); and *American Indian Policy in the Formative Years: The Indian Trade and Intercourse Acts, 1780–1834* (Cambridge, 1962).

Broadax and Bayonet

FRANCIS PAUL PRUCHA

The significant contribution that United States troops made to the development of the frontier was possible only because they constituted, above everything else, directed manpower. They were a labor force unequalled in compactness and unity of purpose by any group of frontiersmen. What they lacked in numbers they made up for in availability; they could be used for military and civilian projects that pioneer families had neither time nor equipment to undertake. This factor must be remembered in evaluating the army's role on the

From Francis Paul Prucha, *Broadax and Bayonet: The Role of the United States Army in the Development of the Northwest, 1815–1860* (Madison, 1953), pp. 34–36. 107, 120–123. Footnotes in the original omitted. Reprinted by permission of the State Historical Society of Wisconsin.

frontier, and it should not be overshadowed by the romantic aspects of Indian fighting.

The average pioneer entering the wilderness beyond the fringes of settlement was obliged to depend upon his family's labors, for he brought little capital with him and had no easily tapped sources of supply in the East. All his energies were directed toward clearing a plot of land, building a cabin and a few outbuildings, and perhaps hunting for game as a staple of his diet.

The army, on the other hand, operated with far greater advantages. True, a substantial part of the soldier's energy, like the pioneer's, was devoted to providing shelter and subsistence. But by no means all. A garrison was always dependent to a large extent on outside sources, which in the last analysis meant the resources of the War Department; provisions and equipment were shipped in from the outside or obtained from local producers, and paid for from the revenues of the federal government. Even the essential military tasks that were the reason for the garrison's existence did not exhaust the men's time and energy. They patroled the Indian country to insure enforcement of the intercourse acts, but often this required only relatively small details of soldiers. In the event of an Indian war the garrison performed the primary function of a military unit, but such wars were infrequent and seldom prolonged. The result was that a frontier garrison had time and energy for tasks other than making a living and holding the Indians in line. For long periods they were free to build impressive fortifications, to cut roads through the wilderness, and to participate in exploratory activities. Such extra-military duties often impaired drill and discipline, but even the military leaders who complained most of the deficiencies did not favor having the soldiers spend all their time in military exercises.

This labor force, furthermore, was not used hit-or-miss. It was directed through a well-knit hierarchy of command, in accordance with specific rules and regulations. Orders were given and executed under military discipline, and the outcome depended only on the wisdom of the commanders and the capabilities of the men.

The frequency and regularity with which the army was called upon to serve as a labor force was striking. Both by Washington officials who needed some task accomplished on the frontier and by pioneer settlers who required labor to supplement their own, the army troops were considered the first possibility. If there were boats to be built for public use, surveys to be made, or roads and canals to be constructed, the army troops could be called upon to do the work without additional expense.

Here, then, was a double-edged tool for developing the West. On the one hand the troops made such positive contributions as the maintenance of order and the development of a wilderness area by lumbering, road-building, and agricultural activities. On the other they stimulated indirectly the economic growth of the new areas by virtue of their purchase of goods and services which they could not produce for themselves.

. . . .

Much of the credit belongs to the corps of officers. Most of them were intelligent and able men, fortified after four years at West Point with the best engineering education that America could offer. The training they had received in mathematics and civil engineering stood them in good stead when they had to choose a site for a fort, plan its quarters and fortifications, and direct the actual work of building. Shortages in the ranks sometimes necessitated the employment of civilians as master carpenters or masons and as superintendents of lumbering activities, but no overall direction of the work was delegated to them. America has not honored these frontier officers as she has her military heroes who have won glory on the battlefield—not even commanders like Major Samuel Woods and quartermaster officers like Captain N. J. T. Dana, who were responsible for building not one but several frontier posts.

. . . .

The frontier army was regularly engaged, likewise, in time-consuming agricultural activity, for the remoteness of the Western posts made some measure of self-sufficiency imperative. Difficult enough was the task of delivering on time the subsistence stores and military equipment which could not be produced in the West. To offset the danger that supply contracts would not be fulfilled, it was highly desirable, if not absolutely necessary, that the Western garrisons have an independent supply of the goods that could be produced locally. From the standpoint of health it was important that the staples of army diet—salt pork and beans and bread—be supplemented by fresh vegetables. Because there was no way to preserve them during transportation, such foods had to be grown in the vicinity of the posts. Moreover, there was the War Department's constant preoccupation with economy. Production by the troops would materially reduce the drain on its coffers and would eliminate the ruinous charges for transportation to the frontier.

Kitchen Gardens and Field Cultivation

Vegetable gardens were therefore established at every permanent Western post. Land on the military reservations close to the forts was assiduously cultivated by the soldiers, who became expert at drawing from the soil a remarkable variety of vegetables. Such gardening had been part of established army policy almost from the beginning, and in 1818, when the advance of the military frontier was dotting the Northwest with remote and isolated garrisons, it became a specific responsibility of the frontier commanders. They had no help from higher headquarters; expenses for seeds, utensils, and fences were met not by army disbursing agents but by the officers and men who were to consume the produce.

. . . .

These gardening activities, however, were merely routine, almost insignificant, as compared with the field cultivation that was undertaken in pursuance of the order of 1818. Garden truck alone represented little saving of War Department funds, for it merely supplemented the basic rations and in only small measure lessened dependence on Eastern sources of supply. Wherever feasible, more extensive farming operations were initiated. The posts on the upper Mississippi, at Green Bay, and at Chicago were directed to begin large-scale farming that would provide wheat for the soldiers' bread, peas and beans, turnips, potatoes, and cabbages for the staples of his diet, and oats and corn for the forage of the livestock. At Fort Snelling in the summer of 1820, only a year after the arrival of the troops, about ninety acres of the bottom and prairie lands was under cultivation, planted chiefly with corn and potatoes. Three years later the acreage had been increased to two hundred and ten, of which about half was in wheat, sixty acres in corn, and the rest in oats, potatoes, and garden vegetables. The post commander had high hopes for the success of the enterprise, and sickles and buhr stones for harvesting the wheat and grinding it into flour were obtained from the commissary officer at St. Louis. With the flour still on hand and that produced from the grain raised by the soldiers, Colonel Snelling was confident that the flour contract for his post could be dispensed with altogether, or at least reduced by three hundred and fifty barrels.

With equal enthusiasm the garrison at Fort Dearborn began its agricultural work. In the summer of 1819 the land was cleared. Oats, corn, peas and beans, and potatoes were planted, and thirty acres made ready for cultivation the following season. The next year fifty acres of corn and thirty-five acres of wheat were planted, which yielded a crop estimated at five to seven hundred bushels of corn and three to five hundred bushels of wheat. Despite the inadequacies of the horse-operated mill, seventy to eighty barrels of flour and cornmeal were produced from the garrison farm. In 1821 more than eight hundred bushels of wheat was raised, and over sixty barrels of flour and forty of cornmeal were manufactured at the garrison. At Fort Armstrong, similarly, a large field was enclosed on which corn, peas and beans, and potatoes were raised in addition to garden vegetables. In 1821 three hundred bushels of corn was produced and the same yield of potatoes and turnips was expected. Lack of milling facilities, however, meant that all the corn had to be fed to the cattle.

Chapter III
THE WISCONSIN TERRITORY

The establishment of Forts Howard (Green Bay), Winnebago (Portage), and Crawford (Prairie du Chien) to control the Indians and regulate the fur trade also stabilized the territory. The frontier continued to attract foreign travelers who sought experiences in the wilderness and were curious about the natives. The newly discovered lead mines along the Mississippi River in southwest Wisconsin and northwest Illinois lured enterprising Yankees—that is, Americans from the east—and Cornish immigrant miners. But the population was transient and the settlements crude.

For a while the United States government tried to maintain the area as Indian land by leasing mineral rights. However, when the bottom fell out of the lead prices, miners pressured the government to allow them to farm their mining claims. The high quality of the region's soil for agricultural purposes turned the transient miners into homesteaders who preempted the ancestral homes of the Sauk and Fox Indians. The growing population along the Michigan lakeshore and in the mining region expected the federal government to negotiate land cessions with the Indians. This would open up the interior for settlement. Surveying teams worked north and west, platting the land in preparation for government land sales.

In 1835, when Michigan began the process of becoming a state, its territory west of Lake Michigan was taken away. It was designated as the Wisconsin Territory by the United States Congress in 1836. A two-house legislature was elected by the voters; the governor and other territorial officers were appointed. The new government primarily concerned itself with political patronage and the great need for federal funds to develop the territory. And the strong personal and political rivalry between Henry Dodge and James Doty was a characteristic mark of this period.

Indians and whites continued to clash in isolated incidents. The Red Bird incident (the Winnebago War of 1827) threw a scare into the lead-mining region. And the Black Hawk War in 1832 convinced the white people of southern Wisconsin that they were right in insisting that the Indians be removed beyond the Mississippi River.

Indian lifestyles changed as tribes became restricted to reservation lands and dependent on government annuities. Most missionaries and settlers justified the consequences of Indian removal with the belief that if the natives just converted to Christianity and settled down as farmers they would become "civilized." The Indians' nomadic ways and lack of a sense of individual land ownership were incompatible with farming and town-building. Age-old animosities between tribes prevented cooperative efforts in resisting government demands. The Indians were out-maneuvered year after year.

1: Travelers and Settlers

Captain Frederick Marryat traveled from Fort Howard to Fort Winnebago with military troops in the late 1830s. As a British officer, he was accustomed to outdoor life and enjoyed his overland trip, the beauties of which he describes with some relish in the first selection.

Albert Ellis, who came to Wisconsin as a young man in 1822, describes Green Bay and its French-Canadian-Indian families in the second selection. He speaks fondly of the maple sugaring, Easter celebration, and other customs of their simple French-speaking way of life. His selection is also interesting for its commentary on Major Matthew Irwin, the fur factor at Green Bay, whose correspondence appears in the preceding chapter.

In the third selection, Daniel M. Parkinson reminisces about his experiences in the lead-mining region. He notes the living conditions, camaraderie, and integrity of the miners, the problems they faced when the price of lead dropped—and the region's subsequent switch to agriculture.

In "Recollections of Wisconsin since 1820," Ebenezer Childs gives an account of the establishment of Madison as the seat of government for the Wisconsin Territory, as well as describing early territorial government in general. His description of the cold and of the elected and appointed officials' less than elegant accommodations is particularly colorful and humorous. Another humorous sketch of Madison, the new territorial capital, written by the upper-class Englishman Morleigh, completes this section. Like Charles Dickens, who was visiting the American frontier at the same time, Morleigh found the raw town and its offerings somewhat difficult to stomach.

Other personal narratives are to be found in the *Wisconsin Historical Collections* (31 vols., Madison, 1855–1931). Travelers who published descriptions of Wisconsin include Charles F. Hoffman, *A Winter in the West* (2 vols., New York, 1835) and Charles A. Murray, *Travels in North America During the Years 1834, 1835, & 1836 . . .* (2 vols., London, 1841).

Green Bay to Fort Winnebago, 1837

FREDERICK MARRYAT

We stopped half an hour at Mackinaw to take in wood, and then started for Green Bay, in the Wisconsin territory. Green Bay is a military station; it is a pretty little place, with soil as rich as garden mould. The Fox River debouches here, but the navigation is checked a few miles above the town by the rapids, which have been dammed up into a water-power; yet there is no doubt that as soon as the whole of the Wisconsin lands are offered for sale by the American government, the river will be made navigable up to its meeting with the Wisconsin, which falls into the Mississippi. There is only a portage of a mile and a half between the two, through junction between the lakes and the far west. It was my original intention to have taken the usual route by Chicago and Galena to St. Louis, but I fell in with Major F———, with whom I had been previously acquainted, who informed me that he was about to send a detachment of troops from Green Bay to Fort Winnebago, across Wisconsin territory. As this afforded me an opportunity of seeing the country, which seldom occurs, I availed myself of an offer to join the party. The detachment consisted of about one hundred recruits, nearly the whole of them Canada patriots, as they are usually called, who, having failed in taking the provinces from John Bull, were fain to accept the shilling from uncle Sam.

Major F——— accompanied us to pay the troops at the fort, and we therefore had five wagons with us, loaded with a considerable quantity of bread and pork, and not quite so large a portion of specie, the latter not having as yet become plentiful again in the United States. We set off, and marched fifteen miles in about half a day, passing through the settlement Des Peres, which is situated at the rapids of the Fox River. Formerly they were called the Rapids des Peres, from a Jesuit college which had been established there by the French. Our course lay along the banks of the Fox River, a beautiful swift stream pouring down between high ridges, covered with fine oak timber.

The American government have disposed of all the land on the banks of this river and the Lake Winnebago, and consequently it is well settled; but the Winnebago territory in Wisconsin, lately purchased of the Winnebago Indians and comprising all the prairie land and rich mineral country from Galena to Mineral Point, is not

From Frederick Marryat, "An English Officer's Description of Wisconsin in 1837," *Wisconsin Historical Collections,* XIV (Madison, 1898), 137–153.

yet offered for sale; when it is, it will be eagerly purchased, and the American government, as it only paid the Indians at the rate of one cent and a fraction per acre, will make an enormous profit by the speculation. Well may the Indians be said, like Esau, to part with their birthright for a mess of pottage; but, in truth, they are *compelled* to sell—the purchase-money being a subterfuge, by which it may *appear* as if their lands were not wrested from them, although, in fact, it is.

On the second day we continued our march along the banks of the Fox River, which, as we advanced, continued to be well settled, and would have been more so, if some of the best land had not fallen, as usual, into the hands of speculators, who, aware of its value, hold out that they may obtain a high price for it. The country through which we passed was undulating, consisting of a succession of ridges, covered with oaks of a large size, but not growing close as in a forest; you could gallop your horse through any part of it. The tracks of deer were frequent, but we saw but one herd of fifteen, and that was at a distance. We now left the banks of the river, and cut across the country to Fond du Lac at the bottom of Lake Winnebago, of which we had had already an occasional glimpse through the openings of the forest. The deer were too wild to allow of our getting near them; so I was obliged to content myself with shooting wood pigeons, which were very plentiful.

On the night of the third day we encamped upon a very high ridge, as usual studded with oak trees. The term used here to distinguish this variety of timber land from the impervious woods is *oak openings*. I never saw a more beautiful view than that which was afforded us from our encampment. From the high ground upon which our tents were pitched, we looked down to the left, upon a prairie flat and level as a billiard-table, extending, as far as the eye could scan, one rich surface of unrivalled green. To the right the prairie gradually changed to oak openings, and then to a thick forest, the topmost boughs and heads of which were level with our tents. Beyond them was the whole broad expanse of the Winnebago lake, smooth and reflecting like a mirror the brilliant tints of the setting sun, which disappeared, leaving a portion of his glory behind him; while the moon in her ascent, with the dark portion of her disk as clearly defined as that which was lighted, gradually increased in brilliancy, and the stars twinkled in the clear sky. We watched the features of the landscape gradually fading from our sight, until nothing was left but broad masses partially lighted up by the young moon.

Nor was the foreground less picturesque: the spreading oaks, the tents of the soldiers, the wagons drawn up with the horses tethered, all lighted up by the blaze of our large fires. Now, when I say our large fires, I mean the *large* fires of *America* consisting of three or four oak trees, containing a load of wood each, besides many large boughs and branches, altogether forming a fire some twenty or thirty feet long, with flames flickering up twice as high as one's head. At a certain distance from this blazing pile you may perceive what in another situation would be considered as a large coffee-pot (before this huge fire it makes a very diminutive appearance). It is placed over some embers drawn out from the mass, which would have soon burnt up coffee-pot and coffee all together; and at a still more respectful distance you may perceive small rods, not above four or five feet long, bifurcated at the smaller end, and fixed by the larger in the ground, so as to hang towards the huge fire, at an angle of forty degrees, like so many tiny fishing-rods. These rods have at their bifurcated ends a piece of pork or ham, or of bread, or perhaps of venison, for we brought some, not having shot any; they are all private property, as each party cooks for himself. Seeing these rods at some distance, you might almost imagine that they were the fishing-rods of little imps bobbing for salamanders in the fiery furnace.

In the meantime, while the meat is cooking and the coffee is boiling, the brandy and whiskey are severely taxed, as we lie upon our cloaks and buffalo skins at the front of our tents. There certainly is a charm in this wild sort of life, which wins upon people the more they practise it; nor can it be wondered at: our wants are in

A drawing of Fort Winnebago

Courtesy of the SHSW [WHi (X3) 1895]

reality so few and so easily satisfied, without the restraint of form and ceremony. . . .

On the fourth day we descended, crossed the wide prairie, and arrived at the Fond du Lac, where we again fell in with the Fox River, which runs through the Winnebago lake. The roads through the forests had been very bad, and the men and horses showed signs of fatigue; but we had now passed through all the thickly wooded country, and had entered into the prairie country, extending to Fort Winnebago, and which was beautiful beyond conception. Its features alone can be described; but its effects can only be felt by being seen. The prairies here are not very large, seldom being above six or seven miles in length or breadth; generally speaking, they lie in gentle undulating flats, and the ridges and hills between them are composed of oak openings. To form an idea of these oak openings, imagine an inland country covered with splendid trees, about as thickly planted as in our English parks; in fact, it is English park scenery, nature having here spontaneously produced what it has been the care and labour of centuries in our own country to effect. Sometimes the prairie will rise and extend along the hills and assume an undulating appearance, like the long swell of the ocean; it is then called rolling prairie.

. . . .

The last night that we bivouacked out was the only unfortunate one. We had been all comfortably settled for the night, and fast asleep, when a sudden storm came on, accompanied with such torrents of rain as would have washed us out of our tents, if they had not been already blown down by the violence of the gale. Had we had any warning, we should have provided against it; as it was, we made up huge fires, which defied the rain; and thus we remained till daylight, the rain pouring on us, while the heat of the fire drying us almost as fast as we got wet, each man threw up a column of steam from his still saturating and still heated garments. Every night we encamped where there was a run of water and plenty of dead timber for our fires; and thus did we go on, emptying our wagons daily of the bread and pork, and filling up the vacancies left by the removal of the empty casks with the sick and lame, until at last we arrived at Fort Winnebago.

A Seth Eastman drawing of Chippewa Indians making maple sugar

Green Bay Society, 1822

ALBERT G. ELLIS

These native settlers of Green Bay lived in primeval simplicity; of all people, they seemed the most innocent, honest, truthful and unsuspecting. They had, moreover, a most perfect immunity from want, their little fields were productive; the River was alive with fish and fowl; summer and winter their food was of the best, and in greatest abundance, and only required the taking. A narrator would not dare state the truth of the abundance of wild fowl, fish and game with which the country abounded, on pain of being held by the listener, an unmitigated Munchausen. Their habiliments were obtained with equal facility. Both sexes, for the most part, arrayed themselves in garments procured from the chase; those of the males were almost entirely of deer skin, while the females indulged in a few cotton stuffs obtained from the traders. All wore the moccasin; not a boot or shoe was to be seen among them.

These simple people inherited their manners from their forefathers, the French of Lower Canada; and politeness and strict "good-breeding" was the rule, from the highest to the lowest. It gave them ease and gracefulness of deportment, often a surprise and reproach to the brusque, abrupt Yankee, rendering their company acceptable and engaging with the most cultivated and polite, and insuring, in their intercourse with each other, the preservation of friendly feeling and good will. They had been sought out by the Catholic ministers, their children were all baptised Christians, had been taught the creed and commandments, and grew up simple-hearted, trusting people. They were strict observers of the seasons of festivals and feasts; from Christmas to Ash-Wednesday, the whole settlement was rife with feasting, dancing, and merrymaking; but, on the approach of Lent, it was suddenly suspended till Easter.

. . . .

The Easter festival was the most joyous of the calendar; with most of them it was celebrated in the deep forests, where they had before repaired, for one of their chief industries, the making of maple sugar: which requires a little more special notice. It was a source of the greatest amusement, as well as profit, occupying two or three months of every year, and engaged nearly the whole population, male and female, children and all. They probably got the art

From Albert G. Ellis, "Fifty-four Years' Recollections of Men and Events in Wisconsin," *Wisconsin Historical Collections,* VII (Madison, 1876), 207–268. Footnotes in the original omitted.

from the Indians, and greatly improved on the savage mode. About the first to the fifteenth of February, preparations were made throughout the settlement for repairing to the *sucrerie,* or sugarbush—for moving from their home cabins on the River bank, into the deep wood, often many miles distant; taking generally most of their household treasures, even to their chickens; and they made the business worthy of their preparations. Some of them had as many as five hundred, eight hundred, and some one thousand sugar trees tapped.

. . . .

The product of those *sucreries* of the better class of the French, was a fair article of sugar, of ready sale, and in some respects preferable to the best muscovado. They had learned to use the utmost neatness and caution to keep out all impurities, and had attained to great perfection in the purifying process. All the sap was strained through a fine sieve into the kettles—the syrup was strained twice before granulating; and here came in the product of the chickens, to-wit, the eggs, the whites of which were broken in the boiling syrup, when all impurities immediately came the surface and were removed. The sugar, when strained off and cooled, was quite fair and pure. Some of the more enterprising and forehanded, bought syrup and coarse sugar of their Indian retainers, and their less able neighbors, and went into the purifying process on a large scale, and thus largely increased their product for the season. A few families of this class had a preference in the sugar market at the frontier trading posts, their mococks, branded with their names, always being first sought, at advanced prices.

As before stated, the Easter festival was generally observed at those *sucreries;* for this reason, those who had the chickens, and could do it, took them into the woods, made houses for them, and saved a store of eggs for this festival. Then it was that their friends at the settlement, the Americans and army officers, were invited to visit them, and the invitations were rarely declined. The American citizens, the gentlemen and ladies of the army, found no greater enjoyment than one of these spring festivals, celebrated among their French and half-breed entertainers in the depth of the great maple woods, in their commodious sugar-houses. There was never-failing good cheer, somewhat enlarged, perhaps, by their visitors in a picnic style; which was followed with strains of the merry violin and the dance, and at length the guests retired with pleasing, vivid recollections of the Easter festival among the French, at the *sucreries.* These frolics were often enlivened by an old fashioned "candy-pull," when the French girls presented their sweet-hearts, on parting, with a cake of candy, folded in a strip of birch bark, which they called their "billet doux."

Apropos of the sugar making. Some years previous, Congress had passed a law prohibiting trade in the Indian country by any but citizens of the United States; and further, had attempted to divest the Indians of foreign influence by the establishment of trading posts by Government agents called factors, one of which was located at each of the several important points in the Indian country. One had been placed at Green Bay, and Major Matthew Irwin, of Pennsylvania, appointed to the office. We found him at Fort Howard, in 1822, the sole occupant of the post, in his stone building, and living under the same roof with his family; the troops having been removed two years before to Camp Smith. Major Irwin was a gentleman of intelligence, culture and integrity, and as well fitted for the trust as any citizen totally unacquainted with the Indian country, its trade and inhabitants, could be—that is, not fitted at all; and moreover, being furnished by the Government with goods unsuited to the Indian trade, and coming in competing contact, with life-long experienced, astute traders, of course the effort to gain confidence, trust and influence with the Indians, was a total failure. His sleazy, woolen blankets, cheap calico, and, worst of all, his poor unservicable guns, were all rejected by the Indians; and during his four years' trade, he did not secure fifty dollars worth of peltries; but the natives, as well as French inhabitants, made quantities of maple sugar; this was not current at New York, for payment of goods, as peltries were; and so not much cared for by the old traders. The Indians resorted with it to the United States factor, Major Irwin, who bought large quantities of it; and had many thousand pounds in store at the time of our arrival in 1822. The experiment of these Government factors for controlling the Indian trade, and extricating the natives from the influence of the old traders—most of them under British rule—having by this time proved a failure in every way, financially as well as politically, an order for their discontinuance was made; and that fall Major Irwin closed up most of the business, shipped his sugar to Detroit, turned over the concern to a young gentleman succeeding him, by the name of Ringgold, and left the country.

Lead Mining

DANIEL M. PARKINSON

I removed my family to the mines in the fall of 1827, and settled at New Diggings, now in La Fayette county. So intent were the new-comers on making money by mining, that they could not take time to erect for themselves and families even a comfortable dwelling place. Instead of houses, they usually lived in dens or caves; a large hole or excavation being made in the side of a hill or bluff, the top being covered with poles, grass and sods. A level way from the edge of the hole at the bottom was dug out, some ten or twelve feet; and this gang-way being closed up on either side, was covered over on top, thus forming a sheltered entrance to the *"dug-out,"* as such places were usually called. In these holes or dug-outs, families lived in apparent comfort and the most perfect satisfaction for years, bouyed up by the constant expectation of soon striking a *big lead*. To these miserable places of abode, men were compelled to carry upon their backs every thing they and their families required for food and fuel. The miners all lived in similar or worse places, or encamped upon the open ground.

What was then called *prospecting,* was the general business of the country. This consisted in digging *"succor holes,"* in all imaginable shapes and depths, and in all manner of places. When a *lead* was struck, then all would flock to that vicinity to mine; and hence, in the course of a few years, mining was concentrated, in some considerable degree, in certain localities, such as New Diggings, Hard Scrabble, Coon Branch, Fair Play, Platteville, Mineral Point, Dodgeville, Blue Mounds, &c., places still of considerable note. During these few early years, the mines were worked chiefly by men from the Southern and Western states, who possessed and practised many of the noblest traits of our race. As an illustration of their innate integrity of character, it is perhaps only necessary to state, that locks and keys were unknown in the country; and all places of abode were always left unfastened, and open to the reception of all, who received a cordial welcome, and a free invitation to partake of every hospitality the dug-out or shanty afforded. Upon the return of the lone miner to his "hole in the ground," after a hard day's work, we would frequently be cheered with the sight of some weary prospecter, who had, in his absence, there taken up his lodgings for the night. Having passed a pleasant night, they would separate in the

From Daniel M. Parkinson, "Pioneer Life in Wisconsin," *Wisconsin Historical Collections,* II (Madison, 1856), 326–340. Footnotes in the original omitted.

morning, perhaps never to meet again. Mining tools, and every thing of this description, were left out, and nothing ever stolen or disturbed.

Debts were contracted without reserve, at the first interview with a new-comer, and he seldom ever failed to meet his promises of payment. The mode of doing business was something like this: A young man would enter a store, or go to a smelter, who usually kept miners' supplies, and would say: "Sir, I have just arrived in the mines, am out of money, and wish to go to mining; if you will let me have some tools and provisions, I will pay you as soon as I strike mineral, which I hope will be in a few days, or weeks at the most." The prompt [and] friendly reply would be—"Yes, Sir, you can have them;" and the pay, sooner or later, was almost sure to come. This custom was so universally prevalent, and men were so prompt to pay their debts, that I have often heard business men of that day declare, that they never knew debts so promptly paid, even in States where they had stringent laws to enforce their collection.

I did not remain long at New Diggings, but soom moved out to Pecatonica, and kept a tavern, which was, for a considerable time, the only house between Gratiot's and the Blue Mounds.

. . . .

After this apparent prosperity, business very much declined, and in the fall and winter ensuing, the inhabitants experienced the severest times that they ever had in the country. Lead and mineral fell in value from a good price, to almost nothing—lead depreciating to one dollar or one dollar and a quarter per hundred, and mineral only brought no more than four dollars per thousand, and often but three. And not only was our great and exclusive product so depressed, but provisions rose to a very high price. Flour commanded from fifteen to eighteen dollars per barrel, pork thirty dollars per barrel, coffee fifty cents and sugar twenty-five cents per pound. At these ruinous prices for lead and mineral, and high prices for provisions, it required a desperate effort on the part of the miner to secure even a scanty living. It took from four to five thousand pounds of mineral to pay for one barrel of flour; I gave four thousand pounds for a barrel. In consequence of the great depression of the times, many persons became discouraged and left the country, many more gave up business, and the country at that period, and during the years 1830 and 1831, presented a most gloomy and unpromising appearance, and was, in fact, any thing but flattering to inhabitants or strangers.

During all this time, the people were compelled to pursue the uncertain and precarious fortune of mining as a means of liveli-

Courtesy of the SHSW [WHi (X3) 8420]

An illustration showing a cross section of a
lead mine, from the Owen report of 1844

hood, the cultivation of the soil being expressly prohibited by the laws and regulations governing the mines. But in the spring of 1832, however, the Superintendent of the mining country, seeing the absolute necessity of the thing, signified to the inhabitants, that he would not take any measures to prevent them from cultivating the soil; but could not, under his instructions from the General Government, give them any special permission to do so. Up to this time, it was necessary, under the mining regulations, to procure a permit even to mine. The regulations governing the mines, were of the most rigid character, and they were sometimes rigidly enforced, sending officers with instructions to remove persons from certain localities. An instance of this kind, I believe, occurred in which Gen. DODGE was the person sought to be removed. He was then mining at Dodgeville, a region to which the Indian title had not been fully extinguished. This was in the year 1828; but these instances were, however, quite rare.

In consequence of the inhabitants being partially permitted to cultivate the soil, there was an evident appearance of increasing improvement and prosperity throughout the country, and the settlers everywhere were looking forward to a season of plenty and comfort. The country now began once more to hold out inducements to immigration, and the population was evidently on the increase from this source.

Territorial Government

EBENEZER CHILD

Delegates were elected, in 1835, to form a State Constitution for Michigan; which being effected, left the region west of Lake Michigan, to be organized into the separate Territory of Wisconsin. The new Territory was organized July 4th, 1836, with Gen. HENRY DODGE for Governor, JOHN S. HORRER for Secretary, CHARLES DUNN for Justice of the Supreme Court, and WM. C. FRAZIER and DAVID

From Ebenezer Child, "Recollections of Wisconsin since 1820," *Wisconsin Historical Collections*, IV (Madison, 1859), 153–195. Footnotes in the original omitted.

IRWIN, JR. for Associate Justices. The first election held for members of the Territorial Legislature, was in September, 1836. According to the apportionment, Brown county was entitled to two members of the Council, and three representatives in the House of Assembly; and HENRY S. BAIRD and JOHN P. ARNDT were chosen to the Council, and EBENEZER CHILDS, ALBERT G. ELLIS, and ALEX J. IRWIN to the House—GEO. MCWILLIAMS contested IRWIN'S seat and gained it. When I was nominated for a seat in the Legislature, I resigned the office of Sheriff of Brown county, and was elected without opposition.

The Governor convened the first Legislature at Belmont, in what is now La Fayette county, and we met there on the 25th of October, 1836. What is now the State of Iowa, then formed a part of Wisconsin Territory. Wisconsin proper then had a little over 7,000 population, and Iowa proper a little over 5,000. The representation from the Iowa side of the Mississippi was nearly as large as that from Wisconsin proper—what for convenience sake, I will call Iowa, had six Councilmen and twelve Representatives, while Wisconsin proper had seven Councilmen and fourteen representatives. The accommodations at Belmont were most miserable, there being but a single boarding-house. The whole of the Brown delegation lodged in one room, about fifteen by twenty feet, and our lobby friends roomed with us. Our beds were all full, and the floor well-spread with blankets and over-coats for lodging purposes. The session lasted till the 9th of December. At that session a bill passed locating the seat of government at Madison; but the Legislature appointed Burlington, in Iowa, as the place of the meeting of the next session, until proper buildings could be erected at Madison.

A majority of the members from Wisconsin proper were opposed to making, at that time, a permanent location of the seat of government; we contended for a temporary location in Green Bay or Milwaukee, or any other place, until the country should become more settled. We contended that the members representing the region west of the Mississippi, though they had a legal right, yet they had no just right to vote on and determine the permanent seat of government for Wisconsin Territory, as they expected soon to be set off into a separate Territory of their own—as they were in 1838. I labored hard to prevent a permanent location at that session; but those who favored the measure from Wisconsin proper had some interest in Madison, and the members from the west side of the Mississippi were bought up to go for Madison. Thus the measure was carried by a small majority. As soon as the Governor signed the bill, there was a great rush for the Land Office at Mineral Point, to purchase land in the neighborhood of the newly located capital. The town plat of Madison was divided into twenty shares; I was offered one share for the small sum of two hundred dollars—I presume that was done, thinking, if I accepted it, that I would vote for Madison for the capital; I rejected the offer with disgust, and felt better satisfied than I should to have sold myself for the twentieth part of Madison. When I returned to Green Bay, my friends were well pleased with the course that I had taken.

The year 1837 brought with it a large increase to the population in all parts of the Territory. Early in November the Legislature met at Burlington, and held a session of some ten weeks. All the members had to travel by land on the west side of Mississippi. There were then but few settlers from Burlington to Dubuque; we had to camp out on the prairies, when the weather was intensely cold. It was the 10th of January, 1838, we adjourned. I was on a committee to investigate the affairs of the old Dubuque Bank. There was then but one public house in Dubuque, and some five hundred inhabitants. I remained there two weeks on this business, and then started alone for Green Bay. At Mineral Point I met a brother of Col. A. A. BIRD, of Madison, who had recently come from there; I waited for him to return, and accompanied him. We started, and went as far as my old Worcester County friend, Col. E. BRIGHAM'S, at the Blue Mounds, with whom we staid all night. The next day we started for Madison, but lost our way and traveled all day and most of the night, when we came to a log shanty, where we tarried the remainder of the night, without, however, anything to eat.

In the morning we renewed our journey, and went to Madison. We found Col. A. A. BIRD there; his mother was quite ill, and attended by the army surgeon from Fort Winnebago. The house or shanty that BIRD lived in was a miserable cold affair. There were then but three other families in Madison. The doctor from Fort Winnebago designed to return the next day, and wished me to wait for him. I concluded to do so, and crossed Fourth Lake to its head, near Pheasant Branch, and spent the night with Col. W. B. SLAUGHTER, who then lived on the west bank of the Lake. The next morning the doctor came over. We started for the Fort, between SLAUGHTER'S and which, there was not a single house. I had my conveyance and the doctor had his, with a driver. When about half way, I asked the driver how the doctor stood the cold—for it was a stinging cold day; the doctor, who was completely covered up with buffalo robes, made no reply, and the driver, of course, could not answer for him. I drove past them, and on reaching a grove of timber, I stopped and made a fire. When the other conveyance came up, I went to see the doctor, took the robes off, and found him completely chilled through, and could not speak. We took him out of the sleigh, carried him to the fire, and rubbed him a long time before he could speak. I had a little brandy with me; he drank some of that, and after a while he was able to walk, when we again started for the Fort. When we arrived at the Fort, as we did without further mishap, we found that the thermometer stood thirty-two degrees below zero. I did not suffer at all with the cold, as I ran the most of the way.

The next day I left alone for Green Bay. There was not then a house between Fort Winnebago and Fond du Lac; the snow was deep across the prairies. I overtook two Stockbridge Indians nearly exhausted from fatigue and cold. I carried them in my jumper to the first timber, when we stopped and made a large fire, and left them. The snow was so deep, that my horse could not draw them. They staid there until the next day, and got home safe. If it had not been for me, they would undoubtedly have perished on the prairie. I arrived at Green Bay safe and sound. There was then but one house between Fond du Lac and Green Bay.

In June, 1838, the Territorial Legislature again met at Burlington. We had a short session, commencing on the 11th and closing on the 25th of June. During the session we received the news that Iowa had been separated from Wisconsin, and formed into a distinct Territory; as soon as this intelligence reached us, we adjourned to meet at Madison in the autumn. While at Burlington, Gov. DODGE appointed me Commissary General, with the rank of Colonel—that was perhaps, the first military commission issued in Wisconsin; I still retain it as a memento of the olden time.

The next Legislature met, for the first time, in Madison, on the 26th of November, 1838. The new capital edifice was not yet in a suitable condition to receive the Legislature; so we had to assemble in the basement of the old American House, where Gov. DODGE delivered his first message at the new seat of Government. We adjourned from day to day, until we could get into the new capital building. At length we took possession of the new Assembly Hall. The floors were laid with green oak boards, full of ice; the walls of the room were iced over; green oak seats, and desks made of rough boards; one fire-place and one small stove. In a few days the flooring near the stove and fire-place so shrunk on account of the heat, that a person could run his hands between the boards. The basement story was all open, and JAMES MORRISON's large drove of hogs had taken possession; they were awfully poor, and it would have taken two of them, standing side by side, to have made a decent shadow on a bright day. We had a great many smart members in the House, and sometimes they spoke for Buncombe. When members of this ilk would become too tedious, I would take a long pole, go at the hogs, and stir them up; when they would raise a young pandemonium for noise and confusion. The speaker's voice would become completely drowned, and he would be compelled to stop, not, however, without giving his squealing disturbers a sample of his swearing ability.

The weather was cold; the halls were cold, our ink would freeze, everything froze—so when we could stand it no longer, we passed a joint resolution to adjourn for twenty days. I was appointed by the two houses to procure carpeting for both halls during the recess; I bought all I could find in the Territory, and brought it to Madison, and put it down after covering the floor with a thick coating of hay. After this, we were more comfortable. The American Hotel was the only public house in Madison, except that Mr. PECK kept a few boarders in his old log-house, which was still standing not long since. We used to have tall times in those days—times long to be remembered. The Forty Thieves were then in their infancy; stealing

An 1835 broadside advertising a political rally

Courtesy of the SHSW [WHi (X3) 33858]

DEMOCRATIC
MEETING.

A Meeting of the Democratic Republicans of the County of Brown, will be held on *Thursday next, at* **6** *o'clock,* **P. M.** *at the School House, in Navarino,* for the purpose of nominating four additional Candidates to be supported at the coming election, in October, with the

HON. JOHN LAWE

for member of the Legislative Council; and also to nominate a suitable person for Assessor; and to take such measures in relation to the support of

JUDGE DOTY,

for the Delegacy as may be found expedient.

LEWIS ROUSE,   LINUS THOMPSON,
S. W. BEALL,   J. W. CONROE,
JOHN P. ARNDT,   DAVID WARD,
                Committee of Vigilance.

A. G. ELLIS, *Secretary.*

Green Bay, Sept. 15, 1835.

was carried on in a small way. Occasionally a bill would be fairly stolen through the Legislature; and the Territory would get gouged a little now and then.

Madison, the New Capital, 1840

MORLEIGH

It was night before we wended our way through the magnificent streets, squares, and avenues of the young capital of Wisconsin. My companions, favoured by the darkness of the night, amused themselves by telling me the names of the various streets we passed through, on our way to the hotel, while I strained my eyes into the oak openings, right and left, in quest of balconies, piazzas, stoops, and colonnades.

Mr. Morrison, the innkeeper, welcomed us to Madison, led the way into his bar, volunteered whisky and water, or a cobbler, to drive the night dew out of our throats. Moreover, the good man accommodated me with a single-bedded room, a luxury I had not enjoyed for sometime. Sunday morning: rose refreshed, and marched out to look at the city, which had vanished like a dream, leaving that great unsightly fabric, the capital, with its tin dome glittering in the sun, and some forty houses, of all sorts, shapes, and sizes, rained about here and there sparingly, at the corner of the *projected* streets and thoroughfares of this embryo town. Entered the capital, which I found full of chips, shavings, and mortar: from the door and raised platform, *en revanche,* we have a splendid view of third and fourth lakes—for, as yet, the lakes have been only numbered, it would seem—and there is a chain of beautiful little lakes about Madison. There is nothing grand about the scenery, but all that quiet beauty of wood and water, frequently seen in the old settled country at home. Return to the hotel, which is the largest house in the place, save the capital, and no great shakes after all. In

From *A Merry Briton in Pioneer Wisconsin:* A contemporary narrative reprinted from *Life in the West . . .* extracts from the Note Book of Morleigh in Search of an Estate [London, 1842] (Madison, 1950), pp. 15–18. Reprinted by permission of the State Historical Society of Wisconsin.

the parlour, I found two spry-looking men seated on a sofa, covered with coon-skin. One of them hailed me directly; he said we had met before, down east, in a steam-boat, though, for my part, I never recollected having had that honour. He began, by telling all he knew about the country; and his calling or profession being that of barrister, or advocate, I did not feel inclined to woo his acquaintance; nevertheless, he resolved to cultivate mine, and we soon jogged along, like sworn brothers. Breakfast, and indeed all our meals, are taken in the cellar, or basement story of the house, where our hostess, who is said to be a blue, deigned to preside over the teapot. Our party was made up of lawyers, their wives, and certain hangers-on, employed and expectants at the seat of government, a doctor, and an exquisite from Chicago, in a very severe blue coat and plucky waistcoat. He held his head very high, as best became him, being employed to cover the dome of the capital with new tin, in his capacity of tinker. Last, not least, at our table, sat the major. The colonel, captain, or squire, as he was called by the guests, Bildad Morrison, our respected host—an original root from the American bottom, as he was wont to boast, when people spoke of their homes down east or south—"I'm from the richest soil in the known world—the American Bottom, in Illinois." Then followed a grandiloquent account of the wondrous vegetation, the fruits, roots, and shoots of that bottom of rich vegetable matter, where common blackberries were as big as peaches—peaches as big as cocoa-nuts, and pumpkins grew as big (you may stare gentlemen!) as the insignificant elevations called hills in this country. Wisconsin is rather flat, but then her pumpkin hills were more than I could swallow; and I left the table, before the forest of Indian cornstalks and the rest of the monstrosities of the American Bottom were paraded. By way of dessert, it was a fortunate circumstance that our host possessed such a garden in his luxuriant brain as enabled him to dispense with the rich productions of Illinois at his table, without a murmur; but how he had reduced himself and family to enjoy a tomato, was beyond my comprehension. Tomato was the word—the theme—the song, from morning till night—from night till morning. The first morning I descended to the bar, there sat the colonel in his white and black chip hat, set jauntily over his round, heavy, swelled face, his crooked foot resting on one knee, his twisted hand resting upon that, (he had been blown up at the Diggins, near Mineral Point,) and his expressive mouth full of red tomato. That swallowed, he held up another love-apple tantalizingly, to a feeble little child, and, mincing his voice, he would exclaim, "Who'll have a tomato? Who'll kiss me for a tomato?" In truth, not I; having in the early part of my days looked upon that grovelling fruit as poison, and never having tasted it even as a pickle with much gusto, I was not prepared to enjoy the tomato feast, at the capital of Wisconsin.

The garden at the rear of the house seemed to produce no other fruit or vegetable. At breakfast we had five or six plates of the scarlet fruit pompously paraded and eagerly devoured, with hearty commendations, by the guests. Some eat them with milk, others with vinegar and mustard, some with sugar and molasses. I essayed to follow suit, and was very near refunding the rest of my breakfast upon the table, the sickly flavour of flat-tongue grass, sour milk, and raw cabbage, being concealed under the beautiful skin of the love-apple I had the temerity to swallow.

At dinner, tomatoes *encore,* in pies and patties, mashed in side dishes, then dried in the sun like figs; at tea, tomato conserves, and preserved in maple sugar; and to crown the whole, the good lady of the hostel launched forth at night into the praise of tomato pills.

2: Indians

The Menominee Indians' ancestral lands were in eastern and central Wisconsin, including the Fox River Valley. This waterway was a vital link in the water route from the Great Lakes to the Mississippi, and the white settlers wanted control of the territory. First the Menominee were asked to give a small tract of land along the Fox River to eastern Indians known collectively as the "New York Indians" (Oneida, Stockbridge, etc.). The first meeting in 1822 between the easterners and the Menominee was described by Albert Ellis in his recollections.

The arrangement soon caused ill feelings on both sides, and the Menominee began to protest the treaty. Whites saw it as a hindrance to their acquiring the coveted lands for settlement. Finally in 1831 a treaty with the federal government settled the issue. The Menominee were pushed back into the interior of the territory. The excerpts from this treaty reprinted in the second selection indicate the payments to be made by the government in exchange for the land.

Personal narratives by Indians are not numerous for this period. But one of the most well known is the autobiography of the Sauk chief Black Hawk (a recent reprint is edited by Donald Jackson, Urbana, 1964), in which he explains his actions that resulted in the Black Hawk War. The recollections of Winnebago chiefs Spoon Decorah and Walking Cloud were transcribed in old age, but they are valuable selections for their points of view. Neither of them agreed to be relocated in the reservation lands given to the Winnebago west of the Mississippi River.

The final selection describes the scene at an annual payment to the Chippewa bands who came to La Pointe on Madeline Island in 1855. It contains a speech by Chief Na-naw-long-ga-be, expressing his bewilderment at the changes that were occurring and his frustration in not being able to provide for his band.

Menominee and Winnebago Meet the New York Indians, 1822

ALBERT G. ELLIS

The first business of . . . the delegates, after housing themselves and the goods, was, to assemble the Indians—the Menomonees and Winnebagoes, and in compliance with stipulations of their treaty made the year before, pay them $1500 in goods. In less than a week both tribes, to the number of three or four thousand, were assembled, and camped along the River bank, A day being appointed, and the American and French citizens, with the officers of the garrison, notified the grand council; the New York delegates, the Menomonees and Winnebagoes, were gathered in front of the old Agency house; the spectacle was quite imposing. Solomon U. Hendricks, chief of the Stockbridges, or, as he styled them, the Mohickanucks, a man of education, and of more than common ability, made the opening speech. He addressed the Menomonees and Winnebagoes as his grand children—told them that the few goods before them were presented not so much in fullfilment of their treaty stipulation, as a testimonial of their love and affection for their grand children. The Menomonees and Winnebagoes made suitable replies, acknowledging the relationship, by calling the New York Indians grandfathers. The goods, consisting of blankets, calicoes, blue cloths, guns, powder, lead and shot, barrels of pork and flour, with a liberal supply of tobacco, were carefully divided in two equal piles, and presented to the two tribes. The treaties were produced, the proper receipts drawn on them, when the chiefs of each tribe signed, and the officers of the army, citizens, agents, and interpreters witnessing. Not a drop of liquor was seen; and the remaining part of the day was devoted to feasting.

On re-assembling the parties the next day, when the deputies of New York Indians made an effort to procure an extension of the session, the Winnebagoes were ready instantly with a reply, declining most positively to grant it. They were already being crowded; white people below Chicago were beginning to pass northward. The Menomonees' answer was scarcely more encouraging; they could not sell any more.

The Winnebagoes were preparing to leave for their fall hunts; but before starting, they would treat their grandfathers to a dance. The whole tribe assembled in front of the house in a large circle, the

From Albert G. Ellis, "Fifty-four Years' Recollections of Men and Events in Wisconsin," *Wisconsin Historical Collections*, VII (Madison, 1876), 207–268. Footnotes in the original omitted.

Courtesy of the SHSW [WHi (X3) 8435]

Albert G. Ellis

dancers, and drummer—the master of ceremonies—in the center; first they gave the pipe dance, an amusing affair, a single one dancing at a time, the trick of which seemed to be to keep time to the drum, and especially to suspend action instantaneously with the cessation of the instrument—the dancer to remain in the exact attitude in which the cessation of the drum caught him; frequently the attitude was ridiculous in the extreme; and the maintaining it for a moment, till the drum commenced again, formed an exciting tableau. Next followed the begging dance, preceded by a speech of the drummer, setting forth the extreme want of some of their very old, poor people, and asking charity in their behalf.

The whole concluded with the war dance, a sight to test the nerves of the stoutest heart. The Winnebagoes at that time, fifty-four years ago, were in all their perfection of savage wildness; two thousand of them, men and women, old and young, were massed in a circle, standing fifty deep; the whites, army officers, in the inner ring, and the warrior dancers, drummer, and singers in the center. Twenty of their most stalwart young warriors took their places with not a thread of clothing save the breech-cloth; but all painted in most gorgeous colors, and especially the faces, with circles of black, white, red, green and blue, around the eyes, giving the countenances expressions indescribably fierce and hideous, all armed with tomahawks, knives, and spears. At first the dance was slow, to measured time of the drum and song; for there were a hundred singers, with the voice of the drummer, both male and female—the latter prevailing above the former. Soon they began to wax warm, the countenances assumed unearthly expressions of fierceness; their tread shook the solid earth, and their yells at the end of each cadence, rent the very heavens. None could endure the scene unmoved—unappalled. This tribe at that period, with their stalwart men, Amazonian women, and independent mien, athletic figures, and defiant bearing, can hardly be recognized as the same race, in the degraded Oneidas, who are now seen in our streets, whose abject mien, attenuated, shrunken forms, half-starved, naked, destitute, miserable, mendicants, half civilized though they be, furnish a painful commentary on our Indian civilization.

When the dances were concluded, a shaking of hands, with a grand "bosho," all round, the Winnebagoes prepared to leave the ground; and in an hour, there was not a sign of one to be seen. The Menomonees lingered; they felt more kindly disposed toward their grand-fathers; negociations were soon renewed, resulting finally in a further treaty, granting the New York Indians a right in common with them, to all their country without reserve; the which treaty, though no doubt made in good faith, became subsequently the source of almost endless trouble, terminating at last in confining the New York Indians to two small reserves; one for the Stockbridges, Munsees and Brothertowns, on the east shore of Lake Winnebago, of some eight by twelve miles; and the other twelve miles square on Duck Creek, for the Oneidas; and from this last, the whites are just now moving heaven and earth to dislodge the Indians.

Treaty with the Menominee, 1831 [February 8]

Articles of agreement made and concluded at the City of Washington, this eighth day of February, one thousand eight hundred and thirty-one, between John H. Eaton, Secretary of War, and Samuel C. Stambaugh, Indian Agent at Green Bay, specially authorized by the President of the United States, and the undersigned chiefs and head men of the Menomonee nation of Indians, fully authorized and empowered by the said nation, to conclude and settle all matters provided for by this agreement.

The Menomonee Tribe of Indians, by their delegates in council, this day, define the boundaries of their country as follows, to wit;

On the *east* side of Green Bay, Fox river, and Winnebago lake; beginning at the south end of Winnebago lake; thence southeastwardly to the Milwauky or Manawauky river; thence down said river to its mouth at lake Michigan; thence north, along the shore of lake Michigan, to the mouth of Green Bay; thence up Green Bay, Fox river, and Winnebago lake, to the place of beginning. And on the *west* side of Fox river as follows: beginning at the mouth of Fox river, thence down the east shore of Green bay, and across its mouth, so as to include all the islands of the "Grand Traverse;" thence westerly, on the highlands between the lake Superior and Green bay, to the upper forks of the Menomonee river; thence to the Plover portage of the Wisconsin river; thence up the Wisconsin river, to the Soft Maple river; thence to the source of the Soft Maple river; thence west to the Plume river, which falls into the Chippe-

From Charles J. Kappler, comp., *Indian Affairs: Laws and Treaties*, I (Washington, 1904), 319–324.

way river; thence down said Plume river to its mouth; thence down the Chippeway river thirty miles; thence easterly to the forks of the Manoy river, which falls into the Wisconsin river; thence down the said Manoy river to its mouth; thence down the Wisconsin river to the Wisconsin portage; thence across the said portage to the Fox river; thence down Fox river to its mouth at Green bay, or the place of beginning.

The country described within the above boundaries, the Menomonees claim as the exclusive property of their tribe. Not yet having disposed of any of their lands, they receive no annuities from the United States: whereas their brothers the Pootowottomees on the south, and the Winnebagoes on the west, have sold a great portion of their country, receive large annuities, and are now encroaching upon the lands of the Menomonees. For the purposes, therefore, of establishing the boundaries of their country, and of ceding certain portions of their lands to the United States, in order to secure great and lasting benefits to themselves and posterity, as well as for the purpose of settling the long existing dispute between themselves and the several tribes of the New York Indians, who claim to have purchased a portion of their lands, the undersigned, chiefs and headmen of the Menomonee tribe, stipulate and agree with the United States, as follows:

First. The Menomonee tribe of Indians declare themselves the friends and allies of the United States, under whose parental care and protection they desire to continue; and although always protesting that they are under no obligation to recognize any claim of the New York Indians to any portion of their country; that they neither sold nor received any value, for the land claimed by these tribes; yet, at the solicitation of their Great Father, the President of the United States, and as an evidence of their love and veneration for him, they agree that such part of the land described, being within the following boundaries, as he may direct, may be set apart as a home to the several tribes of the New York Indians, who may remove to, and settle upon the same, within three years from the date of this agreement, viz: beginning on the west side of Fox river, near the "Little Kackalin," at a point known as the "Old Mill Dam;" thence northwest forty miles; thence northeast to the Oconto creek, falling into Green bay; thence down said Oconto creek to Green bay; thence up and along Green bay and Fox river to the place of beginning; excluding therefrom all private land claims confirmed and also the following reservation for military purposes; beginning on the Fox river, at the mouth of the first creek above Fort Howard; thence north sixty-four degrees west to Duck creek; thence down said Duck creek to its mouth; thence up and along

Green bay and Fox river to the place of beginning. The Menomonee Indians, also reserve, for the use of the United States, from the country herein designated for the New York Indians, timber and firewood for the United States garrison, and as much land as may be deemed necessary for public highways, to be located by the direction, and at the discretion of the President of the United States. The country hereby ceded to the United States, for the benefit of the New York Indians, contains by estimation about five hundred thousand acres, and includes all their improvements on the west side of Fox river. As it is intended for a home for the several tribes of the New York Indians, who may be residing upon the lands at the expiration of three years from this date, and for none others, the President of the United States is hereby empowered to apportion the lands among the actual occupants at that time, so as to assign to any tribe a greater number of acres than may be equal to one hundred for each soul actually settled upon the lands, and if, at the time of such apportionment, any lands shall remain unoccupied by any tribe of the New York Indians, such portion as would have belonged to said Indians, had it been occupied, shall revert to the United States. That portion, if any, so reverting, to be laid off by the President of the United States. It is distinctly understood, that the lands hereby ceded to the United States for the New York Indians, are to be held by those tribes, under such tenure as the Menomonee Indians now hold their lands, subject to such regulations and alteration of tenure, as Congress think proper to adopt.

Second. For the above cession to the United States, for the benefit of the New York Indians, the United States consent to pay the Menomonee Indians, twenty thousand dollars; five thousand to be paid on the first day of August next, and five thousand annually thereafter; which sums shall be applied to the use of the Menomonees, after such manner as the President of the United States may direct.

Third. The Menomonee tribe of Indians, in consideration of the kindness and protection of the Government of the United States, and for the purpose of securing to themselves and posterity, a comfortable home, hereby cede and forever relinquish to the United States, all their country on the southeast side of Winnebago lake, Fox river, and Green bay, which they describe in the following boundaries, to wit: beginning at the south end of Winnebago lake, and running in a southeast direction to Milwauky or Manawauky river; thence down said river to its mouth; thence north, along the shore of lake Michigan, to the entrance of Green bay; thence up and along Green bay, Fox river, and Winnebago lake, to the place of beginning; excluding all private land claims which the United States have heretofore confirmed and sanctioned. It is also agreed that all the islands which lie in Fox river and Green bay, are likewise ceded; the whole comprising by estimation, two million five hundred thousand acres.

Fourth. The following described tract of land, at present owned and occupied by the Menomonee Indians, shall be set apart, and designated for their future homes, upon which their improvements as an agricultural people are to be made: beginning on the West side of Fox river, at the "Old Mill Dam" near the "Little Kackalin," and running up and along said river, to the Winnebago lake; thence along said lake to the mouth of Fox river; thence up Fox river to the Wolf river; thence up Wolf river to a point southwest of the west corner of the tract herein designated for the New York Indians; thence northeast to said west corner; thence southeast to the place of beginning. The above reservation being made to the Menomonee Indians for the purpose of weaning them from their wandering habits, by attaching them to comfortable homes, the President of the United States, as a mark of affection for his children of the Menomonee tribe, will cause to be employed five farmers of established character for capacity, industry, and moral habits, for ten successive years, whose duty it shall be to assist the Menomonee Indians in the cultivation of their farms, and to instruct their children in the business and occupation of farming. Also, five females shall be employed, of like good character, for the purpose of teaching young Menomonee women, in the business of useful housewifery, during a period of ten years.—The annual compensation allowed to the farmers, shall not exceed five hundred dollars, and that of the females three hundred dollars. And the United States will cause to be erected, houses suited to their condition, on said lands, as soon as the Indians agree to occupy them, for which ten thousand dollars shall be appropriated; also, houses for the farmers, for which three thousand dollars shall be appropriated; to be expended under the direction of the Secretary of War. Whenever the Menomonees thus settle their lands, they shall be supplied with useful household articles, horses, cows, hogs, and sheep, farming utensils, and other articles of husbandry necessary to their comfort, to the value of six thousand dollars; and they desire that some suitable device may be stamped upon such articles, to preserve them from sale or barter, to evil disposed white persons: none of which, nor any other articles with which the United States may at any time furnish them, shall be liable to sale, or be disposed of or bargained, without permission of the agent. The whole to be under the immediate care of the farmers employed to remain among said Indians, but subject to the general control of the United States' Indian

Agent at Green Bay acting under the Secretary of War. The United States will erect a grist and saw mill on Fox river, for the benefit of the Menomonee Indians, and saw the lumber necessary for building on their lands, as also to instruct such young men of the Menomonee nation, as desire to, and conveniently can be instructed in the trade of a miller. The expenses of erecting such mills, and a house for the miller to reside in, shall not exceed six thousand dollars, and the annual compensation of the miller shall be six hundred dollars, to continue for ten years. And if the mills so erected by the United States, can saw more lumber or grind more grain, than is required for the proper use of said Menomonee Indians, the proceeds of such milling shall be applied to the payment of other expenses occurring in the Green bay agency, under the direction of the Secretary of War.

In addition to the above provision made for the Menomonee Indians, the President of the United States will cause articles of clothing to be distributed among their tribe at Green bay, within six months from the date of this agreement, to the amount of eight thousand dollars; and flour and wholesome provisions, to the amount of one thousand dollars, one thousand dollars to be paid in specie. The cost of the transportation of the clothing and provisions, to be included in the sum expended. There shall also be allowed annually thereafter, for the space of twelve successive years, to the Menomonee tribe, in such manner and form as the President of the United States shall deem most beneficial and advantageous to the Indians, the sum of six thousand dollars. As a matter of great importance to the Menomonees, there shall be one or more gun and blacksmith's shops erected, to be supplied with a necessary quantity of iron and steel, which, with a shop at Green bay, shall be kept up for the use of the tribe, and continued at the discretion of the President of the United States. There shall also be a house for an interpreter to reside in, erected at Green bay, the expenses not to exceed five hundred dollars.

Fifth. In the treaty of Butte des Morts, concluded in August 1827, an article is contained, appropriately one thousand five hundred dollars annually, for the support of schools in the Menomonee country. And the representatives of the Menomonee nation, who are parties hereto, require, and it is agreed to, that said appropriation shall be increased five hundred dollars, and continued for ten years from this date, to be placed in the hands of the Secretary of War, in trust for the exclusive use and benefit of the Menomonee tribe of Indians, and to be applied by him to the education of the children of the Menomonee Indians, in such manner as he may deem most advisable.

Sixth. The Menomonee tribe of Indians shall be at liberty to hunt and fish on the lands they have now ceded to the United States, on the east side of Fox river and Green bay, with the same privileges they at present enjoy, until it be surveyed and offered for sale by the President; they conducting themselves peaceably and orderly. The chiefs and Warriors of the Menomonee nation, acting under the authority and on behalf of the tribe, solemnly pledge themselves to preserve peace and harmony between their people and the Government of the United States forever. They neither acknowledge the power nor protection of any other State or people. A departure from this pledge by any portion of their tribe, shall be a forfeiture of the protection of the United States' Government, and their annuities will cease. In thus declaring their friendship for the United States, however, the Menomonee tribe of Indians, having the most implicit confidence in their great father, the President of the United States, desire he will, as a kind and faithful guardian of their welfare, direct the provisions of this compact to be carried into immediate effect. The Menomonee chiefs request that such part of it as relates to the New York Indians, be immediately submitted to the representatives of their tribes. And if they refuse to accept the provision made for their benefit, and to remove upon the lands set apart for them, on the west side of Fox river, that he will direct their immediate removal from the Menomonee country; but if they agree to accept of the liberal offer made to them by the parties to this compact, then the Menomonee tribe as dutiful children of their great father the President, will take them by the hand as brothers, and settle down with them in peace and friendship.

The boundary, as stated and defined in this agreement, of the Menomonee country, with the exception of the cessions herein before made to the United States, the Menomonees claim as their country; that part of its adjoining the farming country, on the west side of Fox river, will remain to them as heretofore, for a hunting ground, until the President of the United States, shall deem it expedient to extinguish their title. In that case, the Menomonee tribe promise to surrender it immediately, upon being notified of the desire of Government to possess it. The additional annuity then to be paid to the Menomonee tribe, to be fixed by the President of the United States. It is conceded to the United States that they may enjoy the right of making such roads, and of establishing such military posts, in any part of the country now occuped by the Menomonee nation, as the President at any time may think proper.

As a further earnest of the good feeling on the part of their great father, it is agreed that the expenses of the Menomonee delegation to the city of Washington, and of returning, will be paid, and that a comfortable suit of clothes will be provided for each; also, that the United States will cause four thousand dollars to be expended in procuring fowling guns, and ammunition for them; and likewise, in lieu of any garrison rations, hereafter allowed or received by them, there shall be procured and given to said tribe one thousand dollars worth of good and wholesome provisions annually, for four years, by which time it is hoped their hunting habits may cease, and their attention be turned to the pursuits of agriculture.

In testimony whereof, the respective parties to this agreement have severally signed the same, this 8th February, 1831.

John H. Eaton,	[L. S.]	Ah-ke-ne-pa-weh, earth standing, his x mark, [L. S.]
S. C. Stambaugh,	[L. S.]	Shaw-wan-noh, the south, his x mark, [L. S.]
Kaush-kau-no-naive, grizzly bear, his x mark,	[L. S.]	Mash-ke-wet, his x mark, [L. S.]
A-ya-mah-taw, fish spawn, his x mark,	[L. S.]	Pah-she-nah-sheu, his x mark, [L. S.]
Ko-ma-ni-kin, big wave, his x mark,	[L. S.]	Chi-mi-na-na-quet, great cloud, his x mark, [L. S.]
Ko-ma-ni-kee-no-shah, little wave, his x mark,	[L. S.]	A-na-quet-to-a-peh, setting in a cloud, his x mark, [L. S.]
O-ho-pa-shah, little whoop, his x mark,	[L. S.]	Sha-ka-cho-ka-mo, great chief, his x mark, [L. S.]

Signed, sealed, and delivered in presence of—

R. A. Forsyth,
C. A. Grignon,
    Interpreters,
A. G. Ellis,
Richard Pricket, United States Interpreter, his x mark,

William Wilkins, of Pennsylvania,
Samuel Swartwout, of N. York,
John T. Mason, Michigan,
Rh. M. Johnson, Kentucky.

Spoon Decorah[1]

[An interview[2] conducted by Reuben G. Thwaites, editor of *Wisconsin Historical Collections*. All footnotes retained in this excerpt are Mr. Thwaites'.]

I was born at my father's village near the Caffrey schoolhouse at the mouth of the Baraboo River, a few years before the Tecumseh war. My father's name, among the French, was Zhuminakha [Firewater], which I am told is from a French word having something to do with wine. His Winnebago name was Warrahwikoogah, or Bird Spirit. The Americans called him Grey-headed Decorah. He was a brother[3] of One-eyed Decorah, or Big Canoe.

I remember hearing of the British attack on the American fort at Prairie du Chien [in 1814]. Some of our relatives joined in it. Their names I do not now remember; I am getting very old; my memory is not as good as it was. My father's party were at Little Green Lake at the time of the attack. My father was a peaceable man. He did not like to be at war with the whites. So our people did not go. I was only a boy, then. I think the first time I ever went to Green Bay, was when I was eight years old. I went to visit my aunts, who were living there. I went twice to see them.

[1]Spelled also: Day Korah, Dacorah, DeKaury, DeKauray, Day Kauray, and De Corrah; I have retained the orthography of the neighborhood.

[2]At the home of Spoon, in the town of Big Flats, Adams county, some ten miles north of Friendship, March 29, 1887. Moses Paquette, of Black River Falls, acted as interpreter. Spoon, who died in a cranberry marsh northwest of Necedah, Oct. 13, 1889, was a tall, well-formed, manly-looking fellow, with a well-shaped head, pleasant, open features, and dignified demeanor—quite superior in appearance to the majority of Wisconsin Winnebagoes. He was living with his aged squaw in a reasonably neat small frame cottage, while his progeny, reaching to the fourth generation, were clustered about the patriarchal lodge in family wigwams. The old man told his story in a straightforward, dignified manner, his memory being occasionally jogged by Doctor Decorah, his nephew. The Doctor is a medicine-man, held in high esteem by the Decorah, or mixed-blood element of the Wisconsin Winnebagoes, who live chiefly upon homesteads in Adams, Marquette, and Jackson counties. Spoon took pride in exhibiting a well-thumbed and much-battered copy of vol. vi of these *Collections*, presented to him by Dr. Draper in 1879. He regarded it as "big medicine," and it was his constant companion upon the hunt as well as at home.

To those familiar with the Indian character, it is not necessary to explain that much of the material in this interview, as well as that with Walking Cloud, *post*, was obtained by means of elaborate cross-questioning. Paquette is a faithful and intelligent interpreter, and in each case carefully rendered both questions and answers. The result I have formulated into two continuous narratives, following as closely as possible the Indian manner of speech; as here printed, they meet with Paquette's approval. It is not because of any fresh data herein contained, that these simple "talks" are awarded a place in the *Collections:* but they present the Indian view of several important historical events, thus giving us an insight into what Wisconsin savages themselves are thinking and talking about, in their camp-fire reminiscences of early experiences with the white man.

[3]Cousin, in fact. The Winnebagoes make no distinction, in common speech, between brother and cousin.

From "Narrative of Spoon Decorah in an Interview With the Editor," *Wisconsin Historical Collections*, XIII (Madison, 1895), 448–462. Some footnotes in the original omitted.

Courtesy of the SHSW [WHi (X3) 12668]

An 1887 picture of Spoon Decorah

During what the whites call the Winnebago War, at Prairie du Chien [in 1827], I was living with my people on Little Green Lake. There was among us no general hatred of the whites. Red Bird had some private revenge to satisfy, and murdered the white family at the prairie of his own accord. We were all very sorry. We had no sympathy with him. We felt that he was a bad Indian. He tried to get the rest of his tribe into trouble. I have heard of some white people who enjoy getting their neighbors into any trouble they have themselves got into. There was no feeling among the rest of the tribe, over Red Bird's conduct, except that of anger. We willingly gave him up to the whites.

During the Black Hawk War [1832], I lived at the Portage. When we heard of the trouble, I wanted very much to go and join the Americans. I knew the officers at Fort Winnebago, and was friendly to them. But my friends got around me and said that the Sacs were friends of the Winnebagoes. So I was persuaded not to go. In July, ten families of us started out on our summer's hunt, on the Roche-a-Cri River. We had got as far as Friendship, when Ochpiyoka (The Spaniard), one of our friends, came into camp much excited and told us what had happened down in the Illinois country, saying that the Sacs were headed our way. We had gone out on our hunt in strong numbers. Knowing that the war was going on, we feared that the Sacs might come into our territory. For there was some fear of the Sacs, all the while, although we had been told of their friendliness. They knew that some of our people were with the Americans. We felt that if the Sacs were driven into our hunting-grounds they might be revengeful, and then it would go hard with our hunting parties unless we were prepared for attack. So when The Spaniard came and told us that the Sacs were really headed our way, we were much afraid. He told us that the center of attack would be Portage. We had left many of our old people and women here. So we at once returned to Portage. The other hunting parties, to which runners had also been sent out, did so too. This was a few days before the battle on the Sauk bluffs [Wisconsin Heights].

Our party camped on the rise of ground just back of what is now the city end of the Wisconsin River bridge, in Portage. Nearly the whole tribe was camped about Portage. There were three large camps, on both sides of the river, about where the bridge now is. The principal chiefs in these camps were: Black Wolf,[4] his son Dandy, Tahneekseeickseega (Fond of Tobacco), White Eagle, White

---

[4]Black Wolf's village was on the west shore of Lake Winnebago, south of the site of Oshkosh. He served under the British in the War of 1812–15, being at the captures of Mackinaw and Prairie du Chien. He died at Portage, previous to 1848.

Crow,[5] and Ahsheeshka (Broken Arm). Black Wolf was the uncle of
Gray Eagle's Eye, my present squaw; Dandy was her cousin; White
Crow was a one-eyed chief, who had a village at the Four Lakes,—
he died a few years after the Black Hawk war; Broken Arm fought
under Tecumseh, and also died a few years after the Black Hawk
War.

Pierre Paquette was the trader at the Portage, in those days. He
was a large, powerful man. His squaw was a daughter of Joseph
Crélie. Our tribe had great respect for him. His mother was a Winnebago woman, and he was a good man in every way,—very
friendly to our people. I was his friend, and he once gave me a pony.
The white captains [Dodge and Henry] were in Portage when we
got there; they had brought the news from White Beaver's [General
Atkinson's] camp, that caused our return. Paquette was engaged by
the white captains to take them across the country to Black Hawk's
camp, on the headwaters of the Rock River. Paquette wanted a
party of Winnebagoes to go with him as guides. He sent Nahheesanchonka (Man Who Thinks Himself of Importance) into
the camp to get volunteers. Nahheesanchonka told us that if we
would go into the war we would make a name for ourselves, and get
presents; also win the good opinion of White Beaver, and the Big
Father in Washington. But there was still among us a strong feeling
of friendliness toward the Sacs. This feeling was of friendly pity, not
a desire to help them fight. So only six young men, none of them
chiefs, went with Paquette as guides. Of these were Pawnee (Pania
Blanc), Nahheesanchonka, Notsookega (Bear the Breaks up the
Brush), Ahmegunka, and Tahnichseeka (The Smoker). As I think
again, perhaps White Crow went with Paquette on this expedition,
but of this I am not sure.[6] Anyway, White crow fought on the
American side, at the Sauk bluffs [July 21, 1832].

The return of Paquette's party, a week or so later, told us of the
defeat at the Sauk bluffs. We heard that those Sacs who had escaped
the white bullets had crossed the Wisconsin River in a body. There
was now great excitement in our camp. We feared that Black Hawk,
thinking us now to be his enemies, would turn up the river and
attack us at Portage. Our sympathies were strongly with the whites.
Our trading interests were with them, and we were bound to them

[5]Kaukishkaka (White Crow), a Winnebago chief, who had but one eye, and something of a
reputation as an orator. His village, which comprised about 1,200 persons, housed in tepees
covered with red-cedar bark, appears to have been situated about where is now the little
village of Pheasant Branch, at the west end of Lake Mendota, Dane county; the paper City of
the Four Lakes was to have occupied about the same ground, a few years after the Black
Hawk War. Major Henry Dodge held a council with White Crow at the latter's village, May
25, 1832, and secured his promise to be friendly to the whites, or at least neutral.
[6]All white narrators agree that he was with Paquette's party.

by treaties. Yet we did not like to be fighting old neighbors like the Sacs. Some of our people wanted to move out of the way, but others wanted to stand ground against Black Hawk. And thus we argued the matter between ourselves, till the danger was passed. Black Hawk fled before White Beaver, on his way to the Bad Ax. Two men from our camp went as guides to White Beaver, on this chase. They were Nahreechsecochkeshica (Lame Ankle) and Mahheenibahka (Double Knife). These were the only guides that White Beaver had.

It was only a day's trip with fast ponies between Portage and Prairie la Crosse. There was much traveling between the two places during all this great excitement. So we soon got news of the battle at the Bad Ax [Aug. 2, 1832].

. . . .

I never saw White Beaver, but have always heard he was a big warrior among the whites. My father knew General Dodge very well, and he always claimed him as his brother, in talking with him,—which was a great honor; but General Dodge was a good friend to our people, and deserved to be well treated by them. I met the general twice, and spoke a few words with him each time. The first time was at Blue Mounds, during the Black Hawk War. He had come to the Mounds for supplies. After the war I met him there again.

. . . .

My father gave me good talk about our tribe. He liked to speak of those things. Now the Winnebagoes are poor. They have not so much pride. Very few of them care about the old times. Most of them care only for firewater. We get a very poor living, now. Our farms have not good soil. The game is not as plenty as it was. The white traders cheat and rob us. They make our young men drunk. It would be better if we had an agent.[7] We think the Big Father does not care for us any longer, now that he has all our best land. Perhaps it will not be long before he will want the poor land we now live on. Then we must go to the reservation.[8] Life on the reservation is hard. The Winnebagoes in Wisconsin do not want to go there. They want to die on their own land. They like best the streams and woods where their fathers and uncles have always hunted and trapped. If we had an agent given us, we would do better. My people are

[7] In 1886, the Commissioner of Indian Affairs recommended to Congress the appointment of an agent for the Wisconsin Winnebagoes, but no action was taken. See remarks on this subject, in article, "Wisconsin Winnebagoes," in *Wis. Hist. Colls.*, xii.
[8] In Dakota county, Nebr., where about half of the Winnebago tribe are now living.

like children, and need to be looked after. They want to be encouraged. I am too old to travel much; but some day I will go and see the captain at the Four Lakes.[9] I will ask him to see the Big Father, and procure for us an agent who shall be a good man.[10] We had better have no agent, than such as I hear they sometimes have on the reservation.

[9]Meaning the governor of Wisconsin, at Madison. "Taychoperah" (literally, *four lakes*) is the old Winnebago name for the country round about Madison.
[10]In June, 1887, Spoon Decorah, Four Deer, and Doctor Decorah, with a half-breed interpreter, John la Ronde, of Portage, came to Madison upon this errand, but Governor Rusk was not in the city at the time, and they failed to see him. The party spent the day in the State Historical Society's rooms in the capitol, and then left for home. This was Spoon's last visit to Madison, for in the succeeding autumn he died.

Walking Cloud

[INTERVIEWED BY REUBEN G. THWAITES]

My name is Mauchhewemahnigo (Walking Cloud).[1] I was born on the Wisconsin River. I was about ten years of age when the treaty was held at Prairie du Chien,[2] where they fixed the boundaries between the Winnebagoes and the Chippewas and our cousins the Sioux. I went with my father to that treaty. My squaw's name is Champchekeriwinke (Flash of Lightning). Her uncle was Hootschope (Four Legs). She was born at his village on Lake Winnebago.

During the Black Hawk War, my father had his lodge near La Crosse. I did not go to the war; I was too young. But my brother did. His name was Seeorouspinka. General Dodge sent a messenger down to Prairie du Chien, and said he wanted the Winnebagoes to

[1]The interview took place May 18, 1887, at the Winnebago settlement in the town of Albion, Jackson county. Moses Paquette was the interpreter, and afterwards revised the MS. of the narrative, which I have given as nearly as possible as it fell from Walking Cloud's lips. As with that given by Spoon Decorah, this story has ethnographical rather than historical importance. I think that these two narratives are the last of any value which may be obtained from the Winnebagoes of Wisconsin, for the reason that the younger generation of men have no traditions to which we can attach any scientific importance. Spoon and Walking Cloud were regarded by their fellows as practically "the last of the Mohicans," and their offspring are allowing the old tales to die with them. Spoon died in 1889, but Moses Paquette writes me (Black River Falls, Nov. 6, 1895) that Walking Cloud still lives; his squaw, however, is dead.
[2]Aug. 19, 1825.

From "Narrative of Walking Cloud in an Interview With the Editor," *Wisconsin Historical Collections*, XIII (Madison, 1895), 463–467. Some footnotes in the original are omitted.

go into the war and help the Great Father punish the Sacs. Our people, who were named in this call, did not want to go to war. But the messenger, after we had all arrived in Praire du Chien, picked out Winnebago Black Hawk (my father), and my brother, and they went up the Wisconsin River with a party of white soldiers and officers from Fort Crawford. They met a number of Sacs coming down on a raft made of canoes tied together. The Winnebagoes and the whites killed most of the Sacs in this party.[3] Winnebago Black Hawk was the guide of this expedition.

After the battle of the Bad Ax, the Winnebagoes went on their fall hunt. My father, Winnebago Black Hawk, had a hunting village on the La Crosse River, near where Bangor now is. There were about eighteen hunters in the camp. One day a party of young men were on the chase, having gone up one of the branches of the La Crosse River, towards the head of the Kickapoo. On their return, they came across the camp of the Sac chief, near a little lake. There was much excitement among the hunters. They knew the Great Father had ordered all Winnebagoes to capture the head man of the Sacs; and they did not at first know what to do. They concluded, without talking to the Sacs, to go to their village and report to Winnebago Black Hawk. There was a council held that night in the Winnebago village. It lasted all night and all next day. I remember this council very well. Both Red Wing, here, and I were young men and stood by while the old men talked. The day after the council was over, Winnebago Black Hawk asked three young men to go to the Sac chief, Black Hawk, and tell him that the Winnebagoes had been ordered by General Street, the agent at Prairie du Chien, to take him whenever they saw him and bring him in to Fort Crawford. The three young men were Nenohamphega (Lighting the Water), Wakuntschapinka (Good Thunder), and Chatschunka (Wave). Wave was an interpreter, being one-half Sac and one-half Winnebago. These three went through the woods to the camp of the Sac Black Hawk, and delivered to him the speech of Winnebago Black Hawk. They advised the Sac chief to go peaceably to Prairie du Chien, and doubtless he would not be harmed. The Sac chief said: "You want us to be killed by the whites; as you so wish it, we will go."

So the Sac Black Hawk, and those who were with him, were brought back to our village; and a number of our warriors went down to Prairie du Chien with them, and delivered them up to General Street. One-eyed Decorah was not of this party. I am posi-

[3]During the interview, an old Winnebago named Red Wing was present. He said that he took part in this affair, and killed four Sacs. In the recital of his alleged achievement, he seemed to take a lively satisfaction. See reference to this butchery, in *Wis. Hist. Colls.*, xii., pp. 254, 255.

tive of it. He remained at our village all the time. He was not a good man, and not then a chief. After the treaty and the payment, he was made a chief through the influence of the American Fur Company and the Indian agent, General Street. The agents and traders had a way of putting aside old chiefs, for new ones whom they had gained to their interest. After the Black Hawk War, One-eyed Decorah married two women, and then went off and started a village of his own, on the Black River. He was always afraid somebody would entice his women away. He was ugly and jealous.

H. M. Rice got me [in 1850, or 1851] and many of my friends to go to Long Prairie, Minn., and make up our minds about that country. We were to see if we would like it as a home. We went there and did not like it, so returned home that same fall.

Captain Hunt got us [in 1873] to go to Nebraska. He promised me a span of horses, a wagon, and $200; and said I should get them when I arrived in Nebraska. But I never received them. We soon came back.

I have been living for thirteen years on my present homestead, in the town of Albion, Jackson County.

The Winnebagoes came from the sky, the old Indians say. They settled first at the Red Banks. They first met the French, who came in large boats to trade with them, near Green Bay. The French were always our good friends. We never had any trouble with them.

All of the other tribes of Indians have tried to kill off the Winnebagoes. The Sioux were the most ugly towards us, though I am told they are our cousins. In old times we had much fighting with the Chippewas, but not in my recollection. We have been at peace with everybody, since the Great Father at Washington commanded us to be at peace or he would take away all our guns. The Menomonees have always been our good friends.

Our fathers used to fast and pray, that the spirits might appear to them. Sometimes they would pray that the water spirit might come and wet the corn-fields. This he would do when he was in good humor; but when he was in bad humor we would bring a good deal of water on the land and make a flood. The water spirit, I am told, has a long tail winding around his body, and has two horns. But in my day he has not appeared to any of our people, and we no longer pray to him.

You ask me about a future life. I cannot see how a person may be taken to another world and come back and tell about it. Old people used to tell us that the dead, when washed clean by the Great Spirit, could be sent back to earth. And some believe this, even now.

One thing is certain. The body rests in the earth four days. During that time we take food and place it on the grave, that the body [soul] may not starve. After four days, the body rises and starts out alone, to the happy hunting-ground. A spirit comes to guide the body on its way, unseen. They come to a swift-running stream. They must cross it on a slender pole. If the body is that of a bad Indian, it sinks in the river and never lives more. If it is a good Indian, it walks steadily and crosses the pole. A woman stands on the farther bank, and receives the new comer. The woman asks the stranger his name. When she receives it, she says: "You are good; you shall always live in the happy hunting-ground." This woman is neither old nor young, nor will she ever be old; for the Great Spirit placed her there at the beginning of the world, and she has always looked the same.

Chippewa Payment at La Pointe in 1855

RICHARD MORSE

It may be remembered that the payment to the Chippewa Indians at La Pointe, in August and September, 1855, was necessarily deferred during weeks, waiting for the remote bands to come in.

The department had sent express and timely orders to persons at La Pointe, to have the Indians gathered, and to be in waiting for the Commissioner or Agent, with goods and money for the payment, as per treaty, when we arrived. The persons failed to carry out the orders.

The officers of the commission, and persons connected with the payment, must remain from the time we arrived, (11th August), until messengers could be despatched for the bands at a distance. To Grand Portage, North Shore, and over 200 miles in the wilderness towards the Mississippi and other directions. Consequently the Indians from the interior were weeks arriving. The interval of time being occupied by the Agency in taking the census of—and in putting up packages of goods for, and distributing to, the Indians, as they arrived, and in holding councils with the chiefs in relation to affairs of unsettled business, directing in regard to the payment of

From Richard E. Morse, "The Chippewas of Lake Superior," *Wisconsin Historical Collections,* III (Madison, 1857), 338-344. Some footnotes in the original omitted.

their debts as per appropriation from Government of $90,000 for that purpose. Many sittings and councils were held, and speeches made between those of the commission and the chiefs. A long time, it seemed, had transpired.

The bands from the vicinity of *Lac Court Orielle* were yet to come. Finally news of the arrival of some 200 of these Indians upon the shore of the Bay, about 12 miles from La Pointe, had the evening before reached the Commissioner, who promptly employed three or four little sail boats, the only craft at hand, to bring the Indians over.

· ·

The day was bright and warm. It was nearly noon that the three or four little sail boats which had been despatched to fetch *these forest children* across the Bay to La Pointe hove in sight, and nearing the shore, laden almost to the water's edge with men, women and children. There was a general gathering on shore to see them as they came in.

A scene of the like poverty and abject wretchedness, we hope we may never witness again. Some of these poor creatures, especially the children, were literally naked.

They had but shreds for blankets. Birch bark baskets, and dishes the same, were their chief wares—rude and untanned deer and other skins, their principal wardrobe and baggage. Clothing, they could not be said to have had. Some of the men had what were once shirts—some had not—some, parts of leggings—others none. Most of the women had on them some kind of a miserable excuse for a garment.

The children nearly, some quite naked, were, as if to hide them from sight, mostly inside of a circle made of their effects, and what was a sad apology for baggage.

Several of these poor wretches were so feeble from hunger and sickness, that they needed supporting. A number were lame, others partially blind. All had, for some time, been on scanty rations of nought but wild rice, as they could neither fish nor hunt while hurrying with their sick and children, and fearing their enemies in ambush—to meet their "Great Father." Commissioner MANY-PENNY, Gen. H. L. STEVENS, and many others who were present, can bear testimony to these truths.

Of these interior bands, NA-NAW-ONG-GA-BE was the head. They were from within 30 to 60 miles of the Mississippi; on the opposite side of which is the country of their old and implacable enemies, the Sioux. Between these tribes, deadly feuds and exterminating wars have existed for more than a century, defying all efforts from their

A turn-of-the-century photograph of La Pointe Village,
established early as a French military and trading post

white neighbors, and the means *which have been employed* by the
U.S. Government, to arrest them. Hence these people have good
reason to be in continual fear, and on constant watch for their lives.

The warriors of these bands, it was conceded, excelled those of
any and all others at La Pointe, in their noble features and fine, erect
statures. Nor were they inferior in their sprightliness of mind; their
head chief was the smartest orator on the ground. Not long after
they arrived, the Commissioner sent a request for these bands to
meet him at the council-ground, for the purpose of receiving rations. In two or three hours we saw some 80 to 100 stately warriors, NA-NAW-ONG-GA-BE at their head, marching in more regular
order than those bands less accustomed to the war path, to meet the
Commissioner. These Indians came late last year also, and the
goods mainly having been distributed, they received but very little.

The head chief, NA-NAW-ONG-GA-BE, we should say, had seen
about fifty-five winters. He is rather less than the medium height
and size, an intelligent face and mild expression, a very keen eye,
and then animated in speaking, a sort of fiery look or twinkle. Like

Courtesy of the SHSW [WHi (D488) 5449]

most of the warriors, his face is highly colored with vermillion. At the head of his warriors and in council, he wears an elaborate turban of turkey feathers over his head and shoulders—giving him a fuller appearance in person than he really has, an *unique* look even for an Indian.

It was not long after this chief arrived, before he became the favorite orator and chief. We saw and noticed much of him and his people. We believe they have innate impulses as exalted as in human bosom ever dwelt. We saw tears of sympathy over the scene of misery before us, when these people landed at La Pointe. On the ground, the day they arrived, by the side of NA-NAW-ONG-GA-BE, stood AW-KE-WAIN-ZE, his principal, a tall and majestic chief, and a full head and neck above the red warriors seated around on the grass. The Commissioner addressed them, JOHN JOHNSON, of the *Soo*, a half Chippewa, and a man of intelligence and character, interpreting.

The Commissioner having said that he was very glad to see him and his people, though they had come late; that he felt pained to see

Courtesy of the SHSW [WHi (X3) 12939]

U.S. government officials making an annuity payment to the Chippewa at La Pointe

them in such a sorrowful condition, looking so poverty stricken, &c.

NA-NAW-ONG-GA-BE, in a manner dignified and earnest, readily replied: "My father, we are very happy to see you also. We have reasons for not coming immediately after we heard your voice echoing through the wilderness. We were all roused by the sound of your voice. It created glad feelings and rejoicings among all my people. I lost no time to give orders to all my young men to collect before me. I then informed them that your words had reached me, desiring us to come immediately to you. I took the second thought, and concluded it would not be proper to advise my young men to leave immediately, while we were all busily engaged in collecting wild rice, to provide for my people against hunger and famine. After making all haste to do this, and provide for our sick old women and children, with four of my best warriors to defend them from my troublesome and dangerous neighbors, the Sioux, I and my people with me, hastened upon the path-way to the shores of the Chippewa Lake (Superior). I have obeyed your call—I am now before you.

"You say, my father, you are sorry to see us in our state of poverty. * * No wonder, my father, you see us in poverty and showing so much of our nakedness. Five long winters have passed since I have received as much as a blanket for one of my children.

"My father, what has become of your promise? You probably have sent what you promised to us, but where it has gone, is more than I am able to say. Perhaps it has sunk in the deep waters of the lake, or it may have evaporated in the heavens, like the rising of the mist—or perhaps it has blown over our heads, and gone towards the setting sun. Last year I visited our father (Indian Agent GILBERT) who came here, and gave goods to a portion of his red children—but I could not get here in time—I got nothing. I turned round to some of our traders, no doubt who are now standing among us here, and asked them for some clothing to take to my poor children, but they refused me. Therefore I had to retrace my foot-steps over a long road, with empty hands, to my home in the woods—just as I had come.

"In your words to me, you ask me not to use the fire-water; and after my traders refusing me, as I said before, I do not intend to accept their *fire-water* in case they offer it to me.

"I returned to my home. I endured the severity of the long, cold winter with what nature had provided for me—relieved only by the skins I have taken from the beasts of the forest. I had to sit nearer to my little fire for want of what I did not get of my father, and could not get of my traders; I requested my father the next year to bring me what I needed very much. I am not like your red child that lives on the borders of the Chippewa Lake—he desired you to bring him the irons to spear the fish, and small twine he uses in dropping his hook into the water. I told you, my father, I live principally in traveling through my home in the forest, by carrying the iron on my shoulder,—that whenever I aim at the wild animal, he falls before me. I have come with my young men, and we have brought most of our families on the strength of your promise last year, that you would give us good portions for our wants this year. And like all your children, my father, after a hard day's labor, or walk, I am hungry—my people need something to give them strength and comfort. It is so long since a gun was given us—we have only a few stubs, bound together by leather strings, with which to kill our game, and to defend ourselves against our enemies.

"My father, look around you upon the faces of my poor people; sickness and hunger, whiskey and war are killing us fast. We are dying and fading away; we drop to the ground like the trees before the axe of the white man; we are weak—you are strong. We are but foolish Indians—you have knowledge and wisdom in your head; we want your help and protection. We have no homes—no cattle—no lands, and we will not long need them. A few short winters, my people will be no more. The winds shall moan around the last lodge of your red children. I grieve; but cannot turn our fate away. The sun—the moon—the rivers—the forest, we love so well, we must leave. We shall soon sleep in the ground—we will not awake again. I have no more to say to you, my father."

The Commissioner evinced sympathy for his red children on several occasions, upon hearing earnest appeals addressed to him by their chiefs.

NOTE—We append the following appreciative remarks from the *Lake Superior Miner,* of October, 1855, which close with a reference to NA-NAW ONG-GA-BE, or as the *Miner* has it, NA-GON-A-BI: "It is supposed by many, that the language of the Indians is barren of the poetical expressions, common in the French and English. But what can be more beautiful than the following, which the writer has heard uttered by chiefs of the Chippewas in council. At a treaty made on the Mississippi, last year, the chief, WIDE-MOUTH, made the following remarks, in answer to the refusal of the Government's Agent to accept a proposition of the chiefs, to sell their land at a price double that offered them by the Agent. WIDE-MOUTH said to the Agent: 'My father, I live away north, on the head waters of the Mississippi; my children (band) are poor and destitute, and as it were, almost naked, while you, my father, are rich and well clothed. When I left my home to come to this treaty to sell my lands—for we know that we must sell for what we can get—the whites must have them—my braves, young men, women and children, held a council and begged of me to do the best I could in selling their homes; and now, my father, I beg of you to accept of the proposition I have made you, and to-morrow I will start for home; and then you count the days which you know it will take me to reach there, and on the day of my arrival, look north, and as you see the northern light streaming up in the sky, imagine to yourself that it is the congratulation of joy of my children ascending to God, that you have accepted of the proposition I have offered you.' At the payment made at La Pointe this fall, the chief NA-GON-A-BI, made the following remark, in answer to the question asked him by the Agent, if he understood the articles of the treaty which he had signed at La Pointe last year. He said: 'My father, I was here last year, when the treaty was made, and I swallowed the words of the treaty down my throat, and they have not yet had time to blister on my breast.'"

[Lyman C. Draper]

Chapter IV
WISCONSIN PIONEERS

The rich farmlands, virgin forests, long lake coast, numerous lakes and rivers, and healthful climate of Wisconsin Territory attracted immigrants. All of western Europe seemed seized with "America fever." Overland across the prairies of Indiana and Illinois, and by sailing ship and steamboat through the recently completed Erie Canal across the Great Lakes, the people began to flood into the territory.

Yankees moved west seeking cheap farmlands and fewer people. Europeans, especially English, Scots, Irish, Germans, and Scandinavians, fled overpopulated homelands where jobs were scarce and poverty was spreading. Some also came as political refugees from the unrest in France and the Germanic provinces.

Once in the territory, settlers competed with speculators for choice land. The Yankees, who often brought capital and aggressiveness, settled along the lakeshore and at strategic points along the rivers. The foreign immigrants, with their willingness to work but difficulty with the English language, found they had to push into the interior, clearing forests and settling for less desirable land. Their sense of bewilderment and uneasiness in the new land led them to seek out and settle near acquaintances from the homeland. The old hands eased the adjustment of the new arrivals. Old world customs were continued, and ethnic churches and fraternal organizations were quickly founded.

The economy of territorial Wisconsin was principally agricultural. Wheat was a natural crop in the prairie openings of southern Wisconsin. And because transportation to markets along the lakeshore was costly and slow, the settlers clamored for improved roads and waterways. These pressing needs caused ordinary people to rashly invest in canal projects, waterway improvements, plank roads, and railroads. Most of these schemes fell through, however, and many farmers lost their farms.

The climate of Jacksonian America, with its distrust of banks and paper specie, was certainly evident among territorial citizens. Despite the need for capital, the hard currency flowed out of the territory in payment of goods imported from the east.

Gradually the newcomers settled down, clearing their lands, building churches and schools, finding jobs, and writing to friends and relatives urging them to come to Wisconsin Territory.

1: Immigration to Wisconsin

Handbooks with advice for the emigrant were common. This first excerpt warns against the evils of New York, urging new arrivals to proceed west with measured speed. The second selection is a letter written by a German immigrant to his friends in Bavaria with practical advice for those who might follow him to Wisconsin.

Emigrant's Handbook, 1851

SAMUEL FREEMAN

GENERAL INSTRUCTIONS.

Having now given as clear an outline of the subject as the limits of this work will permit, and I trust fulfilled the promise made at the outset, that the emigrant should be supplied at a cheap rate, with information valuable both for present and future application, I shall draw to a conclusion by offering a few general observations to the emigrant, to guide him to this western country, and be useful to him in time to come.

New York being the principal landing place, and a large city, the emigrant is apt to be surrounded on all sides if he does not keep a sharp look out, by a set of men who, under pretence of being his friend or his countryman, allure him among strangers, with all the snares and temptations that such a large city affords, which are

From Samuel Freeman, *Emigrant's Handbook and Guide to Wisconsin . . .* (Milwaukee, 1851), pp. 90–92.

Irish and General Emigration
LAND AGENCY OFFICE.

Established in Milwaukee, Wisconsin, 1849.

D. G. POWER, Agent.

The Emigrating Public intending to buy lands in Wisconsin, are offered *inducements to purchase* through this office, unequalled by any Land Agent in the United States; and for the following reasons. I have, after immense labor, completed a MAP OF WISCONSIN, four times larger than ever published, on which is represented the *prairies, openings, timber land, rivers, plank and common roads, villages, &c.*, so that the entire features of the State will appear at a glance. I have also marked on this Map over 250,000 *acres of choice lands*, which I am authorized to sell from $1,50 per acre upwards, and in most instances *only a portion of the money* required down.   Included in the above 250,000 acres are several valuable village and mill sites, wild and improved farms with good dwelling houses, saw and grist mills, taverns, &c., located in the best portions of *Wisconsin*, viz: near the cities of *Milwaukee, Kenosha, Racine*, and the flourishing villages of *Madison, Beloit, Janesville, Watertown, Waukesha, Mineral Point, Fond du Lac, Green Bay, Sheboygan, Ozaukee*, &c.; with about 20,000 acres contiguous to the Fox and Wisconsin rivers; also some first rate locations between the Mississippi and Wisconsin rivers.   My map shows the exact position of all these lands; also, the Government land, so that an emigrant wishing to purchase a farm, or locate a land warrant, can see the exact position of the land with regard to roads, water, markets, &c.: also, whether it be opening, prairie or timber land.

I have a book of reference which shows the price, time of payment, and gives a general description of the land, which I have in most instances taken from actual observation.   A large number of Lots for sale in Milwaukee, and in most of the villages in the State.   *Houses and Stores* to rent in Milwaukee. Genuine Land Warrants always on hand, with instructions where to locate them, (a matter of very great importance.)

I am always ready to assist with my advice Emigrants in search of farms, employment, &c., and give them such information as I think they most require, FREE OF CHARGE.

Horses and Waggons on hand to take Emigrants to see farms before paying their money.   Also, taking them and their families to any part of the State they may wish to go to.   Cheap Houses and rooms on hand for the accomodation of Emigrants.

Emigrants having frauds practiced upon them on their route to Milwaukee, by letting me know the facts, I will ensure them redress.   On your arrival at Milwaukee enquire for D. G. POWER, *Irish and General Emigrant Agent*, and you will have no cause to complain.   By enquiring of the *Emigration Commission* at New York, the *Irish Emigrant Society* at New York or Boston, you can satisfy yourselves as to my standing with them.

☞ PASSENGERS forwarded from any part of the Old Country, to New York or Milwaukee; and Money remitted to Ireland, England or Scotland, cheapr, than by any agent in the West.

D. G. POWER, General Emigrant Agent.

Courtesy of the SHSW [WHi (X3) 33833]

A land advertisement appearing in Samuel Freeman's 1851 *Emigrant's Handbook and Guide to Wisconsin*

calculated, in a very short time, to use up all his means before he is aware of it. I would guard him to avoid these men and shun them as he would a serpent, for their only object is to get his money and introduce him to places of resort where gaming and drinking are carried on to an endless extent; and in the end calculated to bring ruin upon himself and his family. One of the many temptations that beset the emigrant, is the numerous gambling houses there are in New York; and one of the most tempting forms of gambling is found at some of the low saloons, where raffles are constantly going on, to a great extent, either for watches, jewelry, guns, pistols, or other bogus articles; and any quantity of liquor indulged in during the intervals of the game. The stake usually put up is not more than the value of a dollar, and is divided into shares of a shilling or sixpence each—the winner being expected to stand treat for the whole company.

It is supposed that in over two thousand grog shops and fashionable drinking saloons in New York, this game is going on every night of the week, attracting throngs of young people, broken-down gamblers, greenhorns from the old country in pursuit of the elephant, idle loafers about town, and others who are always on the scent for whatever gives promise of sport. Such places of resort and allurement I would advise the emigrant to keep away from.

The emigrant's chance of employment and good wages is much increased by removing from seaboard towns,—New York being the principal landing place, and from the influx of strangers continually pouring in there, it is impossible for merchants, traders and others, to give employment to one-tenth that arrive there.

Under these circumstances, I strongly advise the emigrant, both mechanic and laborer, after they have spent a day or two inspecting the city, to lose no time in quitting that place whilst they have the means of so doing to assist themselves. The facilities for travelling in the United States are cheap and good. Steamboats, railroad conveyances and coaches, start daily for all parts. This you will find to be the most profitable way of laying the foundation of your future happiness. Lose no time, then, in working your way out of New York and directing your steps westward, where labor is plentiful and sure to meet with its reward.

Advice to Homeland Friends, 1847

GEORGE ADAM FROMADER

Jefferson City, Jan. 15, 1847

For a long time I have been wanting to write to my dear good friends but I have waited until I had information about various things. As to the trip, my friends, the first day was the hardest of all since with one last handshake we had to say farewell to our good brothers and sisters, friends and neighbors. Our first night we spent at the Inn at Juchhoh, four hours ride from Hof. Then we began to cheer up and console one another. Our journey to Bremen took 13 days, our wagon was too heavily loaded and the horses were not equal to the load. However the trip was not tedious since the passengers got along nicely.[1]

The voyage from Bremen to Quebec took 77 days. It was very tedious, but we may say it was not very uncomfortable and still less dangerous. On the whole trip we had good wind on only 5 or 6 days, when we were able to make 5 hours [fifteen miles] distance in one. The rest of the time we had mostly contrary winds but no storm for even one hour. In the same week most of the passengers became seasick, with headache and vomiting usually lasting two weeks. When we caught sight of America everybody was well and happy. The 120 passengers began singing happy songs and thanked God for the safe voyage.

Three children were born at sea, of which the first was dead, but the two others were sound and well. We arrived at Quebec in the evening and spent the night on our sailing vessel, called the *Petrel*. It was early on the morning of July 30 when the luggage was landed and the landing boats came to take the passengers to town. We were impressed with the splendid order in this city. Our captain Henry Seth of Sunderland was going to make an extra charge of one dollar to each passenger, or delay the unloading until later. Then several passengers went to the German Consul who immediately ordered a steamboat to come and take off the passengers' possessions. The captain had to prove that he had treated the passengers with due consideration, and we really had no complaint.

[1]Beginning in 1827, Bremen became the leading port of emigration in Europe. The Fromader party traveled from Bernstein to Bremen, a distance of over 300 miles, at a rate of approximately twenty-three miles a day.

From George Adam Fromader, "I Live Here Happily; a German Immigrant in Territorial Wisconsin," Jack J. Detzler, ed., *Wisconsin Magazine of History*, L (Spring 1967), 254–259. Some footnotes in the original omitted. Reprinted by permission of the State Historical Society of Wisconsin.

The trip from Quebec to Milwaukee on the steamer cost 11 dollars or 27½ fl. per person.[2]

On Aug. 20 we arrived in Milwaukee and rented a room where we could do our own cooking and keep our boxes. We stayed 8 days and looked at land here and there and bought property on the road from Milwaukee to Jefferson. The road is in the same condition as the one from Bernstein to Pegersgrum. I bought the land 1½ miles from Jefferson from a man named Sam. 3 miles is a German "hour." The land is called a "Fratsche," that is 60 acres or 75 days work in Bavaria. On the land is a good frame house with a shingled roof and a stone lined well with very clear and fresh water. Ten acres of this farm have been cleared, from which I got the crops. The wheat had already been harvested and stacked. A "stack" is a round mound. From it we threshed 110 bushels; a bushel is a Bavarian Metze. We harvested 100 bu. of corn and some buckwheat. On our arrival we were able to dig potatoes; we had been wanting some very much. They are very large and quite good. For the digging we also get 50 bushels of pumpkins, called Kurbis in Germany, 5 wagon loads, very good fodder for pigs and cattle, some cabbage, cucumbers, beets, onions and radishes, also small sweet melons, both in quantities. Also 22 pigs and 60 chickens.

This land, including what is on it, cost 212 dollars that is 530 fl., but is the very best and cheapest purchase. Of all those who bought property in the wooded country the Land Office charged 10 schillings, that is 1¼ Thalers or 3 fl. 7½ Kreuzer, that makes 75 Thalers for 60 acres. It may be that the land will cost 20 schillings. This is not quite certain until word comes back from Washington, the capital where the President lives. It's common talk in America that the land should not be sold for more than 10 schillings [$1.25] an acre, the market price. Most buyers have not paid anything yet. By 1848 the land is to be paid for. So my land with the above mentioned crops costs me $287 or 717 fl. 30. No one ought to expect to buy a farm for less in America, for in this region such farms are known to have sold for from 1000 to 1100 fl. I immediately bought a pair of oxen for $60. They are very large and fine. I bought a new wagon for $52, so that I could transport my baggage and myself from Milwaukee to here. I then bought two cows for $32, a plow for $10, a harrow for $4, 6 chairs for $5, a sleigh for $4, a table for $3, 2 bedsteads $5, washing, drinking, and milking equipment $5,

[2] In the course of his letter, Fromader uses the following table of monetary equivalents:
  One dollar = one thaler or 2½ florins
  One cent = 10/125 schillings
  One schilling = 12½ cents
  One florin = 40 cents
  One kreuzer = .7 cents

butter making equipment $4, an iron stove with pans and kettles $16, a large kettle and pans for boiling sugar, with a box for drying $6, a pair of scales, fire shovel, and ax $8. So our whole property with all equipment costs us $501 or 1252 fl. 30. We are as well equipped as we ever were in Germany and our present possessions represent material far superior to what we had before. The traveling expenses from Bernstein to here for our family of five amounted to 626 fl., so the whole expense is 1877 fl. 50 [$752].

For that we own a fine stretch of land that is both beautiful and good. The most splendid fruits grow on it. The remaining woodland is covered with large trees, oak, linden, walnut, elm, cherry, ash and maple, a kind of oak that is very hard, a kind of larch which grows very tall and is used for building material. One can also sell firewood and boards.

There are stretches of land extending 100 miles where there is no timber at all, where the farms are immense and are called home-steads. This is called openland; timberland is called "bushland." On the openland there are farms with 100 acres sown in wheat, clearing being easy there. I do not want to buy there, because I know what a scarcity of wood means for I experienced that in Germany. People come 20 to 30 miles for boards. Unless I want to clear land I do not cut down trees. Clearing one acre costs $10, but the the wood once

The sidewheel passenger steamer *Milwaukie*, 1832

Courtesy of the SHSW [WHi (X313) 2335]

cut brings returns. But I do not like to clear much more land. There are 20 acres adjoining mine, 13 of which are already cleared. This is owned by an American who wants to sell it to me. He wants $200 for the 20 acres. I have offered him $150 since the land was bought for 20 schillings at the Land Office. If it cost 10 schillings you would get 20 acres of government land besides. I could, of course, easily buy 60 acres for $150, should it cost 20 sch. but it would not be as close to town and would not yet have been cleared. I will get it some time because here people don't like to snatch somebody else's bargain. We could soon establish two homesteads on this land, since we do not want to move away from each other. It is much better here for me, and for my children, ten times better than in Germany. We need not suffer want, having this home which is as good and complete as we had in Germany. We sold two mother pigs for $11½ and slaughtered nine others. Now we have let two young ones grow up and have again 24 head.

Here in America one eats meat every day, sometimes twice—mornings and evenings we have coffee. The Americans have meat on the table three times a day and many kinds of vegetables which we do not know of in Germany. The bread is made of the finest wheat flour,[3] baked with leaven, and there is no trouble in getting yeast to bake fried cakes. On Saturday evening everybody makes fried cakes for Sunday. For coffee we usually exchange eggs, for 1 doz. eggs you get a pound of coffee. One egg costs 1¢ or 1½ sch. A pound of fine wheat flour costs 2¢, a pound of pork 3¢, beef 2½¢ in summer, but 6–8 [in winter]. You can sell anything here but not just when you want to. You must always bide your time. We sold 3 cords of wood in town for 10 schillings, but it must be chopped before taken to market. A schilling is 18 Kreuzers. At this price the chopping and hauling is paid for, but you cannot charge for the wood because it would have to be burned anyway.

I have built a threshing floor. I traded logs for the boards I needed for it. I traded 100 ft. of logs for 50 ft. of boards. I paid the carpenter with 6 bu. of wheat, 2 bu. potatoes, 25 lbs. wheat floor. In summer it would have cost me again as much.

On Oct. 25, our son John and his betrothed Elizabeth Zeidler were married. Also John Adam Jahn was married, both of the weddings were at our house. So we had a joyful wedding celebration. On November 21 our young wife gave birth to a girl, to our great joy. They are both quite well and sound. We are all well and live very happily together. We do not care to be back in our unhappy Germany. There we would have had to waste many words and coax

---

[3]Obviously considered a luxury, since the staple flour of Bavaria was rye.

the law court and community officials to give permission for the marriage. In this country everybody is free to do as he pleases as long as he remains orderly and respectable. Hunting is permitted for everybody in places not fenced in, even on Sunday in the country. Hunting is forbidden in town during church hours.

In Germany we hear strange things about being hanged in America for stealing 5¢ worth of goods, but nobody here knows anything about that. Unless blood is shed, there is little conflict with the law. Everything is very closely investigated before any one is sentenced to prison. Few people let things go that far, for they cherish personal honor and like to have the confidence of their fellow men. An American is ashamed even to quarrel with others, let alone to resort to violence. If a person finds something, he avoids taking it home, but takes it to the nearest house to make it public. So there is the greatest order in everything.

In art and science the land is astonishingly far advanced, and in all things the Germans are far behind and acknowledge it readily. The country at large has already made great advancement in arts and science, over which the people rejoice generally. But the Germans have much to learn.

For church and school we can go to Jefferson. Every 2 weeks a clergyman comes to us and preaches in some private home, which, of course, seems very strange to us.

I can tell you, friends, whoever can bring into the country $200 in cash can become a prosperous farmer. He can buy 40 acres of land. If it is priced at 10 schillings, $100 is enough. For another $100 he can buy the most necessary equipment. And if he has grown-up children they can easily help their father, for here there is no scarcity of work and income, especially for women and girls. A girl of 9 or 10 years can earn a few dollars a month, at the same time she attends school. A good hired man or maid, here called help, each can earn monthly 8, 10, to 12 dollars, the sum depending on how he adapts himself to the work. Men and women have the same opportunity. In this country there is no distinction between master and servant at the table. Caste is unknown in this country. Nothing is known about nobility and different names and titles. Everybody enjoys the same respect, whether he be a servant, a farmer, a minister or a president. Honor is granted to all if deserved. Everybody works. People work for each other, all for pay. Nothing is known about the forester's work, which is considered the hardest in Germany. Every man here is a marksman and carries his gun.

On 80 acres of land you pay $1 tax and 2 days road work, if the land is occupied as a home and is properly worked.

I can assure you, friends, a man who brings 500 fl. can buy a farm on which 50 to 75 acres are sown in winter wheat, where there are 10 to 12 cows, 6 to 8 oxen, 4 to 6 horses, 60 to 70 pigs, 50 to 100 sheep are kept. And all this without a shepherd since all tilled acres are fenced in, so nothing can be destroyed. Whatever I look at, I find everything is easier and more practically managed to earn a living in this country than in Germany.

. . . .

What I am writing to you and am going to write is true. Often our letters are regarded as untrue. I can vouch for all my statements. Anyone who has a desire to follow us may do so confidently if he can bring a little money along, whether it be a father or a family or a single person, man or woman. A skilled and industrious woman even though she brings no money into the country may soon become a housewife. Women are highly respected in this country. They do not work in the fields and may be quite genteel. Whoever wants to make the trip need not bring a great deal except a supply of shirts and woolens. Do not bring tools of any kind, nor extra shoes, for the German ones are not worth carrying across the sea. No matter what you need or want, it is much better than in Germany. The cost may be higher, but they are sure to be worth twice as much as the German product.

The best route, also the cheapest, is via Bremen and New York. The provisions to take on the trip are: good rye bread, cut small and toasted, oatmeal fried in lard, dried pork, dried noodles, coffee and sugar three parts, dried prunes, salted butter, white hard tack. All this you buy in Bremen at the lowest price. You have no need of more advice, for I have told you all that is necessary.

. . . .

Now I wish this letter may reach you in as good health as we were when it was written.

I do not advise a father of a family with many little children to move to this country unless he has money, for things are not as they were a few years ago when you could have cleared a piece of land. Now if a man wants land, he must be able to pay for it. The distance from Milwaukee to Jefferson is 16 German "hours" [forty-eight miles]. Five years ago this was a dense forest with only two small towns just started. Now all this land is thickly settled and there is not an acre of government land along that road to be had. In many places you cannot believe that it once was timberland. The towns and farms spring like mushrooms from the ground.

I want to tell you or anyone who may wish to come to make the drive to Bremen in your own wagon and arrange to take only a limited number of persons and only as many trunks and boxes as are necessary so that you can sleep nights on the wagon. Inns are expensive and of poor quality. I read in German newspapers that food there is high priced.

Now please let us hear from you as soon as possible, for our little Margaret speaks daily of her godmother. Please tell our relatives and friends about this letter or make a copy of it, for it is impossible to write such a long letter to each one. We again send cordial greetings to all and beg you to answer us. . . .

> *You dear friends, good night!*
> *I have accomplished the voyage*
> *That I intended to take*
> *And have come to a good land.*
> *I thank God for this way*
> *Of getting a free life.*
> *I have much wood and good land,*
> *Were you here you would have it, too.*
> *I live here happily*
> *And wish you could have it the same way.*
> *Good night, all you friends!*
> *Germany is a vale of tears.*

Jefferson, January 15, 1847
    The address to:
        George Adam Fromader,
        Jefferson City
        Post Office, Jefferson City
        North American Territory
        Wisconsin

2: The New Home

Letters from new settlers in Fond du Lac to relatives in England, as seen in the first selection, are filled with descriptions of the town, countryside, food, bartering, and prices of goods—as well as the optimism of a growing nation. A second descriptive selection is from the autobiography of John Muir, naturalist and inventor. As a young boy he immigrated with his family to a central Wisconsin farmstead. Years later he was still able to remember his initial wonder and amazement at the natural beauty around him.

Mathilde Brinker came to Wisconsin from France as a young girl. Her father and friends opened a merchandise store in Waubeka; but it failed, and Mr. Brinker was forced to seek work as a tailor in Chicago, leaving his wife and children on their farmstead. In her reminiscences Mathilde relates a child's first memories of home and school during the French family's first years in the state.

Warren Cooke's family were Yankees from the east. They settled on land in present Buffalo County, turning virgin prairie and forest into a farm. His reminiscences recount the poverty, hard work, but also good times of those early years.

This period of Wisconsin history is well documented. The *Wisconsin Historical Collections* (31 vols., 1855–1931) and *Wisconsin Magazine of History* are full of narratives and correspondence telling of pioneer experiences. Many articles and books trace the immigration of specific ethnic groups. Especially useful for information on pioneer women are the Wisconsin State Historical Society's booklets *Famous Wisconsin Women* (Madison, 1961–   ); *Uncommon Lives of Common Women* by Victoria Brown (Madison, 1975); and *The Story of Wisconsin Women* by Ruth de Young Kohler (Madison, 1948).

Letters from Fond du Lac, 1850–1852

December, 1850

Dear Grandmother,

Thinking by this time that you and Uncle John will be saying Ah Clara is gone and forgot all about us, but I hope not to deserve this acuseasation, but I thourt it better to defer writing a few weeks after Mother's letter. Dear Grandmother, we had rather a rough passage across the ocean but we enjoyed ourselves very much barring the difficulties we met with, but Mother says she should know better how to manage if she had to travel again, and we should not think much of such a journey again.

. . . .

I must say something about Fond du Lac. Fond du lack formerly belonged to the Indians. The Government has bought the land of them and they come yearly to recover there pay. There is the Frames of several wigwams which mother has been to see. They go up in the woods in the winter and come here and hunt for Fish in the summer. If they want some Tobaco and you give them some they are sure to bring some Cranberries or Fish as a present. They paint there faces red and have a sort of a Blanket dress. The sqaws as they call the women do most of the work. They are very ingenious, they talk the Indian language but most of the old settlers can understand them enough to trade with them. Father is known all over Fondulac and all came to see and welcome us. We like the place and the People very much, we think them free and generous and they seem willing to lend you any assistance they can. For instance they will help Father with his house which he is getting the timber for now. We have to take all the work we do out in barter. Mother as made 2 coats for Mrs. Hornby which we take out in firewood. Mother as 6 and 8 shillings and pence for of this money, and a dollar goes much further here than it would in England. Harricot beans a dollar a Bushel. Father brought home for half dollar 2 pounds of sugar, quarter of a pound of tea, a pound and 1/2 of coffee, this seemed a good deal to us for 2 english shillings. We have to roast and grind our own coffee, bake our own Bread. We mostly have meat for Breakfast. The Yankees generally live well, we have three meals a day, they [call?] the third Supper. They do not have 3 trays like they

From "God Raised Us Up Good Friends, English Immigrants in Wisconsin," *Wisconsin Magazine of History*, XLVII (Spring 1964), 224–237. Footnotes in the original omitted. Reprinted by permission of the State Historical Society of Wisconsin.

do in england, they have apple sauce, preserves, meat and several kinds of cakes on the Table at one time. At every meal they have tea or coffee. Dear Grandmother, I think you may see it is much easier to get on here than in England. We are in expectation of a rail road coming near us in the spring, which will make the place very Flourishing and money more plentiful. We are invited to dinner Christmas day by that mans brother that mother took the letter for. Mother and I went with a person from England who are Cabinet makers in the Town to see Mrs. Smiths farm who are also english. These Smiths have not been here two years, they came without a penny but now they are in a Flourishing condition. They rent the farm at 2 hundred dollars a year, but there corn that they grow pays there rent and a hundred dollars over. They have 14 cows, 10 calves, and 2 sheep, 23 pigs, 20 fowls. They have 100 acres of land, 50 in cultivation and the rest in pasture. They made us very welcome. I made a Chrochet cap for which we take out in butter. We have several invitations to different farmers when it is good sleaighing, that will be when the snow gets a little deeper on the ground.

The frost set in about the begining of December, it was very severe for a few days, and frose the lakes and rivers up. The weather is dry and clear and fine sunshiny weather. Teams which are drawn by oxen and mools, sleaighs, cutters, all cross the river and lakes on the ice. The inhabitants look forword with pleasure to deep snow and kalaclate on many pleasant visits. The winter last about six months, snowing and freeseing, snowing and freeseing all the winter.

Dear grandmother, the stoves are very different here to what they are at home, they are in sort of iron box with oven and a pipe going up through the ceiling. They mostly stand in the middle of the room and throw out a great heat. There is no coals burnt here, all wood. The men go up in the woods to get it, and chop or saw it at there own place.

We killed the sow and salted it down, now we have three young ones left which Father means to keep. We give them very little food. They run about the prairies and pick up anything they can eat. Sometimes they will go away for days together.

Dear Grandmother, when you write again please to put James Frederick instead of Mr. Chaney as the letters stop at the post office until called for, and they make a peice of work if they are not directed so.

Dear Grandmother, I have not room for any more, but hope you will write directly you receive this, and I will write directly I receive your answer. We are all in good health, as we hope you are also.

Mother and Father send their love to you and Uncle John, Uncle Charles, Aunt Sarah, Phil, Sally and the baby and all inquiring friends. The children send their love.

I am your ever affectionate [grand]daughter, Clara Chaney.

March 1st, 1851

Dear Mother and Charles,

We received your last letter and was very sorry to hear you was so poorly, we hope you are better. We should be glad to have a long letter from you. If you cannot write it, ask Charles to send us a long letter.

We thought you would like to know how we are getting on. We are all in good health, thank the Lord, Ann, Emma and Clara are getting fatter than my Pigs, and no wonder if you could see how they go into it. Plenty to Eat and plenty fine fresh Air. Eliza and Jane are growing very fast and in good health. We have just agreed with a Carpenter to put our House up, we have got the principle of the Materials and expect to have it up very shortly. We are going to have the Ground plowed up and sown with Potatoes, Greens, etc., which will supply us through the Season. We have 3 Pigs and all in thriving condition, expecting every day to be confined. I hope we shall have a Score of Young ones. We have been pretty well off for Work, the Weather is now very fine and we expect to be very Busy this summer. We have had a very fine Winter, not too Cold, we all stood it like trumps.

We have just received a letter from Frank and was very glad to hear he was doing very Comfortable, and expects this summer to do better still. He has written to us to say if we was not doing well where we are to go up to New York, he believes we should do well there. But as a rolling stone gathers no moss we think we can do better hear at least we intend giving it a fair trial. We shall have no Rent to pay here, can grow all our own vegetables, and fatten the principle of our Meat. All this we must pay for at New York. We have several good Ministers here and several Chapels, they are now Building one within a quarter of a Mile of us, Congregationist. Our Neighbours are all very kind and we [get] many invitations. . . .

We have heard and read a good deal about the Worlds Fair, we have just seen a Hansome Engraving of it Gilt in Gold. Suppose it will be a spendid [*sic*] Affair.

Frank says he has written two Letters to England and received no answer. He has lost his last young one 11 months old. I think the California Mania is now at an end. We hear of Numbers that have starved to Death there, and Numbers that have perished in coming home. The Oregon Fever as now started and Numbers are going from this part of America, there, they are giving 320 acres of Land to all that go there. It is 6 Months travelling across the Land about Two Thousand Miles from this part of America. By Sea it is Nineteen Thousand Miles. I do not think I shall ever go there.

We have nearly got rid of the Indians, they will receive their last payment from the Government the latter end of this Year, as the Government Bought them out. They will have to go a Hundred Miles further west, but they are very Quiet peaceable and Good Natured, we never hear any bad accounts of them. They are what are called Civilised, but further West and South they are Savage, Murderous and Cruel. They bring into the Town a good deal of Venison, Sugar, Honey, Fish, etc., etc. We expect we shall have a Railway running through our Town this Summer, if so it will be a busy place. We all like the Country well, we have no wish to return to Old England again, altho some say with all her faults they love her still—Trash—Trash—certainly we should like to see Old Friends and Old Faces, but as that cannot be, God grant we may all Meet together in Heaven.

It is a Beautiful Country, I have travelled about 16 Hundred Miles from East to West, and Ann has travelled about the same distance from North to West. We have seen some fine Citys and Towns, and has to the Views of Scenery it cannot be surpassed, if it can be equalled anywhere.

We all join in our best love and Esteem to you and all Friends and Remain

Yours Affectly
J. F. Chaney

. . . .

June 24, 1852

Dear Grandmother,

We received your letter about four weeks after your date. Mother got Mr. Burroughes to ask his brother to call on you which we have since heard he as done, or we should have written before. We are very sorry to hear that you are so unhappy, I often think you would be quite comfortable here. We are sorry to hear of Uncle Charles Illness and hope he is quite recovered, and also Aunt, I hope she has recovered.

I am Real glad that you have been out in the Country. I could not endure to be shut up in a town from Morning to Night after living here on the open praries.

We are very glad to hear that Uncle John as so far recovered, and trust that he will get quite Hearty and Robust. We have not heard from Uncle Frank lately, our last two Letters remain unanswered.

We have heard from Mrs. Arnold, she called on Uncle while on a Visit to New York. Uncle had been poorly but had recovered and they were all doing well. He had bought a lot, and was building. Mrs. A. thinks of returning to England for the benefit of her health.

We have had such times here, they have made Fond du Lack a city and there has been great excitement with the Olectionering (and Father has become a Citizen). They are making great improvements here now it is a City—side walks, plank roads, and to get it plastered [?], I will send a sketch of it in my next letter. And the Mayor is going to bring steam boats right up the river. The Rail Road is going Ahead. Mr. Walker as been to England to get Loans for that purpose and has Returned successful. People say the towns will soon join, for buildings are going up Rapidly. I guess I told you in the last letter that Father bought a heifer, gave 5 dollars for her. He as sold it for 9 dollars and bought a Cow, gave 14 dollars in trade. She calved but Father knocked the Calf on the head as it did not get along very well, and took all the New Milk, so we have plenty of Milk now and plenty of Butter which latter we make ourselves. What Milk Remains we use for cheese and to make Biscuits. We have had rather a severe Winter but it [is] a delightful Spring. We have got all our garden planted. It contains Potatoes, Beans, Pease, Summer and Winter Squash, Beet, Pumkins, Mush and Water Melons, Citrons, Carrots, Parsnip and Cucumber, onions and Lettuce and Cabbage. An a nice lot of Tomatoes and a little Indian Corn which is Real good to eat green.

I have a Flower bed, but I mean to have a First Rate one next year as we have got the ground Fenced in front of the House. And if you will be so kind as to put one or few Flower seeds in your next letter, if you have got a few by you, I shall be Real glad and I will send you some wild Flower Seeds in Return, some of which are very beautiful.

. . . .

The Children all go to the district school where they teach them everything that is necessary, Grammar, Geography, Arithmatic, and Writing, Composition, etc., etc. We have been hireing Rooms during the Winter at 50 Cents per week, but now we have got into our Building. We expect to get it Finished this Fall.

I had a fine Sleaigh Rid 8 miles out in the country. We are all in excellent health, Mother and all.

[Unsigned, but probably from Clara]

The Wonders of Wisconsin, 1849

JOHN MUIR

Everything about us was so novel and wonderful that we could hardly believe our senses except when hungry or while father was thrashing us. When we first saw Fountain Lake Meadow, on a sultry evening, sprinkled with millions of lightning-bugs throbbing with light, the effect was so strange and beautiful that it seemed far too marvelous to be real. Looking from our shanty on the hill, I thought that the whole wonderful fairy show must be in my eyes; for only in fighting, when my eyes were struck, had I ever seen anything in the least like it. But when I asked my brother if he saw anything strange in the meadow he said, "Yes, it's all covered with shaky fire-sparks." Then I guessed that it might be something outside of us, and applied to our all-knowing Yankee to explain it. "Oh, it's nothing but lightnin'-bugs," he said, and kindly led us down the hill to the edge of the fiery meadow, caught a few of the wonderful bugs, dropped them into a cup, and carried them to the shanty, where we watched them throbbing and flashing out their mysterious light at regular intervals, as if each little passionate glow were caused by the beating of a heart. Once I saw a splendid display of glow-worm light in the foothills of the Himalayas, north of Calcutta, but glorious as it appeared in pure starry radiance, it was far less impressive than the extravagant abounding, quivering, dancing fire on our Wisconsin meadow.

. . . .

We reveled in the glory of the sky scenery as well as that of the woods and meadows and rushy, lily-bordered lakes. The great thunder-storms in particular interested us, so unlike any seen in Scotland, exciting awful, wondering admiration. Gazing awe-stricken, we watched the upbuilding of the sublime cloud-mountains,—glowing, sun-beaten pearl and alabaster cumuli, glorious in beauty and majesty and looking so firm and lasting that birds, we thought, might build their nests amid their downy bosses; the black-browed storm-clouds marching in awful grandeur across the landscape, trailing broad gray sheets of hail and rain like vast cataracts, and ever and anon flashing down vivid zigzag lightning followed by terrible crashing thunder. We saw several trees shattered, and one of them, a punky old oak, was set on fire, while we

From John Muir, *The Story of My Boyhood and Youth,* pp. 71–72, 75–77, 199–205. Copyright 1913, renewed 1941. Reprinted by permission of Houghton Mifflin Company.

wondered why all the trees and everybody and everything did not share the same fate, for oftentimes the whole sky blazed. After sultry storm days, many of the nights were darkened by smooth black apparently structureless cloud-mantles which at short intervals were illumined with startling suddenness to a fiery glow by quick, quivering lightning-flashes, revealing the landscape in almost noonday brightness, to be instantly quenched in solid blackness.

But those first days and weeks of unmixed enjoyment and freedom, reveling in the wonderful wildness about us, were soon to be mingled with the hard work of making a farm. I was first put to burning brush in clearing land for the plough. Those magnificent brush fires with great white hearts and red flames, the first big, wild outdoor fires I had ever seen, were wonderful sights for young eyes. Again and again, when they were burning fiercest so that we could hardly approach near enough to throw on another branch, father put them to awfully practical use as warning lessons, comparing their heat with that of hell, and the branches with bad boys. "Now, John," he would say,—"now, John, just think what an awful thing it would be to be thrown into that fire:—and then think of hellfire, that is so many times hotter. Into that fire all bad boys, with sinners of every sort who disobey God, will be cast as we are casting branches into this brush fire, and although suffering so much, their sufferings will never never end, because neither the fire nor the sinners can die." But those terrible fire lessons quickly faded away in the blithe wilderness air; for no fire can be hotter than the heavenly fire of faith and hope that burns in every healthy boy's heart.

. . . .

At first, wheat, corn, and potatoes were the principal crops we raised; wheat especially. But in four or five years the soil was so exhausted that only five or six bushels an acre, even in the better fields, was obtained, although when first ploughed twenty and twenty-five bushels was about the ordinary yield. More attention was then paid to corn, but without fertilizers the corn-crop also became very meagre. At last it was discovered that English clover would grow on even the exhausted fields, and that when ploughed under and planted with corn, or even wheat, wonderful crops were raised. This caused a complete change in farming methods; the farmers raised fertilizing clover, planted corn, and fed the crop to cattle and hogs.

But no crop raised in our wilderness was so surprisingly rich and sweet and purely generous to us boys and, indeed, to everybody as the watermelons and muskmelons. We planted a large patch on a sunny hill-slope the very first spring, and it seemed miraculous that a few handfuls of little flat seeds should in a few months send up a hundred wagon-loads of crisp, sumptuous, red-hearted and yellow-hearted fruits covering all the hill. We soon learned to know when they were in their prime, and when over-ripe and mealy. Also that if a second crop was taken from the same ground without fertilizing it, the melons would be small and what we called soapy; that is, soft and smooth, utterly uncrisp, and without a trace of the lively freshness and sweetness of those raised on virgin soil. Coming in from the farm work at noon, the half-dozen or so of melons we had placed in our cold spring were a glorious luxury that only weary barefooted farm boys can ever know.

Spring was not very trying as to temperature, and refreshing rains fell at short intervals. The work of ploughing commenced as soon as the frost was out of the ground. Corn- and potato-planting and the sowing of spring wheat was comparatively light work, while the nesting birds sang cheerily, grass and flowers covered the marshes and meadows and all the wild, uncleared parts of the farm, and the trees put forth their new leaves, those of the oaks forming beautiful purple masses as if every leaf were a petal; and with all this we enjoyed the mild soothing winds, the humming of unnumerable small insects and hylas, and the freshness and fragrance of everything. Then, too, came the wonderful passenger pigeons streaming from the south, and flocks of geese and cranes, filling all the sky with whistling wings.

The summer work, on the contrary, was deadly heavy, especially harvesting and corn-hoeing. All the ground had to be hoed over for the first few years, before father bought cultivators or small weed-covering ploughs, and we were not allowed a moment's rest. The hoes had to be kept working up and down as steadily as if they were moved by machinery. Ploughing for winter wheat was comparatively easy, when we walked barefooted in the furrows, while the fine autumn tints kindled in the woods, and the hillsides covered with golden pumpkins.

In summer the chores were grinding scythes, feeding the animals, chopping stove-wood, and carrying water up the hill from the spring on the edge of the meadow, etc. Then breakfast, and to the harvest or hay-field. I was foolishly ambitious to be first in mowing and cradling, and by the time I was sixteen led all the hired men. An hour was allowed at noon for dinner and more chores. We stayed in the field until dark, then supper, and still more chores, family worship, and to bed; making altogether a hard, sweaty day of about sixteen or seventeen hours. Think of that, ye blessed eight-hour-day laborers!

Courtesy of the SHSW [WHi (X3) 609]

Harvesting grain on a frontier homestead, ca. 1848

In winter father came to the foot of the stairs and called us at six o'clock to feed the horses and cattle, grind axes, bring in wood, and do any other chores required, then breakfast, and out to work in the mealy, frosty snow by daybreak, chopping, fencing, etc. So in general our winter work was about as restless and trying as that of the long-day summer. No matter what the weather, there was always something to do. During heavy rains or snow-storms we worked in the barn, shelling corn, fanning wheat, thrashing with the flail, making axe handles or ox-yokes, mending things, or sprouting and sorting potatoes in the cellar.

No pains were taken to diminish or in any way soften the natural hardships of this pioneer farm life; nor did any of the Europeans seem to know how to find reasonable ease and comfort if they would. The very best oak and hickory fuel was embarrassingly abundant and cost nothing but cutting and common sense; but instead of hauling great heart-cheering loads of it for wide, open, all-welcoming, climate-changing, beauty-making, Godlike ingle-fires, it was hauled with weary heart-breaking industry into fences and waste places to get it out of the way of the plough, and out of the way of doing good. The only fire for the whole house was the kitchen stove, with a fire-box about eighteen inches long and eight inches wide and deep,—scant space for three or four small sticks, around which in hard zero weather all the family of ten persons shivered, and beneath which in the morning we found our socks and coarse, soggy boots frozen solid. We were not allowed to start even this despicable little fire in its black box to thaw them. No, we had to squeeze our throbbing, aching, chilblained feet into them, causing greater pain than toothache, and hurry out to chores. Fortunately the miserable chilblain pain began to abate as soon as the temperature of our feet approached the freezing-point, enabling us in spite of hard work and hard frost to enjoy the winter beauty,— the wonderful radiance of the snow when it was starry with crystals, and the dawns and the sunsets and white noons, and the cheery enlivening company of the brave chickadees and nuthatches.

French Immigrants, 1854–1855

MATHILDE BRINKER

By spring (1853) all hopes of making a living by means of the store had vanished. None of the men were farmers. Not one, before he had arrived in the wilderness, had ever wielded an ax. Francois, as said before, was a cabinet maker, L'Esprit and Redding had worked in the city, Audier was a druggist and my father was a tailor.

What else could be done but to separate and each one look for another means of livelihood. Young Audier taught school for a term or two in the neighborhood. Francois, who was a jack of all trades, went to Appleton and was said to have started a furniture store later on. My father, Uncle Redding and the family L'Esprit went to Chicago to find employment, while Mother and we children remained on the land.

. . . .

Mother had by this time learned to bake bread, and had made arrangements with nearer neighbors to get milk and other necessaries. There was the new store in Waubeka and the Post Office was nearer, still she, off and on, had to make the longer trip to Farmington for things she could not secure nearer home. And as there seemed no one else to take Katie's place when she took that trip, I was the one that was left in charge of the two younger children.*

This proved to be an unenviable ordeal. It was usually right after the noonday meal that Mother would leave, so the first hour sister and brother could easily be amused with our dolls, playdishes, and some other playthings. But they soon tired of even the improvised puppet show I would put on. Nor were my little stories more successful in entertaining them. Then I would put water in a dish and sprinkle the window panes, telling them that as soon as the drops were dry Mother would come. This had been the method employed by Katie and, as I remembered, had usually been successful in bringing Mother home. When the drops were drying I sent them to the other window, telling them they could probably see her better from there. Then I would quickly sprinkle the pane anew.

At last their patience ended. Marie opened the door and ran out.

---

*Mathilde was 6 years old. Her sister and brother were 4 and 2. [editors' note]

From M. Brinker Kuechenmeister, *Backwards From Ninety: the Autobiography of Marie Mathilde Brinker,* Martha M. Kuechenmeister, ed. (West Bend, Wis., 3rd ed., 1970), pp. 11, 30–31, 43, 77.

Henry followed up to the big stump near the road. They stood yelling their loudest, "Mama, mama, come, come." This seemed to have the desired effect, for Mother hearing them half a mile away, and thinking something awful had happened, hastened her steps and reached home almost out of breath. She found her two babies with their hands and feet almost frozen and I in tears. O, wretched day! This was the first but not the last that we endured.

. . . .

The Fourth Fall (1855)

And now, too, Mother was getting Marie and me ready for school, for Marie had passed her fifth year in June and I my seventh in August. The term of school did not begin until very late in the fall. There were only three months of school as a rule. For some reason there was no school in our district this winter. Instead, school was held in a vacant frame house in Waubeka.

Mother had visited the school to learn what books we would need. So one morning in late fall, when it was already cold, our little friend Charley Meyer, came to escort us on our new venture.

The schoolroom was filled with pupils, both young and old, probably because two districts had merged. By recess we were sure we had been there half a day, so at noon all three of us started for home, without having eaten our lunch.

When we reached home, Mother opened the window and put out her head calling, "What are you coming home for already? It is only noon." "No, no" we said, "It is evening and school is out," and we burst into tears. When she saw we had not eaten our lunch and we told her we couldn't eat, again I would have liked to say, "Never again school", but didn't dare.

The next morning when Mother was again getting us ready for school, combing Marie's hair, she was crying and fussing terribly. I was taking new courage, determined to stick it out to the last. Again Charley came and again we walked the mile to the place of learning. On the way we decided to stay all day. He told us he had almost gotten a licking the day before for coming home at noon.

At recess, while the other children were having a hilarious time jumping on tables and benches and yelling, we three huddled together in a corner. At noon, when lunches had disappeared, those who did not go home or play outside, but stayed indoors, were playing kissing games. When they threatened to kiss us, we shrank even deeper into the corner. They never got us to play kissing games.

So we stayed the whole afternoon for one more recitation. Still our little slates and pencils were some pastime and consolation. After this we seemed to be "broken in" as the saying goes.

We were all three in one class and when I kept at the head, being the one who learned to read first, the other two wondered how I could do it, not realizing that I was almost two years older than they.

· ·

This fall [1856] Mary*, Henry and I as well as Charley and Ernst Meyer were attending the Little Kohler school (Neumann District) west of us, where the teacher was a Mr. Haskell, a middle-aged man from New York City. How and why so fine a man should have come to this region nobody knew. Rumor had it he must have done something which forced him to leave his former home. His clothes and manners were far superior to those of anyone else in these parts. He taught us how to bow, explaining that if we ever got into high society we would have to know how to do so. He taught us to say "Yes sir" and No sir" and when we did not understand, not to say "What?" but to say "Sir?" He knew how to keep us busy all day for there were classes not only in reading, spelling and arithmetic, but also in geography, although we did not have books in geography.

The first time Mr. Haskell asked us in what country we lived, we said "America". Then he asked in what part of America; there was no response. He showed us where the United States was and also that we lived in Wisconsin, pointing to it on the map. Next he showed us Ozaukee County and Fredonia, the township. As time went on he taught us a great deal more.

There were others who came to school from other districts who had already been teachers—like Marion Keefe and two of her cousins. During that winter there was always a good attendance, the little schoolhouse being rather crowded.

· ·

This was an especially cold winter with much snow. It was hard to go to school and hard to come back. Usually at noon we would find our lunches frozen stiff and all around that long stove, we would be standing, thawing out our bread on top of it. Then we could see the differences in the breads. The Irish, the Regans and the Keefes had pure wheat bread, light and fluffy, probably salt rising bread, with plenty of yellow butter on top. The Germans had pure rye bread made with sour dough, not so fluffy, with lard or pork gravy on it. Ours was half and half, also raised with sour dough.

*That is, Marie. [editors' note]

Whichever it was, it did not seem to make much difference, for we were all a healthy lot.

At noon and at recess, the Germans instead of learning to speak English from the Irish, the Irish learned to speak the German from us, so it was that language which predominated here.

Western Wisconsin Homestead, 1856

WARREN W. COOKE

It was well into the late fall before the cabins, the cattle's enclosed shed, and horse stable were thought to be fitted for the coming winter. Our hay crop was stacked, some of it near the stable and sheds, more at the head of the valley, a mile or more distant. A little breaking of sod land was done for the next summer's vegetables. Flour and salted meats we could get at far-away Fountain City in one single hauling, but for potatoes, cabbage, beets, onions, and rutabagas, we had to have broken sod land the first summer in which to grow them. In October, father went to Fountain City and brought home flour, potatoes, sugar, coffee, and tea in a quantity he thought would last until the following spring. He feared the long winter season, promised us by the earlier settlers, might make it impossible to make a long trip to any market. Before the smaller cabin was built that we called the kitchen, a hole—about five feet square and four feet deep—was dug into the ground in the center of the house plat. Into this hole were dumped the potatoes; then when the kitchen floor was put down, a door about two feet square was cut through the floor. This hole through the floor was made for us children to jump into the cellar and get a raw potato to eat, now and then, which was considered a real luxury for us. Mother said it was a medicine for us, for it would keep us from having scurvy.

The Indians I told you about were camped for some time across the creek from the cabins. They shot some deer and an elk; they cut meat into ribbon-like strips and dried and smoked it on poles over a

From Warren W. Cooke, "A Frontiersman in Wisconsin," *Wisconsin Magazine of History,* XXIII (1939–40), 281–303, 406–426. Footnotes in the original omitted. Reprinted by permission of the State Historical Society of Wisconsin.

low fire. They would have liked to trade their bear, deer, and elk meat for our stock of flour. A little flour was spared, but little meat was taken in trade. They moved away after a time where there were no white settlers and then they got a good, fat bear, the oil of which made the finest of dressing for other meats that they could get. You may be sure we were all glad to see them move away although they were quiet and civil in all ways. Mother and sister did not like the way they cooked their meat and fats, so there were no exchanges of things to eat between mother, sister, and the Indian squaws.

In the November following our settling, the snow began to fall, and father, then free from camp work, took his rifle and shot a number of deer. He gave the fore quarters to the dogs and kept the saddles and hind quarters for our winter supply. You will all say, 'How foolish, how extravagant!' And so it was, for we were just entering the coldest weather and the deepest snowfall of any in the history of our state. The snow fell to the average depth of four feet, which made it impossible to travel afoot anywhere without snow-shoes, the making of which father knew nothing about. Mornings the snow was blown so high about the cabins that it had to be shoveled from all the lower windows before any daylight could enter. Father would often declare at such times that, if the next winter should be like this one, he would pull up stakes and trek back to Indiana. We were snow-bound until late in the following April before we could get out into the open country and look about us.

. . . .

We were all blessed with good health throughout the long, hard winter of 1856–57. The stock had to be turned out to browse as soon as the snow was gone, which was late in April. This was necessary, for the hay was nearly used up and the little yet on hand had to be kept for the horses. We had no grain for them, having grown neither wheat nor oats the summer before. Father cut down many trees, so the cattle could get the oak leaves and small twigs on the oak branches. The old grass and weeds on the meadowland kept them from suffering, but they were far from being fat, as you may suspect. New land was broken up as soon as possible, and potatoes and garden vegetable seeds were planted. At a very early age we children were assigned certain duties or work to carry on, according to our understanding and strength. Mother at one time had many different kinds of plants growing in the garden, and it was my job to see that the new grass and weeds did not get the start of the plants in growing. On looking over my work one day, to her grief and great disappointment, she saw that I had pulled up all the onion seed sprouts. This error on my part made it necessary for her to plant all new seeds and take the risk of a poor crop so late in the fall. But for this one mishap, the good Lord was on the side of mother, and we had a good crop of onions that fall.

. . . .

It was two years before a crop of grain was harvested; the yield was small, and the grain in proportion. In the few earliest years of our stay on the Beaver valley farm, clothing, wraps, quilts, and blankets for bedding were sometimes sorely needed before new supplies could be purchased. Cotton grain sacks were made over into men's pantaloons; the clothing of the older boy or girl, when it became too worn or small for the first wearer, was made over to fit the next child in size. Father and mother could make garments from furred skins as well as from cloth. We learned to tan such animal skins as were made into wearing apparel. My sister had a large cape made from two glossy black beaver skins which in that day would bring a price but little above the value of a heavy woolen cloth cape made of like size. Our winter caps, collars, mitts, and cuffs were made usually from muskrat, mink, and squirrel skins. Buckskin was used as facing for mitts.

We were very poor, and having grown but little grain at the start, it was necessary for us to catch, for their skins, muskrats, mink, beaver, and racoon when cold weather came, or in the season suitable for trapping such. We would have had to go without many real necessities if we had not trapped. These animals were in the streams near and about us. My older brother was a skillful trapper. He early learned how to set traps and what bait, if any was needed, was the best. I remember clearly that on a certain cold winter day he had to go some two miles from home to tend all his traps, but on his return his game bag was found to be well loaded with mink. He threw them from the game bag upon the cabin floor, stepped over to the stove, and grumbled about the weather, but not a word boastfully about the bunch of dead mink he had caught.

. . . .

I was voted the chief and best fox hunter of the family. In one season's trapping I caught eleven red foxes, most of them caught along the trail mentioned. The value of their skins added to that of some dozen muskrat skins enabled me to purchase my first ready-made suit of store clothes.

Winter seasons came and went with us usually quite well. Our household comforts in the way of clothes and bedding were worn to the last scrap of cloth, but through the sale of grain, furs, and now

Courtesy of the Portage County Historical Society

Pioneer homestead

and then live stock, needed articles were purchased. Overshoes were unknown to us; a double thickness of grain sacking was sometimes worn over shoes or boots.

Father and mother were experts in fitting, cutting, and sewing the articles before mentioned for family needs. I look back over those early years and I can see us all seated in the little, log cabin kitchen, some in chairs, some on home-made stools, all are near or about the table. Father may be reading, as it was his wont to read to us when so gathered some article in the last weekly paper that he thought might be interesting to us, or he may be sewing on an article similar to the one mother is engaged upon. The lights we had were tallow candles or a little iron pot filled with bear or coon oil. The wick was a twisted cord made from cotton batting. It was father's job to trim off the burned ends of the oil wick or candle at his right. On the table lies a big brass snuffer, and every five or ten minutes he has snuffing to do; thus were we busy, from oldest to youngest, in all the long evenings of winter doing some useful and needed work.

It was two years after we were settled before a crop of grain was grown sufficient to supply needs for our home and a little besides to sell. The land had first to be cleaned of brush, timber, and grubs;

there was no machine known at that time for doing such work. A good stout boy, eight or ten years of age, was expected to do a bit of grubbing if he was a good chopper, and most of them were skilled in the use of an ax. Not many acres could be cleaned in a year's time for reasons stated, and in addition a large cutting of wild grass for hay for stock was needed. All this was cut by hand with scythes.

· ·

Our cows gave us milk and cream a-plenty; we children were not allowed tea or coffee. There was a *wee puckle*—Scotch—tea and coffee, laid to one side for the serving of ourselves and travelers who sometimes stopped with us. I have often seen the floor of one of our cabins covered with blankets, coats, and the like, in and on which a half dozen or more men would stretch themselves out for the night. Our place for some years was quite a hostelry—it being midway between Winona, Minnesota, and Eau Claire, Wisconsin. Our bill of fare in wild meats seemed to be a drawing card. It was venison or prairie chicken, commonly served in the fall, winter, and spring seasons. Mother was a master chef in the cooking of wild game meats and in the making of butter. Her butter always brought the highest price going. We had a milk-house built of tamarack logs, near the creek, but a few steps from the house. Butter was packed in stone jars and set on large pieces of lime rock that covered the floor of the house. That insured cool and pure air.

· ·

As I vividly recall those days, the sum total of the vacation trips consisted in taking the team of horses or oxen with wagon, loading in the family old and young, and going to some neighbor for a day's visit. There was plenty of the right spirit and joy in such a vacation, and it was sure to bring a like return from the neighbor.

If the late spring frosts did not kill the blueberry crop—which too often was the case—it was sure to be celebrated in name or whatever one might call it, by two or more families in a blueberry camping group. Some scout would first report where the most favorable berry grounds were. From the middle of July to the middle of August, berry picking was eagerly carried on. Two or three of our neighbor families would join with us in an outing trip to the berry grounds. Home provisions, with a good tent or two to sleep under or protect us from rainstorms, were loaded into wagons. Then off we would go! The course would be taken largely through parts where no road was ever made, and the fun of holding that certain seat partner from being thrown out of the wagon when the wheel bumped over a stone or grub added much to the milder pleasures of the trip. The week spent in camp in the blueberry season was a relaxation from the everyday work on the farm, and it pleased all to go to the camp and rest. You could eat berries at will, and with berries at the dinner or supper hour we often had fried prairie chicken, for they liked the berries, and there were always pickers who had shotguns and knew how to shoot and shoot straight. Thus were plain, sober duties of that pioneer life broken for a short time each year for us youngsters.

3: The Economy and Business

George Smith, a Scotsman, knew the need for banking services on the frontier. He circumvented Wisconsin territorial laws to provide these services, as shown in the first selection, an excerpt from Theodore Andersen's *A Century of Banking in Wisconsin*. A book-length narrative of his accomplishments is found in *George Smith's Money: A Scottish Investor in America* by Alice E. Smith (Madison, 1966).

The second selection describes the generally defensive and hostile position of the people of territorial Wisconsin toward the business corporations, or "monopolies." The chapter ends with an example of an enterprising steamboat captain determined to make his fortune on the Fox River. He had to settle for less than his goal but was able to adapt to the situation and bring to the interior of Wisconsin cheap transportation when that was a vital necessity for the developing territory.

Other sources of information on the territorial economy are Margaret Walsh's *The Manufacturing Frontier; Pioneer Industry in Antebellum Wisconsin, 1830–1860* (Madison, 1972); Alice E. Smith's *James Duane Doty, Frontier Promoter* (Madison, 1954); Louis Pelzer's *Henry Dodge* (Iowa City, 1911); and Kenneth W. Duckett's *Frontiersman of Fortune; Moses M. Strong of Mineral Point* (Madison, 1955).

Territorial Banking

THEODORE A. ANDERSEN

Despite the prohibition of banking, a certain amount of illegal banking was carried on between 1841 and 1853. The leaders were George Smith and Alexander Mitchell, who gave a striking demonstration of brilliant banking operations. Smith, an ambitious and successful young farmer, had left his home in Scotland in 1831 to investigate business opportunities in America. Recognizing the potentialities of Chicago and Milwaukee, he speculated in the real estate of these two communities. By 1837 his success encouraged him to expand his business activities and he returned temporarily to Scotland to raise more capital. When he came back in 1838, he brought with him twenty-one-year-old Alexander Mitchell, who had obtained banking experience in Scotland and who had been highly recommended by the large Scottish investors in Smith's new enterprises. Smith planned to set up a chain of banks which would distribute and redeem notes for one another and thus be of assistance when one of them suffered heavy drains on its specie. Since the Panic of 1837 had destroyed almost all the banks in the Middle West, he would have a clear field. He knew that growing communities needed credit and he was confident that he was the person to supply it.

The banking laws of Illinois prevented him from setting up a bank in Chicago, so he obtained a charter for an insurance company, under which he did a banking business until the legislature put a stop to it. He then set about organizing a bank in Milwaukee. Aware that once again it would be impossible to obtain a bank charter from the legislature, he instructed his friend Daniel Wells, a member of the territorial Council and one of Milwaukee's first settlers, to get him a charter with a franchise as much like a bank franchise as possible and to call it what he wanted. Wells studied many charters and finally in the public library of Madison came across one that would serve the purpose: the charter of the Utica Insurance Company of New York. With this document as his model he formulated the charter of the Wisconsin Marine and Fire Insurance Company and succeeded in obtaining the approval of the legislature early in 1839.

The charter granted the usual privileges enjoyed by insurance companies, including the right to accept deposits and make loans. It

From Theodore A. Andersen, *A Century of Banking in Wisconsin* (Madison, 1954), pp. 7–12. Footnotes in the original omitted. Reprinted by permission of the State Historical Society of Wisconsin.

Courtesy of the SHSW [WHi (X3) 22172]
George Baxter Smith

specifically prohibited the exercise of any banking privileges, as did even the charters granted to churches after the failure of the banks in 1837. The provisions of the charter were obviously contradictory, but Smith knew how he was going to proceed. He told Wells that he knew banks were hated by the people of Milwaukee. "The name is a bug-bear they detest, but the thing is a boon they need and will welcome. I will sugar the pill and it will prove sweet."

Milwaukee was growing with great rapidity. By 1839 it already had a land office, two sawmills, a foundry, and an ironworks. Soon to follow were the city's first brewery, its first tannery, its first meat-packing plant, and the little shop that was to grow into Allis-Chalmers, Wisconsin's largest manufacturing concern. With the same foresight which in 1833 had envisioned the future growth of Chicago and Milwaukee, Smith helped to finance many small enterprises which eventually prospered beyond all expectations. It was inconceivable to him that anything should prevent him from using Scottish capital to help finance Milwaukee's surging economic growth, least of all the legislature's hostility toward banks.

The Marine Fire and Insurance Company was authorized to issue $500,000 worth of common stock at a par value of $25 per share. Of the 4,052 shares subscribed to, all but 29 went to Smith, who was subsequently elected to the board of directors and then made president of the company. A month later Alexander Mitchell was also elected to the board and became secretary. The initial paid-in capital of the company totaled $8,104.

The company sold some fire insurance policies to allay suspicions about its main business of banking, the amount of property insured being $770,000 in 1843. To provide currency for its customers in the face of the prohibition on the issuance of notes, Smith issued certificates of deposit to employees and friends and then loaned out the certificates, which served as money. Gradually they acquired the reputation of being as "good as gold," inasmuch as the company was always prepared to redeem them in gold.

A Chicagoan expressed in 1842 the general attitude toward George Smith's money when he wrote a friend: "If you have disposed of the county order I left with you of $7.35, I should like to have you send me $5; and if you send western money, please send fire insurance Milwaukee or something as good. Illinois is worth $.50." One of Milwaukee's leading merchants recalled that it was the Mitchell bank which had originally attracted him to the city.

To meet the pressing demand for loans, the insurance company gradually increased its issue of certificates of deposit to $1,500,000. They circulated throughout the Middle West and were redeemable in gold at Chicago, Detroit, St. Louis, Galena, Buffalo, and New York. As early as 1841, for example, some of them turned up in La Porte, Indiana, where no paper money was in circulation. One hundred dollars of the new type of money was gathered up by suspicious persons and dispatched by messenger to Smith's Chicago offices. Prompt redemption in gold followed, to the amazement of the people of La Porte. Their increased confidence in the notes soon spread to the surrounding communities.

The Marine Fire and Insurance Company was of great assistance to settlers who wished to buy farm land but lacked specie. The firm would buy the land from the government with gold and then sell it on a contract basis to the settlers. The aid thus furnished made many friends for Smith and Mitchell, friends who were to help the two men in the trying days ahead.

The operations of the insurance company revealed some of the advantages paper money had over gold. For example, a purchaser of wheat in Wisconsin might go to Smith's bank for funds with which to finance his purchases. He would give Smith his promissory note and receive in exchange certificates of deposit. With these certificates he would buy wheat. The certificates might change hands many times and ultimately fall into the hands of some merchant who wanted to purchase bolts of cloth in New York. He would present the certificates to Smith and in exchange receive a draft on a New York bank. The cost of the draft, of course, was far less than the cost of shipping gold to New York.

The farmers who accepted certificates of deposit when they sold their wheat profited in that they did not have to wait until the purchaser of wheat had resold it in Eastern markets and obtained gold with which to pay them. The purchaser who shipped the wheat to a consignee in New York would be likely to draw a draft on the consignee, attach a bill of lading, and give both instruments to George Smith in payment of his promissory note. Smith, after collecting on the draft from the New York consignee, would then turn the bill of lading over to the consignee. In collecting on the draft Smith would augment his holding of New York exchange, which in turn would offset the draft he gave to the merchant who presented the certificates of deposit for payment.

Thus the insurance company developed a type of paper money which facilitated the exchange of goods between Wisconsin and the East. It also extended credit to the person selling the wheat in the East and provided a medium of exchange for the Wisconsin settlers and a negotiable credit instrument for the merchant wishing to buy goods from the East.

Territorial Corporations

GEORGE J. KUEHNL

Governor James Doty addressed the legislature of Wisconsin Territory on December 6, 1841, with alarm on the subject of legislative grants of corporate charters:

> The monopolies which have been created within this territory, by acts of incorporation granting exclusive privileges to certain indi-

From George J. Kuehnl, *The Wisconsin Business Corporation* (Madison, the University of Wisconsin Press; © 1959 by the Regents of the University of Wisconsin), pp. 3–6. Footnotes in the original omitted. Reprinted by permission.

viduals, have, from their number and character, justly excited alarm in the minds of all men who are friendly to equal rights, and the establishment of all such institutions as are most favorable to democracy. These combinations of political power and wealth, these petty aristocracies—the offspring of the last four years—have been planted in almost every neighborhood; and although they may now give temporary benefits to a few individuals, we may expect the time will soon arrive when they will yield only bitter fruit for the people. Many of them appear to have been granted to favor particular persons, by creating a value for their property over that of their neighbors, or by thus distinguishing it to render it more saleable. They are incorporations to aid in speculation. Your attention is respectfully invited to all the acts of incorporation which have been passed, that all such as are not lawfully in existence, may be repealed without delay.

Governor Doty's address was delivered after he had held office only two months. His official views did not differ substantially from those of Henry Dodge, who both preceded and followed him as Governor of the Territory. Doty's statement reflected the popular attitude in the Territory, an attitude shaped by turbulent experience with the corporate form of enterprise. Subsequent experience reinforced this attitude. Much of the conflict and debate in the two Wisconsin Constitutional Conventions, prior to Wisconsin's admission as the thirtieth state, centered on this hostility. It partly explains why Wisconsin acquired a general incorporation act only in 1872, after referendum and constitutional amendment.

The attitude concerning corporations indicated by Doty's legislative address was neither abstract nor confined to lawyers; it was a popular view which received wide circulation in the territorial press as well as in the legislative and executive branches of government. It was a view derived from experience. In 1841, when Doty spoke, the population of the Territory of Wisconsin was about 46,000 with farming, fur trapping and lead mining the major industries. Transport was the overwhelming problem confronting this large but thinly settled area. If the Territory were to grow, greater transportation facilities were essential. The chief obstacle was lack of capital.

In attempting to meet the problems of transporation and capital the business and political leaders of the Territory resorted often to the corporate form. Of the thirty-five corporations granted special charters of incorporation by the territorial legislature between 1836 and 1840, seven were for banks and eleven were for canals and railroads. Of the remaining seventeen charters, eight were for lead and copper mining and six were for insurance companies. In the subsequent territorial period (1841–48) the legislature enacted thirty-eight special charters for business purposes. Twenty-nine of the thirty-eight were directly related to internal improvements:

piers, bridges, canals, steamboats, railroads, plankroads, and turnpikes. Six insurance companies were incorporated but no banks were chartered. For the entire territorial period (1836–48), a total of seventy-three business charters were enacted by the legislature: forty of these related directly to internal (transportation) improvement; seven were for banks. Seventeen of the transportation charters were enacted in 1848 and all were plankroad and turnpike companies.

While the problems of the environment dictated the purposes to which legislatively chartered business enterprise was devoted during the territorial period, this does not explain why promoters selected the corporate form instead of some other. It is difficult to determine motives 100 years after the fact, but the evidence has not vanished entirely.

Nearly all of the seventy-three business corporations chartered by the legislature during the territorial period were, by contemporary standards, large undertakings. All required more money than could be obtained from a handful of venturesome capitalists and the corporate form was best suited to collect capital in a money-poor economy. Many projects, particularly the canals and railroads, required government subsidy (land grants) and other aids if they were to succeed, while unusual powers had to be obtained to make other ventures possible. The special aids, subsidies, powers, privileges, exemptions and sanctions could only be obtained from the legislature. The corporate charter was the accepted device for distributing such favors.

If the corporate form met the practical needs of the capitalist of the territorial period, why did it have to be by special charter? Why was it necessary to set into motion the ponderous machinery of a legislature to incorporate a company? Why did it take until 1872, and a constitutional amendment, to secure for Wisconsin a general incorporation law for business ventures?

The answers, at least in part, lie in the following considerations: Most obvious is the public interest attribute of most of the seventy-three territorial corporations. The routes and terminals of canals, turnpikes, plankroads, bridges and railroads were more than casual, or private, affairs; they were vital matters of widespread public interest. A sound currency and easy credit were matters of much more than occasional, individual concern since banks and banking affected everyone. And the exploitation of natural resources (lead and timber) was a matter affected with great public interest. What more natural, then, that the legislature should retain, if not jealously guard, its power over corporations—to create them, to destroy them, to interfere directly in their affairs?

The attitude toward corporations, epitomized by Governor Doty's message of 1841, had a great deal to do with the retention until 1872 of the "special" character of corporate charters. In territorial Wisconsin corporate enterprises frequently proved to be failures—sometimes public scandals and calamities. Certain corporations usurped authority not granted; others openly defied the legislature.

Governor Doty referred to the business corporations as "monopolies," "petty aristocracies" and "incorporations to aid in speculation." This style of invective perhaps indicates familiarity with the Statute of Monopolies and the "Bubble Act," but the attitude itself did not derive from tradition. The enactment of general incorporation laws in Wisconsin was not delayed until 1872 because of abstract or technical notions about partnerships and joint stock companies. The depression of 1837 and the territorial bank failures had more genuine effect. The enactment of the general incorporation laws in 1872 cannot be simply summed up as legislative capitulation to the persistent businessman.

A Steamboat on the Fox, 1843

MARCUS A. McCORISON

In the spring of 1843, Captain Peter Hotaling of Buffalo, New York, brought the steamboat *Black Hawk* to the Fox River of Wisconsin with the intention of operating it between Fort Winnebago and Green Bay. The lead trade, then enjoying prominence in the economic structure of the Territory, was the basis of his seemingly foolhardy decision.

Green Bay merchants were actively emphasizing that port's key position in the short water route between the lead diggings at Galena and New York City. Lead had been coming up the Mississippi, the Wisconsin, and the Fox for many years. In 1822, a Philadelphia newspaper had announced the arrival in that city of 12,000 pounds of lead which came by way of the "Fox and Ouis-

From Marcus A. McCorison, "Peter Hotaling Brings a Steamboat to Lake Winnebago," *Wisconsin Magazine of History,* XL (Winter 1956–57), 117–120. Footnotes in the original omitted. Reprinted by permission of the State Historical Society of Wisconsin.

consin rivers, Green Bay and Detroit." The route had been long
established and was feasible, but from Fort Winnebago to Green
Bay Durham boats had to be used because of the rapids. This was
the weak spot in the chain. Captain Hotaling hoped to bridge this
gap. In addition, he had good reason to believe that in the near
future the entire length of the Fox River would be cleared and that a
canal would be built between the Wisconsin and Fox rivers at what
is now called Portage.

In the 1830's, the Army engineers had completed a survey of the
river. They estimated that, at a cost of $448,470.18, the
Wisconsin-Fox route could be opened to navigation and so recommended. In 1841, during the second session of the twenty-third
Congress, Henry Dodge attempted to introduce a bill in the House
of Representatives for the construction of harbors in Milwaukee,
Racine, and Southport (Kenosha), as well as for the improvement of
navigation on the Neenah and Wisconsin rivers. A similar bill was
introduced in the Senate by Oliver H. Smith of Indiana during the
same session. This was presented on January 28, 1842, and referred
to the Committee on Commerce. Despite active support, the bill
failed of passage. Ultimately a bill was passed, three years after
Hotaling began his venture, which granted a considerable quantity
of land as a basis for financing the improvement of the Fox River.

. . . .

To prepare for his venture in the West, Hotaling outfitted an Erie
Canal boat with a steam engine which one authority states was
given to the Captain by A. D. Patchen, a well known steamship
owner of Buffalo. The craft was christened the *Black Hawk*. Hotaling left Buffalo in May of 1843 in the company of his son Stephen, a
man identified only as John, James Worden, and George M. Man-
sure and family, the first settlers of Neenah. When he arrived in
Detroit, the appearance of the boat called forth from Morgan Bates,
editor of the Detroit *Daily Advertiser,* this comment:

> "A Strange Visitor.—There is now lying at the wharf of Messrs.
> Lawson, Howard & Co. the queerest looking steam water-craft that
> ever condescended to pay us a visit. She came in from Buffalo on
> Wednesday evening at the rate of ten miles per hour. She is nothing
> more or less than an Erie Canal boat, propelled by a small but
> powerful engine with a paddle wheel astern, and a smoke-pipe in the
> centre. She is commanded by Capt. P. Hotaling, who proceeds with
> her to Green Bay and from thence up the Fox River, over the rapids
> of the Fox River, (twenty miles above Green Bay) and will be adapted
> to carrying passengers and towing the Durham boats laden with lead,
> which is transported up the Wisconsin river to within one mile of

Fort Winnebago; and this one mile is all the portage required between Galena and New York, by way of the Lakes. The enterprise is
a novel and a laudable one, and we have no doubt it will be crowned
with entire success. Mr. Hotaling is a man of probity, and untiring
energy and perseverance. We have known him from our earliest
boyhood, and we confidently believe and ardently desire that his
most sanguine anticipations may be realized."

Captain Hotaling apparently left his son Stephen, then fourteen
years old, in Detroit and steamed to Green Bay. The men at Green
Bay were overjoyed to have him and the *Black Hawk* in their midst
and supplied a sizeable crew of Indians and Frenchmen to help him
negotiate the rapids. In addition, they gave him provisions,
"enough to come to nearly 100 dollars."

When he and his crew reached the Kaukauna rapids, they faced a
tremendous task. The *Black Hawk* was hauled over flat rocks for
forty rods and then could be moved no farther. In a letter, dated
July 9, 1843, to his wife, Hotaling described the work as follows:

"I determined to haul her out and take her by land one mile and put
her in above the rapids which I have accomplished. . . . We took her
on rollers such as they move houses with and took her up hill and
down. . . . I worked so hard in laying ways and launching her and
prying her off the rollers that after she was afloat I laid down completely wore out. It took us ten days to cross over this point of land.
We had a fine time you may think in getting her over. . . . We have
lighted the boat of everything we could take from her. We took even
the water wheel off and rolled it on the bank whare it now lies. Took
our sail which I had made in Detroit and formed a tent in which Mr.
Mansur and family still live."

There are no more of Hotaling's letters describing the trip but a
correspondent of the *Neenah Times* stated that Hotaling then
realized he could go no farther up the Fox River. The *Black Hawk*
was hauled back around the rapids and put in commission. The
remainder of the open water season was spent in service between De
Pere and the rapids.

That winter Hotaling supervised the construction of a new hull at
Whitney's Landing in Stockbridge. The Brothertown Indians
supplied the labor, and Daniel Whitney produced the lumber from
his saw mill on Mill Creek. Thomas Cammuck, a Brothertown
Indian, described the part his fellows played in the building of the
boat as follows:

"It may be interesting to know . . . [the steamboat] was built in our
county by the Brothertown Indians, under the superintendance of
Peter Hotaling, who was a white man, and the captain of said steam-

Courtesy of the SHSW [WHi (X313) 1899]

The Grand Chute on the Fox River. The locks were built to make the river navigable for the lumbering interests.

boat. She was called the Manchester, and is still running on the lake under the name, I think, of Fountain City. . . . Manchester, April 29, 1851."

After the hull had been completed in the spring the *Black Hawk* was dismantled and the boiler and useful parts shipped by Durham boat up the Fox River to Lake Winnebago and then to the ways on Mill Creek. There the machinery was installed in the *Manchester*. She was approximately seventy-five feet long and thirteen feet abeam, powered by sidewheels and an engine that generated about twenty horsepower.

. . . .

The steamship *Manchester* began its career as a "mixed freight" carrying passengers and goods between the towns rimming the lake and along the river. W. A. Titus reported that in 1847 passengers were carried from Taycheedah to Brothertown for twenty-five cents, and from Taycheedah to Neenah for seventy-five cents. A barrel of whiskey was sent any place on the lake for twenty-five cents while flour went at twelve cents a barrel. Grain was transported for six cents a bushel.

The run of the *Manchester* was part of a regular network of steamboat service between Galena and Green Bay. The *Milwaukee Sentinel* of July 23, 1845, noted that the steamer *Enterprise,* running between Green Bay and Lake Winnebago, the *Manchester,* covering the lake and part of one way to Fort Winnebago, and the *Maid of Iowa,* plying the Wisconsin and Mississippi rivers down to Galena formed a nearly continuous chain of waterborne traffic over the route. The article quoted a price of $1.35 per hundredweight as freightage and credited Captain Hotaling with founding the transportation system.

. . . .

Peter Hotaling's life was a useful and constructive one. He brought to the interior of Wisconsin, surmounting really great obstacles, a steamboat which, despite its limitations, provided cheap transportation at a time when it was a vital factor to a developing pioneer area. He had the wisdom to defeat failure by organizing a system of steam transportation over a route which he had hoped to dominate but, because of the geography of the river, could not. He thus made the all-water route from Galena to Green Bay nearly a reality. His part was a pioneering one in the development of the state's economy and life.

Chapter V
STATEHOOD
AND THE CIVIL WAR

The citizens of Territorial Wisconsin finally approved a state constitution in 1848, after rejecting an earlier one in 1846. Ratifying a state constitution was the first step toward gaining statehood. Interest in becoming a state had increased during the 1840s as the population grew. But the constitutional convention of 1846 had taken a strong stand on the prohibition of banks and paper money. In addition, several of its other provisions had offended certain groups, and the voters were persuaded to reject the constitution. When the second constitutional convention convened, it had fewer members and was more balanced politically. It revised the earlier constitution to meet voters' objections, and the second constitution passed easily in 1848. Wisconsin was admitted to the Union soon afterward.

The 1850s was a period of rapid population growth as settlers followed the railroads into the interior. Many immigrants from foreign countries came to Wisconsin; they tended to congregate in ethnic groups, seeking help and encouragement from fellow countrymen. Liberal voting laws did encourage all men to participate in government, and the assimilation of the foreign-born proceeded steadily, if slowly.

The economy continued to be shaky, with little credit and little industry. Better roads, railroads, and canals were badly needed to improve transportation. Lumbering was only beginning, and agriculture was facing competition from the opening of the Great Plains to farming.

Wisconsin's citizens responded to the call of the Civil War enthusiastically and in a variety of ways. Immigrant and Yankee sons from all over the state volunteered to serve in the militias. The state's enthusiasm outran its preparedness for some months, and the supplies and training facilities were inadequate. Women in the state joined the war effort by sewing, knitting, packing boxes of supplies for men on the front, serving as nurses, and filling in for men whenever necessary in agriculture, business, and industry.

After training at Camp Randall, the troops were sent north to quell the Sioux uprising in Minnesota, southwest to guard the Mississippi Valley, and southeast into the heart of the fighting. When the initial rush of patriotism wore off, the United States Congress passed a draft bill to fill the Union armies, placing responsibility for implementation on the state governors. Draft quotas in Wisconsin fell particularly heavy on some German communities north of Milwaukee, and a few riots resulted.

As the war dragged on, some Wisconsin Democrats began to object to Lincoln's policies. These Copperheads became convinced that the war was ruining the North and that Lincoln was a despot. Only the eventual victories of 1865 quieted their opposition. When the war was finally over, everyone was happy to return to peacetime activities, even though the war's impact was felt everywhere, and for many it was the most memorable time of their lives.

1: The Politics of Statehood

Rufus King, Whig editor of a Milwaukee paper, represented the sort of opposition which defeated the 1846 constitution. He was also elected as a delegate to the second convention.

The second selection illustrates the difficulties the newly formed Wisconsin Republican Party had in retaining its foothold in Wisconsin government when the prohibitionists demanded legislative action in exchange for their support.

Wisconsin statehood is comprehensively covered in Milo M. Quaife's four volumes published by the Wisconsin State Historical Society between 1918 and 1928: *The Movement for Statehood, 1845–1846; The Convention of 1846; The Struggle Over Ratification, 1846–1847;* and *The Attainment of Statehood.*

Rufus King, 1846–48

PERRY C. HILL

King immediately set out to defeat the 1846 draft constitution with all the considerable powers at his command. He not only wielded his editorial pen against it, but took a personal role in the political campaign, as we will later find his foes attesting.

He was shrewdly able to combine two objectives in the campaign—as a constitution maker, to scrap "a wicked and worthless instrument" as a Whig politician, to disrupt the Democratic

From Perry C. Hill, "Rufus King and the Wisconsin Constitution," *Wisconsin Magazine of History,* XXXII (June 1949), 416–435. Footnotes in the original omitted. Reprinted by permission of the State Historical Society of Wisconsin.

Party. He played upon a division of Democratic opinion to defeat the constituion and, conversely, used the constitutional issue to widen the Democratic split. It was neat strategy, and it worked both ways.

The newspaper campaign took the usual form, in that heyday of personal journalism, of a running feud with the Milwaukee *Courier*, mouthpiece of the proconstitution Democrats. Almost daily for weeks on end, the rival editors referred to the opposition print and to each other by name and by various names. Each advanced his own views by refuting and ridiculing the most recent expression by the other.

. . . .

On March 30 King was among twenty-two leading Whigs who published a ringing exhortation to the electorate to rise up and smite the constitution. A week later they did, by a vote of 14,119 for it and 20,231 against it. This was an astounding victory for King and his cohorts, in view of the minority situation of the Whigs.

. . . .

Editorial post-mortems continued through May. King listed the main issues on which the constitution fell: the homestead exemption clause; the bank article, especially its extraordinary attempt to outlaw foreign currency in denominations under $20 while permitting circulation of larger bills; the provision that married women could hold property separately from their husbands, which was viewed as sacrilege against the marriage bond and an open door to swindling; the lack of a single district system, and too short judicial terms. Then spoke the man of letters as he added (May 6): "Its language was inelegant; the arrangement clumsy; and the entire instrument cumbersome and involved."

The Second Convention

Once the first draft had been rejected, the writing and ratification of a second were anticlimactic. The public were too tired to get excited again so long as the features they had so clearly frowned upon were removed or modified and no other "ultra" notions were added.

. . . .

Governor Dodge called the Territorial Legislature into special session in the fall of 1847, and it decreed a new convention to meet December 15. The *Sentinel* masthead daily listed the Whig

Courtesy of the SHSW [WHi (D489) 1490]

General Rufus King (1861)

nominees for the seven delegate seats from Milwaukee County, with Rufus King heading the list. Being himself a candidate, King confined his editorial comments to urging election of sound men, especially Whigs. His dual role was criticized anyway, and he felt obliged to spell out his policy (November 29): "The *Sentinel,* from an obvious dictate of propriety, has scrupulously abstained from any and all allusions to the candidates on the Democratic ticket."

The election November 28 resulted in a Milwaukee County delegation of six "Locofocos" and one Whig. King outran the rest of his ticket to win seventh place, barely nosing into the delegation. Elsewhere in the Territory, however, the Whigs made heavy gains. The first convention had comprised 124 delegates and only 18 were Whigs—a futile minority. The second convention had only 69 members and 25 were Whigs—better than a third.

. . . .

King himself apparently acted as the *Sentinel* correspondent at the second convention. Although the reports refer to Delegate King in the third person, they are written with a delegate's knowledge and in King's style. But this time they are completely objective reporting, except for occasional remarks on the fine weather and how nicely everything is going and the prospects for early conclusion of the business.

This last type of comment was characteristic of King. He was a hustler and expediter. Way back before the first convention he had written (October 1, 1846): "If the business is properly cut out, and distributed among a sufficient number of working committees during the first week, and a resolute purpose evinced from the start not to tolerate long talking merely for talk's sake, we are not without hopes that the work may all be done up in four or five weeks."

That proved a forlorn hope; the first convention lasted ten weeks and labored in vain. After three weeks, King was already impatient with its dawdling and most unkindly remarked (October 29, 1846): "Two dollars a day is a good deal more than some of the members can earn at home, and they seem disposed to hang on to their perquisites as long as they can."

In the second convention he was appointed on the rules committee, and it made its report the same afternoon. He was on the committee to draft the executive, legislative, and administrative articles of the constitution. The executive article was ready by the sixth day, the administrative on the seventh. The legislative article had to await the census report; that came in December 29, and the article was reported out of committee on the thirtieth.

. . . .

The convention, it is true, had the first draft for a starting point. But it was so extensively overhauled, reorganized, and rewritten that the product was in effect a new document. Ornate language was reduced to simplicity (wherein we can presume Editor King's influence), and the number of articles was cut from nineteen to fourteen. All this was done, and fully debated, in just seven weeks.

King was more fluent with his pen than with his tongue. He did not himself indulge in the "long talking" that he rebuked in others. He presumably did his best work in the cloakroom and the committee chamber. Not a single major speech by him is recorded in the journal. Two other yardsticks have been used, therefore, to appraise the extent of his influence on the product of the convention: (1) comparison of his votes with the outcome on significant roll calls; (2) comparison of major features in the 1846 and 1848 drafts with King's known views.

Out of 242 selected roll calls tabulated by Quaife, King found himself in the majority 69 percent of the time, in the minority 31 percent (he was absent only once). In view of the fact that he was in a one-third political minority, it is significant that he and the majority of delegates were in accord more than two-thirds of the time.

Much more significant is the fact that his minority position on many roll calls ultimately came to be the judgment of the convention. Six times he voted in vain, for example, to beat down a homestead exemption provision, but finally it was omitted. At various times majorities voted against having a lieutenant governor, providing two-year instead of one-year senate terms, submitting the bank issue to referendum, increasing judicial terms, letting Negroes vote; but in the end King's view prevailed on all these points.

King really got steam up over just one big issue on which he could not prevail. He felt strongly aggrieved that Congress, in creating the states of Michigan and Illinois, had given them some territory plainly assigned to Wisconsin in the Northwest Ordinance. Four times he tried to obtain a proviso that Wisconsin's acceptance of the admission act would not prejudice her right to claim indemnity for the misplaced acreage. But the majority feared Congress might not accept the constitution with such a proviso in it, and they were willing to resign themselves to the shrunken boundaries.

King was an advocate of limited state participation in internal improvements, and lost that point, too. He voted in vain for higher public salaries, for a weak executive whose veto a majority could override, a more ambitious militia organization, an even smaller Legislature than was provided. Being in the printing business himself, he was on the short end of eleven roll calls that awarded convention and State printing by contract to the lowest bidder.

From Smith, History of Wisconsin, Vol. I. Courtesy of the SHSW

Wisconsin settlements at the time of statehood, 1848

Nevertheless, from King's standpoint the 1848 constitution contained these major improvements over the earlier draft:

Separate property rights of married women—omitted.
Homestead exemption—no specific provision, merely an injunction upon the Legislature to enact "wholesome laws" on the subject.
Banks—"bank or no bank" referendum authorized; if carried, general banking laws authorized subject to referendum.
Legislature—reduced from a maximum of 160 members to 133.
Judicial terms—increased from five to six years.

Election districts—single districts substituted for countywide elections.

Amendments—by two consecutive Legislatures, instead of one, subject to ratification.

Suffrage—Legislature authorized to extend suffrage subject to referendum.

So little public heat was generated by the second convention that King contented himself in the ratification campaign with the usual editorial appeals to "get out and vote."

....

A relatively light vote on March 13, 1848, overwhelmingly ratified the new document, 16,799 to 6,384, and King wrote a glowing last line to the story of the two-year struggle (March 21): "No state has ever entered the Confederacy with fairer character, maturer growth, or brighter prospects, than Wisconsin."

Republicans and Prohibition

FRANK L. BYRNE

In hailing their state as the birthplace of the Republican party, Wisconsinites have sometimes considered that the sole factor involved in the creation of that organization was the anti-slavery agitation of the 1850's. Yet prohibitionism was also a factor in the formation of the new party, since many voters who became Republicans had previously united behind candidates pledged to end the liquor trade. By their presence in the Republican ranks, such prohibitionists drew the fire of the state's liquor dealers and consumers, thereby posing for their political leaders the dilemma of having to woo voters thirsty for strong drink, while simultaneously seeking to retain the loyalty of the numerous advocates of cold water.

From Frank L. Byrne, "Maine Law Versus Lager Beer: a Dilemma of Wisconsin's Young Republican Party," *Wisconsin Magazine of History*, XLII (Winter 1958–59), 115–120. Footnotes in the original omitted. Reprinted by permission of the State Historical Society of Wisconsin.

Wisconsin prohibitionists, so important in the party's founding, were strongest in the state's south-central counties where the settlers were, either by birth or extraction, largely New Englanders. Since the 1830's, many of these Yankees—as they were often called—as well as their influential evangelical churches, had warmly supported the temperance movement. By 1851, after mixed success in curbing the liquor traffic through legislation, they and other Wisconsin prohibitionists had learned of a new panacea, introduced by Mayor Neal Dow of Portland, Maine, who had induced the Pine Tree State to impose the first strict prohibitory law. In widely circulated temperance newspapers, Wisconsin's anti-alcohol men, like their counterparts in other states, read Dow's sweeping claims for his law's success, and were quick to demand that their own legislature enact a version of the "Maine Law."

After unsuccessful appeals to Democratic and Whig lawmakers, the prohibitionists decided to elect politicians more sympathetic to their cause. On June 9, 1853, in Madison, a State Temperance Convention advised delegates to vote only for their co-believers—a recommendation that principally benefited the Wisconsin Free Democrats. A day earlier at another Madison convention, the state's third party had already nominated for governor a prohibitionist and abolitionist, Milwaukee merchant Edward D. Holton. In his late thirties, the wealthy Holton was a Yankee and a pious Congregationalist whose political supporters had originally organized to oppose the extension of slavery. However, since the Compromise of 1850 had temporarily settled the controversy over slavery in the territories, both he and the Free Democrats were willing to campaign on the Maine Law issue. Many Whigs, tired of their minority status in usually Democratic Wisconsin, later endorsed Holton and a fusion People's Ticket pledged to prohibition. A referendum on the Maine Law to be held at the fall election heightened interest in the campaign. Through the *Wisconsin Temperance League,* a weekly newspaper which Holton controlled, the prohibitionists and politicians co-ordinated a powerful campaign to win majorities for both the Maine Law and the People's Ticket.

But in the state's large German-born population the prohibitionists met their nemesis. The Germans, who dominated several counties near Lake Michigan, had already introduced to Wisconsin the brewing of lager beer, and the lighter, milder European beverage was quickly gaining general popularity. To the distress of their Yankee neighbors, merry drinkers and dancers crowded the German beer gardens, even on the Puritan Sabbath. Vigorously opposed to any prohibitionist interference with their pleasures, the numerous lager-loving Germans, Democrats in the main, put great pressure on the state's leading party to adopt their own *Bier-Anschauung*.

Though himself a Connecticut Yankee, the Democrat's 1853 nominee was willing to placate the Germans. Candidate William A. Barstow of Waukesha, under attack for his conduct in previous state offices, could use the fumes of lager to offset the corrupt odor of his political reputation. The unscrupulous Barstow sought to gull his fellow Yankees with a promise to sign a prohibitory law, provided a majority of voters in the 1853 referendum opposed liquor selling, but carefully stipulated that the legislature must pass a "constitutional" act. German Democrats assured their countrymen that Barstow would curb the "temperance fanatics."

On November 7, 1853, the friends and foes of alcohol met at the ballot box. The prohibitionists sometimes supplemented their dry arguments with the persuasive presence at the polls of ardent temperance women. But at Milwaukee, already the brewing capital of Wisconsin, kegs of beer piled on wagons and strapped to the backs of men walking near the polls offered a counterinfluence. Germans, quaffing lager from long oxhorns, cast their votes against prohibition and prohibitionists, and, in the state-wide referendum on the Maine Law, held their opponents to a small majority. The prohibitionist People's Ticket was drowned in an amber tide of Barstow votes, and the Free Democratic and Whig politicians discovered that in Wisconsin the Maine Law issue could loose a flood of opposition.

Early in 1854, to add to the prohibitionists' frustration, the Democrat-controlled legislature balked at abiding by the result of the Maine Law referendum. Nevertheless, the Whig and Free Democratic assemblymen, aided by a few Democrats, were able to steer a prohibitory bill through the lower house. But in the Senate, a block of Democrats, mostly from the lakeshore, insisted upon a provision submitting the bill to the people. "If they were insane enough to go for it again," shouted a senator from Milwaukee, "in God's name let them have it." The Assembly, refusing to provide for a new referendum, let the prohibitionists' bill die, prompting a prohibitionist editor to suggest, "Perhaps the legislature are waiting to have the people talk in *German* upon this question."

Calling for the election of prohibitionist legislators, the Whigs and Free Democrats prepared to readopt the issue of the previous year's unsuccessful campaign. However, the opponents of the long-dominant Democracy found a new and more promising platform than the advocacy of the Maine Law. Early in 1854, the Democratic national administration endorsed a law to organize the territories of Kansas and Nebraska and permit their voters to decide whether they would be free or slave. In Wisconsin, as in other

CHAMPAGNE.

Heidsieck, Piper & Co., quarts... 2 00
Do.   do.   pints... 1 00
Mumm, quarts... 2 50
Do.   pints... 1 25
Piesel, quarts... 2 00
Do.   pints... 1 25
Charles Heidsick, quarts... 1 25
Do.   do.   pints... 1 25
Creme de Bousee, quarts... 2 00
Do.   do.   pints... 1 25

NATIVE WINE.

Longworth's Sparkling Cataw-
ba, quarts... 2 00
Do.   do.   pints... 1 25
Corneau's Still Catawba... 1 00

PORT.

Old Port... 2 00
London... 2 00
Queen's... 2 00

HOCK.

Sparkling Hock... 2 00
Hockheimer, 1846... 2 00
Rudesheimer... 2 00

GAME.

Rabbits Roasted

SIDE DISHES.

Haricot of Turkeys Wings garnished with Vegetables—ancient style
Giblet Pie—according to Gunter.
Beef Kidneys, stewed with champagne sauce, John Bull fashion.
Mutton Chops, broiled—with Mushroom catsup for sauce.
Tenderloin of Beef, with sauce a la Meurice, and potatoe border.
Spring Chickens fricasseed, with salt pork, and garnished with Rice.
Turkeys' Livers, with salt pork, breaded and broiled, sauce Marsaillaise
Forms of Macaroni, with cheese. a la Hippolita.
Rabbits broiled on Toast.
Vermicelli Cake baked, flavored with lemon sand smothered in sugar

RELISHES.

Pickled Beets,   Pickled Cucumbers,   Pickles,   Cold Slaugh,

VEGETABLES.

New Potatoes,   Rice with Cream,   Onions,
Hot Slaugh,   Boiled Cabbage,   Potatoes Mashed,
Potatoe Balls Baked,   Boiled Rice,   Turnips Mashed,
Onions browned whole.   Beets sliced and stewed,
Carrots,   Summer Squash.   Parsnips browned.

PASTRY AND PUDDINGS.

English Plum Pudding, Brandy sauce,   Variety Pie.
Peach Pie.   Bird's Nest Pudding, Cold sauce.
Mince Pie.   Apple Pie.   Green Apple Pie.
Yankee Squash Pie,   Pumpkin Pie,   Frosted Pie.

DESSERT.

Ginger Snaps,   Ladies' Kisses   Vanities,
Plain Cake,   Follies,   Jelly Cake   Sponge Cake,
Queen Cakes,   Almonds,   Fruit.   Raisins.
Apples, Jamaica rum jelly, Madeira Wine jelly, Rose jelly, Port wine jelly

NOTICE

Gentlemen having friends to dine, will please give notice at the Office.
Meals, Lunches, or Fruit sent to rooms, or carried from the table by guests, will be charged extra.
Children occupying seats at the first table, will be charged full price.
Waiters are furnished with Wine cards and pencils.

HOURS FOR MEALS—by Office Time.

Breakfast from 7½ to 9 o'clk—Dinner at 1 o'clk—Tea from 6 to 8.

SUNDAY.

Breakfast from 8 to 10 o'clk—Dinner at 1½ o'clk—Tea from 6 to 8

CLARET

St. Julien Est... 1 00
La Rose... 1 00
Leoville... 1 00
St. Emelien... 1 00
St. Julien Medoc... 1 50
Chateau Marguax... 2 50

BRANDY

United Vineyard Proprietors... 2 00
Martell... 2 00
Old London Dock... 2 50
Old Hennessy... 2 00
Page & Sons London Particular... 2 00
Thomas Hines & Co.... 2 50
Otard, Dupuy & Co.... 2 00
Pints of the above... 1 25
Q. very old and fine... 3 00
Corneau's Catawba... 2 00

PORTER.

London Brown Stout, quarts... 0 75
Do.   do.   pints... 0 40
Byas   do.
Guinness   do.

SCOTCH ALE.

Younger s, quarts... 0 75
Do.   pints... 0 40
Reynold's...
Byron's...

A broadside bill of fare from the Capital House, Madison (1855)

Northern States, Free Democrats and Whigs proclaimed that the Kansas-Nebraska Act had revived the question of slavery in the territories, but they observed that the meetings which they called to protest the measure attracted some Germans and other Democrats. With the experience of the previous year's People's Ticket behind them, anti-Democratic editors began to talk of organizing a party to meet the slavery menace. On March 20, 1854, a meeting at Ripon first suggested the name "Republican" for the new political organization. Throughout the state, the same groups who had earlier united behind the Maine Law, began to melt into the Republican fusion.

Unlike the People's Ticket, the new party did not commit itself to prohibition. On July 13, 1854, when a convention met at Madison to organize the Wisconsin Republican party, the delegates carefully avoided the Maine Law issue, confining themselves instead to denouncing the Kansas-Nebraska and Fugitive Slave Acts. The men who had suffered in the 1853 election at the hands of the lager-quaffing Germans concluded with an appeal for the support of the foreign born.

. . . .

One of the first victims of the politicians abandonment of prohibition was the weekly *Wisconsin Temperance League*. After the 1853 referendum campaign, the newspaper had continued its attack on the monsters who owned glittering bars and drew up beer from their "vaults of death." The *League's* motto was "Woe unto him that giveth his Neighbor Drink." Its editor supported the formation of the Republican party and commented, "Temperance men are Anti-Nebraska men." By the beginning of September, 1854, however, the editor had ceased praising the Republicans. Instead, he complained of the apathy of temperance men, and begged his ex-supporters not to allow him to be inundated by the "rising tide of intemperance and political treachery." On September 20, with a final, piteous plea for assistance, the *Wisconsin Temperance League* expired. Since its former political friends had found an issue which promised to recruit the very group antagonized by the Maine Law, the prohibition paper had lost its utility.

As was to be expected, the Democrats challenged the Republican leaders' disavowal of their recent interest in prohibition. One Democratic editor asked, ". . . Do they expect by silence to get the German vote . . ., [and] then tell the Germans to go to grass?" A German Democrat attacked the new party as a *"Holy Alliance* of the Abolitionists, Whigs, Know-Nothings, Sunday and Cold Water Fanatics." On being forced into the open, the Republicans retorted that the slavery question was the most important issue before the nation. Although failing to promise that their legislators would not take a stand on prohibition, they called on the voters to "lay aside all minor differences of opinion for the present." Thus the Republicans had decided to stake their campaign entirely on the issue of keeping the territories free of slavery.

This strategy of silence concerning prohibition but stressing the slavery question proved a complete success, resulting in the new party's winning a clear majority in the State Assembly. Although hold-over Democrats held a slim lead in the Senate, some were also pledged foes of the Kansas-Nebraska Act. By sweeping almost completely the central area of the state, the Republicans made the Democracy more dependent upon the lakeshore Germans and rendered it even more subservient to their interests. Conversely, despite their bid for German votes, the Republicans continued to derive most of their strength from the central stronghold of the prohibitionist Yankees.

Almost every Northern state except Wisconsin had already enacted, or was considering, prohibition. Therefore, when the legislature met in January, 1855, Republicans who owed their elections in part to prohibitionist votes were determined to win the prolonged struggle for the Maine Law. On March 3, the Assembly passed by a vote of nearly two to one a bill prohibiting the manufacture and sale of intoxicating drinks. Over 80 per cent of the affirmative voters were Republicans, the opponents mostly lakeshore Democrats. In the Senate vote on March 16, about 40 per cent of the Democrats sided with the Republicans. But, to appease the Germans, the upper house insisted upon exempting Wisconsin beer, wine, and cider from prohibition. Reluctantly the temperance lawmakers in the Assembly agreed to the Senate's change and sent the bill to the desk of the Democratic Governor William A. Barstow.

Although the governor had pledged himself to sign a constitutional prohibitory bill, anti-Maine Law men had predicted that he would veto any such measure, and Barstow, whose administration was under attack for corrupt handling of state funds, needed their support. While the prohibitory bill was in his hands, a Republican editor reported that Frederick W. Horn of Cedarburg, the state immigration commissioner, was seeking pledges from other leading Germans to back Barstow's renomination, in return for a veto. On March 24, 1855, the Democratic governor announced his disapproval of the Maine Law Bill. He mentioned, but did not discuss, his "constitutional objections" to the measure. He also piously objected to the exemptions granted to beer, wine, and cider as "an unwise and unwarranted compromise between principle and expediency."

Immediately the Assembly attempted to override Barstow's veto. But, since the Democrats mustered almost all their forces to uphold the administration, the prohibitionist Republicans failed to obtain the needed two-thirds majority, whereupon the temperance men grimly revised their bill to meet the governor's complaints and on March 27, 1855, rammed it through both houses of the legislature. Four days later, wielding his carefully reserved "constitutional objections," Barstow pounded the measure to death, contending that the bill provided for unreasonable searches and illegal seizures of property, and once more the Assembly failed to override his veto. With the twin slashes of his veto pen, Barstow, the Democrat, had made complete the partisan cleavage over prohibitions.

Temperance advocates raged at what they regarded as the governor's betrayal. A few Dane County women presented him with a box containing thirty pennies, a bottle, a cigar butt, and a piece of crepe. The Republican press was at first inclined to take the issue to the voters at the next election. Referring to Barstow's first name, William, the *Mineral Point Tribune* predicted that the people would veto a "Liquor Bill." The Republican's Madison organ defiantly stated, "If this administration supposes that a baptism in whiskey will wash away the stains of their past misdeeds, . . . we hope the experiment will be tried."

But the anti-prohibitionists and especially the Germans gave Barstow's veto a thunderous reception. In Madison and Milwaukee, they held torch-light processions and fired salutes, while at Watertown a group of paraders celebrated by smashing a temperance man's windows. The proprietor of Best's Beer Hall, one of Milwaukee's usual polling-places, hung the "veto pen" in an honored place. Milwaukee's leading German newspaper proclaimed that the issue in the fall would be Republicans and "temperance-despotism or Democracy and personal freedom." At the end of August, 1855, Governor Barstow won renomination on a platform opposing the Maine Law, demonstrating that the Democrats, while giving lipservice to the suppression of intemperance, had begun to exploit to the hilt the strong public dissatisfaction with the Republicans' prohibitory bills.

Almost too late, the Republicans saw their peril. In the summer of 1855 at Portland, Maine, a riot against the original Maine Law had turned the tide against prohibition, and in Wisconsin, as in other Northern states, a wave of revulsion against the law was mounting. Hurriedly, the Wisconsin Republicans abandoned their intention of making an issue of the Barstow vetoes. While they nominated for governor Coles Bashford, a prohibitionist, they avoided committing their party against liquor selling. Charles Roeser, the German Republican candidate for state treasurer, even published a report that the ambitious Bashford had agreed to set aside prohibition in favor of the "great issue of freedom." In the subsequent gubernatorial election, the Democrats claimed victory, but Bashford charged them with counting fraudulent returns. And the Republicans, who had easily carried the state in the previous year, won him the governorship only with the aid of the courts.

Republicans realized that the prohibition issue had been one of the principal causes of their near-disaster in the state election. As the Milwaukee *Daily Sentinel* of December 21, 1855, put it:

> *"Some, uninformed, may wonder at the cause,*
> *Why beer elects the men who make our laws.*
> *Perhaps to them, the reason seems abstruse,*
> *Though very plain to us residing here;*
> *For we, where every second neighbor brews,*
> *Preserve our liberties in LAGER BEER."*

Throughout 1856, while political physicians labored to restore Republican strength in preparation for the forthcoming presidential election, the party's gravediggers buried its connection with prohibition. In September at a special legislative session, Republicans joined Democrats in voting to postpone indefinitely the consideration of a Maine Law bill. Republican editors and orators, including prohibitionist Edward D. Holton, sought to direct the voters' attention to the controversy over slavery in Kansas. Well might the Presbyterian-Congregational Convention lament in October that, "Under the intense political excitement, the cause of Temperance has been losing ground. . . ."

After sweeping the state in the 1856 election, the Republican politicians did not reassert their loyalty to prohibition. They had no wish to antagonize the growing host of brewers and beer drinkers. In February, 1857, Milwaukee's first carnival celebration demonstrated the strength of beer's backers. For the occasion, the city's breweries poured out a torrent of bock, and a leading brewer, Phillip Best, was Prince of Carnival. Reeling behind him in the carnival parade, two mock "apostles of Temperance" aided "Bacchus" and "King Gambrinus," mythical inventor of lager, in laughing to scorn the defeated prohibitionists. Even the *Milwaukee Sentinel*, which in 1853 and 1854 had endorsed Maine Law candidates, hailed the beery fun.

By the late 1850's, 127 breweries were supplying thirsty citizens of Wisconsin. And in Chicago and other nearby places, signs advertising "Milwaukee Lager Beer" were already beginning to make famous the state's largest city. In 1858, recognizing the brewers' importance, Republican Governor Alexander Randall commissioned Phillip Best a brigadier general of militia. Beer had become, as a journalist remarked, an accepted "institution."

2: The Civil War

The first two selections in this second section document the opposition to President Lincoln that existed in Wisconsin. Marcus M. ("Brick") Pomeroy, editor of the La Crosse *Democrat*, was violently and vociferously opposed to Lincoln's war policies. The abusiveness of his editorials shocked his readers. The second selection is a general examination of Wisconsin Copperheadism. The biography *Edward G. Ryan, Lion of the Law* by Alfons J. Beitzinger (Madison, 1960) and Frank Klement's *The Copperheads in the Middle West* (Chicago, 1960) shed more light on Wisconsin's anti-war Democrats.

The best way to understand the Civil War soldiers' lives is to read their letters and diaries. Many have been published, and among the more interesting letters are those written by Chauncey H. Cooke, younger brother of pioneer Warren Cooke. Chauncey joined the army at the age of sixteen, with his parents' permission. His letters describe daily activities and occasional battles, and they reveal his feelings and attitudes as well. Other narratives include *Jenkin Jones, An Artilleryman's Diary* (Madison, 1914); *A Wisconsin Boy in Dixie: The Selected Letters of James K. Newton,* edited by Stephen E. Ambrose (Madison, 1961); and *Private Elisha Stockwell Sees the Civil War,* edited by Byron R. Abernethy (Norman, Okla., 1958).

The final selection, by Ethel Alice Hurn, gives an account of the contributions that Wisconsin women made to the war effort. Mary A. Livermore, *My Story of the War* (Hartford, Conn., 1909) is also useful for descriptions of nursing in the Sanitary Service.

"Brick" Pomeroy

FRANK KLEMENT

Emotional oratory, mixed with vicious charges and counter-charges, provided fuel for the presidential campaign of 1864. As the political pot boiled more vigorously, Marcus M. Pomeroy, editor of the La Crosse *Democrat,* fed the flames with searing attacks upon the Lincoln administration. The arrogant editor amazed his friends and aroused his foes by placing the caption "The Widow-Maker of the 19th Century" over a front-page picture of President Lincoln. Then, several weeks later, Pomeroy employed his pointed pen to administer the editorial *coup de grâce:*

> The man who votes for Lincoln now is a traitor and murderer. He who pretending to war for, wars against the constitution of our country is a traitor, and Lincoln is one of these men. . . . And if he is elected to misgovern for another four years, we trust some bold hand will pierce his heart with dagger point for the public good.

Even an epigrammatic epitaph was suggested in that issue:
Beneath this turf the Widow Maker lies,
Little in everything, except in size.
Pomeroy's thirst for Lincoln's blood made the assiduous editor a marked man. It won for him the notoriety he sought. Attention was focused on La Crosse, and men queried, "What manner of man is this?"

*   *   *   *   *

A score of Wisconsin citizens would have ventured an answer to that question. Many had more than a passing acquaintance with Pomeroy. In Horicon they spoke highly of the young entrepreneur who had come to town in 1857 with a few dollars in his pocket, a newspaperman's know-how, and the will to succeed. He built the Horicon *Argus* into one of the better small town papers in the State, acquired the sobriquet "Brick," and served as deputy United States marshal. He shifted his base of operations to Milwaukee, where he served as city editor of the Milwaukee *Daily News* and watched the circulation of that enterprising journal double. Pomeroy's support of Stephen A. Douglas rather than President James Buchanan cost the Milwaukeean his slice of the patronage pie, and the marshalship

From Frank Klement, "Brick Pomeroy: Copperhead and Curmudgeon," *Wisconsin Magazine of History,* XXXV (Winter 1951), 106–113, 156–157. Footnotes in the original omitted. Reprinted by permission of the State Historical Society of Wisconsin.

Courtesy of the SHSW [WHi (X3) 17968]

"Brick" Pomeroy

passed into other hands. An out-of-state newspaper venture dissipated his small stake, so he returned to Wisconsin in 1860 and selected La Crosse as a city with a future. On credit he purchased a one-third interest in the office and equipment of the La Crosse *Union and Democrat*. Pomeroy promoted Douglas' doctrine aggressively, both in the editorial offices and in the hotel lobbies. He took a recess from his newspaper duties to attend the Baltimore Convention which named Douglas of Illinois as the standard-bearer of the Northern wing of the Democratic Party.

While Pomeroy directed his editorial efforts in behalf of Douglas, another firm partner preached Buchanan's views. A six-month civil war within the editorial sanctum of the La Crosse *Union and Democrat* endangered the life of that party paper. Sheriff's suspensions and sales, coupled with stock transfers, ended the legal existence of the *Union and Democrat,* and in November of 1860 the ambitious Pomeroy emerged with his own La Crosse *Democrat,* debt-encumbered and circulation dwindling.

. . . .

Pomeroy's spirit of patriotism remained keyed to a high pitch during the early months of the war. He tried to organize his own company, to be named "The Wisconsin Tigers" and to do business in "Marion's style," but that dream faded into nothingness. When the opponents of war raised their voices after the Union debacle at Bull Run Creek, Pomeroy promised vigilante action to quash treason. Truly, he appeared to be an ardent patriot!

But when time combined with realism to cool the ardor of the North, Pomeroy's patriotism also cooled. The cloud of Abolition cast its shadows over the issues preached by the party in power, so the Democratic editor issued a warning:

> There is not today half the enthusiasm in the country there was two months since. . . . A chill has already set in. . . . We are willing to fight till death for the common good of a common people, but will not be forced into a fight to free the slaves. The real traitors in the north are the Abolitionists, and they are the ones who will do more to put off the day of peace than all the soldiers of the South.

Pomeroy endorsed a nonpartisan ticket in the county elections, although he espoused the Democratic slate in the State elections. Slowly it dawned upon the energetic editor that the Union Party ticket represented Republican Party strategy, and he denounced it as a political swindle—a political feast wherein Lincoln's party took the turkey and gave the Democrats the buzzard. He condemned the Abolitionists in general and Sherman M. Booth in particular. "He is to respectable people," Pomeroy wrote of this Milwaukee editor and abolition agitator, "what a blooming pole cat would be in a ballroom." When General John C. Frémont proclaimed the freedom of the slaves of rebels within his jurisdiction, the La Crosse editor showered him with epithets. Pomeroy did not endorse slavery as a desirable institution, but its existence was a *fait accompli,* and the United States government lacked authority to intervene when states accepted and protected it. Furthermore, the freed Negroes, moving northward, threatened the position of free white labor in the North.

The Abolition crusade dampened his enthusiasm for the war. Lincoln's preliminary emancipation proclamation of September 23, 1862, irritated him. It seemed to be proof that the administration was perverting a war to save the Union into one to free the slaves. Lincoln had surrendered to the "abolition hounds"! Republican agitators seemed to be fiddling while Rome burned—for "nigger is a never ending theme."

Yet Pomeroy was patriot enough to oppose the "Ryan Address." This statement of Democratic beliefs and policy—based upon states rights, conciliation, reason, and humanitarianism—disturbed the editor of the La Crosse *Democrat.* "This is no time for drawing party lines... ," pleaded Pomeroy. "Partisan agitation will not subdue the rebellion." He refused to publish the Ryan address in his paper, and he justified his opposition in many columns of type.

Pomeroy's endorsement of the war obviously was not the blind or blanket type. Administration policy often received the stamp of disapprobation on the editorial pages. The suspension of the writ of *habeas corpus* and the wholesale arbitrary arrests drew criticism. He expressed disgust with Lincoln's "bungling" and "experimenting." McClellan's removal seemed to be based upon political motives and the pressure of the Radical Republicans. Soldier voting-in-the-field drew a barrage from the editor, for it was a political stratagem which stifled the Democratic revival. And Abolition as national policy horrified him.

A three-week tour of the St. Louis sector of war and a two-month term in Arkansas at the headquarters of the Army of the Southwest undermined Pomeroy's devotion to war and wrecked his respect for Lincoln's administration. It ended, eventually, his qualified support of the effort to subdue the South by military might. It changed Pomeroy from a protester into a full-fledged Copperhead.

At St. Louis the touring editor had become acquainted with army contractors and army quartermasters who had cooperated to build private fortunes—"making money by the cord." Discontented officers and friends explained army politics and practices to the eager editor and unloaded upon willing ears their tales of political patronage, rank favoritism and widespread frauds. He noted the demoralizing aspects of army life—hordes of "unlawful wives and prostitutes accompanying the army," gambling condoned on every hand, liquor shipments and sales at army bases, and stealing sanctioned as confiscation. "The horrors of war will not end on the battlefield," wrote the editor in a letter to his readers, "nor will habits so easily formed by a large mass of officers and men ever be shaken off." His visits to the field hospitals seared his soul. He saw dying men, pained and disillusioned—shell-shattered bodies writhing in the shadow of death. War was a creator of cripples and beggars. "How a hospital strips the damnable crimson glory from a soldier," he wrote. Watching a lot of 500 pine coffins being unloaded at the St. Louis wharves brought forth the humanitarian's reaction: "These rough, brown, cheap, worm-eaten coffins, piled up there like oyster cans, silently waiting to fold their wooden arms about our sons, brothers and fathers, rather took the poetry out of the shoulder straps and gold-covered cord to be seen strutting around, giving orders to the glory-hunters in plain blue."

. . . .

The La Crosse malcontent became convinced that the South could not be whipped, that the officers were more concerned with promotions than with warfare, that the administration had ceased to command the respect so necessary to success, and that the war had degenerated into a "murderous crusade for cotton and niggers."

His obsession drove Pomeroy to the brink of treason. He recognized that Patrick Henry's pronouncement "If this be treason, make the most of it"—a statement made a hundred years earlier—paralleled his own:

> The people do not want this war. Taxpayers do not wish it. Widows, orphans and overtaxed working men do not ask or need this waste of men, blood, and treasure. There is no glory to be won in a civil war, no more than in a family quarrel. If politicians would let this matter come before the people there would be an honorable peace within sixty days. But so long as blind leaders govern and fanaticism rules the day, so long will there be war, tears, and desolation. It might be treason to write this. But we cannot help it. If the truth be treason, this is the heighth [sic] of it, but such treason will find a cordial "Amen" in thousands of hearts both in and out of the army.

. . . .

By reprinting articles from Copperhead sheets like the Chicago *Times,* the New York *World,* the Cleveland *Plain Dealer,* the Cin-

cinnati *Enquirer,* and the Milwaukee *News,* Pomeroy advocated his
views through indirection. The "Ryan Address," which he had rejected a year earlier, he now endorsed. When President Lincoln set
aside August 5, 1863, as a day for fasting and prayer, Pomeroy
printed a plea he presumed appropriate: "Remove by death the
present Administration from power and give us in their place
Statesmen instead of jokers and clowns—honest men instead of
speculators—military ability instead of conceit and arrogant assumption."

La Crosse Unionists tried to combat Pomeroy's influence. They
tied the tail of treason to Pomeroy's kite. They used "Copperhead"
as a smear term. Unsigned letters threatened Pomeroy's life and
property. Republicans urged that "loyal men" cancel their subscrip-
tions to the La Crosse *Democrat* and that businessmen cease use of
that paper as a medium of advertising. Social boycotts, too, could
be effective. A. P. Blakeslee launched the La Crosse *Democratic
Journal* to lure Democratic Party patrons from Pomeroy's quarters
and to direct editorial blasts at the "treasonable doctrines of those
who sympathize with the rebellion." "Wisconsin Democracy,"
Blakeslee warned, "has a few dangerous men, seeking to be leaders,
whose counsels should be spurned."

Tactics of intimidation and the State election fever of 1863 spur-
red "Brick" Pomeroy to double his accusations and intensify his
charges. He dedicated a poem to Lincoln and army plundering:

> There's blood upon your garments,
> There's guilt upon your soul,
> For the lust of ruthless soldiers
> You let loose beyond control:
> Your dark and wicked doings
> A God of mercy sees
> And the wail of homeless children
> Is heard on every breeze.

"Abraham Lincoln is the traitor," charged Pomeroy. "It is he
who has warred upon the Constitution. We have not. . . . He has
broken his oath—lent himself to corruptionists and fanatics. . . ."
When the patriots shouted, "Copperhead!" Pomeroy retorted,
"Blowsnakes!"

Democratic defeats in the November, 1863, elections perplexed
Pomeroy. He made the "Ryan Address" the scapegoat, forgetting
that his diatribes were even more intemperate. His failure to sell his
bill of goods irritated and angered him. His sincerity and his courage drove him farther to the left, and in the months that followed he
reloaded his canons with more explosive shells. He labeled the draft
a "cruel failure" characterized by "inefficiency, expense, and worth-

lessness." He searched the dictionary for denunciatory derivatives. "Lincoln," stated the abusive editor, "is but the fungus from the corrupt womb of bigotry and fanaticism." In that same issue of April 23, 1864, Pomeroy fastened the phrase "widow-maker" to President Lincoln. When Lincoln sought renomination, Pomeroy's protests were filled with rancor: "May Almighty God forbid that we are to have two terms of the rottenist, most stinking, ruin-working smallpox ever conceived by fiends or mortals, in the shape of two terms of Abe Lincoln's administration." In successive issues he expanded that same theme. "The energy of the administration," he critically averred, "is devoted to secure Lincoln's re-election—to rear the widow-maker to the top of his monument of skulls—to the apex of his heap of national ruin." Dejectedly he added: "God only knows where we are drifting.... A once proud nation is in tears, trouble and mourning.... Patriotism is played out.... All are tired of this damnable tragedy.... Each hour is but sinking us deeper into bankruptcy and desolation...."

. . . .

Pomeroy's fantastic yet serious censure won him national notoriety. He gloried in that publicity—it was food for his vanity. It was then that he became more abusive and asked for the assassination of the President—trusting that "some bold hand will pierce his heart with dagger point for the public good." That was the peak of Pomeroy's denunciation.

Pomeroy received, in full measure, abuse of the same variety which he so savagely distributed. The circulation of his weekly La Crosse *Democrat* dropped to 360 copies—proof of the unpopularity of Copperhead sentiments in western Wisconsin. The social boycott was extended. Intimidation, as the Union Leagues widened their influence, became a more popular policy. Soldiers, writing from camp sites and by campfires, threatened to shoot Pomeroy when they returned. Indignant La Crosse Unionists threatened bodily injury and mob action. The Third Minnesota Regiment, passing through La Crosse, attempted to "clean out the *Democrat* office." Only the prompt action and the cool head of Mayor Pettibone restrained the rioters.

These constant threats infuriated Pomeroy. He feared no one—he would fight fire with fire, so he answered in kind: "When this office is destroyed, a hundred buildings in this city will keep it company. Matches are cheap and retaliation sweet. If anyone wants a little riot, they shall have a big one—one to last them forever." Pomeroy advised his followers, "When they ignite the match, let us apply the torch."

Pomeroy often expressed his feelings in poetry. A satirical stanza, in the closing minutes of the 1864 presidential campaign, pleaded for anti-administration votes:

> And Father Abraham, it's no joke if you again split rails;
> The Constitution you tried to split—in this we think you'll fail—
> We'll swap you off, though in the stream—we're sure to make a raid,
> McClellan is our motto now—free speech, free press, free trade!

The election results repudiated Pomeroy's poetry, McClellan's candidacy, and the Copperhead-sponsored peace policy. The disconsolate editor regretted Lincoln's election "more than words can tell," predicting that the union of the states was "gone forever," that the South "would never be subjugated," and that thieving army generals would work with renewed effort.

· ·

But, increasingly, national news and issues received less space in the editorial columns—local news absorbing the editor's attention. Lincoln's belated removal of General Butler, whom Pomeroy had abused unmercifully, drew a word of approval and a column of applause. A four-month circuitous tour of the East—to New York and points northeast—dulled the Copperhead's sharp criticisms. He found the country not nearly as ruined nor so war-weary as he had earlier imagined. He was convinced that General Grant was dealing the rebellion its death blow and that powder and blood had cleansed the army of the corruptionists and plunderers.

Lincoln's dramatic death—at the hand of an assassin as Pomeroy had earlier suggested—shocked the country. Even the irascible editor of the La Crosse *Democrat* showed regret. He decked his newspaper in mourning garb by turning the column rules and clamored for the assassin's blood. The culprit ought to be "hung in chains to starve to death" in true pirate fashion, suggested Pomeroy. Perhaps, added the editor, Ben Butler's hand lay behind the diabolical plot—the La Crosse curmudgeon knew no one more wicked and less principled. But Pomeroy, too, was under suspicion as the threads of the conspiracy were slowly unraveled; his enemies recalled that he had hoped that "a daggerpoint pierce Lincoln's heart." Weakly the editor defended his editorial excesses of the war years. He reminded his readers that others, too, had been critical and that many comments were the product of "the heat of a fierce political campaign."

The capitulation of the Confederate forces to General Grant and Sherman cancelled, as well, the commissions of the Copperhead captains. The war discredited them as prophets, so Pomeroy and his compatriots stood disgraced. Theirs, too, was a period of readjustment and the struggle to leave behind their wartime reputations and build new ones. In this rebuilding, Pomeroy enjoyed a sweeping success. By 1868 he inflated his subscription list to nearly 100,000—"even his enemies could not resist buying his paper." Then he sought new fields to conquer. At "Boss" Tweed's invitation, Pomeroy set up headquarters in New York and edited the New York *Democrat* until the scrupulous scribbler laid the charges which exploded the notorious "Tweed Ring." He returned, then, to the Midwest, editing *Pomeroy's Democrat* in Chicago while rising to become one of the top chieftains in the Greenback wigwam. Next, Pomeroy heeded Greeley's advice and moved to Denver, where he edited the *Great West,* invested in mines, and reestablished himself financially through organizing and promoting the Atlantic-Pacific Railway Tunnel Company. He spent his last years in the state of his birth, enjoying plush offices in New York City; there he promoted his tunnel company, edited *Advance Thought,* and talked of La Crosse in which he first won notoriety and national recognition.

*   *   *   *   *

Pomeroy's participation in the Copperhead movement can be attributed to his personality and to his predilections. His audacity and unconventionality were fathered by his vanity and his search for notoriety. He was not adverse to complimenting himself in his own newspaper. "If they [the people] wish to read the opinion of a man who fears nothing but his God," he wrote, ". . . the *Democrat* will suit them." A friendly critic insisted that exhibitionism and impulsiveness underwrote Pomeroy's pronouncements, adding: "He neither means nor believes half what he says, politically, in the *Democrat.*"

His political and social philosophy, too, drove him into the Copperhead camp. He was essentially a Jeffersonian Democrat at heart, readily lending his sympathy to the underdog. His individualism prompted him to stress personal rights and freedom of action. Human rights he regarded superior to property rights. Like a sage he passed on advice on values: "We are rich, my boy, in our hearts—not in our breeches pockets. Coffins have no money drawers, and if they had, it is too dark to make change down there." He claimed that employers were morally obligated to pay a living wage, that the sweatshops of New York were a national disgrace, and that God did not sanction the suppression of truth and justice by the money powers. "The hand of an honest laborer, calloused though it may be," read a Pomeroy epigram, "is softer than many a palm kid touched today." Like Jefferson, the editor of the *Democrat* had great faith in man, a respect for constitutional government, and a reverence for individual rights; sovereignty, Pomeroy insisted, rested in the people.

His opposition to war as a means to an end was rooted in his humanitarianism. Visits to hospitals embittered Pomeroy, buzzards over battlefields horrified him, crosses in cemeteries turned his thoughts to distress in far-away homes. Succinctly he stated his thesis: "Truly war is frightful. Its glories are those of death and grief—its pomp and vanities, those of crazed ambition; of sorrow and ruin."

Sectionalism, too, forced his hand. He regarded the Morrill tariff as a monstrous tax upon the agrarian West. He claimed that "rivers of blood" would be shed, "mainly to extend and expand New England puritanism by force upon an unwilling people." It was his loyalty to the debtor West which dictated acceptance of the treasury notes in 1862, and which directed him into the Greenback movement after the war.

"Brick" Pomeroy had predicted that history would vindicate his views and sanction his course of action. Little did he understand the force of nationalism and the unfolding of events! In the popular mind—even today—he lives as a Copperhead and curmudgeon. A rival's evaluation dominates: "He out-jeffed Jeff Davis in treasonable utterances and out-deviled the Devil in deviltry."

Wisconsin Copperheads

FRANK KLEMENT

The word "Copperhead" possessed several different meanings midway in the Civil War. Radical Republicans and Lincoln's loyal supporters gave it a dark and damning definition. They compared

From Frank Klement, "Copperheads and Copperheadism in Wisconsin: Democratic Opposition to the Lincoln Administration," *Wisconsin Magazine of History*, XLII (Spring 1959), 182–185. Footnotes in the original omitted. Reprinted by permission of the State Historical Society of Wisconsin.

the persons whom they called Copperheads to the venomous snake with the copper-colored head, insisting that both were to be detested or dreaded—that the Copperheads were traitorous and the copperheads poisonous.

On the other hand, those who were condemned as Copperheads tried to give their own interpretation to that term. They cut the liberty head out of the old copper cent, and they claimed that the copper-head badge should be worn with honor by the critics of the Lincoln Administration and the opponents of radicalism. A Democratic critic of Lincolnian policy defined a Copperhead as "a man who designs to maintain our system of free government as our fathers founded it, as their successors administered it, and as we and posterity are bound by every motive of interest, patriotism, and honor to continue it."

In the darkest days of the Civil War—the first six months of 1863—there was a question whether Lincoln's supporters or Lincoln's Democratic critics would have their way, keep control of the machinery of government, control policy, and direct the ship of state in the direction they would have it go. In the end, of course, the policies of Lincoln and the Republican party prevailed, and the critics were discredited and ground into the dust—Lincoln's supporters dictated the peace and wrote the definitions for words like justice, honor, and treason. So the definition Lincoln's supporters devised for the term Copperhead was written into history nigh onto a hundred years ago.

Although the efforts of Lincoln's Democratic critics to view the words "Copperhead" and "liberty" as synonymous came to naught, their arguments against Lincolnian policy survive in the pamphlets, letters, and editorials they wrote. These source materials prove that the Copperheads of Civil War years were sincere, capable, and determined—and it is both unfair and unhistorical to view them as men whose hearts were black, whose blood was yellow, and whose minds were blank.

Midwestern Copperheadism (a term applied to the anti-Administration movement in the Midwest as the word Copperhead refers to the individual anti-Lincoln critics of the Democratic political faith) was a complex and intangible thing. Its ingredients were many and varied, and they differed slightly from state to state. Midwestern sectionalism colored the movement in the upper Mississippi valley—there were many in Wisconsin who believed that the Lincoln Administration had sold its soul to New York capitalists and New England manufacturers. Some Copperheads believed that the economic ties of the upper Mississippi valley were more closely bound to the plantation South than to the industrial Northeast.

Partyism or Democratic partisanship was another chief ingredient of that concoction called Copperheadism, for at times Lincoln's critics flavored it with political opportunism and sordid party tactics. Midwestern Copperheadism also possessed some social aspects—in most of the Midwest the Copperhead country was characterized by smaller homesteads, poorer soils, and more widespread illiteracy; in the cities the workingmen tended to express Copperhead views while their employers generally supported the Lincoln Administration. Copperheadism also possessed a religious element, for Know-Nothingism (an anti-Catholic movement of the '50's) colored the Republican party, and many Midwestern Catholics feared that New England Puritanism would try to establish itself as a national church and foist its dogmas upon the rest of the country.

Many Midwestern Copperheads viewed themselves as conservatives who opposed the many changes forged in the workshop of war; their slogan, "The Constitution as it is, the Union as it was," proved that they looked toward the past rather than the future. Some Wisconsin Copperheads viewed themselves as Jeffersonian Democrats and they felt compelled to oppose the centralization of the government and the nationalization of business. A few called themselves humanitarians, and they opposed war and bloodshed as a means to an end. Still others developed a mistrust of the man who occupied the President's chair in the White House, and their hate prompted them to misunderstand Lincoln and misinterpret his intentions. Truly, Midwestern critics of Lincoln mixed emotionalism, realism, partyism, and rationalization in different ratios: each wrote his own recipe.

. . . .

Those midwestern sectionalists who claimed that their area was linked economically more closely to the South than to the East pointed to the economic recession of 1861–1862 as proof of their partisan contention. An economic crisis engulfed the upper Mississippi valley in the first year of the war, and that depression was hydra-headed. The Mississippi river trade collapsed, farm prices spiralled downward, and state bank currency was wiped out.

Wisconsin lumbermen who had rafted logs or lumber down the Mississippi River in the spring of 1861 were forced to sell their products at ruinous prices. The Mississippi River blockade, imposed later by the War Department, closed the down-river produce trade and farm prices dived downward: corn commanded less than ten cents a bushel, potatoes could be had by the hundred bushels for the asking, butter was a drug on the market, and hog prices were more than halved in 1861. Business and professional men complained of the hard times. The unemployed paraded the streets of Milwaukee and blamed the war for their plight. A bank panic swept over Wisconsin; state banks which had based their paper money upon Southern bonds closed their doors and declared bankruptcy. By July 1, 1861, thirty-eight of Wisconsin's 108 banks became insolvent and a score more balanced on the brim of bankruptcy. Financial hocus-pocus, which substituted Wisconsin state bonds for the worthless Southern securities in the hands of the state auditor, saved the banks further embarrassment although that action later received the condemnation of a legislative committee.

The hard times undermined the patriotism which had swept over the country like a tidal wave after Fort Sumter's surrender. When the economic shoe pinched, men transposed their economic grievances into political arguments, into personal pessimism, and into open opposition to the Lincoln Administration. Patriotism lost its appeal when avenues of profit disappeared, when mortgages and interest payments fell due, when taxes drew upon empty pocketbooks, and when hard times engulfed the Midwest of 1861 and 1862.

The fall elections of 1861 and 1862 jolted the Lincoln Administration and threatened the political power held by Lincoln's party. Democratic critics—later denounced as Copperheads—knew that the "general ruin," the "coming oppressive taxation," and the military failures were silent partners in the contests at the polls. The election of November, 1862, for example, was a virtual Democratic landslide—the opposition party polled nearly 20,000 more votes in Wisconsin than it had in the gubernatorial contest of 1861. Lincoln's critics rejoiced. They considered the election returns a repudiation of Lincolnian policy. The editor of the Sheboygan *Journal* announced that "Democratic Victories" were the latest "Fall Fashions."

Although economic grievances and sectional arguments aided Democratic politicians to build an anti-Administration following, as political strategists they also played other aces. Military failures in the early years of the war far out-numbered battlefield victories. Wisconsin Democrats, therefore, claimed that President Lincoln was a failure as the nation's commander-in-chief, and they laid every military defeat at his doorstep. They also bitterly assailed the Administration's emancipation policy, and then accused Lincoln of bowing to the pressure exerted by the abolition wing of the Republican party. Moderate Democrats who had given the Lincoln Administration qualified support early in the war became violent critics after President Lincoln decided to sail the ship of state upon the seas of abolition.

Nearly every Democratic editor condemned the Emancipation Proclamation. The editor of the Oshkosh *Courier* labeled it "political medicine" which he predicted "would kill both the patient and the doctor." Embittered by the Administration's turn toward abolition, the same editor had earlier written: "If this is a war . . . of ABOLITION, then, the sooner the Union goes to the devil the better."

The observant correspondent of the London *Times,* touring the Middle West, stated the case succinctly: "The jealousy of the Low Germans and Irish against the free Negro was sufficient to set them against the war which would have brought four million of their black rivals in competition for the hard and dirty work which American freedom bestowed upon them." Milwaukee Irish workers broke into a jail and seized a Negro who had been imprisoned for fighting with and killing an Irish laborer. The mob's lust for blood was partially satiated by lynching the victim, and the Milwaukee mobsters continued to parade and shout "Kill the damned niggers!" and "Damn the niggers and Abolitionists."

Although religious prejudice, Western sectionalism, economic grievances, and anti-abolitionism all nurtured the Copperhead movement, the basic ingredient of the anti-Administration sentiment was partisan politics and political opportunism. Both of the political parties maneuvered for position. The Republicans wanted to control policy, and they demanded an unqualified support for all Administration measures and policies. They devised political strategems like soldier-voting-in-the-field, Union party tickets, and Union Leagues to keep their party in power. They labeled all who opposed their various and sundry measures as "traitors," "rebel sympathizers," or Copperheads; they pinned the tail of treason upon the Democratic donkey; and they generated nationalism and patriotism to aid their cause.

On the other hand, Democratic party members tried to turn public opinion to political advantage. Resorting to sordid party tactics to get the "ins" out and the "outs" in, they made hay in the field of war weariness by talking of peace and compromise in order to gain votes at the polls. They sought votes in the reaction to conscription and in the fears which a military draft casts over a people, and they hoped that the many military failures would cause people to lose faith in their President.

Letters Home

CHAUNCEY H. COOKE

CAMP SOLOMAN, LA CROSSE, WIS.,
HD. QUARTERS 25TH WIS. VOL. INFT.
Sept. 15th, 1862.

DEAR PARENTS: I am sitting on the straw in my tent with my paper on a trunk for a desk, this is Monday, before breakfast that I am writing you. This has been a very busy week for the soldiers.

We did not get through mustering until last evening which as you know was Sunday. The mustering officer was here all day, and he was a fierce looking fellow. Anyhow that's the way he looked to us younger boys that couldn't swear we was 18. We had to muster in all the same, if it was Sunday. Some of the boys tho't it was a bad omen, and meant bad luck. We were not exactly mustered in because we did not get our pay, but the companies were drawn up in line, one at a time, and the officer with his hands behind his back walked along ten feet or so in front of the line looking every man in the face. Every one he suspicioned of being under 18, he would ask his age. He turned out a lot of them that were not quite 18. Some of them that might have been old enough, were getting homesick and was glad to get out of it by fibbing a little. Seeing how it was working out with the rest, I did not know what to do. I went to see our captain but he said he could not help me. He said his interceding would do no good. I saw our Chaplain and he told me to tell the truth, that I was a little past 16, and he tho't that when the mustering officer saw my whiskers he would not ask my age. That is what the boys all told me but I was afraid. I had about made up my mind to tell him I was going on 19 years, but thank heaven I did not have a chance to lie. He did not ask my age. I am all right and the boys were right. Say do you know the sweat was running down my legs into my boots, when that fellow came down the line, and I was looking hard at the ground fifteen paces in front.

I suppose I am a full fledged soldier now. I have got my uniform and that awful mustering officer has gone. While I am writing, the fife and drums are playing again; how I wish you could come down and see the soldiers. To see a thousand soldiers on regimental drill or parade is what visitors call a splendid sight. Hundreds of people in

From Chauncey H. Cooke, "A Badger Boy in Blue: the Letters of Chauncey H. Cooke," *Wisconsin Magazine of History*, IV–V (1920–21), 75–100, 208–217, 322–344, 431–456; V, 63–98. Footnotes in the original omitted. Reprinted by permission of the State Historical Society of Wisconsin.

La Crosse come out to see us every evening. There was about five hundred visitors here last night to see us on dress parade.

....

St. Cloud, Minn., Oct. 2, 1862.
Co. G. 25th. Regt.

Dear Parents:

In my last I wrote you of our arrival at Fort Snelling and that we were to march into the Indian Country in a day or two. Fort Snelling is a fine place and I hadn't got tired of it when orders came to divide our Regiment, the right wing to go up the Minnesota River and the left wing up the Mississippi. Our Co. is in the left wing so we came up the Mississippi River. The first night after quitting Ft. Snelling we camped in the edge of Minneapolis, a pretty town at the Falls of St. Anthony. St. Anthony, just across the river, has some nice big buildings and is the biggest place. It was awfully hot the day we left the fort and our extra blankets and belts full of ammunition made a load. But we felt good and after supper I scuffled with Casper Meuli and Max Brill till bed time. I know father advised me not to do any wrestling but a fellow can't say no all the time. A lot of women or girls from town came into camp and walked over us as if we were logs. I thot they were pretty fresh. Some of the older soldiers talked pretty plain to them but they didn't seem to care. After awhile they were ordered away and then we went to sleep. The next night and the night after I slept in barns on the hay. The people seemed to be Germans but they were good and gave us all they had of milk and bread. The boys would gather like pigs round a milk pan, three or four drinking at the same time. We came into St. Cloud last night. We crossed the Mississippi here. It isn't the mighty stream here that it is at Alma, I could throw a stone across and hit a dog up here. These people gave us a warm welcome. Some of our boys came down with the measles and will go into hospital quarters until they get well. I have a queer sort of feeling, perhaps its measles with me. You know I never was sick. When the surgeon examined me in La Crosse he hit me a slap and told me I had a constitution like a horse. I told him my living for some years had been buck meat, beaver's tail and bear flesh. He said, "You are a tough one, that is plain to see." I am sitting on a big rock on the bank of the Mississippi. It seems strange that this clear, beautiful stream is the same yellow, broad river that runs so near my home. As I write I am using a fine-tooth comb and I am finding bugs. I don't know where I got them, but I've got them. I was ashamed to be seen combing in camp so I came down behind the big rocks by the river. The other boys must have them. No Indians yet. The old settlers tell us the buffaloes were here but a few years ago. I have seen some of their horns, sharp, black wicked things. Their trails can be seen on the prairies and along the river banks. I remember father saying the buffaloes and Indians would disappear about the same time. Pot hunters would slay the buffaloes for their skins, and the white man's whiskey was as surely slaying the Indian. Tomorrow we take up our march to Richmond, twenty miles away. I will write you then.

Your son
CHAUNCEY.

P.S. Tell father not to brag so much on Webster as a speller. I know I am not in his class quite, but I have bought me a pocket dictionary and I am studying it every day. Our Chaplain came along

Camp Randall (Madison) as it appeared in 1862

last night and saw me with it. He stopped and looked at it; well, he said it is next thing to a testament anyhow.

Good bye.

ST. CLOUD HOSPITAL, ST. CLOUD, MINN.
Oct. 20th, 1862.

DEAR MOTHER, FATHER AND ALL THE REST:

I am writing you from a sick bed propped up on the back of a chair made soft with pillows. You must think it strange that you have got no letters these three weeks but if you knew how fearfully sick I have been you would understand. I have been a mighty sick boy with the measles all this time in a big room in the city building along with ten other of my comrades. Three others of my Co. are

here. Andy Adams, one of my chums from Mondovi, is one of them and he has been very sick. I tell you mother it is a terrible thing to be sick among strangers anyway. I've tho't of home and you so many times. Maybe if I had ever been sick before it would not have seemed so bad, but I want to tell you my dear mother, I never want to be sick away from you. The women of the town came in every day to give nice things to eat and make lemonade for us but they were all strange and new ones came nearly every day. They were kind, of course but O, I don't know. I felt if they were thinking more of their nice clothes and how fine they looked than of us. They wouldn't give me all the water I wanted, and I was always so thirsty. I just dreamed all the time. I don't want to talk like a baby, mother, and the boys say, "Don't write any bad news to your father and mother," but you have always told me I should tell the truth and I believe its all right. God knows I never felt before what it meant to have a good home and a kind father and dear mother. And for these nearly three weeks on my back, I have thought of you all more than a hundred times. What a nice thing is a good home. Don't think I am homesick, mother, you know I can say all these things and still not be homesick. When a fellow is sick and all broke up he can't help saying soft things. But I know if you had been here or I had been there I should not be where I am. Some of the fellows here are awful rough in their talk. They wasn't very sick and they were joking me and a young fellow in Co. E. because we are talking so much about our home and our mothers. I don't deny that I long to see my dear mother, and when the tears come into his eyes I know the poor boy that lays next to me is thinking of home too.

Don't think for a minute, mother, that I am dying. I am getting better and in a few days will rejoin my Co., which is now at Richmond, about 20 miles from here. It will seem like going home almost, to get back to my dear old Company. The nights are getting freezing cold and they tell me the lakes are covered with ice, and lately I dreamed of laying on my stomach and drinking cold icewater through the air holes. I suppose it's because I am always so dry.

They say that a few days ago three hundred soldiers came down from St. Abercrombie, 130 miles from here. They left everything quiet; in fact the Indian war seems at an end unless the upper Sioux turn on us.

Colonel Sibley has recovered all the white prisoners and nearly 2,000 Indian prisoners. The question seems to be whether to let the Sioux remain or drive them from the homes of their ancestors into some western reservation. It seems likely that they will be driven away. Mother, this whole Indian question is wrong. Lying on my sick bed here, I can't help thinking of the wrongdoing of the government toward the Indians. I am losing heart in this war against the Indians. When you come to think that all this beautiful country along the Minnesota River was bought for 2 cents an acre and that the government still owes them this pitiful sum for it, I am sorry for them. The boys tell me I am no better than an Indian when I talk about it, but I can't help it. God made this country and gave it to the Indians. After a while along comes Columbus with his three cockleshell boats, takes possession of all the continent in the name of the Almighty, Queen Isabella of Spain, and the Indians are treated as wild beasts. I often think as I have heard father say, "if this is the spirit of the present Christianity, God will damn it."

. . . .

COLUMBUS, KY., March 5th, 1863.
25TH WIS., VOL. INFANTRY

DEAR FOLKS AT HOME: I sent you a letter a day or two ago and maybe I will hear from you soon. I hope I shall. I am well and we are hearing and seeing things and the days are not so heavy as at Madison. The weather is fine—most of the time warm and clear.

We drill every day, do police work, cleaning round the camp, and take a stroll now and then back in the country, far as the pickets will let us. We are really in the "Sunny South." The slaves, contrabands, we call them, are flocking into Columbus by the hundred. General Thomas of the regular army is here enlisting them for war. All the old buildings on the edge of the town are more than full. You never meet one but he jerks his hat off and bows and shows the whitest teeth. I never saw a bunch of them together but I could pick out an Uncle Tom, a Quimbo, a Sambo, a Chloe, an Eliza, or any other character in *Uncle Tom's Cabin.* The women take in a lot of dimes washing for the soldiers, and the men around picking up odd jobs. I like to talk with them. They are funny enough, and the stories they tell of slave life are stories never to be forgotten. Ask any of them how he feels and the answer nearly always will be, "Sah, I feels mighty good, sah," or "God bress you, massa, I'se so proud I'se a free man." Some are leaving daily on up-river boats for Cairo and up the Ohio River. The Ohio has always been the river Jordan to the slave. It has been the dream of his life even to look upon the Ohio River.

The government transports returning from down river points where they had been with pick up free men on every landing and deliver them free of charge at places along the Ohio and upper Mississippi points.

The slaves are not all black as we in the North are apt to suppose. Some of them are quite light. Those used as house servants seem to have some education and don't talk so broad. A real pretty yellow girl about 18 was delivering some washing to the boys yesterday. She left her master and mistress in December and came to Columbus. In answer to the questions of the boys she said she left home because her mistress was cross to her and all other servants since Lincoln's emancipation. She said her mother came with her. One of the boys asked her why her father did not come with her. She said, "My father hain't no colored man, he's a white man." When the boys began to laugh she picked up her two-bushel basket of clothes, balanced it on her head and went her way. That girl must have made fifty stops among the tents leaving her basket of clothes. I wonder if she heard the same dirty talk in each of them. The talk wasn't clean, but some of us who tho't so just let it pass and kept still.

. . . .

COLUMBUS, KY., May 12th, 1863,
HD. QUARTERS 25TH WISC.

DEAR MOTHER: At last we are under marching orders for the South. Hurrah. The orders came yesterday and I am just writing to tell you the glad news. I don't know why, but the boys are clear gone wild about it. They say they enlisted to fight and they want to fight. We have some rebel prisoners down town and they have been talking pretty saucy to the guard. They say one Butternut (that is the color of their uniform) is good for four Yanks. Poor ignorant devils. * * * They don't know but little more than the negroes, they use the same brogue. If you shut your eyes you would think from their jargon you was talking to a lot of "niggers" as they call the blacks. A call for dress parade. I suspect some important order will be read. Will finish later.

May 13th. This morning we were relieved from further marching orders and told to resume our former quarters. Last night came a rush order to strike camp and march double quick to a boat lying at the wharf. I had just gone to bed like the others and was asleep. Orderlies were rushing from one tent to another calling the boys to up and dress and fall in. In ten minutes time or less every tent along the ten company streets was struck and the match applied to everything of bedding and bunk boards that would burn. Eck Harvey and Bill Anderson, the twins, as they were called, the two biggest men in the company, had just come up from town and were feeling pretty well. They were swearing and calling it a rebel scare. After everything was in a blaze and the companies lining up for orders a cavalryman came dashing along bound for the Colonel's tent. What did the messengers mean? Was it a countermanding order or was it a hurry order? The order came to return to camp, and the camp all in a blaze. Such a howl as went up from a thousand mad men you never heard. I am sure it must have looked to the hundreds of negroes who were watching us as if the devil with all his fireworks and his imps had come to Columbus. This is but one incident of that suspense peculiar to the life of the soldier. Here we had packed up our movables and burned the rest, and it was midnight and dark but for the fire. We lay down and pulled over us for the rest of the night the tent cloth and we went to sleep and dreamed of home and of father and mother just the same.

While we were eating our breakfast our good Lieut. Colonel ordered us to lose no time in falling in without arms. We were in line in a twinkling and waiting for further orders. The colonel then told us that Gen. Hooker had won a victory and he wanted us to give three great big cheers and a lot of tigers. And they were loud and long. Before this letter reaches you, you will have heard of Hooker's victory. Old Hooker is a fox, Old Hooker is a coon, is the praise heard on every side. And he deserves it all if what we hear is true. I heartily wish he had the bloody 25th in his command. If he had I kind of think we would have a chance to work off some of our conceit and surplus patriotism. Though we never met the enemy it is our belief no thousand rebels ever stood in line of battle that could take our colors.

The 11th Missouri came through here yesterday from Clinton 12 miles from this place. They are a hard favored set of war worn veterans. They had seen service. I never saw in my life such a sight as followed in their rear. Such human beings, once slaves. Some were black as ebony with great pitiful, white, rolling eyes, and some nearly white and as pretty and polite as any woman I ever saw. I wonder mother if you ever thought what it is to be a slave, that is for the women, the mothers and daughters. I have thought it all out and I will tell you some time if I ever come home.

Some sardine of a scamp pulled the rope out of our flag pole the other day. Ten dollars was offered anyone who would climb the pole and put it in the pole again. As I write there is a daring fellow on the tip top of the pole putting the rope in the pulley. As Lieutenant Brackett has skipt, our orderly has been promoted to second lieutenant and our second to first lieutenant. Sergeant McKay of Mondovi takes the first sergeant's place and Adam Heinbeaugh of Mondovi comes in as 8th corporal. I think we have the best set of officers in the regiment. We have a bully captain even if he did try to resign at one time. Captain Dorwin is a real good man. I would rather go into battle with him than any other man on the job. He can't keep step to the music, but he aint to blame. It just happens there is no time or music about him. The boys make fun of him but they like him just the same.

The fellows that were promoted had to set up the beer, and the way some of the brave lads drank to their health was a bit saddening to see. Of course your son had to drink some beer, not to be out of fashion, tho to tell the whole truth he had joined the cold water society. My excuse is I was told I could drink cider, and I find I can't so I was deceived. But I promise you, mother, I have not touched a drop of whiskey nor will I while I am in the army. I have never forgotten the firm stand father took soon as he found he liked the taste of drink, and I never shall. I never took a swallow of beer but I felt as guilty as a thief. I wrote sister D. only the other day. Love to the boys and father.

Your son,
CHAUNCEY.

Wisconsin Women in the War

ETHEL ALICE HURN

The Chicago branch of the Sanitary Commission, because of its convenient location, became the channel through which most of the supplies from Wisconsin were sent to the front. On October 17, 1861, this branch was organized, and almost immediately the women of the Northwest began to send large donations to its quarters.

. . . .

Shortly after war was declared, Wisconsin women began to meet to make garments for the soldiers. These gatherings were at first spontaneous and could hardly be given a name. They were prompted by the exigencies of the time and animated by the thought that several enthusiastic, industrious women could accomplish more when working together than separately. As time went on, and the

From Ethel Alice Hurn, *Wisconsin Women in the War Between the States* (Madison, 1911), pp. 20, 22, 25–29, 42–46. Footnotes in the original omitted.

influence of the Sanitary Commission grew stronger, such gatherings became regular aid societies, with officers, rules, and a definite scheme of operation. This was accomplished all the more easily, because many Wisconsin women were used to similar church organizations, and like their New England sisters had long worked in missionary and sewing societies. As a rule the women who had been prominent in the earlier organizations, became the leaders in the aid societies, so that the movement in Wisconsin went rapidly forward.

. . . .

The work done at these meetings was of all sorts; but first and foremost lint was scraped, and for this purpose old table-cloths, rags, and even linen brought from former homes in the old country were used. One method of preparing the lint was to lay a plate bottom upward, on a table or on the lap of the operator, and to place a piece of linen on it; this was vigorously scraped with a case-knife until it was transformed into a fluffy mass of fibre. Another method, which was to ravel the linen, was perhaps less strenuous. Thousands of bandages were likewise sewed and rolled up, ready for use. At the beginning of the war these were the two chief occupations; the women realized that bales of lint and bandages would be needed after each battle. It is needless to say, that had absorbent cotton been in use at that time, much labor might have been saved for other duties.

. . . .

The comfort-bag or housewife, familiarly known as "hussy," was so much a necessary part of every well-provided soldier's equipment, that a detailed description may not be out of place. It was a small bag or needle-case containing half a dozen assorted needles, a skein of white cotton, a skein of black linen thread, half a dozen horn or procelain shirt buttons, a dozen trouser buttons, a small ball of yarn, a darning needle, and a few pins. Occasionally some careful mother or wife would add a small bottle of cayenne pepper, a package of court-plaster, or perhaps a bottle of quinine, which was thought at that time to be a panacea for all the ills that flesh is heir to.

It would be impossible to overestimate the value of such a bag to a soldier in active service. One Wisconsin aid society received five hundred letters of thanks for the two thousand three hundred bags which it had sent out. Among these correspondents was one who declared that his housewife had been "worth ten dollars" to him.

. . . .

Blankets, quilts, and comfort-bags were not the only articles made by the aid societies; all kinds of clothing, such as shirts, dress-

Thomas Nast's woodcut depicting women of the Sanitary Commission, printed in *Harper's* magazine, April 9, 1864

ing gowns, underwear were prepared, the material for such articles being bought with the society's money. Flannel shirts seem to have been especially popular, for the women of Watertown made five hundred for the local company. In a few cases the aid societies even made uniforms for the soldiers, but this was only done occasionally during the first few months of the war. The Milwaukee Zouaves, for instance, were presented with fatigue uniforms consisting of brown trousers, hickory shirts, and red caps.

. . . .

A very popular as well as a necessary occupation was the knitting of socks, mittens, and gloves, especially a peculiar kind of mitten, which had a forefinger as well as a thumb, so that it could be used in shooting. This knitting occupation was kept up in public as well as in private, for women knitted while traveling, during spare minutes at home, or at the meetings of the aid society. One patriotic woman threw her religious scruples to the wind, and knitted a few rounds on Sunday before the church-bell rung. Even young girls knitted socks, and their grandmothers toed and heeled them. In fact there was a perfect epidemic of knitting, which lasted throughout the war.

. . . .

Another line of aid society work grew up in the spring of 1863; namely, the sending of vegetables to the army as "anti-scorbutics" or preventatives of scurvy—a dreadful disease, caused by a lack of fresh fruit and vegetables. On March 4, 1863, the Chicago Branch issued an appeal to the Northwest for vegetables for Grant's army. The short, but urgent circular read, "General Grant's army in danger of scurvy. Rush forward anti-scorbutics." This message was sent to Milwaukee, Beloit, Madison, Racine, Sheboygan, Whitewater, and other towns, and the response was characteristic of the spirit of Wisconsin women. Although it was March, the weather rainy, and the roads very muddy, committees went abroad wherever telegrams were received or newspapers read, begging anti-scorbutics for the soldiers.

The movement was well organized; towns were divided into districts, every house was visited, and a central depot of supplies established. In the country these committees drove round in wagons, begged as they went from house to house, and took with them what was given. This was done day after day, first in one direction, then in another, through mud and rain, by men and women of all classes. Delicate women who could scarcely endure exposure, farmers' wives who could ill afford the time, tradesmen, and even clergymen went out on this generous mission. To remarks which were made, deprecating such effort, the answer was, "Our soldiers do not stop for the weather; neither must we."

A fearful drought during the preceding summer, and a rot caused by the following wet winter, had greatly affected the supply of vegetables. In Illinois and Michigan there was a great dearth of them, but Wisconsin and Iowa were fortunately better off. So whatever supply there was in a home, was cheerfully divided with the soldiers. In quantities, descending from bushels to pecks, from pecks to quarts, from quarts to handfuls, the precious stores were gathered. Pickles were brought out, cabbage pits opened and rifled, horseradish was dug up and forwarded.

Consignments were rushed to Chicago from Wisconsin, which filled the depot, overflowed on to the sidewalks, and even encroached upon the street in front of the Commission rooms. As fast as the vegetables arrived, they were sent South, and their places taken by other consignments. Milwaukee, West Milwaukee, Racine, and Whitewater were especially energetic, and hurried on carload after carload of precious, homely vegetables; a few farmers from Windsor, Bristol, and Spring Prairie forwarded 228 bushels.

The activity of the aid societies was astonishing. Besides the regular meetings, extra ones were called. The neighborhood was canvassed, and the begging-committee was ordered to report on certain days, when the members of the society gathered, anxious to hear the result. Whoever was present, was courteously asked to assist in preparing the sauerkraut and the horseradish, and in packing and forwarding these articles, as well as onions and potatoes.

The reunions of the aid societies were turned into pickling meetings. Barrels and kegs were begged and purchased, sauerkraut cutters were borrowed or hired, and men were employed to use them in cutting the cabbage to the requisite fineness; then aids packed it with layers of salt, and poured vinegar over the whole. Grating committees, amid much rallying, and with many tears, courageously attended to the horseradish.

Soon a "line of vegetables" connected Chicago and Vicksburg, maintained by the shipment of a hundred barrels a day. The importance of this movement on the part of the loyal women can hardly be overestimated, as it was an emergency which the Government could not have successfully met without the aid of the Sanitary Commission. This movement did more to establish its reputation for usefulness, than all previous efforts in other directions.

It was not only Grant's army that was threatened with scurvy, but also the Army of the Cumberland, and there is no doubt that the fresh vegetables and dried fruit sent from the North acted as a successful preventive. But the disease was not yet conquered; in April, 1864, another call was made for anti-scorbutics, and again the rooms of the Chicago Commission were inundated with vegetables; the shipments from Wisconsin were so great, that a special mention of the Wisconsin aid societies was made in Mrs. Livermore's communication of July, 1864.

Not only vegetables came in numbers, but "rivers of blackberry-juice" flowed in from all parts of the country; the supply was not sufficient, however, and a call was therefore again issued for dried fruits of all sorts. The circular reads: "The army is leading the same life, eating the same food, and incurring the same risks." The Commission goes on to express its strong disapproval of canned fruit, and gives directions for drying peaches by dividing them into halves, and placing them on sloping boards in the sun or in slightly-heated ovens; this was such a simple task, that even children were urged to do it. The latter were also asked to have little gardens, where they could raise fresh vegetables for the soldiers. The whole crusade against scurvy shows the efficiency of the Commission machinery, as well as the splendid generosity and enterprise of the women of the Northwest.

Chapter VI
WISCONSIN INDUSTRIALIZES, 1860–1900

Although the Civil War did not industrialize Wisconsin, the forces were present which, when unleashed after the war, resulted in a great leap forward for the state's industrial growth. Dominated by agriculture in the 1860s, the economy of the state broadened to include a substantial amount of manufacturing by the end of the nineteenth century.

Until the 1880s, flour milling was the most important industry in Wisconsin. But wheat, the major agricultural crop, diminished in importance as cheaper lands on the prairies of Kansas, Nebraska, and the Dakotas were opened to wheat production. Consequently, Wisconsin's wheat acreage fell by more than 50 percent during the two decades following the Civil War. Wisconsin's farmers found their salvation in other grain crops, beef, and dairying, but the change severely reduced the importance of the millers in the industrial life of the state. Lumbering and lumber milling, a relatively small industry until the 1850s, grew rapidly along with the expansion of the transportation system in the state, and it quickly surpassed flour milling. Alexander Mitchell's railroad empire, which was organized in 1859 and built around the Chicago and Northwestern Railway, and the Milwaukee Road, organized in 1863, proved beneficial to Wisconsin's industrial transformation. By 1870, Mitchell controlled most of the railroad mileage in the state. The Wisconsin Central and the Soo Line also served the pinery area.

From about 1890 until 1910 lumber and timber products outnumbered all other manufactured goods produced in the state. Yet by the end of the century diversification was expanding the state's industrial economy, with concentrations of heavy industries in the Milwaukee, Racine, and Kenosha areas, meat packing and brewing in Milwaukee, and paper mills in the river valleys of the pinery areas. By 1900 the northern cutover areas stood as a lasting monument to the once-dominant lumbering industry.

The decline of wheat farming led to the slow but steady development of the state's dairy industry. Although the pioneer dairymen stressed the production of butter, cheese-making soon outranked butter-making in importance. The newly founded College of Agriculture at the University of Wisconsin in Madison placed great emphasis on improved means of dairying, and agricultural publications urged farmers to employ modern techniques and processes. One of the major themes espoused by William D. Hoard, editor and publisher of *Hoard's Dairyman* and governor of the state from 1889 to 1891, was that dual-purpose cows—and general incompetence of the farmers—were the undoing of most of the unsuccessful dairy farmers.

By the end of the nineteenth century, farming was still of major importance because of the growing dairy industry. Flour milling, the dominant industry until the 1880s, continued to decline, while lumbering, though still the single most important industry, was in relative decline when compared with other emerging industries. It is clear that Wisconsin, like the rest of the nation, enjoyed a period of tremendous industrial growth and development during the generation immediately following the Civil War.

1: From Flour to Lumber: Wisconsin's Industrial Changes, 1870–1900

As the most important industry in the state until the 1880s, flour milling moved west to the Twin Cities as railroads made those cities more attractive because of their proximity to the new western wheat lands, and as developers poured capital into milling operations there. The rapid growth of Minneapolis as a milling center forced some Wisconsin communities to look for new sources of prosperity. The twin communities of Neenah and Menasha on the Fox River provide an example of this change, as is illustrated in the first selection below. With the westward movement of the wheat culture, industrialists like John Kimberly and Ruben M. Scott shifted most of their capital into papermaking. The second selection illustrates this industrial transformation taking place in the state during the post-Civil War years.

Flour Milling in Wisconsin

CHARLES N. GLAAB AND LAWRENCE H. LARSEN

By the end of the Civil War community leaders had begun to take steps to exploit these natural advantages. They had obtained railroad connections that supplemented their waterway to the Great Lakes; they had built facilities to harness the waterpower; they had subsidized the building of a first-class hotel; they had connected Neenah and Menasha with a series of bridges.... But local efforts

From Charles N. Glaab and Lawrence H. Larsen, "Neenah-Menasha in the 1870's: The Development of Flour Milling and Papermaking," *Wisconsin Magazine of History*, LII, 1 (Autumn 1968), 19–34. Footnotes in original omitted. Reprinted by permission of the State Historical Society of Wisconsin.

alone could not create a city. In an increasingly interdependent economy, urban growth would be influenced by a variety of forces outside Neenah-Menasha and outside the Fox Valley—by national political decisions, regional and national economic conditions, technological developments, and patterns of population movement. In a sense, the tide of growth had already passed by Neenah-Menasha, for the real possibilities of spectacular success in city building through commerce now lay in the underdeveloped areas farther west, along the lines of the rapidly building east-west railroad network. Already local spokesmen had largely abandoned the possibility of Neenah-Menasha becoming an important commercial center on the main lines of transportation, but they did foresee the possibility of duplicating the success of a Rochester, a Pittsburgh, or some other large manufacturing city through the combination of power and readily available raw materials.

They initially pinned their hopes on the development of flour milling, an industry which could take advantage of a locally available product, wheat.

. . . .

Like most frontier communities, Neenah-Menasha had milling facilities from the earliest days of settlement. In the 1830's the federal government as part of its services to the Winnebago Indians had built a mill at Neenah, which was later sold to private investors. By 1850 this mill produced over 17,000 barrels of flour a year valued at over $30,000. During the next decade, as the Fox River region was rapidly settled, the local industry grew substantially. Before the railroads came, Neenah-Menasha millers already controlled a sizable local market and could ship surpluses to other markets by way of the Lower Fox to Green Bay. Numerous millwrights and millers were among the settlers who migrated into the twin communities, providing the limited amount of skilled labor necessary in the industry. Profits from milling were high most of the time; even the depression that followed the Panic of 1857 did not seriously check the growth of the industry. By 1860 Neenah had six mills and Menasha two, which together produced nearly 50,000 barrels of flour valued at a quarter of a million dollars. This output made Neenah-Menasha the second largest flour producer in the state. Only Milwaukee outranked the twin communities, but this could be attributed, local leaders argued, simply to the fact that the industry in Milwaukee was considerably older.

By the last half of the 1860's milling in Neenah-Menasha was becoming big business, with over half of the available local capital invested in the industry. The Civil War had stimulated demand, and despite serious price fluctuations, several new mills were constructed and older ones enlarged their operations. Railroads built into the Valley allowed millers to ship their surpluses during the winter months when navigation was closed on the Great Lakes and prices on the eastern market were higher.

. . . .

During the period, Neenah-Menasha promoters consistently exaggerated the importance of local flour milling in relation to other cities, but there was no doubt of the industry's accelerated growth in the twin communities during the last three years of the 1860's. By 1870 there were fifteen mills, eleven of them in Neenah, representing a capital investment of $232,000—an increase of $143,500 over 1860. During 1870 the mills turned out 233,850 barrels of flour—a 300 per cent advance from 1860—valued at $1,069,000. This meant that Neenah-Menasha mills were already producing half as much flour as Rochester had in its most productive years. Neenah-Menasha, although of course not challenging St.

The Jackson Milling Company

Courtesy of the Portage County Historical Society

Louis, rated on a par with such important western milling cities as Toledo and Akron. Neenah-Menasha was now far ahead of all other Wisconsin cities save Milwaukee, whose industry had also grown rapidly during the decade. The lake port's ten mills produced about three times as much flour as Neenah-Menasha in 1870, 656,000 barrels valued at $3,306,345.

. . . .

Neenah-Menasha leaders had great hopes for their apparently thriving flour-milling industry. That these hopes were not realized, that flour milling did not provide the means of building a great city, was not the result of a failure of local initiative or of any forces over which local leaders had any control. The rise of a rival milling capital, 300 miles to the west in Minneapolis, dictated the failure of this aspect of urban aspirations in Neenah-Menasha. The dramatic growth of Minneapolis flour milling in the 1870's forced Neenah-Menasha businessmen and promoters to adjust their plans radically and to search for a new basis for future prosperity.

. . . .

The rise of Minneapolis occurred in less than two decades. In fact, in one decade, the 1870's, the flour industry there reached a point that assured the city's continued importance. This dashed the hopes of other milling centers like Neenah-Menasha which in 1870 had booming industries.

. . . .

Neenah-Menasha millers could possibly have surmounted some of these problems had they been willing to make the effort. But flour milling was largely forgotten as local entrepreneurs were swept up in a wave of optimism created by a new kind of manufacturing—papermaking. The shift of large amounts of Neenah-Menasha capital from flour milling to papermaking had already started in the 1870's, and the substantial profits made by a few of the early mills aroused the hope that papermaking might be the industry that would enable Neenah-Menasha to fulfill its urban destiny. Many nineteenth-century ventures in city building failed wholly or in part because community leaders were unwilling to risk shifts from one kind of transportation, commercial, or manufacturing activity to something more promising. But one of the characteristics of the essentially small-scale enterprise that prevailed in the frontier communities of Neenah and Menasha was flexibility; in a new region such as the Fox River Valley the profits to be made in finding the right economic base for the growth of cities were potentially so great that entrepreneurs were ordinarily willing—particularly if their lines of activity did not involve great fixed capital investment—to shift rapidly from one endeavor to another. Neenah-Menasha business leaders, seeing their high hopes for flour milling destroyed by the rise of Minneapolis, turned confidently in the 1880's to a new industry.

Changes in Industry, 1870–1900

J. H. ALEXANDER

There is no record of what industries were represented among the 7,013 factories in the state in 1870, but it is certain that in this number were many flour mills and lumber mills.

. . . .

The census of 1880 credits Wisconsin with $128,255,480 in value of manufactured products, 57,109 factory workers and 7,674 manufacturing establishments. This census sheds the first light upon the more important industries then established in the state and the relative importance of each, as shown in the table on p. 230.

This tabulation contains no industry that did not have its genesis either in the pioneer needs of Wisconsin or in the raw materials that were ready and waiting for utilization. Flour mill and grist mill products ranked first by a margin of about 50 per cent over lumber and timber products. Carriage and wagon making, foundry and machine shop products, and the manufacture of agricultural implements, ranking 8th, 9th and 10th, respectively, have far outgrown the pioneer blacksmith shop where each had its beginning.

Particularly noteworthy is the growth of the farm implement manufacturing industry which sprang into prominence through inventions and improvements inspired in the main by farm labor shortage due to the Civil War. Let it be remembered that Wisconsin at that time was primarily a wheat raising state, with a production

From J. H. Alexander, "A Short Industrial History of Wisconsin," *The 1929 Wisconsin Blue Book* (Madison, 1929), pp. 34–39.

Twenty Leading Industries in Wisconsin in 1880

Rank in State	Industry	Value of Products
1.	Flour Mill and Grist Mill Products	$27,639,430
2.	Lumber and Timber Products	18,471,162
3.	Leather:Tanned, Curried and Finished	8,821,162
4.	Liquors, Distilled and Malt	6,614,386
5.	Iron and Steel Manufacturing	6,580,891
6.	Slaughtering and Meat Packing	6,539,920
7.	Clothing Manufacturing	4,883,707
8.	Carriages, Wagons and Materials	4,768,474
9.	Foundry and Machine Shop Products	3,965,652
10.	Agricultural Implements	3,742,069
11.	Planing Mill Products	2,975,687
12.	Tobacco: Cigars and Cigarettes	2,325,201
13.	Furniture Manufacturing	2,177,173
14.	Boots and Shoes	1,736,773
15.	Cooperage: Barrels and Barrel Staves	1,563,208
16.	Butter and Cheese	1,501,087
17.	Woolen Goods (Textiles)	1,480,069
18.	Paper and Wood Pulp	1,277,736
19.	Printing and Publishing	1,093,510
20.	Saddlery and Harness	1,064,235

of 28,000,000 bushels of wheat in 1860. Let it be remembered also that the tools of an ancient civilization, the scythe and cradle, the flail, the walking plow, were still in use as late as 1860 side by side with the early mower and reaper which also placed a heavy demand upon hand labor at a time of stringent labor shortage.

Passing to the census of 1890 shows that the value of industrial products manufactured in Wisconsin had grown to $248,546,164, or almost double the 1880 figure. The number of factory workers had more than doubled to 132,031 and the number of factories had increased to 10,417. Interesting indications of growth and change are contained in the table on page 231.

Several striking disclosures are contained in this table. Of these, the decline of the flour milling industry to 2nd position among the state's industries, while lumbering climbed to 1st place to more than double the value of flour mill products marked the rise to eminence of the lumber industry of the Badger State and the end of the state's supremacy in wheat raising and flour milling. A sure sign of the changing trend of agricultural practices in the state is found in the fact that the butter, cheese and condensed milk industry climbed to 7th rank among our industries in 1890 from 16th in

Twenty Leading Industries in Wisconsin in 1890

Rank in State	Industry	Value of Products
1.	Lumber and Timber Products	$60,966,444
2.	Flour Mill and Grist Mill Products	24,252,297
3.	Liquors, Malt	14,193,057
4.	Leather:Tanned, Curried and Finished	11,161,850
5.	Foundry and Machine Shop Products	8,467,290
6.	Slaughtering and Meat Packing	8,393,754
7.	Butter, Cheese and Condensed Milk	6,960,711
8.	Iron and Steel Manufacturing	6,501,761
9.	Planing Mill Products	6,295,810
10.	Carriages, Wagons and Materials	5,947,499
11.	Agricultural Implements	5,015,512
12.	Paper and Wood Pulp	4,475,368
13.	Knit Goods and Textiles	4,100,201
14.	Clothing Manufacturing (Men's)	3,909,726
15.	Tobacco: Cigars and Cigarettes	3,737,577
16.	Furniture Manufacturing	3,616,517
17.	Printing and Publishing	3,256,897
18.	Boots and Shoes	2,973,233
19.	Malt (for Remanufacture)	2,472,018
20.	Car and General Construction and Repairs	2,221,152

1880. No single statement could more clearly reveal the fact that the wheat farmer had become a dairyman.

. . . .

The census of 1900 credits Wisconsin with $360,818,942 in value of industrial products, or nearly 50 per cent more than the 1890 figure. Though the number of factory workers had increased only slightly to 142,076, the number of industrial establishments reached a total of 16,187 and this high record number has never been even closely approached since that time. Notable examples of advance in relative industrial rank are typified by butter, cheese and condensed milk, by foundry and machine shop products and by the paper and wood pulp industry in the table on p. 232.

This table shows the butter, cheese and condensed milk industry to have advanced from 7th to 4th place among the state's industries with about three times the 1890 value of products. Foundry and machine shop products have climbed from 9th position in 1880 through 5th place in 1890 to occupy the rank of 3rd in point of value of products. This industry is one that would receive special treatment if the scope of this brief outline permitted.

Twenty Leading Industries in Wisconsin in 1900

Rank in State	Industry	Value of Products
1.	Lumber and Timber Products	$57,634,816
2.	Flour Mill and Grist Mill Products	26,327,942
3.	Foundry and Machine Shop Products	22,252,730
4.	Butter, Cheese and Condensed Milk	20,120,147
5.	Leather:Curried, Tanned and Finished	20,074,373
6.	Liquors, Malt	19,394,709
7.	Slaughtering and Meat Packing	13,601,125
8.	Paper and Wood Pulp	10,895,576
9.	Iron and Steel Manufacturing	8,905,226
10.	Furniture and Refrigerators	8,721,823
11.	Planing Mill Products	8,400,695
12.	Agricultural Implements	7,886,363
13.	Carriages, Wagons and Materials	6,956,341
14.	Car and General Construction and Repairs	6,306,823
15.	Tobacco: Cigars and Cigarettes	4,888,030
16.	Boots and Shoes (other than Rubber)	4,791,684
17.	Clothing Manufacturing (Men's)	4,393,092
18.	Knit Goods and Textiles	4,238,242
19.	Printing and Publishing	4,103,415
20.	Malt (for Remanufacture)	4,089,715

The paper and wood pulp industry found in 8th position in 1900 advanced from 18th place in 1880 through 12th rank in 1890....

2: The Rise of Lumbering

One of the most heavily researched subjects in the history of Wisconsin is the pine-logging business in the later years of the nineteenth century. Robert Fries, *Empire in Pine: The Story of Lumbering in Wisconsin, 1830–1900* is the best one-volume account. And numerous articles have appeared primarily, though not exclusively, in *Wisconsin Magazine of History*.

Rafting lumber down the Chippewa, the Wisconsin, or one of several other rivers was for many years the main source of transportation of the pine logs. Competition became fierce, and sometimes open warfare between competing logging firms broke out, such as the Battle of Beef Slough in 1868. After the Civil War, consolidation occurred, and the railroads intruded on the rafting process. Among the most successful of those effecting consolidation in the industry was lumber baron Frederick Weyerhaeuser.

Some early concern was expressed over the rapid depletion of the state's forests. One of the leading scientists, Increase A. Lapham, was invited by the State Horticultural Society to prepare a case and a plan for restoring some of the lost woodlands. The final selection in this section presents some of the findings of Lapham and his committee.

Courtesy of the SHSW [WHi (X3) 14697]

Logging crew on the Chippewa River

Lumber Rafting

W. H. GLOVER

The manifold uncertainties of the river absolutely precluded any attempt by lumbermen to exercise control over their market.

· ·

There was always hope that the river might be tamed so that the rafts could run at the lumberman's convenience. The Stevens Point *Pinery* in 1856 declared: "Great efforts have been made . . . in nearly fruitless endeavors, so to improve these numerous rapids by deepening the channel, removing rocks and other obstructions, as to enable rafts to be passed at all stages of the water."

· ·

Control of the task of creating a satisfactory channel finally fell into capable hands with the setting up of the Wisconsin River Improvement Company. The organization was first attempted in 1853. The legislature enacted a charter of incorporation giving full power to make dams and piers and to charge tolls.

· ·

The Wisconsin River Improvement Company became the hope of the industry. Its ideal was to work "until a Wisconsin raft can be run to market by two men over all rapids." It spent from $3,000 to $10,000 a year on dams, booms, and removal of obstructions. The expenditures were financed by tolls of about 10 cents per thousand feet of lumber at Big Bull Falls (Wausau) and Little Bull (Mosinee) and 7 ½ cents at Grand Rapids and Lower Rapids.

· ·

But the Improvement Company did not succeed in turning the "old Wisconse" into a placid canal. It had its triumphs, as when two men took a rapids piece over turbulent Grand Rapids. But it too often happened that it only changed the nature of the hazard. Its dam at Little Bull Falls covered and tamed the terrible maelstrom there but itself smashed many rafts and drowned many men. A $35,000 project at Big Bull Falls did not end the destruction of lumber there. And frequently enough, floods or the spring breakup

From W. H. Glover, "Lumber Rafting on the Wisconsin River, Part II," *Wisconsin Magazine of History*, XXV,3 (March 1942), 308–324. Footnotes in original omitted. Reprinted by permission of the State Historical Society of Wisconsin.

of the ice swept away these costly works. The river remained hazardous and uncertain to the end.

. . . .

The long-awaited railroad finally arrived to break the grip of the river. Railroad service to Stevens Point began in November, 1871, and the Wisconsin Valley Railroad reached Wausau through Grand Rapids and Mosinee, October 31, 1874. For years the lumbermen had discussed the railroad, raised funds, given grants of county lands, cajoled railroad officials, and declared that "the great difficulty of this country is, want of facilities for shipment when the river is low." With the railroad dream at last realized, the citizens of the pinery began to reminisce without regret of the plank roads and stage lines and steamboats which got them to Milwaukee or Chicago in three days. Many of them remembered deep snow that isolated them and sent food prices to dizzy heights. The lumbermen sat down to figure out what to do about shipping their product.

. . . .

One by one the lumbermen quit rafting.

. . . .

The last rafts probably left the mills above Grand Rapids in 1883. The date may be accepted as that of the realization that there was no longer any purpose in making the long and dangerous journey to the Mississippi River markets. The lumberman whose experience clinched the matter was John Redfield, who operated in the neighborhood of Knowlton, about four miles from the Wisconsin Valley Railroad. The Stevens Point *Journal* reported fully:

> Two fleets of lumber passed through the city . . . this week. They are owned by John Redfield, who every year markets his lumber in the old fashioned way. . . . Mr. Redfield, with the exception of R. P. Manson . . . is the only man who ships wholly by water on this river, while only a few years ago it was the sole dependence of every lumberman in Northern Wisconsin.

Within two months he was back, somewhat disillusioned, and reported that "the days of the Mississippi, as a market for lumber from the Wisconsin are drawing to a close."

The Battle of Beef Slough

Wisconsin had no cowboys or range wars to glorify her legend of the past, but brawny, flannel-shirted lumbermen have given the state a unique place in American folklore. Riding logs in the day time and creating the fantastic tales of Paul Bunyan around the fire at night, they roared, bullied, chopped, sawed and guffawed their way through the north woods during the last half of the 19th century.

One of the wildest episodes in Wisconsin's logging history was the Beef Slough "war" on the Chippewa River.

. . . .

Beef Slough, a backwater channel from the Chippewa River into the Mississippi, was only part of the vast complex that made the swift Chippewa the center of the largest lumbering operation in the United States. Although neither Buffalo nor Pepin county was located in the timber belt, the river's many sloughs, bends, and branches provided ideal storage pools for logs waiting to go to the local mills, while the rapid current of the main stream could not have been better for shunting timber to more distant mills.

Beef Slough itself appeared quiet enough. A broad, swampy area below Durand, it was in fact so quiet that it was almost stagnant and thus a perfect open-air warehouse. Here logs were stored and sorted before being sent to rafting works above Alma on the Mississippi. At Alma a small percentage were strung together and floated "in the bark" to the mills of Iowa, Illinois, Missouri and Mississippi.

Wisconsin mill owners above the slough, however, were losing business to the "foreigners" down the Mississippi. Some Wisconsin loggers decided to get better prices by selling to the mills down the river; the slough for them was a valuable storage harbor for their logs. To protect themselves against this outside competition, Eau Claire millmen secured special rights to the slough from the Wisconsin legislature. Their intention was not to use the slough themselves, but to keep it out of the hands of the competition.

But the southern millmen retaliated by forming the Beef Slough Manufacturing, Booming, Log Driving and Transportation Company, and the strength of their combined capital gave the company power as impressive as the length of its name. In 1868 it petitioned the legislature for a charter to erect in the slough the piers and booms (log blockades) necessary for its work. And while the Beef

From "The Battle of Beef Slough," *Wisconsin Then and Now*, Feb. 1964, pp. 4–5. Reprinted by permission of the State Historical Society of Wisconsin.

Slough Company's lawyers were busy with that problem, its management contracted to deliver 60 million feet of logs to the mills down the Mississippi in the spring.

Local mill owners were furious. The Eau Claire *Free Press* objected vehemently. The bill, it contended, was opposed by nine-tenths of the resident property owners of the Chippewa Valley. "Its principle supporters are foreign capitalists who ... entered large tracts of pine lands on the Chippewa (and) now propose to ruin the country by stripping it of its wealth and conveying the same to other states. . . . The legislation will effectually ruin us in less than two years. . . ."

The bill was killed 47 to 36. A large crowd turned out in the streets of Eau Claire to raise thankful cain, and the victorious millmen of the city hustled a crew of several hundred "river rats" down the Chippewa to dam up the entrance to the menacing slough. An injunction, sworn out against the millmen by the Beef Slough Company, did not come through in time to halt the dam's hasty construction.

But the "foreigners" were not dead yet; their next step was both shrewd and more effective. With the help of friendly local authorities, the lawyers of the Beef Slough Company dispossessed the millmen of their ownership of the head of the slough by having it condemned on the pretense that a public highway had to be built on the land. Shortly thereafter the dam was ripped down.

But the removal of the dam still left the problem of getting logs past the Eau Claire millmen and down to Beef Slough. Having found it financially impossible to erect sorting booms through which every company might get its own logs, local lumbermen had relied on an exchange system to stock the various mills. All that came downstream was held at or near Eau Claire; when freshly-cut timber came down the river from company logging fields to the north, a corresponding amount would be let through the lower booms and sent to the mills.

The Eau Claire millmen used their control over the river's log-flow as a weapon in their war against the Beef Slough Company, holding back its logs on the pretense that it was impossible to tell whose logs were whose. Further animosity was stirred when an agent for the company, a man identified by the Eau Claire *Free Press* as Mr. Bacon, refused to submit to the custom of exchanging logs. At stake were the profits from the sale of 60 million feet of timber, and he openly stated that he would have his identical logs and, if necessary, cut every boom on the river to obtain them.

On Friday, May 1, 1868, Bacon carried out his threat. Backed up by a crew of one hundred of his toughest log drivers, some armed with guns as well as axes and peavies, he stomped up the river and begun hacking away at the mill booms, opening storage ponds, and sending all the logs down to the Mississippi.

One boom, that of the Hodgins and Robson Company, was located about six miles above Eau Claire. It was stocked with seven to twelve million feet of logs, only a tenth of which belonged to Bacon. But when his task force ripped into the booms, the whole lot was swept down the Chippewa on the swirling current. Bacon got his one million feet of logs, but in the process he destroyed $20,000 worth of Hodgins and Robson property and took with him millions of feet of timber belonging to the other lumbermen of the valley.

The furious local property holders issued a call to arms. By Saturday morning 200 rugged and angry men, led by the sheriff, had been organized to persuade Bacon and his band to stop their thievery and destruction. It appeared as though the Beef Slough war was about to come to a head.

Bacon and his crowd of one hundred were, however, reasonable men. Carefully weighing the logic in the arguments of their two hundred opponents, the invaders agreed that retreat was the safer part of valor. A few of the more sporting gentlemen came to blows, but there was no general bloodshed. The Beef Slough boys were arrested, a truce was arranged, and they were shortly released.

It was reported later that Bacon, not the millmen, had first offered to exchange logs at the Eau Claire booms, and that the millmen, not Bacon, had refused. The *Free Press,* of course, defended the millmen. It was also debatable which side could rightfully claim victory in the nearly bloody encounter that Saturday morning. No more booms were "busted up," but the company fulfilled its contract that spring, and it would do so again the following year.

In 1870 there was again hope for the Eau Claire interests. The Beef Slough Company's stormy career on the Chippewa had cost a fortune, and even while it was securing confirmation and extension of its charter it was on the edge of bankruptcy. It was beginning to look as though the war would indeed be won by the Chippewa millmen when Frederick Weyerhaeuser arrived on the scene.

Weyerhaeuser and his Mississippi Logging Company took over the operation of driving logs to the downriver mills. He poured seemingly unlimited capital into the area and crammed the Chippewa full of more logs than could be stopped at Eau Claire. Eau Claire mill owners fought in the legislature and the courts. They tried to get the booming company outlawed on the grounds that it obstructed navigation of the Chippewa. They persuaded steamboat owners to sue the company for damages by floating logs.

But they could not fight indefinitely. The Beef Slough war ended in a compromise—of sorts: in 1880 a logsharing plan brought timber cutting and transportation in the Chippewa Valley largely under control of the same parent company. For the local millmen it was a choice between joining and going out of business entirely. Still to come were thirty years of logging on the river before the lumbermen moved west. The war had not killed the industry; it only made it change hands.

Frederick Weyerhaeuser

WILLIAM F. RANEY

The greatest consolidation of interests to appear in the history of Wisconsin lumbering was that headed by Frederick Weyerhaeuser. His career as a lumberman began in Illinois, and ended in Minnesota, but in the middle period of his activity he invaded Wisconsin. Mr. Weyerhaeuser was born in Germany in 1834. He came to the United States at the age of eighteen, and in 1856 he was employed in a sawmill at Rock Island, Illinois. Soon he acquired a small mill for himself, and in 1860 he took his first partner. At first his firm purchased logs from river jobbers, but later they invested heavily in lands on the Black and Chippewa rivers.

In 1870 Mr. Weyerhaeuser led in forming the Mississippi river logging company. They leased the boom and storage rights from the Beef slough company and two years later bought a majority of its stock. Mr. Weyerhaeuser next made peace along the Chippewa by arranging a great 'pool,' and each firm got out of the river a definite share proportionate to what it had put in; it meant a gigantic exchange of logs. The Mississippi river logging company bought great amounts of pine lands. In 1875 they purchased 50,000 acres of Chippewa lands from Cornell university, which had received them from the federal government. Up to 1881 the company merely furnished logs to its members. In that year, however, it bought a majority of the stock in the Chippewa lumber and boom company,

From William F. Raney, "Pine Lumbering in Wisconsin," *Wisconsin Magazine of History*, XIX,1 (Sept. 1935), 71–90. Reprinted by permission of the State Historical Society of Wisconsin.

which had recently been formed at Chippewa Falls. This latter company continued under its old name, but with Mr. Weyerhaeuser as president. It owned, among other things, the properties of the defunct Union lumber company, which had gone into bankruptcy in 1879, and which owned the old mill built by Brunet, already enlarged and rebuilt several times. Thus the Mississippi river logging company became a manufacturer of lumber in Wisconsin. The old mill burned in 1886, but was immediately rebuilt, and became, so it was said, 'the largest mill in the world,' with a capacity of 2,000,000 feet a week. In 1887 the Mississippi river logging company bought out the Eau Claire lumber company for something over a million dollars. By this and other purchases its resources in pine lands became enormous, and it controlled as well the water highways for transporting logs. In 1887 it made it a rule to ship all sawed lumber by rail.

The Beef slough began to choke up with sand, and so the West Newton slough opening into the Mississippi river six miles lower down at first supplemented and then supplanted it. In 1890 both sloughs were used to handle more than a billion feet of logs which the company was moving for its own mills and mills of outsiders who bought of them. For years a thousand men were employed at the West Newton slough to handle upwards of half a billion feet of logs annually.

At length even the pine resources of the Chippewa were exhausted. In 1909 the original Mississippi river logging company was dissolved. The next year saw the last drive down the Chippewa, and in 1911 'the largest mill in the world' sawed its last lumber.

Some Early Conservation Concerns

INCREASE A. LAPHAM

SUMMARY VIEW OF FACTS AND CONSEQUENCES

While there is no doubt but that these very decided changes of climate can be produced by man, by the rearing or by the destruc-

From Increase A. Lapham, et al., Report on the Disastrous Effects of the Destruction of Forest Trees, Now Going on So Rapidly in the State of Wisconsin (Madison, 1867), pp. 23–37, 100–101.

tion of forests, it must be remembered that after all, they do not materially change the great climatic laws due to the latitude in which we live; though we can protect the ground occupied by our growing crops from the fierce winds; those winds will not cease to blow; though we can secure shade, the piercing rays of the sun will in no wise be abated, and though we may prevent the undue evaporation of water from the soil, the quantity of rain will be but little if any changed. We here have the ready explanation of the great differences of opinion upon this subject among men; the changes being local and not general. It may be true that the annual quantity of heat received from the sun upon a given quantity of land is the same through all time, yet it will be found to make a vast difference with the condition of that land, whether this heat is, or is not, permitted to strike the ground.

From the facts already given above it must be quite evident that clearing away the forests of Wisconsin will have a very decided effect upon the climate and productions, and therefore upon the inhabitants themselves. The summers will become hotter and more oppressive; the winters colder; both the cold blasts of winter and the hot winds of summer will have full unobstructed sweep over the land; the dryness of the ground will be increased; springs dried up; rivers cease to flow at some seasons of the year, and become great floods at others; the soil on sloping hills washed away; loose sands blown over the country preventing cultivation; snow will accumulate in great drifts in some places, while other places are left bare and unprotected; the ground become frozen to great depth; vegetation retarded in the spring; the productiveness of the soil diminished; thunder-storms will be increased in number and violence; and there will be more hail and more heavy, damaging rains.

Under these changes of climate and productiveness, the people being deprived of so many of the means of comfortable living, will revert to a condition of barbarism!

While we are holding out inducements for the oppressed of all the earth to make new homes in our midst we are planting the seeds of decay, that will sooner or later render their homes miserable; and send these people and their posterity to other, more favored lands, for that home they will have failed to find here.

Of the consequences of the destruction of the forests to the future inhabitants of the state we can only judge from the experience of other countries where selfishness, folly and want of proper appreciation of the wants of the future, have already brought upon them the evils that may soon be looked for here. Consult the history of Egypt, of Palestine, of Greece, of Italy, and we shall see that the original fertility and productiveness of a country may be destroyed;

a country capable of sustaining a dense population of happy, prosperous and civilized people, may be converted into one of comparative sterility where the scanty population living in tents, or rude huts, are but little above the lowest of the human family. Such may be *our* future unless we profit by their example.

. . . .

THE DUTY OF THE STATE

In view of the dangers thus shown to be threatening the future welfare of Wisconsin, it surely should be the duty of some competent authority to make such efforts as may be deemed necessary to avert them. Should an enemy appear upon our borders threatening us with these disasters, money would be at once raised without limit, men would be pressed (if necessary) into the service, and every effort made to repel the invasion; and surely it can be no less the duty of the state to interpose its authority for the same object when no such extraordinary exercise of power is needed. The labor of the wise and good for many generations past, has resulted in the civilization of the nineteenth century, and shall it be said, that for a want of prudent foresight, the men of that century neglected the means necessary to prevent its destruction. The eminence now secured is certainly worth preserving; and if it is the duty of the government to so shape its policy as to secure the greatest good to the greatest numbers, it surely cannot be deficient in authority to act in a matter of so much importance.

A state that finds authority to regulate the times and seasons when its citizens may catch fish, or shoot game, may certainly assume such as may be needed to preserve the civilization of the present times; it would require no greater stretch of power to regulate the cutting of timber where it would obviously entail a public calamity, or to encourage its production where it is so much needed for the public good.

One of the most serious evils this state has to contend with is the purchase of large tracts of land by persons who reside in some other states, or who, if residing here, still have no permanent and living interest in the land. It is purchased by such persons, not for the ordinary, legitimate and proper purpose of converting it into a farm or homestead for himself and family, but solely with a view of stripping it of its valuable timber. Leaving the worthless trees and bushes to encumber the ground, he sells it for what it is worth, and renews his depredations upon other lands. He builds fine houses in a distant place—he destroys the fair face of nature here. Surely there should be some means devised to compel such men to spare at least a belt of these noble trees for the purposes contemplated in this report. Their interest should be made to yield to that of the men who are to become the permanent occupants of the land, and whose interest in the state will induce them to improve and adorn it, rather than to injure and destroy it.

. . . .

IN CONCLUSION

The Commissioners having brought their work to a close, will state again that in their opinion, no other interest so much demands the immediate attention of the legislature of Wisconsin, as does that of increasing and preserving so much timber as shall be needed for use by her people.

3: Life in a Lumber Camp

Many accounts of life in a lumbering camp have been recorded. John Nelligan's story, published in *Wisconsin Magazine of History*, provides one of the most detailed statements. Part of that account is reproduced below. Lumbermen developed a language of their own, and the second selection provides a few examples of that language. An account of a lesser-known phase of life in a lumber camp is presented in the third selection. Edith Dodd Culver, daughter of a physician who located in Ashland in 1889, recounts life in a hospital set up primarily for lumbermen.

How Lumbermen Lived

JOHN E. NELLIGAN

The daily routine of life in a lumber camp began long before the break of day. At about four o'clock in the morning the chore boy, awakened by an alarm clock or, more often, by that sixth sense which warns a man that the designated hour of awakening is at hand, would crawl from his cozy nest of warm blankets into the chill early morning atmosphere and start the fires—one in the cook's camp, one in the men's camp, and a third in the camp office, where the foreman and the scaler and perhaps one or two others slept. When a good healthy blaze was roaring in each of the three stoves and waves of warmth were attacking the blanket of cold

From John E. Nelligan (as told to Charles M. Sheridan), "The Life of a Lumberman, Part II," *Wisconsin Magazine of History*, XIII,2 (1929–1930), 131–185. Reprinted by permission of the State Historical Society of Wisconsin.

which lay over the camp like a pall, the chore boy would go into the men's camp and shake the teamsters into wakefulness, being careful not to disturb the sleep of the other men. The chore boy's popularity among the jacks depended largely upon his discretion in this matter. The teamsters would sleepily and noiselessly arise, pull on their outer garments, and depart for the barns, where they fed, cleaned, and harnessed their horses in preparation for the day's work. This done, they returned to the camp, dressed their feet fully, washed for breakfast and, perhaps, took a chew of plug tobacco as an appetizer.

Chewing tobacco reminds me of Ed Erickson. Ed was one of the best woods and river foremen we ever had and he was a gentleman to boot. He started his career as a teamster and he was as good a man at handling horses as he later became at handling men. Like most Scandinavian woodsmen, especially teamsters, Ed loved his chewing tobacco. Whenever he pulled his plug of tobacco out of his pocket, the horses would turn their heads expectantly towards him and he always had to give each of them a chew before putting the plug back. They loved the stuff and Ed, being a gentleman, always treated them, but it ran his tobacco bill pretty high.

By the time the teamsters were ready for breakfast, the camp reveille, blown on a big tin horn, had roused the rest of the camp at about 4:35 A. M., and the jacks had rolled out of their blankets, pulled on the clothes they had taken off the night before—few enough, in truth—taken their heavy socks from the drying racks, donned them and were washing for breakfast. At 4:50 or 5:00 A. M. the "gaberal" would blow the breakfast horn as a signal to the jacks to "come and get it." There would be a rush for the long tables in the cook shanty and a pitched battle would ensue between the lumberjacks and the marvelous products of the cook's culinary efforts, with the jacks invariably the victors. Breakfast in a lumber camp was no such light meal as the morning fruit, cereal, and coffee titbits eaten by modern business men. It was as large and important a meal as any other and the bill of fare would read more like a dinner than a breakfast to the average person of today. Flapjacks or pancakes, sometimes of buckwheat, fried as only a lumber camp cook can fry them, stacked in great piles along the oil cloth covered tables, were favorite items of fare among the jacks. But there might be baked beans, or fried meat and potatoes, or hash, or any other dish which could be prepared from the extensive larder. All this washed down with great draughts of coffee, coffee with such fragrance that one's nose crinkles with remembrance at the thought of it. And there were tasty cookies and cakes. The men were never given an opportunity to complain about the bill of fare in our camps, nor in any other camps for that matter. Lumberjacks were always fed well. They demanded it and it paid the camp operators to feed them well. The better they were fed, the better work they did.

Breakfast over, the men pulled on their outer working clothes and departed for their various posts. Most of them wore wool caps, heavy flannel shirts, mackinaw cloth jackets and pants, heavy German socks and low rubbers. This was the warmest, most comfortable, and most efficient costume for woods work. When the scene of the cutting wasn't too far from the camp, the men returned to the cook shanty for their midday meal, but when it was some distance away, the "flaggin's" were carried to them on a large sled by the chore boys. Great, thick sandwiches, large cans full of hot food from which the jacks filled their tin plates, and great, steaming cans of hot tea satisfied the midday hunger. Back to work they went and labored until after dark. Conditions are somewhat changed now, but in those days there was no eight hour day and while there was day-light the work went on. Then they would straggle into camp and eat their evening meal with appetites such as only tired and hungry men can develop. The teamsters put away and cared for their horses before eating. After supper the jacks would gather around the great red-hot stove in the bunkhouse, pull off their wet, stinking socks and hang them on the drying racks around and above the stove, where they steamed away and emitted an indescribably atrocious odor which permeated the bunkhouse atmosphere.

For several hours the jacks enjoyed themselves to the best of their various abilities. A few, perhaps, read, but there was little to read aside from a few old newspapers and the *Police Gazette,* which was always very popular. In all my experience in logging camps, I remember only one man who ever had a Bible. He was a young fellow spending his first winter in the woods who came of pious parents. They had given him the Bible when he left home and told him to read it faithfully every Sunday he was in camp, but after watching the lumberjacks enjoy themselves doing the stag dance, the jig dance, and playing games, he put the Bible aside and said, "I'll read it in the spring."

Wherever and whenever men's work is strenuous, their recreation is the same. Reading the Bible wasn't generally considered the sort of thing with which to prepare one's self for another week of hard labor.

A Lumberjack's Story of His Accident

L. C. SORDEN

An Irish lumberjack was brought into a hospital, in the early logging days, with a few broken ribs. The nurse, full of sympathy, asked him how it happened. He replied, "Well sister, I'll tell you how the whole thing happened. You see, I was up in the woods aloading one cold morning, when I was sending a big burly school marm up on fourth tier, and I see she was going to cannon, so I glams into it to cut her back, when the bitch broke and she comes and caves in a couple of my slats."

A lumberjack in another hospital, when asked by the nurse how he got hurt, replied, "The ground loader threw the beads around a pine log. He claimed he had called for a Saint Croix but he gave a Saginaw; she gunned, broke three of my slats and one of my stilts and also a very fine skid." The nurse said, "I don't understand." His reply was, "I don't either. He must have been yaps."

Glossary

adam's fruit—dried apples; pregnant women.

adze—a tool used in hewing logs to flatten them on one side, it had a handle long enough to enable the worker to use it while standing; same as shin cutter.

alibi day—payday in camp when many loggers developed tooth-aches or other ills requiring trips to town.

beads—chain used in loading logs.

cannoned—a log being sent up skids to a rollway, or a load when it got out of control and pointed skyward, similar to a cannon.

gabboon—spittoon or cuspidor; found only in better bunk-houses.

gandy dancer or *gandy hand*—pick and shovel man; a road monkey or worker on a railroad track crew.

gangway—the incline place upon which logs are moved from the water into a sawmill; same as jack ladder, jack, log way, slip.

garbage can—a camp with poor accommodations.

From L. C. Sorden, *Lumberjack Lingo* (Sauk City, Wis., 1969), pp. 1, 7, 21, 46, 50, 51, 93, 102, 104, 110, 112, 135, 138, 145. Reprinted by permission of Stanton & Lee Publishers, Inc., Sauk City, Wisconsin.

ground loader—a member of the crew who attaches the tongs or loading hooks to the logs or guides the logs up the skids; same as bottom loader, hooker, hooker on, sender.

gunned—1) to fail to get a log on a car or a sleigh so that one end rests on the ground thereby resembling the barrel of a cannon; a log that goes up endways in loading. 2) to direct the fall to a tree.

rack—a sled body for hauling short bolts such as pulpwood.

raft—a unit or raft of logs on a river or lake.

rafted out logs—no more logs; river drive completed.

Saginaw—to retard the larger or butt end of a log in loading it up on a car; opposite of Saint Croix.

Saint Croix—to retard the small end of a log in loading, generally by using a cant hook on the underside; opposite of Saginaw.

school marm—a crotched log or tree with two main trunks.

skid—1) to drag logs from the place they are cut to the skidway, landing, or mill; same as drag in, dray in, snake, twitch. 2) a log or pole, commonly used in pairs, upon which logs were handled or piled. 3) the log or pole laid in a skid road to reinforce it. 4) a piece of hardwood about six feet long with studs on one side and two hooks on one end. It was placed on edge of dray to roll logs onto dray with a cant hook. The studs kept the log from slipping back.

slats—a man's ribs.

twitch—1) to skid logs or full-length trees to yarding area; same as snake. 2) a short chain.

twitch road—a narrow road or trail for twitching logs.

wampus cat—an imaginary animal to which night noises were attributed.

yaps—crazy, out of his mind.

Medical Care for Lumbermen

EDITH DODD CULVER

Papa was an orphan of the Civil War who grew up on a farm near Fordyce, a small town on Frosty Run in Greene County, Pennsylvania. He was a self-made man who worked his way through college and medical school as a carpenter's helper. His cousin, Dr. William Rinehart, fifteen years older than Papa, had encouraged and helped him to become a physician. In the 1880's, when Dr. Will left a lucrative practice in nearby Waynesburg for a more adventuresome life out West, Papa began to consider that too, especially when he was later invited to join him out there. Dr. Will became the supervisor of a company which owned several hospitals that catered to lumberjacks: the American Hospital Aid Association, whose headquarters were at Eau Claire, Wisconsin. Dr. Will had special charge of the one in Ashland. These hospitals were crude affairs, actually little more than boardinghouses, with few modern conveniences. There were cots for beds in the sparsely furnished rooms, and the fare was simple but adequate. There were no women nurses, and even the male "nurses" were convalescent patients who took care of each other. Patients were usually surgical cases, although there was an occasional pneumonia or typhoid case. But these so-called hospitals met the need of that day and they were a great training ground for a young surgeon.

Lumberjack patients were admitted to these hospitals on the hospital ticket plan, an insurance plan by which a lumberjack bought a ticket for from $3 to $10 from agents who traveled among the camps selling tickets for his particular hospital. It entitled the ticketholder to up to six months' care in a hospital, including surgery and bed care. Since the lumber barons accepted no responsibility in case of accidents, virtually every lumberjack bought a ticket, and the agent's commissions were well worth traveling through cold and snow from one camp to another.

. . . .

A typhoid fever epidemic struck Ashland in 1893 and 1894, and in March, 1894, both Papa and Mama were stricken with it in its most virulent form. The hospital was closed to all but their nurse, Miss Ellen Peterson, and her two patients, who hovered between life

From Edith Dodd Culver, "610 Ellis and the Hospital Children," *Wisconsin Magazine of History*, LX,2 (Winter 1976–77), 116–137. Reprinted by permission of the State Historical Society of Wisconsin.

and death for months; and but for the care of the faithful nurse they would not have survived.

When, after months of illness and convalescence, Papa felt able to resume his practice, he was faced with new problems. He had lost his residence because he could not make the payments, his money had been all used up, and the hospital building (a rental) had been sold over his head. So was he simply to open an office downtown, or should he seek quarters for another hospital? Feeling so keenly that his recovery had been due to good nursing, it was almost a calling that he should have a hospital and establish a training school for nurses. It was then that he began in earnest to search for a building that would be suitable.

Papa had, of course, noticed the long, low white building partly hidden in the underbrush, as he made his way up and down Ellis Avenue on his bicycle or on foot; but he had paid no more attention to it than to a number of abandoned warehouses along the nearby railroad tracks. It had never entered his mind to see any possibilities in a building which everyone knew had long ago been one of the most notorious sporting houses in northern Wisconsin. The *Ashland Sunday News* had carried a story on March 23, 1890, which left no doubt as to the status of 610 Ellis: "Mrs. Sadie Mahoney, wife of Jack Mahoney, proprietor of a dance house on Ellis Avenue, who was shot by Jack Linsey about two years ago, died last night about 11 o'clock." So this dance hall and brothel had been the haunt of murderers! No wonder that the citizens of Ashland had wanted it torn down, and its infamous history obliterated. Why this had not been done years earlier was the question.

One day early in 1895, desperate for a building in which to house his hospital, Papa decided to have a look at it, in spite of its reputation.

. . . .

And so it was that Dr. John Morris Dodd of Ashland recommenced his medical career at 610 Ellis, an address which was to serve for ten years as both a haven for the sick and injured and a home for his family.

. . . .

Because we lived so close to one of the nation's most important pineries, and because the logging trade was inherently dangerous, many of Papa's cases involved lumberjacks and millhands.

. . . .

Papa's zeal for teaching, and his concern for victims, of such accidents in the woods and mills of northern Wisconsin, prompted him to institute a kind of correspondence course or "crash program" in first aid. He recognized that many loggers knew nothing at all about what to do in a medical emergency, and that accident victims were often mistreated by their well-meaning but ignorant colleagues. He therefore had booklets printed for Frank Davis, the hospital's field agent, to distribute among the lumber camps during his ticket-selling tours. The booklet was simple and direct, and although it may now seem somewhat quaint, it is perhaps worth quoting at some length for what it tells us about the state of medicine and medical knowledge in an area that was but one step removed from the frontier as late as 1905.

THE DODD HOSPITAL
Ashland, Wisconsin

Have you a ticket? No one is exempt from sickness or injury, and misfortunes are most liable to come when we are least prepared for them.

A hospital ticket provides you with a home with the best of care in case you become sick or injured, at a price which is so low as to leave no excuse for a man to be without one. The hospital is the best place for you, and it is better for you to pay seven to ten dollars for a ticket, than to pay that much per week, which would be the charge if you had no ticket.

It is safe for you to buy a ticket on this hospital as it is now in its third year and has lived through all kinds of opposition from its competitors. It has gone ahead doing good work believing that to be the surest foundation on which to build.

The success of hospital work depends a great deal on the nursing. Trained nurses are a special feature of this hospital, it being the only one in Ashland employing them, and one of the objects of this hospital in its beginning was to give its patients the benefits of trained nurses. . . .

The hospital building is large and comfortable and everything is kept neat and clean. When coming to the hospital bring a change of underclothing if possible, as all patients are required to take a bath and change clothing on admission.

While the hospital is not a boarding house or a loafing place for men out of a job, it is your home when you are injured or sick, and we will be glad to have you come in when it is necessary. It is an old saying that a stitch in time saves nine, and this applies equally well to sickness. When unwell, it is best to see a physician and some simple treatment may keep off a serious sick spell. It is money saved to both you and the hospital to attend promptly to what may seem to be slight ailments.

If not convenient to come in when you feel that you need medicine, write to the hospital, describing your symptoms as best you can and medicine will be sent to you by return mail or express. Much of our medicine is put up in tablet form as these are more easily mailed and you can be more accurate in the doses. . . .

Venereal diseases will be treated on our ten dollar ticket, but patients with these diseases will not be admitted to the hospital unless the case is one that requires absolute rest.

Directions for the care of the injured while removing to the hospital:

Do not neglect an open wound no matter how produced, as even a very slight wound will sometimes cause death from blood poison.

Open wounds should be covered with the piece of tissue which will be found in the pocket in the back of this book, and a bandage bound closely about the part. Do not put tobacco, flour, salt pork, or any other substance in or on the wound but bind it up at once in the way described and come direct to the hospital. Some men prefer to lay up in camp with a cut, but this is not the best way. A cut if properly dressed will heal in a few days, while if left to itself will always gap and the space must fill in with new tissue which takes weeks. Some of our worst hospital cases are those who wait too long before coming to the hospital.

You may sometimes have bleeding, which will be alarming. Keep your head, and it is easily stopped. If you learn the following points you may be the means of saving some poor fellow's life. Blood in the arteries flows *from the heart* and is bright red in color, and when an artery is cut, spouts out like water from a hose. To stop it make pressure *between the wound and the heart.* You can stop it with a thumb or finger if you press deeply just over the vessel. The so-called Spanish Windlass is something easily made on the spot, and when properly applied will always stop the bleeding. To make it, take a piece of rope or a handkerchief or any similar piece of material, tie it loosely around the part and run a stick through it and twist until the bleeding stops. Blood from the veins is dark red in color and flows in a steady stream like water from a spring. It can easily be stopped by pressing on the side *opposite the heart.* In the veins the blood is flowing toward the heart. . . .

In case of a broken leg, place it in the position in which it is the most comfortable and take strips of wood or bark about eighteen inches long and lay them lengthwise around the leg and bind them on with a bandage or with cords which may be tied separately. Place the patient flat upon his back upon a stretcher and remove him to the hospital as quickly as possible. A stretcher of some kind can always be gotten up on short notice by some one of the crew. . . . For sprain or bruises you will need no special instruction, but always keep the part from hanging down as much as possible.

Whenever possible, notify the hospital in advance by telephone or telegraph when a patient is coming, and free transportation from the depot will be provided, and a physician will meet and superintend the transfer of serious cases.

If we have given you some points which will enable you to render intelligent assistance to your unfortunate fellowmen, this little book will not have been written in vain.

Respectfully
THE DODD HOSPITAL

4: Other Industrial Development

Railroads spread rapidly across Wisconsin during the post-Civil War period, as they did in other states, particularly during the six years from 1867 to 1873, and again between 1875 and 1890. Railroad mileage in the state grew from 891 miles in 1860 to 5,583 in 1890. Federal land grants and the exploitation of eager communities and individuals aided in the rapid growth, as is illustrated in the first selection below.

Less information is available on industries other than lumbering and railroading. Brewing became Milwaukee's most famous industry during this era, illustrated in the second article. The needs of the brewing and meat-packing industries in both Milwaukee and Chicago led to a temporarily flourishing ice trade in Wisconsin, as explained in the third selection below. In the fourth item, Richard N. Current traces the development of the typewriter, another important product of the Badger State. Appleton's pioneer experience in the use of hydro-electric power is the subject of the final selection.

The Railroad Boom

WILLIAM F. RANEY

In the early days of Wisconsin railroad building, much of the state was still in the frontier stage. The new communities needed the railways desperately to get their surplus products to market. At the

From William F. Raney, "The Building of Wisconsin Railroads," *Wisconsin Magazine of History*, XIX,4 (June 1936), 387–403. Footnotes in the original omitted. Reprinted by permission of the State Historical Society of Wisconsin.

same time the frontier was poor. The constitution forbade the state to lend money or credit for internal improvements, whereby Wisconsin was spared some of the woes experienced by Michigan, Illinois, and Minnesota. But if the state might not help, there were still local agencies on the one hand and the federal government on the other. There was no prohibition nor effective limitation resting on counties and towns, villages and cities. When a railroad was projected, the localities along the route were expected to borrow to pay for it; and for the most part they did so, readily and rather recklessly. For example, when, in the winter of 1860–61, the Northwestern extended its line from Oshkosh to Appleton, a distance of some twenty miles, the 'company issued $184,000 of Appleton Extension first mortgage seven per cent bonds and $30,000 in common stock in exchange at par for city bonds of Appleton and Neenah.' Eastern capitalists were often interested in Wisconsin roads, but regarded them as highly speculative, and until after 1870 they never carried more than a small part of the investment; the localities and individuals served by the road paid for it.

Besides the municipalities the railroad companies exploited private citizens, especially the farmers who so much desired their facilities. Between 1850 and 1857 some 6,000 Wisconsin farmers mortgaged their farms for a total of nearly $5,000,000. The agents of the companies gave stock certificates to the farmers in exchange for the mortgages which they immediately sold to investors in the eastern states. Then in the panic of 1857 every railroad in the state went into bankruptcy, and the farmers were left with a lot of worthless paper. Compromise and legislation did something to remedy this situation during the decade of the Civil war, but it has remained one of the most painful episodes in the history of Wisconsin railroad finance.

The federal government had a great reservoir of wealth in the public domain, and since the lands belonged to the people and the people wanted railroads, congress made large grants of these lands to aid in financing railroads. These grants were all made between 1850 and 1872. Sometimes they were made directly to the railroad companies; at other times the lands were given in trust to the state governments. The grants were in some cases not well administered by the states nor honestly earned by the companies that received them, and only a third of the lands granted were finally patented to the railroads. Yet the railroads received in all the United States some 49,000,000 acres, and in Wisconsin they ultimately got 2,874,000 acres, or nearly one-twelfth of the area of the state.

Brewing in Milwaukee

Given the ingredients of an ever increasing German population, abundant natural resources, and a magnificent harbor, the inevitable result could only be a developing industry—beer—and a city—Milwaukee, Wisconsin—whose reputation and history would come to be intrinsically linked.

That beer was ultimately "to make Milwaukee famous" was not so evident in 1840 when the only brewery in operation produced ale. Besides, Milwaukee had already become known as "Cream City" due to the manufacturing of cream colored bricks.

With the influx of German immigrants in the middle forties, however, "Teutonia" began to challenge the predominantly Yorker-Yankee village. By 1850, some 64 per cent of the population were of foreign birth, and of the total population, more than one-third was German. With the increase of Germans came a demand for their favorite beer, lager beer. Besides increasing the demand for lager, the Germans, drawn to Wisconsin because of the cheap farm lands and low taxes, provided the new industry with a growing supply of barley. In addition, the immigration brought with it men who were skilled in the art of brewing, having centuries of family experience to draw upon.

Up to the 1840's, American brews were all of the type known as top-fermentation beer, in which the yeast stayed on the top of the beer until it was skimmed off. The alcoholic content of this beer ran high, and it did not keep for very long periods. With the German influx came men skilled in making bottom-fermentation beer (lager beer). Lager, which did not spoil quickly, was first discovered by monks in the seventeenth century.

The first lager brewery in Milwaukee was established in 1847 by a German immigrant with a name of various spellings—one Herman Riedelschoefer (Reutelschoefer, Reuthlisberger, or Reidelschofer). The venture proved unsuccessful, but, as history would have it, the plant was to come into the brewing picture again in 1870 when it was purchased by Best and Company for $30,000.

Considered one of the earliest brewers of lager in Milwaukee, Best and Company was established in 1844 by Jacob Best, Sr. Best, a brewhouse and winery owner in Mettenheim, Rheinshessen, was persuaded to sell his business and start anew by his oldest son, Jacob, Jr., who with his brother, Charles, had become sold on Milwaukee when they were sent there to establish a vinegar factory in

From "Milwaukee Beer—It Made a City 'Famous'," *Wisconsin Then and Now*, XIV,7 (February 1968), 1–5. Reprinted by permission of the State Historical Society of Wisconsin.

1842. During their first years in business, Best and Company sales were limited to 200 to 300 barrels per year—just enough to meet the local demand.

Although there were only five firms making beer when the Bests began their venture, by the 1850's, Milwaukee could boast of 14 or 15 breweries.

. . . .

The increase in the number of breweries was due to a number of factors. One obvious reason for the increase in the local markets was Milwaukee's population which was now approaching the 40,000 level. In addition, the beer market was gaining friends among the non-Germans who were acquiring a taste for lager. Better transportation also contributed to the boom as new markets could be opened due to the railroad and harbor facilities. The first year in which there is evidence of out-of-town shipment of beer is 1852, when 645 barrels were "exported" from Milwaukee. By the following year, shipments totaled 3,639 barrels. At the top of the boom in 1857, it is reported that the Cream City was shipping beer at the rate of 25,000 to 30,000 barrels a year.

Besides bringing economic power to Milwaukee, the industry's most important contribution, the brewing business had a marked effect on the social life of the city. Although German beer halls and gardens were sometimes attacked by moralists, these beer gardens and lager-beer halls were among the first centers of singing, instrumental music, and drama in the city. "It was in these fields," explains Thomas C. Cochran, author of *The Pabst Brewing Company,* "that Milwaukee reached Midwestern eminence by the 1850's and was known as the German Athens." He continues, "Although it may have lacked something of the literature, sculpture, and painting of the ancient city in its Golden Age, Milwaukee tried to compensate for this by a lusty enthusiasm for the livelier arts."

Local historian William George Bruce believed that the old-fashioned saloon not only had its definite place in the social life of the community, but also served a useful purpose of introducing new world conditions to the immigrants.

. . . .

The post-Civil War period saw the resumption of heavy German immigration, the boom of 1868, and an increased demand for beer among native-born Americans. One explanation of this new drinking trend was that factory workers could not drink hard liquor and hold their jobs, but a glass or two of beer wouldn't impair their efficiency.

Courtesy of the SHSW [WHi (X3) 33861]

The Pabst Brewing Company wagon, Milwaukee

Between 1864 and 1873, the nation's consumption of beer was to increase by 140 per cent. In Milwaukee, a relatively moderate progress occurred from 1865 to 1868, and then sales increased 260 per cent in the next five years. This increase stemmed from the fact that about 30 to 50 per cent of the production was being shipped to other markets. According to a Chamber of Commerce bulletin, by 1872, the "relatively small city of Milwaukee had overtaken such great brewing centers as New York, Philadelphia, and St. Louis as the greatest beer exporting center in the nation."

The Chicago Fire of 1871 also contributed to this surge of exporting since the fire caused many of the Chicago brewers to go out of business. "Milwaukeeans coming to the aid of thirsty Chicago increased their total sales 44 per cent the following year." It was after the fire episode that Schlitz adopted the merchandising slogan, "The beer that made Milwaukee famous."

With the increase in beer exports, Milwaukee was discovering that brewing had become "big business" and that more than any other product, it was beer which was spreading her reputation. The next 40 years were to see a 26-fold expansion raise the annual beer output from 142,000 barrels in 1871 to 3,700,000 in 1910. The industry was to experience consistent growth and become, at the turn of the nineties, the city's first industry. The factors which led the industry to this pinnacle were many—broadened financial foundations, new processes of manufacture, exploitation of wider markets, and recourse to high-powered techniques of advertising.

The Ice Business in Wisconsin

LEE E. LAWRENCE

In Wisconsin the primary reason for the rise of a large-scale harvesting and shipping of natural ice was the expansion of the brewing and packing industries in Milwaukee and Chicago. The development of a large beer-drinking public, and the transfer of popular preference from heavier and more alcoholic malt liquors to lighter and more effervescent beers, at once helped to make Milwaukee famous and created an important demand for ice. In the early 1880's, for example, Milwaukee breweries were storing 335,000 tons of ice for use in their operations. The largest—the Best Brewing Company—was estimated to have used 21,000 tons in 1879 and 60,000 tons in 1880. In the absence of mechanical cooling, ice in these quantities was required in the manufacturing of light or lager beers and in the maintenance of low temperatures during the aging process. It was also indispensable in preserving these beers, unless pasteurized, in transit and in packing the coils which cooled the beverages to the temperature popular with Americans, already regarded as curious in Europe for their preference for iced drinks.

Even more significant to the increase in the harvesting of Wisconsin ice and its shipment to industrial cities and transportation centers was the growth of the great meatpacking firms of Chicago and, to a lesser extent, of Milwaukee. The development of an efficient refrigerated railroad car was a long, haphazard, and murky process, but the success of Gustavus Swift, the Chicago packer, in devising a practical system for shipping refrigerated meat by rail rapidly brought about the wide use of fresh meats. The meat was

From Lee E. Lawrence, "The Wisconsin Ice Trade," *Wisconsin Magazine of History*, XLVIII,4 (Summer 1965), 257-267. Footnotes in original omitted. Reprinted by permission of the State Historical Society of Wisconsin.

now processed in Chicago and kept unspoiled in storage, during shipment, and while awaiting sale to the consumer by ice refrigeration. Swift's success was quickly imitated by Armour and other meat packers.

. . . .

The tapping of the lake country of southeastern Wisconsin, still close to Chicago but north of and colder than the area around the southern end of Lake Michigan, was made economically possible by the widespread lines of the primary ice carrier, the Chicago, Milwaukee, and St. Paul Railroad, the expanding tracks of the Chicago and North Western, the north-south line of the Wisconsin Central (later the Soo Line), and the extension of the Illinois Central to Madison in 1891. Lakes near railroad lines throughout this whole region were only overnight from Chicago, a vital consideration for the summer transportation of ice.

. . . .

At times the men employed by the ice companies left the neighboring communities anything but quiet. During stoppages brought about by thaws or prolonged subzero weather, they poured into

Ice harvesting

Courtesy of the Portage County Historical Society

the village saloons, often became highly boisterous, and sometimes precipitated near riots. With telephones available only in the later years of the trade, and often with no faster means than horses to bring in aid, maintaining order among several hundred excited young men in a strange village or in company boardinghouses was a problem. There were also similar problems in hard times when men, desperate for jobs, showed up at the plants in greater numbers than were needed.

. . . .

During the harvesting season, unless stopped by intense cold or thaw, activity was often incessant day and night. Cakes of ice 22 inches by 22 inches were conveyed in a steady procession up the inclined elevators from the lake and along the galleries for switching into the rooms of the ice-house, or along platforms for switching into railroad cars waiting eight to ten at a time to be loaded, four to five cakes high, by tongmen in the cars. When ice was short to the south, the steady, tedious, and dangerous labor was interrupted only by breakdowns and by blasts of the whistle of the 65-horsepower steam engine, signalling dinner time in the boarding-houses or the change of the ten-hour shifts. Meantime, switch engines pulled the comparatively small cars of the turn of the century—20-tonners—away from the platforms when filled, and pushed in strings of empties. The cars—sometimes as many as two to three hundred a day—blocked country roads and village streets as they were slowly moved across the railroad scales at Pewaukee and then gathered into trains to go south to empty ice-houses in Chicago, or to those in scores of railroad-division towns throughout the Midwest, and in warm winters even farther afield in the country. Indeed, in these years of shortages, the cutting went on relentlessly until the ice was no longer safe to work upon.

Wisconsin and the Typewriter

RICHARD N. CURRENT

The typewriter came out of Wisconsin. In its first practical form, it was developed in Milwaukee, between 1867 and 1873. The two men who did most in its development, the inventor C. Latham Sholes and the promoter James Densmore, had been publishers of Wisconsin newspapers. As pioneer journalists, both Sholes and Densmore had got to know all phases of the task of converting words into type—they had become familiar with the challenge of the deadline in a region where experienced printers were not always easy to find. It was natural for these men, with such a background, to turn eventually to the problem of making a machine to write with types. The story of their success adds a footnote to a familiar thesis: throughout the history of technology new labor-saving devices have appeared most often in relatively unsettled, "frontier" areas of the world, where there has been a chronic manpower shortage.

. . . .

An article in the *Scientific American* gave the Milwaukee enterprise its start. The editors of this periodical, one of whom, A. E. Beach, was himself the inventor of a writing machine, made it their policy to stimulate all kinds of mechanical invention in the United States. In their issue for July 6, 1867, they published an account of a "type writing machine" which an Alabaman by the name of John Pratt had recently exhibited in England. This device carried all its types on a movable "solid electrotype plate." In front of this plate a vertical framework held a piece of paper and a "carbonized sheet," and a "minute hammer" striking the paper from behind knocked it against the carbon and one of the types to make the impression. After describing this machine of Pratt's, the *Scientific American* went on to say: "The subject of type writing is one of the interesting aspects of the near future." Writing was about to be revolutionized—"the laborious and unsatisfactory performance of the pen must sooner or later become obsolete for general purposes," and the "weary process of learning penmanship in schools" must be "reduced to the acquirement of writing one's own signature and playing on the literary piano above described, or rather on its improved successors." These words came to the attention of C. Latham Sholes, and he got an inspiration from them.

. . . .

From Richard N. Current, "The Original Typewriter Enterprise, 1867–1873," *Wisconsin Magazine of History*, XXXII,4 (June 1949), 391–407. Footnotes in the original omitted. Reprinted by permission of the State Historical Society of Wisconsin.

Sholes and his co-workers completed their first model in September, 1867. It looked something like a cross between a small piano and a kitchen table. In fact, Sholes had brought down from his attic an old kitchen table on which to hang the mechanism, and he patterned the keyboard on that of a piano, arranging figures and letters in numerical and alphabetical order. Awkward and cumbersome though it was, the thing worked—it actually wrote, but only in capital letters. Sholes sent this machine or one like it to his friend Charles Weller in St. Louis, and Weller used it for nearly two years (until he could get a new and improved model) to transcribe the notes he took as a shorthand reporter. Meanwhile, though the inventors continued to work on refinements, they were confident their basic job was done. They thought it was time to find someone to finance the manufacture of their machine. So Sholes typed out a letter and sent it to his former newspaper associate of Kenosha, Wisconsin—James Densmore, now of Meadville, Pennsylvania. [Densmore soon invested in the project.]

. . . .

Though Sholes was steadily improving the invention, Densmore did not yet consider it perfected when, in the summer of 1870, the two men received an invitation to exhibit their machine with the object of selling out their interests in it. Sholes, having neither aptitude nor taste for business affairs, left the decision to Densmore, who made up his mind to sell if his price could be met. In September he got a testimonial from Weller in St. Louis, told Sholes to bring a model from Milwaukee, and went himself from Washington to join Sholes in New York. There he found that the prospective buyers were D. N. Craig and George Harrington, officers of the newly formed Automatic Telegraph Company. Craig brought in, as an expert to appraise the machine, the young Thomas A. Edison, whom he had recently hired to perfect the automatic telegraph. Edison was not very favorably impressed. "The alignment of the letters was awful," he was to recall long afterward. So Craig and Harrington decided not to buy the invention, but they did give Densmore an order for several machines.

Others also gave him orders, and so the following summer (1871) he undertook to manufacture in Milwaukee enough typewriters to "supply the present demand, pay up the debts, and have one or two over to sell."

. . . .

Ultimately the typewriter was to make possible the growth of both big business and big government. Yet neither businessmen nor

Courtesy of the SHSW [WHi (X313) 2865]

Lillian Sholes, daughter of the inventor of the typewriter, C. Latham Sholes, experiments with an early model

government officials showed much interest in a writing machine in the beginning. The early demand came from stenographers (court reporters) and from telegraphers. With such men Densmore placed most of the several dozen machines he made—at a time when he could induce very few government bureaus or mercantile and manufacturing firms to try them out. Stenography and telegraphy provided the "felt need" for the invention, and telegraphy and stenography helped to inspire it in other ways as well. For instance, Sholes put together his first partial model out of parts of telegraph apparatus. Both he and Densmore were interested in shorthand as amateurs, and as early as 1869 he conceived the idea of a stenotype. So there was from the start a close relationship between typewriting, on the one hand, and shorthand reporting and telegraphy on the other.

Appleton's Pioneer Electric Plant

G. W. VAN DERZEE

In July [1882] H. F. Rogers, successful paper manufacturer, went fishing with his friend H. E. Jacobs, remarkable salesman for the Western Edison Electric Company. No one knows whether or not H. J. Rogers landed any fish on that trip, but the star salesman landed a contract for an Edison central station. So successful was Jacobs' selling that Rogers, though he never had seen a light bulb, bought a complete plant.

Three years before, Edison had conducted his now famous experiments in which he created incandescent light, using a piece of carbonized sewing thread as a filament. In the three succeeding years Edison improved the existing generators and a distribution system, and found bamboo a better filament than thread for his incandescent light. In order to prove his lighting equipment, he planned to erect a power plant to generate electricity from steam power in the investment district of New York.

From G. W. Van Derzee, "Pioneering the Electrical Age," *Wisconsin Magazine of History*, XLI,3 (Spring 1958), 210–214. Footnotes in original omitted. Reprinted by permission of the State Historical Society of Wisconsin.

Rogers returned from his fishing trip so enthusiastic about the miracle of incandescent light that he did not wait for Edison's system to be proved. He persuaded A. L. Smith, who was also a personal friend of Edison, H. D. Smith, a blast furnace owner, and Charles Beveridge, a banker, to join him in forming the Appleton Edison Light Co., Ltd. The new company entered into a contract with Samuel Insull, Edison's secretary, for the exclusive franchise to use the Edison system in the Fox Valley. Rogers' new home on the bluff overlooking the Fox River, and two paper mills were wired. The house, by the way, still stands, and some of the original wiring may still be in use. Copper wire was used, usually with insulation of cotton or tape, sometimes bare. Mechanics fastened the wires between floors, in walls, and to the walls with wooden cleats.

While Edison was building his New York power plant, using steam, the Appleton paper makers, long experienced in utilizing the power of the Fox River, were preparing to use the power of falling water to generate electricity. The generator and water wheel had arrived, and the little hydroelectric central station was nearing completion.

Word came that the Edison plant in New York City was in successful operation on September 4, 1882. Efforts in Appleton were redoubled. "We will start operating in the morning," said one of the Edison experts. On the morning of September 30, 1882, everybody was present at the appointed moment—Rogers, the two Smiths, Beveridge, and their friends. The leather drive belt was connected to the water wheel, and everyone drew a long breath of anticipation. Nothing happened. "Change the connections," was the order. They changed and changed and changed; the generators turned, but the lamps did not light. Noon came and afternoon dragged on. The five o'clock whistles blew and still the specialists tinkered with the mysterious thing, electricity. It was getting dark when suddenly, whimsically, something happened: the carbonized filaments slowly became dull red, then bright red, then incandescent, and Glory Be— there was light! It is recorded that the men jumped up and down and screamed like school boys. The man who had made the final connection then speeded up the dynamo and the lights brightened. Water power was making light. Triumphantly the *Appleton Post* reported that "the lamps produced a beautiful soft white light absolutely steady and constant, and equal in intensity or exceeding, if desired, the illuminating power of a gas jet of the best quality. The electric light is perfectly safe and convenient, and is destined to be the great illuminating agent of the near future."

This tiny plant of 12.5 kilowatts capacity on Vulcan Street in Appleton was the first central station in the world to convert the power of falling water into electric power; and this plant was a grandparent of hydroelectric central stations all over the world that now put rivers to work making electricity. H. J. Rogers' home in Appleton which received electric service from the Appleton Edison Light Company on that memorable September evening, bears the distinction of being the first house in the world—devoted exclusively to residential use—to receive electric service from an electric central station.

This was but the beginning. If the first moment of operation was a dream, the next twenty years were a nightmare. Sometimes the voltage was so high that all the lamps in the circuit burned out; and, with lamps costing $1.60 each, this was an expensive fault. Because regulators had not yet been developed, the intensity of the light was governed by the operator at the power house, who depended on his own eyesight to judge if the voltage was adequate. There were no volt meters or ammeters, no lightning protection, no fuses, nor instruments of any kind. Any disturbance would short out the circuit. When this happened, all hands went out tracing the wires, and service was suspended until the trouble was located. Although the electric light often did not work, it was judged a success. It was a novelty and—perhaps as important—it was inexpensive. In fact, the company knew so little about the economics of its business that for some time it actually sold its service below cost.

Despite a great increase in the number of customers, the company lost money, and only through such unorthodox methods as applying stock subscription payments to operating expenses instead of plant investment, was it able to meet expenses during those early years. By the end of 1885 it was overdrawn at the bank by more than $1,000. In practice, the company never audited its books or knew exactly where it stood. In the first three years the stockholders had invested nearly $24,000 in the company. They owned a plant worth only $18,700, and had neither received a cent in dividends nor would they expect any in the foreseeable future. It should be remembered that the service was only for lighting—from dusk to dawn—since motors and other uses of electricity were yet to be discovered.

In 1884, the company launched a bold, imaginative, and decisive program to solve its problems. An extensive promotional campaign was initiated. Early in 1886 a new plant was built with a capacity of 190 kilowatts. The new plant incorporated all the advanced features of the Edison system, including various regulatory devices, fuses, and a three-wire distributing system. In 1888, electrolytic meters were added, and in 1890 twenty-four hour service was begun and some customers installed and operated electric motors.

By 1890, the number of customers had increased 6,000 per cent, from only three customers ten years before, to a total of 182.

In 1886, during the company's expansion program, an even more revolutionary development was taking place. The Appleton Electric Street Railway Company was incorporated by three other Fox Valley residents. A 60 kilowatt generator, driven by water power, furnished the electricity for the trolleys. This company, too, had its difficulties, and when the novelty wore off in 1891, the street car company was put on the block.

To the investors in the lighting company the street car system looked like a golden opportunity. An electric street car system, they reasoned, would provide a daytime revenue for their electric plant which was a full-time investment working only at night. Furthermore, the street car company could be cheaply bought. Accordingly, A. L. Smith and C. A. Beveridge purchased the street railway company and formed a new corporation to consolidate the lighting and street railway companies. This, they learned later, was a mistake. Revamping the street railway system cost much more than anyone had anticipated. If the company had remained exclusively in the lighting and power field it would have been a thriving success, but the street railway operated at a net loss of over $4,000 for the year 1893. Then in 1894 the local gas company cut its rates, and in addition a competing electric company was formed. The Edison company was forced to cut its rates; some of its electric light and power business slipped away; and receipts of the street railway department dropped, instead of rising as anticipated. The company lost its credit at banks and the "roof fell in."

In January, 1896, the Appleton Edison Electric Company formally went into bankruptcy. But A. L. Smith, president, never surrendered. At a foreclosure sale in 1896 Smith bought the property of the defunct enterprise and formed a new company. In 1897 the new company acquired the competing electric company which had also run into financial difficulties due to its inability to secure new capital for expansion. The new Appleton Electric Light and Power Company seemed at last to be on solid ground. But just as the future was beginning to look promising, a fire destroyed the entire generating plant in 1897. The new company limped along until 1900 when it was merged with the Neenah and Menasha Electric Railway Company, and the Wisconsin Traction, Light, Heat & Power Company was formed.

The enthusiastic salesmanship of H. E. Jacobs and the expectations of the original investors had been too optimistic. Though thousands of dollars had been poured into the venture of electrical power for the Fox Valley, the venture had never paid a dividend.

But out of the nightmares and ashes of nearly twenty years of labor had risen a potentially great electric utility which was to become the backbone of Wisconsin Michigan Power Company in 1927.

From the consumers' point of view, the extent and quality of electric service in this area in 1901 were equal to, perhaps better, than in any other cities of comparable size in the world.

5: Agriculture

Farming remained a primary factor in Wisconsin's economy throughout this period despite the simultaneous growth of industry. In fact, the number of farms increased, due at least in part to the efforts of promoters to sell the lands cleared by the lumber companies. Individual speculators, railroads, and the lumber companies all got into the act. Many farmers willingly supported the lumber companies in their policies of land clearing. They eagerly settled some of the cutover lands, as illustrated in the first selection below.

Dairying replaced wheat farming as the leading agricultural activity by the end of the century. Butter production was initially emphasized, but cheese soon became more important. An account of the early and successful cheese producers Lucy and Nicholas Pauly is given in the second selection. Those wishing to know more about the rise and development of the dairy industry are urged to read Eric E. Lampard, *The Rise of the Dairy Industry in Wisconsin* (1962).

One of the state's leading proponents of modern dairying was William D. Hoard, journalist and politician. An outspoken critic of those who did not agree with him and his methods, Hoard is noted for his journalistic contributions to agriculture. Some of his more picturesque suggestions are presented in the final selection of this section.

Selling the Stump Lands

ARLAN HELGESON

Several kinds of enterprisers engaged in colonizing northern Wisconsin before 1900. There were large scale speculators and the land grant railroads, with thousands of acres to dispose of. Many lumbermen turned to colonizing their cutover lands. A host of real estate dealers also attempted to bring settlers to the stump lands. This paper is intended to describe some of the typical colonization activities. Every village and hamlet in the cutover area had someone engaged in selling land to settlers. . . .

. . . .

Railroads played a great part in the attempt to make northern Wisconsin a land of farms. Perhaps foremost among them in the nineteenth century was the Wisconsin Central Railroad. From its earliest days that company worked closely with state immigration agencies in advertising low-priced lands and the advantages of building homes in the northern forests. Potential settlers were shown displays of northern grown grains and vegetables at the Milwaukee offices of the road. A number of testimonials by actual settlers bolstered the company's propaganda. Thus they published such stories as "What John Welch Has Done." In 1873, this pioneer, so the story ran, purchased eighty acres of timber land and began to clear it. Having cut off the timber in the fall, he logged and burned off the tract in the spring, then planted potatoes. The harvest netted him 756 bushels of potatoes from the two and one-half acres he had been able to prepare. This was sufficient, the company stated, to bring a profit of $270 over the cost of land, labor, and seed.

In the eighties the Wisconsin Central pursued both American and European settlers diligently. The road employed Kent Kennan to spend much of his time in Europe obtaining settlers for north central Wisconsin. A great mass of literature was produced for both native and foreign consumption, Kennan writing and distributing much of it. He also distributed, and the company no doubt inspired, such publications as that of a Pastor W. Koch, written in 1883, praising lands along the railroad and urging readers in Germany and Switzerland to join him in building a German Evangelical settlement in northern Wisconsin.

The Wisconsin Central had agents not only in large cities in

From Arlan Helgeson, "Nineteenth Century Land Colonization in Northern Wisconsin," *Wisconsin Magazine of History*, XXXVI,2 (Winter 1952–53), 115–121. Footnotes in original omitted. Reprinted by permission of the State Historical Society of Wisconsin.

Europe and America, but employed a number of local agents on a commission basis in northern Wisconsin. These agents sold to the settlers on the usual company terms of approximately $5.00 an acre, $50 down payment, and the remainder in three yearly payments at 7 percent interest. The company paid such agents a 10 percent commission. Since railroads benefited not only from the sale of their own lands but from the colonization of any lands to and from which they might obtain the "haul," the Wisconsin Central and other lines sought to promote the settlement of other northern lands almost as eagerly as their own. Consequently company officials acted as "go-betweens" without commission where deals might affect the welfare of their road. They sought particularly to encourage stock grazing and other experiments that might lead to large scale agricultural enterprise in the stump lands.

Like many other railroads the Wisconsin Central deducted the price of a "land seeker's" fare if he purchased a tract from the road. Moreover, he paid only half the freight rates ordinarily charged for moving household goods to his new home.

By 1890 directors of the Wisconsin Central Company reported that they disposed of 250,000 acres of their 838,628 acre grant.

. . . .

If speculators and landholders like . . . the land grant railroads came early to a belief in the agricultural possibilities of the Cutover, no such unity of conviction appeared among the individual lumbermen who possessed the greater portion of northern Wisconsin lands. Nevertheless, a number of factors turned the attention of lumbermen toward agricultural settlement. For instance, dwindling forests caused some to move to other fields of operation or search for other means to exploit their cutover acres. Equally important was the fact that, by 1890, much of the choice farming land of the West had been settled. Thus the stump lands of Wisconsin had less competition in the movement to gain settlers. Moreover, the nation's rapid growth in population made the eventual settlement of the Cutover seem all the more certain. Hence, more lumbermen tended to keep their stump lands, with an eye to selling them for farms.

Where lands had been cut over, their owners could adopt one of several courses: allow them to lie idle, let them be taken by counties in lieu of taxes, sell them to speculators, or attempt to induce settlement themselves. Each year long lists of tax delinquent lands in the local newspapers testified to the common practice by which many lumbermen forfeited cutover lands through failure to pay assessments. However, lumbermen who planned to continue working in a given area might elect to lessen their taxes by increasing the number of taxable landholders in that area. In most cases agricultural settlement appeared sooner or later as one solution to the problems of the cutover tracts.

The attitudes of lumbermen varied greatly as to the disposal of stump lands. Some were unwilling to sell, being inclined to hold their lands for future rising prices, except in those counties where taxes seemed excessively high. Even when they felt convinced that lands should be sold, some lumbermen felt a certain reluctance toward entering the land business. Some timber owners frankly declared themselves against settlement. One northern editor quoted a lumberman as saying: "So long as we have standing pine of any considerable quantities in a county, we want the settler to keep out, for as soon as the farmer appears he wants school houses, roads, and other improvements, for which we, as large holders of land in his neighborhood must pay in increased taxation."

. . . .

Selling cutover lands and developing hardwood manufacturing industries proved to be a happy combination in many parts of the Cutover. The non-floating hardwoods demanded new techniques of logging and manufacture in which seasonal use of local laborers and the growth of small sawmill towns played a prominent role. Thus colonizing farmer-lumberjacks became a feature of the hardwood areas: summer farming and winter logging proceeding hand in hand.

Easily the most exciting figure to come to the fore in the nineties, and the personification of big business in stump land colonization, was James Leslie Gates. Too long neglected by Wisconsin biographers and historians, this audacious speculator combined the advocacy of free silver in the 1890's with the reputation of being one of the nation's twelve most heavily insured capitalists. At his peak he controlled half a million acres of Wisconsin stump lands. In the midst of his tireless campaign to interest anyone and everyone in a farm or a ranch in northern Wisconsin, he also found time to suggest to J. P. Morgan that they form a billion dollar corporation to corner all the timber on the West Coast.

Gates reflected the optimism that was felt by most of the colonizers of northern Wisconsin at the turn of the century. Sales of slightly over a million acres in 1899 rose to double that amount in 1900. Surely northern Wisconsin would become a land of farms.

A Pioneer Cheese Company

HAROLD T. I. SHANNON

In the autumn of 1953 the Pauly Cheese Company was seventy-five years old. It is possibly the first Wisconsin cheese company to attain to a Diamond Jubilee. It is certainly the only Wisconsin cheese company which has been operated for so long a time by the founder's family. In seventy-five years the Pauly family's one-room, one-vat cheese factory has grown to be one of the three or four largest cheese companies in the world. It is a big factor in natural cheese production since its business is about equally divided between processed cheese and natural cheeses. Other giants in the cheese business process a much greater percentage of their volume.

William H. Pauly manages the company, which now centers all of its activities in Green Bay. The general offices and the main processing and packaging operations are here. Pauly is one of seven sons of the founder, all of whom followed in the cheese-making business. The Green Bay man's immediate predecessor as president was his brother Felix, who held the office from the time of incorporation until he retired two years ago in California.

. . . .

Nicholas Pauly, the father, was the founder of the huge enterprise. It was the boys' mother, Lucy Pauly, however, who made the first cheese in the Pauly cheese factory in 1878.

Nicholas Pauly was a very young man when he came to Wisconsin from Luxembourg in 1874 upon the advice and at the insistence of a youth of his same age, who had arrived some few years before. Pauly had mastered the carriage maker's trade in the old country. His friend was a good blacksmith. They did not become partners, but they became closely associated at Knellsville, one and one-half miles north of Port Washington, in the manufacture of surreys, cutters, and farm wagons. They had no models. Each vehicle was custom-made. They were doing every bit as well as the friend had written to Pauly that he predicted they would. Pauly had married an Ozaukee County girl, and by 1878 they had two sons and two daughters.

Though cheese was being made in Wisconsin in small quantities, it was produced profitably. Chester Hazen had produced the first commercial Wisconsin cheese in Fond du Lac County, whose fac-

From Harold T. I. Shannon, "The Pauly Cheese Company," *Wisconsin Magazine of History,* XXXVIII,4 (Summer 1955), 234–236. Footnotes in the original omitted. Reprinted by permission of the State Historical Society of Wisconsin.

tory was perhaps the first one established in the State, in 1864. Now rumor had it that somebody in nearby Sheboygan Falls was making and selling cheese. The successful wagon maker was fascinated. He and his wife closed shop and drove over to investigate, the journey consuming most of one day to travel the twenty-five miles and another day to return. But it was worth it, history now relates, because it was the beginning of the Pauly Cheese Company.

Hardheaded Nicholas Pauly determined he and his wife should learn this cheese-making business. He was convinced that every pound they'd make would be grabbed up by the Chicago buyers, because he would make a premium cheese. His wagons were the best that money could buy. He'd go into the cheese market with a demonstrably better cheese. However, he had no intention of giving up his profitable carriage business. In 1878 he made a deal with a cheesemaker instead to come to Knellsville and to stay there until the Paulys had mastered the cheese-making techniques. And he was to be quartered and fed and paid for this service.

More than a billion pounds of Pauly Cheese have been made by the Pauly family since Lucy Pauly produced her first seventy-pound Cheddar, more generally known as American cheese, in 1878. Mr. Pauly did the heavy lifting and the getting-things-ready every day. His wife then took charge of the one-vat and one-press cheese factory and made the cheese with the same care and native skill she employed in making the bread loaves and the gingerbread the same day. The factory was a two-room addition to the wagon shop.

Nor did the senior Pauly ever give up the wagon works. He witnessed his cheese business grow and his able sons develop it into one of the best known names and powerful influences in the cheese trade. Yet he remained the expert custom carriage builder until his retirement in 1910.

. . . .

By 1915 the company was selling 10,000,000 pounds of cheese a year. (By 1950—50,000,000!)

The Plymouth market established the price of cheese, based upon the amount of cheese on hand and what the market would pay for it. The Pauly Cheese Company actively traded on the Plymouth Exchange and other exchanges in the State.

By 1912 the company was engaged in vast expansion. It bought or erected warehouses in many places in Wisconsin. The company presently owns and operates more cheese factories in Wisconsin and Upper Michigan than any other company.

The cheese business not only saw many changes in Pauly's seventy-five years—it was completely revolutionized. Once Wisconsin had about 3,600 cheese factories. This was during the horse and buggy age when milk could not be transported far. Then came motor transportation, and the bigger, better located factories got bigger. Many of the little factories closed. Today there are not more than 1,200 cheese factories in Wisconsin. In 1917 cheese processing was introduced. In another seventeen years Pauly added processing at Manitowoc.

. . . .

The founder, Nicholas Pauly, lived to see most of the company's expansion. He lived until 1921—until he was seventy-nine. And Wisconsin's first woman cheesemaker, his wife, lived until 1926— until seventy-six.

Hoard and the Dairy Industry

GEORGE WILLIAM RANKIN

The Temperament of Cattle

One of Hoard's earliest and most valuable contributions to dairy knowledge consisted in his demonstration of the following proposition, "Temperament determines form and form governs function."

Up to the time he made this somewhat radical declaration, no particular attention had been given temperament in determining the function of an animal, brute or human.

Most dairymen were just milking—giving little or no thought to breeds and breeding, with the result that many of them were keeping cows instead of having cows keep them.

Not so with Hoard.

. . . .

"The dairy function in cows," he said, "is like the speed function in horses, all very largely a matter of temperament. In the human family we have the same types: those with the phlegmatic tempera-

From George William Rankin, *William Dempster Hoard* (Fort Atkinson, Wis.: W. D. Hoard and Sons, Co., 1925), pp. 147–148, 150–153, 179–180. Reprinted by permission.

Courtesy of the SHSW [WHi (X3) 14802]

The original Babcock milk tester, 1906

ment and those with the nervous temperament. The former are the flesh-forming type. They usually have a short, thick neck, large trunk, and short limbs. The nervous temperament type, of which I am an example, are tall, slender, and angular. You can't any more put fat on the bones of a man like me than you can fatten a fanning mill by running oats through it, and thus it is with the brute animal."

. . . .

Hoard's Description of a Good Dairy Cow

"A good dairy cow should have a large nostril, because milk is evolved from the blood, and the blood is vitalized by the air the cow breathes. She must have a large muzzle, because she must be a good feeder. She must have a full, prominent eye, because this indicates strong nervous force and energy, and this is vitally necessary for large milk production. She should be long from the eye to the top of the poll, because this indicates a large brain. The backbone should come up strong against the head. A good backbone is one of the most essential things in the requisites of a good dairy cow. The jointure of the backbone to the head should be strong—if there is a falling away at this point, avoid that cow. The spinal marrow is but the continuation of the brain, and it is most important that strength and power in this particular be well indicated. The backbone should be rugged, showing large and heavy processes. A good cow will, as a rule, show larger spinal processes than an ox. Furthermore, there must be strong navel development, else the cow will be lacking in vitality. The Yorkshire soldiers understood this latter point when they said of a fighter, "e is nae gude, 'e 'as nae belly.'""

. . . .

"I have given years of study to the dairy cow, and I believe that I know a good deal about her, but more and more I am becoming convinced that the darkest place on earth is the inside of a cow. Chemists have their laboratories for research and investigation; mechanics have their mechanisms to aid them in the search for truth, but no human agency has been devised to enable us to discover how the dairy cow transforms the hay and grain that she eats into milk. I never look at a cow but that I think of her with humility and a feeling of awe and inspiration."

. . . .

The Dual-Purpose Cow

"The man who hazards his success in the business of dairying upon the dual-purpose cow," he said, "reminds me of a certain

Courtesy of the SHSW [WHi (D485) 6815]

William D. Hoard

backwoodsman who, being subjected to the constant depredations of wild animals, conceived the idea of setting a spring gun to catch the marauders. His few head of stock ranged the woods and clearings, and so he said to himself, 'I must set this gun so that it will hit if it's a bear and miss if it's a calf,' which he accordingly did—but unfortunately his best calf sprung the trap. So you farmers who are keeping dual-purpose cows may well take a lesson from the experience of this simple backwoodsman. You seem to think you can breed your cows so that all the bull calves will be profitable steers and that all the heifer calves will be profitable cows. It can't be done."

. . . .

Hoard Sayings

"Remember that a cow is a mother, and her calf is a baby."

"All things shall be added to him that loveth the cow."

"Honor be to me as I honor thee." (In reference to the cow.)

"If you want a cow to do well for you, get her confidence."

"Show me a successful dairy cow that a woman has not had a great deal to do with."

"Nothing on earth, save the virtue of a woman, is more susceptible to scandal than butterfat."

"If cows could talk, they would be heard all over this country calling for an improved breed of dairymen."

"To him who loveth the cow, to him shall all other things be added—feed, ensilage, butter, more grasses, more prosperity, happier homes, and greater wealth."

Chapter VII
ETHNICITY AND POLITICS, 1865–1900

To say that politics and ethnicity were inseparable in post-Civil War Wisconsin would be an oversimplification. Yet all the major issues the state faced were influenced by concern for and by the various ethnic concentrations. Issues such as liquor control and English language teaching in the schools, the two issues most disruptive to the state's political situation during that period, were of utmost importance to substantial elements of the immigrant community.

Republicans dominated state politics throughout the era except for two brief periods, both essentially aberrations from the normal political situation. In 1873 a reform coalition consisting of Democrats, Liberal Republicans, Grangers, and many non-Catholic Germans who were upset over the Republican-passed Graham Law, managed to sweep the Republicans out of state offices. The German element in this coalition was particularly angered by the Graham Law, a liquor-control bill they viewed as a threat to their traditional culture and values.

In office, the coalition led by Governor William R. Taylor repealed the Graham Law, but it promptly began its own self-destruction in the controversy over railroad regulation. The Grangers (Patrons of Husbandry), organized in part to counteract the influence of the railroads, found themselves in a strange alliance with Democrats led by Alexander Mitchell, *the* leading figure in Wisconsin's railroads. Republicans, with little to lose on the issue, forced passage of the Potter Law, which provided for the establishment of a railroad commission, financial reporting by the roads, and rate-setting guidelines. This issue divided the reform group. Those who were already well served by railroads favored tough regulations, while those seeking to lure railroads into their communities opposed any action tending to limit further growth of the railroads. The return of Republicans to control after 1875 brought repeal of the Potter Law, and the collapse of the reform coalition led to the restoration of the conservative Bourbon (industry-oriented) element's control of the Democratic Party.

The only other serious breach in the Republican hold on the state's voters came in 1890. Wisconsin's school laws of 1849 permitted instruction in a foreign language; laws passed in 1852 and 1867 required that traditional subjects had to be taught in English, although later modifications allowed for some training in a foreign language. In 1889 the legislature passed the Bennett Law, the state's first compulsory education law. The law made it mandatory for the schools to teach the subjects of "reading, writing, arithmetic, and United States history in the English language." Both Catholic and non-Catholic Germans, supported by many Lutherans of Scandinavian background, protested this measure. Despite appeals from some Republican leaders, Republican Governor William D. Hoard campaigned squarely on the justness of the Bennett Law—and took the entire ticket down to defeat with him. Once again Republicans were swept from their control of the state on the strength of an opposition coalition formed essentially around a single issue.

The ethnic influences on the development of the state went beyond the impact of immigrant voting. Certain industries—for example, brewing, tanning, furniture making—were dominated by immigrants, while both rural and urban work forces depended on the continued influx of immigration. Germans and Scandinavians remained the dominant groups, though later waves of immigration brought large numbers of immigrants from Poland, Italy, Greece, and other areas of eastern and southern Europe. These "new" immigrants were often resented by their predecessors, and this resentment was at times expressed in the activities of anti-Catholic groups such as the American Protective Association, a nativist group which played upon fears of the unknown.

In investigating the role of minorities in Wisconsin's history, one must be cognizant of the part played by "native" minorities, though their influence was not strong during the post-Civil War period. The Indians of the state remained outside white society for the most part. After the passage of the Dawes Act in 1887, the Oneida and Stockbridge voluntarily relinquished much of their land; the Menominee, on the other hand, resisted and maintained most of their collective holdings. Blacks were few in number in the state and had little impact during this time. In the area of equal rights, the supporters of women's suffrage made few noticeable gains.

The ethnic diversity and the resultant competition between various groups often worked to the disadvantage of the laboring class. Unions remained small and weak and nearly disappeared after the "Bay View Massacre" of 1886. That episode, which occurred at the same time and for many of the same reasons as the more celebrated Haymarket Riot in Chicago, severely crippled the labor movement while it made a national hero out of Governor Jeremiah ("Uncle Jerry") Rusk. Much of what was left of the labor movement after this crisis followed Victor Berger into Socialism in the 1890s.

Politically, the state ended the immediate post-Civil War period much as it had started it. Republicans were back in control and apparently immovable except in reaction to specific issues such as those raised in 1873 or 1890. Yet the party would soon be overtaken by reform from within.

With acculturation proceeding at a steady pace, ethnicity was declining in importance by the end of the century. Islands of ethnic exclusiveness remained, but the outward signs indicated that the process of Americanization was well under way in the state.

1: A Melting Pot?

Although immigration to Wisconsin was dominated by Germans and Scandinavians, many other ethnic groups settled within the state. The English and the Irish came in large numbers in the early years, while emigrants from the nations of southern and eastern Europe came during the latter third of the century. Many sources of information concerning the impact of various ethnic groups on the state do exist, but a fertile and virtually untilled field remains for the serious historian of Wisconsin's ethnic past. Gerd Korman's *Industrialization, Immigrants and Americanizers: The View from Milwaukee, 1866– 1921* is the most thorough recent study. Most of the other available material is to be found in periodical literature. The selections which follow are taken from representative portions of that literature.

The German Immigration

GUY-HAROLD SMITH

At the time Wisconsin was admitted into the Union in 1848 the revolutionary movement in Germany had initiated a trans-Atlantic migration of liberals who sought in America the freedom that was lacking in Prussia and Austria. Between 1844 and 1854 over a million Germans emigrated to the United States. The great migration, and later the Jacksonian migration, had already peopled Ohio, Indiana, Illinois, and the southern sections of Michigan and Wis-

From Guy-Harold Smith, "Notes on the Distribution of the German-Born in Wisconsin in 1905," *Wisconsin Magazine of History*, XIII (1929–1930), 107–120. Footnotes in the original omitted. Reprinted by permission of the State Historical Society of Wisconsin.

consin. Much of the good land was gone or was being held for high prices, so the German immigrants naturally sought the new lands along the frontier, which by 1850 had reached the lower Wisconsin-Fox Rivers. Beyond the frontier lay the wilderness only recently invaded by the lumbermen who were to alter materially the physical landscape; behind the wavering frontier line the thin film of population had left untenanted large blocks of land. To this sparsely populated pioneer area the Germans emigrated and began at once to carve their homes from the forests of maple and pine.

In the early fifties the Wisconsin Bureau of Immigration rendered valuable aid to prospective German settlers, and no doubt indirectly persuaded many more to migrate to Wisconsin. The glacial landscape, not unlike the homeland, was another condition that favored the choice of Wisconsin as the future home of these German pioneers. A quotation from one of the creditable news journals of the time gives a fair conception of the beginning of this peaceful German conquest of new lands in America. "About 30,000 old Luthern [sic] subjects of Prussia, from the borders of the Baltic, are shortly to come over and settle in these United States. It is a religious movement, these people preferring the good old orthodox doctrines to the modern philosophy of Berlin. There are men of very large fortunes among them; old German noblemen whose pedigrees date back to the thirteenth century. They will make excellent western farmers and are about to settle in Wiskonsin—the coolest spot they can select."

. . . .

Between 1840 and 1850 the total population of Wisconsin increased from 30,749 to 304,756. Only 17.82 per cent of the population at the latter date had been born within the State. The other states of the Union had contributed 139,166 persons or 45.66 per cent of the population. Or considering both groups collectively it is evident that Wisconsin entered the Union as a typical American state with 63.48 per cent of the inhabitants as native Americans. However, the Germans had begun to arrive in such numbers that they constituted an important foreign element. In 1850 the census reported 38,064 Germans in Wisconsin, a number greater than the total population of the Territory in 1840. The only other foreign element to exceed the Germans was the British, represented by 18,952 English, 21,043 Irish, 3,527 Scots, and 4,319 Welsh, a total of 47,841. This should certify beyond a doubt that, while the Germans became very important from the beginning of statehood, Wisconsin was preeminently British-American, or in reality Yankee-British in 1848.

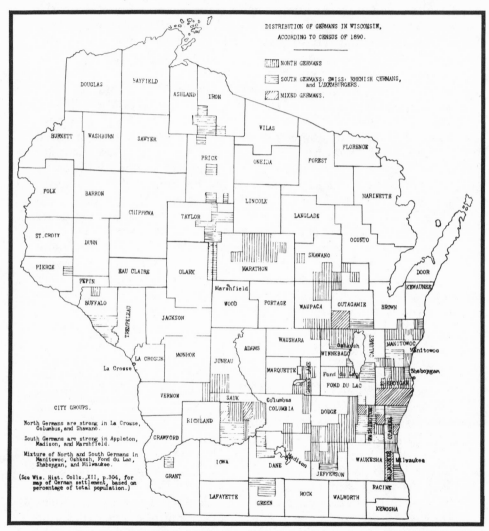

From Wisconsin Historical Collections (1898), Vol. 14. Courtesy of the SHSW [WHi (X3) 33835]

Distribution of Germans in Wisconsin (Census of 1890)

While the Germans constituted the second largest foreign element in 1850 the number increased so rapidly in the fifties that by 1860 they numbered 123,879, including 7,081 credited to Austria. The British element had increased to 93,860 almost double the number in 1850, but the great number of Germans made them, from sometime in the fifties, the dominant foreign-born element. The table presented below gives the number of German-born residing in Wisconsin at each decennial census from 1850 to 1920.

THE GERMAN-BORN IN WISCONSIN

1850	38,064	1890	259,819
1860	123,879	1900	268,384
1870	162,314	1910	233,384
1880	184,328	1920	151,250

Wisconsin Czechs

KAREL D. BICHA

Czech-speaking immigrants from Bohemia and Moravia, most of whom settled in Wisconsin between 1848 and 1880, were both pioneers of Wisconsin farmland and primary instruments in shaping the contours of the Czech-American institutional life which flourished from the 1880's through the 1920's.

· ·

Czech settlement in Wisconsin (and elsewhere in America) was the earliest of any of the Slavic-language peoples, roughly contemporary with the main body of German rather than Slavic immigration. It consisted largely of farmers and skilled tradesmen, as well as a considerable number of refugee intellectuals, and in terms of skills represented an abler group than the more numerous Czech immigrants who arrived later and settled in other states.

· ·

From Karel D. Bicha, "The Czechs in Wisconsin History," *Wisconsin Magazine of History,* LIII,3 (Spring 1970), 194–203. Footnotes in the original omitted. Reprinted by permission of the State Historical Society of Wisconsin.

Like German settlement in Wisconsin, the location of early Czech settlements was quite disparate and widely diffused throughout the southern half of the state.

. . . .

The largest of the western Wisconsin establishments was commenced in 1855 in the town of La Crosse, a settlement which later took cohesive shape around the society and church of St. Vaclav. In the late 1870's a major influx of immigrants from the region of Ceske Budejovice increased the number of Bohemian-born in the city to nearly 500. By the end of the century Czech life was well developed, and the community possessed a weekly newspaper, *Vlastenec* (Patriot), a Catholic church and school, lodges and social clubs, dramatic facilities, eight stores retailing "mixed goods" (groceries), ten taverns, a butcher, baker, saddler, barber, furrier, tinsmith, plow maker, cigar maker, tailor, several coopers, and artisans specializing in grave markers and billiard tables.

Contemporary with the La Crosse foundations, Czech families from the Plzen (Pilsen) region began to occupy the isolated ridge and valley country of northern Richland and southern Vernon counties, establishing themselves around the village of Yuba in Richland County. Their principal settlement, Champion Valley, attracted other immigrants and by 1861 nineteen Czech family names were represented in the valley. As an isolated outpost, household manufacture was employed for most purposes, and the men of the community made an annual journey to Lone Rock to mill the year's wheat and to convert surplus corn, maple sugar, and some butter into tools, coffee, and cloth. Dairy products posed a major disposal problem for the community, and until the Yuba cheese factory commenced operations in 1892 the products of the butter churn often served as a lubricant for machinery. Yet the colony flourished, and by 1900 some 233 families of the first and second generations farmed the ridges, bluffs, and valleys of the Yuba area.

The last of the sizable Czech settlements in western Wisconsin was founded in Crawford County, especially in the village of Prairie du Chien and the townships of Eastman, Bridgeport, Mariella, and Wauzeka. Except for isolated cases, the earliest of the main bodies of immigrants arrived in 1857, settling on federal land, and coming principally after a brief residence in Chicago. Crawford County Czechs acquired a reputation for exclusiveness and parochialism, even in the broader Czech-American community. These attitudes were later reflected in secessionist tendencies from Catholic fraternal bodies. Nonetheless, the colonies experienced considerable growth, and by 1890 about 1,400 immigrants and their children lived in the vicinity of Prairie du Chien.

In summary, all of the major Czech settlements in Wisconsin were founded in the 1850's, and by 1880 the bulk of Czech immigrants who would come to Wisconsin had already arrived. Increased demands on the immigrant lines operating from Hamburg and Bremen permitted a drastic drop in fares, and by the 1870's an immigrant could come on a single ticket from Prague to Racine, Milwaukee, or Kewaunee for fifty dollars or less. Other Czech immigrants, after unsatisfactory experiences in the mushrooming Chicago Czech community, filtered after 1876 into the newly cutover areas to establish farms. Small settlements were made near Phillips in Price County, and many of the early arrivals reflected the success of unscrupulous Chicago land promoters. A larger number located, with greater advance knowledge, near Antigo in Langlade County.

Yet the dominance of Wisconsin as the principal attraction of immigrants from Bohemia and Moravia was at an end by the 1870's. Though little is known of the internal mobility of immigrants in the United States, it is a certainty that even in the 1860's outmovement was commonplace among Wisconsin Czechs. Grant County, owing to the relatively unfavorable conditions of initial settlement, was perhaps most affected, but Manitowoc County also experienced some losses. The Nebraska prairie became the magnet for Wisconsin Bohemians intent on using the new Homestead Act.

Poles in Wisconsin

FRANK H. MILLER

The causes of Polish immigration are not difficult to find. Previous to 1872 they were chiefly economic. The low wages paid in Europe and the great difficulty of obtaining land drove many Poles

From Frank H. Miller, "The Polanders in Wisconsin," in *Parkman Club Papers, 1896* (Milwaukee, 1896), pp. 239–246.

to this country. Those who came to this country sent for their friends, frequently sending them money with which to come. To the economic causes was added in 1871 the religious. Bismarck determined that all of the inhabitants of Prussia should speak the German language and laws were passed to give the government a control of the parochial schools which was very irritating to the Catholics, and especially to the clergy. Another decree banished the Jesuit priests from the empire. About the same time the severe military law began to operate as a cause of emigration. Every Polish youth was obliged to serve in the German army for four years.

The effect of these laws is seen almost immediately upon the Polish immigration in Wisconsin. There had been a very gradual immigration since 1855. In 1872 there was a large immigration of priests and through their influence a great impetus was given to the movement. That there was not a wholesale emigration from Prussian Poland at this time was due partly to the efforts of the government to restrain it, but more largely to the lack of funds to make the necessary journey. Most of the emigrants were young, as few men had the money to transport a large family to America, even if they had the courage at an advanced age to begin the battle of life over again in a New World.

The terms Polish colony and Polish settlement, so frequently used in regard to the Polish districts of our large cities, might indicate that the Poles came in large numbers and immediately established a Polish colony, Polish churches and schools. This has not been the case in any of the large settlements in Wisconsin. In Milwaukee the first Polish family came about 1855. It was ten years before there was a church and at that time there were only about thirty families. The growth of the Polish colony was evidently slow. Even these few Poles did not live close together. Some of them were on the West and East sides, but the location of the church at Grove and Mineral streets fixed a center around which the Polish element tended to settle. Just as among other nationalities, the tendency of the Poles to gather around this church drove others away from the vicinity, especially as it soon became necessary to speak the Polish language in order to do business in this locality.

By 1872 the old church was not large enough to hold all of the Poles, and two new ones were erected—St. Stanislaus on the corner of Grove and Mitchell, and St. Hedwig's, on the corner of Franklin and Brady, on the East side. The former is the center of the settlement of the Twelfth and Fourteenth wards; the latter of the First and Eighteenth wards. Every effort was made by the settlers to induce immigration. August Rudzinski had lithographs made of the

St. Stanislaus church which he had sent to his friends and distributed in the old country.

The process of settlement was similar in other cities. Neither in
Stevens Point nor in Berlin was there a large original settlement, and
in Marinette the Poles are so scattered that with a population of
about 500 there is no parochial school.

I have already mentioned the establishment of the two earliest
churches in Milwaukee. There are now seven Polish churches in
Milwaukee and a parochial school connected with each one. The
aggregate attendance at these parochial schools is 4,605.

Besides these parochial schools, which correspond roughly in
grade to the ward schools, there is a Polish High School for boys—
St. Josephat's High School. This school is more like a business
college than a public high school. There are 78 pupils. In Milwaukee there are very few Polish children in the public schools. This
was demonstrated last spring, during the controversy over the introduction of the study of Polish into the public schools in Polish
wards. It is noticeable that this proposition was opposed by the
priests.

Outside of Milwaukee there are a few cities which have Polish
parochial schools, Berlin, Stevens Point and Menasha having the
largest attendance. In these places very few Polish children attend
the public schools. But in places where there are no Polish parochial
schools, the children attend the public schools largely even though
there are German and English Catholic schools in the place.

In Marinette, for instance, there are 76 Polish children in the
public schools out of an estimated population of 500. This must
include nearly all of the children who attend school, as the proportion is as large as that in the parochial schools here in Milwaukee.
This would indicate that the desire to send the children to the parochial school was more a matter of nationality than of religion.

The Polanders have been Democrats both in Milwaukee and outside in the state. In Milwaukee they exercised very little influence in
politics previous to 1885. In that year they were represented in the
Common Council by Theodore Rudzinski and succeeded in electing
Peter Sytowski supervisor. Both of these men were on the Democratic ticket and from the Twelfth Ward, which was largely Polish.
In the spring of 1886 occurred the riots in which the Poles were
active. This caused a breach between the Poles and the Democratic

party, especially as John Black, who had been foreman of the jury which indicted the leaders in the riot, became the Democratic candidate for congressman in the fall of 1886.

The Poles bolted and joined the People's party, which nominated Henry Smith for Congress. The district had previously been Democratic, but so great was the loss by this bolt that the Democrats came out third in the race. The vote was as follows: Henry Smith, People's, 13,272; Thos. H. Brown, Rep., 9,754; John Black, Dem., 8,300. In the state election, also, the People's party was successful and elected Theodore Rudzinski to the assembly, leaving the Democrats third in the race. Rudzinski was the first Pole elected to the State Legislature. The Poles also succeeded in electing in the county John Czerwinski as coroner. In the city election in 1887 the Democrats and the Republicans fused and put up a Citizens' ticket, which was elected. The Poles succeeded in electing an alderman on the People's ticket, Stanislaus Hanizeski in the Fourteenth Ward. Peter Pawinski in the Twelfth Ward was defeated by the Citizens' ticket. In 1888 the Democrats and the Republicans again united and elected their city ticket. In the Fourteenth Ward the Poles were again successful and elected Michael Huntowski as alderman and Stanislaus Hanizeski as supervisor. In the Eighteenth Ward, also, a Pole was elected, John Weiher. In the fall election of 1888 there were three county tickets—Republican, Democratic and Labor party. In the two last the Poles were given places, but the Republican ticket was elected. There was a Democratic Labor fusion ticket for Congress with Henry Smith again as candidate, but he was defeated. E. J. Slupecki was elected to the Assembly on the Democratic ticket. The importance attached to the Polish vote is shown by the fact that Rudzinski was put on the ticket for register of deeds, an office worth at that time $30,000 per annum.

In 1889 the Poles elected aldermen and supervisors for the Twelfth, Fourteenth and Eighteenth Wards. In 1890 they again elected three aldermen and comptroller. In the fall election Michael Kruszka was elected to the assembly on the Democratic ticket. Ignatz Czerwinski was elected clerk of the courts.

F. J. Borchardt, the captain of the Kosciusko Guards at the time of the riots, who had been so severely boycotted in 1886, seems to have regained the goodwill of his countrymen, as he is elected justice of the peace.

In 1892 Michael Kruszka was elected to the State Senate—the first Pole to sit in that body. Michael Blenski was elected to the Assembly. He became famous by supporting Bragg for United States Senator to the bitter end when the rest of the Milwaukee delegation had gone over to Mitchell. Out of gratitude for this, Gen. Bragg secured Blenski a position in the civil service at Washington. In 1894 the Poles attempted to get C. J. M. Malek on the state ticket for insurance commissioner, but failed to do so. He was placated, however, by a place in the state land office.

Enough has been said to show how the Poles have been working into a place of influence that necessitates their recognition on county and city tickets by the Democratic party. Undoubtedly the riots of 1886 and the bolt which followed were of service to them in showing them their strength and demonstrating to the Democratic party the necessity of obtaining the Polish vote if they wished to win in city and county elections. They are now—1896—represented by five aldermen, three school commissioners, two members of the County Board, one assemblyman and a state senator. Another recognition of the Polish element is the fact that the state laws and city ordinances are published in Polish since 1891, *The Kuryer Polski* being the official organ.

. . . .

The large majority of Poles are common laborers. They are employed in the factories and upon the streets. In every large Polish settlement there are Polish shopkeepers of all kinds. The majority of them are in the cities, but these are forming communities in the vicinity of all of the larger settlements. Their industry and thrift are evidenced by the fact that a large number of Polish workmen in Milwaukee own their homes, although their wages are less than $1.50 a day.

Italians in Milwaukee

ALBERTO C. MELONI

Gastronomically speaking, the early Milwaukee Italians did not parallel the popular picture of a Roman feast bedecked with innumerable main courses, all stoically savored by Nero-type gluttons. A

From Alberto C. Meloni, "Italy Invades the Bloody Third: The Early History of Milwaukee's Italians," *Historical Messenger,* XXV,1 (March 1969), 34–46. Footnotes in the original omitted. Reprinted by permission of the Milwaukee County Historical Society.

typical Third Ward dinner consisted of macaroni with tomatoes or soup with vegetables. Once or twice a week, meat and potatoes may have been eaten with an occasional green smothered in vinegar and oil. Here in Milwaukee, beer became a substitute for the usual wine consumed at all Italian meals, but the immortal fame of the ward's "Dago Red" attests to the fact that much of the liquid must have been mysteriously bountiful. Thus, the typical Italian family numbering eight spent $7.13 a week for groceries. All purchasing was done at the one or two Italian stores often poorly equipped and miserably unhygenic [sic]. But the familiarity of language and the easy extension of credit were two alluring features irresistible to Italian housewives.

Whatever the dietary habits of Milwaukee's Italians might have been, they gained an early reputation in Milwaukee's Third Ward for having a cooking odor all of their own. A Milwaukeean described the situation as follows:

> The corner grocery and the saloon lend their odors to the mingled smells that float from many kitchens where strange dishes of which garlic is a component part are being prepared. The odor is unclassifiable and defies definitions, but it is all persuasive and is a characteristic of the quarter that one remembers long after one has passed into less odoriferous regions.

In view of the surroundings in which he lived, the conditions under which he survived and the food with which he sustained himself, it is understandable why Milwaukeeans feared the new waves of Italians principally because of disease and crime.

Tuberculosis, pneumonia and rheumatism were the chief sicknesses overcoming the Italians in the city. Statistically, however, in contracting the three diseases, Italians were outnumbered by all other immigrant groups as well as all of the native population. The most frequent causes of ill health among the Italians were: the difference between Milwaukee climatic variances and the steady Mediterranean type weather to which the Sicilian was accustomed, occupational hazards of exposure to dusts, poisonous fumes, excessive humidity and heat, frequent periods of idleness from employment which necessitated deficient diets and excessive overcrowding. Sick Italians never proved to be a burden upon the community since they either quickly left for Italy or most often refused to attend American hospitals but rather cured themselves at home.

The romance and adventure of such figments of the imagination as the Mafia, the Camorra, and the Black Hand were just too tempting for either the Milwaukeean or even the Italian to resist exploiting. In 1897 after an Italian crime in the Third Ward, Milwaukee logically surmised that the area was a center for Black Hand and Mafia activity. Since both organizations were bred in Sicily, and since Third Warders were mostly Sicilians, it seemed to naturally follow that all members of the ward were Mafiosi. For years, everyone tip-toed about the Italian district whispering, constantly glancing behind their backs, and fearing to open their mail or strange packages delivered by strange black-coated violinists. It can be safely estimated that at some time between 1900 and 1910 all Italians and many Americans in Milwaukee received a letter bearing the Black Hand daggers crossed upon writing demanding insurance money. The majority of these were only childish pranks perpetrated by playful Italians in the hope of benefitting from the mass hysteria. The few notes which were genuine were never traced to any set organized body; and to this day, any such tracings remain only wild and imaginative speculations. It became safe to assume that Milwaukee during the early years of Italian settlement was not a center of any large scale Mafia or Black Hand organization. If any representative dwelled in the city, he was solely one isolated individual.

By 1902 Milwaukeeans began to understand that organizations like the Mafia arose only because people could no longer trust their own government for protection. The realistic and logical remedy for the Mafia seemed to be a series of legal and social reforms as well as a hope of economic betterment. The *Sentinel* understood the Mafia to be "a noxious plant bred of local conditions, and will not bear transplanting to the generous soil and free atmosphere of America." Perhaps this was not to be true in all of the United States, but Milwaukee was left relatively free from any such evil. Finally, one must always remember that when alone, unwanted, and oppressed it became a convenience for the poor Italian to claim a membership in one of these fictitious organizations. Yet, these innocents were as much overcome by the mystery and romance as were all other Milwaukeeans.

Milwaukee's Italians were often jailed for carrying concealed weapons or for violating a city ordinance. The former offense was a carry over from the days of brigandage in Southern Italy while the latter was a mere lack of knowledge. Concerning all other crimes, ample evidence exists depicting the Italian to be as law abiding as any other member of the city. And as far as cases of abandonment, drunkenness and prostitution, Italians were even more law abiding.

If not the Mafia or the Black Hand, there were certain organizations to which the Italians of Milwaukee most assuredly belonged. These were the mutual benefit secret societies named as follows: Liberta Siciliana, Vespri Siciliani, Cristoforo Colombo, Galileo

Galilei, Vittorio Emanuele III, San Giuseppe, Madonna Del Lume, Santa Croce, Garibaldi, Naso-Capo D'Orlando, Trinacria, Duca Degli Abbruzzi, Tripoli Italiana, Fratellanza Toscana, and Madonna Di Custonai. Each contained from fifty to 100 members, all of whom paid approximately an individual $15.00 a year fee. The members were usually from the same province or in some cases from the same village, such as those of Santa Croce, all emanating from Santo Stefano Camastra in Sicily.

These societies served much the same purpose as did insurance companies. After the first three days of sickness, a member would receive $1.00 a day for three months. If ill health persisted, he would receive 50c for an additional three months. Funeral expenses were taken care of by the organization, and $2.00 were collected from each living member for the benefits of the decedent's family. However, payments were never issued when sicknesses was a result of crime or wounds gained in illegal fighting. When a member had failed to pay dues for three continuous months or had contracted venereal diseases, he was also refused aid. Though usually working towards a good, these societies sometimes prevented the various members of the numerous Sicilian villages represented from ever uniting into a solid and effective Italian colony.

Politically, the Italians, following much the same pattern of all ghetto immigrants, were solid Democrats.

Greeks in Milwaukee

THEODORE SALOUTOS

The settling of Greeks in Milwaukee is part of the broader picture of Greeks settling in the United States, and their establishment in a city of a predominantly German population, if anything, displayed a willingness and an ability on their part to root themselves in a community far different from what they had known at home and to commingle with people of diverse ethnic and cultural origins. Arriving in small numbers after the opening of the twentieth century, and

From Theodore Saloutos, "The Greeks of Milwaukee," *Wisconsin Magazine of History*, LIII,3 (Spring 1970), 175–193. Footnotes in the original omitted. Reprinted by permission of the State Historical Society of Wisconsin.

especially after 1905, they chose to locate themselves in the urbanized areas of Wisconsin's lakeshore district. Small colonies emerged in Sheboygan, which in the early years boasted of the largest Greek population in the state, Milwaukee, Kenosha and Racine; still others found themselves in Waukesha, Fond du Lac, Oshkosh, Green Bay, Madison, and La Crosse. But the largest and most permanently rooted Greek colony in Wisconsin was that in Milwaukee.

In part the reasons for coming to Milwaukee are traceable to the general causes of emigrating from Greece and arriving in the United States. They were primarily economic, for political and religious oppression—except among the Greeks living in the Ottoman Empire—was almost unknown in Greece. The Greek immigrants more or less were pushed out of their native land by the niggardliness of her soil, the periodic crop failures, the lack of opportunities, and a stratified class structure that made it difficult, if not impossible, for them to escape from its repressive clutches. Some naturally sought to escape from military service, a practice known to people of many lands, and also a practice that the more patriotic Greeks would deny vehemently.

Greeks were attracted to Milwaukee by the opportunities it offered. The demand for skilled labor was great, and unfamiliarity with the English language hardly was an obstacle in a land which needed men with strong backs and strong arms. There was no waiting as in Greece for the annual harvest that often brought a small crop. Here a man worked for wages in the factory, a store or an industrial plant; the pay, relatively speaking, was high and he received it at the end of the week and sometimes at the end of the day. The opportunity for saving money by retaining Old World living standards and receiving New World wages could be seized upon, and many a Greek with the cost of passage, courage, and determination seized the chance to capitalize on these prospects.

· ·

Once a small nucleus established itself in the city, relatives and friends from the same or nearby villages joined them. As a rule, the newcomers planned their voyage with greater care than frequently was realized. Some came direct from their home villages to brothers, sisters, cousins, uncles, aunts, fathers, and friends. Others came to Milwaukee after working and living temporarily in other cities, being encouraged to come by the desire to be near friends and relatives or by the job opportunities. The arrival of one or two from the Tripolis-Megalopolis area, for instance, triggered the arrival of still others, especially after it had become known their relatives or friends were established in the city. A Greek description of Milwaukee in 1910 referred to it as "a large city, beautiful, commercial and industrial . . . the acropolis of the socialists . . ." whose people spoke the language of the Kaiser and drank beer.

Statistics on the number who came to the city are fragmentary and must be viewed with caution. In 1906 a special committee of the Greek Chamber of Deputies placed the number of Greeks in Sheboygan, a furniture-making center, at 410 and in Milwaukee at 314. Another report by a Greek Ministry stated that in 1900 the state of Wisconsin had a Greek population of sixty-three and in 1910 of 2,810, while the City of Milwaukee had twenty-six and 1,122 respectively in the same years. In all probability the Greek population of Milwaukee, at its peak, never exceeded 4,000 to 5,000.

The tanneries which furnished employment for many of the early Greeks were built, owned, and operated by members of pioneer German families such as Guido Pfister, Frederick P. Vogel, August T. Gallun, and Albert O. Troestel. These men early had gauged the potential of Milwaukee as a tanning center and helped convert it into one of the prominent industries of the city and nation. In 1916 the manufacturer of leather, an end product of tanning, ranked third in the economic life of Milwaukee. Only iron, steel and heavy machinery, and packed meats ranked ahead of it; leather-making even was more important than beer, which mistakenly was assumed to be the principal staple of the city.

The tanneries offered jobs the Greeks could perform with a minimum knowledge of English and experience. The first ethnics employed in the tanneries were Germans; then came the Irish, a few Englishmen and Scotsmen, with the Germans predominating. By 1910 about eighteen nationalities were working in the tanneries, including Poles (with whom the Greeks were at odds in the beginning), Russians, Italians, Croatians, Slovaks, and Lithuanians; the Greeks who were employed in the industry in 1898–1899 were among the last to be hired.

Just what precisely attracted the Greeks to the tanneries of Milwaukee is hard to say. In all probability the availability of jobs—for jobs in the tanneries were hardly choice ones—and the tendency of those few Greeks who got jobs there to pull in more of their compatriots perhaps explains their presence. A number of Milwaukee's Greek pioneers can be counted among the alumni of her tanneries. William Helis, who later achieved fame and fortune as an oil magnate, horse breeder, and racetrack owner elsewhere, once was an employee of a Milwaukee tannery.

Other Greeks found jobs in iron and steel mills; restaurants and hotels as waiters, dishwashers, and handymen; shoeshining parlors and hat-cleaning establishments; factories and industrial plants of various kinds; and on railroad construction gangs. Their lack of technical skills, formal education, and professional training facilitated rather than handicapped their occupational adjustment. For what was required was not culture and refinement but physical endurance, patience, reliability, and a willingness to work hard at any available labor. The Greek immigrant would have been lost without these qualities.

2: The Liquor Control Question

One of the major issues that disturbed some of the ethnic voters in the state was the question of liquor control. Some saw the matter as an attempt by Yankee elements to bridle the social habits of the Germans. Between 1872 and 1874 the focus of the issue was the Graham Law, passed by the legislature in 1872. The first selection below recounts the state's experiences with that law. After 1874, the temperance movement was not supported directly by either of the two major parties, but it continued to make its presence felt, as indicated in the second selection.

The Graham Law

HERMAN J. DEUTSCH

The movement for the curtailing of the liquor traffic was sponsored by the Good Templar Lodge, whose first chapter in Wisconsin was organized at Sheboygan Falls in 1855. It varied in strength but at one time was said to constitute 500 lodges and 20,000 members. Naturally it was a force with which Badger politicians had to reckon, especially at times of close contests, also because sporadic attempts were made by Templars to create separate political organizations who, with their third ticket, might upset the equilibrium in state politics.

From Herman J. Deutsch, "Yankee-Teuton Rivalry in Wisconsin Politics of the Seventies," *Wisconsin Magazine of History*, XIV (1930–1931), 262–282. Footnotes in original omitted. Reprinted by permission of the State Historical Society of Wisconsin.

The sixties were quiet from the standpoint of temperance propaganda, possibly because of the Civil War and its aftermath, but
towards the end of the decade agitation was renewed. In his message of 1872, Governor Washburn recommended the subject of
liquor control to the legislature for its serious consideration. The
response was a bill introduced by the gentleman from Rock County,
Alexander Graham, by whose name the bill was henceforth known.
Significant among its provisions were: the requirement of a bond of
$2,000 as a deposit for the issue of a license to sell liquor; a civil
damage clause with a large list of eligible claimants; and a heavy
penalty for drunkenness. These provisions, together with iron-clad
safeguards against circumvention, made the bill a rigorous measure.

. . . .

More effective in determining the legal force of the law than
speeches or resolutions was a test case resulting from the peculiar
enforcement program of the officials of the city of Milwaukee. Har-
rison Ludington, mayor, in May, 1873, requested of city attorney,
Emil Wallber, an opinion as to the bearing of the Graham Law
upon that clause in the charter of the city of Milwaukee which
delegated to the common council the right to grant licenses and to
regulate the sale of liquor. The gist of the attorney's opinion was
that the Graham Law was unconstitutional and that in regranting
licenses, which had expired April 30, the mayor should follow provisions of the city ordinance. Thereupon, the executive issued permits to saloon keepers without requiring the bond prescribed by the
recent state law. The city council was evidently in full sympathy
with Ludington's program since it refused to restrain the mayor and
ordered Wallber's opinion printed.

. . . .

A trial case was had, and Chief Justice Dixon, upholding the law,
declared any license issued in contravention to it to be null and void.
The forces of law and order had won their point, but Ludington
also scored when the court refused to issue a writ of mandamus
restraining him from issuing permits; for, the judge held, it would
be useless to restrain the mayor since his permits had obviously no
legal force. As the later Chief Justice of the State Supreme Court, E.
G. Ryan, who had anticipated such a decision remarked, a munici-
pality had been permitted to assume sovereign powers and had set
itself in defiance against a state law for a period of months without
suffering rebuke by the courts. Ludington not only escaped judical
[sic] discipline but saw his prestige actually enhanced to the extent
that, when the Republicans were searching for a likely candidate for

governor, in the contest of 1875, they hit upon the mayor who had won the favor of Milwaukee Germans.

· ·

Much as the temperance question stirred the political atmosphere in 1873, it did not become the paramount issue of the campaign. The question of railroad control by the state was more conspicuous and probably of greater importance. The Republican platform made no mention of the liquor issue and the clause in the platform of the Reform party which was composed of Democrats, leaders in agricultural politics, and anti-temperance men, was far from outspoken on the subject. Curious also was the fact that Taylor, who contested Governor Washburn's reëlection was a member of the Good Templars. Though not the most agitated issue, the liquor contest was probably the determining one; for an analysis of the voters of 1872 and 1873 shows clearly that the disaffection from the Republican party was greatest in the cities, especially those with a large German population, not in the rural districts where one would expect the railroad issues to have had the greatest effect.

· ·

The experiences of the years 1872 and 1874 were sufficient to deter either of the major parties from again waging war on demon rum. Agitation among the Germans had died down and in the late seventies the Republicans who had formerly leaned toward the native element discovered that the German vote could be won on questions which did not directly concern national prejudices, namely, that of honest money. When the temperance men discovered that they could no longer expect support from their former ally, they decided to form a separate organization which would act for itself at least in local elections. Had the balance of power between the two major parties not been so slight, the separatest [sic] movement would have been of little consequence, for the tendency of temperance folk was to vote the old party ticket. In this respect they were unlike most antitemperance folk who showed little compunction about breaking old party ties when their party took an unfavorable stand on the liquor question. Fully cognizant of this peculiarity among their kind, leaders among the Good Templars decided, nevertheless, that since the old parties were competing for the liquor vote, an independent organization remained their only weapon. This decision was not made without protests; many felt that the Republican party even though not committed in their favor, was preferable to the Democratic. "It seems that when temperance is in, brains are out, just as when whisky is in," concluded one politician, otherwise sympathetic with the anti-liquor crusaders. Local politicians in strong temperance communities were especially frightened. "For God's sake, put a stop to it [separate temperance ticket]. Cold water cannot win this fall," cried one of them. Despite all, however, separate state tickets were put into the field in 1875, 1877, 1879. The votes polled were negligible, but these tactics helped to sustain interest in the question and bore some fruit. In 1878, a joint resolution to amend the constitution by an article providing for the total prohibition of the sale of liquor in the state was lost by one vote in the senate, and in the two following years certain minor regulatory measures were put on the statute books: one dealt with the sale of liquor to spendthrifts; the other punished treating.

Convinced that the older parties were "appealing to the cupidity of the weakest and basest elements of society," the temperance folk in 1881 decided upon a distinct party organization and not to rely only upon a separate party ticket. The result was an appreciable cut in the Republican vote, but the Prohibition party never achieved the position even of a group of irreconcilables wielding the balance of power between the old parties.

The peculiar character of the controversy over liquor control in Wisconsin during the seventies was undoubtedly due to the reaction of Germans toward the place of alcoholic beverages in social life.

Temperance in Milwaukee

DANIEL F. RING

In many ways, the temperance movement spilled over into Milwaukee politics, precipitating quarrels among the leading politicos which at times assumed the characteristics of a battle between the "blue-nosed puritan" and the libertine.

The "blue-nosed" element was led by John Stowell, a businessman turned politician. Stowell came to the mayor's office in

From Daniel F. Ring, "The Temperance Movement in Milwaukee: 1872–1884," *Historical Messenger*, XXXI (Winter 1975), 98–105. Footnotes in the original omitted. Reprinted by permission of the Milwaukee County Historical Society.

1881 largely through the support of the working classes, and his views on drink are therefore somewhat of an anomaly. Like those in the Women's Christian Temperance Union, he visited the homes of people arrested for public drunkenness, admonishing them of the dangers of alcohol. As a public official, he took a strong stand on the issue of licensing saloons which he felt were detrimental to public order.

The city charter vested the common council with the power to license saloons, but under certain ordinances the mayor possessed the power to issue and revoke licenses. Soon after assuming office, Mayor John Stowell refused to issue licenses to certain saloons which he felt were nuisances. Possession of a license, he believed, was not a legal right but a discretionary privilege resting with the mayor. Stowell further recommended the passage of an ordinance that would define what activities could be permitted in saloons. All amusement devices that would induce men to stay longer than necessary would be forbidden. The ordinance would also include a provision that saloons close at a "seasonable hour" [sic] or that the maximum $200 license fee be paid by "all night saloons," which Stowell felt were the causes of crime and pauperism. Small wonder that the *Evening Wisconsin* said he was acting more like a "republican moralist" than a Democratic mayor.

Alderman William J. Brisby countered Stowell's revocation of licenses with a proposal that would take the power of issuing saloon licenses away from the mayor and place it with the common council's committee on licenses. The committee on licenses added that Stowell's proposed ordinance was " dictated more in the interest of temperance fanatics than by a desire to benefit the city."

Stowell was not opposed to Brisby's proposal as such. The mayor advised the council that he would support the proposal if the committee that reviewed licenses were composed of men with "broad views," but he feared that the bill was "special legislation" in the interest of a few individuals. He further threatened to resign unless he was supported by what he called the "better class" of people and if the ordinance were passed. While Brisby's proposal was indefinitely postponed, the common council made another effort to obtain for itself the power of granting and revoking licenses.

In this second venture, the common council's standard was carried by the adroit John Hinsey, a shrewd politician who opposed not only license reform but almost all types of reform. Hinsey was not nicknamed "Boss" for nothing. His ordinance, which was accepted by the council, provided that an applicant apply to the mayor for a license, with the mayor having the power to grant or refuse it; if the mayor refused, an appeal could be made to the common council which by a majority vote, would have the final decision. The same procedure followed if a mayor revoked a license. In a caustic interview with the *Journal*, Hinsey said that the motive behind his ordinance was to "protect everybody's interest in the matter of granting licenses." Since Hinsey later became a member of the Wisconsin Protective Association, an anti-prohibition organization, it is likely that he believed Stowell's moves were in the direction of temperance or prohibition.

Stowell vetoed the ordinance because he objected to the precedent it would establish in giving the common council the right to supervise the actions of the mayor. He also disliked that portion of the Hinsey ordinance which allowed a majority vote to override the mayor's decisions because it reduced the executive office to a "nonentity." Stowell based much of his argument on the police power given to the mayor in the charter. The mayor concluded his message by stating that the veto was not the abridgement of a right but the "defining of the limitations of a privilege."

Stowell's veto was overridden by the council, and his legal arguments were overturned by the courts. In *Miller v. Holtz,* Judge Mallory decided that the defendants must be given hearings before a license could be revoked; licenses could not be revoked without sufficient cause; only the common council could issue licenses, and it could not delegate that power to the mayor. In *Wagner v. Stowell and Watson,* Circuit Judge Charles A. Hamilton also held that the council alone had the right to grant and revoke licenses. In the light of these decisions, Stowell refused to issue any more licenses.

The courts' decisions did not represent a strategic loss for the "better element" of Milwaukee's citizens, but merely a tactical setback. In the years following the Stowell administration, Milwaukeeans voted overwhelmingly to double the license fee for saloons. "High license," as it was called, was intended to drive "disreputable" saloons out of business. In this respect, the influence of the temperance societies on the Citizens' League, John Stowell, and high license proponents cannot be minimized. While differing in their aspirations, the temperance followers defined the issues that other groups addressed themselves to: the relationships among liquor, poverty and crime, and between the liquor interests and city politics. The temperance advocates then were "gadflies" in that they brought the scientific, social and political implications of alcohol abuse to the attention of the public and thus produced some limitations on the liquor traffic.

3: The Failure of Railroad Regulation

The reform coalition which swept the Republicans out of office in 1873 included elements favoring strict regulation of the state's railroads. The minority Republicans, seeing that the party would lose nothing by getting in on the act, startled the opposition by sponsoring legislation even more regulatory than that introduced by the reformers. The Republican legislation, referred to as the Potter Law, was enacted by the legislature in 1874. The selections that follow deal with the passage of the legislation and the efforts of the newly created railroad commission.

The Potter Law

ROBERT T. DALAND

The legislature of Wisconsin enacted the Potter Law during the session of 1874. The law sought to regulate various railroad practices, including the rates charged. By some historians, this law has been characterized as "Granger Legislation." Others allege that it was written or supported by the railroads for the purpose of preventing the enactment of any railroad legislation at all, on the theory that the act was so extreme that it would not only fail, but would carry similar measures down with it.

. . . .

From Robert T. Daland, "Enactment of the Potter Law," *Wisconsin Magazine of History,* XXXIII,1 (Sept. 1949), 45–54. Footnotes in the original omitted. Reprinted by permission of the State Historical Society of Wisconsin.

In his first annual message to the Legislature Governor Taylor took a firm stand that railroads should be controlled. In addition he enumerated a ten-point program of railroad legislation. This included the prevention of discrimination among shippers, the classification of freight, and rates and fares which would be subject to revision and modification by state authority. The message reflected every major point of the Granger program and carried it a step farther by going into detail.

The Democratic-Reform group was not alone in advocating railroad regulation. The Republicans were even more specific in their platform which urged:

> ... the creation of a Board of Railroad Control, whose duty it shall be to examine the whole subject of transportation and freights, and report the facts in relation thereto, and prescribe and adjust such regulations as will be fair and equitable both to the people and the railway companies. ... We claim, nevertheless, the right under our constitution to regulate their conduct, or, if necessary, to repeal the charters under which they exist.

To these seemingly overwhelming pro-regulation forces, the railroads were opposed.

The Legislature of 1874 first met on January 14. The two protagonists of railroad regulation lost no time in getting their programs before the Legislature in the form of bills. A joint select committee on railroad tariff and taxation was appointed in January. This committee recommended a bill which did not specifically set rates, but which provided for maximum rates which would be those of June, 1872. On February 6 Assemblyman Francis H. West, Liberal Republican, introduced into that body a bill which defined maximum railway rates in specific terms. The select committee report had been submitted on February 17. Ten days before, another bill had been introduced into the senate by R. L. D. Potter, Republican senator from Waushara County. This was the bill which became notorious after its enactment as the "Potter Law." Authorship of the Potter bill is in doubt. One view holds that the railroads wrote the bill, making it so bad that it couldn't possibly pass, but would at the same time deadlock the Legislature so that no legislation at all would be enacted. On the other hand, it is possible that Potter sincerely favored his bill. During the spirited attack on the bill by senate Democrats, no charge that the railroads authored the Potter bill was made. In fact, Senator Burchard charged that Potter himself wrote it, and that, furthermore, Potter was a man of little experience in the affairs of railroads, which was why the bill was so bad. In reply to Senator Burchard, Potter exclaimed that in seeking information to assist in writing the bill, he had been completely rebuffed by railroad men who, said Potter, wanted no legislation on the subject at all. In light of this exchange, it appears that either Burchard was trying to get Potter to admit the influence of the railroads and Potter countered with an imaginative lie, or else Potter wrote the bill.

A comparison of the various bills on rate regulation indicates surprisingly few differences—particularly between the two major contenders, the Potter bill and the select committee bill. In both the Potter bill and in the committee bill the constitution of the railroad commission itself is identical. The West bill, provided for no commission at all.

. . . .

The select committee and West bills both provided against discrimination, while the Potter bill omitted such provisions. This is the first real difference, and, from the point of view of the farmers, a real defect in the Potter version. A second significant difference concerns the method of changing the classification of freight. Here the West bill provides no method of change. The Potter bill gives the railroad commission some independent power of classification, but bars board action on some classes of freight, notably that including grain and flour. The select committee bill goes farther and allows the commission to reclassify all freight. Thus the West bill at least protected the railroads from arbitrary action of the commissioners while it also left them no chance of applying for relief. The select committee bill allowed the commission greater powers of freight classification than did the Potter bill, presumably to the advantage of the farmer, since the railroad commission was not to include a representative of the railroads.

The third and remaining major difference between the bills concerns the rates set, and more important, the provision for modification of such rates. The select committee bill adopted as the maximum rates those of June 1872, while providing for revision by the commission subject to approval of the governor. The Potter bill specified some maximum rates, and the remainder were to be the higher rates of 1873. Here, however, the commission could reduce, but not raise the rates. Thus it can be seen that the select committee bill provided for commission action which might favor either the railroads or the farmers. On the other hand, the Potter bill commission could favor the farmer, but could not favor the railroads.

. . . .

The senate-assembly struggle as between the Potter bill and the select committee bill, then, was by no means a struggle between the forces of reform agrarianism and the vested interests of the railroads. The railroads had lost the first skirmishes of that fight before the Legislature had convened, if not even before it had been elected. The real battle was now a political one between the Republicans and what even the *Wisconsin Legislative Manual* of 1874 officially termed "the opposition," a term which referred with apparent seriousness to non-Republicans.

. . . .

When the railroad bills came before the senate for final action on February 25, the Potter bill was adopted. The debate indicated that part of the Republican vote consisted of persons who felt that the select committee bill was preferable to the others, but since it could not pass the senate for political reasons, the Potter bill should receive support. Others were voting in opposition to the Potter law. In any case, the vote divided along party lines.

On the following day the assembly passed the select committee bill by a resounding 69 to 14 majority. In this case, both the majority and the minority groups were bipartisan in nature.

In the senate-assembly contest a vital factor in the outcome was the fact that the session was rapidly drawing to a close. As it turned out, the date of adjournment was March 12, only nine days away. The railroads had cause for optimism. In neither the assembly nor in the senate had the contest been really close. A deadlock till the end of the session could be hoped for. The senate could wait longer than the assembly, since the danger of no railroad legislation at all could hardly reflect upon the opposition. But the governor, with a majority in the assembly would be discredited if no law were passed. There were pledges to live up to. The technicalities of the bill did not impress the farmer. The senate awaited the action of the assembly.

. . . .

On March 5 the senate voted to substitute the Potter bill for the assembly bill. But now, half of the senate Democrats broke from their party to accept the Republican sponsored bill.

In the assembly, sentiment was slowly growing that the railroads were a greater menace than the Republicans. Primary necessity called for the certain enactment of some legislation to control railroads. There appeared in the assembly, in no less person than Speaker Bouck, the attitude that the Potter bill was the best bill that could be gotten. The assembly concurred in the Potter Law.

Ardent reformers fought on, however. Another caucus was held invoking party discipline, and the next day concurrence was withdrawn. The senate again refused to stall. It immediately took up the

Potter bill, amended it in one minor point, and returned it to the assembly. The session had only five days more to run. Clearly, now, it was the Potter Law or no law at all. The assembly concurred in the bill, and on March 12 the act became law with the signature of Governor Taylor.

What is the significance that we can attach to the events just described? (1) It is clear that the majority in both houses of the Legislature, as well as the majority in both major political parties, sought the passing of railroad regulation legislation.

(2) The Potter Law was not a piece of "Granger" legislation, having been enacted as a result of the Republican battle against reform-Democratic forces. Yet to say the law would have been enacted even if there had been no Granger agitation during the 1873 electoral campaign, would be unjustified.

(3) There is no proof of authorship of the Potter Law. While some evidence suggests a partisan Republican origin, a letter to the Republican "Boss" Keyes suggests at least the possibility of a railroad origin.

(4) The attitude of the railroads, once the Potter bill was introduced, can be clarified. The director of the railroad lobby was H. L. Palmer of Milwaukee. His leading lobbyist at Madison was George B. Smith, an attorney for the Chicago and North Western Railroad Company. When the debate on the railroad bills was in its earliest stages, Palmer wrote Smith a revealing letter. Palmer implied that although the original hope had been that the assembly would reject the Potter Law, and thereby all legislation, this now appeared unlikely. Perhaps it would be better to attempt improvement of the law itself, through senate amendments, in case it might be passed.

This new strategy of the railroads can be reconstructed with the benefit of hindsight. In 1873 the railroads had no alliance with either of the two dominant political parties. During the legislative session of 1874 the necessity to form an alliance with one party against the other became apparent. This alliance was made with the Republicans, but not because the Republican sponsored Potter bill was radically worse than the reform-Democrat bill. The reason should rather be sought in the fact that the Republicans had little to lose should no bill be passed, while the Reform Party, as long as it should remain in power, was firmly committed to railroad regulation. This was in no small measure due to the events of the fall of 1873 when the Grangers "threw their hat in the ring" by joining with the Democratic Party. Both party platforms of 1873 presented the same policy of railroad regulation—but the Democrats were allied with the militant Grangers.

The new alliance between the railroads and the Republicans

worked well. Having cooperated with them in calling off the fight against the Potter Law, the railroads were repaid two years later when, in 1876, the newly elected Legislature, again dominated by Republicans in both houses, repealed the Potter Law.

The First Railroad Commission

WILLIAM L. BURTON

As for the pertinent features of the Potter Law itself, they may be summarized under the following areas:

1. Railroads in the state were divided into three classes. Class A included the Chicago, Milwaukee, and St. Paul Railroad, the Chicago and North Western Railroad, and the Western Union Railroad; class B included the Wisconsin Central, the Green Bay and Minnesota, and the West Wisconsin; class C included all other roads.
2. Passenger rates were set for each class, ranging from three cents per mile for class A to four cents per mile for class C.
3. Freight rates were established for each of several different classifications of freight.
4. Justices of the Peace were given legal jurisdiction to enforce the law, with power to impose fines on violators.
5. A Commission of three men was given the power to ascertain railroad construction costs, net earnings, classify freight and rates, and require lengthy reports from each of the railroads in the state.

. . . .

At the very moment the new commission came into existence the major railroads in Wisconsin were embarking upon a deliberate plan to violate the Potter Law. Their object was to check both the determination of the state to enforce the law and the constitutionality of the statute. The Milwaukee Road fired the first shot of the

From William L. Burton, "Wisconsin's First Railroad Commission: A Case Study in Apostasy," *Wisconsin Magazine of History*, XLV,3 (Spring 1962), 190-198. Footnotes in the original omitted. Reprinted by permission of the State Historical Society of Wisconsin.

campaign when it published a new schedule of fares, higher than those permitted under the Potter Law, on the day before the law went into effect. The first official act of the three commissioners was the publication of legal passenger and freight fares. Thus the battle was joined. Governor Taylor threw his support behind the commissioners and the law with a blistering attack upon the two major roads. Taylor informed the railroad executives that in ordering their agents to collect illegal fares they were forcing the agents into acts of criminal disobedience. The railroad presidents, declared Taylor, ". . . have set up another law than that of the state." Public opinion, as measured by the state's newspapers, was solidly behind the Governor and against the deliberate disobedience of the railroads. Since the railroads could not be prosecuted until complaints were lodged by citizens against specific violations of the law, Governor Taylor urged citizens to make complaints, and forms printed for that purpose were given wide distribution.

It did not take long for the struggle to reach the courts. Railroad practice called for passengers paying the legal maximum fare to be forcibly expelled from a train if they refused to pay the railroad's own fare. A Jesse Hinkley, seventy-three, of Fond du Lac, after having been thrown off a Milwaukee train for refusing to pay more than the legal fare, signed a complaint and lodged a suit against the railroad for $25,000. Before long, suits were filed against agents throughout Wisconsin. A test case decided in the Madison Municipal Court found an agent guilty of selling a ticket at a price above the legal fare, thus setting the pattern for lower court decisions all over the state. Railroads counterattacked by refusing to let trains stop at any station where an agent had been convicted of violating the Potter Law. At the same time, the two principal railroads made plans to check the constitutionality of the law in the state Supreme Court.

At this time of crisis, Luther S. Dixon, Chief Justice of the Supreme Court, retired. Governor Taylor was gravely concerned over the replacement. To meet the "irrepressible conflict" that was at hand, the Governor felt that the primary qualification for the office would be the right attitude toward the constitutionality of the Potter Law. Before he appointed Elisha G. Ryan to fill the vacancy, Governor Taylor ascertained Ryan's opinion on the railroad question. The eventual appointment of Ryan virtually guaranteed victory to the state in the subsequent court battle.

. . . .

In the Wisconsin courts the railroads relied heavily on the Dartmouth College Case as a basis for their claim that the Potter

Law violated the sanctity of a contract; railroad attorneys also insisted that the law confiscated private property without just compensation and without due process. But court decisions consistently went against the roads. After their defeat in the municipal courts the railroads went to a circuit court, where again they met judges favorable to the law. Finally, on September 15, 1874, the Supreme Court of Wisconsin gave its verdict. A large crowd of interested spectators, including the Governor, heard the new Chief Justice read through a forty-page judgment fully sustaining the Potter Law. The administration had won a complete victory over the railroads, whose stock promptly dropped several points in the market.

. . . .

Commissioners Osborn, Paul, and Hoyt found their job far from easy. Being pioneers in the field, they had to feel their way through many a legal and procedural snarl with little or no precedent to guide them. To add to the many difficulties of coping with the normal tribulations of such a position, the three commissioners found themselves with two additional foes to face—their own doubts about the Potter Law and the commission idea, and state politics. Each of the three commissioners had doubts and reservations about his own position. All three men believed that the law had deficiencies and they labored for its revision or repeal. The correspondence of the three commissioners—and they appear to have been quite frank in their letters to each other—reveals the extent of their discontent with the Potter Law.

Then, too, as the November elections drew closer the commissioners dropped all official business and turned to campaign work. The three men circulated campaign literature, while Commissioner Paul, who was chairman of the State Democratic Committee, was responsible for organizing and directing party activities. Since no state administrative offices were at stake, both parties concentrated their attention on the Potter Law, which was a major campaign issue. The Republican Party, basing its fight on support of the Potter Law, won the election. State Senator Potter was re-elected, and the head of the Democratic Party admitted that the law's popularity was responsible for his party's defeat. Results of the 1874 election indicate that the voters of Wisconsin were solidly in favor of the Potter Law.

What happened next is the most surprising link in the whole chain of events. The Republican-controlled legislature of 1875 promptly examined the Potter Law and began a series of amendments that left the commission unchanged but altered the rates in favor of the railroads. In part, at least, these changes were the result of the work of the three commissioners themselves. Commissioner Paul, whose Milwaukee newspaper consistently and vehemently attacked the whole commission idea, had some peculiar conceptions of the position he held. In a letter to President Mitchell of the Milwaukee Road, Paul expressed his personal opinion on the eve of the new legislative year. "It gives me great pleasure to assure you," he wrote, "that the Governor and at least two of the commissioners (Osborn and Paul) favor great alterations in railroad legislation the present winter, and that a fair compromise of sentiment, based upon justice and reason, is not impossible. Much is due to the conciliatory disposition manifested by you for whatever is accomplished in this direction." Some of Paul's friendly attitude toward the roads may have been based on favors extended to him and his family by the railroad managers. Despite a law to the contrary, the Paul family received free passes on the railroads.

As a result of their experience and investigations the commissioners lost faith in the original Potter Law and commission structure. From control of the railroads in the interests of Wisconsin farmers and lumbermen, the attitude of the commission changed to the promotion of fares high enough to assure a fair return to investors in railroad stocks. The commissioners' report for 1875 condemned the Potter Law and recommended a return to more conservative practices.

And that is precisely what happened. The Republican legislature of 1876 promptly attacked the Potter Law and completely emasculated it. The old rate schedules were discarded and the regulatory commission was stripped of virtually all its powers and reduced to one elected official. The experiment with reform had ended; thenceforth for several decades the Wisconsin Railroad Commission played only a minor role in state politics.

4: The Bennett Law: Ethnic Voters and the Election of 1890

For only the second time since the end of the Civil War, Wisconsin's Republicans were voted out of office in 1890 by a wave of protest centered almost entirely among the state's ethnic voters. Angered over passage of the Bennett Law in 1889 and Governor Hoard's defense of the law in the campaign of 1890, German voters, both Catholic and non-Catholic, gave their support to the Democrats because of that party's stand in opposition to the hated school law. Scandinavian voters, traditionally Republican, faced the election with mixed emotions and, as a result, voted in smaller numbers than before. As the following selection suggests, the decisions of German and Scandinavian voters swung the election to the Democrats.

The Election of 1890

ROGER E. WYMAN

The Bennett Law controversy of 1889–1890 was one of the most exciting chapters in Wisconsin's colorful political history. The furor over this law, a seemingly innocuous child labor and compulsory education act which also stipulated that certain subjects had to be taught in the English language, created a brief but major upheaval in Wisconsin politics, and the debris left in its wake cast a shadow over the political life of the state for a decade.

From Roger E. Wyman, "Wisconsin Ethnic Groups and the Election of 1890," *Wisconsin Magazine of History*, LI,4 (Summer 1968), 269–293. Footnotes in the original omitted. Reprinted by permission of the State Historical Society of Wisconsin.

The ethnic and religious antagonisms that the Bennett Law aroused were the bitterest ever experienced in Wisconsin. Defenders of the law asserted that it was necessary for the preservation of the public school system, but Germans saw it as an attempt by Americanizing Yankees to extinguish the German language in the United States; Catholics and Lutherans viewed it as a direct threat to their system of parochial education. As a result, in the election of 1890, a unified German and Catholic vote handed the Wisconsin Republican party its worst defeat until 1932; and in 1892 the lingering emotions among the law's opponents enabled a Democratic presidential candidate to carry the state for the first time since 1852.

. . . .

In light of the furor it created, it is ironic that the Bennett Law passed virtually unnoticed through the 1889 legislature. Republican Governor William D. Hoard had advocated a compulsory education law in his inaugural address, and the subsequent bill, introduced by young Iowa County assemblyman Michael J. Bennett, passed through the legislature without debate. The law was enacted on April 17, at the end of the session, and signed by Governor Hoard the following day. It required compulsory attendance for each child of school age in "some public or private day school in the city, town or district in which he resides" for at least twelve weeks. The heart of the law, in the eyes of its opponents, was section five:

> No school shall be regarded as a school, under this act, unless there shall be taught therein, as part of the elementary education of children, reading, writing, arithmetic and United States history, in the English language.

The last four words—"in the English language"—ignited the political explosion which followed.

Concerted opposition to the Bennett Law did not develop for several months. In June, 1889, three German Protestant bodies denounced the law as an attack upon German churches, schools, and language, but the undercurrent of opposition remained below the surface until early in 1890. The Republican *Milwaukee Sentinel* was largely responsible for fomenting much of the bitterness of the ensuing battle. It undertook an aggressive and belligerent campaign to defend the law as necessary for the preservation of the common school system and the speedier assimilation of all immigrants. It wrapped the law in a mantle of Americanism and patriotism, belittling the opponents of the law as enemies of the public schools, narrow-minded clerics, or self-seeking politicians. Day after day the *Sentinel* filled its editorial pages with defenses of the law, strongly worded attacks on its opponents, and exposés of American-born adults who could not speak, read, or write English.

The *Sentinel's* intransigence made it impossible to keep the issue out of the spring municipal elections. In Milwaukee, anti-Bennett Law clubs were formed in several wards; individual German Lutheran parishes established their own political organizations. Three weeks before the April 1 election the state's three German-born Catholic bishops, who had been content to let the Lutherans lead the assault, entered the fray. They issued a Bishops' Manifesto which contended that the real object of the law was to bring parochial schools under state regulation and ultimately to destroy the parochial school system altogether. They denounced the law as unnecessary, offensive, and unjust, and advocated the support of candidates who favored its repeal.

In an atmosphere of such agitation, neither party could avoid the issue. Despite the efforts of state Republican chairman, Henry C. Payne to effect a compromise, the Republican platform upheld the law. The influential Protestant German weekly, *Die Germania,* usually staunchly Republican, then deserted to the Democrats, who had denounced the law unequivocally in their platform.

The Bennett Law was the only issue of consequence in the ensuing campaign. The Democrats assailed the law but denied they opposed public schools. Their main target was the consequences of the law; the Democratic mayoralty candidate, humorist George Peck, the author of *Peck's Bad Boy,* went so far as to call it a forerunner of prohibition. The *Sentinel,* still outwardly confident and aggressive, finally realized the gravity of the situation when German Lutheran clergy and lay leaders applied religious fervor to political activity. As the campaign closed, the *Sentinel* attempted to hold Lutherans in the Republican fold by arousing anti-Catholic feelings. It warned Lutherans of the evil consequences of an alliance with their Catholic enemies and denounced the political activity of both Catholic and Lutheran clergymen. It also exaggerated support for the law among Irish, Polish, Bohemian, and American Catholics.

The election results shattered the *Sentinel's* illusions of support for the Bennett Law. Peck and the entire Democratic ticket won in a landslide, carrying all but three of the city's eighteen wards.

. . . .

The Republicans, stunned by their Milwaukee defeat, were bitterly divided over the course to pursue regarding the Bennett Law. For Governor Hoard and his associates, vindication by standing firm on the issue was the answer. Hoard had stated earlier that he would stand or fall on the school issue if necessary, and he refused to adopt a more conciliatory position. The day after the Milwaukee election Hoard delivered a speech to a teachers' group in which he stoutly defended the law and denounced its enemies.

. . . .

The attitudes of Haugen and Hoard dominated the Republican convention, which stood firmly for the law. The entire Republican campaign effort centered on the Bennett Law as necessary for the preservation of the common school system. The slogan became "The Little School House—Stand By It." A picture of a school, with an American flag flying above it and the slogan written on its roof, decorated the editorial pages of Republican newspapers and the stationery of campaign committees. In letters and speeches full of Biblical rhetoric and imagery, Hoard insisted that the public schools were in danger and defended the necessity that "the poor little German boy" learn English if he were to become a useful American citizen.

As early as the autumn of 1889 Democratic party leaders realized that they might profit by the dissatisfaction of German Lutherans with the law but were afraid to inject such an emotion-laden issue into the campaign. Even after the landslide for Peck in April, party leaders were still divided as to whether or not the issue should be exploited.

The younger and bolder party managers, particularly former state chairman Ellis B. Usher and new chairman Edward C. Wall, denounced such indecision. They saw a golden opportunity to capture the predominantly Republican German Protestant vote by a strong stand against the law.

. . . .

Wall and Usher decided to press the issue immediately by opposing the law as paternalistic and undemocratic. This would put the Republicans on the defensive, forcing them to "defend their child." A firm stand would force the Republicans either to desert Hoard or else to defend the law. In either case, Wall felt, the Republicans would lose the Lutheran vote.

. . . .

The anti-Bennett Law plank of the Democratic party was scrutinized carefully by religious leaders. After the Catholics approved it, Wall showed it to the Lutherans who made a few changes but called the platform a masterpiece.

. . . .

STAND BY IT!

Courtesy of the SHSW [WHi (X3) 33856]

The Bennett Law dominated the campaign. The Democrats nominated Milwaukee's "happy mayor," George W. Peck, for governor and demanded the law's repeal. Both parties, plus the Lutheran and Catholic organizations, kept up an incessant torrent of charges and countercharges concerning the law. In the last weeks of the campaign, Vilas, who had stressed national issues in most of his speeches, delighted Wisconsin German audiences with his comment that it did not matter whether a person said "two plus two makes four" or *"zwei und zwei machen vier."*

The 1890 election campaign witnessed the most blatant ethnic and religious appeals in the state's history. The Germans called on their brethren to defend the mother tongue and Germanism; pro-Bennett Law advocates charged the Germans with reverse know-nothingism. Much of the pro-Bennett Law literature and press had a distinct antiforeign and anti-Catholic tone. The *Sentinel* and other Republican papers attacked the Lutheran clergy almost as vociferously as the Catholic hierarchy. Latent nationality and religious prejudices were aroused on both sides.

Ethnic campaigning rose to a peak in both parties. By fall the Republicans were resigned to losing most of the German vote, but they hoped to offset it by gains among native and Irish-American Democrats who supported the law. The Irish, engaged in an often bitter running battle with German Catholics over the use of English or German in individual parishes and for control of the state Catholic hierarchy, were strong supporters of the public schools. Most Irishmen educated their children there, and many served as teachers and administrators. John Nagle, superintendent of Manitowoc County schools and editor of the Manitowoc *Pilot,* was a leader of the largely Irish-American Democratic Bennett Law League. The League received a big play in the Republican press but was numerically weak. Despite Republican overtures, most Irish-Americans, loyal Catholics, and their clergy opposed the law because of the possibility of its use against parochial schools.

More important to Republican success was the usually solid Scandinavian vote. The Scandinavian Lutheran churches which operated parochial schools usually did so in the summer months, when public schools were not in session. Only in rare instances did they compete with public schools. Scandinavian opposition to the law centered on the district clause and the implications of the law for all parochial schools. Scandinavians generally approved of the law's Americanizing features, but rumors of breaks in their support for the Republicans persisted. The Republicans made a concerted effort to keep them in line, and leaders such as Haugen were kept scurrying around the state mending fences among the dissidents.

The Democrats' main efforts were aimed at securing the German Protestant vote and at keeping their usual support from German, Irish, Polish, and Bohemian Catholics. Wall also set up a special Scandinavian bureau to proselytize among the Norwegians. Expecting considerable defection from Scandinavians over both the Bennett Law and the tariff, the Democrats sent speakers and literature into Norwegian areas at an unprecedented rate. Wall relied heavily on the Catholic hierarchy to keep the Polish and Irish vote solidly Democratic, but extra efforts were made in Irish wards and townships. In addition to the earlier Bishops' Manifesto, the three bishops spoke against the law, and circulars opposing it were read from Catholic pulpits. In an Oshkosh speech, Bishop Frederick X. Katzer even intimated that those Catholics who failed to vote against the law were traitors to the church.

The earliest returns left no doubt about the outcome: it was a Democratic landslide. Although Governor Hoard ran 6,000 votes ahead of the Republican ticket, he was inundated. Hoard's 1888 plurality of 20,273 was transformed into a 28,320 vote margin for Peck, and the entire Democratic state ticket was swept into office. The cruelest blow to the Republicans came in the congressional and legislative races. Nils P. Haugen, secure in his heavily Scandinavian district, was the only one of seven Republican incumbents to survive. The Democrats also captured a solid majority in both houses of the legislature, thus assuring that a Democrat would replace John C. Spooner in the United States Senate.

The Democrats registered large gains in all parts of the state. In 1888 they had won only fifteen of sixty-eight counties, most of which were concentrated in the traditionally Democratic eastern and lakeshore counties. In 1890 Peck captured forty-one counties; in the entire eastern half of Wisconsin, only six counties remained loyal to the Grand Old Party. The Republican percentage of the total vote declined in every single county in the state. Except for four heavily Anglo-American counties along the southern border, the great majority of Republican counties in 1890 were in the western and northwestern part of the state, in areas populated largely by Scandinavians and native Americans.

It was obvious that the Bennett Law was at the root of the upheaval in the state's political composition. In the heavily German areas, rejoicing over the results was unparalleled.

5: "Native Minorities"

Although often unmentioned, there were early contributions by Indians, blacks and women to Wisconsin's history. These "native minorities" are discussed in the selections which follow. Dr. Willard H. Titus, a government physician who labored on the Menominee reservation for four years, provides in his notes an insight into the attitudes of a significant part of educated white society toward the native Americans in 1875. Paternalism and racism prevailed in the white responses to problems faced by Indians and blacks, a view illustrated in the second selection, which discusses the attitude of a prominent member of the United States Senate.

Civil rights movements of the late nineteenth century were small when compared to those of the mid-twentieth century; but they did exist in many states after the Civil War. The selection by Leslie H. Fishel, Jr. provides an account of the successful effort to obtain a civil rights law in Wisconsin in the 1890s.

Although Wisconsin was not one of the leading states in the movement for women's suffrage, some notable efforts were made. Olympia Brown, a minister of the Universalist Church, was the state's most prominent advocate of suffrage, as the selection by Charles Neu illustrates.

The Menominee Indians

WILLARD H. TITUS, M.D.

It has frequently been contended that the government has not always dealt fairly with the Indian in the matter of granting him lands which should continually revert to his posterity. It must be remembered, however, that tribal rights can never be made freehold rights. No law was ever enacted that would deprive him of citizenship once attained but he must be considered an alien to the government until he declared his intention to be otherwise. The privileges and advantages of citizenship the Indian was slow to comprehend and to accept, preferring rather to be a dependent ward with the risk of being removed from one locality to another as time made his lands more desirable. This has been done time after time and in every instance he is the loser. He takes no lesson from his experience or those of his forefathers, preferring to sit lazily down and grumble at his wrongs or to menace some innocent citizen by malicious thieving, by threats of bodily harm or other lawless acts that make him continually obnoxious.

It can be concluded then at this period of writing (1875) that the Indian is a shiftless, ignorant, and almost homeless vagabond with the traditions of his ancestors converted into the most malignant superstitions. In writing thus, I am taking the Indian collectively. Exceptions can be made to this statement showing some truly manly characters.

The Indians whom I shall attempt to describe are the Menominee located in the southern part of Shawano County, Wisconsin, although I may also allude to the Chippewa and Stockbridges located only a short distance west of here.

The reserve is forty by fifty miles square with a population of about 5,000. It is heavily wooded, undulating and interspersed with beautiful lakes and streams, well stocked with fish and fur, while game abounds in this and the surrounding country. The soil needs only to be tickled to make it produce abundantly. Some of the finest tracts of pine to be found in the country are also within its limits. In fact, there is everything here to give rise to a thrifty peaceful settlement. The government has furnished an English school, and a farmer to teach them how to cultivate the soil. Their religious customs are in no way interfered with although a Catholic church is located on the reservation. The headquarters are at Keshena in the

From Willard H. Titus, "Observations on the Menominee Indians," *Wisconsin Magazine of History*, XIV (1930–1931), 92–105. Footnotes in the original omitted. Reprinted by permission of the State Historical Society of Wisconsin.

southern part of this tract of land on the east bank of the Wolf River.

Previous to their location here in 1850, they were a wandering band scattered over the central eastern part of the Territory of Wisconsin with their center at Lake Winnebago, their number being much in excess of what it is now. Tradition has it that they were at one time very numerous, but wars, internal feuds, and pestilence, which was the direct outgrowth of slovenly habits combined with exposure to a very rigorous climate, decimated them to the number above stated. It may be mentioned, also, that in spite of better hygienic conditions with which the government has tried to surround them, with better clothing, shelter and food, the decimation still goes on. The latest cause of their decrease is wholly due to their contact with the whites. Contrary to the usual results where foreigners intermarry, the cross with the whites breeds the most fatal of maladies. This is due more to the lawlessness of the whites with whom they come in contact than to the Indians themselves. Nevertheless, the Indians suffer the decrease. Scrofula, consumption, and other diseases canker in their veins where the pure aboriginal blood should be flowing.

These Indians are divided into two distinct classes by their religious beliefs, the Christians who have renounced the old customs and modes of worship and the pagans who still hold to the traditions and religious customs of their forefathers. The Christian Indian adopts the civilian dress while the pagan clings to his blanket, breech clout, and leggings.

It is a fact worth mentioning and one that should excite grave consideration, that the loathsome diseases are almost wholly confined to the Christian class. The pagan, firm in his faith with chastity a leading feature in his creed, has escaped largely the curse of these diseases, but he is sadly in the minority. This fact may not be and probably is not due to the acceptance of a new creed; it is largely the disaffected and the weakest ones who have been first to embrace a new idea. The susceptible character of the Indian has furnished a striking field for the exhibition of human frailities.

The Indian is naturally a strong robust fellow, but no more able to stand hardships than his white competitor; in fact, it is a question whether the modern Indian is his equal, for it is a hygienic law that the best physical condition can never be produced by alternate fasting and feasting as the Indian is wont to do. His hardihood is due to another cause which has so far not received proper attention. When his robustness is referred to as an example of simple living, no greater mistake could be made. When people deny their children the proper amount of clothing to keep them warm, and compel them to sleep in cold and illy prepared beds with a view to toughen them, using the Indian as an argument for so doing, a mistake is made which is little less than crime. The fact is the Indian reproduces more rapidly than the White, but the hardships to which he is early exposed soon kill off the weaker ones. An Indian child is surely tough who can stand the rigors to which his early life is subjected. Therefore, no wonder those who grow up are hardy. For the past few years more attention has been paid by the government to the needs of the Indian mothers with the result of late that more of the feeble infants have been able to survive this destructive period. They are most sure, however, to fall victims to consumption in adult life. The average mortality, therefore, is not radically changed.

Senator Spooner and Minorities

JAMES R. PARKER

Legislative advocates of expanded rights for American minority groups were few and extremely limited in their attitudes at the beginning of the twentieth century. Within the United States Congress, one Senator who posed as leading spokesman and champion for equal rights was Republican John C. Spooner of Wisconsin. In fact, however, Spooner's achievements fell short of his pretensions. He usually confined his efforts to the rhetoric of expanded political rights for black Americans. While Senator Spooner attempted to reflect the traditional egalitarian principle of the Republican party, which relied for electoral support partly on its human rights record of the Reconstruction era, he and his party ultimately avoided the execution of the ideal and substituted empty words and gestures.

. . . .

Spooner began his career as a railroad lawyer and lobbyist for the West Wisconsin and North Wisconsin railroads, which were later

From James R. Parker, "Paternalism and Racism: Senator John C. Spooner and American Minorities, 1897-1907," *Wisconsin Magazine of History*, LVII,3 (Spring 1974), 195-200. Footnotes in the original omitted. Reprinted by permission of the State Historical Society of Wisconsin.

Courtesy of the SHSW [WHi (X3) 3102]

Senator John Spooner

absorbed by the Chicago and North Western Railway. He was elected to the Wisconsin Assembly for one term in the 1870's, and attracted the attention of Senator Philetus Sawyer who brought Spooner into his machine. In 1885 Spooner earned the Republican caucus nomination, and was elected to the United States Senate. During his first term Spooner developed a close political relationship with the powerful Senate leaders: Nelson W. Aldrich of Rhode Island, Orville Platt of Connecticut, and William B. Allison of Iowa. Spooner's conservative political philosophy, and legal and oratorical talents, enhanced his value to their group. In 1891 he lost his Senate seat and became a counselor for the Northern Pacific Railroad receivers, during which time he cultivated new relationships with influential New York lawyers and investors.

When the state legislature of Wisconsin returned Spooner to Washington in 1897, the Senate's leadership immediately placed him on a number of powerful committees, and he became one of the dominant policy makers for the Republican command, developing close ties to both William McKinley and Theodore Roosevelt. Between 1897 and 1904 he exercised important influence in many phases of both domestic and foreign policy. Through his privileged position on committees and close relationships with the executive he, in fact, had abundant opportunity to take the initiative for positive action on the question of minority rights.

At best, Spooner was a paternalist who, like most politicians of his time, did not genuinely accept the concept of equality for all Americans. He gained his notoriety on the civil liberties issue because he was prepared to argue the case for human rights and to consult, however infrequently, with black Americans in his Wisconsin constituency—this in an era of relatively unrestrained southern racial violence. When his party's interests required defense, Spooner like other leaders, abandoned the flowery phrases of idealism and abetted gross injustices.

. . . .

[In 1902] Spooner responded to Mississippi Senator Hernando Money's accusation that black Americans were incapable of being educated. "To those who develop ability, honor, a sense of responsibility and possession of gifts," Spooner responded, "I want to give a chance without regard to the race." Spooner's willingness to address the issue seemed to stem from his desire to attack the Democrats, for no action followed his words.

Even Spooner's casual interest in the civil rights issue seemed to decline after 1902, and he became even more skeptical of a solution. He thought that southerners had presented the racial question "in a

new form, revolutionary, impudent, and impossible." "If it were
not for the black problem there would not be a solid South any-
more," he observed in the spring of 1904, "but the black problem is
there to stay. God only knows if it can be solved. I fear it cannot
be." By 1904, Spooner appeared to abandon the issue: "I took great
interest in it [the Civil rights issue] for years, until it seemed hopeless."

. . . .

Senator Spooner also subscribed to the various racial myths
about American Indians, which gave comfort to those who exploited them. From colonial times forward, during which the government seized Indian land in spite of treaty guarantees, most
Americans took the view that they were barbaric savages, an interpretation which Spooner shared. At the turn of the century, after
the policy of genocide had destroyed Indian resistance, the Senator,
like many Americans, took a paternalistic view that assumed that
Indians had not the intelligence to determine their own futures; this
permitted a subtle and devastating repression of human dignity.

During an 1898 congressional debate relating to the restoration
of annuities to selected groups of Sioux, which they had lost after
certain bands had raided Minnesota towns in 1862, Spooner used
the barbaric myth. Senator Richard F. Pettigrew of South Dakota
noted that the Indians under discussion had not been in the raiding
party. Spooner replied that he agreed, but that only thirty-nine of
the guilty Indians were hanged where "we ought to have hung
300." On another occasion Spooner responded to a critic of the
government's Indian policy, asserting "I am quite certain that your
theory that the Government has treated the Indians in any other
than a perfectly honorable and just way is incorrect."

While Spooner could apologize for the use of violence against
Native Americans as a necessity for the growth of civilization, he
did recognize the results of the policies with which he concurred.
"We have pressed the Indians whom Mr. Jefferson said loved independence and liberty," he said in 1902 "until today we have nearly
all who are left in 'concentration camps' called reservations."

Essentially, as with black Americans, Spooner was a benevolent
paternalist. He refused to permit Indians to alienate their land al-
lotments, because he feared that white speculators might take the
land for much less than its real value. "You cannot change an
Indian by making him a citizen," Spooner told his Senate colleagues
in 1905. "The Indian never ceases to need a certain degree of paternalistic interest and protection." Indians were too improvident and
callous to the needs of their families to use money wisely, he

thought. A declaration of citizenship would not, he believed, "instill into the Indian the prudence and care and business judgment of a white man...," for they were too childlike.

The pressure for land alienation mounted in 1906. Although there were undoubtedly corrupt land speculators in favor of it, many Indians wanted the freedom to decide the issue. One full-blooded Creek lawyer complained that while Indians lived under white laws and paid white taxes, they had no freedom to grow and learn or determine for themselves a place in the society.

Spooner remained adamant in opposing land alienation, for fear the railroad companies might exploit the Indians. "He [the Indian] needs a guardian," the Senator held. To change him from a dependent status would clothe him with a dignity that he was "not fit to appreciate," and would make him "easy prey to the white man." In his last month in the Senate, Spooner made his most extreme statement on the Indians, suggesting that their intelligence varied in direct proportion to the amount of white blood in their veins.

Thus, while Spooner thought he was protecting American Indians, he provided for their continuing dependency, creating a culture of despondency, based on an attitude of racial discrimination. While it was more pronounced in this case than others, it was the same basic attitude with which he viewed other American minorities.

Spooner viewed the Mexican-American population of the southwestern territories in the same distorted way. Early in 1906 when the Senate debated statehood proposals for Arizona and New Mexico, Spooner partially based his opposition to Arizona's admittance on the ethnic background of its residents. "It is nothing against those people that they are Spanish," declared Spooner, "far from it; it is nothing against them that they do not understand English; far from it"; it was that they were so highly illiterate in any language that Spooner opposed Arizona's admission. His 1906 speech recalled his racial attitudes of February, 1905, when he objected to "60,000 Mexicans" becoming eligible for citizenship in the southwest and declared that the census of the area "reads like the muster roll of a Spanish military company."

Thus, Spooner's attitude toward the three largest nonwhite groups in American society, blacks, Indians, and Mexican-Americans, was consistently paternalistic and sometimes repressive. Outside of the narrow sphere of the question of political rights for black Americans, the only area that could prove politically productive, Spooner demonstrated a gross misunderstanding of the problems of American minority groups in a white society, a weakness which he shared with most of his political associates. Like them, he lacked an essential sensitivity to the plight of American minorities. Yet he considered himself a leading defender of human rights at the turn of the century. It was indicative of the tragedy of his era that he gained an unearned reputation as one of the more enlightened politicians on the issue of civil rights.

Civil Rights Act of 1895

LESLIE H. FISHEL, JR.

... in December of 1889, a bill had been drawn up to protect Wisconsin's Negroes in their civil rights, but it was not until January, 1891, that the legislature convened and the bill was introduced. The bill was comprehensive, listing "inns, restaurants, saloons, barber shops, eating houses, public conveyances on land and water, theaters and all other places of public accommodation or amusement" as open to all persons alike, even specifying that no person could be required to pay more than the regular rate for these services. Violators would be charged with a misdemeanor and fined no less than $25 nor more than $500 and/or imprisoned for up to one year for each offense.

The bill was undoubtedly drafted by Milwaukee Negroes or their friends immediately after their 1889 civil rights convention. It was introduced by a Milwaukee assemblyman, Orren T. Williams, who was serving his first and only term in the legislature and represented the fourth ward, where William T. Green resided. A Republican, Williams was in the minority as a result of the Democratic landslide the previous November. He was a minority member of the judiciary Committee, to which the bill was referred. At the committee hearing at least one Negro testified; he was probably William Green, who was then attending law school in Madison. His appearance was effective enough to make a favorable impression on a legislative leader who was opposed to the bill, but it did not change his vote. The committee emasculated the bill by striking out the entire list of

From Leslie H. Fishel, Jr., "The Genesis of the First Wisconsin Civil Rights Act," *Wisconsin Magazine of History,* XLIX,4 (Summer 1966), 324–333. Footnotes in the original omitted. Reprinted by permission of the State Historical Society of Wisconsin.

public places, except inns, and reported back. On Wednesday, March 11, the lower house devoted most of the morning to a spirited debate on the bill, the partisan nature of which was revealed in the headlines of the Madison *Democrat:* "Republicans seek to make capital out of the Civil Rights Bill, but their game is blocked and they themselves placed on record."

Williams opened the debate by citing the examples of Michigan and Minnesota, which had already passed civil rights acts, and by using the case of Howell *v.* Litt as proof of the need in Wisconsin. He read portions of Judge Johnson's charge to the Assembly. The opposition called the original bill "too broad" imposing "extreme exactions" on businessmen. Prejudice is here to stay, one assemblyman stated. "There is no member of the house who desires to be placed upon an equality with the negro. . . . The negro in Wisconsin had . . . all the rights he can reasonably expect." Other assemblymen argued that there was no need for a law of this type and that this bill was a Republican trick to embarrass the Democratic majority. The Republicans, one Democrat taunted, had had more than two decades of legislative control in which to enact a civil rights statute. Assemblyman John Winans, a member of the Judiciary Committee, asked, "Where is the man on this floor who will say the colored man is the equal of the white man? God did not create them equal," he added, and legislation to make them equal would do them harm. Occasional colored men deserved "that highest consideration," but not the rank and file. It was too much to ask "that the wives and daughters of the members of this legislature shall mingle with the black men. . . ." Orren Williams made a final unsuccessful effort to enlarge the bill to approximate its original meaning; then the assembly, with Winans absent, approved the emasculated version.

The Winans speech had "a deal of moss on it," the *Wisconsin State Journal* snorted the next day and ridiculed the assemblyman for raising the intermarriage bogey. But the senate would not even have the watered-down version, and the bill failed. Wisconsin's Negroes needed a good deal more political leverage, and they now set about acquiring it within the Republican party.

. . . .

The Democrats maintained their control over the 1893 legislature and no effort was made to introduce a civil rights bill. The elections of 1894 brought the Republicans back to power, and a former Milwaukee assemblyman, William H. Austin, returned as a freshman senator. A young man with a distinguished legal and civic career still before him, Senator Austin introduced in February of

1895 the original 1891 civil rights bill, by request, on the last per-
missible day. On the same day, Assemblyman Reinhardt Klabunde,
a liquor dealer from Milwaukee, did the same in the lower house. It
was February 12, Lincoln's Birthday.

Unlike the bill of four years earlier, this civil rights bill moved
through both committee and legislature without public notice of
any kind. The senate committee amended the bill by reducing the
penalties. The assembly passed its bill without amendment, but
finally concurred in the senate bill. On April 20, 1895, Governor W.
H. Upham signed the bill and Wisconsin had its first civil rights act,
prohibiting racial discrimination at inns, restaurants, and a long list
of other public places under penalty of a fine from $5 to $100 or six
months' imprisonment. For Wisconsin, and for the period, it was a
good law.

. . . .

By the turn of the century, the Wisconsin Civil Rights Act was
firmly and substantially the law of the state. Its passage had depended upon the initiative and persistence of Negroes, a pattern
which had developed in other Northern states which enacted civil
rights legislation after the 1883 Supreme Court decision. At a time
when Southern whites were cresting their campaign for stringent
segregation and Northern whites busied themselves with other concerns, this form of Negro resistance to discrimination and subordination suggested both the restlessness and the power of Northern
Negroes. While their restlessness was largely unharnessed and their
power limited and still bound to and channeled through the Republican party, Northern Negroes actively worked to erode their
second-class citizenship and to achieve parity with whites. The Atlanta Compromise of Booker T. Washington has tended to obscure
their dissatisfaction with their status and has minimized their successes. Wisconsin's civil rights achievement, in the year of the Atlanta Compromise, testified to the conviction and the capabilities of
the Negro group in the North.

Woman's Suffrage

CHARLES E. NEU

In 1878 the Reverend Olympia Brown arrived in Racine, Wisconsin, where she took charge of a small Universalist group—the Church of the Good Shepherd. Her arrival should have received more recognition than it did, for Mrs. Brown personified the kind of emancipated woman that the country was to see more of in the years ahead. At forty-three she was in the prime of a life devoted to Universalism and woman's freedom, eager to turn her fellow men to righteousness and to reveal to them the grave inequalities in the American social and political system. Already prominent in woman suffrage circles in the East, she had now come to the Midwest, the place of her birth, believing that in this section of the country lay the greatest opportunities for reform.

. . . .

She was ordained to the Universalist ministry in June 1863, the first woman in America to be ordained to the ministry of a regularly constituted ecclesiastical body.

. . . .

Mrs. Brown had no illusions about the position and attainments of American womanhood. Although women were more sensitive to the religious experience they were on the whole "feeble, abject being[s]" lacking knowledge, education, and purposeful lives. Their morals were appalling, as was their physical degeneracy. They were, in short, "mere butterflies sporting in sunshine." But "amid this wreck of intellect, this waste of God-given powers, this ruin of moral character," Mrs. Brown could "see the trace of what might have been a noble being," and she was determined to bend every effort to the realization of woman's potentiality. The keys to the revolution in woman's character were the ballot and formal education, both of which would teach women to think and form independent opinions.

. . . .

In 1866 Mrs. Brown met Susan B. Anthony and became an ardent suffragist. She participated in the innumerable campaigns, conventions, and petitions through which women were expressing

From Charles E. Neu, "Olympia Brown and the Woman's Suffrage Movement," *Wisconsin Magazine of History*, XLIII,4 (Summer 1960), 277–287. Footnotes in the original omitted. Reprinted by permission of the State Historical Society of Wisconsin.

Courtesy of the SHSW [WHi (X323) 1674]

Olympia Brown

their discontent, but her real baptism into the woman's suffrage ranks came in 1876 when she toured Kansas in the first state campaign for a woman's suffrage constitutional amendment. Her travels across the hot grasslands, interrupted by two or three meetings a day at widely separate settlements, were an arduous but exhilarating experience. Mrs. Brown later recalled the "Grand, rolling prairies stretching far away . . . hospitable homes . . . brave and earnest women; kind and true men; and . . . some of the most dishonest politicians the world has ever seen." She left Kansas with an abiding love of the West and its people.

Mrs. Brown was a charter member of the American Equal Rights Association, created at the close of the Civil War presumably to advance the right of both Negroes and women. Soon abolitionists and suffragists were at odds over which reform should come first. Abolitionists claimed it was "the Negro's hour" and supported the Fifteenth Amendment, even though it did not include woman's suffrage. Some suffragists acquiesced in this, but Mrs. Brown, like Miss Anthony and Elizabeth Cady Stanton, bitterly denounced the abolitionists and opposed the Fifteenth Amendment.

. . . .

In 1873 Mrs. Brown had married John Henry Willis, thus thwarting the popular stereotype of suffragists. She had, however, been deeply impressed by the arguments of Lucy Stone, and continued to be known throughout her life by her maiden name. Five years later, when she received her call from the Universalist Church, the Willis family moved to Racine where Mr. Willis became part owner and business manager of the Times Publishing Company, while Mrs. Brown, in addition to her ministerial duties, plunged into local suffrage work. She was elected president of the state association, and by 1886 seemed to have secured a significant victory—the approval of a law whereby women could vote in elections pertaining to school matters. The law appeared so promising that Mrs. Brown resigned her pastorate in 1887 and devoted all of her energies to a campaign to awaken women to their new voting rights. At the same time, dissatisfied with the narrow interpretation of the law by local officials, she instituted a suit which reached the Wisconsin Supreme Court. The court in effect invalidated the whole law, leaving the suffrage cause in Wisconsin precisely where it was prior to 1886, except for the addition of an onerous debt and the effects of a heartbreaking defeat. Many old workers now felt that woman's suffrage was a "mathematical impossibility."

. . . .

Mrs. Brown considered it "unbearable" that women were "the political inferiors of all the riffraff of Europe that is poured upon our shores." "There is no language," she said, "that can express the enormous injustice done to women." She deplored the subservience of political conventions to foreigners. Nevertheless, her thought remained fairly coherent until the arduous woman's suffrage campaign in drought-stricken South Dakota in 1890. After her experiences in that campaign, where once again recent immigrants were marshaled to defeat woman's suffrage, a real element of paranoia began to appear in her speeches. Now she claimed that foreign intriguers (perhaps the Maffia), who aspired to control our state governments, were behind the increase in the number of voting-age immigrants (not from the most energetic parts of the European population) coming to America after 1886. The greatest threat in Wisconsin was the preponderance of foreign-born citizens at the polls. The crux of the danger to republican institutions caused by the ignorant foreign and Negro vote was the "corruption of the ballot box," which allowed "aliens, paupers, tramps [and] drunkards" to vote while shutting out "teachers, church members, preachers [and] mothers of the republic." This corruption, Mrs. Brown claimed, was preparing the way for a national catastrophe, a war of labor and capital complicated by religious and race questions such as that predicted in the *Arena* of August 1890.

The solution to the impending catastrophe was, as expected, woman's suffrage via a constitutional amendment. This would throw the voting balance to native-born Americans since women were scarce among the foreign born, and would also ease tension in the South by returning the whites to power. The corruption of the ballot box would be diminished, especially if states were forbidden to enfranchise noncitizens, and Protestant domination would be assured. With these reforms, Mrs. Brown predicted, the "evils that now beset us would vanish like the winter's snow before an April sun."

. . . .

While Mrs. Brown was searching for "the mistake" and for new justifications for woman's suffrage, the two rival suffrage associations—the National Woman Suffrage Association and the American Woman Suffrage Association—united in 1889, ending a twenty-year split. Voting in the New National American Association's conventions would be by delegates sent from state auxiliary associations, and the organization would undertake both state and federal work. Mrs. Brown, a firm supporter of the National Association, was disturbed by the union, for she believed that the National should continue to agitate only for an amendment to the federal constitution, allowing each state suffrage unit complete autonomy.

She correctly foresaw the almost exclusive concentration of the new association upon state campaigns. Moreover, in the National American Association the rights of individual suffragists were diminished; they could no longer cast a vote at national conventions without representing any state auxiliary. Mrs. Brown's protests were those of a pioneer and individualist who could not adjust to the increasing organization and subordination that younger workers thought necessary for the success of the cause.

Mrs. Brown was not a woman to make idle protests, for through her initiative the Federal Suffrage Association was founded in Chicago in 1892. It was pledged to work for federal suffrage. . . .

. . . .

But personal tragedy cut short Mrs. Brown's protest. In 1893 her husband died and her beloved mother was stricken with a lingering illness. "Sickness and death," she wrote, "have entered my home and endless sorrow has fallen upon my heart." Life became harder for her, and she was forced to give up most of her suffrage work and pleasant travels throughout Wisconsin in order to concentrate upon running her husband's printing firm. The one sermon surviving from this period, emphasizing as it does the terrible justice and judgment of God, gives some hint of her suffering.

At the turn of the century her mother died and Mrs. Brown, at about the same time, gave up the printing business. She once again was able to work intensively for the suffrage cause, and in 1902 with the aid of Clara Colby reshaped the defunct Federal Suffrage Association into the Federal Woman's Equality Association. Mrs. Brown was attempting to broaden the former's base of support by emphasizing woman's economic as well as political advancement and by stressing the organizational simplicity of the Equality Association—its lack of red tape, auxiliaries and delegates.

. . . .

After 1889 Mrs. Brown's alienation from the National American Association continued to grow. In 1893 it rejected the federal suffrage idea and in 1902 showed little interest in Mrs. Brown's proposal for concentration upon Congress. She felt that National-American leaders no longer needed or desired her services. There may have been some truth in this, for both National-American leaders and some local suffragists were increasingly dissatisfied with the progress of the cause in Wisconsin.

. . . .

The tension between Mrs. Brown, her co-workers, and the National-American leaders was brought to a head by the submission of a woman's suffrage amendment to the voters of Wisconsin, to be voted upon in 1912. Some younger Wisconsin suffragists, claiming that Mrs. Brown was too old and decrepit to lead a vigorous campaign, formed a rival suffrage association called the Political Equality League, and proceeded to organize with such energy that Mrs. Brown found many of her customary financial sources diverted.

. . . .

The Wisconsin suffrage campaign of 1912 was lost, Mrs. Brown resigned from the presidency of the Woman's Suffrage Association, and the two factions reunited soon afterwards. Her days of active suffrage work in Wisconsin ended.

6: Nativism and Labor

Organized labor in Wisconsin—as was true in the nation as a whole—faced severe trials and experienced numerous ups and downs during the post-Civil War period. Growth in the 1880s led to a confrontation with the National Guard in Milwaukee in 1886. The first two selections below tell of this "Bay View Massacre" and the role of the Wisconsin National Guard in it.

Labor troubles, along with other pressures, led many to seek quick and simplistic solutions to the problems of society. One such effort was that of the national organization known as the American Protective Association, a secret society with an anti-Catholic emphasis organized in 1887. Fearing the influx of immigrants from southern and eastern Europe, members took oaths not to hire Catholics, to keep them from political office, and to do all they could to protect the public schools, labor, and other American institutions from "Romanism." The role of the A.P.A. in the Middle West is discussed in John Higham's *Strangers in the Land* and in Donald Kinzer's *An Episode in Anti-Catholicism: The American Protective Association.* The selection that concludes this section deals with the A.P.A. in Wisconsin.

The Guard Prepares for Trouble

JERRY M. COOPER

The development of the Wisconsin National Guard generally parallelled the national trend. The antibellum volunteer militia system,

From Jerry M. Cooper, "The Wisconsin National Guard in the Milwaukee Riots of 1886," *Wisconsin Magazine of History,* LV,1 (Autumn 1971), 31–48. Footnotes in the original omitted. Reprinted by permission of the State Historical Society of Wisconsin.

practically destroyed by the war, revived slowly during the late 1860's and early 1870's but always remained ephemeral. The state began providing financial assistance to militia companies in 1873, but the evolution of the modern Wisconsin National Guard, not officially designated as such until 1879, did not reach maturity until the early 1880's. For the most part, the general populace and most state legislators took little interest in the organization. The impact of nationwide labor strife had not yet been felt in Wisconsin and most people saw little need to spend money on the militia. Nonetheless, Guard advocates relied mainly upon the threat of labor disorders as the main justification for financial support of the institution. In 1880, for example, Governor William E. Smith made a strong appeal for a well organized state force, noting that it was always best to be prepared, for "We cannot hope always to escape disorders and tumults similar to those which have arisen in other states and nations." Guard officials serving under Smith, his successor Jeremiah M. Rusk, and other militia advocates all relied upon this argument to gain public and legislative support for the force. A year after Smith made the statement, he sent 300 Guardsmen to Eau Claire to break a strike of lumbermill hands.

By the mid-1880's, this appeal and the diligent work of Rusk's adjutant general, Chandler P. Chapman of Madison, had produced an organized Guard force of about 2,400 officers and men.

. . . .

The efforts of Adjutant General Chapman and his aide Charles King, a colonel and chief of inspection by 1885, to give a sense of direction to the Wisconsin National Guard illustrate the fact that the Guard lacked a central purpose.

. . . .

At the same time that Chapman and King sought to remake the Guard in the image of the Army, and thus by implication make it a reserve military force, they also relied upon the argument that the Guard constituted a state constabulary force as the surest means of gaining financial support from the legislature and of maintaining a more immediate sense of mission in the ranks. Chapman continually stressed this function of the Guard in his annual reports, sometimes referring to the strike duty of National Guards in such states as Pennsylvania and New York.

Charles King also discussed this aspect of Guard duty. A much more outspoken man than Chapman, King indicated his pointed views on riot duty in a stirring lecture to a gathering of Wisconsin Guard officers. Ostensibly King's remarks on riots were to have been merely tactical, but he talked at length on the political and social aspects of labor strikes, strongly implying that these were the main sources of riots. The motives of all strikers, regardless of their actions, were questioned by King. He saw most strikes as "... outbreaks in which law, order and property are arranged on the one hand against a faction or class, driven to temporary insanity, it may be by fancied wrongs, blind fanaticism, the specious arguments of designing demagogues or uncontrollable passions. ..."

His recommendations for dealing with mobs were quite simple. A Guard unit should make a demonstration of force, and if this did not dispel the group, "Two volleys by battalion, low, cool, steady, well aimed, will knock the fight out of any ordinary mob. ..." King ended his lecture with speculations on the possibilities of riot duty for the Wisconsin Guard. He did not foresee any likelihood of riots or labor strife of any consequence in the state except in Milwaukee, where, King believed, "... from whose dregs can be swept up the constituents of a mob [on] whom it might be a municipal blessing to fire. ..." The city was, in his opinion, woefully unprepared to cope with such an occurrence, as was the Guard. He made several suggestions for preparing both the city and the Guard for such an eventuality, noting that "I speak of this only as illustrative of the apathetic condition of the Milwaukee mind on matters of this character, and while it is to be hoped no rude awakening may come, it is best to be prepared." Two years later, the rude awakening came.

[Editors' note: Conclusions about the guard's role in the May 1886 riots contained in the above article appear following the next selection.]

The Bay View Labor Riot of 1886

The "merry, merry month of May" wasn't so merry in Milwaukee in 1886. From May 1 to May 11 of that year the city was in confusion as agitation for the eight-hour day for labor resulted in

From "State Scene: Milwaukee in May, 1886," *Wisconsin Then and Now*, V,10 (May 1959), 1–3. Reprinted by permission of the State Historical Society of Wisconsin.

National Guardsmen prepare to fire into a crowd of strikers during the May 1886 strike at the Allis Reliance Works, Milwaukee

the first general labor strike in the city's history, and what was later to be called "the Bay View Labor Riot of 1886."

The outbreak was the Milwaukee phase of labor's nationwide struggle for broader rights—a struggle which in Chicago took the form of the more widely publicized Haymarket bombing.

In Milwaukee, getting employers to reduce the working day from 10 hours to eight was not the heart of the issue. Labor was attempting to force management to accept the eight-hour day and still pay for 10 hours' work.

Two newspaper editors figured prominently in the struggle, Paul Grottkau, editor of the *Arbeiter Zeitung* and leader of the Central Labor Union, was prepared to use violence if necessary. Robert Schilling, editor of the *Volksblatt* and leader of the Knights of Labor, sought a peaceful means for winning the struggle.

These men were bitter rivals and expression of their differences frequently found its way into the columns of their newspapers. Despite this, they tried to join their efforts in winning an eight-hour day for labor.

By May 1 thousands of men throughout the city were already on strike. Reports list the number at anywhere from 7,000 to 15,000. These workmen belonged mainly to the following classes: railroad and brewery workers, carpenters, shop tailors, clothing cutters, cigarmakers, broommakers, and common laborers.

May 1, the day appointed for the eight-hour rule to go into effect, dawned with unrest and suppressed excitement in the air, but passed without incident.

Sunday, May 2, was the day of the big labor parade, and the gigantic picnic planned by the Central Labor Union.

The parade promised to be the biggest in the city's history and was witnessed by some 25,000 people. Certain of the parade banners and the display of the red flag (there was a Socialist element in the movement) caused some excitement and objection, but parade and picnic began and ended without violence.

Some of the parade banners carried these slogans:

> *Eight Hours! Our Password and Battle-Cry!*
> *The Working Man does not Beg, He Demands.*
> *Capital is the Product of Labor; not its Master!*
> *Humbug, your name is Robert!*

This last slogan referred, of course, to Robert Schilling, and reveals more of the animosity between him and Grottkau.

Monday, May 3, saw the strike become more general and the first lawlessness occur. It seems the Polish workmen of the city had thrown themselves into the eight-hour movement with great enthusiasm. They had been deluded into thinking all wage-earners would quit work the same day and would not return to work until all returned together. When they loyally carried out their end of the bargain only to find that hundreds of workmen had not gone on strike, they felt betrayed and were "fighting mad." They were fertile ground for the few anarchists in the city, and were easily persuaded to take action.

They marched to the Reliance Iron Works, owned by Edward P. Allis for a showdown. There the nonstriking workers grabbed hoses and met the angry strikers with pounding streams of water that sprawled them back and to the ground.

Just at this time two patrol wagons arrived with about 20 policemen who "jumped into the midst of the crowd . . . hammering right and left with their clubs of stout hickory." The strikers were eventually dispersed, and Allis was promised protection for his plant.

The city was now duly alarmed. Indeed, "the authority of law trembled in the balance." So grave the danger seemed that Governor Jeremiah Rusk was summoned from Madison.

He arrived in Milwaukee by special train and met that night (May 3) with Mayor Emil Wallber and other city officials. During this meeting "delegations of merchants called on the governor, requesting him to immediately call out all of the available militia."

Although the city officials did not feel troops were necessary at this time, several companies of militia from Milwaukee, Madison, and Darlington were alerted.

Governor Rusk and Mayor Wallber agreed that the workers of Milwaukee had the right to strike when they and their employers couldn't agree on the terms of service, but on the other hand, they felt that a man willing to work should be allowed to do so, and property should be protected from damage. The Knights of Labor acquiesced in this policy, but not so the Central Labor Union members.

Tuesday, May 4, day of the Haymarket bombing, saw the conflict progress to even greater violence. Central Labor Union members marched on certain factories—forcing one to shut down and tangling with militiamen at another.

At another point in the city a band of almost 1,000 strikers, said to be made up mostly of Polish people, gathered. They marched, clubs in hand, to the Bay View rolling mills where the workers had refused to strike.

Rolling mills officials telephoned for help, and stalled the angry mob for a time. As the strikers became impatient and violence seemed imminent, Robert Schilling appeared and counseled the men to make no lawless demonstration—an act that later won him praise from Mayor Wallber.

Schilling had just finished speaking when a train sped into the midst of the astonished strikers and four companies of state militia stepped to the ground.

One of the companies—the Kosciusko guard—immediately caused great concern! The Polish strikers became "wild with anger" when they saw their own countrymen taking sides against them. In an attempt to keep the strikers controlled, the militia fired a volley into the air—and though no one was hurt, the strikers offered no further resistance that day.

The militia camped at Bay View and had orders to "shoot to kill" if the mob threatened again.

May 5 dawned—and the battlefield was once more the Bay View rolling mills. The strikers this day did not heed the command to halt—and attempted to rush the armed militiamen. A volley was fired into the mob, and many men were killed and injured. Reports list the number dead at anywhere from one to 10. This ended the riot.

There was sadness in the city that night, but many people felt "law and order" had won a victory. As the labor riots of 1886 ended so, for the time, did agitation for the eight-hour day.

The strikers returned to their work without renewing their demands, and factories and workshops resumed operations. The last of the militia was withdrawn on May 13.

The scar, however, would be long in healing. For many months a boycott was maintained—especially against members of the Kosciusko guard. It took years to end the enmity evolved by their response to duty when the call to arms was a summons to face neighbors and friends with leveled rifles.

The riots had been costly, not only in human life, but in dollars as well. The loss in wages, business losses, expense to the executive and adjutant general's offices, police, and militia was estimated at not less than $2,000,000.

The two newspaper-labor leaders, Schilling and Grottkau, were discredited, with the hand of justice falling more heavily on Grottkau. Their respective labor organizations also lost prestige "thus making way for a new national organization, the American Federation of Labor."

Governor Rusk came out of the ordeal a hero in state and nation for his prompt suppression of the riots. He was unanimously re-nominated for a third term, and was re-elected. He received his

Courtesy of the SHSW [WHi (W6) 5977]

Governor Jeremiah M. Rusk

praise modestly with the now-famous statement, "I seen my duty and I done it."

The Role of the Guard

JERRY M. COOPER

It is highly unlikely that the individual Guardsman in the ranks thought of himself as a strikebreaker. It is just as unlikely that

From Cooper, *loc. cit.*

Governor Rusk, Adjutant General Chapman, or Colonel King saw themselves in this role. To most of these men, the issue had been, from the beginning, a simple one of law and order, although King later rumbled about smashing anarchists and rebellious foreign rabble.

. . . .

Not surprisingly, the shooting at Bay View on May 5 brought forth the most serious criticism of the National Guard. Robert Schilling wrote in his *Milwaukee Volksblatt,* "The firing was unjustified and cruel, and to say it in plain German, it was cowardly, premeditated murder." The Central Labor Union issued a public statement which accused the police and militia of unnecessary and harsh action throughout the strike and called the killing ". . . over-zealous, unjustifiable and damnable." Indignation and outrage were particularly acute in the Polish wards, again not surprisingly, because except for Franz Kunkel, all those killed or wounded at Bay View had been Polish. Alderman Theodore Rudzinski was caustically critical of the National Guard, charging that it precipitately fired on a peaceful crowd which had a perfect right to demonstrate in front of the Bay View plant.

The Milwaukee Sunday Telegraph, along with most of the English-language papers in the city, deplored the fact that, ". . . demagogues who hope to gain a little political preference will make sneering remarks about the National Guard. . . ." But, the paper pointed out, the shooting at Bay View " . . . had a most wonderfully purifying effect." Praise for the Guard and Governor Rusk's stand during the riots came from these Milwaukee papers, most papers around the state and much of the national press. The Governor received memorials from several business groups in Milwaukee lauding his recent actions, one of which assured him that: ". . . it comes from the hearts of that class which has the best interests of the State and country at heart, and who are interested to so great an extent in the commercial welfare and mercantile interests of the country. . . ."

. . . .

Most of the city's newspapers and many of the state officials had made much of the ethnicity of the strikers, as though to explain away the troubles by blaming foreigners and outsiders. The *Sentinel,* in particular, continually referred to "Polack" strikers as the real troublemakers. This paper, other segments of the press, and state officials could not resist pointing out that the two leaders of the strike, Robert Schilling and Paul Grottkau, were German-born

350 ETHNICITY AND POLITICS, 1865-1900

and Socialists to boot. As noted earlier, many state officials and businessmen believed the troubles arose because Germans dominated local politics and were spineless and untrustworthy. Charles King, almost obsessed with nativism, later condemned all foreigners in the affair, regardless of the role they played. He attacked city and county officials, contemptuously referred to Traeumer as that "German major," criticized the discipline of the Kosciusko Guards, "mainly Polanders, but of a better class," and asserted that the only decent Guard troops in the fray were the cavalry troop and the battery, "all dashing young Americans." Undoubtedly this antiforeign attitude explains in great part the harsh policy laid down by Governor Rusk and pursued by General Chapman and Colonel King.

Paradoxically, the immigrant companies of the Fourth Battalion carried out the Governor's policy, but the severity of their actions came from poor preparation not antiforeign bias. The Fourth Battalion consistently received the lowest efficiency ratings of all units in the Guard and their performance at Bay View indicates the outfit was poorly trained. The Guard as a whole lacked riot training and the Fourth, often torn by political and social conflicts, frequently performed poorly even at dress parades. Their first day's action at Bay View, when they displayed a total lack of knowledge concerning crowd control, indicated their poor preparation. Furthermore, although Traeumer was under orders to fire if the strikers attempted to enter the plant grounds, he made no effort to determine fully the intentions of the crowd before firing into it. Traeumer displayed indecision throughout the disorders and relied upon ultimate force to cover his indecision. A comment in the *Milwaukee Journal* partially bears out this conclusion, as it noted: "The general opinion of the people of Bay View is that the action of the militia was hasty, and that bloodshed could have been prevented by drawing the militia in line outside the works and menacing the crowd without shooting."

Poor training, lack of discipline, and incompetent leadership, then, were as much a cause of the killing as the resolute stand of the state officials. It is clear that the men of the Fourth were poorly trained for riot duty. Many served throughout the strike in their dress-parade uniforms and went without blankets, overcoats, or hot food for two days when the nights were damp and chilly. On the night following the killing at Bay View the troops remained very jumpy. Twice during the night of May 5–6, nervous sentries awoke other Guardsmen at Bay View by firing at imaginary skulkers in the shadows. Finally, at least some of the Guardsmen, already in an overexcited state, were told by their officers to be ready to kill. Prior to leaving the Armory for Bay View, the captain of the Sheridan Guards gave a short speech to his men, stating in part: "I don't want any of you to show the white feather. . . . Above all things, keep cool. Don't lose your head, but wait for the order to fire before you pull a trigger. And when you do fire, take an aim; pick out your man and kill him." No one in authority bothered to consider these factors, and on May 7 a coroner's jury absolved the militia of any responsibility for the killings at Bay View.

The American Protective Association in Wisconsin: Immigrants and Labor

K. GERALD MARSDEN

In Wisconsin, the organization seems to have been well developed, though not as extensive as in neighboring Michigan, Minnesota, and Ohio, states in which the movement was strongest. Over 170 local councils were scattered throughout more than twenty-five Wisconsin cities. In 1893 even a Milwaukee Catholic newspaper said that in that city A.P.A. membership had reached 4,215 although the A.P.A. set the local membership at 15,000; by late 1894 there were more than twenty councils. Indicative of the increasing importance of the Wisconsin A.P.A. is the fact that Henry M. Stark, a Milwaukeean, was elected treasurer of the national council in 1894 and was made a trustee of the organization in 1895, the year the annual national convention was held in Milwaukee.

In May, 1893, a weekly newspaper, the *Wisconsin Patriot,* was established in Milwaukee, with A. C. Macrorie as its first editor. Though the *Patriot* denied being the official organ of the A.P.A., it readily admitted being its unofficial spokesman—"the only strictly A.P.A. paper in Wisconsin."

. . . .

From K. Gerald Marsden, "Patriotic Societies and American Labor: the American Protective Association in Wisconsin," *Wisconsin Magazine of History,* XLI,4 (Summer 1958), 287–294. Footnotes in the original omitted. Reprinted by permission of the State Historical Society of Wisconsin.

Although the A.P.A. was primarily an anti-Catholic organization, in Wisconsin, at least, it was more than that. It believed, as the *Patriot* made evident, that the country was in the midst of a struggle for power, a struggle between free government—defined as rule by will of the people expressed through a system of manhood suffrage—and various forces seeking to destroy free government. The *Patriot's* position in this struggle was inflexibly on the side of the people. "Allow no special privileges . . . to any corporation, sect, creed or class," it demanded editorially. "Allow no power to have supremacy above the state. Always remember that the voice of 'the people is the voice of God.'"

"The people" referred to were those for whom the paper was written, namely, the A.P.A. membership which the evidence shows tended to belong to the lower reaches of the professional and white-collar classes and the upper levels of the laboring class. It was, the *Patriot* believed, the middle and lower classes which led the way "in all movements to advance the interests of the people," and it further believed that the "interest of the working c[l]asses is the interest of the American people." Emphasis on the workingman and small businessman as the bulwark of American democracy and liberty was a common theme in the paper's columns.

. . . .

The *Patriot*, though it never spoke in favor of labor unions, opposed them only to the extent that they were under the influence of the church hierarchy. The most favorable comment it could muster in the unions' favor was at best neutral, as when in late 1894 it asked hopefully:

> "DID IT EVER OCCUR TO YOU . . . that demagoguery in labor unions, as well as political parties, has seen its last days. Americanism will kill it as easily as it is stamping out Romanism."

. . . .

On August 11, 1894, the *Patriot* noted that there had been several complaints about its assertion that Eugene V. Debs, president of the American Railway Union, was a Catholic. "The bulk of evidence so far goes to show that he is not at present a communicant of that faith, but he is an uncompromising enemy of the American Protective Association, therefore he is to all intents and purposes in antagonism to the principles on which this nation is founded. . . . If he is not a Romanist he is very closely in touch with the hierarchy and a willing worker for Rome's ends." The tendency to identify anything anti-A.P.A. with the Catholic church was common; and that Eugene V. Debs was opposed to the A.P.A. there can be little doubt.

. . . .

From the beginning the A.P.A. cautioned American workingmen against the Knights of Labor because Terence V. Powderly, its leader, was a Catholic. The Knights of Labor was never referred to by the *Patriot* except as a radical or Catholic union in the worst sense of those terms.

. . . .

Why the AF of L was not condemned as were the A.R.U. and the Knights of Labor is open to question, since all three apparently condemned the A.P.A. Powderly was a Catholic; Debs, though charged with being a Catholic, was not. It may be that the A.P.A. actually believed he had close Catholic affiliations and for that reason condemned him along with Powderly. Or it may have been that the greater conservatism of AF of L policies, its refusal to enter the arena of partisan politics as well as its emphasis on skilled labor—which would automatically eliminate a good many immigrants from its ranks—made it appear to be a more typically "American" union than either of the others.

The *Patriot* blamed the immigrant for many of America's ills and more specifically for many of America's labor problems. It must be borne in mind that the immigrants of this period were largely southern European Catholics. In nearly every issue of the paper a platform of A.P.A. principles was printed, including one plank that said: "We demand for the protection of our citizen laborers the prohibition of the importation of pauper labor and restriction of immigration to all persons except those who can show their ability and honest intention to become self-supporting American citizens." Indeed, the *Patriot* insisted, "Protection to American industry— YES, AND PROTECTION TO AMERICAN LABOR, TOO. Let protection bear on all alike. Protect . . . by restricting immigration. . . ." It was further held that unrestricted immigration jeopardized the success of strikes and displaced an "equal number of our laborers" who could not exist on the wages paid to immigrants. An additional factor to be taken into account was "the gross ignorance, superstition and treasonable principle which should exclude them." The *Patriot* went on to rationalize that "low wages, the store order system, the company house and all the numerous schemes of the operator to grind labor should never have prospered . . ." were it not for the presence of the "foreign element." As a result of these convictions it concluded that "our country is virtually in the hands of foreigners..." and proposed a system of rigid exclusion, plus a fifteen-year naturalization program involving payment of several twenty-five to fifty-dollar fees.

In addition to laying the blame for most of the difficulties of industrial strife at the door of the Catholic immigrants, the *Patriot* also held them responsible for the violence and bloodshed of strikes and riots. It employed two lines of attack: the immigrant laborer was first indicted for being radical and lawless in such statements as, "the anarchistic and hoodlum element that so seriously menaces the stability of our government comes from the unassimilated foreign immigrants." The second indictment was that the immigrant laborer was the tool of the Catholic hierarchy and was to play a part in the coming revolution.

Chapter VIII
PROGRESSIVE INTERLUDE, 1890–1919

The rise and fall of progressivism is the major theme in the political history of Wisconsin during the period from the early 1890s through World War I. Traditionally and appropriately, much of the attention has been focused on the role of Robert Marion LaFollette. LaFollette, elected to the United States Congress for three terms between 1885 and 1891, became the spokesman for Wisconsin progressivism. Yet, as recent scholarship has suggested, LaFollette was not a rebel during his Congressional career, and in many instances he was only carrying forward ideas voiced previously by Nils Haugen, Albert R. Hall, and others.

LaFollette's effort to gain control of the Republican party really began after an 1891 meeting in Milwaukee with Senator Philetus Sawyer, one-third of the Sawyer, Spooner and Payne triumvirate controlling the party in the state. Sawyer, according to LaFollette's account, attempted to bribe him to gain influence in a judicial matter being presided over by LaFollette's brother-in-law, Judge Robert Siebecker. Sawyer denied the accusation, but LaFollette's disillusionment with party leadership grew from that point.

Although he gained fame as a reformer, LaFollette actually moved cautiously in the direction of reformism. He was not in sympathy with the Populists and worked hard to defeat William Jennings Bryan in 1896. Thwarted by party regulars in his own bid for the governorship in 1896, LaFollette bided his time and made conciliatory gestures to gain the nomination and the election in 1900. As governor, LaFollette's demands of the legislature included a direct primary election law, increased taxation of the railroads, and a strong state railway commission. Passage of the direct primary referendum by the state's voters in 1904 satisfied the first demand, while the legislature passed a bill in 1905 that provided for a watered-down railway commission.

Following LaFollette's departure for the United States Senate in 1906, progressivism temporarily lost momentum in the state. However, 1910 was a progressive year, and with his Senate seat on the line, LaFollette formed a temporary political alliance with Francis McGovern, who won the gubernatorial race. McGovern, who was never LaFollette's man, took the reformist tide well beyond the point reached by LaFollette. In 1911 a workmen's compensation law was passed, an industrial commission was established, a successful state income tax law was implemented, and the State Life Insurance Fund was developed. McGovern's administration also encouraged further development of the "Wisconsin Idea," which involved cooperation and support between the state government and the University of Wisconsin.

McGovern's second term was not successful, and troubles among the Progressives increased in 1914, when McGovern lost his bid for a Senate seat. Conservative Emmanuel Philipp was elected governor; he was pledged to a program of economy and rolling back progressivism. A conservative trend was apparent as the zeal for reform declined. Internal dissension further hurt the cause of the Progressives.

More crucial to the fate of Progressivism than the threat of a return to conservatism by a gubernatorial candidate was the onset of World War I. Wisconsin, with its heavy German population, was deeply divided over the war and experienced a traumatic situation. Senator LaFollette and nine of the state's congressmen voted against President Wilson's declaration of war in 1917. LaFollette, who never strayed from a position of strict neutrality, opposed preparedness measures and called for nationalization of the arms industry. Ultimately, an unsuccessful effort was started to remove him from the Senate; yet, neutrality had been so popular in 1916 that he had won an easy re-election victory.

The other source of embarrassment to patriotic organizations in Wisconsin was the antiwar position espoused by Milwaukee's Socialists. Under the leadership of Victor Berger, socialism appealed to many in the German working-class wards in Milwaukee. So strong was the neutrality sentiment in 1916 (coupled with the mess in city hall created by the two major parties) that Socialist Daniel Hoan was elected mayor of the city. Berger, the first Socialist elected to Congress (in 1910), was again elected to Congress in 1918, but was charged with violation of the Espionage Act of 1917 and sentenced to a long prison term. When the House refused to seat him, Wisconsin elected him again—and again he was refused admission into Congress. After the espionage verdict was overturned in 1921, Berger was elected again in 1922 and seated without incident.

Patriotic groups such as the Wisconsin Defense League and the Wisconsin Loyalty Legion were formed to prove to the rest of America that Wisconsin was not a traitorous state; their propaganda attacked Germans and Socialists indiscriminately. Small towns were the real centers of super-patriotism, but no part of the state completely escaped this nationalistic jingoism and hostility.

The pressures of war and the conservative trends in evidence by 1914 resulted in less legislative effort at reform. By 1919 many Progressives had become discouraged; as with the rest of the nation, "normalcy" had set in in Wisconsin, and reformers spent the next decade in retreat and confusion. LaFollette himself emerged to lead the Progressive party nationally in 1924, but reform in the state diminished substantially by that time.

1: LaFollette and Progressivism in Wisconsin

Central to the history of the Progressive movement in Wisconsin is the role of Robert M. LaFollette. In the first selection, David P. Thelen discusses LaFollette's emergence as a spokesman for the reformers in Wisconsin's Republican party. Thelen's account of the Sawyer-LaFollette encounter in 1891 leaves confusion about what actually happened. Readers may wish to consult LaFollette's *Autobiography* to get his version of the incident, while Sawyer's role is reported in Richard Current's *Pine Logs and Politics: A Life of Philetus Sawyer.*

Nils Haugen, author of the reminiscences in the second selection, was the only Republican congressman to survive the disastrous election of 1890. Originally numbered among LaFollette's supporters, Haugen became disillusioned with him in later years.

The final two selections deal with two specific issues facing the state during the peak of Progressive success. The effort to gain public support for road building is described in the first of the two. In 1911, the legislature voted to submit the question of woman suffrage to the voters in a referendum. Suffragettes took to the road in an unsuccessful attempt to gain support for the referendum. The last selection chronicles some of their efforts.

LaFollette Becomes a Reformer

DAVID P. THELEN

The popular legend of how ex-Congressman LaFollette became an insurgent progressive gives credence to Napoleon's famous dic-

From David P. Thelen, *Robert M. LaFollette and the Insurgent Spirit* (Boston, 1976), pp. 16–21. Reprinted by permission.

358

tum that history is the agreed-upon myth. In 1911 friends and enemies alike considered LaFollette the nation's oldest and most courageous progressive, and they readily accepted the account that he wrote in his autobiography that year. He described his life as a constant struggle against special interests and depicted the offer of a bribe in 1891 as the point at which he had resolved to convert the state of Wisconsin to progressivism. By 1900 he had accomplished his goal when Wisconsin voters, inspired by his speeches, elected him governor.

In fact, however, when the 1890s began, LaFollette was a more or less typical politician whose main distinguishing quality was his receptivity to the mood and feelings of voters. When the economic depression that began in 1893 generated widespread popular unrest in Wisconsin and elsewhere and led voters to demand changes, LaFollette sensed the popularity of insurgency—of challenges to privilege and concentrated wealth and power—and saw in it an opportunity to advance his career. When he began to champion insurgent measures in 1897 it was not as a longtime progressive but as a politician who was unusually responsive to grassroots attitudes.

LaFollette never could have imagined these developments in 1891 when he settled into the life of a lawyer in Madison, Wisconsin. University students and state employees gave Madison a more intensely political and intellectual climate than that of most villages. Madisonians came to like their short, clean-shaven ex-congressman who worked so hard that he would annually collapse from nervous exhaustion.

· ·

LaFollette could not return to the state capital and expect to retire from politics. He gladly spoke for the ticket when Republican leaders asked him. He cherished the applause of the audiences, and he met—and charmed—dozens of politicians as he travelled all over the state to promote the party. Now, however, there was a difference in his relationship to the leaders—a difference that had grown out of a conversation he had on September 17, 1891, with United States Senator Philetus Sawyer. As he answered Sawyer's summons to Milwaukee's Plankinton House, LaFollette knew that the senator would lose $300,000 if he lost a case that was about to be heard before LaFollette's brother-in-law, Judge Robert Siebecker, in Madison.

What they actually said to each other must remain a mystery forever since Sawyer and LaFollette told radically different stories. LaFollette dashed home to Madison and told his family and friends that Sawyer had flashed a large roll of bills and promised more if

LaFollette could persuade Siebecker to decide the case "right." LaFollette recalled that he had angrily told Sawyer: "If you struck me in the face you could not insult me as you insult me now." LaFollette then told this story to Siebecker, who promptly withdrew from the case. Editors speculated that someone, probably Sawyer, had tried to bribe Siebecker. Sawyer immediately released his version. Sawyer explained that he had not known that Siebecker was LaFollette's brother-in-law and was only trying to retain LaFollette to help the defense lawyers.

The public battle between LaFollette and Sawyer seriously affected LaFollette's ambitions. Party leaders insisted publicly that the controversy was insignificant, but LaFollette knew that the leaders closest to Sawyer would never forgive him for raising the whole issue. If he were ever again to run for office, he would need a personal organization.

Even during the 1880s he had relied for his elections on loyal friends and his zealous defense of popular causes more than on party leaders. In the 1890s, when he emerged as the leader of a new faction within the Republican Party, he again built a personal organization and championed popular issues as he sought to wrest control of the state party from Sawyer. His organization, like others across the country, battled the dominant faction only because it did not promote ambitious politicians rapidly enough. Reaching for power, they charged that wicked bosses controlled the ruling "machine" and pledged to throw the rascals out, while differing very little on matters of principle. Victory meant only that a different group would administer the state and distribute the patronage. There was nothing very reformist about LaFollette's faction before 1897.

Although LaFollette had alienated Sawyer's friends, other politicians turned to him because he was a "rattling campaigner" and charming person. "One can't shake hands with the man without a quiet feeling that he can get on the payroll any time he pleases," observed one editor. LaFollette spoke at school picnics, county fairs, and church gatherings. In sharp contrast to the leaders of the ruling faction, he sought direct contact with voters.

He attracted individuals and groups with grievances against the "machine"—the Sawyer faction. Ambitious young men who thought they could rise faster in his organization than in the machine's joined him. Dairy farmers, who hated the machine for its subservience to the oleomargarine interests, also turned to LaFollette, and their statewide leader, ex-Governor William D. Hoard, became one of LaFollette's leading champions. In fact, dairy farmers colored his organization so completely in 1896 that one editor urged LaFollette to learn that "there are more momentous issues involved in the present campaign than the dairy cow."

Scandinavians, living mainly in the rural western part of the state, had overwhelmingly supported the Republican Party since its formation and believed that the machine took their loyalty too much for granted and denied them long overdue political recognition. In the election of 1890, Sawyer and Henry C. Payne, who courted German Protestants, believed that Governor Hoard and the Republican 1889 legislature had blundered badly by sponsoring the school language law. Hoping that the Germans would soon return to the GOP, the machine leaders gave Hoard and the party only lukewarm support. Since Scandinavians did not particularly care about the law, they interpreted the machine's inaction in 1890 as proof of its indifference to them and preference for Germans. LaFollette recognized the Scandinavians' desires and rewarded them. He chose Norwegian-born Nils P. Haugen as his organization's first gubernatorial candidate in 1894 because "I knew [the Scandinavians] felt a certain national pride in Congressman Haugen's prominence and success, and I counted on their giving him very strong support." LaFollette wooed Scandinavian voters further by urging friendly state and federal officials to appoint Scandinavians to patronage jobs.

After the machine beat Haugen in 1894, LaFollette and his friends began planning for 1895. LaFollette decided to run for governor himself. He mailed more than a thousand letters to local politicians, most of them young, urging them to pack their caucuses with voters who would elect LaFollette delegates to the state nominating convention. Ex-Governor Hoard appealed directly to voters to support his friend. LaFollette was delighted with the results. He would go to the Milwaukee convention on August 5 with twelve more delegates than he needed to win the nomination.

Sawyer's friends had one thing LaFollette lacked: money. On the night before the convention would nominate its governor, twenty delegates told LaFollette that they had been offered bribes to support the machine's candidate. The next day the convention chose Edward Scofield.

LaFollette's loyal delegates, many of them participating in politics for the first time, were furious. Though they urged him to run as an independent, LaFollette knew that he could not possibly win. He sent the disappointed delegates home, determined to win in 1898. In the meantime, LaFollette proved his loyalty by speaking for the entire GOP ticket in the fall.

In private, however, LaFollette and his close friends brooded deeply over the 1896 defeat. As a responsive politician, LaFollette began looking for issues to promote his candidacy for 1898. In 1897 he decided to advocate a program with which voters could associate him, one that fitted his own ambitions and style of popular politics. He took his new ideology directly from reformers who had been battling political establishments in towns and cities across Wisconsin and the nation. The obvious popularity of these grassroots reformers converted Robert M. LaFollette into an insurgent progressive.

LaFollette Viewed by a Contemporary

NILS P. HAUGEN

My own course being so closely interwoven with the political life and ambitions of LaFollette, I feel it necessary to give him more space and attention than might otherwise be warranted. No sooner had LaFollette taken his seat in the Senate than he discovered a star still higher in the political firmament, and the presidency became his consuming aspiration. I first became aware of this in the autumn of 1907. The presidential election of the following year was attracting public attention. While the press naturally gave much space to the subject, very little, however, was devoted to LaFollette, except an occasional notice in the state newspapers. There was certainly no apparent popular demand. I was therefore surprised when on a Saturday afternoon I called at his farm home at Maple Bluff and found a number of his friends consulting with him as to his prospects of obtaining the nomination. I was about to withdraw, not having been invited to the apparently private conference, when Bob asked me to "sit in." I did so, but listened only, until asked by him what I thought of it. I frankly stated that thus far I had discovered no apparent demand for his candidacy, that I thought the efforts as outlined would be in vain; adding that I feared he would go into the convention with the Wisconsin delegation only, and might not have

From Nils P. Haugen, "Pioneer and Political Reminiscences, Part 6," *Wisconsin Magazine of History*, XII,3 (1928), 271–293. Reprinted by permission of the State Historical Society of Wisconsin.

Courtesy of the SHSW [WHi (X3) 7855]

Robert M. LaFollette

that entire; that if he aspired to that high office the way to attain it, in my opinion, was to make the best record possible in the Senate, and, "if you please, on the Chatauqua Circuit," where he had acquired some repute; but that his candidacy at the time seemed premature and hopeless. At any rate, that was the substance of my answer. It was the last time I was asked to "sit in." The result confirmed my forecast. Bob went into the convention with the Wisconsin delegation, except one delegate from the Wausau district. It may have given him some advertising. He continued to pursue this ambition with the same persistence that he had pursued the governorship in the nineties. I certainly gave him my honest opinion, and feel now that his burning ambition was unfortunate for himself; and that if the office had been more modestly sought he might have been more successful. But his impatience would brook no delay. I believe, too, that his service in the Senate might have been more effective for the good of the country, and incidentally better for himself, if he could have forgotten his higher ambition. There was no breach in our friendship because of my failure to give unqualified approval to his candidacy at the time referred to; at any rate, none came to my notice. I have not been able to consider his presidential aspirations otherwise than as unfortunate for himself and for others, as there was at no time a reasonable hope of his success. He met with repeated disappointments, and was a poor loser, as manifested at each repeated defeat. They made him unhappy. When I first knew Bob in Washington, he was a cheerful and happy individual. From his general attitude and expressions in his magazine and elsewhere it is fair to presume that after 1912, and perhaps after 1908, he never voted for the Republican nominee for president.

. . . .

He became a carping critic of each and every administration. He was entirely unable to do teamwork, which is so necessary in legislation. Perhaps he was better adapted to executive than to legislative service. In legislation, in order to progress at all, there must be compromises. To that necessity LaFollette was entirely oblivious. He must have his way, or stop the machine. He, who in old times had aided Tom Reed to break up filibustering in the House, became the greatest obstructionist in the Senate. He had earned his early laurels as an opponent to "boss rule" but became the supreme type of the "boss" in his later years. He made friends easily, but discarded them without a scruple when he thought it to his political advantage. Many of them were good and faithful friends, ready to give him honest advice, but perhaps giving it too disinterestedly; advice that would have served him well in the end. In this manner he estranged many of his early and most loyal friends and earnest supporters; men like Isaac Stephenson, Gen. George E. Bryant, Herman Daley, James Davidson; yes, even his early political foster father, Eli Peterson, did not come up to the mark. Later Senator Lenroot and Governor McGovern were added to the number of cast-off friends; each one sacrificed for no apparent reason, except that LaFollette desired more subserviency in his supporters. He is too important a character in Wisconsin history, and his imprint upon its political development was such that discussion of him cannot be omitted. He should be treated fairly, but truthfully, and that I aim to do. There is certainly no one in sight to take his place in the leadership of his clique; believing that term fully justified. But, for the present I would say:

> "No farther seek his merits to disclose,
> Or draw his frailties from their dread abode."

The Struggle for Roads

BALLARD CAMPBELL

During the transformation of public opinion toward the acceptance of state-financed highways, the automobile age dawned in Wisconsin. Although various Wisconsinites claimed to have built motor vehicles in earlier years, gasoline-powered motor cars first appeared regularly in the state in 1899. At the opening of the state fair that year in Milwaukee, a newspaper reported that "automobiles dashed hither and thither." Three years later the Milwaukee city council passed an ordinance to regulate autos, limiting their speed to a reckless four miles per hour. Around 1901 cars were seen in Madison, and soon afterward in other cities. When LaFollette rode in an auto during part of his 1902 gubernatorial campaign, his use of the new mode of transportation symbolized the emergence of the motor era in Wisconsin.

Motoring was not only a new travel experience for people in the

From Ballard Campbell, "The Good Roads Movement in Wisconsin, 1890–1911," *Wisconsin Magazine of History*, XLIX,4 (Summer 1966), 273–293. Footnotes in the original omitted. Reprinted by permission of the State Historical Society of Wisconsin.

state, but Wisconsin also became a regional center of the automotive industry. By 1906 Thomas Jeffrey in Kenosha, George Kissel in Hartford, and Lewis Mitchell in Racine—names best remembered now among antique automobile buffs—all were producing cars. Like the other early automobile manufacturers in the state, Jeffrey, Kissel, and Mitchell failed to weather the rigorous competition in the new industry, and only the KisselKar survived until the Great Depression. Jeffrey's operation, however, was continued by Charles Nash, and at mid-century, the Nash-Kelvinator Corporation introduced a modern version of the old Jeffrey "Rambler." Other manufacturers during the same period turned to the production of motorcycles and auto parts, and shortly afterward, trucks. The A. O. Smith Corporation of Milwaukee, for example, now the principal manufacturer of automobile structural parts, made its first auto frames in 1903 and by the end of the decade captured the major share of that market.

Like the bicycles of the previous decade, the automobilists' newly formed acquaintance with country roads aroused their interest in highway improvement, and through the vehicle of their automobile clubs they added their voices to the chorus that already preached the good roads message. The first auto club in Wisconsin was organized in Milwaukee in 1902, the early center of auto activity in the state, and the next year another was formed in Madison. Through the energetic leadership of the Milwaukee Auto Club and its active secretary, James T. Drought, the Wisconsin State Automobile Association was created in 1907, with road improvement included among its avowed objectives. Members of these clubs and others established in urban areas during the first decade of the twentieth century pioneered the motor age. Not only did they contend with roads unsuited for rapid speeds, and sometimes for any speed, but they also faced roads that were poorly marked, if at all. After motoring from Milwaukee to Madison in 1907, James Drought commented that "we 'blazed the trail' by putting up yellow signs and arrows along the route on fence and telegraph posts marking the way."

The appearance of motor vehicles on Wisconsin's roads prompted the state to establish automobile regulations. After attempts failed in the senate in 1903, a law passed in the next legislative session which limited the speed of autos to twenty-five miles per hour in the country and twelve miles per hour in the city, and required the registration of all vehicles with the Wisconsin secretary of state. In compliance with the law, 1,492 autos were granted licenses in 1905, a ratio of approximately one car to every 1,400 citizens. Because horses, as well as many of their owners, reacted unfavorably to the new "machines," the law also stipulated that every person operating an auto must "stop all motor power and remain stationary" upon a signal from a person riding or driving a horse. While the confrontation between horse and horseless carriage is far less frequent now than it used to be, the basic structure of this portion of the 1905 auto regulation law is still a part of Wisconsin's statutes.

Most motorists favored registration and other reasonable regulations, but they were annoyed by the widespread hostility to their vehicles. One form of this opposition appeared in a law proposed in 1907 which would have reduced the legal speed limits to eight miles per hour in the city and twelve miles per hour on rural roads. Fortunately for motorists the bill failed to become law, in good part because of the active lobby against the measure by James Drought and the Milwaukee Auto Club. Realizing that many lawmakers had little understanding of reasonable auto speeds, Drought gave numerous legislators their first automobile rides by driving them around the state capitol. But the autoists received a setback two years later, however, when Governor James O. Davidson vetoed a bill that raised the legal city speed to eighteen miles per hour, a rate which he contended was "highly improper and dangerous."

The bulk of the opposition to the new horseless carriages came from farmers, who displayed their resentment by denouncing motorists as "road hogs" and "joy-riders." Some rural inhabitants considered automobiling on the public highways as trespassing upon their own private property. Not all farmers spread nails on the roads or shot holes in auto tires as occasionally occurred, but those who had their horses frightened by a car often viewed the vehicles as unneeded nuisances, a situation which probably reinforced some rural resistance to road reform. The upshot of rural resentment to automobilists in the early years of the twentieth century was a strong demand for legal curtailment of auto freedom. Even though some farmers used gasoline engines for farm chores, few farmers could afford to purchase a car during the first decade of the twentieth century, and many of them considered autos an expensive luxury. While a few auto producers offered relatively inexpensive models, such as Ford's $600 Model N which appeared in 1907, the average retail price of a new car in 1909 was $1,719, a figure beyond the reach of all but wealthy farmers. The popularity of motor vehicles did gain momentum among farmers around 1908 and 1909, but other factors prevented widespread use of motor transportation during most of the first decade of the century. Inexpensive one- or two-cylinder models were too frail to last long on bad country roads, heavier autos were too expensive, and foul weather frequently prohibited motor travel altogether. One dairy farmer, while recognizing the potential of auto transportation, suggested their limitations by complaining that motor vehicles were too unreliable and too costly. "We as farmers," he remarked in 1912, "could get along without the autowagon, but we could not dispense with the horse."

During the years that the automobile made its debut in Wisconsin, both the state and federal governments inaugurated campaigns for state road aid. The federal government officially began its good roads work in 1893 through the creation of the Office of Public Roads Inquiry (Office of Public Roads after 1904). Beginning in the twentieth century the federal road agency did a small portion of its educational and demonstration work in Wisconsin. Besides its lecturers and publications which broadcast arguments for state aid to Wisconsin's rural residents, the Office of Public Roads occasionally built model roads in the state and sent technical advisers to local areas that requested expert assistance in improving their highways.

Paralleling the work of the federal highway agency were the activities of Wisconsin's Geological and Natural History Survey, created in 1897. At first the Survey's highway work consisted only of testing road materials. Later, however, with the creation of a Highway Division within the Geological Survey in 1907, the Survey exhibited practical examples of professional highway maintenance through model road, consultant, and educational work. Probably the most significant contribution which the Highway Division made to the good roads movement was demonstrating to skeptical rural residents and officials the improvements that were possible when trained engineers, using modern machinery, supervised road construction.

Shouldering the responsibility for the Highway Division's work was its director, William O. Hotchkiss, a civic-minded geology instructor at the state university and later the state geologist. Hotchkiss not only supervised the activities of his small staff of engineers, but he also was a vociferous advocate of state-aided roads. While his chief objectives lay in convincing farmers and rural governmental officials that a co-ordinated system of good roads depended upon state financial assistance, Hotchkiss also made frequent speaking appearances after 1906 before automobile clubs, conventions of rural mailmen, municipal organizations, and urban-sponsored good roads associations. His energetic publicity campaign, plus his later contribution of helping to create a centralized highway commission, earned Hotchkiss the complimentary though not entirely accurate epithet of "father" of the good roads movement in Wisconsin.

While the work of Hotchkiss and the Highway Division put the prestige of the state behind professional highway improvements, their role in hastening acceptance of state aid to roads was marginal, as growing numbers of farmers already endorsed state-financed roads. This change of opinion was evident when two successive legislatures easily brushed aside token opposition and passed resolutions in 1905 and 1907 to submit an internal improvement amendment to the people for referendum.

. . . .

By a decisive mandate of 116,107 to 46,762, the people of Wisconsin registered their approval of the constitutional change in 1908.

. . . .

When Governor Francis E. McGovern signed the bill into law on June 14, 1911, Wisconsin joined thirty-eight other states in providing financial assistance for highway construction.

Suffragettes Take to the Road

KENNETH W. DUCKETT

In 1911 the State Legislature had voted to submit the question of woman suffrage to the electorate at the next general election on November 5, 1912. As soon as Governor Francis McGovern signed the bill, the officers of the Political Equality League began organizing county suffrage groups. The officers, for the most part, were uninitiated amateurs in political affairs, but what they lacked in skill and experience they more than made up in imagination and enthusiasm. Early in their attempts to organize the counties they concluded that their strongest opposition came from the women themselves, the "prigs in petticoats" who felt that "womenly women" should not be concerned with politics. After deciding that

From "Suffragettes on the Stump: Letter from the Political Equality League of Wisconsin, 1912," with introduction and notes by Kenneth W. Duckett, *Wisconsin Magazine of History,* XXXVIII,1 (Autumn 1954), 31–34. Footnotes in the original omitted. Reprinted by permission of the State Historical Society of Wisconsin.

I intend to vote for Woman Suffrage Nov. 5, 1912.

Name _Teddy Roosevelt_

Address _Washington D.C. (after nov 5/12)_

If you are with us, please fill out this card and return it to

THE POLITICAL EQUALITY LEAGUE,

518 Colby-Abbot Bldg., 445 Milwaukee St.

Milwaukee, Wis.

We want to remind all our friends just before election.

I am with you Girls! Heart & Soul!

Courtesy of the SHSW [WHi (X3) 33854]

Teddy Roosevelt's campaign endorsement of the Woman Suffrage Movement (card found in the Ada James papers)

more than staid polite little speeches would be necessary to startle their disinterested sisters out of their complacency, the officers of the League embarked upon a campaign deliberately patterned on the spectacular appeal of the circus sideshow.

. . . .

By airplane and by boat—colorful but limited methods—the suffragettes carried their message to some of the people, but it was by automobile tours that they reached the voters in Wisconsin's many hamlets and at the crossroads. In 1912 it was considered quite daring for a group of women to travel alone by car about the countryside, and, as a concession to public opinion, men chauffeured the first tours. Later, as campaign funds dwindled and expenses mounted, the women began to drive their own cars. In the letter printed below Crystal Eastman Benedict, campaign manager of the Political Equality League, instructed a suffragist worker how to organize an automobile tour.

July 12, 1912

Mrs. C. W. Steele,
Whitewater, Wis.
Dear Mrs. Steele:

I certainly am proud of the Whitewater League. The way you all stiffened up under that rebuff and found yourselves stronger than ever as a result of it was perfectly splendid and now how beautifully it has come out. I am sure Miss King will be equal to the occasion, and that you will have a fine time tomorrow night.

Now Miss James and I have been discussing your letter and have decided to make this suggestion very strongly to your Whitewater organization. We advise you to keep Miss King right on for four or five days and organize with an automobile with her help, and that of your local speakers. I will tell you exactly how we have done it in Milwaukee this week because I think you can follow the same plan. We have borrowed a different automobile every day and made one big town every night. The machine with two speakers and three or four good lively workers would start out about 2 o'clock or any time to reach the destination by 4. The machine would be decorated with a great big *Votes for Women* banner and two or three little flags. It would be driven up and down the streets of the town a great many times so that everybody in town would have a chance to see it. Then all the workers in the machine and speakers, would get out and each take a different street and leave a dodger like the enclosed at every house, speaking with the women also, and urging her to come and bring her men folks. They would have time to tack up dodgers in stores and on telegraph poles and every available place also. If you could get a cornet or some musical instrument to travel up and down with the machine, it would be even better. After advertising yourselves thus in a thorough way, the party would go to the hotel and eat their supper and rest a little while and then they would find their crowd assembled around the machine.

After trying many ways of conducting an automobile tour this seems to be the most successful. To do one big town a day get up your own meeting by advertising yourselves the way the circus does with its parade. This avoids depending on newspaper advertisements, etc. for drawing a crowd.

Besides holding the meeting our girls were able to form a little committee in each town through their canvassing in the afternoon and to get a good many voters' pledges signed in the crowd at night. If you can do this, especially if you can leave a little responsible committee it makes the trip eminently worth while.

Now if you can get the machine for all day and your workers are equal to a long trip, you can start out at ten or eleven and take in the smaller towns at noon, but speaking in the afternoon when the men are all at work doesn't seem to me of much use.

Now don't you think you could borrow automobiles enough to do your county in this way next week, or at least to touch the towns that have no organization? No doubt you could rent a machine for a day or two to fill in if you needed it and pay for it out of collections taken on the trip. Miss Henderson should surely go with Miss King and speak also, and as many more of you as could get in the machine should go along to do the work. If you can follow this plan just keep Miss King as long as you need her. If not, drop me a line and we will be glad to get her back of course or to send her somewhere else.

Your plan of speaking at the band concerts is splendid and if you run out of speakers we will send someone.

To be very definite in regard to the expenses of the auto trip, I would come back to your headquarters every night. I believe you can reach every point in your county in this way. Then there is no expense unless you have to rent a car, except, of course, having the dodgers printed. These are very cheap and very important.

I am glad you are looking forward toward county organization. It would be a good idea to get Sharon, Elkhorn, Lake Geneva, and Whitewater representatives to meet and divide up the work of the County and perhaps to appoint County officers. I am sure we could send Miss Curtis. Miss Judd has been married and left us. Miss Curtis is way out in the western part of the State and may be obliged to stay there for some time, but we can surely send you someone who will be equal to the task whenever you need her if you can give us a few days warning.

I believe the canvassing blanks and pledge cards and literature you ordered have been sent.

With best wishes for your work.

Cordially yours,

Crystal Eastman Benedict
Campaign Manager.

2: Milwaukee Socialists, the "Other Progressives"

Socialists gained control in Milwaukee in 1910 just as Progressives were reaching the zenith of their power in the state. The origins and growth of the movement are discussed in the first selection which follows. The role of organized labor in the success of Milwaukee Socialism is the subject of the second selection.

Daniel Hoan, who served as mayor of Milwaukee from 1916 to 1940, and Victor Berger, the nation's first Socialist congressman, are the best-known Socialists from this era. Hoan's role in municipal reform is the subject of the third selection, and his attitude toward World War I is discussed in the fourth. The final article in this section describes Congress's almost unanimous refusal to seat Berger in the congressional sessions of 1919 and 1921; his re-election each time by his Milwaukee district; and his eventual seating in 1923 after the Supreme Court threw out the espionage conviction.

The Origins of Milwaukee Socialism

FREDERICK I. OLSON

Socialist doctrine was brought to Milwaukee as early as the 1840's with the arrival of German immigrants, especially the Forty-Eighters, and was nurtured in liberal German societies such as the Turners. The Marxian version reached the west side of Lake Michigan by the late 1860's, and in the next decade and a half

From Frederick I. Olson, "Milwaukee's Socialist Mayors: End of an Era and Its Beginning," *Historical Messenger,* XVI,1 (March 1960), 3–8. Reprinted by permission of the Milwaukee County Historical Society.

Milwaukee witnessed slow growth of socialist thought and organization. During the 1880's local radicalism was channeled into the eight-hour day agitation and the Knights of Labor, and in the 1890's into an urban Populism, with labor leader Robert Schilling providing continuity. The leading socialist agitator was Paul Grottkau, whose jousts with the more conservative and unpredictable Schilling were offset by his effective debates with anarchist Johann Most.

In the early 1890's Austrian-born Victor L. Berger assumed leadership of an informal group of German-speaking socialists, holding them together by his editorship of the "Wisconsin Vorwarts," formerly Grottkau's organ. Possessed of a keen mind and extensive European education, Berger moved forward from a temporary flirtation with Henry George's single tax to outspoken advocacy of Marxian socialism but with strong political interests. So pronounced was the German cast of Berger's cohorts when they gathered to discuss socialist theories that the late Frederick Heath, a Mayflower descendant, was promptly labeled a "Yankee socialist" when he volunteered to join.

One of the strengths of this study group was its close relation with organized labor. Frank J. Weber, a seaman who was a prime mover in the Wisconsin State Federation of Labor for a quarter of a century after its founding in 1893, gravitated into the socialist camp. Berger himself gained the confidence of trade union leaders sufficiently that his "Vorwarts" and later his English-language paper, the "Social Democratic Herald," became official union organs. Fred Brockhausen, who worked alongside Weber during the first decade of the twentieth century in the WSFL, also favored socialism. The State Federation went so far as to imbed into its constitution a declaration of principles of socialist inspiration.

Marxian socialist thought implied that the evolution of the capitalist economy would ultimately produce socialism, but it also sounded a call for revolution to overthrow the present system and end its attendant human misery. Milwaukee's socialists talked in orthodox fashion, but they believed strongly in the use of the ballot box. In Berger's case, revisionism went so far as to include advocacy of remedial legislation, thus softening the alleged evils of capitalism instead of permitting conditions to deteriorate until revolution became inevitable.

In the middle 1890's Berger and company expressed their political interests through the Populist party. In Milwaukee this involved some cooperation with Schilling, whom they distrusted, but it avoided the hated Socialist Laborites, now under Daniel De Leon.

The fiasco of the Populists in the Bryan campaign of 1896, however, led Berger and his closest friends to conclude that the time had come for independent political action. Nationally their opportunity arose when Eugene V. Debs, labor's hero in the Pullman strike of 1894, announced his conversion to socialism. Now, in Chicago in 1897, Berger helped Debs convert his Brotherhood of the Cooperative Commonwealth into the Social Democracy of America. The latter was committed to a western colonizing scheme, a variation on the contemporary form of communitarianism, but the Milwaukeeans had no interest in it whatsoever.

The first branch of the Social Democracy of America, organized in Milwaukee soon after the national founding in Chicago, was so impatient to try politics that it obtained a special dispensation to run candidates in the city elections of 1898. While the entry of Social Democrats into Milwaukee politics took on great significance later, their mayoralty candidate did poorly in 1898, whereas the Democrats, now formally joined by Schilling's Populists in a "Popocrat" ticket, swept all before them. The new mayor, elected on a platform of reform, public ownership, and business hostility, was David S. Rose. Handsome, goateed, dapper, an attractive campaigner, Rose captured the city's attention so well that he was re-elected in four of the next five campaigns and served ten years as the city's chief executive.

Between 1898 and 1910 the Milwaukee Socialists steadily gained in political power until they captured control of the city and county governments from the Democrats and Republicans. To be sure, their success in the April 1910 elections, when they won the mayoralty and other city-wide offices plus a majority of the Common Council and the County Board, came in a three-party contest by a plurality, not a clear-cut majority of the votes. That it was not political accident was demonstrated in the fall elections, however, when the Socialists increased their representation in the state legislature, won county offices, and, most significantly, sent Berger to Washington from the Fifth District as the party's first Congressman.

How can we account for these sweeping victories of a 12-year old party which bore a foreign label and advocated the political and economic doctrines of European thinkers? Only by reference to three levels of explanation: first, the quality of local Socialist leadership and the capacity of its supporters for party work, that is, factors lying within the party; second, favoring circumstances within the local political scene; and third, the existence of a strong reform spirit in state and nation which was not deflected by the socialist label.

Socialists and Labor

FREDERICK I. OLSON

On April 19, 1960, when Frank P. Zeidler retired from the Milwaukee city hall, Socialist party members had occupied the mayor's office for thirty-eight of the previous fifty years, making of Milwaukee one of the most successful and durable examples of local Socialist party strength in the nation. To name some of the party's former leaders of the past half-century is to prove a point: Emil Seidel, first Socialist to become chief executive of a major American city; Daniel Webster Hoan, for twenty years mayor, and city attorney during the preceding six years; and Victor L. Berger, the nation's first Socialist Congressman.

Although as a party Milwaukee's Socialists never commanded the dependable allegiance of a majority of the city's voters and at their peak had hardly even a numerous membership, their candidates, beginning in 1904, could and did win election and re-election to selected local, state, and Congressional offices. Their electoral successes were particularly marked until the mid-1930's when they chose to join a broader movement with the LaFollettes and their labor farm allies, and thus lost their identity.

It is possible to find a convincing explanation for the remarkable political success of the Socialists in Milwaukee. During the nineteenth century the city received a large migration of Germans, many of them familiar with and some quite sympathetic to socialist ideas. Among the convinced socialists, all of whom were friendly to labor and to union organization, were such leaders as Berger, who advocated political action and the revisionist doctrines of Eduard Bernstein. Early in the twentieth century these politically-conscious leaders found their opportunity in Milwaukeeans' increasing awareness that Democrats and Republicans alike shared in local corruption and incompetence. The national trend toward municipal reform in the Progressive era, and particularly the increasing respectability of Socialist party activity, helped to make Milwaukee's Socialists acceptable. Increasing public confidence in the record of party members elected to the state legislature, the common council, the county board, and the school board was stimulated by constant party agitation and a sound political organization. Berger's publishing enterprises, in German and English, though privately controlled, provided a form of party press. The successes of 1910, when So-

From Frederick I. Olson, "The Socialist Party and the Union in Milwaukee, 1900-1912," *Wisconsin Magazine of History*, XLIV,2 (Winter 1960-1961), 110-116. Footnotes in the original omitted. Reprinted by permission of the State Historical Society of Wisconsin.

cialist pluralities won control of the common council and county board, elected a mayor and Congressman and sent a fourteen-man delegation to the state legislature, surprised only those who had ignored the meaning of election returns since 1904.

Thus no single factor can account for Milwaukee's emergence as a Socialist stronghold. The character of the party, both in its leadership and in its rank and file, was important. The city's ethnic pattern and its low political estate provided the opportunity; national reform trends co-operated. But our concern here, however, is solely with one aspect of these factors—the relationship of the Socialist party to the labor unions. It is my contention that this relationship was essential to the party's success.

From 1893 until his death in 1929, Victor Berger dominated the Milwaukee Socialist movement, setting forth its philosophy, defining its objectives, and determining the means it would employ. Its trade-union policy, in particular, was largely of his making.

. . . .

In Berger's view, the economic activity of the trade union was complementary to the political activity of the Socialist party. As a practical matter, the most important trade-union relationship which the Milwaukee Socialists maintained from their formal organization as a party in 1897 until they achieved temporary control of the city's government in 1910, was with the Federated Trades Council and a few of the American Federation of Labor-affiliated locals represented in the F.T.C. The Council, associated with the AF of L since 1887, had evolved from the labor strife of the 1880's when union leadership recognized the value of an organization to serve the common local needs of internationally affiliated unions.

The Milwaukee Socialists began their political activity with city and county tickets; and while they always offered candidates for statewide offices and supported the national party nominee in presidential campaigns, their successes were basically local, and so were their significant trade-union relationships. The Wisconsin State Federation of Labor, organized in 1893 when Berger was active in union politics, fitted to some extent into the Socialist scheme of action, especially to the degree that Milwaukee supplied much of its strength and many of its leaders. But just as the Socialist party failed to match party growth in Milwaukee, so Socialist strength in the Wisconsin State Federation of Labor never equalled its hold on the Federated Trades Council. Although until 1910 Berger and his Milwaukee cohorts sought to influence the AF of L in the direction of socialism and their own philosophy of reform, Samuel Gompers kept control and gradually reduced Socialist effectiveness within the Federation.

Given the F.T.C. as the prime target and the W.S.F.L. and AF of L as lesser objectives, what policy guided the Milwaukee Socialists in their union relations? Basically, their aim was to preserve a single trade-union movement as the economic arm of the working class, while developing the Socialist party as the political arm.

. . . .

It is clear, then, that the Socialists, at first more openly and formally than later, gained a foothold in the major organs of the trade-union movement in Milwaukee and to a lesser degree throughout Wisconsin. While no direct evidence on the subject is available, it would appear that the increase in Socialist voting strength from 1898 to 1910, when they captured the city and county with over 40 percent of the vote in three-way balloting, was attributable in part to the support of trade-union members. Socialist voters were concentrated in working-class districts, more obviously when these districts were German rather than Polish, and less clearly whenever Catholics predominated. On the other hand, the Socialists themselves as early as 1904 had apparently concluded that they could not win exclusively by a Marxian appeal to class-conscious workingmen. Consequently, they modified their stand on public utility franchises and adopted more of the progressive reform program with its middle-class appeal. Indeed, they probably gained most by posing as incorruptible while grand juries brought forth hundreds of indictments against Democratic and Republican of-ficeholders and the people they dealt with. Never a truly doctrinaire Marxian, Berger led his party from proletarian revolution to Bern-stein revisionism, and then to practical middleclass reform.

. . . .

In the period under review, it is not possible to determine accurately the union membership status of all Socialist candidates for public office, but evidently far more than half belonged to a union. More significantly, Socialists elected to office were overwhelmingly union members and the majority were labor functionaries. Milwaukee's Socialists, by helping trade unionists to be elected as a matter of course to the common council, county board, school board, state legislature, and in 1910 to city and county-wide offices and to Congress, gave labor unions a stature hitherto denied them by the Democrats and Republicans who had ignored labor candidates, except in very special cases where they were needed chiefly for display or for ticket-balancing.

As a minority group, Socialist trade unionists found legislative office prior to 1910 an admirable opportunity to set party and union platforms before a wide audience. When the Socialists captured control of the common council and the county board, they elected union leaders as presiding officers and used their votes to benefit union labor and trade-union objectives. Capture of administrative positions, including the mayor's office at the top of the city system, afforded opportunities not only for certain forms of patronage, which in the past had generally been denied members of the working class and their leaders, but also for administrative action favorable to union principles. Mayor Seidel's administration from 1910–1912 foreshadowed for Milwaukee the increasing recognition accorded organized labor nationally by the Wilson Administration and on the part of state and local governments during and after the first World War.

Although the Milwaukee Socialists were to retain their political vitality for another quarter of a century, their success of 1910 was reversed by the fusion of Democrats and Republicans two years later. After 1912 new conditions affected Milwaukee politics— nonpartisan elections pitting Socialist against anti-Socialist, new issues generated by municipal housekeeping problems and the War, and the emergence of new party personalities like Daniel Webster Hoan.

On the national scene the Socialist party had passed its peak by 1912. But in Milwaukee, because of Socialist support, the trade-union movement had gained new stableness and stature; one might even say, respectability. In fact, no sharp break between Milwaukee's Socialists and their union allies occurred until the CIO episode of the 1930's. On the surface, the Berger concept of the two arms of the labor movement and the reality of an interlocking directorate served reasonably well. But the ideal relationship of party and union that had helped Milwaukee Socialists to victory in 1910 was lost beyond recovery.

Daniel Hoan and Municipal Reform

ROBERT C. REINDERS

Hoan was approached in 1909 with an offer to serve as the Socialist Party candidate for city attorney in the forthcoming city elections. With some reluctance he accepted. Berger and other party leaders considered him their weakest major candidate.

· ·

Hoan ran against John T. Kelley and John Runge, the present and past city attorneys respectively. During the campaign an event occurred which has become part of Milwaukee's political folklore. Arriving a few minutes early for a noon hour speech at a factory, Hoan was told by a policeman not to loiter. His Irish temper up, Hoan informed his worker audience of the incident and stated that his opponents would not be subject to police harassment and that the men would be forced to listen to them. Prophetically a few days later City Attorney Kelley appeared at the plant and the men were requested by the company to listen to his campaign speech. Kelley had hardly started when a laborer began to sing a popular song, "Slide Kelley, Slide" and was joined by his fellow workingmen. Poor Kelley; at his next factory appearance he was met with the strains of "Has Anybody Here Seen Kelley." Years later Hoan stated that Kelley's plight lent an element of humor to the campaign and undoubtedly benefited the Socialists.

(I might add that Hoan in this campaign made use of his favorite pollsters, street car motormen, whom he felt were more aware of political trends than any other group in the community. When I mentioned Hoan's practice to my Uncle Jacob Manthey, his admiration for Mayor Hoan rose even greater. Perhaps the fact that my Uncle Jake was a street car conductor for forty years had something to do with his attitude.)

Being a reform-minded city attorney in the Progressive Period was a bit like being a "fighting D.A." in more recent times. The embattled city attorney was called on to grapple with the powers of darkness; he was to tackle the "invisible government" of the trusts and to defeat the "malefactors of great wealth." To do this Hoan gathered around him a group of young, talented, underpaid (and non-Socialist) lawyers ready and eager to enter the fray against the "interests."

From Robert C. Reinders, "Daniel W. Hoan and Municipal Reform in Milwaukee, 1910–1920," *Historical Messenger*, XXI,2 (June 1965), 33–44. Reprinted by permission of the Milwaukee County Historical Society.

Courtesy of the SHSW [WHi (X3) 33862]

Milwaukee Mayor Daniel Hoan

No company more nearly epitomized the "evil of big business" than the Milwaukee Electric Railway and Light Company and its subsidiary the Milwaukee Light, Heat and Traction Company; they were part of J. P. Morgan's North American Company and had been originally purchased by Wall Street financiers Henry Villard and Thomas Fortune Ryan. Even the Milwaukee "Sentinel" was hard pressed to defend the street car company, and attacks on the company's rolling stock by aroused citizens were common events.

The several confrontations of the city attorney's office with the street railway company may be observed in one area: cases involving paving by the street car line. Shortly after the 1910 election Hoan and his special assistant, Clifton Williams, made a study of municipal franchises and ordinances, discovering that the city could force the street railways to pave between tracks. Paving requirements were generally written into each street franchise, therefore necessitating legal action on every line. In 1911 the city placed asphalt over wooden blocks on Walnut Street and insisted that the street railway company do likewise, but the latter refused. Supported by a common council resolution Hoan opened a suit in February, 1912 to make the company pave its portion of the street. The Milwaukee County Circuit Court ruled in favor of the city and the case went to the Wisconsin Supreme Court. The street railway attorneys pointed out that the Walnut Street franchise of 1887 ordered the company to repair, not to repave. Chief Justice Winslow was critical of the company's subtleties and stated that where the language is capable of dual meanings, the meaning that benefits the general public takes precedence. He added laconically that after thirty-seven years the pavement must need more than incidental repair. The company was accordingly ordered to pave its section of the street, though not necessarily with asphalt. After losing three more paving cases to the city attorney, the company decided to pave without the benefit of legal counsel.

The efforts of the city attorney to have the Milwaukee Road depress their tracks on the northwest side of the city—one of several such cases instituted by Hoan—is worth noting in detail. When Hoan came to office hearings on track depression were already before the Railroad Commission. Hoan was fearful that the Commission would adopt the Milwaukee Road plan of raising its track level four feet and thus require the city to place its streets below the track level. To counter this possibility Hoan led John Roemer, a Railroad Commissioner, to state for the record that the Commission would never urge the city to lower its streets. Nothing further was accomplished until 1913 when engineers employed by the Railroad Commission compiled a report favoring track depression and on March 24, 1914, a tentative order was issued calling for track depression; a permanent order was delayed until interested groups could study the plans.

The Milwaukee "Leader" and several civic organizations on the strongly Socialist northwest side supported track depression. The Northwest Side Manufactures and Shippers Association opposed the order; they feared that track depression would mean an added expense in rebuilding spur lines. This group and the influential Merchants and Manufacturers Association prevailed upon the Railroad Commission to grant a stay of action. (In October, 1913 the city engineer, George Staal, came to Hoan's office and informed him that Mayor Gerhard Bading had asked him to change his testimony and favor street depression. Hoan advised him not to unless so ordered by the common council.) The Railroad Commission on

October 12 evaded the issue by ordering track depression if the common council approved. Hoan immediately informed shop keepers near the tracks that if the city had to depress its streets customers would enter their stores by step ladders. Almost to the man they came out for track depression. Meanwhile public meetings were held nightly throughout the area and aldermen, always keen to the winds of public opinion, quickly passed a resolution calling for track depression.

Hoan was elated and on January 28, 1916 he went to Madison to arrange for the final signature of the Railroad Commissioner, John Roemer. To Hoan's amazement the Commissioner refused to sign the order. The City Attorney returned to Milwaukee, gathered a group at the Globe Hotel from whom he obtained a list of couple of hundred friends of Roemer. Hoan then telephoned or sent telegrams to each of these individuals urging them to contact Roemer and protest the Commissioner's action. It worked; at eleven the next morning Hoan received news from Madison that Roemer had signed. Thirty years later Hoan recorded that this was his "most important victory" as city attorney.

Hoan's experience with the railroad commission led him to question the basis of state regulation of public utilities and common carriers. Accordingly he wrote a pamphlet, published in 1914, entitled "The Failure of Regulation." Hoan analyzed the weaknesses of regulatory commissions abroad and, using his own experiences, he presented a case by case criticism of the operation of the public service commission in Wisconsin. Since in Hoan's mind regulation was a failure—it fostered rather than deterred monopolies—the only practical answer was public ownership of municipal utilities. The City Attorney's attack was the first serious left-wing critique of the regulatory idea. The book was hardly a "solar plexus [blow] for the LaFollettes and the Progressives," as the Socialist Wisconsin "Comrade" saw it, but it aroused interest among some municipal reformers and undoubtedly strengthened the public ownership movement.

With the approach of the mayoralty campaign of 1916 Hoan could view his years as city attorney with a considerable sense of satisfaction. His work had attracted the admiration of Socialists and non-Socialists alike—one reason he was re-elected in 1914 when other Socialists were defeated. In 1948, looking back on a long and noteworthy career, Hoan told me that his six years as city attorney were his happiest in office.

Daniel Hoan, Socialists, and World War I

ROBERT C. REINDERS

A more serious crisis for Hoan was soon forthcoming. By the winter of 1916–17 the outbreak of war was obviously only a question of time. Would the Socialist Party follow the lead of the European Socialists and endorse their nation's war, or would it adhere to the traditional Marx-Engels position and condemn the war as capitalist inspired and oppose its operation? Hoan favored the former stand, writing two months before the war: "While I personally believe every living soul would regret to see our country involved in a war, still if war should come, then the loyal support and assistance of every citizen will be absolutely necessary." The party was to favor the traditional Socialist position. In order to determine the American Socialist stand an emergency convention was held at St. Louis on April 7. A majority report, drafted by Morris Hillquit, Algernon Lee, and Charles E. Ruthenberg, unequivocally proclaimed: "We brand the declaration of war by our government as a crime of our capitalist class against the people of the United States and against the nations of the world. . . . There has been no war more unjustified than the war in which we are about to engage." It pledged: "Continuous active and public opposition to the war, through demonstration, mass petition, and all other means within our party," and "consistent propaganda against military training." In the party referendum the majority report was adopted and became, thereby, the official "party line" to be accepted by all Socialist Party members.

The "line" was not, however, universally followed. On May 18, 1917, President Wilson signed the conscription bill, authorizing the mayors of all cities of over 30,000 population to administer the draft registration. On the advice of Victor Berger, Hoan decided to carry out the provisions of the law. The day after the act was in force the voting booths were set up to be used for draft registration. Begun on May 27, the draft was completed by June 6, Milwaukee being the first major city to finish the task.

· ·

Hoan urged that a local council of defense be organized to cooperate with the recently established State Council of Defense. The pro-

From Robert C. Reinders, "Daniel W. Hoan and the Milwaukee Socialist Party During the First World War," *Wisconsin Magazine of History*, XXXVI,1 (Autumn 1952), 48–55. Footnotes in the original omitted. Reprinted by permission of the State Historical Society of Wisconsin.

posed council, Hoan contended, should represent all factions in the community in order to convince the people "that this was not Morgan's war." He suggested that the council of defense deal with three types of problems: (1) industrial, involving problems of employment and distribution of labor in industry; (2) financial, raising funds for wartime emergencies; and (3) welfare, looking after those in want due to the war.

. . . .

The Council of Defense was financed by a small state tax and by grants from the city and county governments. Functioning through 1,500 voluntary workers, the council established a food control board to handle food shortages and emergency relief; it set up a labor board to adjust employer-employee differences; and it publicized and secured the cooperation of local organizations in "Hooverizing" Milwaukee. The council also investigated rent profiteering, endeavored to secure an adequate supply of coal and reasonable coal prices through a fuel board, and participated in all the various programs involving the war effort: staging going-away parties for soldiers, furnishing four-minute speakers for Liberty Loan drives, endorsing relief societies, and launching a program of vacant lot cultivation.

. . . .

To the orthodox Socialist, Hoan's attitude toward the St. Louis platform, judged by his war work, was all but scandalous. On the other hand his relations with the Socialist Party were correct and, at times, invaluable. He had protested to President Wilson the Post-Office Department's cancellation of the Socialist *Leader's* mailing privileges; he had protested the imprisonment of Kate Richards O'Hare; he had invited the much maligned anti-war Peoples Council to find a haven in Milwaukee; he had acted as an intermediary between outside Socialists and the *Leader* staff; and he had undergone two personal investigations, one by the Chicago district attorney, and the other by federal authorities. This policy appeased neither the war enthusiasts nor the followers of the "party line" as dictated by the St. Louis platform. The inevitable conflict arose during one of the most turbulent periods in Wisconsin's political history, the winter and spring elections of 1918. Hoan was the first to feel the lash of the party whip.

. . . .

Necessarily, the major campaign issue of the 1918 election would be the war. In Berger's words it was "whether the elector wants to register his vote in favor of an immediate, general, and democratic peace for which the Socialists stand—or whether the electors prefer the vote for a bloody, long drawn-out plutocratic war." The "big and vital issue of unswerving loyalty," as the other Milwaukee papers, with one pro-German exception, defined the campaign, was accepted.

Opposing Hoan were Theodore Dammann, William Park, and Percy Braman, all asserting their loyalty to the war effort. On March 1, at *Bahn Frei* Hall, Hoan began what he expected to be his most difficult campaign. In his opening speech, Hoan stressed the central arguments which he used constantly throughout the campaign, varying only as subsequent events necessitated. He emphasized the need of peace, he condemned the "paytriots" hiding behind the loyalty issue, endorsed Berger's candidacy, and reviewed his program as mayor. On March 5, Hoan's principal opponent, Braman, started his campaign, preaching loyalty and promising to foster a law against seditious talk in Milwaukee. "The true blue Americanism of Mr. Braman is unquestionable," the *Journal* editorialized approvingly the following day. The campaign had not quite begun in earnest, when the executive committee of the council of defense asked Hoan to resign on the ground of his disloyalty to the country.

This was the last group that Hoan had reason to believe would question his loyalty. As recently as January 5, 1918, when the advisory committee was doubting Hoan's devotion to the propagation of the war, Wheeler Bloodgood, speaking for the council of defense, had affirmed Hoan's cooperation with the council in carrying out its war work. However, on March 8, Bloodgood was more critical, declaring that: "Mr. Hoan can neither stand upon nor straddle the St. Louis platform and at the same time head an organization which has for its object doing its part in the winning of this war...." On March 11, the executive council of the defense agency met in Hoan's office and asked Hoan to resign. Hoan refused, and two days later was asked to resign before the full membership of the council. The meeting began with a statement by Bloodgood that the council of defense executive committee had accepted Hoan's stand until the adoption of the Socialist municipal platform, which had rendered his position on the council of defense untenable. Hoan then read a prepared statement to the council. He recounted that when the executive committee had asked him to resign he had inquired of that body a single instance in which he had not supported the war effort and that the committee could offer none. "I then informed the committee that it was clear that the issue they presented was this. . . . They have no objection to either myself personally or my conduct, nor did they claim that I had not supported the program of work outlined by the government. . . . In short . . . the committee . . . does not like my politics." Hoan then took the offensive by challenging the moral and legal right of the council to depose him; morally, because he had organized the group and had preserved its unity; legally, because the group was using taxpayers' funds and should, thereby, represent all the people and not a faction. "I say you cannot get rid of Dan Hoan so easily," he warned them. The vote to depose Hoan was sixteen in favor to five opposed—to depose the four Socialists, thirteen to seven. After an acrimonious debate further action was delayed by a successful move to reconsider the measure on April 2.

With the matter deferred until after the election, Hoan began campaigning again, speaking at from three to five meetings a day. Nor was the opposition quiescent, constantly berating Hoan and the Socialists for their lack of patriotism. The press viewed the election as a noble crusade to vindicate Milwaukee in the eyes of the nation. The March 20 primaries did little to justify their faith. Hoan received 28,493 votes to Braman's 22,374, Dammann's 6,211, and Park's 1,567. The rest of the Socialist ticket was nominated with totals from four to five thousand below Hoan's. Bloodgood, in particular, was not enthusiastic over Hoan's primary vote. Writing to the *Free Press*, he announced fatally: "If the people of this country are ready—as the primary votes would indicate—to . . . abandon the honor of the nation, and stab in the back the boys in France, then we should be treated as an enemy stronghold . . . a province of the German Imperial Government."

. . . .

A less serious incident associated with the war and one which catapulted Hoan for a time into unsought national prominence was his reaction toward a proposed invitation to King Albert of Belgium to visit Milwaukee on his proposed postwar tour about the United States. On September 16, 1919, A. T. Van Scoy of the Milwaukee Association of Commerce requested Hoan to submit the association's invitation to the State Department which was arranging the King's tour. Hoan in his answer to Van Scoy agreed to serve as the medium by which organizations might send invitations, then indiscreetly, if not nonsensically, added:

> Please do not ask me to invite any king, kaiser, or czar. While I mean no disrespect to the Belgium people whom I love, nor discourtesy to you, yet these are days that try men's souls. We must take our places with kings . . . or line up with the rights of common man.
> I should go to my grave in everlasting shame were I to boost one

iota the stock of any king. Mr. Van Scoy, remind your associates, I STAND FOR THE MAN WHO WORKS, TO HELL WITH KINGS.

Papers throughout the country printed the letter in whole or in part. The local *Journal* called it "good campaign stuff," the *Sentinel*, an indication of Hoan's "genius for doing the wrong thing at the wrong time." An editor in dry Kansas moralized: "Only a man capable of so coarse a remark could in the first place have been elected mayor of Milwaukee." The Chicago *Herald-Examiner* headlined: "Milwaukee No Place for Kings." A Southern paper reported that Hoan: "Profanely Scores Gallant Belgium in Letter." The New York *Times* expressed its state of outraged propriety.

As a result of this unsuspected publicity, letters of praise and protest were sent to Hoan, amounting to as many as fifty letters daily. The hundreds of letters Hoan received present a fascinating picture of the over-exaggerated patriotism of the time, and of the anti-monarchial (a more accurate term would be anti-British) feeling which characterized the age. Most of the letters were laudatory, a few comparing Hoan's statement to the famous remarks of Patrick Henry, Thomas Pinckney, and General Grant, some even suggesting that Hoan run for President on the strength of his patriotism. There were critical letters as well, ranging in vituperation from describing Hoan as a "sow-pig" to "misguided."

By 1920 the wartime issues had largely disappeared.

Victor Berger and Congress, 1918-1923

EDWARD J. MUZIK

Muzzled by public opinion, or paralyzed by their own fears and prejudices, or consumed by overwhelming ambition, Congressmen too frequently have acted in ways calculated to insure re-election. This tendency is dramatically illustrated in the case of Victor L. Berger, the Milwaukee Socialist, who twice was prevented from

From Edward J. Muzik, "Victor L. Berger: Congress and the Red Scare," *Wisconsin Magazine of History*, XLVII,4 (Summer 1964), 309-318. Footnotes in the original omitted. Reprinted by permission of the State Historical Society of Wisconsin.

taking his House seat by congressional action during the national hysteria accompanying the Red Scare of 1919–1920.

Berger's exclusions from Congress occurred in November, 1919, and January, 1920, climaxing a long career of left-wing journalism and politico-economic reform.

· ·

When the United States entered the war on April 6, 1917, Berger and the Socialists were in a dilemma. To support the war would mean the denial of their principles and convictions. But to oppose the war might kindle accusations of disloyalty, entail long prison sentences, and perhaps even provoke the dissolution of the Socialist party. This dilemma was resolved by a convention held in St. Louis April 7–14, 1917, which issued an anti-war proclamation roundly denouncing the United States' entry into the war, condemning American participation as "unjustifiable," and rashly avowing the party's "unalterable opposition" to the conflict. In its program of action the party foolhardily promised "continuous, active and public opposition to the war, through demonstrations, mass petitions, and all other means within our power...."

After some hesitation, Berger subscribed to the entire document and asserted that in time it would rank with the Declaration of Independence in its importance for the working people of the country. In the *Milwaukee Leader,* an English-language newspaper which he had begun editing in 1911, he so stanchly opposed the war that the Post Office Department, in an informal hearing in September of 1917, termed the paper a disloyal publication and revoked its right to second-class mailing privileges. Berger fought strenuously and in vain to have the mailing rights restored and also to preserve his paper which, though greatly weakened, continued to exist.

Under these circumstances, Berger ran for the U.S. Senate in March, 1918. Branded as traitorous and un-American, he nevertheless received 110,487 votes out of a total of 423,393 cast for three candidates, even though in the midst of the campaign he had been served an indictment formally charging him with violation of the Espionage Act of June 15, 1917. Despite his defeat and additional indictments, in November he sought the office of Congressman from the Fifth District, consisting largely of the city of Milwaukee, and was elected against split opposition by a 5,500-vote plurality just six days before the Armistice was signed.

One month later, on December 9, 1918, the famous Chicago trial of Berger and four other Socialists charged with conspiracy to hinder the war effort began before the Federal District Court of the

Courtesy of the SHSW [WHi (X3) 17921]

Congressman Victor L. Berger

doughty but intemperate Judge Kenesaw Mountain Landis. The trial lasted four weeks, resulting in the conviction of the defendants on January 8, 1919. Landis sentenced each of the four to twenty years' imprisonment at Fort Leavenworth, but all were freed on a total bail of $625,000 and the case was appealed to higher courts. In April Berger received another blow. The Court of Appeals of the District of Columbia, which had considered the case of the *Milwaukee Leader,* upheld the Post Office Department's disloyalty charge and rejected a plea for a writ of mandamus compelling Postmaster General Albert S. Burleson to return the second-class mailing right. Judge Charles H. Robb declared that the *Leader* was "a hostile or enemy publication" and that no person could read its editorials "without becoming convinced that they were printed in a spirit of disloyalty to our government and in a spirit of sympathy for the Central Powers; that, through them, appellant sought to hinder and embarrass the government in the prosecution of the war." This was the situation in May when Berger appeared before Congress to take the oath of office.

When Berger presented himself before the speaker's desk on May 9, 1919, to be sworn in, Representative Frederick W. Dallinger of Massachusetts challenged his right to a seat, whereupon a resolution was offered and passed without dissent, suspending Berger from all rights as a member of the House until final action was taken. His efforts to gain recognition were futile and a special committee of nine was appointed to hear his case. This group also decided to judge the election claims of Berger's chief opponent in the election, Joseph Carney, a Democrat, who argued that those who voted for the Socialist had thrown their votes away and that Carney should be adjudged the winner. Berger remained in Washington throughout the late spring and summer of 1919, drawing his congressional pay and drumming up support for his cause. Nationally and in his own state, he received the full backing of his party as well as that of the Milwaukee Federated Trades Council and the Wisconsin State Federation of Labor.

In an executive meeting on May 26, the committee decided to try Berger on a general charge of disloyalty under the Fourteenth Amendment which excluded from Congress any state or federal official who had previously taken an oath to support the Constitution and had subsequently given aid or comfort to the country's enemies.

. . . .

On October 24, 1919, the committee reported to the House, with one member recommending a delay until the conviction of Berger was finally decided by the courts, since reversal would remove the main reason for denial of his seat. The eight-man majority agreed that "Victor L. Berger . . . did obstruct, hinder, and embarrass the Government of the United States in the prosecution of the war and did give aid and comfort to the enemy." Since Berger had previously taken an oath as a member of Congress to support the Constitution of the United States, he was "absolutely ineligible to membership in the House of Representatives under section 3 of the fourteenth amendment to the Constitution of the United States." However, Carney's contention that Berger's supporters had thrown their ballots away was categorically denied and the committee's recommendation that the governor of Wisconsin call a special session to fill the vacancy was later approved.

The report was well received in the House, which acted on November 10, 1919. As this was the first case of disloyalty to come before Congress since those arising out of the Civil War, Berger was, as in 1911 when he was the country's first Socialist Congressman, an object of great curiosity. He was allotted one and a half hours out of five and a half of debate before a packed gallery. Leading the opposition was Representative Dallinger, who accused him of being "the head and front of this organized conspiracy to prevent this Government from winning the war" and declared that the Department of Justice regarded him as "one of the most dangerous men in the United States."

Remembering the happy effects of his maiden speech eight years earlier, Berger again pleaded with the House to overlook his accent but nothing else. He made a long, rambling, and intemperate plea for representative government, although well aware that he could do nothing to change the hard set of the members' opinions. Discussing at length the causes of the war, the unjustness of the Chicago trial, and the distinction between socialism and communism, he declared that "it would be foolish and criminal to deprive the Socialist Party—a party casting over a million votes—of its sole representative in Congress." He justified his views and actions by quoting from Wilson's speech of September 5, 1919, that "The real reason that the war we have just finished took place was that Germany was afraid that her commercial rivals were going to get the better of her, and the reason why some nations went into the war against Germany was that they were afraid that Germany would get the commercial advantage of them." "Was it a crime," he asked the restless members of the House, "to tell the truth until Mr. Woodrow Wilson permitted it to be told?"

Berger refused to recant, boasting that "under the same circumstances I would say and write it all over again, only I would make it a great deal stronger, because I have been justified by the events since the armistice was concluded and the war practically ended." He did not endear himself or his cause when he accused Congress of being a "rubber stamp" and not "truly representative of all the people." The report of the committee was "prejudiced," false in its premises, and its conclusions were "crooked, perverse, and dishonest." If adopted, he declared, it "will put a lasting blot upon the pages of the parliamentary history of our country" and would be "an extremely vicious precedent." Some members he said, had assured him privately that in a secret ballot he would be seated, and recognizing the potency of the Red Scare he asserted that "this fear has America in its grip just now. And fear is always evil."

In conclusion he threw a challenge at the House that he later was to recall with extreme pleasure. "Remember, gentlemen, you may exclude me once. You may exclude me twice. But the fifth district of Wisconsin can not permit you to dictate what kind of a man is to represent it. If representative government shall survive, you will see me or a man of my kind, let us hope many men of my kind—in the Nation's Legislature. Therefore, whatever decision you may make, I will just say 'Au revoir.'" His speech was interrupted four times by individuals who objected to his line of argument or his language, and at its conclusion numerous Congressmen rose to question and attack his remarks. There was no applause at any point and the speech was listened to with disapproval and growing anger which vented itself in a determined but futile effort to expunge his remarks from the *Congressional Record.*

Fourteen members of Congress spoke against the seating of Berger. Representative Joe Henry Eagle, a member of the investigating committee, while declaring that the Socialist party was not on trial, condemned it as "one branch of the German propaganda in the United States." Berger, he averred, "was treacherously disloyal" and had "practically endeavored to hoist the flag of the Germans on every foot of ground in this country. . . ." Such wild hysteria echoed and re-echoed as others invoked the ghost of Theodore Roosevelt, raked the hot coals of Berger's relationship with the I.W.W., recalled his inflammatory "Ballots and Bullets" editorial of 1909, and denounced his "authorship" of the St. Louis proclamation.

Only one representative, Edward Voigt of Wisconsin, rose to defend Berger. This progressive Congressman denounced the prejudice of Judge Landis and his refusal to heed the testimony of a juror named Nixon, who swore that one of the bailiffs who had charge of the Chicago jury had sought to inflame it against Berger. Voigt also declared that the excessive bail imposed by Landis violated the constitutional rights of the defendants. His speech availed nothing, for when the final vote was taken Berger was excluded by a vote of 311 to 1 with 119 absent. Immediately after this, Representative William W. Rucker of Missouri voiced the opinions of the throng, declaring that Berger had repeatedly, "boldly and defiantly refused to retract, qualify, or apologize for the disloyal and unpatriotic utterances for which he at this very hour stands convicted in the courts of our country. He audaciously denounced the President, abused and vilified the judiciary of this Nation, ridiculed, jeered, and laughed at you Members of Congress, arraigned you for lack of backbone and manly courage. . . ." He was aghast at his colleagues for permitting to remain in the *Congressional Record* the "untrue, unjust, unpatriotic, un-American ravings of one who would destroy our system of government."

The press of the country almost unanimously approved the action of the House, and national and local organizations attacked the Milwaukee Socialist. The *Washington Post* asserted that no "finer or more impressive demonstration of Americanism" could have been given by the house, while the *Toledo Blade* declared that the members had "preserved their self-respect." The *Baltimore Sun,* like many other papers, decried the fact that even one vote had been cast for Berger. Assembled in national convention, the American Legion called for the cancellation of his citizenship papers and deportation. Echoing its parent, the local Milwaukee Legion asked all loyal Americans to unite against Berger, claiming that the issue in the forthcoming election was Americanism versus disloyalty.

Two days after Berger's exclusion from the House, the Milwaukee Socialists unanimously renominated him for Congress, endorsing and approving his "every act, word and writing," an action which the *Milwaukee Journal* deplored as "insolently defying the spirit of Americanism in Milwaukee. . . ." The national executive committee of the Socialist party denounced the House's decision as "an affront to the Socialist movement . . . a challenge to millions of American citizens," and caustically claimed that the House had seated Timothy D. Sullivan in 1912 while he was in an asylum mentally incompetent "to do anything." To assure Berger's defeat in the special election called for December 19, 1919, the Democrats and Republicans fused behind the candidacy of H. H. Bodenstab who was also supported by the Good Government League. In full-page advertisements the latter, associating Berger with the Bolshevism of Lenin and Trotsky, asked, "Is Milwaukee Red or Red, White, and Blue?" and presented the issue as simply "Americanism or Just Plain Hell."

While the anti-Socialists stressed the issue of Bolshevism and

Berger's inability to be seated, Berger emphasized his pro-Germanism as well as his opposition to prohibition, the war, and high prices. In this ill-tempered and ugly campaign District Attorney Clyne threatened to revoke Berger's bond because of his utterances about a "packed jury" and "the patrioteer judge," but the Socialist sneered at him, claiming that Clyne was angry because Berger had called him a liar in the hearings. Berger, the favorite, won the election handily, 24,350 to 19,566, gaining, in every ward except the silk-stocking eighteenth, more votes than he had received in the 1918 race. The Fifth District of Wisconsin thus replied to Congress and the nation. The issue of Bolshevism was recognized by many as fraudulent, and Berger, known and respected throughout his district, achieved a momentous personal victory, receiving 40 per cent more votes than in 1918, most of which came from non-Socialists.

. . . .

Victor Berger's second exclusion from Congress was conceded even by himself, and he deliberately delayed his appearance until January 10, 1920, four days after the opening, when Representative Dallinger again led the fight, declaring that Berger should be excluded because of the previous facts before the House. Nothing, he asserted, had changed except that Berger had been re-elected, and he implied that the House would reject him as often as he was elected. Dallinger offered him ten minutes for a speech, but the members refused to hear him; a second attempt near the end of the proceedings was objected to by Representative Thomas Blanton of Texas.

When Representative Edward Voigt defended the Socialist leader in an impassioned speech as "a high-minded and honorable gentleman," the House laughed jeeringly. Voigt then turned angrily on his colleagues: "You may laugh and scoff, gentlemen, but I know Victor Berger. No man can devote his whole life and fortune to the great cause of endeavoring to better the conditions of a toiling millions, stand by his principles like a rock of Gibraltar, regardless of personal consequences, without being morally great . . . Victor Berger's name will stand in the future as that of a martyr to a great cause—the rights of free speech, free press, and representative government." Declaring that the people of the Fifth District had "spoken in no uncertain terms," he asserted that "you may say that Victor Berger is a traitor, but if you do, you have got to say that there are 25,000 traitors in the fifth district of Wisconsin." To which some member cried, "There are."

. . . .

Despite these protestations the House excluded Berger by a vote of 330 to 6, with one voting present. Ninety-one were absent.

"Lynched again," was Berger's simple description of the proceedings. "Twelve men, it is true, convicted me of disloyalty, but 25,000 voters vindicated me, and it was the duty of the House to seat me." He promised to run again and again if necessary, contending that his exclusion as "only one link of the immense chain of oppression" in an "official conspiracy" to destroy the Socialist party. Within thirty minutes after hearing of the action of the House, the Milwaukee Socialist county executive committee renominated him, issuing a statement that "We'll keep on nominating Berger until hades freezes over if that un-American aggregation called congress continues to exclude him."

Whatever semblance of legality might have hovered about the first exclusion, none whatsoever could be conjured to explain the second. Berger's case is a prime example of the hysteria of the Red Scare, and the House action gave courage to the New York Assembly which expelled five Socialists a few days later. Peace had been in effect for exactly fourteen months when Berger was excluded on a wartime charge which had not yet been finally decided by the courts. The principle of representative government was beclouded by the momentary hysteria, the vaunted democracy of the lower house suffered a severe blow from its fear-filled action, and a dangerous precedent was set.

In the 1920 election Berger, again the favorite, lost because of the Harding landslide which carried his opponent, William H. Stafford, to victory. But in the non-presidential year of 1922 Berger once more opposed Stafford and was successful in his bid for re-election by a majority of 3,771. Congress was informed shortly thereafter by Representative Dallinger that nothing had changed since Berger's last exclusion and that he was still ineligible. However, the Supreme Court had thrown out his conviction in 1921 on a technicality, and when Berger appeared in Congress in December, 1923, to take the oath of office, he was warmly welcomed. The hysteria of the Red Scare had dissipated and the Congressmen who had so strongly and so self-righteously opposed him as disloyal could now lift their heads from the sands of intolerance and with perfect equanimity throw their arms around his shoulders in a cordial embrace. Though his remaining years in Congress were of little significance for the moribund Socialist movement, he continued to be successful in his efforts for re-election until the presidential election year of 1928 when he was again overwhelmed in a Republican landslide. In 1929 he died.

3: The Impact of War

With its heavy German population, Wisconsin was almost inevitably headed for dissent and unrest with the approach and onset of World War I. Legislative unrest reflected the uneasiness of the people, as shown in the first selection below. An attempt to coordinate the war effort was made with the establishment of the State Council of Defense. The council's work is the subject of the second selection.

Not all of Wisconsin's congressional delegation opposed the war. Senator Paul O. Husting, Democrat, who served only a brief period, took a strong prowar position, as evidenced by the letter cited as the third selection.

Patriotic groups were formed to attempt to influence the state's behavior. The Wisconsin Loyalty Legion (originally known as the Wisconsin Defense League) was one such group. Its role is discussed in an article by Lorin L. Cary. The final two selections deal with the hysteria and irrationality that accompanied such outbursts of patriotism.

Wisconsin and the War

DAVID A. SHANNON

Perhaps the best index to Wisconsin popular opinion about the decision to go to war in April, 1917, was the vote of Wisconsin delegates in Congress. Wisconsin's two senators divided on the war

From David A. Shannon, "The World, the War, and Wisconsin: 1914–1918," *Historical Messenger*, XXII,1 (March 1966), 43–56. Footnotes in the original omitted. Reprinted by permission of the Milwaukee County Historical Society.

vote. Senator LaFollette, who spoke at great length during the Senate's debate, voted against the declaration of war and Senator Paul O. Husting, Democrat of Mayville, Dodge County, voted for it. Nine of the eleven Wisconsin members of the House of Representatives voted against the declaration of war: Henry Allen Cooper of Racine; Edward Voight of Sheboygan, who was born in Bremen; John M. Nelson of Madison; William Joseph Cary and William H. Stafford of Milwaukee; James H. Davidson of Oshkosh; John J. Esch of La Crosse; Edward E. Browne of Waupaca; and James A. Frear of Hudson. Two Wisconsin Representatives voted yea on the war resolution: David G. Classon of Oconto and Irvine L. Lenroot of Superior. (The entire Wisconsin delegation in the House was Republican, either Progressive or Stalwart.) Thus nine of the fifty votes against the war in the House of Representatives and one of the six in the Senate were from Wisconsin.

There is not much solid evidence on the subject, but what there is suggests that these politicians in Washington reflected the opinion of the state's voters rather accurately. A group of peace proponents in Monroe persuaded the city council to include a special referendum on war in the spring election of 1917. On April 3, the day after Wilson asked Congress for a war resolution, the voters of Monroe responded to the referendum's question, "Under existing conditions, do you favor a declaration of war by Congress?" by a vote of 954 to 95 against war. However, three days later when the United States officially declared war, Monroe held a huge mass meeting and parade to demonstrate its acquiescence in the decision. In Sheboygan ballots in both English and German were distributed through the churches asking, "Shall the United States enter the European War?" Congress declared war before the balloting could be completed and it stopped at that point; the count was 4,112 against war to 17 for war at the time. Another unofficial vote in Manitowoc showed similar results.

With such a start in the war, it would not have been surprising if the war effort in Wisconsin had lagged considerably behind that of other states. But such was not the case. The state had an excellent record on the war work that really counted. For example, in the first few months of the war Wisconsin had a higher percentage of volunteers to draftees than any other midwestern state. Michigan was lowest with 31.4 per cent; Wisconsin had 54.5 per cent. Wisconsin led the forty-eight in recruiting and equipping its National Guard. State governments administered registrations for military conscriptions, and Wisconsin's conduct of the four separate draft registrations during the war months was so efficient that each time it was the first in the Union to complete the task. The state exceeded its quota in every Liberty bond drive. Proportionately to population, Wisconsin contributed more doctors to the armed services than any other state. It was the first state to organize a State Council of Defense and the first to create a county defense council scheme. Wisconsin was the first state to grant financial aid to soldiers' dependents, as it was the first to inaugurate "wheatless" and "meatless" days to conserve food and the first to make it possible for its soldiers to vote. These achievements were substantial. On the other hand, they were not dramatic achievements that attracted popular attention. To the person who did not have data before him on the comparative contributions of the states toward the war effort, the vote against the war by ten of the state's thirteen representatives and senators was more impressive.

Thus some Wisconsin citizens were hypersensitive on the question of loyalty and support of the war. The upper house of the state legislature demonstrated this hypersensitivity less than three weeks after America became a belligerent. At a session of the state senate the night of April 24, 1917, Senator Frank Raguse, a Socialist from Milwaukee, addressed himself to the question before the chamber, a bill to appropriate funds to print and distribute President Wilson's war message. In the course of the discussion another senator from Milwaukee had remarked that he was willing to spend a million dollars to promote patriotism. Senator Raguse delivered a wandering attack on spending for patriotism, arguing that people would be patriotic and protect their country only when they had a stake in their country. "How can a man have any patriotism when he has not got any land, for I claim that unless a man owns land he has not got any country, and I am one of them who don't own no land. Eighty-five percent of the people in this country have got no land and what we ought to do to make patriotism is to find some way to get them some land. You never can do it by passing resolutions like this." Senator Raguse's speech was not well organized, temperate, relevant, nor even grammatical. But to consider it disloyal, subversive, or harmful to the war effort would require stretching the meaning of words beyond reason. Nevertheless, two days later the senate caucused informally and presented Raguse for his signature a prepared retraction and apology. He refused to sign it. That evening Senator Raguse was the first to get the floor when the senate convened. He clarified his remarks of two nights before, saying he "did not have reference to and [did] not question the true and genuine patriotism of the people. I believe that the people of this country, and particularly the people of Wisconsin, are not lacking in patriotism to their country in the true sense. I directed my remarks at what I considered to be a manufactured form of patriotism and the methods employed and the agencies at work in bringing about an undue state of public mind. . . . If I have chosen words which have been understood otherwise, I regret to have been the cause of such misunderstanding." This statement did not satisfy Senator Timothy Burke, the chamber's president pro tem, who introduced a resolution calling upon Raguse to sign the statement he had refused to sign in the afternoon or be expelled from the senate. The motion passed. Raguse refused to sign the statement. The senate by a vote of thirty to three expelled the Milwaukee member.

From the early days of the war there were some elements in the State Council of Defense that saw threats to the war effort everywhere about them. The State Council of Defense needs a bit of explanation. Soon after the war declaration the legislature created this body, composed of representatives of the various economic interests of the state, to mobilize the state's resources. The Council apparently grew from the suggestion of A.L.P. Dennis, Canadian born professor of history at the University. As noted earlier, Wisconsin was the first state to create such an organization; many other states followed Wisconsin's lead. Governor Emanuel Philipp, a Stalwart Republican of Milwaukee, appointed a Council that was well qualified, reflected all major economic interests, and was nonpartisan. Governor Philipp even appointed a Milwaukee Socialist, Fred Brockhausen, to represent the State Federation of Labor on the Council. However, from the beginning, at the county level of the Council, there were what can be described only as illiberal extremists, and these elements in time converted the State Council of Defense into something quite different. Indeed, it even abandoned its name and became the Wisconsin Loyalty Legion and affiliated itself with the American Protective League, a national vigilante organization that searched out dissent and tried to stamp it out with a blatant disregard for traditions of civil liberties.

The State Council of Defense

R. B. PIXLEY

No more important body took part in carrying out Wisconsin's war program than the State Council of Defense. Created at the very beginning of the war, it laid the foundation for practically all of the war activities which followed its organization. Its influence extending down through the counties to the smallest divisions of the state, it was a power for good which never can be estimated. Much of its work was done quietly, and its value to the state and to the nation can not be stated in figures.

Two of its most important functions were investigation and publicity, and its aid to the food administration and other bodies which operated through headquarters in Washington was appreciated, at least, by those who were charged with such responsibilities. Its members were public spirited citizens, who worked without compensation except that which came to them for having helped Wisconsin and contributed to its war record.

The express function of the State Council of Defense, as designated by the law passed by the legislature, was to "assist the governor in doing all things necessary to bring about the highest effectiveness within our state in the crisis now existing and to coordinate all our efforts with the federal government and with those of other states." Throughout the act, it was evident that it was the legislative intent to create a board which was to supervise the mobilization of the aggregate resources of the state—military, naval, financial, industrial and social.

The council was to consist of the governor, the adjutant general, and ten other citizens to be appointed by the governor and representative of the various industries, organizations and professions of the state, including manufacturing interests, labor, farming, relief organizations, medicine, banking, railroads and engineering.

The council was empowered and directed:

"To adopt such rules and regulations as might be necessary to carry out the law creating it.

"To communicate at once with the National Council of Defense and with the defense bodies of other states, tendering Wisconsin's cooperation.

"To investigate all questions relating to the mobilization of the resources of the state, and in so doing to subpoena witnesses and to require their testimony under penalty.

From R. B. Pixley, *Wisconsin in the World War* (Milwaukee, 1919), pp. 70-71, 204-210.

"To report whenever it was discovered that excessive profits were being made through the manufacture or supply of food, fuel, and other articles necessary for the common defense, so that the governor might secure special legislation making provision for control thereof by the state."

All departments, bureaus, commissions, boards and public institutions, all state, county and municipal organizations and all citizens of the state were expressly commanded to cooperate with and to aid the council in its work.

Gov. Philipp selected as the first chairman of the council Magnus Swenson of Madison, a man who had accumulated a modest fortune through his own efforts.

. . . .

Firmly believing in this plan and in the cooperation of the people of the state, Mr. Swenson issued the following proclamation on Friday, September 14:

PROCLAMATION TO CITIZENS OF WISCONSIN

"Pursuant to the authority vested in him by the President of the United States, Herbert Hoover, National Food Administrator, has urged as a patriotic duty one meatless day and one wheatless day in each week as a means of conserving the food supply.

"Owing to the very great shortage of wheat and meat, and the urgent necessity of conserving the present food supply and of creating a reserve supply for future needs, the people of this Nation have been asked to make personal sacrifices. It is through their cooperation alone that the food administration can be successfully carried out.

"Therefore, acting under the direction of Food Administrator Herbert Hoover, I, Magnus Swenson, Food Administrator for Wisconsin, hereby call upon and urgently request the citizens of this state to set aside Tuesday, September 18, 1917, and each Tuesday thereafter during the period of the war as a meatless day. I ask that all hotels, restaurants and other eating places serve meatless meals upon that day and that this practice be followed in the homes of all patriotic citizens.

"In order, further, that Wisconsin may do its share in the conservation of food I ask that Wednesday, September 19, 1917, and each Wednesday thereafter during the period of the war be set aside as a wheatless day. I ask the people of Wisconsin to abstain from the use of bread and pastries made from wheat upon that day to the end that the wheat supply of the United States may be increased for the time when greater calls will be made upon it."

The response to this proclamation was surprising, even to the most optimistic. Issued on Friday, the following Tuesday and Wed-

DANE COUNTY'S BIG

HOOVER FOOD CELEBRATION

Capitol Building and Grounds

FRIDAY EVE., AUG. 17

6 P. M. Picnic Lunch on the Capitol Grounds.

7:30 Bugle Call and Community Singing.

8:00 Movies of Camp Douglas and War Scenes.

9:00 Flag Ceremony and Band Concert.

Join "General" Hoover's Army of Food Fighters! All Free. Bring your neighbors, and lunch on the Capitol green.

It's the FOOD Bullets that are going to crush the enemy!

DANE COUNTY COUNCIL OF DEFENSE

Courtesy of the SHSW [WHi (X3) 33832]

A Wisconsin Council of Defense Poster, 1917

nesday it was obeyed to the letter by many hotels and restaurants and private homes. In the cases of many eating places supplies had been purchased and to avoid waste these were allowed to establish the days the following week.

One week later found Wisconsin leading the nation in the conservation of the two articles of food most vital to the winning of the war.

· ·

Many amusing incidents enlivened the meatless and wheatless days, all proving the patriotism of the people. Transients afforded most of them, for Wisconsin residents knew that there was no use in ordering meat or wheat, and as a matter of fact, gladly accepted this small way in which to help win the war.

"Give me some shredded wheat," said a patron of the restaurant.

"No wheat today," replied the waitress.

"What's the matter with this state," asked the man. "I asked for meat yesterday in Milwaukee and could not get it."

"That was meatless Tuesday," was the reply, "and this is wheatless Wednesday. We've got to win the war."

"By George, that's so," replied the man. "Give me a cheese sandwich, and, say, put it on rye bread."

· ·

The students of the University of Wisconsin and the other colleges were given an opportunity to assist the food administration. The Wisconsin committee prepared a special pledge card which was circulated and signed by students without exceptions. A copy of that card follows:

> "I promise as a voluntary member of the food administration to keep the meatless Tuesday and wheatless Wednesday pledge, and in addition I promise:
> "1. To have at least 7 wheatless meals a week.
> "2. To have at least seven meatless meals a week.
> "3. To use at least one less pat of butter a day.
> "4. To omit between meals ice cream, candy and other luxuries.
> "5. To cut the use of candy at least one-third."

Senator Husting and the War

PAUL O. HUSTING

Mr. ———— ————,
————————, Wisconsin.

My dear Sir:

Yours of May 16th was duly received and contents noted. In reply I want to say that your letter bears evidence of conscientious thought and your conclusions are, no doubt, honest. I assume you have written me not only for the purpose of giving your own views but also are inviting mine in return. And inasmuch as you have volunteered a doubt as to whether or not your German ancestry has colored or biased your judgment in the premises, I take the liberty of giving you my judgment on that point as I gather it from the context of this and your previous letter.

I believe your reasonings and your conclusions are from the German, not the American, standpoint. In other words, you are holding a brief for Germany and not for the United States. "How important a part" your "German ancestry plays" in this, it may be difficult for you to apprehend but your bias will readily be apparent to anyone who reads your letter. Now, you are an American-born citizen, I take it. You are an attorney-at-law and a member of the bar of Wisconsin. You owe a duty to your country which sympathy for Germany, no matter how genuine it may be, cannot diminish, much less nullify. Now the premises from which you as an American must reason are these: This country is at war with Germany. Your President, my President, our President, backed by a declaration of your Congress, my Congress, our Congress, has proclaimed that war exists. This was done for reasons which appeared sufficient to the President and the Congress to make this declaration imperative. The loyalty and the fidelity of the President and of Congress to the people of the nation has never been questioned or challenged and I do not understand you to challenge or question them now. You are merely attempting in your letter to set your judgment against theirs. Germany is now an enemy of the United States which means that she is your enemy, my enemy, our enemy. Now, it is plain, as the Vice President remarked in a speech some time ago, that we cannot have a hundred million presidents or secretaries of state, meaning, of course, that we can only have one of each at a time and that when these officers, to whom this power has been

From "Documents: Some Letters of Paul O. Husting Concerning the Current Crisis," *Wisconsin Magazine of History*, I,4 (1917), 388–416.

delegated, have, with the aid of Congress, committed this government to a war, that question to all intents and purposes of the war is settled for all men who are citizens of the United States. And when the status of our relations with a foreign country is once fixed as that of war, then the time for argument has ceased and there is no longer any room for controversy between citizens upon that question. The question then, for the time being, that is to say, during the pendency of the war, is a closed and not an open one. And for the sake of your peace of mind as well as in justice to yourself as an American citizen who does not desire his loyalty questioned or to have his honorable reputation permanently impaired, you should respect, obey, and support the mandate of your country in the spirit of true and devoted American citizenship.

Now, I assume you love this country and that you love it because it is a free country and that you are here practicing your profession because of your desire to live in and to practice law in a country where fullest and freest opportunity is afforded you to work out your own destiny in your own way. In short, I assume that you favor a republican form of government and that you are devoted to America and its free institutions. I am sure that you would not have anyone believe otherwise of you because that would impute to you disloyalty and moreover it would impute to you a lack of intelligent enterprise by your remaining in a country that according to your ideas is improperly governed instead of removing yourself to the jurisdiction of another country which more nearly squares with your ideas of good government. So, I repeat that I assume that you are here because you like to be here under a government that suits you and which you love better than any other government on earth. Now, it is evident in your letter that you love and sympathize with Germany but the question arises in my mind whether your love is for the German people or for the German government. You can easily put yourself to the test. If you love the German people then you must desire them to have as good a government as you enjoy here and it ought to make you happy that your country, if it prevails in this war, will make the German people as free and as happy as you are. If, on the other hand, you are mostly concerned in the success of the German government, that is to say, if you are mostly concerned in having the present Hohenzollern dynasty remain in power, then it would seem to be quite clear that your love is not for the German people but for the Hohenzollern dynasty and the German autocracy. In other words, your love would then be of the form and not of the substance. You cannot love this country and its institutions and at the same time love the German autocracy. These are incompatible and repugnant one to the other. They cannot both exist in the same heart at the same time. Your love for the German people, as is your love of mankind generally, is entirely compatible with your love of this country but it must be clear to you, as it must be perfectly clear to every American, that you cannot love your country and the German people and mankind generally and at the same time love the fearful German autocracy which is trying to impose or impress its system, its frightfulness, and its wish and will upon the world and which in its mad lust for power silences the promptings of conscience, scoffs at the weakness of love for human-kind, deafens its ears to the dictates of humanity, and which in pursuit of its fell purpose sets at naught all law human and divine. Now let me ask you to search your heart and see whether your love for the German fatherland is a love compatible with your duties as an American citizen—whether it is compatible with your love of liberty and humanity—whether it is compatible with the principles enunciated in the Declaration of Independence that all men are entitled to the right of "life, liberty and the pursuit of happiness"! If such love is compatible with all these then your love for the German fatherland is a virtue and not a vice. But, if searching deeply into your heart you find that your love of the fatherland means that you love the relentless, ruthless, and despotic Hohenzollern dynasty and its system, pluck it out as you would a cancer, for it is a thing of evil and you cannot love it and be a good and true American.

. . . .

And so I have written this letter in the hope that I might be instrumental in showing you that your position is untenable and in the hope that you will abandon it for one which will reflect credit on your patriotism, your judgment, and your citizenship and which at the same time will afford you the best opportunity for advancing the interests and welfare of your kinsmen across the sea.

Very truly yours,

PAUL O. HUSTING.

The Loyalty Issue

LORIN LEE CARY

As the possibility of United States entrance into the war became clearer, the loyalty issue attracted men of widely diverse and even diametrically opposed views. The April 6 declaration of war hastened this process. Pro-war Socialists such as Algie Simons united with the anti-Socialist, pro-British, and predominantly Stalwart Republican group which had originally spearheaded the movement. LaFollette men who broke with the Senator over his opposition to the war joined hands with such traditional enemies as meat packer John Cudahy and motorcycle manufacturer Walter Davidson. And Democrats like Husting agreed with Irvine L. Lenroot, LaFollette protege, in publicly backing the purposes of the League.

Forged by war, this strange coalition sought to support Wilson and by opposing LaFollette and Socialist critics of the war to dispel criticism of Wisconsin. Warning that antiwar sentiment bordered on treason, the League organized a series of patriotic rallies across the state and undertook a program of education to convert dissenters and sway doubters.

. . . .

By late April the League boasted 5,000 members and branches in all seventy-one counties, though in private Simons and Moriarity admitted to a less complete coverage of the state. Patriotic meetings drew enthusiastic crowds but garnered relatively few members. The chief difficulty was that Governor Emanuel Philipp's creation of a State Council of Defense, the first in the nation, weakened the League's appeal. The SCD duplicated a number of the programs the League had started, such as co-ordinating assistance to military recruiters and the Red Cross. People began to confuse the two Defense organizations and to assume that the state-sponsored one was the more important. Under the circumstances, the League's membership drive faltered and the financial support at first so generously given by large companies began to evaporate. League officials tried to retain a leading role in the state's support-the-war movement by establishing formal ties with the SCD, but Governor Philipp quashed this attempt because of his aversion to the emotionalism which, he felt, distorted League thinking. By July, Defense League membership had fallen drastically, local League leaders

From Lorin Lee Cary, "The Wisconsin Loyalty Legion, 1917–1918," *Wisconsin Magazine of History*, LIII,1 (Autumn 1969), 33–50. Footnotes in the original omitted. Reprinted by permission of the State Historical Society of Wisconsin.

were complaining that they had little to do, and Joseph Moriarity confided that the League was "in urgent need of funds."

With its fortunes on the decline, the Defense League was passing out of existence. Yet fertile fields for watchful patriots still existed and prevented Moriarity's gloomy report on WDL finances from serving as the obituary for the state's patriotic movement. Not only had nine of eleven Wisconsin Congressmen joined Senator LaFollette in voting against the war, but the poor image of the state's loyalty was further tarnished when its citizens subscribed only $34,000,000 of a requested $44,000,000 in the first Liberty Bond drive that summer. On all sides, moreover, there seemed signs of intensified antiwar activity. Socialists stumped the state, the North Dakota-based Nonpartisan League made plans to organize Wisconsin, rumors of Industrial Workers of the World influence spread, and in Milwaukee dissenters founded a branch of the People's Council for Peace and Democracy. To make matters worse, these signs of disloyalty, as the self-conscious patriots interpreted them, did not pass unnoticed outside the state. The *Louisville Courier Journal,* for example, expressed a widely held view when it speculated that Wisconsin would be known as "the traitor state" by the war's end. And a Philadelphian confirmed this attitude by writing that easterners thought of Wisconsin "as either too yellow to fight, or as sold out to German influences. . . ."

To Defense League leaders it seemed apparent that the slurs hurled against Wisconsin could be disproven only by a vigorous show of patriotism.

. . . .

Thus, as their concern for Wisconsin's reputation heightened, it seemed increasingly clear to the state's extreme patriots that although the State Council of Defense had usurped some of the League's original functions, the need for a strong patriotic center still existed.

It was this conviction which motivated League officials to form a new organization.

. . . .

. . . the League held a mass meeting in mid-August which paved the way for officially founding the Wisconsin Loyalty Legion in September.

Though the new organization's name had been carefully chosen to eliminate the confusion which had developed over the Defense League and the State Council of Defense, with few exceptions leadership remained with those who had headed the Defense League.

. . . .

The Loyalty Legion members proved themselves to be as enthusiastically intolerant as citizens in other states. They defined their primary goal as "a broad and vigorous American patriotism" which would be developed through "patriotic education." Beneath the verbiage about "patriotic education," however, there existed an angry and emotional response to dissent, reflected in the pledge required of new members to "hold up slackers to public contempt" and to "seek out and bring traitors to punishment." Legion spokesmen underlined this emphasis by pledging that they would "attack disloyalty to the utmost wherever found." In this view, so typical of World War I emotionalism, there were no shades of gray, only "two classes, those who are right and those who are wrong, those who are loyal and those who are either secretly or openly trying to aid the enemy."

Legion executive secretary Walter Goodland, editor of the *Racine Times Call* and a former LaFollette man, reflected this temper in his statement that every effort would be made "to separate the loyal from the disloyal." He warned patriotic German-Americans to disassociate themselves from those "citizens of German blood who are disloyal in their words and actions" by "openly and emphatically" aligning themselves with the Loyalty Legion. Most Legion officials agreed with Guy D. Goff, who proselytized for the Legion on Federal Government stationery, that this was "no time to take chances ... to permit any element of our population to traffic in our liberties." Those who opposed the war had to be taught "to recognize the clear difference between liberty and license." To Milwaukeean Herman A. Wagner, president of the Wisconsin Bridge and Iron Works and chairman of the Milwaukee Loyalty Legion, Goff's sentiments were translated into action as he rallied to the cause of liberty and became a leading exponent for suppression of dissent.

. . . .

To some extent Wisconsin patriots merely followed a national trend, being swept into the whirlwind spun out of the heightened demand for conformity. But the slurs hurled at Wisconsin because of its delegation's behavior in Congress made the state's patriots particularly sensitive. This sensitivity was evidenced by the Legion's first activity—circulation of a petition to be signed by "grieved and humiliated Wisconsinites." "You know the impression has gone out over the Country that Wisconsin is disloyal," Goodland wrote a prospective signer. All good citizens, he prompted, would "wish to efface this stain from the fair name of Wisconsin." Aimed at LaFollette and other war opponents in the congressional delegation, the petition sought to "repudiate, in the name of Wisconsin, every disloyal word and deed calculated to misrepresent her and her people. . . ." The Legion circulated the petition widely in the fall of 1917, received the endorsement of the State Council of Defense, and claimed 150,000 signers by the end of the year. Like the loyalty petitions sponsored by the Defense League prior to America's entrance into the war, this effort to quell attacks on Wisconsin proved to be of doubtful value.

. . . .

At its peak the Legion claimed 70,346 members, most of whom joined in response to concentrated organizing drives and social pressure. Various individuals utilized the Legion, as they had its precursor the Defense League, to strike at traditional enemies, or joined because they feared the economic effect of the state's poor reputation upon their own businesses. But on the whole those who enlisted and those who led the Legion shared a sincere conviction that Wisconsin's sullied name had to be cleansed by emphatic and outward displays of patriotism.

This defensive response to the intense pressures of World War I was not atypical, although in Wisconsin its manifestations were exaggerated because of the numerous symbols of "disloyalty." The material for an ardent patriotic cause existed in the votes against war, in the large numbers of German-Americans of seemingly doubtful patriotism who threatened national unity, and in the Socialists who though strongest in Milwaukee seemed to threaten the whole state with their antiwar propaganda. But what was most disturbing to those who organized the Legion was the public and national scope of these signs of disloyalty. The attempt to clear Wisconsin's name in the eyes of the union was, therefore, a provincial one in many respects.

So intent were the leaders of the Legion upon improving Wisconsin's reputation that their thinking about means and tactics was distorted. Most important, the Legion consistently exaggerated the extent of superpatriotism. It mistook support of the war for war fervor and acceptance of Legion goals. And often it responded to its own enthusiasm. The black-and-white psychology of superpatriotism compounded the miscalculation, for those who disagreed with the Legion could be disregarded as either misinformed or traitorous. On the other hand, any encouragement for militant patriotism— from *Milwaukee Journal* editorials to the fervent praise of a Madison man—was eagerly seized upon as evidence that the Legion was on the right track.

This kind of support sustained the Legion in its effort to enter the state's political arena and in its campaign of "patriotic education," but it also perpetuated the Legion's illusions about the dimensions of war fervor. This showed most clearly in the Legion's efforts to influence the special election of April, 1918, and the fall congressional elections of that year. In both campaigns Legion chiefs overestimated the extent to which their own criteria would sway voters. Thus they clumsily hammered at a man's vote against war as a symbol of disloyalty, in spite of the fact that many who had voted against war later supported the war effort with as much fervor as any Legion official. They also misjudged politicians' commitment to the loyalty issue and failed to see that in most cases politicians were simply bent upon winning political office. Legion leaders never utilized barn burnings or physical attacks upon antiwar speakers, as did some other patriotic groups elsewhere, but their barrage of propaganda, and the assumptions upon which it was based, generated a sizable opposition group which vented its protest in the privacy of the voting booth.

Though the war did have a profound impact on the thinking of many citizens in Wisconsin, the principles upon which the Loyalty Legion rested did not outlive the war in the Badger state. Once the United States entered the conflict a majority supported the war effort, but even during the war patriots of the Loyalty Legion brand remained a minority. The results of the 1918 congressional elections indicated the limits of Legion influence. Interest in the Legion sagged sharply after the elections and the Armistice of November, 1918, terminated its active life. Within less than a year the Wisconsin Loyalty Legion faded from the scene.

War-Time Hysteria

EDWIN J. GROSS

When I think back at the hysteria that developed during the 1st World War, I sometimes wonder whether some of our public offi-

From Edwin J. Gross, "Public Hysteria: First World War Variety," *Historical Messenger,* XVII,2 (June 1961), 2-8. Reprinted by permission of the Milwaukee County Historical Society.

cials and citizens aren't going a little too far in condemning people who innocently happen to have associated with men who later on are found to be directly connected with the Communist party or with organizations which are now branded as "front" organizations. Many people forget that during the 2nd World War and for some time prior and subsequent thereto Russia was considered by many not only as our ally but as our friend. Under these circumstances it is easy for me to understand why some of our citizens were not discreet enough to pick their associations, and, without having the least sympathy for the Communist party, allied themselves with people and groups that later resulted in their being branded. Many a person who hated Communism to the core still is eyed with suspicion by some people because he happened to attend a so-called Communist "front" meeting or visited with someone who later was found to be a member of the Communist party.

But to go back to the hysteria that developed and grew during the 1st World War—the hate was not directed alone against people but against the German language, the German name and German music and literature.

I remember on one occasion when I was in the diner coming home from Chicago, I ordered what was commonly called German fried potatoes. The waiter, in an insulting tone, told me that he couldn't serve me any German fried potatoes, that all he could give me were Liberty fried potatoes. Since there was no difference in what I wanted I finally bowed to his demand and had German fried potatoes under a new and patriotic title.

In the summer of 1917 a meeting was called in one of the rooms at the Public Library for the purpose of organizing the "People's Council." More than 200 persons attended this meeting. The real purpose of the Council was to induce our Government to announce immediately in concrete terms its war aims and to seize every opportunity to achieve those aims through negotiation unhampered by the ambitions of other governments. In order to become a member it was necessary to sign a card which read as follows:

THE PEOPLE'S CHOICE OF MILWAUKEE
DEMANDS

1. Early, general, democratic peace by negotiations without forcible annexations or punitive indemnities.
2. Immediate statement by our government of its war aims in concrete terms.
3. Defense of constitutional right of free speech, free press and peaceful assemblage.

TO THE CITIZENS OF WISCONSIN

THE WISCONSIN DEFENSE LEAGUE

Endorses the following

DECLARATION

TO THE PRESIDENT OF THE UNITED STATES:

As an American faithful to American ideals of justice, liberty and humanity, and confident that the Government has exerted its most earnest efforts to keep us at peace with the world, I hereby declare my absolute and unconditional loyalty to the Government of the United States, and pledge my support to you in protecting American rights against unlawful violence upon land and sea, in guarding the Nation against hostile attacks, and in upholding international right.

If you endorse these sentiments sign here:

Name_____

Address_____

Do you stand willing to back your country in case of need? If you do fill out the blank below.

Show Uncle Sam where you stand.
This is not an Enlistment.   It is your pledge of loyalty.

Present Occupation:_____

Age:_____Weight:_____ Height:_____

General Health:_____Married or Single:_____

Previous Naval or Military Experience:_____

1.   Are you a Machinist:_____
2.   "   "   " Stenographer:_____
3.   "   "   " Chauffeur:_____
4.   Can you drive a Motorcycle_____
5.   Are you a Locomotive or Marine Engineer:_____
6.   "   "   an Electrician:_____
7.   "   "   a Cook or Baker:_____
8.   "   "   " Plumber, Carpenter, Coppersmith or Boilermaker:_____
9.   "   "   " Horse Shoer:_____
10. "   "   " Packer:_____
11. "   "   " Teamster:_____
12. "   "   " Yachtsman or Boatman:_____
13   ", "   " Aviator:_____
14. "   "   " Blacksmith_____

Will you volunteer for service in any of the military branches of the United States in case of war:_____

Indicate the branch of service you prefer:

U. S. ARMY   U. S. NAVY
U. S. MARINE CORPS   NATIONAL GUARD

Mail to Army and Navy Recruiting Office, Plankinton Arcade, Milwaukee

A Wisconsin Defense League broadside, ca. 1917

4. Maintenance of labor standards, elimination of war profits, taxation of wealth to pay for the war.
5. Amendment of the conscription law.
6. Referendum on war and peace, and democratic foreign policy for world peace.

When the meeting was called to order the members present proceeded to elect a president. Victor Berger and Meta Berger, both Socialists, attended and took a rather active part. Mrs. Berger placed my name in nomination in a speech of very few words.

I didn't like the idea of participating in a movement that was attended by too many Socialists and declined to accept the nomination. Either Victor Berger or his wife then arose and asked me whether I believed in the principles that were written on a blackboard on the stage. I told them that I did believe in those principles. They then said that they were surprised that I should decline to contribute my support to such important principles that I believe in. In plain English, they shamed me out of declining the nomination. The result—I was nominated and elected. From that time on I was a marked man.

The Milwaukee "Journal" of July 31, 1917, in referring to the stand taken by the Council, had this to say:

> "In assuming charge of the meeting Mr. Gross said:
> 'It has always been my opinion, and I think that I speak rightly, when I say that the President and the Administration have always been anxious to have a reflection of public opinion upon all matters that affect the people. We are now engaged in war. The fact that we are engaged in a war should not alter that condition. In fact, it should strengthen that condition. It is people who must contribute money, lives and property; therefore the men at Washington should know the sentiment of the people in relation to legislation and matters pertaining to war. It is because I feel that the men and women came here for that purpose; came here for the purpose of trying to aid the Administration in coping with these great problems that confront us today, that caused me to accept the nomination of temporary chairman. I trust that whatever we do will be done along the lines of law abiding American citizens in an effort to aid the people of this country.' "

That was the position taken by all of the members of the Council and that was the position that was taken by all of the speakers at these Council meetings. Unless you shouted from day to day that you were a loyal American and ready and willing to annihilate anything German, you were considered a traitor to your country.

War Hysteria and the Wobblies

JOHN D. STEVENS

While the Industrial Workers of the World was strongest in the West and in a few industrial centers of the Northeast, the radical labor organization also struck terror in Wisconsin and in Milwaukee. The Wobblies were involved in strikes in the state as early as 1911, and during World War I they took the blame for almost every fire, labor dispute and commotion in the state. They wrote much of their Wisconsin chapter in the cutover pine lands of the north, but they also held sway in Milwaukee.

. . . .

In 1914, the only local listed in Wisconsin was in Milwaukee; however, there was considerable I.W.W. activity in the lumber camps, shipping docks and mining camps throughout the state. Often an organizer would show up, sign up some men, and then flee for his life ahead of the company's guards or local deputies—as often as not, the same men. Although that "local" disappeared, the men left behind might be sympathetic to the next organizer they met.

The Wobblies struck the docks at Superior in 1911 and at Allouez in 1913. They were involved in the strike of quarry workers at Red Granite in 1916 and struck the Superior docks again in 1916. During 1916, the I.W.W. conducted a vigorous recruiting campaign among the lumberjacks of the upper midwest, an effort ending with the bitter strike in the Minnesota forests which the National Guard helped break.

Not all the Wisconsin strikes were confined to the north. In February, 1917—about two months before the United States entered the war—an I.W.W. organizer and six assistants were arrested and fined $5.00 each in Milwaukee city court for disturbing the peace during a strike against a construction company. In that case, when the assistant city attorney asked for a dismissal, the judge instead dismissed the attorney. After passing sentence on the defendants, the judge gave the attorney a tongue-lashing for "casting aspersions" on the arresting policemen.

With the coming of war, the cost of living soared. From August, 1915, to June, 1918, it was up 58 per cent; by the end of the war, the cost of living had climbed another 16 per cent. Wages did not

From John D. Stevens, "Wobblies in Milwaukee," *Historical Messenger*, XXIV,1 (March 1968), 23–27. Footnotes in the original omitted. Reprinted by permission of the Milwaukee County Historical Society.

keep pace with prices, and this explains why there were more strikes during World War I than in any previous 20-month period in American history. This was in spite of a no-strike agreement on the part of the American Federation of Labor, an agreement which the I.W.W. haughtily refused to consider. In Milwaukee, as elsewhere, there were many strikes, but most of them were brief.

War hysteria prodded citizens from all over the state to pour reports of I.W.W. activity—by their definition but not by any legal definition disloyal—to state and federal officials. The state Council of Defense was besieged with such reports, most of which it referred to federal agents. Police and sheriffs often acted on their own to jail men suspected of I.W.W work, and apparently many policemen considered any out-of-town troublemaker a Wobbly.

During July, 1917, an Industrial Workers organizer was jailed at Milwaukee for inciting strikes, for insulting the President and for lying to obtain his naturalization papers. He had a German name. There was no record of any indictment. During the same month, a thirty-four-year-old man was arrested near the armory at Whitefish Bay. When his pockets revealed an I.W.W. dues book, he was charged with vagrancy.

Two incidents in September, 1917, indicate the fear that the I.W.W. evoked in Wisconsin. Police thought it worth an investigation when a Civil War veteran at Portage said he saw a stranger with an I.W.W. button on his vest inquiring about a hotel room; the police found no trace of the man. The other incident involved Albert Wolfe, federal attorney for the Western District of Wisconsin. While working in his Madison office one morning, Wolfe pinned on a red-and-black button confiscated from an I.W.W. member. It was an office joke, but he forgot to remove it before going to lunch. When he returned, there were reports on his desk about the Wobbly seen in that restaurant. There was no local, state or federal law against belonging to or working for the I.W.W.

On September 5, 1918, federal agents raided Wobbly offices in 33 cities, including three branches in Milwaukee. The agents expressed disappointed [sic] that no members were present, but a national officer of the Industrial Workers wrote that all locals knew in advance of the impending "secret" raids. Without warrants, the agents ransacked drawers and safes, hauling off great piles of records and literature. They also swooped down on homes of individual union leaders, in one case seizing a bundle of old love letters. On September 13, they made a second pass at one I.W.W. office in Milwaukee, arresting two local officials and again filling their sacks with records—records which never were returned, incidentally.

. . . .

Unlike most states with Wobbly activity, Wisconsin did not enact an anti-syndicalist law. Such laws punish membership in any group which seeks to use force to bring about industrial and/or political reforms. The laws were aimed directly at the Industrial Workers. Each house of the Wisconsin legislature adopted a version of such a bill in 1919, but they could not agree on a compromise version.

Chapter IX
NORMALCY
AND DEPRESSION,
1920–1940

Wisconsin felt the effects of the many currents and cross-currents of the two decades between World Wars I and II. In many ways the state was a microcosm of the nation. Its populace voted for Warren G. Harding in 1920 and for Franklin D. Roosevelt in 1932. Its state and local politics mirrored the continuing unrest within the traditional two-party structure. The state's population, like that of much of the nation, continued its move away from the farms and to the urban centers. Its industrial base, thriving during World War I, experienced some declines before reaching new heights in 1927–28, just before the crash of 1929. Farm income, as in other rural areas, declined sharply between 1919 and 1921; and it did not recover fully throughout the following two decades. Mortgage foreclosures, mounting debts, and violence occurred throughout the nation's farm belt, including Wisconsin.

Like other states, Wisconsin experienced the era of Prohibition, the debate over evolutionary theories, the revival of the Ku Klux Klan, and the economic uncertainties of these two decades, which produced first economic boom and then bust. The crash of the stock market in 1929 severely damaged Wisconsin's industry. Factories either reduced output or shut down; unemployment rose sharply, and many of those lucky enough to keep their jobs received substantial pay cuts; banks around the state closed.

Politically, although the intensity of the progressivism of the earlier period declined, the LaFollette family provided the dominant political influence on Wisconsin during much of the interwar era. With the death of the elder LaFollette in 1925, Robert M., Jr. took his father's Senate seat, although Progressives lost the governorship the next year. Phillip LaFollette was elected governor in 1930, capitalizing on stalwart Governor Walter Kohler's traditional Republican response to the stock market crash and resulting problems. But in 1932, LaFollette, himself tainted by incumbency during a trying time, lost to Kohler in the primary, and Kohler in turn lost to Democrat Albert Schmedeman, a beneficiary of the Roosevelt landslide.

Moving into a new third party after losing control of the Republican party in 1932, the LaFollettes found support from President Roosevelt, who correctly viewed the state's Democratic party as too conservative to give him much support. By the late 1930s, however, this third-party movement was itself in disarray, at least partly due to Phillip LaFollette's national political ambitions in 1938, illustrated by his abortive efforts to launch a National Progressive party in that year.

The contributions of Wisconsin to the New Deal were considerable. The "Wisconsin Idea," which emphasized the use of experts from the University of Wisconsin as advisers to the government, was seen by some to be influential in Roosevelt's development and use of his brain trust. More specifically, Wisconsin ideas such as the state's old-age pension bill passed in 1925 influenced similar New Deal legislation. And under Governor Phillip LaFollette the state began public works programs to provide work for the unemployed, something tried later by the New Deal. In 1932, Wisconsin passed a state unemployment compensation act. It was the first state to do so.

During his later administrations (1935–1939), Governor LaFollette and the legislature enacted a state New Deal, involving a number of social programs. But this effort came too late in the Depression to win the degree of public approval given earlier to FDR's New Deal.

As Wisconsin approached World War II, the state, like the nation, was still troubled by economic problems: unemployment was too high; factory output was still below that of a decade earlier; political unrest and uncertainty were still apparent. As with the United States in general, it took war to help the state make a complete recovery from the Depression.

Phillip LaFollette's *Adventures in Politics: The Memoirs of Phillip LaFollette* (New York, 1970), and Patrick Maney's *"Young Bob" LaFollette* (Columbia, Mo., 1978) shed much light on the politics of the younger LaFollettes. Periodical literature and dissertations provide most of the other materials available for a study of Wisconsin during this period.

1: Prohibition in the Beer State

Ratification of the eighteenth amendment in 1919 meant a temporary end to the sale of alcoholic beverages. In Wisconsin the response to ratification was not joyous, since brewing was the state's fifth largest industry. For the Anti-Saloon League, ratification of the amendment by Wisconsin was a sweet victory. In its report to the national convention in 1919, and in its *Year Book* for that year, the League made clear its delight with success in the beer state. The first reading traces some of the steps taken by the state prior to the ratification of national Prohibition. The second and third selections illustrate the position of the Anti-Saloon League. Surviving prohibition in the "beer city" is discussed in the final selection.

Sin in Wisconsin

PAUL H. HASS

Alcohol the corruptor, the contaminator of society, the stumbling block to progress: it ran like a thread through the fabric of testimony. A clergyman said that sexual behavior, immorality, and "the liquor question" were one and the same problem. A La Crosse businessman told the committee that Sunday closing laws could not be enforced because most of the city's saloons were owned by powerful brewers. Even a madam could say that "I think liquor is the one great curse of this great world. . . ." The saloons of Wisconsin

From Paul H. Hass, "Sin in Wisconsin: The Teasdale Vice Committee of 1913," *Wisconsin Magazine of History*, XLIX,2 (Winter 1965–66), 138–151. Footnotes in the original omitted. Reprinted by permission of the State Historical Society of Wisconsin.

operated every day of the year, in defiance of state law, and very few witnesses were prepared to state that liquor had nothing to do with girls who strayed.

Here the Methodist teetotaler parted company with the progressive investigator. "I think I may safely say," Teasdale wrote in late 1914, "that 75% to 80% of all the cases of immorality come from the liquor traffic in its various forms and phases, and this is what I of course consider the prime cause of the downfall of girls." He had known it all along. The smoke-filled saloon, full of lounging gamblers and sports; the noisy palm garden, its adolescent customers besotted with drink; the River Street bawdyhouse, with its weekly delivery of beer: these were things against which reformers of every stripe must unite. In the rhetoric of the prohibitionists, these were "the resorts of the underworld," the "stepping stones to white slavery."

And so it was, out of the long, droning hours of testimony and the thousands of pages of transcripts, that the *Report and Recommendations of the Wisconsin Legislative Committee to Investigate the White Slave Traffic and Kindred Subjects* became a weapon in the last great crusade of the Anti-Saloon League to make America dry.

When the report was published late in 1914, with its ringing indictment of the liquor traffic and its recommendations to enforce Sunday closing laws, bar women and minors from saloons, require local as well as federal liquor licenses, revoke licenses of offending barkeeps, prohibit liquor at dances, and request brewers and liquor dealers "to assist in the enforcement of the moral and excise laws," Senator Teasdale was deluged with letters from jubilant prohibitionists. "I can suggest nothing further except an out and out stand for statewide and national prohibition," wrote a Clintonville woman, "and the work that you have done is a great stride toward that end." "Your recommendations are very good," wrote another, "but as liquor is the cause of all the vice and most all of the crime, would it not be better to put liquor out of the state?" A minister in Jefferson tendered his warmest thanks to Teasdale and marveled at the strides that had been made since the turn of the century: "Fifteen years ago Prohibition was considered the dream of the theorist. Today there are many who say that its enactment is near at hand. If so, it is because the people demand it."

The people did not demand it—not yet—but the day was coming. In 1905 only 11 per cent of Wisconsin had been dry; by 1916 the figure had risen to 45 per cent. After June, 1917, when, as a war measure, the federal government prohibited the distillation of alcoholic liquors from grain, the issue was virtually decided. In 1918 the Anti-Saloon League, at the zenith of its power, spent $67,000 to elect a dry-minded state legislature, and on January 22, 1919, Wisconsin duly ratified the Eighteenth Amendment. Five months later, at midnight on June 30, the lights went out in the one hundred thirty seven breweries and nearly 10,000 saloons of Wisconsin.

The Teasdale committee had contributed, however modestly, to the triumph of Prohibition, and Teasdale no doubt savored the role he had played. It had not been without cost: he had left his fences unmended while conducting the vice investigation, and in the fall of 1914 another Republican defeated him in the primary and took his seat in the senate. But he returned in 1918 to cast his vote for Prohibition, and then served four consecutive terms until his retirement in 1931. When he died in 1936, at the age of eighty, he was remembered in the press as a "colorful vice crusader," as a "noted reform leader," and as the man who had "introduced more bills to make it easy for democracy to tread the straight and narrow path than all his colleagues together."

The segregated vice district and the old-time parlor house, like Demon Rum, were effectively dispatched by America's entry into the World War. The massive weight of the War Department largely crushed commercialized vice in camp towns and embarkation centers, and this, combined with the spate of state and municipal legislation, carried the day for the reformers. The telephone, the automobile, and—ironically—the speakeasy would soon revolutionize the operations of the prostitute; but by 1921 a vice crusader could report with satisfaction that "Publicly recognized markets of vice have been largely done away with. Their place, it is true, has partially been taken by new centers of activity, but these latter are furtive and surreptitious. Their blatant air is gone, and the business is not what it used to be."

Wisconsin Goes Dry

Wisconsin ratified the National Prohibition Amendment to the federal constitution by a vote of 19 to 11 in the State Senate on January 16, 1919, and 58 to 35 in the House on the following day, thus being the thirty-ninth state to ratify.

From *The Anti-Saloon League Year Book, 1919* (Westerville, Ohio, 1919), pp. 155–156.

When war-time Prohibition becomes operative on July 1, 1919, 9,636 saloons and 136 breweries in the state will be closed.

Wisconsin is under local option. The law provides for a vote on the liquor question in towns, villages and cities. There is also a residence district law on the statute books.

The dry forces have made a gain of 100 per cent in dry population, and a 50 per cent gain in dry territory, in two years. There are now 1,125 dry units, with a total population of 900,000. Wisconsin is 75 per cent dry as to territory; and 40 per cent of her population live in dry territory.

The city of Milwaukee has over 2,000 saloons, a larger number in proportion to the population than are to be found in any other large city in the United States.

For several years the number of no-license victories in the towns and villages has been constantly increasing. In the spring elections of 1914, 33 incorporated cities and villages previously wet voted dry and only one dry village voted wet, thus making a net gain of 32 dry cities and villages in the state.

In the spring elections of 1915, 35 cities and villages went dry for the first time while only three small villages changed from no-license to license. It is estimated that during 1914 and 1915 the saloon was voted out of territory inhabited by 60,000 people and as a result 400 saloons were compelled to close.

Thirty-one incorporated cities and villages, including Superior, the second city in the state, voted out the saloon in 1916. Four of the normal school cities of the state—Superior, River Falls, Menomonie and Platteville—voted out the saloon. In these four cities 2,200 young people were attending school. A net gain of 85,000 people in dry territory was made at the spring elections in 1916, and 400 saloons closed their doors in July of that year.

A determined effort was made by the liquor interests to induce the Legislature of 1913 to so amend the Baker law as to destroy its effectiveness. The effort failed. The Baker law provides that saloon licenses be granted on a ratio of one for every 250 people or fraction thereof, though where there was a larger number than this doing business when the law went into effect in 1907 they might continue provided they remained in the same location. The law was ignored in many places, and many new licenses given in excess of one for every 250 people. The Anti-Saloon League carried a case to the state Supreme Court. The court decided these places were illegal. The liquor interests then made a great effort to induce the Legislature to so amend the law as to legalize all saloons doing business up to that time. This effort failed. The enforcement of the law has closed over 200 saloons in Milwaukee, and many more in other parts of the state.

The Legislature of 1915 changed the limit on the number of saloons in a given community. Previous to this action saloons were permitted on a ratio of one for every 250 people. The change in the Baker law has raised this to one for every 500 people.

The Cost of Ratification

R. P. HUTTON

Thirty-nine and four-tenths per cent of our males of voting age were born abroad in heavy beer-drinking countries. Thirty-eight and three-tenths per cent were born here, but of foreign parentage from heavy beer-drinking countries. Six-tenths of one per cent are negro and Indian. Seventy-eight and three-tenths per cent had an inherited wet predilection. Only 21.7 per cent of our voters were native-born of native parents, and half of them still had the wet predeliction.

Here was a problem which was complicated by the fact that we made one-sixth of all the beer made in America and had more saloons per capita than any other state.

The present Superintendent took charge June 11, 1917, which left only sixteen and a half months till election, and only fourteen and a half until the primary, which was the real test—for the Republican primary is the only place where there is any doubt in Wisconsin. They said it couldn't be done. Wisconsin did it—just as she has met every demand of loyalty, all of which they said she couldn't do.

We used a million book pages of literature per month; twelve million a year. We put on a country schoolhouse campaign. We put factory experts to speak in the factories, and got the companies to pay the men for listening. We built up a Council of One Thousand to back us—business and labor leaders who opened the factors. We enlisted the Hemlock-Hardwood Lumber Association in its entirety. We sold the factories billboards and posters which were changed bi-weekly, and a monthly educational scientific tract in tabloid form which went into the pay envelope. We organized the drys of every county. We helped to select dry legislative candidates who could get

From "A Sober World," *Proceedings 19th National Convention of the Anti-Saloon League of America,* Washington, D.C., June 3–6, 1919, p. 322.

votes. We listed the two-thirds of our voters who habitually fail to vote in the primary; divided them into blocks of five, put a dry corporal over each five, and got 138,000 of these stay-at-homes to the polls on the primary day, September 3, knowing who was the dry candidate for Senate and Assembly, and absolutely pledged to vote for them. We staged the biggest demonstration in Madison the state has ever seen. We ratified! And in the archives at Washington Wisconsin was one of the first 36 on which the Secretary of State declared National Prohibition. We put it over! As Wisconsin always puts it over.

January 16, 1920, 9,656 saloons must close in this state. Our campaign cost $67,000 approximately—$6.93 for each saloon killed. Talk about the high cost of living! It isn't a "patchin" to the low cost of dying for saloons. Let 'em die while the dying is cheap.

Wisconsin's Ratification Council of 1,000 (now numbering more than 3,000) is the greatest body of business and labor leaders definitely enlisted for law enforcement in any state in the Union, bar none. And while some states unquestionably have greater stars, no state has finer team-play, nor gets greater results per man than the Wisconsin Anti-Saloon League field force. You are getting more for your dollar in the way of Kingdom-building, nation-building and constitution-strengthening by putting a dollar into this fight than you can by putting it anywhere else in the world.

Surviving Prohibition in Milwaukee

JOHN C. EIGEL

On January 16, 1920, the Eighteenth Amendment to the United States Constitution went into effect, making the sale or transportation of intoxicating liquors illegal. Prohibition had begun. It was to last for thirteen years, until it was repealed in 1933. During that period Wisconsin, like every other state, was dry. Milwaukee, with

From John C. Eigel, "Surviving Prohibition in Milwaukee," *Historical Messenger*, XXXIII,4 (Winter 1977), 118–124. Reprinted by permission of the Milwaukee County Historical Society.

its firmly established brewing industry, was greatly affected, as Prohibition included beer.

One of Milwaukee's oldest breweries was the Cream City Brewery, located at Thirteenth and Cherry Streets. Although open production of their beer was impossible, the Cream City Brewery continued to produce soda water and "near beer" for the duration of Prohibition. My great-grandmother, Minnie Edler, was employed throughout Prohibition as the brewery's scrubwoman.

Minnie had come from Germany as a young woman, settled in Milwaukee and married John Edler of the city in the early 1880's.

· ·

She was hired as the scrubwoman and stayed with the brewery until her death in 1933. The brewery outlived her by only a number of years.

· ·

The central character of the Cream City Brewery was its brewmaster, Braumeister Gustav Hanke. He, too, enjoyed rubbing elbows with Minnie. Prohibition was, obviously, particularly obnoxious to a brewmaster, in charge of brewing the near beer. He gave Minnie directions to make it herself, as home brewing was quite common. My grandmother, Emma Edler, claims everyone they knew made home brew, with varying degrees of success.

One could not expect, however, that a proud brewmaster would content himself with the quality of his orange soda and commercial home brew. Braumeister Hanke did not. He continued to make beer of the same quality as before Prohibition. I have no way of knowing how much was produced or how many speakeasies were supplied, but I do know that Minnie was rather generously supplied with regular beer for being only the scrubwoman.

Braumeister Hanke was certainly not the only person with access to beer. Although everyone had their own home brew, no one was satisfied with it. Throughout the city were speakeasies, or "blind pigs," as my grandmother remembers them. The ease of access to alcohol was nothing like the situation in Chicago, where it was generally agreed that liquor was never effectively banned. My relatives, like most Milwaukee residents, were terrified of Chicago and everything that occurred there.

· ·

With some exercise of the imagination, Minnie's eldest son could be referred to as a "rumrunner." In a family cartage business, he

Prohibition ends! The Schlitz train with
the first beer after Prohibition on board,
one minute after midnight, April 7, 1933

owned a truck in which he frequently transported beer. When his oldest daughter was to be married, he had the expensive and risky task of procuring an entire barrel of beer and taking it from the Town of Wauwatosa to his home at Fourth Street and Garfield Avenue. The depression had hit them hard; the wedding reception was to be held in their garage.

. . . .

The Twenty-First Amendment repealing Prohibition was just cause for the breweries of Milwaukee to celebrate, and the Cream City firm was no exception. On the eve of the day the Amendment was to take effect, all the Edlers were at the brewery early in the evening. There, they waited in anticipation with many others for the clock to strike twelve, when beer would be legal once again.

At twelve midnight, whistles blew throughout the city; perhaps even some progressive church bells rang. At the Cream City Brewery, Braumeister Hanke had the beer all ready to flow. When the whistles blew, their operations resumed. Beer flowed freely for the crowd that had been waiting for hours. The whole brewing cycle was in operation, and in no time at all there were hundreds of brown bottles circulating through the crowds.

. . . .

The descendants of Minnie Edler still possess the recipe, typed on official Cream City Brewing Co. stationery, for home brew given to Minnie by Braumeister Hanke. His directions for concocting this Prohibition-era beverage follows; note his cryptic final sentence.

Put 3 oz. hops in 2 gallons of water and boil for an hour and a half. Strain through a cotton sack and add to the liquid 1½ pounds of granulated sugar, 1 quart of malt extract and 3 gallons of boiling water. Boil the mixture for 25 minutes and let it stand in an earthenware crock or wooden tub until it is lukewarm. Dissolve one cake of yeast in a cupful of lukewarm water and add to the liquid in the crock. Set the mixture in a warm place and allow to ferment for 60 to 70 days. Skim off foam twice a day.

Filter through fibre and bottle. Cork tightly and let it stand in a warm room for 2 days. Then remove it to a cool place and keep it there for another week before using. If the liquid foams too much when the bottle is opened, it was bottled too soon. If too flat, it was allowed to stand too long before bottling. Omit fermentation in dry territory.

2: Evolution: "Fundamentalists" and "Liberals"

The controversy over evolution, nationally dramatized by the trial of John Scopes in Tennessee, raged in Wisconsin during 1921 and 1922. William Jennings Bryan, champion of fundamentalism in the Scopes Trial, provoked a lingering controversy with President Edward A. Birge of the University of Wisconsin, in a speech given in Madison in 1921. The following article describes what followed.

Bryan versus Birge

IRVIN G. WYLLIE

At the close of the first World War, William Jennings Bryan was a troubled man, casting about for explanations of the chaos of his world.

. . . .

In his search for the evil force which had unsettled his ideal Christian world, Bryan ultimately fixed upon Darwinism. Implicit in Darwinism was a denial that man was specially created in the image of God, with a status but little lower than that of angels. Darwinism pulled man down from his lofty perch, placed him in the animal kingdom, and made the law of the jungle the rule in human affairs. To Bryan's way of thinking, Darwinism brutalized every

From Irvin G. Wyllie, "Bryan, Birge, and the Wisconsin Evolution Controversy, 1921–1922," *Wisconsin Magazine of History,* XXXV,4 (Summer 1952), 294–301. Footnotes in the original omitted. Reprinted by permission of the State Historical Society of Wisconsin.

social relation. As early as 1905 he had ventured a prediction that Darwinism would seriously weaken political democracy and promote class conflict.

. . . .

Having identified the enemy, Bryan prepared for his own aggressions. The main question was, where to begin? If Mrs. Bryan is to be credited, his decision was made easy by the fact that every visit of the mailman brought word from distressed parents, pastors, and Sunday school teachers, warning that university education was demolishing the religious faith of young America. In no time at all Bryan had convinced himself that the teaching of evolution as a fact, rather than as a theory, was responsible for the bad turn of events. From the moment of discovery he resolved upon a crusade against evolution in the schools.

It is imperative to understand that Bryan's campaign was not simply the offspring of senility and bigotry. Its object was as much social as religious, aiming to preserve orthodox Christianity as a foundation for peace and economic justice. Bryan's objectives were no less worthy now than they had been in the days of the silver and peace crusades. But the difficulty, as always, was that his intentions outran his understanding. In the heat of battle he could never quite distinguish between means and ends; too often he found himself defending theological absurdities, when his intention was to enter a plea for social justice.

The futility of Bryan's methods was amply demonstrated in his long dispute with President Edward A. Birge of the University of Wisconsin, in the year 1921–1922. This battle, one of the earliest and fiercest on the road to Dayton, began on the night of May 5, 1921, when the Commoner lectured on the subject, "Brother or Brute?" before 2,500 students and townspeople in the University gymnasium. Seated on the platform were many dignitaries, including Governor John J. Blaine, and the man who was to be Bryan's principal antagonist for the next year, President Birge. Of Birge's scientific and religious background the Commoner knew little or nothing; had he been better informed, he might have been more wary. The venerable president had come to the University in 1875 as an instructor in natural history, and had served over the years as professor of zoology, dean of the College of Letters and Science, acting president, and president. His intimate connection with the University had given him considerable prestige within the State, while in scientific circles elsewhere he was recognized as one of America's foremost limnologists. In Madison he bore a reputation as a leading churchman; for almost half a century before Bryan cast

aspersions on his faith he had been active in the First Congregational Church, serving for a time as deacon, and for twenty-five
years as the teacher of a large Bible class. During this time he had
succeeded in accommodating Christian doctrine to the findings of
science, and with the utmost sincerity could report:

> I have taken part both in the religious and the scientific activities
> of the world in which I have lived, with no thought of conflict or
> even division between them. I have never found it necessary to justify
> religion to science or to excuse science to religion. I have accepted
> both as equally divine revelations, and both are equally wrought into
> the constitution of the world.

Bryan's remarks on that May evening made it plain that he did
not believe that evolution and religion were equally divine revela-
tions. He devoted the main portion of his speech to developing the
familiar thesis that Darwinism was directly responsible for the
World War, for the plight of the American farmer, and for an
assortment of other national problems. Then briefly, towards the
end of the evening, he took up the scientific and religious aspects of
Darwinism. Scientists had found no facts in fifty years to upset the
Biblical account of creation, he declared, and professors who taught
evolution were guilty of promoting false science and irreligion. He
climaxed the speech with a charge that one Wisconsin professor
regularly told his classes that the Bible was a collection of myths. He
had heard that a Catholic girl once fled this professor's classroom in
tears and, upon meeting a Methodist clergyman who had miracu-
lously stationed himself nearby, revealed the attack upon her faith.
Bryan reported that the girl wept like Mary Magdalene: her professors had taken away her Lord, and she knew not where they had
laid him.

Birge, who was naturally disputatious, fidgeted through the last
part of the speech, his wrath rising all the while. As soon as Bryan
had finished, Birge rushed across the platform to register his dis-
pleasure. Bryan recalled later that he was chatting with Governor
Blaine and other bystanders when Birge stormed up and called him
an atheist. The Commoner claimed that he asked those within ear-
shot to refrain from saying anything about the incident, on the
ground that Birge was terribly excited, and ought not to be embar-
rassed by having his intemperate remarks made public. Birge's recollections were substantially different. According to his version he
merely told Bryan that his antievolution tirades were atheistic in
tendency since they encouraged students to base their faith on untenable scientific doctrines. He also denied having protested to
Bryan in the presence of others and disclaimed any intention of
making the dispute a matter of public interest.

Whatever his original intentions, it was the president and his colleagues who kept the issue alive.

· ·

The most stinging rebuttal was issued by President Birge. Though he praised the clarity, vigor, and moral purpose of Bryan's talk, the president called attention to one fatal flaw: it was "fundamentally mistaken in its methods and conclusions." Recalling that he had heard many similar antievolution harangues in the 1870's, he said that from an educational viewpoint he was pleased that University students should have had an opportunity to hear the kind of tirade heard so often by their fathers and grandfathers. He noted, however, that religion and science had come a long way since 1870, and expressed regret that Bryan seemed ignorant of this fact:

> I must say plainly, that when one attempts to induce young people to unite their religious faiths to discredited scientific doctrines, he commits a very grievous error and endangers the religious life of those he is trying to help. The leaders of religion in general have learned this lesson, and I can only regret that Colonel Bryan has not done so.

Birge undoubtedly hoped that Bryan's charges would pass unnoticed, but in this he was disappointed. Roman Catholic spokesmen quickly put themselves on record in support of Bryan, the Protestant fundamentalist. Father Herbert C. Noonan, president of Marquette University, announced that if Birge's evolution was "of the extreme type that applies not only to the evolution of the human body, but also to that of the human soul from brute matter I must condemn it as subversive not only of Christianity, but of morality itself." At the annual meeting of the Wisconsin Council of Catholic Women a strong resolution was adopted, censuring Birge, Otto, Ross, and Guyer for their stand on the evolution question. The Catholic women, who professed to have been dissatisfied for a long time over the manner in which the University was conducted, pledged themselves to a vigorous crusade to eliminate false teachings at Madison. A month later a Sun Prairie medical doctor, in a letter to the *Wisconsin State Journal,* reiterated the Catholic position and demanded that the University's disseminators of materialism be asked to resign.

· ·

After reading the rebuttal that came from the University, Bryan was convinced that his first charges were well founded. For the June issue of *The Commoner* he prepared an editorial on "The Modern Arena," in which he compared the University of Wisconsin with the old Roman arena: both institutions specialized in the destruction of Christians. He suggested that Birge circulate handbills announcing that "our classrooms furnish an arena in which a brutish doctrine tears to pieces the religious faith of young men and young women; parents of the children are cordially invited to witness the spectacle." By this time it was evident that Bryan had lost sight of his larger objectives, and was ready to engage Birge on the narrow grounds of religious orthodoxy.

The battle entered its second phase when the Commoner returned to Wisconsin on September 2, 1921, to lecture to the citizens of Monroe on the subject of "Man and Brute." It was evident that Bryan had been stung by Birge's charge that he was an intellectual back-number, utterly ignorant of the scientific and religious gains of the preceding half-century. He proceeded to offer a stirring defense of old-time religion and, playing upon the prejudices of his audience, portrayed Birge as a militant atheist who scoffed at the religious convictions of the older generation. He asserted that the president worked endlessly to "undo the work of the Christian home and the Christian church, and set at naught the good work Christian mothers do with their little ones at their knees."

After the Monroe speech, several newspaper reporters arranged for a conference with Birge, hoping to pick up some publishable reaction. But they found the president more adamant than ever on the point of newspaper disputation. After considerable prodding, however, he agreed to share his views on an off-the-record basis. The next morning the Chicago *Tribune* gave front-page coverage to his off-hand remarks. "Bryan is crazy," the president reputedly told the newsmen. "He is seeking notoriety, and I refuse to engage in a newspaper argument with him. No one pays any attention to what Bryan says, anyhow."

. . . .

Outside Wisconsin many people were interested in this controversy, but few knew anything more than that Bryan had denounced Birge as an atheist, and that Birge had declared Bryan to be crazy. For those who had axes to grind that was enough. Fundamentalists generally thought of Birge as an educational representative of His Satanic Majesty. In the nation's capital a father thanked God that his children were attending a college governed by Christian people, and trembled for the day when the atheistic president of the University of Wisconsin would stand in judgment before his Creator. A deacon in the Congregational Church at Princeton, Illinois, told his pastor that the University of Wisconsin was teaching atheism.

. . . .

If Birge's friends had been as reticent as he, the dispute might have ended within six months. By October, 1921, Bryan seemed to have grown weary of the struggle; but a succession of taunts and invitations kept him active against the president until April of the next year. One of the Commoner's chief tormentors was Birge's pastor, Edward F. Worcester, who tried to vouch for the president's soundness without specifying his exact views on the fundamentals of Christianity. Worcester made much of the fact that Birge had promoted religion in the University: he credited him with inducing Dean George C. Sellery to join the church, and with screening new appointees, especially in the philosophy department, to prevent the hiring of Free-thinkers. Admittedly there were irreligious teachers at the University, but they were men appointed by Van Hise and not by Birge.

This defense, however well-intentioned, played directly into Bryan's hands. If the president was sound in his faith, he should have no objection to signing a statement to the effect that he accepted the Genesis account of creation, the Virgin Birth, the Resurrection, and other Biblical miracles. If he was a faculty soul-saver and appointer of Christian teachers, he should be willing to "purge the institution of any who in their teachings discredit the Bible." Bryan agreed to retract all of his charges if Birge would get on with a purge and sign a statement of faith. After waiting four months to get a settlement on these terms, he determined to smoke the president out, using the two Madison newspapers for his purpose. What, he asked, did Birge teach his Sunday school class? If he taught the brute theory, the more he taught the more harm he did. Why was he so reluctant to reveal his faith to the taxpayers of the State? "Teachers are employed to teach what their employers want taught," Bryan asserted. And he thought Birge's salary was "large enough to call for something more than giving his students a monkey ancestry and ridiculing those who defend the Bible before them."

. . . .

The moment for which the president had been waiting for almost a year had finally arrived. Bryan had retired from the field, leaving him free to issue a last word that would be completely unequivocal. To the charge that he had evaded the evolution issue the president replied that he had been teaching evolution forty years before, when Bryan was still studying law, and had continued to teach it ever since. "Evasion would be impossible under such circumstances even if I desired it, and Mr. Bryan knows very well that the charge is buncombe." Birge rejected the demand that he state his theological views for the people of the State, on the ground that his views were none of their business. "I do not believe that they have now designated a Chautauqua lecturer from Florida to start a theological grand jury inquiry in their name. I do not believe that they consider it any of their business to investigate the attitude of teachers toward theological doctrines...." As for the hired-man theory of the teacher, it was too loathsome for contemplation. "Mr. Bryan is at work to make the teacher into the hired man of money—teaching not the truth as he sees it or as God progressively reveals it to the world, but repeating in parrot fashion the doctrines that his paymaster calls for." In conclusion Birge quoted Huxley on the question of ape ancestry:

> "A man has no reason to be ashamed of having an ape for his grandfather. If there were an ancestor which I should feel shame in recalling it would rather be a *man*—a man of restless and versatile intellect—who, not content with equivocal success in his own sphere of activity, plunges into scientific questions with which he has no real acquaintance, only to obscure them by an aimless rhetoric, and distract the attention of his hearers from the real point at issue by eloquent digressions and skilled appeals to religious prejudice."

At the battle's end it was evident that neither contestant had covered himself with honor. Bryan, while trying to undermine the president's influence, succeeded only in undermining his own. Though he professed to defend the Golden Rule as the rule of life, his performance squared better with jungle law than with Holy Writ. Throughout, his crassness and vulgarity did little credit to the idea that man was made in the image of God. On the other side Birge's conduct, though creditable on the whole, was not above reproach. Despite his pose of outraged innocence, it was his own fit of temper that brought him into the battle. Once in, he helped keep it alive by unguarded references to Bryan's sanity and intellectual sensitivity. Through most of the controversy he dodged the main issues; his only unequivocal stand came after Bryan had withdrawn from the contest. To say that men were enlightened or swayed by either disputant would be to stretch the truth. The melancholy fact is that this performance, like the Scopes trial at Dayton, was little more than an exercise in futility.

3: The "New Klan" in Wisconsin

In 1915, William J. Simmons founded a new Ku Klux Klan. Anti-black in the South, the Klan was primarily anti-Catholic in the Middle West. In Wisconsin the Klan found a receptive populace and, as a result, was a force of some importance during the 1920s, as is made clear by the two articles which follow.

The Klan in Wisconsin

In an open field a quarter-mile west of Horlick's Dam on July 26, 1923, thousands gathered to witness an initiation. A seventy-five foot cross studded with electric lights blazed against the darkness with two smaller, turpentine-soaked crosses burning brightly on either side. Laid before the large cross were an American flag, an unopened Bible, an unsheathed sword, and a canteen of water.

Those thousands of witnesses were white-robed and hooded, and they had gathered near Horlick's Dam to initiate new members into their Ku Klux Klan.

Where was Horlick's Dam? Not in Atlanta, Georgia, nor in Tuscaloosa, Alabama, nor in Jackson, Mississippi, but just outside Racine, Wisconsin.

That 1923 Wisconsin gathering illustrates the growth and spread of the Ku Klux Klan since its birth nearly sixty years earlier, on December 24, 1865, in Pulaski, Tennessee. In that small town near the Alabama border, six young former Confederate officers, dis-

From "Wisconsin and the KKK," *Wisconsin Then and Now* (April 1969), 1–3. Reprinted by permission of the State Historical Society of Wisconsin.

couraged not only by the wreckage caused by the Civil War, but by the devastation and death left in the wake of a recent cyclone, and by their personal lack of property and prospects, vowed to form a club "to break this monotony and to cheer up our mothers and the girls."

The six met again one week later and chose a name for their infant organization. One fellow suggested *Kuklos,* a Greek word meaning "circle," and from this came Ku Klux Klan—adopted because of its alliteration and mystical possibilities. Secrecy and disguise became their by-laws, and they clothed themselves and their horses in white sheets and agreed to meet only at night.

. . . .

In the next few years, the Klan gained political influence and effectively lowered Republican margins of victory in some state elections, but economically the Klan did little, and when, by 1875, the South was still insecure and chaotic, the Klan slipped into dormancy.

For forty years the KKK remained dormant. Then in 1915 Col. William J. Simmons, professor of history at Lanier University in Atlanta revived it. Simmons claimed that for many years he had dreamed of creating a fraternal order to stand for "comprehensive Americanism," and when he reached manhood, he had a vision: *"On horseback in their white robes, they rode across the wall in front of me, and as the picture faded out, I got down on my knees and swore I would found a fraternal organization which would be a memorial to the KKK."*

Simmons' "new" Klan stressed "one-hundred-per-cent Americanism," and Kluxers campaigned against Negroes, Jews, Orientals, Roman Catholics, aliens, and against dope, bootlegging, graft, night clubs, roadhouses, violations of the Sabbath, unfair business dealings, marital "goings-on," and all forms of scandalous behavior.

In the mood of national exaltation that swept America after World War I, the movement gained strength. By 1921, 100,000 men had donned white robes and entered into the realm of the Invisible Empire—for a $10 fee or *Klectoken.* The nation was divided into regions, each headed by a *Grand Goblin,* and these regions were subdivided into states headed by *King Kleagles.* on the local level, there were *Klafliffs,* vice-presidents; *Klokards,* lecturers; *Kludds,* chaplains; *Kligrapps,* secretaries; *Klabees,* treasurers; *Kladds,* conductors of members into meetings; *Klexters,* outer guards; and *Klokanns,* advisors. Meetings were *Konklaves;* meeting places, *Klaverns;* and the official manual was the *Kloran.*

During this period in 1920, the Klan came to Wisconsin at a

secret meeting aboard the USS Hawk moored in the Milwaukee River. Eight years later it was defunct, but for those eight years, fiery crosses blazed from Grandad's Bluff in La Crosse to Manitowoc's harbor and from Kenosha to Superior. For an example of Klan strength, Wisconsinites had only to look to Racine where masked Klan guards sported deputy sheriff badges and ruled the city.

The Wisconsin membership reached a peak of 75,000 in 1924, and in July of that year, more than 70,000 Midwestern Klansmen and their families gathered in Klan Park, that ninety-acre field west of Horlick's Dam near Racine, and held the biggest Ku Klux Klan celebration ever in Wisconsin. The Konklave seemed more like a family picnic than a sinister gathering, however, for all events were open to the public. There was a parade, community singing, vaudeville acts, and fireworks. Racine merchants even displayed banners which said "Welcome KKK" on their storefronts.

Other Wisconsin towns, however, were less receptive to Kluxers. Mazomanie citizens pelted a hooded band with eggs. At Waunakee a clanging fire bell summoned 500 citizens to rout a Klonvocation from a pasture. In Waukesha a riled citizen marched down the aisle at a Klan gathering waving a revolver and shouting that there would be no meeting, and when a lug wrench came crashing through a window, the Klan bigwigs decided to leave and barely took their lives with them.

The beginning of the end of Wisconsin's KKK came at the Oshkosh Fourth of July celebration in 1925. Advance publicity in April boasted that 135,000 Klansmen were coming to Oshkosh for the celebration. Feature attractions scheduled were a 52-by-100 foot Stars and Stripes, a fiery electric cross to be displayed from an airplane, an eight-mile long parade, and a lighter-than-air craft used in World War I.

When the Fourth of July came, the huge flag was displayed and a six-mile parade with 2,000 participating was held, but the 135,000 visiting Klansmen, the airplane, and the promised speakers failed to show.

By 1928, the Klan was almost non-existent in Wisconsin. Racine and Kenosha harbored members the longest, but other cities, either disgusted because they could never get a Klan charter from Atlanta or shocked by the hate and bigotry preached from Atlanta by professional Klan rousers, disbanded their Klubs.

Gradually, the Ku Klux Klan again drifted into dormancy....

The Klan in Madison

ROBERT A. GOLDBERG

In 1920 the Propagation Department, in response to a request from a group of Milwaukee men, appointed a king kleagle to organize Wisconsin. That fall, several individuals met secretly aboard the Coast Guard cutter *Hawk* anchored in the Milwaukee River. At this meeting they agreed to form Milwaukee Provisional Klan #1. Because of the king kleagle's failure to expand the organization beyond Milwaukee and its suburbs, the department replaced him in the summer of 1921 with William Wieseman. During his reign the Ku Klux Klan spread into every county in Wisconsin.

Madison, the state's capital, was an early target for Wieseman's kleagles. During the 1920's Madison was not only the site of the Wisconsin state government and its many bureaus and agencies, but also the home of the University of Wisconsin, which drew to the city a student body from all over the United States and from many foreign countries. Although the city never developed much heavy industry, it was characterized by a diversified group of small factories requiring skilled labor. Indeed, manufacturing accounted for nearly a third of the total employment.

Between 1910 and 1920 the population of Madison increased by 50 per cent, to over 38,000 persons. A similar high rate of growth continued throughout the 1920's, reaching 56,000 persons by 1930. The inhabitants were predominantly white and Protestant. In 1920 there were only 259 blacks in the community and in 1926 only 1,000 Jews. The number of Roman Catholics had risen from 6,641 in 1916 to 10,250 in 1926, thus constituting slightly less than 25 per cent of the population. The city was, for the most part, ethnically and culturally homogeneous, and the vast majority of recent immigrants possessed a cultural background closely resembling that of the native-born population.

. . . .

On August 26, 1921, an unusual want ad appeared in the classified section of a Madison newspaper, the *Wisconsin State Journal*. It read, "Wanted: Fraternal Organizers, men of ability between the ages of 25 and 40. Must be 100% Americans. Masons Preferred." Many Madisonians probably never saw the ad; others who read it perhaps thought it innocuous. But some understood its meaning. A kleagle of the Ku Klux Klan was in their city recruiting

From Robert A. Goldberg, "The Ku Klux Klan in Madison, 1922–1927," *Wisconsin Magazine of History*, LVIII,1 (Autumn 1974), 31–44. Footnotes in the original omitted. Reprinted by permission of the State Historical Society of Wisconsin.

men to organize Madison and Dane County for the Invisible Empire. On September 3 the kleagle spoke in Madison and outlined several of the Klan's objectives—the promotion of Anglo-Saxon Protestant solidarity, the maintenance of law and order and white supremacy, the protection of American womanhood, and the extension of justice and liberty to all men. The recruiter described the Invisible Empire as nothing more than "a high, close, mystic, social, patriotic, benevolent association having a perfected lodge system." Catholics and Jews could not become Knights of the Invisible Empire: Catholics because their allegiance to the Pope made it impossible for them to profess sincerely the ideals of 100 Per Cent Americanism; Jews because they constituted an unassimilable racial group whose members, according to the Klan, had spawned the doctrine of Bolshevism. Moreover, since the Jews did not believe in the divinity of Christ they could never become eligible for membership. The kleagle did little more than distribute Klan literature to interested Madisonians and left the city shortly after his arrival.

The *Wisconsin State Journal* immediately voiced its disapproval of the organization. It called upon all Madisonians to consider carefully the claims of the Klan before joining, then pointedly asked, "Do we want here 'an invisible empire,' the very name of which means that it is a force above and beyond the law, for the authority of which as it sees fit it substitutes its own will?" The Masons were angry because of the statement, "Masons Preferred," in the Klan's newspaper advertisement. In the words of Charles E. Whelan, the former Grand Master of Madison's Masons, the ad was an "insidious effort to prostitute the institution of Masonry to a movement entirely out of line with its principles. . . ."

Almost a year later, in July, 1922, F. S. Webster registered at the Monona Hotel in Madison. King Kleagle Wieseman had appointed Webster, a resident of Chicago, as chief organizer for the Klan in Dane County. For the next three months Webster conducted a secret recruiting drive from his hotel room. By early fall he had organized a Madison Klan under the title, "The Loyal Businessmen's Society." The society held weekly meetings in the Woodmen of the World Hall on Main Street in downtown Madison. In order to prevent detection, the Klan used a chain system for sending messages. If, for example, Webster desired to inform the membership of a change in activities, he telephoned one Klansman. That Klansman would then call three others. They in turn would each inform three more. The men repeated this procedure until they had notified all of the members of Madison's Klan of the change in activities. The Klan succeeded in maintaining its secrecy through September, 1922, and few Madisonians were even faintly aware of its presence.

In early October Madison Provisional Klan #7 publicly proclaimed its existence. Webster informed the *Capital Times* that it had secretly initiated 800 men into the Invisible Empire. "We have," he said, "members of the Ku Klux Klan in every important place in the city. We have members among city and county officials. They are also in the state capitol. We have them in the schools." This was not an entirely empty boast, since William McCormick, a former chief of police detectives, recalls that "prety near all the men in the department were Klansmen."

On October 12, two days after the Klan's initial announcement, the kleagle divulged plans for a future outdoor, white-robed initiation and demonstration at which he claimed over 900 men formally would swear allegiance to the Klan. This figure included 100 men who had joined the organization in the previous two days. Later, Webster asked Madison's Mayor I. Milo Kittleson for permission to bring Klan lecturers to the city. The mayor replied, "If they are as they set forth, I see no reason in the world why they should not be given the same consideration as any other organization."

Madisonians joined the Klan for a variety of reasons. Some, attracted by the patriotic image of the organization, were sincere in their belief that America's institutions and values were in danger. The Klan was, these men felt, a vehicle by which the doctrines of 100 Per Cent Americanism could be strengthened and extended. The Wisconsin Klan pledged in its Articles of Incorporation "to conserve, protect, and maintain the distinctive institutions, rights, privileges, principles, traditions, and ideals of pure Americanism." Others believed that the Klan would unite all Protestants under a single banner and restore faith in God and in the supremacy of the Bible. Kleagle Webster also appealed to anti-Catholic and anti-Jewish prejudices. Specifically, Webster promised prospective members that the Klan would eliminate "Catholic control" over the city's government and school system.

. . . .

Probably the Klan's most effective lure was its promise to "clean up" Madison and, in particular, Little Italy. Also referred to as "Greenbush" or more commonly "the Bush," Little Italy was culturally and ethnically distinct from the rest of the city. Triangular in shape, it was bounded roughly by West Washington Avenue, South Park Street, and Regent Street. Within this area lived most of Madison's 484 Italians, the largest unassimilated nationality group in the city. The first significantly large group of Italians to arrive in Madison were construction laborers who helped erect the State Historical Society building at the turn of the century and later the state capitol building. As the years passed more Italians settled in the city, mainly in the Bush, where they clustered together and perpetuated their traditional customs and institutions. Many Madison residents developed suspicions about this growing "alien presence."

Madisonians were concerned about the Italian community for other reasons also. Little Italy was the production and distribution center during Prohibition for the Madison and Dane County liquor trade.

. . . .

Little Italy was, in addition, afflicted with a reputation for violence. According to one Madisonian, "You didn't dare walk down through there. You couldn't even drive a car through there cause you might pick up a shot." Between 1913 and 1923 six men were killed in the Italian neighborhood; in 1924 the total number of murdered men rose to twelve. The newspapers believed that the six slain in 1924 were the victims of a "rum war." The *Capital Times* told its readers that two rival Italian clans were battling for control of Little Italy's liquor trade. When a war erupted in an Italian community, the *Times* remarked, "one must choose between the three S's—*schiopetto, stilleto, strada*: the rifle, the dagger, or flight." The Madison police proved ineffective in combating the violence or apprehending the murderers.

The city suffered from one other major social problem. In early 1924, a private investigator announced to a shocked citizenry his discovery of fifteen houses of prostitution. Although the brothels were, for the most part, scattered around the city, six were located in the vicinity of Little Italy. Again the public wondered why its police force had failed to suppress the activities of the city's criminal elements.

Distrustful of their own police force and court system, some Madisonians turned to the KKK as the only force capable of driving the bootlegger, the prostitute, and the murderer from the community. And the Klan was careful to present itself as an organization of aggrieved citizens, a militant Protestant and 100 Per Cent American fraternal order dedicated to the eradication of crime and corruption. Its stated objectives promised something for everyone, and it is probable that only a few took out membership because of a single feature of the Klan's program.

But in actuality the secret order's crusade for moral reform was narrow and restricted. The real target of the Klansmen was the bootlegger, who they believed to be the root of all corruption in the city. Unlike Klans in some states, the Madison organization did not attack wife-beaters, adulterers, "neckers," or "petters." The rest of the Wisconsin Klans mirrored this stance. As one state Klan leader said, "Sometimes women would want us to go against their husbands for drinking or running around with other women. We refused to do that."

On October 13, 1922, F. S. Webster enunciated the goals of the local Klan. Klansmen were determined, he said, to make Madison again a fit place in which to live. The organization was ready to lend its services to the mayor or the chief of police to accomplish this objective. Later in the year the Klan announced formation of the Klavaliers, a group which the kleagle described as a military unit trained to fight crime, fires, floods, riots, and strikes. The commander of the Klavaliers promised that the unit would serve only in conjunction with and under the command of the Madison Police Department. However, the city's chief of police, Thomas Shaughnessy, rejected this offer of assistance. Webster also vowed that the secret order would protect Madison's public schools from dangerous influences. In particular, the Klan pledged to launch a crusade to strip school textbooks of disparaging remarks about the nation's past actions and leaders.

. . . .

. . . by the end of 1922 the local chapter claimed a membership of 1,000.

The year 1923 was a quiet one for the Madison Klan, highlighted only by sporadic press releases. In March it announced plans to form a female auxiliary. A Klan spokesman claimed that over 1,000 white, Protestant women had expressed a desire to join the order. Four months later the newspapers reported that Klansmen were busy collecting funds for the construction of the first Ku Klux Klan temple in the state. Subsequently the Klan decided to issue stock to finance the structure, but it was never built. However, membership continued to increase, and in the summer of 1923 Wisconsin's king kleagle announced that the Madison Klan now contained 2,500 men.

On March 8, 1924, the Klan made its first public appearance. Twenty-five hooded and robed Klansmen assembled along the shore of Lake Mendota to initiate several men. Before the group departed it burned a wooden cross which drew a large crowd of curious spectators. Ten days later the Klansmen burned another cross which was visible from the downtown area. Klan stickers began to appear on store windows along Capitol Square and even on the door of the governor's office, exhorting Madisonians to join the Klan and to stand by the public schools.

. . . .

As the number of sincere and decent Klansmen declined, the voices of religious intolerance became more influential. In 1925 the only overt anti-Catholic incidents in the history of the Madison chapter occurred. In January the Klan opposed a plan to vaccinate school children against disease because the innoculations were to be administered in Catholic parochial schools. The Klansmen were afraid that Protestant youths would be exposed to the "Vatican Virus" while awaiting immunization. The newspapers, however, never reported that the children would be sent to Catholic schools for vaccination, and children were innoculated in the schools which they regularly attended. Later in the month the Klan charged that the Madison public school system was dominated by "Romanists," after the Board of Education refused to allow it the use of a high school auditorium for a public meeting. The Dane County Klan's endorsement of Edward Dithmar for the United States Senate also reflected anti-Catholic sentiment, since it urged members to vote for Dithmar, a 100 Per Cent American who opposed the "Rome Ring" that controlled Madison. The primary election in September produced one final anti-Catholic incident. A Madison Klanswoman challenged nine Catholic nuns as they cast their votes in the election, contending that the nuns' ballots were invalid because they voted under names they assumed when they entered their order. A Madison court later ruled in favor of the sisters.

The final major Klan event in Dane County took place on Labor Day in 1925 when several thousand Klansmen and their families from all over Wisconsin gathered in Madison for a state konklave and parade. Only a few Klansmen from Dane County participated in either of these activities. The procession through Madison was similar to the Klan parade in 1924; the column consisted of bands, floats, and marching Klansmen. Violence, however, marred the event. A spectator rushed into the line of march, pulled a Klansman from his horse, and threw him to the street, fracturing his collarbone and breaking two of his ribs. Madison police officers intervened quickly but the assailant fled. Later the police arrested Wayne Olson for shouting obscenities at the passing Klansmen. Olson was found guilty of disorderly conduct and fined $25.00.

After 1925 the Klan virtually ceased to exist in Madison, and a year later there were only scattered reports of Klan activity. In August, 1926, the Klan attempted to refill its depleted ranks, but recruitment efforts failed to bring many new members into the organization. One of the last actions of the Ku Klux Klan in the capital city occurred on December 8, 1926, when Madison's Klan leader, M. M. Shirk, asked the city's Board of Education for permission to present a patriotic play in one of the local high schools. The

Board members denied Shirk's request. As the order languished, several men formulated plans to bring a new patriotic society to Madison. On February 8, 1926, "Major General" Lew Wallace McComb and "Major" William Dean announced that they were organizing a regiment of the Minute Men of America, a society established by a dissident faction of the Denver, Colorado, Klan in 1925. Like the Ku Klux Klan, it promised to support the public schools, to encourage the growth of patriotism, and to prevent lawlessness, but it did not, however, imitate the mode of attire of the Nights of the Invisible Empire. Instead of white sheets, the Minute Men adopted the uniform of the colonial soldier. The new group was also less restrictive in its membership requirements; all white, native Americans, regardless of religious affiliation, were eligible to join. But the organization directed its most strenuous recruiting efforts toward the former Klansmen. McComb and Dean told them that the Minute Men could achieve the Klan's ends without inciting racial and religious hatreds. Nevertheless, the recruiting campaign was unsuccessful, and after acknowledging failure, Madison's Minute Men quietly disbanded. Meanwhile the decline of the Madison Klan accelerated. By the end of 1927 its funds were exhausted, its last members were dispersed.

4: The Great Depression and Agriculture

Problems related to the Great Depression dominated legislative concern during much of the period between 1920 and 1940. Agriculture, a key element in the state's economy, was hit first. Special problems confronted the state in the northern cutover areas, about which Vernon Carstensen writes in the first article. The impact of the Depression and the efforts of the Agricultural Adjustment Administration are discussed in the following two selections. The final reading in this section, dealing with the Wisconsin Milk Strike, suggests how some farmers sought to deal with the problems caused by the depression in agriculture.

The Depressed Cutover

VERNON CARSTENSEN

The 1920's was a time of trouble in northern Wisconsin. The decade was ushered in with a sharp decline in agricultural prices. This was followed by a period of slow, uneven, and incomplete recovery, climaxed in 1929 by a disastrous stock market crash and general depression. We need not be concerned here with the several factors involved in this collapse and the ensuing period of depression except to recognize that agricultural depression in the United States in the 1920's was widespread and lasting, and that even farmers in the rich land areas suffered. The analysis on which the

From Vernon Carstensen, *Farms or Forests: Evolution of a State Land Policy for Northern Wisconsin, 1850–1932* (Madison, 1958), pp. 91–114. Footnotes in the original omitted. Reprinted by permission.

A homestead in the cutover region

expectation of large-scale and widespread post war agricultural development in northern Wisconsin was based was fundamentally
wrong. The demand for more foodstuff simply did not appear either
within the United States or abroad. During the 1920's, indeed until
the beginning of World War II, food surplus, not shortage, determined the condition of American agriculture.

Land clearing and farm making in northern Wisconsin slowed
down and almost stopped. Colonization companies went out of
business—some of them into bankruptcy. Tax delinquency, always
a problem, began to assume ominous proportions in the northern
counties.

. . . .

The legislature took a more important step in 1925 by adopting
for the first time a resolution to amend the uniform taxation clause
of the constitution by adding the words "with such classification as
to forests and minerals, including or separate or severed from the
land." The object of this amendment, introduced by the committee
on state affairs, was to permit special taxation for forest lands and

for forest growing. Neither the assembly nor the senate objected to this amendment. More important in terms of the problems which were emerging in the north was the decision of the 1925 legislature to establish an interim committee on administration and taxation with instructions to report to the legislature in 1927. The committee was given $10,000 to conduct the investigation.

This committee was not created specifically for the purpose of looking into the northern Wisconsin land problem, but rather to explore the general problems of state administration and taxation. Yet the plight of the northern country invited special attention. Tax delinquency had increased steadily since 1921. In that year a million acres of land in the 17 northern Wisconsin counties had been offered for sale as tax delinquent. The total area of these counties amounted to a little over 11 million acres. By 1925, the amount of land offered for tax sale exceeded 2¼ million acres and two years later the amount reached 2½ million. Moreover, buyers of tax deeds decreased. In 1921, two-fifths of the tax deeds offered for sale went unsold, in 1927, four-fifths of the tax deeds found no buyers.

Other aspects were as gloomy. In 1925, the 17 counties had less than 1½ million acres of saw timber left. Yet after 40 years of assiduous work on the part of local real estate dealers, county officials, state officials, representatives of the College of Agriculture and of colonization companies—after 40 years of much verbal and some actual farm making—only 6 per cent of the total acreage was in cultivated farm crops. The amount ranged from 11.4 per cent in Burnett county to 1.4 per cent in Vilas county. B. H. Hibbard estimated that it took a decade to put into farms the amount of land deforested in one year, and that it would take 400 years to make the northern cutover areas into farms provided the rate of land clearing proceeded at the same rate.

. . . .

The legislature responded by passing the constitutional amendment for a second time and providing for a popular referendum in the spring election. With its approval by the electorate, the legislature turned its attention to the other remedial legislation proposed by the committee. The first proposition to be considered was the forest crop law under which private landholders could enter into agreements with the state running up to 50 years. The owner of growing timber would pay an annual tax of 10 cents an acre until the trees were cut. He was then required to pay a severance tax of 10 per cent of the value of the crop. Under the terms of this act, the state would reimburse the towns 10 cents an acre for loss of taxes. Thus, the towns would collect a full 20 cents an acre on all timber

Settlers farming the cutover

land put under the forest crop law. This law was enacted, and thus there was placed on the statute books a proposal first presented more or less specifically in 1911. At last the law recognized that special tax provision must be made for growing timber.

A second law growing out of the report of the committee authorized counties to establish county forests. Such an arrangement had been proposed as early as 1898, had been lost sight of, and now when made again in 1927 was easily carried through the legislature. The same legislature provided for the creation of a joint interim committee to study the problem of forestry and public lands in Wisconsin and to report in 1929.

. . . .

The work of the men of the agricultural extension service and their associates in discussing questions of better ways to use northern Wisconsin lands not only underscored the fact that farm making in the cutover land had come to a standstill but served at the beginning to give point to the study by Hibbard and his associates in June of 1928. This study, covering 17 northern counties, recorded the general failure of the big plans of promoter and optimist alike.

The forest was fast disappearing, the counties were becoming more and more burdened with tax delinquent land, and each year fewer buyers of tax certificates appeared at the annual tax sales. Tax delinquency was forcing the town taxing authorities to increase taxes on property that could still pay, because money had to be obtained somewhere to maintain government services that could not be cut in proportion to the loss of revenue. Nearly one-quarter of the land in the 17 northern counties had been offered for sale as tax delinquent in 1927, and only 18 per cent of the amount offered had been purchased by buyers of tax certificates. The investigators predicted that the amount of tax delinquency would increase in the coming years. Time proved they were correct.

Hibbard and his associates could point to no easy way out of the difficulty. They proposed gathering additional facts on the situation, wider use of the new forest crop law, a school equalization law to permit wealthy counties to help support schools in the poorer ones, and creation of county forests. They reported, moreover, that "the counties finding it impossible to collect taxes on large areas of land, and, together with the townships, finding it impossible to provide for schools, roads, and other governmental undertakings, are making plans to relieve the situation. These plans, so far as they are formulated, look toward districting the county. They involve moving isolated settlers located in territory having no immediate prospect of development into more desirable territory where schools and highways can be maintained economically." They also suggested that the counties take title to tax delinquent land and use this county owned land as a means of directing settlement. Some relief might also be expected from the federal government. Federal authorities were already selecting purchase areas for national forest in northern Wisconsin.

The Hibbard report was a systematic presentation of the gloomy situation in northern Wisconsin. The hearings of the legislative interim committee produced hundreds of vignettes of desperation in the testimony of town and county officials, of representatives of organized groups, and of citizens who came before the committee and told their stories.

. . . .

In 1931 the legislature adopted a resolution creating a special joint committee of both houses to investigate the cutover land and tax problems in northern Wisconsin. By this time the term "cutover," which had earlier merely described land with the pine taken off, was beginning to be used as synonymous with depressed area. The resolution pointed to the extensive tax delinquency, the near bankruptcy of local governmental units, and the need for a careful study of the situation. The committee, to be made up of three senators and four assemblymen, was voted $5,000 and directed to consider particularly the cutover land problem, tax delinquency, high taxes. It was also directed to study uses that might be made of the land particularly for forestry and reforestation, problems of fire protection, the removal of isolated settlers, the reduction of costs by consolidation of local government units, the value of economic surveys, and such other matters as might appear to be legitimate within the general purpose of the investigation. Although created as a special committee by the legislature, the committee was authorized and directed to continue its investigation after the adjournment of the legislature as an interim committee.

. . . .

The land of the cutover country was not being made into farms. Both the nature of the soil and the agricultural depression accounted for this. The land, stripped of its resources, was not paying taxes. The plough had not followed the axe into large areas of northern Wisconsin. . . .

Wisconsin Agriculture in the 1930s

WALTER H. EBLING

The United States Census for 1930 covered the crop and livestock production for 1929. It recorded livestock numbers and also data on the number of farms and land values for 1930. It happened that the data collected by the 1930 Census enumeration largely represent conditions as they were just before the present world-wide depression. They, consequently, mark a base point for calculating the extent of the depression and the down-swing in prices which has prevailed since 1929.

The agriculture of Wisconsin is of a rather stable type, and changes in it are somewhat less rapid than in other types of farming. For the most part, the state's farm output is composed of livestock and livestock products. The Wisconsin farmer, though he may find changes necessary and desirable, has almost no satisfactory alternatives which would take him away from his program of livestock production. Changes are rather gradual in Wisconsin, but, nevertheless, adjustments are constantly going on.

Violent price changes are bound to bring adjustments in production. In 1929, Wisconsin farm prices averaged 55% above the pre-war level. In 1931, they averaged 10% below the pre-war level, a net decline of 42%. By June, 1932, the Wisconsin index of farm prices had declined to a level of 60% of pre-war, a decline of over 61% from the average of 1929. This is the most drastic decline in agricultural prices of which we have any record. As a result of it the agricultural income has fallen to the lowest level experienced in many years. Under these conditions, agriculture as an industry is certain to undertake changes and adjustments in order to meet the changed situation.

The gross farm income of the leading agricultural products as calculated for Wisconsin was a little over 254 million dollars in 1931 as compared with 434 million dollars in 1929, a decline of about 41% for the two-year period. Such a change in the state farm income results from changes in prices rather than production, for the total production of the state changes only gradually. Price fluctuations have been very much more marked than changes in production.

Unusually severe and prolonged drought has prevailed in many parts of Wisconsin during the past three years. Weather during

From Walter H. Ebling, "Changes in Wisconsin Agriculture Since the Last Census," *1933 Wisconsin Blue Book* (Madison, 1933), pp. 133–139. Reprinted by permission.

1929 was quite favorable and that year the state harvested a record hay crop. Since then, each succeeding year has seen a decline in hay acreage and a reduction in the hay crop. Since tame hay in Wisconsin occupies over one-third of the cropped land, this shrinking of the hay acreage represents a fundamental change which influences all forms of agricultural production in the state.

Crop Changes Since the Census

These three dry years in succession produced marked changes in crop acreages. The drought affected different parts of the state in different years, and the changes for the state as a whole do not necessarily represent the changes in any particular county. . . .

From 1929 to 1932 Wisconsin lost about 800,000 acres of clover and timothy hay. Of the land made available by this loss, 242,000 acres went to corn production, and this crop reached a high acreage in 1932. Oats in 1932 were seeded on 98,000 acres more land than in 1929. Barley during the period increased 65,000 acres, rye 48,000 acres, wheat 10,000 acres, and potatoes 45,000 acres.

With the extremely large loss of clover and timothy hay from 1929 to 1932 the need for hay has been very marked in the state, and while much of the land made available by the reduction in clover and timothy hay was planted to corn and other feed grains, there nevertheless has been an unusual effort to provide hay by means other than clover and timothy. From 1929 to 1932 the acreage of alfalfa hay increased by 46,000, and the acreage of other minor tame hays, such as grain cut for hay, soy beans, peas, millet, Sudan and other grasses, and sweet clover, increased 159,000 acres. The sharpest increase in these other hays came in 1932 when the clover and timothy acreage had reached its low point and when alfalfa also showed a decline due to unfavorable weather. With the large livestock population on the farms of the state, the need for feed crops is at a high point, and with the destruction of hay and grass acreage, the shift to other feed crops was a necessary adjustment to provide feed supplies for Wisconsin livestock. About half of the state's corn acreage is used for silage, and much silage has been substituted for hay during these years of reduced hay production. In the main, the dry years have been favorable to the corn crop, and corn production, particularly in 1932, was large.

Among the cash crops, the leading one—the potato crop—shows a gain in acreage over the low year of 1929. Nearly all of the other cash crops in 1932 had smaller acreages, largely because of the low prices.

Changes in Livestock Numbers

With the exception of horses, all classes of livestock at the beginning of 1932 were more numerous on Wisconsin farms than at the beginning of 1930, the year when the census was taken. . . .

Horses, unlike the other livestock species, continued their gradual decline in Wisconsin during the past two years. This decline began in 1915 with the incoming of tractors and automobiles in large numbers, and has continued steadily ever since. The number of horses and mules on the farms of Wisconsin on January 1, 1930 was estimated at 557,000 head, and the number on January 1, 1932 at 541,000 head.

. . . .

Reducing all of the livestock population, not counting poultry, to animal units, we find that from January of 1930 to January of 1932 there was an increase of about 4% in the livestock population of the state. This indicates rather clearly that under the conditions of the past two years farmers have shifted to more livestock in their effort to meet the reduced farm income which has accompanied the price decline of the world-wide depression. In this shift toward more livestock, the dairy industry has grown steadily, and the milk production in Wisconsin rose from 1930 to 1932 in spite of the fact that the years were dry and pastures were poor.

Dairy and Other Changes

The dairymen of the state have made and are continuing to make important adjustments within their own industry to meet the changed situations resulting from the great price decline of the last few years. More production of milk in Wisconsin during the last few years has resulted primarily from an increase in the number of cows on farms. Production per cow has not been increased because of unfavorable conditions from the standpoint of pasture, hay, and feed supplies. Given favorable weather and improved feed conditions, further increases in the production per cow are probable in Wisconsin during the next few years. With the low prices of milk which have prevailed, there has been a tendency to feed somewhat more sparingly, particularly during the months of lowest prices in the summer, in spite of the fact that pastures have been poor. Wherever possible, dairymen have depended more upon home grown feeds and less upon the commercial feeds which they had to buy. There has been also a continuation of the tendency long apparent in Wisconsin toward more winter milking so as to level out the flow of milk production in the different seasons of the year. Formerly, milk production was high during the summer months and relatively low in the winter months. For a long time there has been an increasing tendency toward more fall freshening of cows and more winter milking, with the result that the milk flow in the winter has been greatly increased. This tendency has gone forward steadily during the last few years.

There have also been some changes in the outlets of milk available to farmers in the state. The consumption of fluid milk has declined, throwing more milk into the channels of commercial manufacture. During the past few years in particular, there seems to have been a rather marked trend toward the separation of milk on the farm for the sale of cream and away from the sale of whole milk. More recently, this trend seems to have been partly reversed, and somewhat more milk seems to be used by the cheese industry.

Farmers of the state are making such adjustments as they can, both in their methods of living and in the operation of their farms. Expenditures for feed, fertilizer, farm machinery and farm labor have been relatively low during the last few years. Farm labor employed on the farms of the state has declined somewhat, but farm wages have declined a great deal more. The index of wages paid for farm labor in Wisconsin on October 1, 1932, stood at 72% of the pre-war average as compared with 172 on October 1, 1929. This indicates that the wages paid by farmers are now 58% less than they were three years ago. Living standards on a number of the farms in Wisconsin have obviously been reduced during the past few years because of the reduced buying power resulting from the low prices paid for farm products as compared with the higher levels of prices of things which farmers buy. An inquiry in 1931 showed that 2% fewer Wisconsin farmers were taking daily newspapers than was the case in 1928. Likewise, the number of farms reporting telephones has declined, there being 2% fewer farms with telephones in 1931 than in 1928. Other changes of this type are doubtless going on, and will continue until the buying power of agriculture is restored.

The 1930 Census found the farm population in Wisconsin at a low point. With the coming of the depression in industry there has been some tendency for population to flow back into the rural sections from the cities where they had been attracted by the prosperity which followed the war. For the future, this will probably mean somewhat more people on the farms of the state as well as a new increase in the number of farms.

Farm Prices and Income Since 1929

The period since 1929 has been one of extreme price decline. This carried farm incomes far below those experienced since the war. In fact, the farm income for 1932 is below the farm income in 1910 in spite of an increase in production since pre-war days of about 28%....

Farm prices and farm income during this period have fluctuated enormously. During the war, prices reached a high point in 1919, when they averaged 115% above the five-year period from 1910 to 1914. Following this high point came a depression so that in 1921 Wisconsin farm prices were only 28% above the pre-war average. Following 1921, prices again improved, reaching a high point in 1928 and 1929. The price level in Wisconsin in 1928 was 56% above pre-war. Since that time there has been a very sharp drop in all prices, and agricultural prices in Wisconsin for 1932 averaged only 69% of pre-war.

Farm income has very closely followed the trend of farm prices. In 1910 the farm income of the state was slightly under $200,000,000. The average of the five-year period just before the war was about $222,000,000. During the war it rose sharply, reaching a high point in 1919 of $547,000,000. Following the high point of 1919 the gross farm income in the state declined to $320,000,000 in 1921. From that time it again rose, reaching a high point of $438,000,000 in 1929, since which time it has declined to about $190,000,000 for 1932, which is about 15% under the five-year average from 1910 to 1914, and nearly $10,000,000 below the gross income for 1910 in spite of a materially larger farm production. It is quite clear that the periods of prosperity and depression in agriculture in Wisconsin have been very largely the result of changes in the price levels. The production during the period from 1910 to 1931 fluctuated relatively little from year to year, but with the sharp changes in prices the income of agriculture had fluctuations similar to those of prices.

The Agricultural Adjustment Programs in Wisconsin

Beginning in 1933 the United States Department of Agriculture undertook a broad program of adjusting the supply of certain agricultural products produced in the United States, in accordance with the Act of Congress commonly referred to as the Agricultural Adjustment Act. Of the various crops for which programs were initiated under this Act, so far only four have affected Wisconsin.

The first program to be organized in Wisconsin was the tobacco program which got under way in 1933. Under this program there were approximately 7,000 contracts in the state. The farmer was required to reduce his tobacco acreage 50 per cent, and was in turn paid a benefit varying commonly from $33 to $35 per acre for the land taken out of tobacco production. In some cases the payments ran higher because the amounts were calculated on the basis of average yields for the particular farm.

Another tobacco program in 1934 increased considerably the number of contracts in the state, bringing it up to approximately 8,500. In the 1934 program the producer had several choices. He could reduce his acreage one-third or one-half, or if he chose he could grow no tobacco at all. These programs were effective in greatly reducing the acreage of tobacco in Wisconsin. In 1932 the estimated tobacco acreage was 28,000. In 1934 it had been reduced to 7,500 acres. In 1933 the program brought tobacco producers in the state about $524,000 in benefit payments and the 1934 program about $1,097,000. The work continues in 1935.

The wheat program was initiated in 1933, and while the farmers were not required to make any reduction in acreage of that year due to the fact that the program was gotten under way after planting time, they were required to agree to reduce their acreage in 1934 by 15 per cent below the 5-year average, 1928-1932. For this they were paid benefits of about 29 cents per bushel for the acreage to be taken out of production. There were about 1,100 wheat contracts in the state in 1933 and about the same number in 1934. In the 1934 contract a 15 per cent acreage reduction for that year was required but the producer was also required to grow 54 per cent of his base acreage. Benefit payments to Wisconsin wheat growers on 1933 contracts were estimated to be about $39,000 and for 1934 contracts about $41,000.

The corn-hog program was the most important of the adjustment programs in Wisconsin. Work on this program was begun in 1933

From "The Situation in Agriculture," *1935 Wisconsin Blue Book* (Madison, 1935), pp. 56-57. Reprinted by permission.

but the first contracts were offered to cover the 1934 production. A program of reduction in hogs was undertaken in 1933, by the purchase of sows and pigs on the part of the government. In this preliminary program there were sold for slaughter from Wisconsin 3,332 sows and 128,002 pigs. The amount of money paid to producers in the state for these animals was $845,000.

In the 1934 corn-hog contracts producers were required to reduce their hogs produced for market 25 per cent below the 1932–33 average, and their corn acreage from 20 to 30 per cent below the average acreage in 1932 and 1933. Benefit payments on corn could not exceed 30 per cent of the base acreage though the producer could, if he chose, reduce his acreage more. For this they were paid benefits at a rate of $5 per head on 75 per cent of their adjusted average annual hog production during the base period, and at the rate of 30 cents per bushel on the 10-year average yield per acre of the corn land for the acres taken out of corn production. This program was popular in Wisconsin, particularly in those counties where the production of corn and hogs is important. There were nearly 43,000 contracts signed in the state and the benefit payments to Wisconsin producers on 1934 contracts aggregate about $7,879,000. Of the 1934 benefit payments $6,180,000 was paid on hogs and $1,699,000 was paid on corn.

The corn-hog reduction program is being continued in 1935, but the required reduction on hogs is only 10 per cent under the 1932–1933 average production. Corn acreage may be reduced from 10 to 30 per cent and the 1935 corn benefit payments will be 35 cents per bushel for the acres retired, based on the 10-year average yield for all corn land in the farm.

. . . .

In addition, there is also offered in 1935 a sugar beet contract, which while involving only a small portion of the state's farmers, is important in a few localities where sugar beet production is established.

Funds for these reduction programs are provided by the processing taxes levied in the processing of agricultural products, as specified in the Act. The processing tax on wheat is 30 cents per bushel, on hogs the processing tax has been graduated up to $2.50 per hundred-weight, on tobacco 3 cents per pound on cigar type, and 55 cents per hundred on sugar. Funds obtained from these taxes provide the benefit payments to producers as well as for most of the overhead expenditures made to carry out these programs. In all of these programs an effort was made to have the work rest on the producers themselves as far as practicable, and the actual work of having the contracts signed and properly adjusted was largely done by local workers on town and county committees. The administrative responsibility for the state was centered in the Extension Service, and for the corn-hog program partly in the State Board of Review.

Dairy Farmers Strike Back

HERBERT JACOBS

The economists, of which I am not one, take a comforting view of strikes. They call them a product and an indicator of good times. When production and profits are high, that's when the worker decides to hit for his share of the gains. The boss can afford to give a little, rather than have his plant tied up at a time when everybody wants to buy his product, and the workers know it.

But I don't think the economists were thinking about milk strikes when they laid down that rule about strikes being an indicator of prosperity. Rather, I think the Wisconsin milk strikes, concentrated in the year 1933, were a product of desperation. They climaxed a dozen years of falling farm prices, when the farmer saw the prices of the things he sold going down steadily, while the prices of the things he needed to buy remained the same or increased. The strikes preceded the economic upsurge of the New Deal, when an expanding economy gobbled up dairy products at rising prices. This was followed by the booming war years when practically anybody could make money at farming. The dairy farmer still had plenty of troubles preceding and during the war years, but they were not tough enough to make him think of strikes any more.

It was a time of ferment and turmoil. Looking back at it now, it seems almost as if we were close to revolution, and perhaps we were. Milk, the kind that went to cheese and butter factories and condenseries, brought the farmer about 75 to 85 cents a hundred pounds, or slightly over a cent and a half a quart. In some regions

From Herbert Jacobs, "The Wisconsin Milk Strikes," *Wisconsin Magazine of History*, XXXV,1 (Autumn 1951), 30–35. Reprinted by permission of the State Historical Society of Wisconsin.

the farmer only got 60 cents out of which also came hauling charges. The kings in the business were the farmers who supplied the fluid market—bottled milk for the cities. They got a whole dollar and a half for a hundred pounds. Since most Wisconsin milk goes into manufactured products, like cheese, butter, and ice cream mix, these "kings" were less than 10 percent of the farmers.

I'm not certain that the crisis hour calls forth the right man to cope with it, but anyway three colorful and dynamic figures were on hand to translate "farm unrest" into farm revolt. I think there would have been some sort of milk strike even if those three men had not appeared, but they certainly didn't tend to quiet things down.

All around Wisconsin, in the dozen months preceding 1933, the Middle West was aflame with a seething farm violence. Milk strikes, dumping of milk, livestock embargoes, clashes between farmers and law officers were the order of the day, from New York State through all of the Midwest. The only wonder is that Wisconsin didn't join the procession earlier. Many Wisconsin farmers took a hand in trying to keep livestock from being shipped to Iowa when the Farm Holiday Association there called a meat animal strike, and they watched and read about the rural turmoil in Illinois, Indiana, and other states. Wisconsin farmers were spoiling for a fight, and three men were on hand to lead them to it.

One of them was Arnold Gilberts, a Dunn County man who headed the Wisconsin Farm Holiday Association. A gentle, angular, and good-natured man, he gave an appearance of great sincerity and earnestness. But he was capable, under stress, of firebrand statements that surprised his audiences and possibly himself. For instance, at a mass meeting of some 5,000 or more farmers at Marshfield, on September 2, 1932, Gilberts was quoted as saying: "We'll solve our problems with bayonets, and I don't mean maybe."

Another of the three musketeers of Wisconsin farm revolt was Milo Reno, national president of the Farm Holiday. True, he was from Iowa, but he came to Wisconsin frequently for speeches, and he did perhaps more than anyone to lay the groundwork for what followed. He was a short, school-teacherish sort of fellow, with a tremendous shock of white hair, and a wonderful gift of dramatic speech and homely illustration. I have seen him sway an audience of 4,000 to his will, like wind bowing a field of green oats. It all seemed so simple, the way he put it, and they ate it up. Everybody forgot that Iowa was a corn and hog state, where you could withhold farm products for months without hurting the farmer much.

Nobody remembered that Wisconsin was a dairy cow state, and that cows produce milk twice a day, and you've got to do something with it right away.

And then there was Walter M. Singler of Shiocton, president of the Wisconsin Co-operative Milk Pool which had been organized two years before to give small farmers bargaining power with the dairies. He was a giant paradox of a man, a roaring dynamo, where Milo Reno was more a wisecracking salesman. Barrel-chested Singler stood six feet two, and weighed 230 pounds. Atop his head was a light-colored Texas style hat—maybe two gallons instead of ten. His black hair was luxuriant, he had a conspicuous mustache, and a ridiculously small goatee, almost lost in his ruddy complexion. He sported flamboyant, reddish-colored waistcoats, and—crowning affront to Wisconsin farmers—he wore spats. The costume and appearance were those of a circus barker rather than a farmer, and by rights the farmers should have hooted him out of town. Instead, they practically worshipped him. Few of them knew that he had been an oil promoter and land speculator in Texas, and that his farming experience was extremely limited. He talked their language, and he promised action, and that was enough for them. The Fox River valley and nearby territory was the stronghold of his milk pool, but his name was a powerful stimulant throughout the rest of the State.

But it would be a mistake to think of the Wisconsin milk strikes only in terms of these three men. Farm foreclosures, skinny, ragged kids, the realization that each year you were farther behind financially than the year before—all these built up a powerful head of steam. Somewhere between 5,000 and 8,000 farmers turned out for the meeting at Marshfield, September 2, 1932, when the Wisconsin Farm Holiday was organized, while a Holiday strike was then going on in Iowa. In a few months the organization claimed a membership of 130,000 out of Wisconsin's 180,000 farmers. Part of this was merely paper, for the dues were less than a dollar a year, and the organization never became anything but a highly sleepy giant, always threatening action, but never getting up off the ground.

Singler's Milk Pool, on the other hand, had something like 6,700 members, recruited largely from the smaller, marginal type of farmer, shipping milk to small local cheese factories and condenseries. They literally had nothing to lose, and they had the courage of desperation. The more prosperous farmers (if that term can be applied to conditions of 1933) in general those with good herds, supplying the city markets, actively opposed Singler and all he stood for. They had a comparatively good thing, and they didn't want to take a chance on losing it.

Thus the milk strikes were partly civil war among the farmers as well as a fight against the commercial dairy interests, and this internal battle gave them their peculiar character.

The State resounded during the winter of 1932–33 with talk of milk strikes and farm holidays. Milo Reno spoke several times in the southern part of the State, but Singler's star began to eclipse that of Arnold Gilberts and Reno. He brought things to a head at a meeting of the Milk Pool directors, February 8, 1933, when he told them bluntly, "Call a strike or quit."

The directors authorized the strike, to be called at Singler's discretion. But he refused to designate it as a strike. He announced merely that the farm price for milk would be $1.40 per hundred, starting the morning of February 15. Everybody was supposed to hold his milk for that price. But when the strike deadline came, since the Milk Pool was outnumbered at least 20 to 1, a lot of farmers ignored the Singler edict and shipped their milk.

The Milk Pool was able, by persuasion or methods close to intimidation, including dumping of quantities of milk along the highways, to close up most of the small cheese and butter factories of the Fox River valley, where the Pool was strongest. Then the Pool turned its attention to the larger cities, regarding them as the key to break the price deadlock. And here they bucked the non-Pool members. Log chains across the road, barricades of old boxes or logs, and even masses of men in the road were used to halt milk trucks. Those who would not turn back had their loads dumped. Sheriff's deputies used tear gas and clubs to break up the picket groups, but there were too many places, and too few officers. Even private cars, as well as trucks, were stopped and searched, to the great indignation of the public.

Campfires of pickets blazed all night beside crossroads leading to big towns like Milwaukee. But what the pickets didn't see and could not stop were the convoys of milk trucks slipping by them in the dark over side roads, and the trains carrying extra cars of milk. There were many cases, too, of farmers arranging to have their own milk transported, and then dashing out to the picket lines to stop the milk of more gullible farmers. The big cities kept on getting all the milk they really needed. And the rural milk processing plants, even though closed, were not worrying, because there was such a big backlog of manufactured dairy products.

In spite of some rough spots, it was a fairly good-humored strike on both sides, though largely ineffective. Singler called it off February 22, after an all-night mass meeting at Madison, at which twenty-one farm organizations refused to go along with him any farther. Singler claimed a strike victory because Governor

Courtesy of the SHSW [WHi (X3) 27919]

Striking farmers pour out milk on the Soo Line near Burlington, January 10, 1934

Schmedeman promised to "study" the milk price question, but detractors said he quit because he was licked.

They were wrong. Singler and the Pool were just getting started. On April 11, 1933, at Appleton, plans were made for a forty-state strike of farmers, to include other products besides milk. Arnold Gilberts said his 130,000 Holiday members were going to join the strike.

Possibly in view of this threat, many State dairies on April 16 agreed to go along with the governor's suggestion that they increase the price of condensery milk to $1.00 per hundred, by adding 15 cents to the current price.

This failed to pacify either the Milk Pool or the Farm Holiday. They went ahead with plans for a jumbo strike May 12. The governor countered this, on the eve of the strike, by ordering an embargo on all milk movement until each county had a chance to decide whether or not to go along with the strike. On May 12, the day the strike began, the governor lifted the embargo for fifty-two of the State's seventy-one counties, because a majority of the farmers in those counties disapproved of the strike.

Another body blow came to the Milk Pool the same day, when Milo Reno called off the Farm Holiday which he had just ordered. The Milk Pool was going it alone again, but this time it had more opposition from the State. Adjutant General Ralph Immell placed 2,500 National Guardsmen at the disposal of local sheriffs, to be sworn in as special deputies. The State arranged to furnish a more potent form of gas—not merely tear gas this time, but tear gas plus a gas that was an emetic and cathartic, guaranteed to spoil the day for any striker. Both sides had learned a lot from the first Milk Pool strike and were busy putting the learning to use.

The pickets took to cars instead of camping at crossroads. They swooped down on trucks when no guardsmen were present, dumped the loads, and vanished. Near Mukwonago I saw a new wrinkle, when pickets tossed an old harrow in front of a line of trucks to stop them by puncturing the tires. But the authorites were even more forehanded. The lead truck had a snowplow, which brushed the harrow off the road. The deputies wore gas masks when they exploded their triple-action bombs. And the pickets wore leather gloves to toss the bombs right back before they exploded.

. . . .

Other scenes of violence were being enacted elsewhere in the State, notably around Shawano and near Appleton, and blood from noses was flowing almost as freely as milk. Both sides were beginning to play for keeps, when Singler called off the strike May 19. It had cost the State $100,000 for 2,000 troops and incidentals, and the counties $70,000 for 4,000 special deputies, not to mention the loss to farmers from vanished milk checks. The ostensible reason for calling off the strike was to give the new Roosevelt administration time to do something for the farmer. What everybody wanted was "cost of production." Nobody bothered to define it, or put it down in dollars and cents, but the sentiment was unanimous for getting it, preferably by a law which would simply order it for all farmers.

By the fall of 1933 both the Milk Pool and the Farm Holiday Association had concluded that F.D.R. would not come across with cost of production. The Farm Holiday called a strike in several states, to begin October 21. This time the Milk Pool, having seen the Holiday group sit out two strikes, decided to wait until the Holiday proved it meant business.

Reassured that the sleeping giant was really going to get in there and pitch this time, the Milk Pool joined the strike on October 31. Two days later the Farm Holiday called off the embargo just in Wisconsin, leaving the Milk Pool to go it alone again. The announced reason was to give a conference of five Midwest governors in Des Moines time to come up with a plan to save the farmers.

The third strike produced more spectacular violence than its predecessors. At least seven bombs were exploded at cheese factories, one of them resulting in $15,000 damage. Some 34,000 pounds of milk were dumped at one time in Racine. Governor Schmedeman threatened to call out the National Guard. A farmer near Madison was shot and killed by a man in a passenger car who had passed through the picket line, then came back fifteen minutes later to argue and fire at the crowd. A man had been killed in each of the other two strikes in accidents involving trucks.

One bright spot was furnished near Milwaukee when deputy sheriffs cleared a path for a bootlegger's truck, announcing solemnly, "The mail, the milk, and the moon must go through."

The strike "petered out" during the first third of November.

5: Manufacturing and the Depression

Manufacturing in Wisconsin, which boomed in the 1920s, also suffered from the impact of the Depression. The following items illustrate the extent of manufacturing in the state in 1925 and the effect of the first years of the Depression upon the industrial strength of Wisconsin.

Manufacturing in Wisconsin, 1925

J. H. H. ALEXANDER

The census of 1925 presents the latest available picture of the relative size and rank of Wisconsin's industries. Motor vehicle manufacturing has finally surpassed foundry and machine shop products to rank 2nd in the state. This comparatively new industry, if combined with the manufacture of motor vehicle bodies and parts, would exceed the butter, cheese and condensed milk industry in value of products. Noteworthy also in the table on page 468 is the increasing importance of the manufacture of rubber tires, aluminum products, plumbing supplies and stamped and enameled ware:

The complete enumeration of all of the industries found in Wisconsin, with value of product and state and national rank of each, does not fall within the scope of this brief history. The large number and great variety which becomes evident when Wisconsin's smaller

From J. H. H. Alexander, "A Short Industrial History of Wisconsin," *1929 Wisconsin Blue Book* (Madison, 1929), pp. 31–49. Reprinted by permission.

Leading Industries in Wisconsin in 1925

Rank in State	Rank in U.S.	Industry	Value of Products
1.	1	Butter, Cheese and Condensed Milk ...$	209,260,384
2.	4	Motor Vehicles (except Motorcycles) ..	155,944,670
3.	6	Foundry and Machine Shop Products ..	125,063,220
4.	2	Paper and Wood Pulp	97,779,601
5.	14	Slaughtering and Meat Packing	70,793,049
6.	5	Motor Vehicle Bodies and Parts	59,403,191
7.	3	Knit Goods and Textiles	58,086,110
8.	9	Lumber and Timber Products	56,374,735
9.	5	Boots and Shoes (other than Rubber) ..	53,954,002
10.	4	Furniture Manufacturing (except Refrigerators)	53,915,692
11.	2	Engines and Water Wheels	53,174,241
12.	9	Electrical Machinery, Apparatus and Supplies	46,431,351
13.	2	Rubber Tires and Inner Tubes	46,271,447
14.	4	Leather: Curried, Tanned and Finished .	44,591,782
15.	7	Planing Mill Products	32,931,415
16.	8	Canning and Preserving (Fruits and Vegetables)	29,870,848
17.	14	Car and General Construction and Repairs	29,408,902
18.	6	Brass, Bronze and other Nonferrous Metals	28,636,197
19.	11	Bread and Bakery Products	27,986,959
20.	15	Print and Publishing (Newspapers and Periodicals)	22,983,303
21.	18	Flour Mill and Grist Mill Products	22,414,608
22.	3	Plumbing Supplies (except Enameled Ware)	20,149,315
23.	1	Aluminum Manufacturing	19,813,231
24.	11	Iron and Steel Manufacturing.........	18,145,242
25.	3	Agricultural Implements	14,782,355
26.	4	Stamped and Enameled Ware	14,388,486

industries are enumerated indicates that "diversified" may be applied to manufacturing just as it may be applied to farming in the Badger State. In addition to our ten leading manufacturing industries, the census lists 114 other industries that run the range of the alphabet from agricultural implements to worsted goods.

Agricultural implements are manufactured in 21 plants which employ 1,861 workers and pay out $2,616,157 in wages. With $14,782,355 in value of products, Wisconsin ranks 3rd in the nation and is known throughout the world as a source of farm machinery. The manufacture of paper boxes and cartons almost equals agricultural implement manufacturing with $14,215,399 in value of products, and with 27 plants that give employment to 2,096 workers who divide an annual pay roll of $2,174,550. In addition, there are 55 factories manufacturing wooden boxes, employing 2,322 workers, paying out $2,084,840 in wages and producing $8,040,697 worth of wooden boxes. The confectionery industry employs 2,204 candy makers in 48 establishments which pay $1,735,125 in wages and produce $11,741,796 worth of a wide variety of confectionery products. A surprise is found in the fact that 11 Wisconsin factories produce $6,100,303 worth of flavoring extracts and syrups. The fur goods industry employs 961 workers in 34 establishments, with a pay roll of $1,145,431 and products valued at $6,889,986. In this age of automobiles, trucks and tractors, the $1,466,378 worth of horse blankets, fly nets and related products manufactured in 6 Wisconsin factories would, it seems, supply the needs of the nation.

All the way down the alphabet from A to Z the small industries receive but little of the attentive interest and credit they rightfully deserve. Ice cream manufacturing, for example, gives employment to 591 persons in 68 plants which have a total production of $6,995,953 and pay out $845,216 in wages. The manufacture of mattresses and bed springs is carried on in 24 establishments which produce $3,617,626 worth of sleeping comfort and pay out $561,175 to 539 workers. Musical instruments are made in 9 plants employing 539 workers. Piano manufacturers alone pay out $549,280 in wages and produce $2,525,668 worth of pianos. Twelve factories produce $11,613,259 worth of paints and varnishes, employ 573 workers, pay out $783,901 in wages and earn for Wisconsin a national rank of 9th in this industry. Eight refrigerator factories pay out $706,231 in wages and use Wisconsin black ash in the production of $3,520,198 worth of fine grade ice refrigerators. There are 15 ship building and boat building plants in the state, with 1,310 workers and an annual pay roll of $1,745,850, in the production of $4,999,693 worth of wooden and steel ships and boats. Stove and furnace manufacturing has a combined product valued at $11,783,156 or 16 plants employing 2,111 workers who divide $2,854,439 in wages. As a producer of trunks, suitcases and bags, Wisconsin is better known by people in other states than by people here at home. With 19 factories engaged in this industry, 890 workers are employed for $1,008,979 in wages in the manufacture of products valued at $5,833,758. It is only when the numerous small industries are studied as a group, when their combined value of products is summed up, and when the total number of wage earners employed is disclosed that the true worth of these highly diversified "small children" of Wisconsin's industrial family comes to light. Though ten industries of the state account for $940,574,644 of the $1,856,243,930 in value of manufactured products, or slightly more than one-half of the state's output, the remaining industries outrank the ten leaders not only in number of establishments but in number of employes and in total pay roll. Of the 247,341 persons industrially employed in Wisconsin, 134,397 are employed by the small industries, and the 3,803 plants in the small industries group pay out $171,806,744 in wages, or 54 per cent of the state's pay roll.

Where Factories Are Located

A passing glance at the distribution of Wisconsin's factories within the state is interesting and important. In 1925 there were 7,262 industrial establishments of all sizes in the state. Of this number, 2,843 were located in the 21 cities having 10,000 or more population, and 4,419 were located in cities having less than 10,000 population or in rural districts, a large share of the latter being cheese factories or creameries. Thus we see that our 21 larger cities had 39 per cent of the factories and the remainder of the state had 61 per cent, but of the state's total industrial production of $1,859,243,930, factories in 21 cities produced $1,164,721,726 or 62 per cent. The much larger number of factories outside of these cities produced 38 per cent or $694,522,204 worth of our industrial products. Of our total number of industrial employes, the 21 cities claimed 164,423 or 66 per cent, and 82,918 or 34 per cent belonged to the remainder of the state. Likewise, of $314,883,011 which represented our total factory pay roll, $216,543,460 or 68 per cent was paid to the workers in 21 cities and $98,330,551 or 32 per cent took care of the pay rolls of the remainder of the state. Naturally, Milwaukee was responsible for a large share of the total industrial showing made by the 21 cities. Excluding Milwaukee, however, 20 cities produced $622,810,187 in value of products, or nearly as much as the remainder of the state which had $694,522,204.

Twelve of the 21 cities are located in the 27 counties comprising the highly industrialized eastern judicial district of Wisconsin, and 9 of the cities are located in the 44 counties comprising the western judicial district. Milwaukee included, the 12 eastern cities produced $971,094,026 worth or 52 per cent of the total industrial production of the Badger State. The 9 cities in the western judicial district produced $193,627,700 worth or 10 per cent. Excluding Milwaukee, the remaining 11 cities in the eastern district produced $429,182,487 worth or 23 per cent of the state's total, compared to 10 per cent for the 9 western district cities. The 12 eastern cities employed 137,910 of the state's industrial workers, or about 55 per cent, and they paid out $185,261,783, or about 58 per cent, of our total pay roll. The 9 western cities employed 26,513 workers, or about 10 per cent, and paid out $31,281,677, or about 9 per cent, of the total pay roll of the state. The 21 cities of 10,000 or more population, ranked as follows in value of products, wages paid, number of plants and employes in 1925:

Name of City	Plants	Employees	Wages	Products
Milwaukee	1,445	77,432	$105,123,022	$541,911,539
Kenosha	54	11,994	19,168,502	124,748,272
Racine	182	11,102	16,200,593	89,165,253
Janesville	52	2,671	3,400,632	48,093,105
West Allis	43	7,164	10,771,988	45,515,487
Madison	100	4,286	5,461,234	33,286,639
Oshkosh	117	6,911	7,265,300	32,681,683
Sheboygan	108	6,534	7,224,831	30,790,865
Beloit	34	5,032	6,226,886	28,304,514
Green Bay	83	3,880	4,679,695	23,598,506
Superior	61	2,297	3,111,991	21,536,898
La Crosse	112	4,731	4,770,148	21,497,279
Manitowoc	61	3,338	4,010,566	21,281,464
Fond du Lac	67	3,341	3,618,911	20,487,153
Eau Clare	64	2,890	3,186,866	19,980,754
Appleton	67	2,705	3,195,712	17,593,746
Waukesha	46	1,877	2,396,965	14,576,768
Wausau	60	2,926	3,131,731	13,994,649
Marinette	35	1,633	1,605,698	8,743,290
Stevens Point	32	1,101	1,216,952	5,047,575
Ashland	20	578	775,237	1,936,287
Remainder of State	4,419	82,918	98,339,551	694,522,204
State Total (1925)	7,262	247,341	$314,883,011	$1,859,243,930

. . . .

A good impression of the size of Wisconsin's factory pay roll may be reached by assuming that Wisconsin manufacturers used silver dollars in paying $314,833,011 in total wages annually. Five freight trains each half a mile long would be required to carry the pay roll in silver dollars. The 308 box cars would be loaded to capacity with 18,519,588 pounds of silver dollars, about 2,960 tons. A crew of ten men, working eight hours a day, would work 46 days unloading the cars with scoop shovels. But the 247,341 workers in Wisconsin's factories could not wait for an annual pay day. Factory workers and their families represent some 920,061 people; or more than one-third of the population of the state, and factory wages pay their bills. For a pay day every two weeks, 12 box cars would be needed to carry $1,118,042 in silver dollars which would weigh 721,649 pounds or about 350 tons.

Impact of Depression

ORRIN A. FRIED

The industrial growth of the United States, per capita of population, on a long time basis, has advanced rather uniformly at the rate of about 2.8 per cent, compounded annually, for many decades past. Such regularity may be expected in view of the long time and the vast amount of capital required to bring advancements and improvements in the arts into general use. Furthermore, any extensive shift in the occupational attachments of the people is a slow process. It takes time to develop good mechanics, good craftsmen, etc. The momentum of our ways of life, and our inertia to change, brings into relief certain economic tendencies which characterize us over long periods of years.

At any particular time there is, of course, much variability as regards economic trends in different industries. In general, total agricultural production has been increasing at about the same rate as the population, while the rate of increase in total production of fabricated goods has been very much higher. On an average, a net increase of about 0.6 per cent per year in total consumers goods available per capita represents our productive margin for raising the general standard of living of our population.

From Orrin A. Fried, "Wisconsin Manufacturing Since 1929," 1933 Wisconsin Blue Book (Madison, 1933), pp. 141–142. Footnotes in the original omitted. Reprinted by permission.

Courtesy of the SHSW [WHi (X3) 33375]

Governor Phillip LaFollette signs Wisconsin's pioneer
Unemployment Compensation Law, January 28, 1932

Aside from divergent changes in the physical volume of production in various industries, the past decade has seen large changes in
the per capita productivity of wage earners in individual industries.
Agricultural production has continued to increase, with a slight
decrease in the number of agricultural workers. The largest increases in labor productivity, however, have generally been attained
in manufacturing processes where advances in mechanical, chemical
and electrical applications so greatly increased the output per
worker, and opened the way for shorter working hours per day and
per week. This is also one reason why the on-coming workers of the
new generation have found jobs in non-manufacturing industries to
a relatively larger extent than in manufacturing industries during
recent years.

Since 1929 both industrial and non-industrial economic activities
have been ailing seriously; but this is not the place for a treatise on
that subject. This brief note is to point out certain changes in Wis-

consin manufactures since the beginning of this depression which started about as early as April, 1929. Such changes stand in sharp contrast to the long term trends mentioned above.

In terms of employment and pay rolls, the production of factory goods and the financial return to the working population usually devoted to manufacturing lines, may be stated as follows:

In 1929 Wisconsin factories employed a monthly average of 264,745 wage earners at an annual wages bill of $352,490,893. In 1932 corresponding employment averaged approximately 116,525 wage earners at an annual wages bill of only $141,707,338. Within the brief span of 2 years, Wisconsin factory employment dropped 37.1 per cent, and corresponding wage payments decreased 59.8 per cent.

A further observation along this line is that Wisconsin factories employed 50,516 salaried officers and employes at an annual salary bill of $130,913,267 in 1929. In 1932 the number of salaried officers and employes decreased to an estimated average of 37,892 and an annual salary bill of about $72,002,298. There was a reduction of about 25 per cent in salaried workers, while total salary payments decreased about 45 per cent.

Excepting the construction industries, we find that the manufacturing industries as a group have suffered relatively more drastic losses in employment and pay rolls than other lines. For example, in the period from August, 1929, to February, 1933, total factory employment decreased 43 per cent and corresponding pay rolls declined 69 per cent. Losses in total employment and aggregate pay rolls for wholesale trade amounted to 22 per cent and 32 per cent respectively; for retail trade 11 per cent and 34 per cent respectively; for express, telephone and telegraph companies 29 per cent and 38 per cent respectively. In this relation one may also note that the farming population remains at work without serious curtailment of agricultural production irrespective of whether the farming business pays out or not, and regardless of the business tie-up and banking holidays which so largely characterized this industrial depression and forced some 225,000 employes into involuntary idleness in Wisconsin.

A rough estimate shows that total wage and salary payments in Wisconsin decreased from $1,080,864,797 in 1929 to $548,407,234 in 1932, the total reduction being $532,457,563 per year. While wage earners and salaried employees in manufacturing total about 28 per cent of the gainfully employed in Wisconsin, approximately forty per cent of the reduction in total wage and salary payments has been carried by workers normally employed in the manufacturing industries.

6: Wisconsin Politics, 1930s

Weakness of the Democratic party in Wisconsin meant that the real political action was in the Republican primary through much of the 1920s and 1930s. The Progressive faction of the GOP, dominated by the LaFollette brothers, continued to do battle with the Old Guard faction until it made a break with the party in 1934. While enjoying substantial successes, the Progressives' bent for self-destruction led to Phillip LaFollette's abortive national third-party movement in 1938, and to methods of dealing with the legislature that even the normally sympathetic Madison *Capital-Times* was forced to declare objectionable. By the end of the 1930s the end was in view for the Progressives.

Progressives Leave the Party

LEON D. EPSTEIN

In the whole period from 1900 to 1932 Wisconsin politics were fought largely within the Republican party. Never in those years did the Democrats win the governorship, and never except in the early Wilsonian years (when a Democrat won a U.S. senatorship) did they have any serious chance of gaining power in the state. Only in the three-way presidential contest of 1912 did the Democratic party win Wisconsin's electoral votes. At times the Democrats seemed to be little more than a minor party; in 1922 the Democratic candidate

From Leon D. Epstein, *Politics in Wisconsin* (Madison: The University of Wisconsin Press; © 1967 by the Regents of the University of Wisconsin), pp. 37–44. Footnotes in the original omitted. Reprinted by permission.

Courtesy of the SHSW [WHi (X3) 18343]

Governor Phillip F. LaFollette

for governor received only 12 per cent of the two-party vote, and in 1926 only 17 per cent. The Socialist party seemed almost as strong just after World War I, when Socialists were continuing to elect Milwaukee's mayor and were also electing a Milwaukee congressman and casting almost one-sixth of the vote in state-wide contests.

During this period of Republican supremacy, the form of the intraparty contest is of principal concern. The direct primary was instituted in 1906 under the inspiration of the elder La Follette, then serving his third term as governor. Subsequently the struggle between La Follette progressives and anti-La Follette conservatives, or stalwarts, was not for party convention delegates but for voters. In view of the openness of the primary, the relevant voters were practically the electorate-at-large, and not a closely defined Republican electorate. Any voter wishing to participate in the only serious election contest simply chose the Republican primary ballot. Although it can be argued that the state's very one-party situation as of 1906 made the primary especially appropriate (as in the South), nevertheless the opportunity of choice which the primary subsequently afforded the voters tended to obviate any need or desire for a two-party system. Much of the time the Wisconsin electorate was confronted with two alternative slates of candidates, one progressive and the other conservative, seeking the Republican nomination for the state's executive and legislative offices. Both Republican factions had leadership cadres resembling those of separate parties elsewhere in the United States. Insofar as this bifactionalism prevailed in Republican primary contests, Wisconsin escaped the chaotic personal and locally based rivalries which have been found to characterize much of the one-party South.

However, bifactionalism did not always clearly prevail in Wisconsin's Republican primary. At times the progressive-conservative line was loosely drawn, and at other times one faction failed to achieve a consensus with respect to its candidate.

. . . .

But despite multiple candidacies and plurality victories, it is probably fair to say that bifactionalism sufficiently characterized the Republican primary so that the alternatives were more often defined in progressive-conservative terms than they were in many two-party states between 1906 and the mid-1930's.

Wisconsin voters concentrated on the Republican primary in the same manner, if not in the same degree, as have southern voters on the Democratic primary. It was ordinarily the decisive election. In the most extreme instances, 1922 and 1930, the Republican primary vote for governor actually exceeded the total votes cast for gubernatorial candidates of all parties in the subsequent general election. Generally, however, Wisconsin did not thus resemble the familiar southern pattern even in other off-year (nonpresidential) elections.

. . . .

In 1932 Roosevelt won 67 per cent of Wisconsin's major-party presidential vote, and in 1936 the figure was 68 per cent. Both of these percentages were well above Roosevelt's national proportion (59 per cent in 1932 and 62 per cent in 1936). Yet these overwhelming Democratic presidential voting records failed to vitalize the Wisconsin Democratic party. The traditional residuum of state Democrats was ill-suited, and not entirely willing, to become the Wisconsin wing of the New Deal, and the opportunity afforded by Rooseveltian triumphs was largely wasted. Only in 1932, in the wake of the national landslide, did Wisconsin Democrats win

Courtesy of the SHSW [WHi (X3) 2457]
Robert M. LaFollette, Jr. (1895-1953)

state-wide offices (including the governorship and U.S. senatorship), and thereafter Democratic percentages declined continuously
in each gubernatorial election of the 1930's.

The inadequacies of Wisconsin's archaic Democratic organization were not solely responsible for the failure to establish a two-
party system in the 1930's. Prepared to take advantage of the absence of liberal Democrats in a liberal period were the two sons of
Robert M. La Follette—Robert, Jr., an incumbent Republican U.S.
senator, and Philip, who had been a Republican governor from
1931 to 1933. In 1934, when the Senator was to seek re-election
and Philip wanted to regain the governorship, it was plain enough
that the Republican ticket, just then, was not the place for a family
accustomed to winning office. Nor, for different reasons, was the
Democratic party inviting to the La Follettes. For one thing, old-line
Democrats were now officeholders, and they coupled a conservative
antipathy for progressivism to an understandable desire to keep the
La Follettes from taking over the jobs which Democrats had so

Courtesy of the SHSW [WHi (X3) 3101]

Emmanuel L. Philipp (1861–1925)

recently and surprisingly won. Secondly, the La Follettes could hardly avoid the impression that the Democratic label, whatever its value in the early 1930's, was traditionally disreputable in Wisconsin and might well be so again. Thirdly, in addition to estimating the liabilities of the state Democratic party, the La Follettes could also have calculated that the time was finally ripe to begin in Wisconsin what would become a new national party.

Whatever the reasoning, in 1934 the La Follettes took almost all of their following out of the Republican party and into a separate Progressive organization. They managed to secure Roosevelt's blessing for the La Follette senatorial candidacy, and at least a kind of national Democratic neutrality with respect to the gubernatorial contest. National patronage arrangements came, in part, to benefit the Progressives. They competed successfully for Wisconsin's pro-Roosevelt vote, winning the governorship in 1934 and 1936 in addition to holding their Senate seat in 1934. Also in these halcyon days of the New Deal the Progressives were well represented in the state's congressional delegation and in the state legislature. By 1936 the Democrats were reduced to a decidedly third-party status, and in 1938 they almost lost their separate identity when their regularly chosen gubernatorial candidate withdrew in favor of the successful Republican opponent of Philip La Follette. The formal Democratic substitute polled only eight per cent of the total 1938 vote for governor, as many traditional Democrats cast Republican ballots. Such liberal Democrats as there were had little choice, at least temporarily, except to vote Progressive in state politics.

This anomalous situation, in which Wisconsin politics were so out of line with national politics, did not endure. The Progressive alliance with the national Democratic administration cracked under the combined force of Philip La Follette's abortive (and somewhat comic) national third party of 1938 and the subsequent division between the internationalist Roosevelt and the isolationist La Follettes. Then the Progressives were so unfortunate as to have the governor they elected in 1942 (against the inept Republican incumbent) die before he could assume office. In 1944 they proved unable to maintain, without a well-known candidate and in the atmosphere of a presidential campaign, their status as a major party. For the first time since 1934 the Democratic candidate for governor ran second.

It could be said that the three-party system was ended, but it is not so clear that it ever really existed. In only one of the six gubernatorial elections during the life of the Progressive party did each of the three parties receive more than 20 per cent of the vote. And in two elections one party failed to win as much as ten per cent. The system was more like that of two and one-half parties. First one and then another of the three parties was reduced to a plainly minor role as the votes tended to divide mainly between the "ins" and one set of "outs." In the end, it was the originally victorious Progressives, without fixed national identification, who dissolved.

The *Cap-Times* Blasts the Progressives

The Capital Times views the recent special session of the legislature with mixed emotions. There was much on the credit side. There was much on the debit side. Unfortunately there was so much on the debit side that was needless and unnecessary.

The Capital Times has always opposed the placing of time limitations on any session of the legislature. This newpaper believes that such limitations are undemocratic. *The Capital Times* has always stood for the widest freedom in debate and the fullest discussion of every proposal affecting the public interest in the halls of legislation. The limit on legislative sessions will ultimately play into the hands of reactionary interests and their high priced lobbyists who will use the limited session to their advantage.

It was with considerable misgiving, therefore, that we heard of the decision of Gov. La Follette to amend the call and include 11 highly controversial measures on the stipulation that the legislature must adjourn by Oct. 16. That left a little over a week in which to get legislative action on many bills affecting the welfare of the state—more than were acted on at the regular session.

The sequence of events which have been chronicled in the news columns in this newspaper came in logical order. The session ended in disgraceful uproar. During the last few days of the session, orderly parliamentary procedure was thrown out of the window. The presiding officers in both houses made rulings in defiance of all accepted rules of procedure and the speaker of the house, on one occasion, made a ruling, unheard of in Wisconsin, denying the right to appeal from a decision of the chair. The rights of the minority were swept aside. The last few days of the session were characterized by tactics of the Huey Long variety and legislation was railroaded through in shotgun style. Bills were put through the legislative hopper under gag rule that never had an adequate hearing. Members voted on bills they had never read.

It was a week in which we had legislation by executive decree through pressure exerted from the governor's office. It was a week in which democratic processes were abandoned and an executive dictatorship was in the saddle.

The Capital Times is not unmindful of the fact that the dilatory tactics of the opposition during the regular session and at the beginning of the special session provoked the tactics used in the last 10 days of the special session.

From *The Capital Times* (Madison), October 19, 1937. Reprinted by permission.

During the regular session there was a long period of procrastination and delay. There was indefensible stalling and it was apparent that the opposition was determined to drag out the session as the best means of defeating the measures which they opposed.

But the woeful lack of leadership on the Progressive side was responsible, too, for the inability to get things done. Progressives, particularly in the senate, sat for week after week seemingly indifferent to the policy of drifting that eventuated.

On one occasion, Progressives sat glued in their seats, mute and motionless, when bills that would have enacted Progressive party pledges into law were before the senate.

The governor's office, too, seemed indifferent. On many occasions when a major Progressive measure was up for a vote in the legislature the next day, the governor's office was dark the night before instead of burning with activity in preparing for the next day's battle as in the days of Old Bob. During the first week of the special session, every constitutional officer was out of the state,—an incident showing the lack of a united front on a crucial occasion.

If justification for the tactics used during the special session is argued on the ground that the ends attained justified the means, then the question arises: "Why weren't these tactics used during the regular session?" The governor's office exerted enough power in the final 10 days of the regular session to bring about an adjournment. The governor's office then was responsible for the adjournment at a time when many important measures remained unacted upon in the regular session.

In making these observations, *The Capital Times* is aware that they may not be popular because the legislature hasn't many friends. That is unfortunate because members of the legislature are the direct representatives of the people.

The Capital Times is taking this position because we hope the state will never again see such spectacles as characterized this special session. The governor in his Saturday night speech said that the session demonstrated that democracy can be made to work. Democracy isn't advanced through the employment of undemocractic devices. There wasn't much democracy in the special session,—there was too much that smacked of Hitler and Mussolini.

The danger of the special session lies in the dangerous precedents that were set. The brushing aside of parliamentary tradition, gag rule and the denial of parliamentary rights that are historic in the development of representative government were inconsistent with the Progressive philosophy of government.

But the real danger is that two can play this game. The Progressives have now established precedents which will be quickly used if reactionary interests once more succeed in getting control of government in Wisconsin. They need no invitation to use the technique of dictatorship. And they are now furnished with a good excuse to use it if the opportunity is ever presented.

Chapter X
WORLD WAR II AND AFTER

The Depression of the 1930s ended in Wisconsin, as in the nation, with the enormous demands made on both the state and nation with the onset of World War II, which, like World War I, brought prosperity to Wisconsin. Agriculture and industry shared in the benefits of a wartime economy. Labor, never more in demand, was lured into the cities, producing goods required for the defense industry. Chief among the state's contributions to the defense industry was shipbuilding, centered in Manitowoc, Superior, and Sturgeon Bay. With the lure of jobs in industry, and with sons of farmers serving in the armed forces, the need for migratory farm labor increased dramatically during the war years. Unemployment, near 14 percent in 1940, seemed a thing of the past by 1942, and it was still at a low level of around 3 percent in 1950. Although it has climbed somewhat higher since that time, the unemployment level in the state has remained below the national average through the mid-1970s.

There was little antiwar sentiment in the state when war was declared in 1941. In October 1940, Governor Julius Heil established a state council of defense to coordinate various defense programs. In a situation unlike that of World War I, the council did not have to spend much effort to convince the state's populace to support the war effort.

Emerging from the war with a mature economy, the state faced the postwar period with optimism. In the thirty years following the war's end, Wisconsin made impressive commitments to education (including higher education), highways, tourism and outdoor recreation, and, somewhat belatedly, to a cleaner environment. By the 1970s the state led the way in several of these areas, though many of the state's citizens were beginning to question seriously the high level of financial support required.

Wisconsin's economy, with a mixed agricultural and industrial base, continued to expand in the postwar period. Fewer farm families and less acreage farmed reflected the trend away from small family farms. Dairying is still the single most important factor in the agricultural economy in the 1970s. Machinery, paper and allied products, and electrical equipment set the pace in manufacturing.

Politically, the postwar period produced a reversal in the state's political structure. The Progressive party of the 1930s had collapsed in the early 1940s. Some of the followers of the LaFollettes returned with Robert LaFollette, Jr. to the Republican party, which maintained its hold on the state's electorate until the late 1950s. By the end of the 1950s, however, the revitalized Democrats (among them many of the ex-Progressives who had strayed from the Republican fold in the 1930s because of the party's conservative image in the state) began to make their move. And by the mid-1970s, Democrats held the governor's office, both Senate seats, a majority of the Congressional delegation, and control of both houses of the state legislature. One significant factor in the resurgence of the Democrats was Republican Senator Joseph R. McCarthy (1946–1957). Reaction against McCarthy, who attracted national notoriety with his celebrated anti-Communist witch hunts, provided a base around which Democrats could rally support.

As a state with an ethnic heritage, Wisconsin faced some unique cultural problems. The attempts by the federal government to help with development of the native American community provides a good illustration. After years of indecision, the state terminated the Menominee reservation in northeastern Wisconsin in 1961, and the reservation became the state's seventy-second county. But because this was a failure in several ways, termination in turn was ended and the Menominee were returned to reservation status in 1973. Blacks came to Wisconsin in search of wartime employment during both world wars and settled primarily in the urban areas of the state. Milwaukee's population, for example, was 14.7 percent black in 1970, holding about 105,000 of the state's total black population of about 125,000.

Migrant workers, brought into the state in increasing numbers during World War II, have also faced problems common to minorities. The state has made progress in providing decent housing and other protections for this minority, although some problems remain.

Wisconsin gained national prominence in the late sixties and early seventies as a major scene of violent student demonstrations. The war in Vietnam, recruitment on campuses by companies producing controversial military products, and the demand for new courses of study focusing on ethnic and social concerns all contributed to several periods of unrest and uncertainty on many of the state's college campuses.

During the postwar period Wisconsin has mirrored American society for the most part. Yet in some ways the state has provided innovative leadership—in higher education, in outdoor recreation, and in the fledgling conservation movement of the 1960s and 1970s. The state's economy came through the post-Vietnam recessionary periods in better shape than did the economies of many other states. By the mid-1970s many of the social and cultural problems of the state were, if not resolved, in a substantially passive or dormant phase. Questions faced by the late 1970s focused increasingly on such topics as future sources of energy, the need for a better environment, and the continuing question of growth versus stability.

Most of the historical literature on this period of Wisconsin's history is found in periodicals, although the career of Senator Joseph McCarthy is chronicled in studies by Richard Rovere, Robert Griffith, Michael Rogin, and several others. Much remains to be done by historians studying Wisconsin since 1940.

1: Wisconsin in World War II

When war came in 1941, Wisconsin made a substantial contribution. As the demand for food supplies increased, Wisconsin's farmers were encouraged to do their part. As the first selection below indicates, the state's farmers promptly responded to the challenge.

Antiwar sentiment in the state was minimal during this war, and the Council of Defense spent its time coordinating the defense effort. Some of the tasks supervised or encouraged by the council are discussed in the second selection. Much work remains for historians concerned with the war and its impact on Wisconsin.

The Farmers Respond to War

R. S. KINGSLEY

Wisconsin is the key state of the nation in the production of protective foods such as dairy products, meats, eggs, vegetables, and fruits, that are rich in the vitamins necessary for proper nutrition. The important part Wisconsin agriculture plays in producing these protective foods becomes apparent when it is known that Wisconsin farmers produce more than half of the cheese, one-third of the evaporated milk, and one-fourth of the dry milk produced in the United States. Our soldiers, sailors, marines, and aviators, wherever they may be, at home, in Iceland, Panama, and scattered over the broad expanse of the Pacific and its islands, are all fighting on

From R. S. Kingsley, "Wisconsin in the Defense Program," *1942 Wisconsin Blue Book* (Madison, 1942), pp. 151–158. Reprinted by permission.

rations of protective foods coming extensively from Wisconsin farms. Not only the British at home but the various military forces of the democracies in the Near East, in the Orient, and in Africa are sustained in no small part by foods from Wisconsin.

During the last war we were urged to grow more wheat. Today America has a two-year reserve supply of wheat on hand. Now the emphasis is upon dairy products in the production of which Wisconsin is the outstanding leader of the nation. Today the demands for food production fall heaviest on Wisconsin. We are truly the key state in the "Food for Defense" program.

. . . .

In sustaining the cause of our allies through lend-lease as well as in support of our own armed forces, the United States has asked for and has purchased substantial quantities of these protective foods. To be provided for lend-lease purposes during the 15-month period, April 1, 1941 to July 1, 1942, our government asked for 250,000,000 pounds of cheddar cheese; 200,000,000 pounds of dry milk; and 15,000,000 cases of evaporated milk. In slightly more than one-half of this period, from March 15, 1941 to November 22, 1941, government purchases of these products in Wisconsin alone amounted to 60,711,842 pounds of cheese; 9,833,000 pounds of dry milk; 5,915,500 cases of evaporated milk, or 24.3 percent, 4.9 percent, and 35.4 percent, respectively, of the totals requested for lend-lease purposes. In addition Wisconsin provided 142,400 cases of eggs; 5,295,574 pounds of dried eggs; and 570,000 pounds of frozen eggs.

During the first 11 months of 1941 Wisconsin poultrymen produced 1,791,000,000 eggs. Loaded into refrigerator cars, this amount of eggs would have made up a train 94 miles long and consisting of approximately 12,000 cars.

Typical of American agriculture, there had been no letup in the production of food by Wisconsin farmers even during the depression. When asked by the Federal Government to expand production during the present emergency, Wisconsin farmers increased their milk production eight percent over the previous year, which was approximately four times as great as the increase for the nation as a whole. This was accomplished in spite of the draft and the enlistment of farm boys and the draining of much rural population to assist in speeding up other defense industries. Wisconsin's intensive type of dairy farming calls for more labor than most other types of farming. Hence, this record of accomplishment becomes all the more outstanding.

With dairy requirements for lend-lease export centering especially on increased production of cheddar cheese, evaporated and dried milk, it became necessary to use for these products large volumes of milk formerly used for other purposes. Although handicapped by difficulty in getting necessary equipment, many dairy plants installed milk-drying equipment. To make larger supplies of skim milk available for milk powder, thousands of farmers shifted from the sale of farm-separated milk to the sale of whole milk. By the middle of December 1941, 47 creameries, including some of the largest in the state, had shifted to the manufacture of cheddar cheese. Also, tremendously increased quantities of whole milk have been diverted to condenseries.

In making these changes, established markets for established brands of goods often have been sacrificed. As a result, dairy plants in many instances have lost patrons and some have closed their doors.

During 1941, Wisconsin farmers stepped up hog production to 3,519,000 head. This is 10 percent over 1940 and nearly a million head more than the 10-year average.

Wisconsin is also the leading producer of vegetables for canning. In response to defense demands, Wisconsin farmers in 1941 increased their plantings of vegetable canning crops by 33 percent over the 10-year average. The total canning crop acreage in 1941 exceeded 200,000 acres. Wisconsin produces one-third of the total pea pack of the nation amounting to 10,800,000 cases in 1941 or two cans of peas for every man, woman, and child in America. The government purchased about 1,100,000 cases of Wisconsin peas in 1941; mostly for the army and navy, though some were used for lend-lease export.

Wisconsin farmers have increased their sweet corn acreage so that they now rank third in the nation. The 1941 corn pack of 3,200,000 cases is four times the 10-year average. Wisconsin vegetable canning is becoming more diversified, with the state ranking second in beets, cabbage for kraut, and cucumbers for pickles. We rank third in the canning of snap beans. The farm value of Wisconsin canning crops in 1941 exceeded $10,000,000, and cannery payrolls exceeded $5,000,000.

The loyalty of Wisconsin farmers, demonstrated by their response to increased production, has been what naturally would be expected. On top of the 1941 record production of 13,700,000,000 pounds of milk, Wisconsin dairymen are asked to add another 1,500,000,000 pounds to this peak production in 1942. Hog and poultry production is being increased again in 1942. Add to all this the request for a 45 percent increase in pea acreage, as well as substantial increases in other vegetable crops, and one may realize that task that Wisconsin farmers are resolutely facing in 1942. This challenge will be met.

With less help to do more work, Wisconsin dairymen, stockmen, poultrymen, and general farmers will double their efforts to do their important job of food production in defense of America and her allies. They will work even longer hours than in the past. Their wives and their children will labor uncomplainingly from early till late in the greatest all-out production effort in history. Wisconsin will gladly and competently carry her great load in food production. America's people, her military forces, and her allies will not go hungry. Wisconsin's mighty defense industry, so indispensable to victory, so necessary to peace, moves loyally on. Her much needed protective foods will help to "win the war and write the peace."

The Council of Defense and the War Effort

Profiting from the experience of World War I, the Governor, at the request of the Advisory Commission to the Council of National Defense, on October 1, 1940 appointed a council of defense by executive order consisting of representatives of agriculture, commerce, industry, labor, and state and local governments. Its objective, as stated by the Governor, was "to do every necessary thing to develop and to utilize Wisconsin's many resources in the fullest measure possible, the council being authorized to call upon the various departments of the state government for such aid and assistance as will expedite its work; that it shall cause to be created such local or special committees as may be needed, and define the limits and extent of their work."

Its membership was enlarged as time went on and in 1943 by Chapter 22 it was given statutory sanction as the State Council of Defense.

Its early program involved the surveying of potentials. It first made a survey of vacant and unoccupied manufacturing plant space followed by a survey of manufacturing plant capacity. Later, it

From "Wisconsin in World War II," *1962 Wisconsin Blue Book* (Madison, 1962), pp. 189–198. Reprinted by permission.

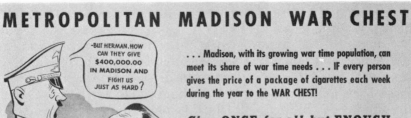

A cartoon advertisement for Wisconsin's war effort

surveyed the needs to protect plants and utilities against sabotage and the pooling of protection personnel and equipment in case of an emergency.

Wisconsin was one of 2 states chosen for a county test of an aluminum collection program. The test, conducted in Dane County, was too successful because it collected 5 times as much material as was collected averagely throughout the nation. The Defense Industry Board created within the council sought to secure an all-out production program within the highly industrialized state. Employment expanded rapidly, especially in the metal industries, because of government contracts. Plants began to work around the clock and problems of wages and hours had to be settled. Payrolls increased because more people were employed, wages went up and overtime increased. Wages of factory workers were higher in 1941 than in any previous time in the history of the state. Layoffs in nonessential industries resulted in the need for shifting of labor and the development of essential industries in such areas.

Wisconsin, as a state with diversified industry, produced a variety of essential materials including uniforms, raincoats, blankets, underwear, sox, gloves, shoes, mess kits, guns, trucks, ships, motorcycles, ammunition, machine tools, and a variety of other items including many items of food.

Wisconsin, as America's great dairy state, was called upon to increase its production of cheese, condensed milk, and dry milk, which resulted in some readjustments in the industry. The production and packing of vegetables increased. Thirty-three per cent more green peas were produced in 1941 than before and sweet corn production went up. This production increase was necessary to provide food for our ever-increasing military forces, for lend-lease to our allies, and for our civilian population which by reason of its greater prosperity and increased employment required more food.

In 1943 when the Wisconsin Council of Defense became the statutory State Council of Defense it was divided into 2 main branches, the Citizens Defense Corps and the Citizens Service Corps.

The Citizens Defense Corps was the forerunner of our present civil defense setup. It was "to effect a passive defense of the state and to augment and assist the regularly established peacetime protective agencies in emergencies." Almost 100,000 trained personnel participated in these programs. An air raid warning system was established and county control centers to receive reports of damage and dispatch help were set up. Practice blackouts were held in many counties and more than 10,000 people were trained in emergency medical service.

The second branch of the Council of Defense, the Citizens Service Corps, had as its primary purpose giving civilian volunteers opportunities to do civilian war jobs. It provided seasonal and permanent farm labor. It provided people to man drives for scrap, fats, grease, wastepaper, clothing, etc. It provided people to encourage car-sharing, group riding, and conservation of tires and gasoline. It provided staff to distribute information on method of coping with food shortages. It encouraged victory gardens to increase the production of food. It provided staff to explain the food rationing system and to man the rationing boards. It supplied volunteers for war bond drives. It provided local clearinghouses for volunteers for civilian defense activities.

State Government Activities

The war and its readjustments put heavy responsibilities on many state agencies. Only a few of the problems to be coped with can be mentioned.

The fear that water supplies might be sabotaged caused the State Health Department to urge their protection by fencing, guards, and lights. Instruction in clearing up contaminated water supplies was given.

The tremendous concentration of people in tents and trailers around industrial plants and army installations led to rules and inspections to prevent unhealthful conditions resulting from congestion under adverse housing conditions. Food and eating establishment inspection was made more difficult, the problems of nutrition were increased due to irregular hours and working mothers, and family care problems among the transient workers were greater. The requirements of proof of citizenship increased the burdens on the Bureau of Vital Statistics.

The state itself had difficulty in securing employes because of the heavy demands on the labor force. One institution had a 58 per cent turnover in attendants. To attract employes to the state, a cost of living bonus was instituted, a retirement system was adopted, and various procedures to recruit were put into operation. In 1943 under the so-called "Sweetheart" law, the Legislature abandoned its 40-year-old prohibition against the employment of female clerks.

The heavy emphasis on the motor vehicle in wartime commerce and in the military establishment increased the need for driver training and for streamlining the authority to haul for others. Convoys had to be escorted and local authorities had to cope with traffic congestion at off hours.

The Beverage Tax Division, one of the state's more effective law enforcement agencies, was placed in control of the suppression of prostitution in congested areas. Wisconsin's army camps led the nation with the lowest rate of venereal disease infection. This organization was also charged with suppressing black market operations. The liquor industry was organized in the promotion of war bond sales and the state ranked fifth in its sales through this medium.

While the work in the conservation of our fish and game population suffered from the loss of men, the protection of our forests, needed for the production of wood products and the vast quantities of paper needed to prosecute a war, was intensified. Forest fire protection became a function of the civil defense organization. Game wardens and forest rangers were given broader scope by direction to observe critical installations such as dams, power plants, bridges, and roads in their patroling activities to prevent sabotage.

The Department of Agriculture was prominent in the drive for greater production of food stuffs by better farming methods, increasing acreage and decreasing diseases, pests, and weeds which affect production. It was also required to investigate substitutes to assure that they were healthful and properly labeled. Weights and measures had to be checked to avoid cheating.

While the aids to certain groups on relief declined with greater work opportunities, other welfare problems developed due to the dependents left by members of the armed forces. Every effort was made to use the manpower in the institutions, such as the school for boys and the prison. The prison was awarded a banner by the War Production Board for their production record.

As a leading manufacturing state, Wisconsin made an all-out effort to increase its output of the commodities which it had been producing and to expand its scope to include the materials required by the war. This expansion not only strained the labor standards such as the maximum hours of work for women and youngsters and the night work of women, but required additional safety precautions because of the intensity of the operation, the number of untrained workers, and the emphasis on output. While industrial accidents increased, every effort was made to keep them at the absolute minimum.

The diversion of critical materials and employes to more essential occupations seriously handicapped the construction of highways. Little new construction was effected, but the heavy use of the roads made it increasingly necessary to keep them in repair.

These are but a few of the many impacts which the war had on the operation of state and local government.

. . . .

State Government Activities in Support of the War Effort

In avoiding the admonition to do as I say and not as I do, the state government itself sought to gear its own operations to conform to the war effort. Not only did state employes participate in war bond purchases, but more than $50,000,000 of the state's funds were thus invested. The state employes reduced their travel mileage by more than 11,000,000 miles in one year, thus saving more than a thousand tires and 750,000 gallons of gasoline. Hundreds of state employes did yeoman service as volunteers in many drives and many held additional jobs. Strenuous efforts to save light, heat, paper, and other supplies were made.

Evidences of Public Support

No one will ever compile all the evidence of public support of World War II. We do not know how many people used less butter and sugar; restricted their driving; kept their old cars rather than seeking to buy new ones; donated scrap of one kind or another; conserved electricity; donated phonographs, records, books, magazines, radios, and other things to army camps; abandoned vacations; worked extra hours; contributed to the many campaigns; and provided volunteer services. Some measuring sticks of the public effort do, however, exist. For example, restricted driving both in terms of distance and speed reduced highway accidents in spite of heavy commercial and military travel. The number of strikes and the man-hours lost were drastically cut. The percentage of the labor force employed rose. War bond quotas were met and there was great response to the pleas for the many drives.

Training of Production Workers

One of the many phases of war activities in which Wisconsin excelled was in the training of war production workers under the federally sponsored and financed war production workers programs. The reduction in the labor force caused by the expansion of the armed forces, the increased production demands, and the development of new products required trained workers. Because it was impossible to train skilled machinists and other craftsmen in the short time allotted, many processes were broken down into a series of tasks for which people could be trained quickly. The vocational school system of the state was admirably suited to this task of training and it is generally conceded that Wisconsin was producing trained employes who were on the job before most states had established a plan for training.

Wisconsin with Oregon led the nation in the development of apprenticeship programs, a function assigned to the Board of Vocational and Adult Education.

Of equal significance was the food production war training program which gave instruction in the use of farm machines, increased food production, conservation of food, and distribution of foodstuffs.

Many hundreds of physically handicapped persons were trained to enter industry in occupations which minimized their handicaps.

The Educational System and the War

The war had several effects upon the educational system. It caused a substantial shortage in teachers due to military service and opportunities in other fields. It reduced the number of male college students. It affected curriculums and it resulted in pupils shifting schools as their families moved.

In the public schools, the students helped in drives for sugar and gasoline rationing, war stamps and salvage drives. Many students had their hours adjusted so they could take part-time jobs to release adults for more important work, and in some cases received credit for work experience. Model airplanes for instructional purposes in the armed forces were made in manual arts classes. Classes in motor repair, radio, welding and similar subjects were started and an intensive physical fitness program was instituted to improve the status of future draftees.

The university not only speeded up its program for training undergraduates, but immediately began a series of service schools.

. . . .

The state colleges conducted training in civil and military pilot training programs, war industry jobs, radio, mathematics, electronics, map-making, and meteorology. Physical education, teacher training, and military drill were stepped up; and the course was concentrated to permit earlier graduation.

Local Government and the War Effort

Counties and municipalities found their activities curtailed by the war as they lost personnel and they could not get the materials with which to work. On the other hand, their work expanded as they had to provide for population changes, the influx of strangers, and a more intense community. Local units, generally unable to expend money for capital improvements, began to build surpluses and to make long-range plans for their ultimate use. Police, health, and sanitation problems arose wherever large groups of people concentrated.

Conclusion

While many homes and businesses displayed blue and gold starred service flags indicating that members of their group were on active duty or had made the supreme sacrifice, there were few outer symbols of the services rendered, often without renumeration, by thousands upon thousands of our citizens who worked in industry or agriculture, solicited for every conceivable cause, or who knitted, sewed, or exerted themselves in scores of other ways to further the war effort. There were some shirkers, some who hoarded, some who profited; but the record made indicates that Wisconsin's citizens, many of whom had relatives among the enemies, gave of their services, their substance and their time, without restraint.

2: Political Developments in Wisconsin, 1940–1970

The demise of the Progressive party in the 1940s and the collapse of Milwaukee Socialism provided a needed infusion of new blood into the Democratic party of Wisconsin. Although Republicans continued their traditional dominance of the state until the late 1950s, the forces of change were at work by the end of World War II, and by 1970 the traditional balance had been reversed.

The best-known (and most controversial) political figure in the state during this period was Republican Senator Joseph R. McCarthy. Opposition to McCarthy's Communist witch hunts was strong in both parties. The first selection below recounts the attempt to defeat McCarthy in 1952. After McCarthy's re-election, the "Joe Must Go" movement led to an unsuccessful recall effort in 1954, which is the subject discussed in the second selection.

The rise of the Democrats is the topic covered by Richard Haney in the third selection, and the state's difficulties with reapportionment during the 1960s are chronicled in the final selection.

McCarthy Faces Opposition at Home

MICHAEL J. O'BRIEN

A Catholic of German descent, Len Schmitt was the third important candidate to enter the race and the only formidable one to challenge McCarthy in the Republican primary. The dynamic,

From Michael J. O'Brien, "The Anti-McCarthy Campaign, in Wisconsin, 1951–1952," *Wisconsin Magazine of History*, LVI,2 (Winter 1972–73), 91–108. Footnotes in the original omitted. Reprinted by permission of the State Historical Society of Wisconsin.

vigorous, but humorless former Progressive announced his candidacy in June under the assumption that anti-McCarthy efforts would be concentrated on his primary battle. His most important backing came from William T. Evjue and *The Capital Times*. Schmitt had known Evjue since childhood and had briefly worked for his newspaper while attending the University of Wisconsin. The two had similar ideological views, both being militant fighters for the "little fellow" against the "millionaire bosses" who ran the Republican party. Against the wishes of most of his staff, who thought Schmitt's candidacy a hopeless cause, Evjue was instrumental in coaxing Schmitt to enter the primary contest and then with single-minded devotion supported him during his campaign. Fairchild's candidacy hurt Schmitt. With a tough Democratic primary [between Henry Reuss and Thomas Fairchild], he could not expect a large Democratic cross-over vote. Republican strategists estimated that Fairchild's entry would cost Schmitt at least 50,000 votes.

As the September primary approached, anti-McCarthy forces were severely divided. *The Capital Times* and a few independent groups urged voters to support Schmitt. Every opportunity, they reasoned, must be made to defeat McCarthy. If Schmitt lost in the primary, McCarthy's opponents could try again in the general election. Evjue blasted Democratic leaders for putting "party and political expediency above a great moral crusade." Fairchild's candidacy was purely a partisan decision, "dictated by the fears of a few party leaders that the party might suffer some loss of prestige if Democrats took the opportunity to place the state's good name above loyalty to party and political expediency and to vote for Leonard F. Schmitt." On the other hand, most labor leaders and journals advised workers to stay in the Democratic primary and for the most part ignored Schmitt's candidacy. Doyle insisted that Democrats remain in their own primary. Only with the strongest Democratic candidate, he argued, could they defeat the Senator in November. Besides, Democrats had many important local elections to decide. In Milwaukee County, for example, seventy Democrats sought the party's nomination for sheriff.

As the primary approached, most attention focused on the Schmitt-McCarthy race. The Merrill attorney followed essentially the same strategy used by the Senator's opponents since he began his crusade, namely, to publicize his unethical conduct and refute his charges of communists-in-government while criticizing his methods. McCarthy's red hunt was a "gigantic hoax," Schmitt asserted; the Senator had done "absolutely nothing to chase Communists out of the government."

Schmitt began a traditional stump campaign of the state, delivering street corner speeches from a sound truck, but this was a failure. Crowds seemed resentful of him and, according to Schmitt, stared at him "like dumb animals." He needed public exposure. When he heard about the amazing success of the talkathon as a campaign device in Arkansas, he decided to base his entire effort on that format. The talkathon was a marathon radio talk in which the candidate answered questions from all comers. In some large cities, Schmitt remained on the air for as long as twenty-five continuous hours, answering questions about himself and McCarthy. With his physical stamina, calm manner, and keen knowledge of the issues, Schmitt seemed ideally suited for this technique. The publicity it received and the interest it aroused seemed to confirm its success.

The talkathon technique, however, was not nearly enough to give Schmitt the victory. Aside from *The Capital Times,* a few citizens' groups, and some segments of the state AF of L, his candidacy received little support. As a whole, organized labor ignored his campaign and urged its members to vote in the Democratic primary.

Senator McCarthy and his wife read the *Communist Daily Worker* of November 8, 1954, the day the Senate was to consider censure charges against him

Courtesy of the SHSW [WHi (X3) 23666]

R. Merrill Rhey, secretary of the Kenosha Trades and Labor Council, argued that Republicans should "put their own house in order."

While ignoring Schmitt's press releases, conservative newspapers were unsparing in their editorial criticism. They reminded their Republican readers of Schmitt's refusal to support Walter Kohler in 1950, after his defeat in the gubernatorial primary, and of his outspoken criticism of the Republican Voluntary Committee.

Nor could Schmitt's vigor and dedication compensate for his lack of finances, party endorsement, and statewide organization—assets which McCarthy possessed. Financial problems frustrated Schmitt. His plan to raise money from the "little people" through a "Dollars for Decency" campaign was a complete failure, and Fairchild's candidacy destroyed his hope of acquiring funds outside the state. Meyer Cohen, a lawyer and Democratic party leader from Green Bay, tried to collect money for Schmitt among contacts in New York and had expected to raise $50,000. About the time Cohen arrived in New York to close the deal, Fairchild entered the Democratic primary. Since most of Cohen's contacts were labor officials and Democrats, they immediately changed their minds and he returned to Wisconsin with only $5,000.

Despite many problems, cautious optimism pervaded the Schmitt camp on the eve of the primary. Some believed that McCarthy's fanatically vocal supporters might have created the impression that his backing among Republicans was greater than it was. Notwithstanding the urging of their leaders, Schmitt's partisans felt that many rank-and-file Democrats and working men would vote for Schmitt.

Anti-McCarthy forces were stunned, therefore, when McCarthy trounced Schmitt by a two-and-a-half to one margin (515,481 to 213,701), winning all but two of Wisconsin's seventy-one counties. Fairchild narrowly defeated Reuss in the Democratic race (97,321 to 94,379), but the two candidates received only 17 per cent of the total vote, compared to 30 per cent in the 1950 senatorial primary. McCarthy received 100,000 more votes than the combined total of all his opponents (five Republicans and two Democrats). He won the labor strongholds of Milwaukee, Kenosha, and Racine. The farm vote, the labor vote, the white collar vote, and some Democratic votes, observers believed, went to the incumbent. Now convinced of his vote-getting power, many of the Senator's critics sought explanations for the debacle in the strength of isolationism in the state, McCarthy's overwhelming Catholic support, his concentration on a single issue, his underdog image, and especially the effective issue of communists-in-government. "I think," a shaken Len Schmitt observed, "that Wisconsin people are voting against

Stalin." Whereas the Senator's opponents were depressed, McCarthy partisans were jubilant and the meaning of the victory was clear to them. As one post-election headline read: "Joe Landslide Shows Faith in War On Reds."

To nearly everyone, McCarthy appeared politically invincible. Actually, however, this was not the case, and anti-McCarthy prospects for the general election were not so gloomy as most observers believed. Democrats traditionally did poorly in the primary. This was particularly true in 1952 when the party would triple its primary vote in the general election while at the same time McCarthy's would increase only fractionally. In the primary, Democrats either abstained from voting, voted in the Democratic column, or voted for Schmitt. McCarthy did best in those counties with the least Democrats and did worst in traditional Democratic strongholds. But only a few Democratic strategists perceived this fact. Many party workers and supporters were demoralized by the primary tabulations, a situation which handicapped Democratic efforts during the general election campaign.

To critics of McCarthy the meaning of the 1952 primary election was clear: it was suicidal to fight the Senator on his communist issue. A minority of his opponents had held this position all along, but after the Schmitt debacle it became the dominant view. After the primary, Aldric Revell of *The Capital Times* again reminded anti-McCarthyites that "it does no good to quote reams of statistics attempting to prove that McCarthy failed to expose Communists in Washington. The people believe that he has."

. . . .

No longer should state Democrats "slug out the campaign on the issue of McCarthyism." Instead, while continuing to publicize his unethical conduct, they should concentrate more on his neglect of farmers, labor, and small businessmen and point out the economic progress of the past twenty years under national Democratic control.

With such slim prospects of defeating McCarthy, it was difficult to raise money for Thomas Fairchild's campaign. For the same reason, there was a noticeable tendency for liberal publications to pay less attention to defeating the Senator in order to concentrate on more promising contests.

. . . .

McCarthy's opponents sought to exploit the tension between McCarthy and Eisenhower, but without success. The Republican presidential nominee was caught in a dilemma. Apart from his personal distaste for the Senator, of which he left no doubt in private conversation, he had an almost obsessive hatred for McCarthy's "smearing" of the Truman and Roosevelt administrations. Eisenhower's blood boiled at the mention of McCarthy's assault on his friend George Marshall. On the other hand, Ike had to appease the rabid pro-McCarthy faction in his party in order to avoid full-scale party warfare on the very eve of the election.

At first Eisenhower attempted to avoid the problem by taking an ambiguous stand on the controversial Senator. At a news conference in Denver, Colorado, on August 22, 1952, he distinguished between a general, party-line endorsement for an entire Republican slate, and a specific declaration of personal support for a particular candidate. He would not support anything which smacked of "un-Americanism" such as "the unjust damaging of reputation." He could not give a "blanket endorsement" to anyone who held views of that kind. He promised, however, to "support" any candidate as a "member of the Republican organization." During his dramatic campaign trip to Wisconsin in early October, 1952, Eisenhower conceded to the wishes of Republican party leaders and refrained from criticizing McCarthy or praising General Marshall.

. . . .

If there was a single thread of strategy for the Fairchild campaign, it was to divert the preoccupation of various groups with McCarthy's communist hunt to issues which normally tied them to the Democratic party. In Milwaukee, for example, Democratic strategy sought to capture the Polish-Catholic-Labor vote which was attracted to McCarthy because of his affiliation with the Roman Catholic Church and his anticommunist campaign. Democrats placed advertisements in Polish newspapers, depicting Fairchild with popular Milwaukee Democratic Congressman Clement Zablocki and stressing the gains of labor under the Democratic party.

Fairchild seldom questioned the veracity of McCarthy's charges of communists-in-government. On one occasion he alleged that the Senator had not exposed any communists, that the only ones "who have been convicted have been rooted out by the FBI, the Justice Department and the courts of the United States." Usually, when he discussed the issue at all, he attacked McCarthy's methods which destroyed "the rights of free speech and free thought."

. . . .

Despite his vigorous efforts, Fairchild could not offset the major advantages enjoyed by McCarthy, namely, better financial backing, stronger party organization, and overwhelming newspaper support and publicity.

. . . .

These handicaps proved too much for Fairchild, as McCarthy swept to victory by a plurality of 870,444 to 731,402. The Senator's adversaries were proud of the "moral victory" they achieved in that McCarthy trailed the state ticket. Nevertheless, he won another six-year term in the Senate. His re-election was a "black day in the history of Wisconsin," *The Capital Times* noted sadly, a day in which the people "with full knowledge of the record—endorsed the cult of McCarthyism." The sentiments of his opponents, and an accurate prediction of the events of the next five years, were probably best expressed by James Doyle's statement following the election:

> To President Eisenhower: Our full and fervent support in the task of building the peace.
> To Gov. Stevenson: Our eternal admiration for the most gallant and eloquent campaign in American history.
> To Gov. Kohler: Our congratulations on your decisive victory.
> To Senator McCarthy: War unto the death.

And so it would be.

McCarthy Recall Fails

DAVID P. AND ESTHER S. THELEN

Oddly enough, the idea of recalling Senator McCarthy did not originate, as might have been expected, in a metropolitan setting; nor did it come from any of the highly articulate civic-minded or reform groups in which Wisconsin abounds. Instead it was conceived in a Wisconsin River village of less than 2,000 inhabitants, and by a man who was anything but a reformer. Leroy Gore, on the contrary, was a mild, fifty-year-old small-town newspaper editor, a Republican and a former supporter of Senator McCarthy. He had been born and raised in Iowa, had graduated from the University of Nebraska's school of journalism in 1928, and for the next twenty years had worked in an advertising agency and assisted the pub-

From David P. and Esther S. Thelen, "Joe Must Go: The Movement to Recall Senator Joseph R. McCarthy," *Wisconsin Magazine of History*, XLIX,3 (Spring 1966), 185–209. Footnotes in the original omitted. Reprinted by permission of the State Historical Society of Wisconsin.

lishers of three Midwestern weeklies. In 1947 he bought the *Sun* in Spring Valley, Wisconsin, and published it for five years; in 1952 he moved to Sauk City, about thirty miles from Madison, where he took over the *Sauk-Prairie Star*. His sense of humor showed in the paper's editorial masthead, which quoted H. L. Mencken: "Every little squirt thinks he's a fountain of wisdom."

In politics Leroy Gore mostly voted a straight Republican ticket. His Republicanism, however, was tinged with the progressivism of Robert M. La Follette and George Norris, whose ideas he did not always accept, but whose honesty and integrity he had admired since childhood. In the mid-1950's Gore espoused the moderate views of Dwight D. Eisenhower, but, as a party regular, he nevertheless supported Joseph McCarthy "with considerable vigor" in the senatorial campaign of 1952.

Gore had drawn statewide attention as editor of the *Star,* not in the realm of politics but as a spokesman for the dairy farmers whose herds grazed the rich pastures around Sauk City.

. . . .

Gore received service awards from the American Dairy Association of Wisconsin in 1953 and 1954, one of which resulted from his flamboyant project of advertising—and selling—a ton of green butter, in order to dramatize the fact that people preferred butter of any color to the low-priced spread.

It was from precisely the farmer's point of view that Gore first began to scrutinize the career of Wisconsin's junior Senator. In December of 1953 he editorialized: "When the dairy business was going great guns . . . Wisconsin could afford a vaudeville comedian at Washington to make faces at the Reds, but now that there's a quarter of a billion pounds of butter in storage voters are beginning to wonder why Joe, if he's the hot number he pretends to be, doesn't peddle that butter." Gore watched television and read the state's daily newspapers, and could scarcely help forming personal opinions about the Senator. Yet his disillusionment with McCarthy was gradual. At first he had simply labeled as "nonsense" McCarthy's well-publicized anti-Communist crusade, and, with a Midwesterner's inbred suspicion of all politicians, had dismissed him as just another example of the breed. He had met and talked with McCarthy, and knew him mainly as an extroverted man who worked hard at his job. But Gore upheld a strict code of personal morality, and this, in his eyes, McCarthy had repeatedly violated. The Senator's harassment of Annie Lee Moss, a State Department employee mistakenly identified as someone else, made Gore feel "sick." McCarthy's attacks on General George C. Marshall and on Wisconsin's

General Ralph Zwicker drove him to anger, and as a regular Republican he resented McCarthy's attempt to undermine the leadership of President Eisenhower. What apparently drove him at last to action was the innocent bafflement of a neighbor's twelve-year-old daughter over one of McCarthy's anti-Communist speeches. Leroy Gore would ride no farther with the Senator.

He began talking with his fellow Sauk Citians in drugstores, coffee shops, and barbers' chairs. Eventually someone mentioned the recall provision in the Wisconsin constitution, and Gore, with the same dramatic instinct that had conceived of a ton of green butter, began to see the great possibilities of a recall campaign. He sounded out a number of sympathetic people, including the editors of several weekly newspapers and Miles McMillin, a liberal writer for the Madison *Capital Times,* but many of them scoffed at the chances for success. After all, more than 1,656,000 Wisconsinites had voted in the gubernatorial election of 1952—a presidential year—and therefore some 404,000 notarized signatures would have to be obtained in order to recall Senator McCarthy. And all this within a period of sixty days. But Gore and his friends, none of whom dreamed that the requisite number of signatures might actually be secured, still believed that if no more than 100,000 voters signed a recall petition, at least the United States Senate, and the nation at large, would be convinced that McCarthy was opposed by a strong protest movement in his home state. At any rate, they concluded, it was worth a try.

Past midnight on March 15, 1954, Leroy Gore sat down to write the editorial which initiated the recall movement. In it he expressed his admiration for the Senator's intellectual vigor and courage, but he asserted that "The Senator Joseph McCarthy of March 1954 is NOT the man the people of Wisconsin elected to the United States Senate in November 1952." He went on to list the ways in which McCarthy had failed his party and the people of Wisconsin. First, he wrote, since 1952 McCarthy had used "his evil genius for blackmail" to subvert the leadership of President Eisenhower—an especially bitter pill for Republicans, since the Senator had ridden to victory on Eisenhower's coattails in 1952. Second, he had vilified the Army and slandered General Zwicker, "one of Wisconsin's most valorous soldiers." Finally, he had remained "silent as a rabbit with laryngitis" when the dairy crisis had struck Wisconsin. "The *Star,*" Gore wrote, "proposes a recall election in which the sole issue shall be the fitness of Joseph McCarthy to serve his nation, his party, and the sovereign state of Wisconsin." Opposite this editorial Gore printed a sample recall petition with space for two signatures and instructions for filling it out.

The editorial appeared in the *Sauk-Prairie Star* on March 18, and almost immediately Gore found himself in the national spotlight. Television and movie camera crews descended on Sauk City; Gore's telephone line was clogged with long-distance calls from newspapers and magazines throughout the country; his quiet office became a bedlam; sacks of mail arrived in avalanches. Within a few days of the publication of the editorial, he received 8,000 letters. And interestingly, those from out-of-state correspondents ran two to one in the Senator's favor; those written by Wisconsin residents ran seventy-five to one against McCarthy. The editorial had clearly struck a responsive chord within the borders of the state.

Most of the Wisconsin writers requested recall petitions, and since Gore had short-sightedly failed to arm himself with additional petitions, he had 4,000 of them cranked out on a small hand press when he discovered that commercial printers could not produce them fast enough. Taking a still-wet petition to the local drugstore, Gore himself obtained the first signatures from the morning coffee-break crowd assembled there, among them the novelist August Derleth. It was a beginning, obviously, but Gore realized from the magnitude of the initial response that it would take more than one small-town editor and a handful of friends to obtain even 100,000 signatures—much less 404,000 of them. Whether or not the campaign remained simply a protest or actually resulted in a recall election, it required the creation of a broadly based state-wide organization.

In forming such an organization, Gore and his companions feared above all else that the movement to recall Senator McCarthy would be branded with the "Communist sympathizer" label. From the outset, therefore, they sought the support and counsel of Republicans and businessmen in preference to McCarthy's traditional enemies, the Democrats and labor leaders. Early in the campaign they announced that the movement would accept no money or support from left-wing groups. But the critical problem was not so much the source of funds as it was to find capable conservative leaders. Providentially, Gore found the sort of man he wanted when a young Amery dry cleaner telephoned to volunteer his services. Few could challenge the orthodoxy of Harold L. Michael, a former Marine captain who had fought in World War II and Korea and who was currently chairman of the Polk County Republicans. It was Michael who suggested that a statewide recall organization could reach more citizens than a mail campaign directed from Sauk City.

. . . .

June fifth came and went, and so did the attempt to recall Senator Joseph R. McCarthy. Exactly how many signatures were obtained

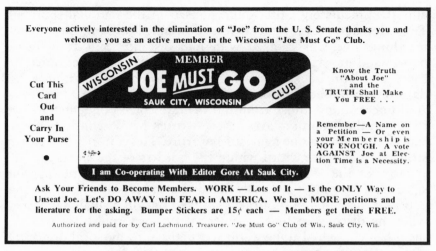

Everyone actively interested in the elimination of "Joe" from the U. S. Senate thanks you and welcomes you as an active member in the Wisconsin "Joe Must Go" Club.

Cut This
Card
Out
and
Carry In
Your Purse

●

WISCONSIN
MEMBER
JOE MUST GO
SAUK CITY, WISCONSIN
CLUB

I am Co-operating With Editor Gore At Sauk City.

Know the Truth
"About Joe"
and the
TRUTH Shall Make
You FREE . . .

●

Remember—A Name on
a Petition — Or even
your Membership is
NOT ENOUGH. A vote
AGAINST Joe at Elec-
tion Time is a Necessity.

Ask Your Friends to Become Members. WORK — Lots of It — Is the ONLY Way to Unseat Joe. Let's DO AWAY with FEAR in AMERICA. We have MORE petitions and literature for the asking. Bumper Stickers are 15¢ each — Members get theirs FREE.

Authorized and paid for by Carl Lachmund, Treasurer, "Joe Must Go" Club of Wis., Sauk City, Wis.

Courtesy of the SHSW [WHi (X3) 33855]

A "Joe Must Go" Club membership card

during the campaign remains a mystery. No exact count was ever made, mainly because the Sauk County district attorney subpoenaed the petitions as soon as the campaign ended, and to keep them out of his hands the recall leaders shipped them to Minneapolis and Chicago or buried them on farms near Sauk City. However, it is known that from March 18 to June 5 Gore and his compatriots collected about 400,000 signatures. When the petitions were later displayed at the Conrad Hilton hotel in Chicago, newspapermen counted 335,000 signatures; another 50,000 were reportedly in Minneapolis. Of these, many were invalid because they had come in too early or too late, or because they were not notarized. Probably the best estimate of the total is that a third of a million Wisconsin voters signed properly legal petitions in the sixty days ending on June 5, 1954.

Failure or no, the Joe Must Go movement had made its point. More people had signed this protest than had ever signed any notarized petition in the nation's history, and they had dealt a massive blow to the myth of McCarthy's invincibility. A Chicago newspaperman summed up the reaction of many Americans when he looked at the huge pile of petitions and exclaimed, "I'd sure hate to have that many people mad at me!"

The full significance of the recall movement was to become clearer in the months to follow. It had given McCarthy the scare of his political life, and for the many Wisconsinites who had signed petitions its most important result was that it forced the Senator to pay more attention to the problems facing his constituents. And coming as it did at the time of the Army-McCarthy hearings, it was one of the factors which produced a change in national sentiment toward Wisconsin's junior Senator, culminating in the United States Senate's vote of "condemnation" on December 2, 1954. McCarthy's colleagues in Washington recognized the significance of the vote of no-confidence from Wisconsin, and the success-in-failure of the recall movement undoubtedly stiffened many senatorial spines. As Harold Michael wired ex-Senator William Benton of Connecticut at the campaign's end: "Movement achieved tremendous success in proving McCarthy no longer represents Wisconsin electorate."

Democrats Return to Power

RICHARD C. HANEY

Wisconsin politics underwent a sweeping realignment in the years following World War II. Although Wisconsin's first territorial governor was a Democrat, and a majority of pre-statehood voters probably considered themselves the same, it was not until the period following World War II that the party achieved extensive political power throughout the state. And when it did, the liberal or moderately liberal organization which came into being in the 1950's bore little resemblance to its predecessor.

. . . .

Scores of the key leaders of the post-World War II Democratic party, who formerly had been Progressives, maintain that the Wisconsin Democratic party of the quarter-century following the war developed largely because of the disappearance of the Wisconsin Progressive party. Rent by dissension over foreign policy and the new priorities brought on by war, the party declined and died, thus

From Richard C. Haney, "The Rise of Wisconsin's New Democrats: A Political Realignment in the Mid-Twentieth Century," *Wisconsin Magazine of History*, LVIII,2 (Winter 1974–75), 91–106. Footnotes in the original omitted. Reprinted by permission of the State Historical Society of Wisconsin.

opening the way for a political realignment which at long last fit Wisconsin politics into the national pattern. Progressive (and some-times Republican) votes of the La Follette period bear a close rela-tionship to the Democratic votes of the late 1950's and 1960's.

. . . . : . . . .

The development began, really, with Daniel Hoan, the colorful and cantankerous former Socialist mayor of Milwaukee. Hoan de-cided to run for governor on the Democratic ticket in 1944 and 1946 and thus provided the impetus which enabled politically unaf-filiated liberals to begin to make a success of the Wisconsin Demo-cratic organization. Hoan became a Democrat for expedient, per-sonal political reasons. He turned to the party as the most promis-ing vehicle to advance his career, and in so doing contributed signif-icantly to its development, while failing to realize his personal aspi-rations.

. . . .

The next step in the rebirth of the Wisconsin Democracy hinged on the ultimately ill-fated decision of Senator Robert La Follette, Jr., to re-enter the Republican fold. La Follette revealed his intention at the final Progressive convention in 1946 at Portage, and brought with him, initially at least, a group of rising young politicians, mostly from outside Milwaukee. Subsequently, the state Republi-cans snubbed La Follette and endorsed State Chairman Thomas Coleman's choice for Senator—then little-known Marine Corps veteran Joseph R. McCarthy. While La Follette, a twenty-one-year veteran of the Senate, over-confidently remained in Washington attending to government business, McCarthy ran an active and victorious primary campaign with the slogan, "Congress Needs a Tail Gunner." The defeat of La Follette—and the consequent triumph of the Coleman-McCarthy-stalwart machine over the un-seated Senator for control of the state Republican organization—left young, former Progressives who had followed La Follette to the GOP with only one alternative: the Democratic party.

. . . .

Leaders of several liberal political groups, including Dan Hoan's Liberal League and the Dane County Democratic Club led by Carl Thompson, met in the Retlaw Hotel in Fond du Lac in May, 1948, to establish formally the Democratic Organizing Committee. Its two-fold purpose was to circumvent the statutory Democratic party organization controlled by Charles Greene, the conservative state chairman who had refused to step down despite a 17½-to-2½ vote by the national convention delegation requesting his resignation, and to create an extralegal body which could accept members and campaign contributions.

. . . .

The Wisconsin Democratic organization established itself during the 1950 campaign as an issues-oriented, Fair Deal party. The DOC campaigned feverishly in support of Truman's Fair Deal, including the Brannan Plan for agriculture, civil rights, extended social security coverage, and repeal of the Taft-Hartley Act; and it called for the defeat of Joseph McCarthy in 1952. Gubernatorial candidate Carl Thompson and U.S. Senate candidate Thomas Fairchild ran ahead of the rest of the ticket. The Wisconsin Democratic vote increased, while nationally the Republican party gained, indicating that the DOC organizational work had paid off. Wisconsin Democrats had come a long way from 1946 when a sign behind the speakers' table at the state convention misspelled the name of the President, "Harry S. Trumann." Yet state Democrats still lacked the organization and the candidates to compete on equal terms with the perennially dominant Republicans.

To its coalition of ex-Progressives and labor unions, the DOC in 1952 added voters who opposed the tactics and positions of Senator Joseph McCarthy.

. . . .

McCarthyism helped expand and unite the state's Democratic minority, but party wheelhorses realized after the 1952 election that further growth depended on more than just anti-McCarthyism. As for the Senator, said John Reynolds, "Frankly, he's not worth a resolution." While some Democrats participated in the 1954 bipartisan Joe-Must-Go Club, the feeling of most party professionals was that the effort was doomed to amateurish failure. The party supplanted the anti-McCarthy crusade with an eagerness to attract more votes, to develop winning candidates, and to deal principally with economic issues.

. . . .

The Democrats anticipated the 1956 election with optimism. They hoped that labor efforts in urban areas together with an increased portion of the farm vote would produce victory, and they concentrated on pocketbook issues. [William] Proxmire, a Harvard- and Yale-educated economist making his third try for the governorship, advocated a broader state income tax base as an alternative to instituting a sales tax, warned of growing unemployment in

urban areas, and met with farmers in their own town halls throughout Wisconsin. President Dwight Eisenhower and Senator Alexander
Wiley, however, led a statewide Republican landslide. Nevertheless
Democratic Congressmen Henry Reuss, Lester Johnson, and Clement Zablocki were re-elected, and there was no major shift of
power in the state legislature. Proxmire lost to Vernon Thomson in
a close race for governor, but in five years of continuous campaigning he had established himself as the Democrat most familiar to
Wisconsin voters.

The special election in 1957 to fill the U.S. Senate seat made
vacant by Joseph McCarthy's death presented Proxmire with a
fourth, and perhaps final, opportunity to win office. Following an
easy primary victory over Congressman Clement J. Zablocki of
Milwaukee, Proxmire faced his two-time conquerer, former Republican Governor Kohler. Kohler won a divisive seven-man GOP primary in which he carefully identified himself as a moderate
Eisenhower Republican and made no effort to disguise his distaste
for McCarthyism. Backed by many McCarthyites, conservative
former Congressman Glenn Davis ran a close second. No major
issue or controversy enlivened the Proxmire-Kohler contest, and
Proxmire capitalized on the division between GOP moderates and
the McCarthyites, many of whom refused to support Kohler's candidacy. Years later, Proxmire admonished: "Never forget the tendency of the Republicans in Wisconsin to save the Democrats."

. . . .

The rise of [Patrick] Lucey to the chairmanship, the Proxmire
breakthrough, and a national Democratic trend made 1958 a banner
year for Wisconsin Democrats. Senator Proxmire easily won re-
election over token Republican opposition. The party won a 55-to-
45 majority in the state Assembly and increased its state Senate
minority. Robert Kastenmeier of Watertown and Gerald Flynn of
Racine won congressional seats to give the Wisconsin delegation a
5-to-5 split. John Reynolds was elected attorney general; Philleo
Nash, lieutenant governor; and Eugene Lamb, state treasurer. Most
important for the Democrats, state Senator Gaylord Nelson upset
incumbent Republican Governor Vernon Thomson.

. . . .

Despite intraparty divisions, Democrats experienced continuing
success in the early 1960's. In 1960 itself, Governor Nelson and
Attorney General Reynolds were re-elected, four of the five incumbent Democratic Congressmen survived, and the party increased its
number of courthouse offices. Republicans, however, regained an
Assembly majority, captured three state constitutional offices, and

Courtesy of the SHSW [WHi (X3) 33860]

Gaylord Nelson campaigning for governor, 1958

carried the state for Richard Nixon over John Kennedy in the presidential race.

· ·

[In 1962] Nelson challenged incumbent Republican Senator Alexander Wiley, a twenty-four-year veteran of the Senate whose advancing age was an insurmountable handicap against a rival who campaigned on his achievements as governor. Reynolds, a staunch opponent of the sales tax, consciously turned his race for the governorship against Republican Philip Kuehn into a virtual sales tax referendum. Wisconsin's Democratic party met the challenge articulated in the *Times* and passed from adolescence to maturity with the election of John Reynolds as governor and Gaylord Nelson as Senator.

· ·

A two-party balance in modern Wisconsin began to evolve when a cadre of youthful ex-Progressives went into the "catacombs" throughout the state and steadily built a new Democratic party. They concentrated on establishing grass-roots support from the time they chose the Democratic party as their political vehicle in the middle 1940's until they created a professional, election-winning organization by the early 1960's. The decline of the Progressives and the subsequent defeat of Senator Robert La Follette, Jr., in 1946 had set the stage for the steady growth of the Democrats to achieve parity with the powerful state GOP. But a number of factors accounted for that achievement. Urban and labor votes, which had buttressed Democratic President Franklin D. Roosevelt and the Wisconsin Progressive party during the 1930's, became Democratic rather than Republican in state contests following the death of the Progressives. Democrats benefited from the political impact upon Wisconsin in the 1950's of McCarthyism, the cost-price squeeze on farmers, and the close alliance between the party and politically active labor union leaders. And they gradually nurtured candidates who could win elections. William Proxmire's breakthrough to a United States Senate seat in 1957 led the way, and was followed a year later by Gaylord Nelson's winning of the governorship. Although nationwide political trends and considerable help from the national Democratic party certainly contributed to the growth of the state's party, these were of secondary importance. The devoted efforts of Wisconsin political leaders acting upon political conditions unique to Wisconsin account for the rise of the state's mid-twentieth-century Democratic party. The result is modern Wisconsin's evenly balanced Republican-Democratic political structure.

The Struggle over Reapportionment

H. RUPERT THEOBALD

1960

Wisconsin's population, as shown by the 18th Census of Population, now numbered 3,952,765. The increase during the decade of

From H. Rupert Theobald, "Equal Representation: A Study of Legislative and Congressional Apportionment in Wisconsin," 1970 Wisconsin Blue Book (Madison, 1970), pp. 255–258. Reprinted by permission.

the 1950's—517,202—was the largest absolute increase ever experienced by the state (the relative increase was, however, only 15.1%). Of the state's total population, 63.8% were now classed as urban. As the first census of population relying entirely on computers for its computations, the 1960 Census had a particularly slow publication schedule. The first printed "preliminary report" for Wisconsin by minor civil divisions—Series PC (P1)/51—was received on September 26; the raw data for Milwaukee block statistics (not yet in printed form) were received by the City of Milwaukee Planning Commission on December 25 and had to be translated into the populations of existing wards before ward line revision could be started.

1961

Assemblyman Glen E. Pommerening (Rep., Wauwatosa) offered *1961 Assembly Bill 578* which retained Milwaukee County at 24 Assembly districts. The Assembly Committee on Rules, at the request of Assemblymen Allen J. Flannigan and Wilfred Schuele, introduced *1961 Assembly Bill 645* which was based on the work of the Legislative Council's Reapportionment Committee (though not approved by the council because the work was completed too late) which would have increased the Milwaukee County Assembly delegation to 26 members, and *1961 Assembly Bill 647*, relating to Congressional districts. On January 12, 1962, the Wisconsin Legislature recessed under *1961 Assembly Joint Resolution 147* until January 9, 1963 (one hour prior to the convening of the 1963 Legislature) without enacting any of these apportionment bills.

Chapter 679, Laws of 1961, reapportioned Menominee County so that all of the county would be in the same Assembly, Senate and Congressional district with neighboring Shawano County.

1962

Attorney General John W. Reynolds brought suit in the Wisconsin Supreme Court to prevent Secretary of State Robert C. Zimmerman from conducting the 1962 legislative elections under the existing apportionment. In March, the court dismissed the petition subject to the proviso that it could be renewed after June 1, 1963 (reported in 22 Wis. 2d 544, 549). On March 26, the United States Supreme Court decided the Tennessee Case of *Baker v. Carr* (369 U.S. 186; 82 S.Ct. 691), holding that legislative apportionment was a justiciable issue, that the citizen's right to equal representation was protected against "invidious discrimination" under the equal protection clause of the XIVth Amendment to the United States Constitution, and that legislative election districts had to be substantially equal in population subject to such minor deviations from

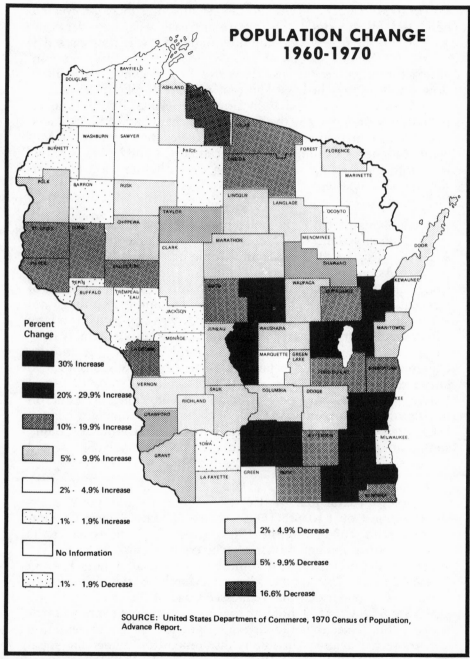

POPULATION CHANGE
1960-1970

Percent
Change

30% Increase

20% - 29.9% Increase

10% - 19.9% Increase

5% - 9.9% Increase

2% - 4.9% Increase

.1% - 1.9% Increase

No Information

.1% - 1.9% Decrease

2% - 4.9% Decrease

5% - 9.9% Decrease

16.6% Decrease

SOURCE: United States Department of Commerce, 1970 Census of Population,
Advance Report.

From Collins, An Atlas of Wisconsin. *Courtesy of American Printing and Publishing Company (Madison)*

Map showing population change in Wisconsin, 1960–1970

the average as flowed from a rational design. The Attorney General renewed his suit in the U. S. District Court for the Western District of Wisconsin, but received a preliminary setback when he was told by the court, on May 26, that the State of Wisconsin was not a "person" whose rights are protected by the XIVth Amendment (205 F.Supp. 673). The court suggested that the Attorney General could amend his complaint to include 5 citizens as parties plaintiff, and suggested that the Legislature should reconvene meanwhile to perform its constitutional reapportionment duty.

Governor Gaylord Nelson called a special reapportionment session to begin on June 18. When the legislators assembled in the Capitol on that date, a majority of the members of each house signed a petition to reconvene the 1961 Session under the terms of the adjournment resolution, *1961 Assembly Joint Resolution 147.* For the first time, the Wisconsin Legislature was simultaneously in regular and special session.

At the session, the Legislature considered 4 bills for Congressional redistricting, 5 bills for legislative reapportionment, and 8 joint resolutions proposing amendments to the Wisconsin Constitution relating to reapportionment. Two bills for Congressional redistricting, and one bill for legislative reapportionment, were passed and vetoed: Congressional—*1961 Senate Bills 814 and 817:* legislative—*1961 Senate Bill 815.* The Legislature tried to repass the legislative apportionment in the form of *1961 Senate Joint Resolution 125,* but the attempt failed in the Assembly. Once more, the Legislature adjourned until January 1963.

Attorney General Reynolds renewed his suit in federal district court. The court appointed Emmert L. Wingert, a former justice of the Wisconsin Supreme Court, as a special master to hold hearings on the issue. On August 14, and based on the master's findings, the court held that the disparities in Wisconsin legislative districts did not amount to invidious discrimination and that, because of the impending 1962 elections, it was impractical to grant any relief at that time. It invited renewal of the suit "after August 1, 1963 if, by that time, the State of Wisconsin has not been redistricted"; *Reynolds v. Zimmerman,* 209 F.Supp. 183.

1963

State Treasurer Dena A. Smith refused to countersign the Attorney General's vouchers for payment of the expenses in the federal court suit. In *State ex rel. Reynolds v. Smith,* decided on April 2, 1963 (19 Wis. 2d 577), the Wisconsin Supreme Court reaffirmed that as a matter of Wisconsin law the state was a proper party plaintiff in an apportionment suit, and ordered release of the voucher.

Chapter 63, Laws of 1963, approved May 20, revised Wisconsin's Congressional districts and reduced the population deviation among the state's 10 districts to the then unheard-of-close range from minus 3.2% to plus 3.4% of the average district population (395,276). The Milwaukee-Waukesha area was given 3 whole Congressional districts, with the 4th and 5th situated entirely in Milwaukee County, and the 9th consisting of Waukesha County and the northern and northwestern suburban areas of Milwaukee County.

1963 Senate Bill 575, which again provided for only 24 Assembly districts in Milwaukee County, was vetoed by Governor Reynolds; passed by the Senate notwithstanding the Governor's objections, but failed in the Assembly.

1963 Senate Bill 627, offered by Senator Jerris Leonard (Rep. Bayside) on the day after the veto, failed in the house of origin. Both houses then proceeded to repass the vetoed legislative apportionment in the form of *1963 Senate Joint Resolution 74*.

1963 Senate Bill 677, designed only to shift the dividing line between the Assembly districts in La Crosse County (it was, therefore, an amendment to the 1951 Rosenberry apportionment), was also vetoed.

Governor Reynolds renewed the apportionment litigation before the Supreme Court of Wisconsin (alleging that the new Attorney General, George Thompson, was not prepared to commence the suit.) He sought to enjoin Secretary of State Robert Zimmerman from conducting the 1964 legislative elections on the basis of the Rosenberry apportionment of 1951, to be held instead under an apportionment plan to be promulgated by the Wisconsin Supreme Court or, on the alternative, at large. The Secretary of State replied that he intended to conduct the elections based on the provisions of *1963 Senate Joint Resolution 74* or (if that be invalid) from the existing districts unless otherwise directed by the court.

1964

In *State ex rel. Reynolds v. Zimmerman* (22 Wis. 2d 544), decided on February 28, the Wisconsin Supreme Court held that Wisconsin Legislative apportionment requires participation by the Governor and, hence, that *1963 Senate Joint Resolution 74* was not a valid apportionment. The court reviewed Wisconsin apportionment law and pointed out that the "county . . . town or ward lines" limitation on Assembly district boundaries made perfect population equality impossible. Nevertheless, the court admonished the Legislature to reapportion the legislative districts to achieve as close an approximation to exact population equality as possible. The court set a May 1 deadline for legislative reapportionment and promised that, if the deadline was not met, it would itself by May 15 devise an apportionment plan for the conduct of the 1964 legislative elections.

Governor Reynolds pledged publicly to veto any legislative apportionment bill which did not give Milwaukee County 26 Assembly districts. When the Legislature returned on April 13 for its regularly scheduled continuation of the 1963 Session, it again gave the apportionment issue full debate. *1963 Senate Bill 679* was passed, increasing the number of Assembly districts in Milwaukee County from 24 to 25, and reducing the population differences among Assembly districts in several other multi-Assembly district counties. Governor Reynolds, true to his pledge, vetoed the bill 4 days later, and the attempt to override the veto failed in the Senate 20 to 11 (short of the required ⅔ majority). As a parting gesture, the Legislature passed *1963 Senate Joint Resolution 109,* instructing the Chief of the Legislative Reference Bureau "to provide such technical assistance as is required by the Wisconsin Supreme Court for legislative apportionment" and to "give precedence to this task over all other tasks" until May 15.

Assisted by the Reference Bureau's maps, statistics and analysis of all legislative apportionment proposals considered by the Legislature since 1960, the Wisconsin Supreme Court on May 14, 1964, promulgated its own "temporary" legislative apportionment plan, to be used for the 1964 legislative elections and thereafter until the enactment of a valid apportionment by the Legislature (none was enacted during the decade of the 1960's).

. . . .

Unfortunately, by 1964 nearly every state in the Nation was engaged in apportionment litigation, and on June 15, 1964, the United States Supreme Court issued a series of *Reapportionment Decisions* which required strict adherence to population equality among districts for each house of a 2-house legislature.

The *Reapportionment Decisions,* led by the Alabama case of *Reynolds v. Sims* (377 U.S. 533; 84 S.Ct. 1362), included 2 other cases from Alabama and one case each from Colorado, Delaware, Maryland, New York and Virginia. Based on these cases, the only constitutionally valid approach to legislative apportionment would be an "honest and good faith effort" to reduce to a minimum the population differences among districts by constructing such districts along town, ward (city or village) or even precinct lines if necessary.

3 : Minority Concerns in the Postwar Era

By the end of World War II most of Wisconsin's European ethnic groups had been assimilated into the social fabric of the state to a reasonable degree. Problems that arose in this period mostly concerned native Americans and migrant farm workers. A Human Rights Commission was established by the governor in 1945 and was given full legislative endorsement four years later.

The problems for native Americans were most pronounced. With the emphasis on self-help during the conservative Eisenhower Administrations, several tribes, including the state's Menominees, were slated for termination of their reservation status. The first two selections deal with this and related problems faced by the state's Indian population.

Mexican-American migrant workers faced harsh living and working conditions and often also the hostility of the local community. The third and fourth selections are from the 1962 and 1965 reports of the Governor's Commission on Human Rights. The fifth selection describes the reaction of a small town to the influx of migrant workers. And the final selection suggests the state's leadership role in the struggle for equal rights for women.

The Native American in the Postwar Period

NANCY OESTREICH LURIE

From treaty to termination the boundaries of the state of Wisconsin encompass an astonishingly representative illustration of the

From Nancy Oestreich Lurie, "Wisconsin: A Natural Laboratory for North American Indian Studies," *Wisconsin Magazine of History*, LIII,1 (Autumn 1969), 3–20. Footnotes in the original omitted. Reprinted by permission of the State Historical Society of Wisconsin.

total development of federal Indian policy and Indian adaptation and resistance to it. The Wisconsin Indian population today—at least 15,000 people—is the third largest east of the Mississippi River. North Carolina and New York have more Indians, but Wisconsin includes a greater variety of tribal and linguistic proveniences and administrative complications. Many western states, of course, have much larger Indian populations than Wisconsin but only a few—notably Oklahoma, Arizona, New Mexico, and California—offer more diversity than Wisconsin's three major linguistic stocks, six broad tribal affiliations, and twelve separately identifiable Indian societies covering the range of experiments in Indian policy from the founding of the republic to the present day.

In Wisconsin, as elsewhere, a quarter to a half or more of the Indian population resides in cities. The intertribal population of Milwaukee alone is in the neighborhood of 4,000 people.

. . . .

Two striking facts emerge from the contemporary Wisconsin Indian scene. First, it appears that no matter what the government tried and no matter which tribe was involved, the result is dismal uniformity and shockingly prevalent low standards of living. Second, although the various kinds of Indian settlements look very much alike to the outsider, the perceptive observer notes that there is something definably and distinctively Indian about these generally poor communities and that each community has its own local distinctiveness.

In terms of general conditions, most Wisconsin Indian children now attend public schools in or near Indian communities.

. . . .

A recent spate of housing projects brightens up the Indian settlements a bit at present, but like many such low-cost units built at earlier dates they are arranged and constructed with little consultation with the people who will live in them. They will soon deteriorate.

. . . .

For all the local Indian groups various forms of public relief are necessary to maintain life. A few tribes have timber resources, but because of the broken nature of their land holdings these cannot be effectively utilized. Some tribes derive income for local welfare from leasing land to whites, but the amount of money is not great.

Guiding, performing Indian dances at tourist centers, and selling handcraft as well as various kinds of wage work contribute in varying proportions to Indian family incomes from time to time and place to place. Wage work is usually crop harvesting, timbering, and road maintenance. Sporadic or regular urban employment is increasingly important. A few people in all the Indian groups still do a little trapping, and many families depend on the deer season to supply the larder with substantial quantities of meat. City relatives are very likely to get home for deer season. A constant controversy goes on with the fish and game authorities, who feel Indians should abide by state game seasons and limits, and the Indians who believe their treaties entitle them to hunt, trap, and fish on their own land.

. . . .

Tribal enterprises which Indian people would really like to develop to create more employment close to home are tried here and there, but the results are disappointing even if the efforts do not fail completely.

. . . .

In regard to religion, Wisconsin Indians have been converted to Roman Catholicism and various protestant denominations, usually managing to make their local churches distinctively Indian, community institutions. However, with the exception of the Oneida and Stockbridge who were long Christianized in the East, all the other major tribal groups in Wisconsin have active factions of traditionalists who hold their ancient rites in quiet but deep defiance of the white man's religions. Furthermore, there are congregations of both the Drum or Dream Dance religion found among the Potawatomi, Chippewa, and Menomini, and the peyote religion, chartered as the Native American Church, which is strongest among the Winnebago but has diffused to the Algonkian-speaking tribes, with the exception of the Stockbridge. These major pan-Indian revitalization or nativistic movements originated farther west during the nineteenth century as self-help efforts to unite and uplift Indians spiritually and morally in a time of crisis and despair. They are still gaining converts.

. . . .

When the United States entered the Second World War in 1941 the Bureau of Indian Affairs, like other offices, had to cut back while a large proportion of the federal budget went into the war effort. But more was involved as Congress turned a deaf ear to Collier's pleas to keep alive programs and prepare for the problems of Indians in peacetime. However, with so many Indians in the armed services or in the cities working in defense industries and sending money home, problems of Indian poverty were temporarily alleviated. Congress considered the Indians' problems permanently solved. But, as Collier knew would be the case, when the war was over the Indians came back home. There had also been an Indian baby boom. Already limited and undeveloped reservation resources were now totally inadequate. But the war had been a mass educational experience and Indians returned with widespread understanding of what could be done on the reservations and how to do it through the mechanism of IRA. All that was needed was adequate funding to get started.

It gave Congress pause that Indians were obviously worse off than ever and that vast amounts of money would be needed to get communities on their feet and regain ground lost during the war when nascent programs were allowed to atrophy without funds. Congress conveniently blamed John Collier for the crisis in Indian affairs because he had turned aside from the time-honored principle of assimilating the Indians. The cry was on to "desegregate" and even "free" the Indians and "get the government out of the Indian business." Ironically, as the Black Movement for civil rights gained momentum, the words of new hope for black people were a chilling threat to Indians. The reservations were not segregated ghettos— allowed to deteriorate by indifferent landlords—but Indian property they had struggled to protect from illegal appropriation by whites and which they wanted to develop as a basis of healthy community life. No one denied the Indians the vote. Quite the contrary! Indians experienced little racial prejudice. They had always been free as individuals to be dropped from the tribal rolls by their own choice.

Collier was finally forced to resign in 1946 and by 1950 a total change had occurred in Indian policy, based on the pre-Collier philosophy. Two major endeavors were mounted as the final solution (again!) to the Indian problem: termination of the reservations and relocation of Indians in cities. Wisconsin, as usual, was a primary laboratory to tinker around in.

Noting that Indians went to the cities and adapted well to industrial work although they kept returning home and maintaining tribal ties, the Voluntary Relocation Program (dubbed "Operation Relocation" by the Indians) provided fare to cities, preferably as far from the Indian's home community as possible, as well as a first job and housing. Little screening was done and with the slight recession of the mid-1950's many Indians were left in destitute condition, unable to get local public relief because of residence requirements, no longer a responsibility of the relocation offices, and unable to get back home. Old intertribal organizations in cities were swamped with hardship cases and many new Indian centers were established with church and other private funding, and in some cases with help from local universities. Gradually, many people drifted back home. Fortunately, Indian resistance to the termination program meant that for most tribes there still was a home community where they could get help. However, the government was determined to push termination wherever possible, and it happened that in 1928 the Menomini in Wisconsin, as well as the Klamath in Oregon, were singled out as soon ready to manage their own affairs without federal supervision. Developed lumbering enterprises had forestalled allotment as inappropriate to these reservations. In 1951 the Menomini had won a judgment of $8,500,000 on proof of mismanagement of their forests by the government. They voted to invest a good part in community development and reserved part to divide into per capita payments, about $1,500 per person. Organized under the Indian Reorganization Act, the Menomini were just beginning to grasp the principles and potentialities of real self-government, but despite the Brookings Report recommendation, the Bureau had made no effort to train Menomini in business management or gradually turn tribal affairs fully over to the Menomini people. The Brookings Report had envisioned a self-sustaining tribal community free of federal interference, but the objective of termination proceedings in the 1950's was to destroy tribal entities. Although they had misgivings, the Menomini actually voted for termination, understanding that it would be along lines intended in the Brookings Report and also because they were deceived into believing that payment of their per capitas depended on termination.

When the true nature of the situation became apparent, they played for time, getting the date for termination moved from 1958 to 1961. Co-operation by the state in designating the reservation a new county also helped to maintain community identity. But the state was less experienced than even the Bureau in dealing with Indian communities and brought in private industry, even less informed about Indians, to help the Menomini make the transition to terminated status. It is not possible to cite here all the legal and social complications, and it must also be said that at least some of the misguided efforts by outsiders, ostensibly in behalf of the Menomini, were not done viciously. But the worst abuses arising out of the Allotment Act and resulting in land loss, Indian impoverishment, and personal and social despair and demoralization pale in comparison to what is happening to the Menomini—the oldest continuously resident tribe in the state.

By the time of the presidential campaign of 1960, both major parties recognized that Indian affairs were in a terrible mess and required study and new direction. When John Kennedy was elected, he appointed a task force to meet and talk with Indians as a basis for future policy. Philleo Nash, who headed the task force, was subsequently appointed Commissioner of Indian Affairs. Nash, an anthropologist, inspired real hope as a new Collier. Moving cautiously at first in the face of continuing assimilationist sentiment in Congress, Nash nevertheless operated on the principle that Indians were here to stay. He stressed community development and humanized the relocation program for Indians who desired to avail themselves of it. Nash understood that Indians were interested in raising the general community level and needed to explore opportunities to reach consensus on plans. But he was deemed too slow by his superiors, who saw Indian community development in terms of cheap labor pools for white capital. Nash's tenure lasted just half as long as Collier's. His successor, Robert L. Bennett, a mixed-blood Oneida, was committed to the Indian interest in his public statements but could do little to forward it, given the powerful forces which had succeeded in ousting Nash. With the change in party administration, Bennett, too, was obliged to resign, leaving the situation very unstructured. There was a long delay in choosing a new Commissioner of Indian Affairs, and during a six-month period half a dozen candidates promoted by such organizations as the National Congress of American Indians were rejected. On August 8, 1969, it was announced that Louis R. Bruce, a New York Mohawk, had been appointed. Mr. Bruce, a Republican, has lived and worked in Manhattan as an advertising executive with little active involvement in national Indian affairs.

Nash's brief tenure had a profound effect for at least one Wisconsin tribe. In 1961 the Winnebago developed an acting business committee out of a claims committee which had been established by election at the time the tribal claim was filed in 1949. Seeing the advantages of formal organization, they became the first tribe in the entire country since the early 1940's to apply for and be granted the right to organize under the Indian Reorganization Act. Permission to organize was delayed because they were not a reservation tribe, but the discovery that an individual homestead had reverted to tribal trust land status because the owner died without heirs qualified them with a forty-acre "reservation."

This curious technicality inspired the new Wisconsin Winnebago Business Committee to acquire land in order to avail themselves of housing programs undertaken on the reservations in co-operation between the BIA and PHA during the 1960's. Their efforts included petitioning for a change of title of federal land which the Winnebago had been given the use of for a WPA housing project during

Collier's administration, soliciting donations of land, and raising money to buy land. The Nash administration was agreeable to having the acreage declared tribal trust land. Thus, a year after termination had become a fact for the Menomini, the Winnebago were in a process of extending federal responsibility over new Indian land. The attitude of the Nash administration also benefited the Oneida, who in the mid-1960's began procedures whereby a share of an old allotment, just under thirty acres, was transferred from individual Indian land to tribal trust status. Located in the Green Bay area, it is valuable property and the tribe is drawing up plans for an industrial enterprise.

The 1960's saw another important development in Wisconsin, typical of what is happening across the country where there are concentrations of different tribal groups. In 1961, the Great Lakes Inter-Tribal Council was formed by the governing bodies of the various tribes in the state. Fearful of the Menomini experience they desired to retain their federal ties, but hoped that through intertribal unity they could develop their own community programs, seek outside funds, and gain some real leverage in dealing with the Indian Bureau. While still in its formative stage and handicapped by the fact that its component governing bodies did not always command the confidence of their local constituents to carry out promises of community development, GLIT responded to the request of OEO to act as the central agency for work among Wisconsin Indians.

The Menominees and Termination

STEPHEN J. HERZBERG

The passage by Congress of the Menominee Restoration Act of 1973 constitutes a significant and in some respects a dramatic reversal of American Indian policy. By thus repealing the Menominee Restoration Act of 1954, the federal government rejected its avowed policy of the 1950's—forced assimilation through termina-

From Stephen J. Herzberg, "The Menominee Indians: From Treaty to Termination," *Wisconsin Magazine of History*, LX,4 (Summer 1977), 267–329. Footnotes in the original omitted. Reprinted by permission of the State Historical Society of Wisconsin.

tion of tribal status—and reconferred upon one of Wisconsin's historic Indian tribes the perquisites of recognition as a tribe. Expressly and symbolically, the Restoration Act reaffirmed the principles of Indian self-determination and self-government, and, to a degree, redressed two decades of economic and social distress suffered by a Native American people whose wants, needs, and aspirations had largely been ignored or misrepresented by the United States government.

. . . .

By 1951, the 2,957 Menominee of Wisconsin had reached a level of economic development and stability which, although it did not put them on a par with non-Indian Americans, made them appear to be relatively prosperous when compared to the members of other tribes. Although the reservation economy was somewhat artificial—it was run for full employment rather than for profit, and was subsidized by exemptions from both federal and state taxation—the good chance of long-term capital investment made possible by the $8.5 million judgment gave reason for tribal optimism. In addition to providing an extensive array of services, the tribe had developed an acclaimed law-and-order system. In fact, at this time the tribe's only major weakness was its general inability to govern itself. In 1951 the lack of self-government did not appear to be a major problem; the tribal government was rarely called upon to make a quick, difficult decision. Unfortunately, in the years to come this pattern was to be reversed; and the Menominee were to pay dearly for their inability to self-govern.

. . . .

In the early 1950's the Menominee were a highly literate people; only fifty adults were unable to read and write, and only twenty were unable to speak English. They had attained a level of education equal to the average of eight years' schooling among their non-Indian neighbors. However, they lacked training in the specialized skills and professions necessary to make theirs a self-sustaining community. There were three grade schools on the reservation, but no high school. The tribe owned all three, two of which were run by the Catholic church, the other by the state. After completing the eighth grade, Menominee children could go on to high school in Shawano County. In 1954, 80 per cent did so, and 75 per cent of these ultimately were graduated. But in 1950 only five Menominee were found to have been graduated from college, and in 1955 only three were attending college.

Supported by the mill, which was run so as to maximize employ-

Courtesy of the SHSW [WHi (X3) 9633]

The Neopit sawmill on the Menominee reservation, ca. 1950

ment rather than profits, the vast majority of working Menominee families were able to find jobs on the reservation. In the late 1950's there were 410 working families; 60 per cent were employed by the mill; they shared, through their wages, more than $1,200,000 of the $1,600,000 annual mill budget. Only 10 per cent of the mill employees were not Indians; most of them were hired because they had special skills. Thirty Menominee families supported themselves through commercial agriculture. Non-mill and non-agricultural reservation employment was limited to work at a small garment factory and to jobs with the Indian Bureau. About 100 families were employed off the reservation. The non-agricultural family median income was $2,225, compared to a $2,800 median income for the non-Indian families in the surrounding area. The median for agricultural families was $649.

. . . .

At the end of World War II a new generation of conservatives "was quick to attribute the ills of the Indian communities to the peculiar policies of the New Deal. . . . Isolation from national, social and economic life was seen as the fundamental obstacle to Indian progress. The nostrums proposed were private ownership and rapid integration." Congress also wanted to rid the government of the "burden" of administering the Indian programs. These concerns set the stage for a new Indian policy: termination.

Beginning with the congressional session in 1947, and for a period of six years thereafter, a continuous stream of legislation was introduced to repeal the Indian Reorganization Act, terminate either individual or all tribes, and eliminate the Indian Bureau.

. . . .

The dominant legislative objective—that Congress should rid the federal government of the costs, burdens, and risks of trustee management—was carefully understated. The subcommittees did not jeopardize the legislative package by disclosing that along with the "rights" they would be getting, the tribes would have to give up the benefits of essential programs and the exercise of tribal rights, many of which were guaranteed by treaty.

. . . .

Senator Watkins attended the Menominee General Council meeting of June 20, 1953. He dropped the liberal rhetoric, calling for "Indian freedom," that he was using successfully in Congress and presented a new hard line:

> He told the tribal members that they were going to be terminated whether they liked it or not, that they would be allowed no more than three years to prepare a plan "for termination, and that unless they agreed to termination their own tribal funds would not be released for the requested, and much needed, $1,500 per capita payment. He further stated that the United States was unwilling to continue paying interest on the Menominee funds held in trust in the Treasury.

. . . .

One hour after Watkins' departure, the General Council reconvened. Fortuitously, the Menominee had previously drafted a termination resolution. While in Washington lobbying for the per capita payment legislation, the tribal delegation was repeatedly asked to draft a resolution showing that the Menominee were considering self-management. The following resolution, drafted in response to those demands, was placed before the tribe:

RESOLVED, that the Menominee General Council instruct the tribal attorneys and a tribal planning officer (to be appointed by the Advisory Council or the General Council on such terms and for such period as decided by the Advisory Council or the General Council) *to present to Senator Watkins for introduction in Congress as an amendment to the per capita Bill a draft containing the following:*

1. A three year period during which the tribe may arrange for such planning as it deems desirable;
2. Authorize the Secretary of the Interior, at the end of such three year period, to transfer so-called agency functions to the Tribe in accordance with a plan to be submitted by the Tribe and as amended by the Secretary;
3. Authorize the Secretary to transfer to the Tribe, or an organization designated by the Tribe, responsibility for operation of the Menominee forests and mills in accordance with a plan submitted by the Tribe as amended by the Secretary, after five years following the enactment of the bill;
4. Authorize the disbursement of such tribal funds as may be requested by the Tribe for the planning necessary to carry out the intention of the legislation;
5. Provide for the closing of the Menominee rolls as of a date to be designated by the Menominee General Council;
6. Provide that individual interests in the tribal assets shall pass by inheritance under the laws of Wisconsin;
7. Provide that the Tribe may, within the five year term provided, indicate its desire that the Reservation be sold in one or several units, and that such requests shall be carried into effect by the Secretary.

After a short discussion, the resolution was adopted by a vote of 169 to 5.

For several reasons the passage of this resolution cannot be viewed as an act of tribal consent to termination. The vote was not the product of reason and careful consideration, but rather of misunderstanding, coercion, and the Indians' need for the $1,500 per capita payments. It was not accepted by a majority of the tribe, but rather was passed by a small group that represented neither a cultural cross-section nor the desires of the Menominee as a whole. The vote was not the result of the traditional tribal consensus—the format usually used to reach important tribal decisions—but rather of a short, hurried meeting whose procedures reflected the white man's method of governing more than the Indians'.

. . . .

The chairmen of both subcommittees, Senator Watkins and Congressman E. Y Berry, decided that 1954 was to be the year in which termination legislation would pass. Both were in a hurry for fear that the Republican party might, in the forthcoming elections, lose its slim majorities in and subsequent control over the congressional committees. To expedite the matter, they employed a rare congressional procedure: the joint hearing.

. . . .

Three days of hearings were held on the Menominee Indians of Wisconsin. The most salient feature was the total lack of opposition to termination of tribal status. Both the tribe (which believed termination inevitable) and the State of Wisconsin instead sought modification of the bills to give both more time to prepare for withdrawal. In fact, there was so little controversy or excitement during the hearings that on the third day only one of the nineteen joint committee members—Senator Watkins—attended.

. . . .

Although it is now clear that some Congressmen would have voted against the Menominee termination bill had they known of the tribe's opposition to withdrawal and the true reason for its "consent," this information was not brought forth during the hearings. Instead, it appeared that both the Menominee and the state favored termination, and that their only disagreement with the proposed legislation was with the termination date set by the Watkins bill.

After the hearings, each subcommittee drafted its own Menominee termination bill. The Senate chose the Watkins bill; the House adopted the Laird bill. Both were sent to a conference committee which reported a bill containing the major provisions of the Watkins draft. Watkins, who wanted the legislation to be passed on the consent calendars, knew that Laird's negative vote could defeat the legislation in the House. He called for a second conference committee meeting. This committee reported a bill that contained the major provisions of the Watkins bill but included the more generous time period allotted by Laird's proposal. The Menominee were to be given four and a half years until their termination, which was to take effect on December 31, 1958. This bill was passed, without dissent, by both houses, and was signed into law by President Eisenhower on June 17, 1954.

The mechanics of termination were not complex. On the termination date, the Secretary of the Interior was to publish a termination proclamation in the *Federal Register*, in which he was to announce that the individual Menominee were no longer entitled to "any of the services performed by the United States for Indians because of their status as Indians," that "all statutes of the United States which affect Indians because of their status as Indians shall no longer be applicable to the members of the tribe," and that "the laws of the several states shall apply to the tribe and its members in the same manner as they apply to other citizens or persons within their jurisdiction." On that same date the Secretary was to transfer to a tribal corporation or trustee the title to all property held in trust by the United States.

Two steps were to be taken upon the enactment of the legislation. First, the tribal rolls were to be closed. Menominee children born after June 17, 1954 (four years before termination), were not to be enrolled as members of the tribe. These, the first victims of the forced assimilation, were to lose their paper status as Indians. Second, on that same date, the Secretary of the Interior was authorized to distribute the $1,500 per capita payment to each enrolled Menominee.

During the four-and-a-half-year interim period, the Menominee were to prepare for withdrawal. The most difficult task they faced was the formulation, for presentation to the Secretary, of a "termination plan"; this plan was to be filed by December 31, 1957. The entire burden of co-ordinating the studies and planning for termination was placed upon the tribe.

. . . .

Within a short time it was obvious that the Menominee had neither the resources nor the time to meet the planning and termination deadlines. The tribal treasury account had been depleted by two sets of per capita payments; the tribe had but 20 per cent of the funds that had been available to it when the termination bill was passed. In an effort to help, in 1955 the State of Wisconsin created the Menominee Indian Study Committee which was to study withdrawal and formulate specific proposals.

In the years that followed, the Menominee repeatedly called upon Congress for amendments to the termination act which would allow them more planning time, and for legislation to reimburse the tribal treasury for planning expenditures. These efforts were only partially successful.

. . . .

On January 17, 1959, the General Council approved a proposed termination plan. In it, the tribe called for the creation of a business corporation to hold title to, and manage, the tribe's property. In accord with the mandate of a previous tribal referendum, the plan called for the creation of a separate county to govern the area that would no longer be the Menominee reservation.

Courtesy of the SHSW [WHi (X3) 14973]

Governor Nelson signs the bill for Menominee County, upon termination of the Menominee reservation, July 31, 1959

However, the Menominee still did not feel prepared for termination. At the June 25, 1959, General Council meeting, 105 voters unanimously passed the following resolution:

> ... that it is the sentiment, expression and will of the tribesmen present at this General Council, the situation being as it is, and the tribe helpless under P.L. 399, as amended, to do anything about it, that the Congress of the United States be importuned and begged (if you please) to take all steps necessary in the field of required legislation to extend the termination requirements and dates, and all interim deadline dates presently contained in P.L. 399 for a period of ten years; and in particular extend any present deadline dates under said law necessary to the welfare, and well-being of the Menominee Tribe of Indians, to the end that the economy and welfare, and destiny of the tribe be preserved, this Tribe being bitterly opposed to any transfer of tribal property, and the administration thereof, to a Trustee of the Secretary of Interior's choice.

No action was taken to implement this resolution.

On July 31, 1959, the Assistant Secretary of the Interior approved the termination plan in principle. The tribe and the Department agreed upon a final plan on October 31, 1959.

. . . .

At midnight on April 30, 1961, the Menominee Reservation—all that had remained of the extensive tribal lands—ceased to be. At that same hour, the Menominee people, whose ancestors were among the original inhabitants of the Wisconsin region, were stripped of their official recognition as an Indian people. Termination was a reality.

It is not hard to understand why the tribe co-operated with the forces of termination, but it is difficult to understand why the State of Wisconsin, if it truly opposed the policy, followed the same strategic approach. There are other possible explanations for the state's actions. First, it may have believed in the so-called "public position" taken by the Menominee in support of termination; if so, the state evinced a lack of sensitivity to, and knowledge of, its Indian citizens. Second, the state may not have testified against the legislation because it actually supported the termination-assimilation policy. Or, third, the state may have underestimated its ability to defeat the termination bills; but it is hard to believe that Wisconsin failed to learn from the other successful opponents of termination. In any event, whether by conscious design or strategic mistake, the position taken by the State of Wisconsin subjected the Menominee to great hardship and suffering.

Migrant Labor in Wisconsin

ELIZABETH B. RAUSHENBUSH

Then came the acute farm labor shortage of World War II. A nationwide farm labor program operated under Agricultural Extension brought to Wisconsin German prisoners of war and foreign

From Elizabeth Brandeis Raushenbush, "The Migrant Labor Problem in Wisconsin," pamphlet (Madison, 1962), pp. 11–13.

workers from Mexico and the British West Indies to harvest a variety of fruits and vegetables. Texas Mexicans continued to be brought to the state by the sugar companies and attempts were made to put them to work in other crops between the two seasons of sugar beet work. It seems probable that 1947 was the first year that Texas Mexicans were used in substantial numbers in cultivating and harvesting crops other than sugar beets. The number of Texas Mexicans in the state that year was about 5,000. In addition, foreign migrants numbered about 2,800. It was probably assumed that the use of migrants in Wisconsin agriculture would diminish from then on. Instead it increased. Wisconsin State Employment Service (WSES) reported nearly 9,000 domestic migrant workers in 1953 and nearly 12,000 in 1954. The 10-year average for 1950–1960 was around 11,000 workers (not counting children under 16, though many of them work.) Perhaps due to exceptionally good crops the number reached 12,686 in 1961. Mechanization of one harvesting operation after another which has occurred in the past decade does not seem to reduce the over-all demand for migrant labor. At least up to 1961, mechanization has been offset by other factors which increase demand.

In 1961 WSES counted 12,686 domestic migrants working in Wisconsin plus 5,039 children under 16, many of whom worked, too. Most of these were Texas Mexicans—10,770 out of the 12,686. How many additional migrants worked in the state without using the Employment Service, we don't know. The sugar refining company recruited directly in Texas without using the Service, but WSES believes that most of these Texas Mexicans registered with them after beet cultivation was over and thus got into their count. Figures for 1960 indicate that migrants worked in 28 of the 71 counties of the state. The largest concentrations were in Waushara, Door, and Oconto—in Waushara and Oconto mainly to harvest cucumbers for pickling, in Door to pick cherries. Smaller numbers were used in harvesting peas and sweet corn for canning, to thin and block sugar beets and to work in miscellaneous vegetables, including mint—much of this in mucklands. The migrants stayed in one location for lengths of time varying from over five months in vegetables, where they plant, weed and harvest, to four weeks in cherries where they merely pick. In sugar beets, migrants in recent years were used only in the early season—late May to early July—to thin and block. The harvesting was done by machine without the use of migrants.

In addition to these domestic migrants the WSES brought to Wisconsin in 1961 approximately 1,300 foreign workers. Most of this group were Mexican Nationals.

Problems of Migrant Workers

GOVERNOR'S COMMISSION ON HUMAN RIGHTS, 1965

Wages and Hours of Migrant Workers in Wisconsin

Information about wages earned by migrants is difficult to obtain since most of them are paid on a piece-rate basis and the family often works as a unit. In 1960 the U. S. Department of Agriculture cited 85¢ an hour as the average for all farm labor in Wisconsin and $6 per day for the North Central Region including Wisconsin. Compare these figures with the lowest non-farm rate of $1.34 per hour or $9.74 per day for laundry workers.

When weather is good and the crop ready, farm workers may work from sun-up to sun-down with no additional time-and-a-half for overtime. On the other hand, there is underemployment or no employment at all during adverse crop conditions, and, of course, there is no reimbursement for time required in transit from job to job.

Living Conditions of Migrants

Texas Mexicans are often hired through a "crew leader", a fellow Texas Mexican, who contracts for them with an employer and transports them in trucks from Texas to the site of employment, or the family happily drives its own car. Housing is supplied by the employer, and in the past, has often been make-shift with few conveniences and sanitary facilities. However, Wisconsin Bill 597S was passed in 1951, setting up standards for migrant housing. In 1957 and 1961 the law was strengthened and now is in need of further amending since in a few cases State Board of Health inspectors have been denied admission to camps. Standards as set by law are somewhat better than minimal, yet there are frequent complaints by visitors to some camps, particularly concerning the water supply, toilet facilities, and refrigeration of food.

Migrant Children, Their Employment and Education

About 4,000 migrant children under 16 accompanied their parents to Wisconsin in 1964. The older children worked in the fields with the adult members of the family. Wisconsin's Child Labor Law covers agriculture to only a very limited extent. Although the Industrial Commission has the power to regulate the employment of children under 16 in certain kinds of agriculture, it has used this

From Governor's Commission on Human Rights, "Migrant Labor in Wisconsin," 1965, pp. 1–3.

power only once. In 1960 at the request of the Governor's Commission on Human Rights, the Industrial Commission set 12 years as the minimum age in all kinds of agriculture to which its power extends.

Migrant children are covered by the state compulsory education law and should be in school if it is in session. Although most educators in areas of migrant concentration make an effort to carry out their responsibility, each year there are a few cases in Wisconsin that are prosecuted by federal authorities under the Fair Labor Standards Act, which prohibits children from working during school hours.

Because of their frequent moves, cultural deprivation, and the language barrier, children of migrants have been found to be educationally retarded. This retardation increases with age. A seven year old may be a year behind in school, but by eleven, he is frequently three or more years behind. To counteract this, a number of public and parochial summer schools have been set up in the state in the past five years. In 1961, Bill 48A providing state aids to summer schools operated by local school districts, was vigorously supported by the Governor's Committee on Migratory Labor in hopes that it would benefit migrant children as well.

Demonstration summer schools were operated in Manitowoc County in 1960 and 1961 at the request of the Governor's Committee on Migratory Labor and the Governor's Commission on Human Rights. In Lake Mills, the public school system at first maintained a special rural school for migrant children in the fall and spring of the year, then in 1962 operated a special summer school. However, after weighing the advantages and disadvantages, it was decided to integrate all migrant children into the regular school classes and to conduct an integrated summer school as well. The children have been well accepted, and the program has been successful in improving both their cultural and educational levels. Moreover, it has acted as an incentive for them to continue to high school.

A number of the Catholic dioceses in the state have operated educational programs for migrant children, both during the regular school year and in the summer. A spokesman for the parochial summer school at Endeavor, said that their school concentrated on spoken English, reading, and spelling, the areas of the children's most glaring deficiencies. They found that most of the children had been able to keep up with their age group in mathematics.

. . . .

Day Care for Migrant Children

Using federal funds from the Department of Health, Education and Welfare, the Division for Children and Youth in the State Department of Public Welfare operated a number of Day Care Centers for migrant and local children, with the help of local advisory committees. In 1964 there were seven such centers in Waushara County and four in Door County. Besides freeing the parents to work and providing supervision for the children, these centers taught migrant and local children to play and learn together. The older children, up to the age of 12, were given training in the language arts, including reading and English. The Department of Public Instruction cooperated in setting up the curriculum.

Health Care for Migrants

Because of poor diet and crowded, sometimes unsanitary conditions, and because of lack of medical and dental attention, the health problems of migrants are more pronounced then those in the average community. The Day Care Centers require medical examinations and immunization shots for all children who attend. This has helped to pick up medical problems among the children. The State Department of Public Health has supplied extra public health nurses in Waushara and Door Counties at the time of the heaviest concentration of migrants. The Catholic Diocese of Green Bay with the help of local doctors has set up a health clinic for migrants in Door County.

In 1962 Congress passed the Migrant Health Act, providing federal funds for migrant health projects.

. . . .

Although health insurance for migrants is badly needed and unpaid bills are a problem to some hospitals, there are a number of difficulties in trying to provide it. Growers feel that they are working on such a small profit margin that they cannot contribute to the costs. Migrants are not interested because of their low income and because coverage would be so limited at the rate they could afford. The Governor's Committee on Migratory Labor, in conjunction with health insurance companies has been working on the problem, so far without success.

Wautoma Reacts to the Migrants

VERNA KING GRUHLKE

Wautoma had changed in another way long before the Ed Gein affair came to light, and that was when it was discovered that the sandy soil of Waushara County was suited to the growth of cucumbers for pickles. Prior to that time it was supposed that potatoes, corn, and a few grain crops were all that could grow even moderately well there; but suddenly, almost overnight, Wautoma became the Pickle Capitol of the United States.

A new, thriving industry sprang up with the rapidity of a mushroom, and farmers were quick to respond to the challenge. The big trouble turned out to be that Wautoma was not prepared for such a radical change, especially in the field of labor. Picking cucumbers is long, hard, dirty work during the hottest, driest months of summer weather and the people of Waushara County—lank, lean Yankees and fat, rotund Germans—simply are not geared to such backbreaking endeavor. Picking up potatoes for a couple of weeks in the fall, hoeing corn, riding a tractor, operating a combine, they could and would do; but spending hot hours bent over endless rows of cucumber vines was a completely different kettle of fish. Some of them tried it for a few weeks and gave up screaming bloody murder; the complaints of rheumatism, "cricks" in backs, and weak kidneys must have been heard as far away as Washington, D.C.

The answer to the problem of the harried land-owners, who were trying to get their precious crop harvested before it was too late, came sneaking up on most of the citizens of Wautoma and Waushara County in such a way that they were overwhelmed by it even before they realized what was happening to them and their community. Suddenly fleets of trucks whose licenses bore such foreign names as Texas, Mexico, New Mexico, and Jamaica began to disgorge hundreds of men, women, and children into the downtown streets of our village. It was an inundation which shocked the natives of Wautoma no end and for which they were completely unprepared physically, morally, and socially; for to their unsophisticated eyes the newcomers were all "niggers."

Wautomaites were shocked, outraged, and flabbergasted. From the very first, and in fact, for several seasons, the migrant workers were barred from all but a very few places of business; even owners of general stores treated them summarily if they deigned to wait on them at all, and it took years for them to wake up and realize that

From Verna King Gruhlke, *Small Town Wisconsin* (Spring Green, Wis., 1971), pp. 163–168. Reprinted by permission of Stanton & Lee Publishers, Inc., Sauk City, Wisconsin.

these foreigners were the best customers they had—of necessity they had to spend most of the money they earned in Wautoma right in the town in order to keep alive.

Nobody wanted the poor, bewildered Mexicans (for that is what they turned out to be—most of them United States citizens from Texas), and they must have had a lonesome disillusioning time of it. The movie house refused them admittance, taverns spurned them; and even the churches, which should have been among the first to welcome strangers in a hostile land, turned a cold shoulder to them should they dare to venture toward a house of worship.

. . . .

Until the state authorities intervened, many of the living quarters provided for the imported workers were so sub-standard that they were actually sub-human. Area farmers hastily converted pig-pens, chicken houses, turkey shelters, canvas tents, corn cribs, and old machine sheds into bunk houses and make-shift living quarters. There were no toilet facilities visible to the eyes of passers-by (except for the one small wooden privy leaning crazily against a barn). Running water was a luxury unheard of. The Mexicans came too suddenly and the farmers simply were not ready for them.

The odd part of it all was that the Mexicans themselves came into town looking beautifully clean and well dressed, with their clothes washed spotless and pressed to perfection. How they achieved such immaculateness in their miserable quarters is anybody's guess, but they would have put most any man to shame.

I am happy to report that when living conditions among the migratory workers became flagrantly wretched in a few cases, the State Department of Public Health stepped in to demand that conditions be improved. At the present time each farmer's quarters for his itinerant help are carefully inspected; and if they don't meet certain standards, the farmer is given a definite period of time in which to improve, clean up, or renovate—all depending on what is lacking in his accommodations. If he fails to comply with the state requirements within the allotted time, his workers are taken away from him. I know of several instances in which this very thing has happened; thus it is plain to see the state does more than make idle threats.

. . . .

On rainy days the streets of Wautoma are jammed with Mexicans. They walk up and down the street outside the stores waiting for the sun to come out, dry out the fields, and make it possible for them to go back to work.

In spite of the hundreds and hundreds of strangers downtown, the streets are quiet during these wet, gloomy days which often drag out into wet, gloomy weeks. One can be excused for wondering if Americans in a small Mexican town under similar conditions would show the same restraint and patience the Mexicans do in my hometown.

One of the most shocking features about the treatment of Mexican workers in Wautoma was the way in which they were at first disregarded (even snubbed) by the guardians of the local public institutions, and especially the churches.

They had been in town for several summers, and none of them were attending church services. It was becoming increasingly evident that they must be afraid. If they weren't welcomed in such mundane places as stores and taverns even when they had good money to spend, what kind of treatment could they expect if they should have the fortitude to approach a place as sacrosanct as a church on a Sunday morning?

Anyone who knows anything at all knows that men of Spanish origin are apt to be Catholics; hence it was only reasonable to expect that the Mexican workers and their families should be attending the local Catholic church. But they did not, and surely it must have been a deprivation which tore at their hearts and nagged at their consciences through many lonely, bitter hours. Deprive a man of his right to worship in the church of his choice, and you have deprived many a good man of his reason for existing.

The whole thing came to a head when a group of businessmen, who must have been suffering from twinges of their own consciences, went around town asking for donations to finance a non-sectarian Sunday school for the Mexican children. Everything went well until they approached a young Catholic businessman and asked him for a contribution.

"A non-sectarian Sunday school! What in hell are you talking about?" he roared. "Those Mexicans are Catholic and should be going to my church, I'm ashamed to admit. Until we Catholics wake up and make them welcome where they belong, I'll not contribute a damned cent to anything. Non-sectarian, my eye!"

Beginning in the summer of 1957 the diocese of Green Bay began to operate a summer school in the Catholic Church at Wautoma for about eighty Mexican children, who were picked up each weekday morning from twenty-eight locations along a fifty-five mile route by private cars and a specially-donated bus. At noon the women of the parish served the children a hot lunch.

Two young priests and several Spanish-speaking nuns were sent to Wautoma by the bishop to aid the local priest who did not speak

Spanish, and it is to these young men and women that much of the success of the project was due. Mexican parents and their children clustered around the priests and sisters, chattering happily in Spanish, laughing and joking in a truly uninhibited, friendly fashion.

Wisconsin and Women's Rights

GOVERNOR'S COMMISSION ON THE STATUS OF WOMEN, 1975

Wisconsin has a long tradition of progressive legislation and was the first state to record its ratification of the Nineteenth Amendment, which extended the suffrage to women. Soon after women achieved full citizenship in 1920, Wisconsin passed an equal rights statute. Now, more than half a century later, the state and the nation are still engaged in the process of defining and instituting full equality under the law for all people.

The Wisconsin Equal Rights Statute

Women shall have the same rights and privileges under the law as men in the exercise of suffrage, freedom of contract, choice of residence for voting purposes, jury service, holding office, holding and conveying property, care and custody of children, and in all other respects. The various courts, executive and administrative officers shall construe the statutes where the masculine gender is used to include the feminine gender unless such construction will deny to females the special protection and privileges which they now enjoy for the general welfare. The courts, executive and administrative officers shall make all necessary rules and provisions to carry out the intent and purpose of this section.

This statute, virtually unchanged since its enactment in Wisconsin in 1921, was the first equal rights statute passed by a state legislature. Women in Wisconsin do not, however, share equal rights and responsibilities with men as the provision might lead one to expect.

From Governor's Commission on the Status of Women, "Wisconsin Women and the Law," 1975, pp. 4–5. Footnotes in the original omitted.

Employment laws, family laws, criminal laws, taxation and retirement laws, and reproduction control under the law treat women and men differently, in ways that would appear to be in clear violation of Wisconsin's unique statute guaranteeing equal rights to women. Still, women do have considerable rights under the law as it now exists, and continuous pressure is being applied to the legislature and the courts to eliminate the inequities that still remain. The Equal Rights Amendment (ERA) to the United States Constitution will nullify most of these unequal laws or will permit both women and men to receive the benefits of those laws that now benefit only one sex.

The Federal Equal Rights Amendment

The Equal Rights Amendment to the Constitution of the United States is regarded by many as the most comprehensive contemporary legal change affecting women—and thus, of course, men. When finally ratified by 38 states it will become the Twenty-seventh Amendment and a part of the fundamental law of our nation.

The Constitution was designed to be broad and general enough to cover many circumstances and many years. It is made current by interpretive court pronouncement and by statute. By setting forth principles that must be adhered to by federal and state governments, the Constitution, with its amendments, serves as a yardstick by which the validity of laws is measured. A statute or other public mandate that is found to be in conflict with the provisions of the Constitution is struck down and is no longer valid.

Therefore, ERA has the potential to invalidate the hundreds of statutory provisions, many enumerated throughout this handbook, that treat women and men differently. Some people argue that equal treatment is already guaranteed by the equal protection clause of the Fourteenth Amendment and that ERA is unnecessary. However, until Congress finally passed ERA and the entire question of sex-based discrimination had become a matter of public debate, the Supreme Court had not applied the Fourteenth Amendment to such cases and had indeed refused to consider such application. While over the past several years the Court has invoked the Fourteenth Amendment as a tool to challenge sex-based discrimination, still some 70 national organizations have continued to work for the ratification of ERA as the preferable, more reliable, and more clear-cut course to follow.

The substance of ERA is a simple one-sentence statement: "Equality of rights under the law shall not be denied or abridged by the United States or by any State on account of sex." It goes on to say: "The Congress shall have the power to enforce, by appropriate legislation, the provisions of this article.

"This amendment shall take effect 2 years after the date of ratification."

In a special session in April 1972, the Wisconsin legislature became the fourteenth state to ratify ERA to the U.S. Constitution. First introduced into Congress in 1923 at the insistence of the National Woman's Party, and reintroduced into each subsequent Congress, the measure in its present form finally passed Congress in 1972. Three fourths of the state legislatures (38 out of 50) must ratify it within seven years for it to become the law of the nation. As this handbook goes to print, 34 of the states have ratified the amendment, two of which have attempted to rescind their ratifications. Precedent indicates, however, that a state that has ratified an amendment cannot nullify its ratification.

4: Student Protest in Wisconsin

Student unrest in the 1960s and early 1970s was a national phenomenon, but the University of Wisconsin campus at Madison was often the center of attraction. The war in Vietnam, the bombing of Cambodia, the use of chemicals in the war, and a general attitude of antimilitarism combined to bring about many of these disturbances. The first selection which follows discusses the reaction in Madison to job interviews conducted in 1967 by the Dow Chemical Company, a maker of the chemical napalm used in Vietnam. The second selection shows the reaction of frustrated city officials attempting to deal with the turbulent campus community. The destruction of the Army Math Research Center on the Madison campus is the subject of the final selection.

1967—Reaction to Dow

JAMES RIDGEWAY

The faculty of the University of Wisconsin, said to run the place, has given the new Chancellor, William H. Sewell, a vote of confidence for the way he handled the peaceable student demonstration here. Sewell brought the Madison police riot squad onto campus to disperse 200 people sitting down outside a room where Dow Chemical Company representatives were holding job interviews. Dow makes napalm used by our forces in Vietnam.

From James Ridgeway, "On Wisconsin," *The New Republic* (November 4, 1967), pp. 8–10. Reprinted by permission.

Instead of clearing the building, the police clubbed, stomped and tear gassed those inside, as well as 1,500 students standing outside. When students called the university hospital and asked for ambulances to take away the unconscious, the hospital refused. When an intern asked for medical supplies so that he might on his own help the injured, the hospital refused. Neither Chancellor Sewell, nor his chief lieutenant, Joseph F. Kaufman, dean of student affairs, appeared at the scene; yet they wasted no time in suspending 13 students; then in the name of safety they called off the Dow interviews.

On the morning of October 18, the demonstrators had proceeded in rag-tag formation to the Commerce Building, a few blocks from where the Dow men were conducting their interviews. The demonstration had an altogether festive air; reporters and cameramen clogged the entranceway to Commerce. The demonstrators had to push their way in. Finally some 200 got inside, solidly packing every bit of space on the main floor. During the morning Ralph Hansen, the campus police chief, called Chancellor Sewell and told him his force couldn't handle the demonstrators; Sewell told him to go ahead and call in the city police. Larry Silver, a graduate student in the Law School was inside the Commerce Building and reports what happened next:

"Approximately at 12:30 Chief Hansen asked to see some of the leaders of the demonstration. He knew them by name. He talked to them and they said over a loudspeaker there was going to be a deal: If Dow would leave, the demonstrators would leave. Everyone cheered with approval ... the protest leaders then left to get confirmation of this offer from Chancellor Sewell. They returned; they announced that their meeting with the chancellor did not produce this result and that Dow would not leave. At this point Chief Hansen took the loudspeaker and addressed the noisy demonstrators: This is an unlawful assembly. If you wish to avoid arrest, leave now. The halls were so packed that there was no possibility of emptying them in less than 10 minutes. Within one minute of Chief Hansen's arrest warnings, at least 20 riot police, helmeted, with clubs swinging, charged the crowd. I could see several assaulted protestors falling. As they fell, police continued to beat them.... There was immediate panic among the protestors; there was no place to go; they were forced to face the police lines. When people tried to leave voluntarily, they were clubbed, tripped and clubbed some more.... [A girl] wanted to get out. She tried to get up, but the police clubbed her to the floor with blows to the head and shoulders. At this point of the pandemonium, I was pushed back by the crowd which was trying to avoid the riot police. I pleaded with a university policeman guarding the office to the School of Commerce, 'Please let me in. I'm an observer. Let me out of this.' This red-haired policeman answered, 'You fink, go out like the rest of them.' He pushed me over the heads of several demonstrators on the floor. The university policemen kicked the people on the floor. The front line of the riot police continued to club people around me. To leave I had to run the gauntlet of the riot police. I was hit four times as I went through the gauntlet."

That description is among 50 or so depositions taken by students and professors at the Law School.

Every so often somebody would sail out the door. A boy was half carried, half dragged out by his friends. He was unconscious. A girl, crying hysterically and holding her head, reeled out of the building; two boys rushed to catch her as she fell. The students outside began to fight the police. A policeman, his billy club flying into the air, went down and there was a roar from the crowd. A handful of students sneaked behind a paddy wagon where six students, under arrest, were being held. They let the air out of the wagon's tires, then pushed cars in front to block its path. The police regrouped, then fired tear gas into the students, rushing in behind the gas clubbing and stomping anybody who couldn't run fast enough to get away. Suddenly police reinforcements appeared, and the crowd broke up.

That evening 8,000 students met and agreed unanimously to boycott classes the next day. It reduced attendance at the College of Letters and Sciences, the largest at the University, by perhaps 25 percent. Three hundred of the faculty supported the students; a number of sympathizing teaching assistants were fired.

The following afternoon, the 1,200 members of the faculty met in special session and squabbled from mid-afternoon till midnight over parliamentary procedures; a few professors spoke up for the students; they made little impression. J. H. Westing, a professor in the Commerce School who had looked into the activities of the police, reported there was "surprising little blood," although he had observed a "trickle here and there." Professor Edward Obert, Engineering, charged "student brutality." Professor Scott Cutlip, Journalism, said the University could not allow "200 nihilists" to paralyze its operations. Chancellor Sewell declared that the faculty should muster "the guts" to face up to the fact that he only was administering the rules they themselves had written the previous spring. The faculty voted two-to-one to back the Chancellor in his handling of the affair. At the same time, a motion to condemn the police for the way they behaved, was beaten off.

While this was going on, Republicans who run the state legislature had whipped themselves into a frenzy. They thought Sewell was too lenient; a committee was set up to get the facts; it subpoenaed students to get the names of others. One representative suggested that future demonstrators deserved to be shot; others wanted the FBI to help find the students who had cut down an American flag from atop Bascom Hall. Among both the faculty and legislators there is a growing conviction that the demonstration was part of a conspiracy masterminded by Students for a Democratic Society and the Du Bois Clubs. The only trouble with this theory is that people who have tried to find the local Du Bois Club chapter can't find it; and SDS was against the demonstration because its members, who at the hard core number perhaps 25, felt the protest did not reach to substantive issues. Bronzon [*sic*] LaFollette, the Democratic state attorney general, at first accused the city police of brutality, but after he was scolded by the city police chief and the Republican lieutenant governor who was acting governor at the time, he backed off and diplomatically suggested that perhaps there was violence on both sides.

The Uneasy Campus Neighborhood—1969

JULIE PREIS

If, as was reported at the time of the street invasion by the police, the Mayor and other city officials actually shook their heads in wonderment because they thought "it couldn't happen here," they must be credited with providing the (somewhat bitter) laugh of the week. For Madison has exactly the atmosphere where it could be expected to happen. The "student as nigger" analogy, which has been kicking around for some time now, is particularly appropriate for a town like this, where there are few blacks and where poverty areas are not so blatantly visible as in larger cities. It does have the University, though, and with it the students, who compose the heaviest population of downtown Madison. Many of the students

From Julie Preis, "Postscript: The Mifflin St. Riots," *The North American Review*, VI,2 (Summer 1969), pp. 20–21. Reprinted by permission.

are ghettoized into high-rent, slum-condition streets (such as the Mifflin-Bassett St. area where the police struck); their moral and political values are often on different planes from other citizens'; physically they are more casual and less restrained by conventional standards of respectability. In short, they are "freaks," the sources of moral decay and civil disharmony, and their trouble-making capacity was proven as recently as the student strike earlier this year. Because "student" is so frequently identified with "disruptive element," and student activism inevitably condemned by authorities as destructive of democracy, one cannot accept as spoken in good faith the assertions by city and police officials that students were treated, during the time of the riots, just as any other citizens would have been. To be a student is to be stigmatized and made a scapegoat. Never was the community's need for finding scapegoats so directly expressed as during the police riot this spring.

That it was a police riot is indisputable. When the students living on Mifflin street planned a block party for Saturday afternoon, they were setting no precedent: such parties had been held in the city in the past, even though city ordinances make no provisions for them. Just the week before, the residents of another University-area street had held a dance, without interference from police. But this time it was impossible not to believe the attack had been planned (with Mayor William Dyke's knowledge, says one reliable city reporter; both the Mayor and the Police Inspector "happened" to be out of town that day); to quote Police Chief Wilbur Emery, the students "aren't looking for a party, they're looking for a fight." The sight of hundreds of club-carrying cops arriving on the scene, armed with tear gas canisters, made it clear who was looking for a fight. The melee that followed was repeated on Sunday and Monday, as police moved onto other mid-city streets in their determination to catch every available student: innumerable clubbings and tear gas explosions, answered with flying rocks and bottles; students forced onto porches, into homes and University buildings, only to be forced out by more exploding canisters of gas; faculty members and other non-students beaten; in all, 107 arrests (simply being on the forbidden streets constituted "disorderly conduct"). It is true that no permit had been granted for the party, although one had been sought. It is not true that the party was designed as a potential confrontation with the law; one does not arm himself for battle with ice cream and oranges.

Because the violence was unprovoked, unnecessary, and so clearly an expression of irrational hatred, the sense of powerlessness and anger it evoked among students was enormous—especially since their living conditions were already such as to create ripeness for violence on their own part. At the same time, few disputed the need to "cool it," recognizing that a rational assessment of the weekend's outbursts was not a cop-out, but rather the only intelligent response to the situation. Ostensibly, of course, Mayor Dyke and the City Council also professed hope for a peaceful settlement and for a rational examination of the issues. To some extent this was achieved, when the Mayor sent a committee of 30 Madison businessmen, lawyers, clergy, and professors into the riot area to interview students.

In the City Council meetings that week, however, it became clear that most of the aldermen intended to react to the riots just as the state legislature had to the student strike in February—*i.e.*, with vituperative attacks on "extremist" students, and legalized restraints against them. Included as objects of criticism were Aldermen Paul Soglin and Eugene Parks, both ex-University students and representatives of Ward 8, where Mifflin St. is located. Both Soglin and Parks were largely responsible for organizing the Mifflin St. residents and suggesting reasonable methods of presenting their grievances. (Both had also been arrested during the riots; Soglin was bailed out by Fire Captain Edward Durkin, who felt that the young alderman was needed to calm the students. Ironically, Durkin's legal action was regarded by many Madisonians as evidence of complicity with subversive parties.) The major subject for debate in the Council was Soglin's motion that a permit be issued for another block party, to be held the following Saturday. The motion failed, 17-3. A yes vote, felt its opponents, would be a concession to extremists, an open invitation to more street fighting, a finger in the eye of law and order. Nevertheless, the Mayor scheduled another hearing for the following week, on the subject of recreational use of the streets. Mifflin Streeters, who had resolved to hold the party regardless of the vote in the City Council, decided instead to accept Captain Durkin's invitation to spend Saturday afternoon at his farm, and the city settled down to at least surface calm.

The student as citizen: the student as nigger. Protection of the community: violent suppression of a minority. In Madison, this is no accident; it is deliberate support of a tradition. During the same week of the riots, the process of vindicating the Wisconsin Way continued throughout the state. For example, the budget offered by the Joint Finance Committee received final approval. Governor Knowles signed into law the anti-student protest bills mentioned in the preceding article. The Board of Regents denied permission to hold the SDS national convention here this summer. President Harrington, appearing before the Legislative Investigating Committee, vowed not to tolerate "disruptive" protests at the University;

Senator Gordon Roseleip, a member of the Committee and a longtime adversary of Harrington, condemned the President as "un-American" for even tolerating the presence of SDS on campus. Two state senators introduced legislation barring Father James Groppi and cohorts from participating in further demonstrations at the Capitol. . . . This is only a partial list. Madison and the state of Wisconsin have no right to be incredulous when the police enact violently the kind of procedure which elected officials, under the aegis of democracy and due process, carry out every day. Not only *can* it happen here, it has—and will again, as long as the reactionary powers last.

The Army Math Research Center—1970

PETER WEISS

People's reaction to a bombing in the midst of denying a war is frightening. The U.S. Army Math Research Center at the University of Wisconsin was blown up, causing $6 million damage and the death of one man. It rattled windows all over town and the walls of Middle American isolation. Some 1,700 pounds of Wisconsin fertilizer, 100 gallons of oil and a stick of dynamite exploded the dream of nothing wrong that a spanking wouldn't cure. The blast was heard for 30 miles, all the way to the county line, but it aroused the people, in the days that followed, only to an angry whimper, a thrashing about in a dog's sleep. America had caught up with itself.

Madison used to be one of the loveliest towns in the country: a regal Midwestern capital on majestic lakes, with shaded streets and city limits that encompassed sensibility and charm. It was a state of mind, a professor's place, a worker's place, in the heart of America and protected by its centrality. Politically, in this land of Machine Gun Kelly, it was heaven. It fought Joe McCarthy during those awful years and still had time to quarrel with Frank Lloyd Wright. It was a refuge for liberals, a redoubt of the La Follette era. You

From Peter Weiss, "Madison, U.S.A.: Bomb Crater in the American Dream," *The Nation* (Oct. 5, 1970), pp. 302–305. Reprinted by permission.

knew it was an American community in the old sense, because the anti-Semitism was genteel.

In the cold-war years, the Madison campus of the University of Wisconsin was fitful but quiet. Its students comprised the "Lost Generation," the "Generation of Jellyfish," who watched the Army-McCarthy hearings on television and rooted for the Army. McCarthy was attacking the universities and the Wisconsin faculty was virile in its defense of academic freedom, scorning the students for their moral lethargy. President Harrington, in an interview just before the August 24 bombing, still regrets "the apathy and indifference which characterized students in the early 1950s"—as the students of today now regret his.

. . . .

By the time the change was becoming apparent, with the smell of today already in the air, the freedom movement had begun in the South. This was the Kennedy period, with its images of tasteful opportunity for reform, Peace Corps and Vietnamese War, and on all sides the young were encouraged to cross the New Frontier of contradictions. The universities were back in favor after their long recuperation from the fifties. The National Institutes of Health and the National Science Foundation were bursting with funds for health and social research, and the Army Math Research Center at Wisconsin was humming. Madison was an intellectual boom town, the Harvard of the West, for the careers it made in Washington. And there was plenty left over for social services.

The good feeling was augmented by the opportunities for social heroism in the South. Bull Connor was still "one of them" and Chaney, Goodman and Schwerner were brothers. Madison was back to its historic quarrels with Mr. Wright. The war in Vietnam was just coming into focus. The hippies were just being born and their problems had not yet been defined by the media. The Kennedy assassination was still "the work of a deranged mind," and Dr. King was having his dream. Madison rested on its liberal laurels and hustled the students.

. . . .

The University of Wisconsin is a large institution in a small state, the politics of which tend to be dominated by the cautions of a rural legislature. The social defection of the young has everybody worried and the campus rebellion is alarming. The public does not understand long hair and drugs and the searing social criticisms of the underground press. It does not understand the university's connection with the war or, indeed, its own connection with it, beyond the frustration of taxes and the deaths of sons. No governor or university president is going to stand up and explain it, so people explain it to one another at Kiwanis and Rotary meetings, and fortify themselves with Yankee epithets about law and order, gathering behind the home guard veterans' groups which never cease in their forage for virtue. To them, the trouble in Madison is caused by strangers who want to "turn the university into a rendezvous for radicals and revolutionaries, a propaganda factory for communism or spawning ground for subversives." It is the return of the Christian Crusade, no longer confined to the Southern regions of dark-age America.

The Dow demonstrations caused a roar in the legislative wind tunnel that brought the lieutenant governor and a Senate committee to the campus with threats of money cuts "to show 'em who's boss." They were confident in their derision that a "good dose of detergent and varnish ... would make her [the university] the grand old gal she used to be." They had their day, this committee of political opportunity, peering blindly across the table at the hairy radicals they had heard about at Kiwanis, who were speaking now about napalm; and at nervous university officials who were pleading for mercy. The Governor returned from a mission of commercial good will to Taiwan in time to apply his balm to the public wound, but notice had been given: the administration had better get tough or the regents would take over. How quaint that seems, now that the regents have had *their* chance and the state is making policy.

The university continued to function in an increasingly sterile way. The faculty did not retreat in the face of new confrontations. They just stood there clucking like the rest of Wisconsin, while the chancellor moved the police around. When they would meet over some crisis like the draft, industrial recruiting on campus, or black studies, the students would gather outside to wait until the P.A. system carried the words of surrender. The meetings would begin with a parliamentary wrangle about limiting debate. The faculty's world was collapsing but they did not want to miss supper. There would be praise for the students, praise for the university, exchanges between old radicals who could not remember the reasons, and a lot of proposals, resolutions, amendments—a lot of parliamentary scratching leading up to the administration's position, the boss's point of view, which would then be accepted along with a motion to adjourn. Outside, the students would line up to form an aisle of silent contempt for the parade of tweed jackets.

It was sad to see such discouragement on the young faces. They still believed that those deaf ears were merely clogged; not that they were tuned in to another station. And they still believed that demonstrations could prop up the sagging liberal center that provided a cushion of hope. On the national scale, it was working in the move to dump Johnson. Disillusionment had not yet hardened into cynical despair. Nihilism was still on the fringe.

. . . .

Public antagonism was growing. The long period of confrontations had shifted the focus of the public eye from the issues of dissent within the university to the battles between students and police. People watch too much television! The police were beginning to look like "our boys" overseas and the students like the V.C., especially since they so identified themselves. The police had enormous stockpiles of riot-control equipment.

. . . .

Between September 26, 1969 and January 5, 1970 there were twenty-five firebombings on and off campus, some of them causing enormous damage. Most of these attacks were against the National Guard, ROTC, the draft board and the Army reserve. In addition, a large supermarket in the student district was burned to the ground. On January 1, 1970, there was an abortive aerial attack on an ordnance plant outside Madison which makes gunpowder and bullets for the Army. Windows were smashed in the shopping district near campus during demonstrations in support of a strike at General Electric, when G.E. was recruiting on campus, and again in opposition to the invasion of Cambodia. In the fall of 1969 mathematicians attending a meeting sponsored by the Army Math Research Center were spattered with paint. Last summer, the Research Center was bombed.

Credit for the bombing was taken by people calling themselves the "Vanguard of the Revolution," and declaring their "solidarity with the San Rafael four" and "each and every peasant, worker, student and displaced person who, in his day-by-day existence, struggles against the oppressive conditions heaped on him by the monster." They went on to demand the "immediate release of the Milwaukee 3 (Panthers), the abolition of ROTC, and the elimination of the male supremacist women's hours on the Wisconsin campus." They threatened "revolutionary measures of an intensity never before seen in this country—open warfare, kidnapping of important officials, and even assassination will not be ruled out."

Index